THE RECONSTRUCTION
OF WESTERN EUROPE
1945–51

THE RECONSTRUCTION
OF WESTERN EUROPE
1945–51

Alan S. Milward

Routledge
Taylor & Francis Group

LONDON AND NEW YORK

First published in 1984 by Methuen & Co. Ltd

Reprinted 2003
by Routledge
11 New Fetter Lane, London, EC4P 4EE

Transferred to Digital Printing 2003

Routledge is an imprint of the Taylor & Francis Group

British Library
Cataloguing in Publication Data

Milward, Alan S.
The reconstruction of Western Europe,
1945–1951.
1. Reconstruction (1939–1951) – Europe
I. Title
940.55'4   D825

ISBN 0–416–04352–6

Printed and bound by Antony Rowe Ltd, Eastbourne

CONTENTS

FIGURES

TABLES

The continent would be a single people, the nations would live their own lives in the life of the community. No more frontiers, customs or duties.

A continental currency would replace and absorb all the absurd different kinds of money we have now.

At the summit of this universal splendour would reign England and France. There has never been an antipathy between them, only the desire to surpass. France is the adversary of England as the better is the enemy of the good.

PREFACE

This book was written only because I wanted to write a quite different one. My intention was to write a history of the greatest economic boom in European history, of that unique, ugly and triumphant experience of the 1950s and 1960s which changed so utterly the scope of human existence and expectations as well as the consciousness of the people of western Europe. But as soon as I really began it became clear that this extraordinary boom had one other attribute as unique as the remarkable length of time over which the growth of output, incomes and wealth lasted. No one knew when or why it had started, and I soon discovered that neither did I. It was in fact not only one of the most unexpected events in western Europe's history, but remains one of the most unexplained.

As the huge armies of America and the Soviet Union met amongst the endless rubble of what had been Europe's largest economy and over the corpses of a government which had mocked the long history of European civilization and culture, no matter how heroic the sentiments expressed scarcely anyone could have believed that the small, shattered nations of western Europe were on the brink of the most prosperous, peaceful and one of the most creditable periods in their history. European capitalism, which many of its staunchest adherents had feared in the 1930s to be in its death throes, was not on the point of expiry but on the brink of more than two decades of remarkable vigour and success. But, although for very many people the immediate post-war years were a time of great hardship, one conclusion of this book is that the great boom started in 1945. What is much more difficult to explain, however, is why it was not interrupted and how it eventually took the form it did. Why did it not come to the savage halt to which the short, fierce post-war booms after the Napoleonic wars and, except in Germany, after the First World War had led? How did a boom whose origins lay in an intensely nationalistic reconstruction of capital goods industries and the national infrastructure turn, without apparent interruption, into an export-led boom in increasingly open economies driven forward by high levels of consumption?

It soon became clear that this particular turning-point was only one of the unexplained aspects of the great boom's long and complex history and that to write that history was impossible without a more searching historical investigation than is at the moment feasible. All that was possible was to try to answer the question, why was Europe's reconstruction after the Second World War so much more successful than after the First, and in answering that question to try also to explain why, at least for that brief period, the post-war boom proved so much more durable than its precursors. In part, it is argued, the answer was because the political reconstruction was more successful. It was based on the settlement of what were usually thought of as lower-level economic issues between the states, all attempts at a grand international settlement of the major political issues having failed. Thus the book became something quite different. It became a political as well as an economic history of Western Europe's reconstruction. Its only contribution to the history of the boom is to explain how it started, why it was not stopped by government action in 1947, why it continued in unpropitious circumstances in 1949, and to make some tentative suggestions about how from 1949 onwards it began to change in nature. Who can be surprised that, so accidentally conceived and so strangely born, it has some of the attributes of a vindictive monster, not easily approachable, threatening to run amok.

I have tried to explain both the economic and political nature of the reconstruction, using the word reconstruction to mean the whole process of political and economic rebuilding. A central argument of the work is that the success of Western Europe's reconstruction came from creating its own pattern of institutionalized, international economic interdependence. This was not the pattern which has erroneously been labelled 'the Bretton Woods system', not the brave new world celebrated by European federalists or other ardent exponents of the irreversible process of integration, and certainly not the emergence of the happy harmony between Western Europe and the United States depicted in so much of the 'Atlanticist' literature of the time. What it was and how it emerged is the matter of the whole book. However, a full account of the arguments is given at the start of the last chapter in such form that the reader who wishes to skip evidence and narrative may turn there first.

It is only fair to draw attention here to what seems to be the work's unavoidable weakness as history. It is a study of western Europe's reconstruction written from above not below. Because it is concerned with the way in which governments shaped the pattern of economic interdependence to suit their own national objectives it concentrates on the international aspects of economic change as well as of government policy. Furthermore, it deals, more or less, with seventeen countries and cannot help but be confined to the macroeconomic level. The work is based on a thorough study of the available statistical information and, for seven of the countries concerned, a long period of archival research. But on the important details of economic activity within the separate countries, as well as on the vital questions of how and why particular domestic economic policies emerged, there is ultimately far more to be written than appears here. I look forward to reading it.

It may be argued by others that the book also has a weakness in so far as it relies so much on the use of government records. Yet in a large, modern, democratic governmental system so much is still set down on paper that those records continue to have great value for historical research. There are several matters in this book of some importance which were effectively kept out of the public eye at the time but could hardly be kept out of official records or subsequently expunged from them. I would readily agree that reliance on such sources is mainly of use for studying the evolution of policy, but that is a very important aspect of a book such as this. In fact it seems to me that it is the abundance of dubiously accurate statistics produced by governments and international organizations in this field, invariably cited as a much more reliable and useful historical source, which should be looked at more critically. Exactly how, and precisely for what purpose, all these figures were compiled is virtually never known to the historian and for the most part is information which may never be recaptured. Although I have also used this evidence very heavily and contributed to manufacturing some more of it I became more sceptical about some of it than about the written record.

The archival materials on which the book draws are the following; the cabinet papers and the records of Her Majesty's Foreign Office and Treasury in the Public Record Office, the decimal files and committee records of the United States Department of State and of the National Advisory Council on International Monetary and Financial Problems in the National Archives of the United States, the archives of the Economic Co-operation Agency and the chronological files of Paul Hoffman in the Washington Federal Records Center, the archives of the President's Committee on Foreign Aid and of the Committee for the Marshall Plan, the personal papers of Dean Acheson, William L. Clayton, Clark Clifford, George M. Elsey and Paul Hoffmann, and the office files of William L. Clayton in the Harry S. Truman Memorial Library, certain papers made available by the United States Treasury, Série Y and Série Z of the archives of the Ministère des Relations Extérieures, formerly the Ministère des Affaires Etrangères in Paris, the Council papers and decisions of OEEC now in the care of the Organization for Economic Co-operation and Development in Paris, the archives of the Ministerie voor Buitenlandse Zaken in the Hague, the archives of Det Norske Utenriksdepartement in Oslo, a variety of materials from the Office of the Military Governor, United States, mainly in the Institut für Zeitgeschichte in Munich, the papers of Jean Monnet in the Fondation Jean Monnet at the University of Lausanne, and the Sunnanå Archiv at the University of Bergen.

So much of the work had to be done away from where I live and teach that I could not possibly have completed it without help from several research foundations. Stiftung Volkswagenwerk generously made it possible for me to take a sabbatical leave and work in United States archives. A grant from the Social Science Research Council allowed me to work in France, the Netherlands and Norway and supported my work in Britain for two years. The Leverhulme Foundation enabled me to complete my work in the Public Record Office and a grant from the British Academy made it possible for me to use the archives of the Fondation Jean Monnet in Switzerland. To all of them I am most grateful and I can only hope that they do not find their support misplaced.

To those who at times helped me to gain access to sources, Professor J.-B. Duroselle, Dr A. Kersten, Professor W. Lipgens, Dr H. Nordvik, Professor H. Rieben, and Professor M. Skodvin, and my friend Helge Paulsen, I would like to express my thanks for their interest. To those who readily and quickly responded to requests for information, Professor J. Bouvier, Professor A. Cairncross, Professor C.P. Kindleberger, Dr H. Pharo, the Bureau of Agricultural Economics in Canberra, the Institut National de Statistique in Brussels, the Netherlands Central Statistical Bureau, the Statistisches Amt of the German Federal Republic, and the United States Department of Agriculture, I am particularly grateful. The book deals with so many countries that without this sort of genuine practical help from those on the spot it would have taken more than twice as long to complete. To Cathérine de Cuttoli for sharing her knowledge of the French archives so readily I wish not only to express my generous appreciation but my hopes that she and others will feel her thesis to be well worthwhile. To my wife, whose puckered brow is always the surest sign that what I have written is incomprehensible, there is not much I can say because I owe her too much. I am overwhelmed by the patience of my close colleague and friend, Dr Frances Lynch who has quietly listened so long to expositions of my more ardent and mistaken ideas about the subject before quietly puncturing them. She also read some of the manuscript for me as did Professor S.B. Saul. An even worse job fell to my admirable secretary, Mrs Liz Diggle, who not only typed it more than twice but kept it all in order while the world seemed to be falling to pieces around us. May she never have to do anything so awful again. To Mrs Maureen Douglas, my research assistant for more than two years, must be credited a substantial share of whatever merit people find in the book. Her assiduous efforts in discovering statistics and other kinds of information at a time when I was too busy to offer any real help at all were a remarkable contribution; I thank her very warmly. I would like to dedicate the book to my daughter Colette with whose life it has exactly coincided. How sick she must be of it!

PREFACE TO THE PAPERBACK EDITION

Because the publishers have allowed me to make a few alterations from the original text for the paperback edition, I would like to explain what I have done. When my book was first written there were few sources available to show the course and nature of the negotiations for the Treaty of Paris. Since then the release of more government records and research into other materials such as industrial archives and private papers have shown how imprecise some of my original guesses were. I have therefore made several important changes to chapter XII. Secondly, more is now known about the Finebel (Fritalux) proposals of autumn 1949 and this has been incorporated into the second section of chapter X. Thirdly, research has made better sense of the first proposals for a Common Agricultural Policy, so that chapter XIII has also been altered to bring it up to date. Much of this new research has been done in association with the research project on 'The Origins of the European Community' at the European University Institute. Where it is the outcome of work by my own research students in that project I have only used it to rectify errors or where not to do so would have made nonsense, for I would prefer them to have the one luxury available to research students, that of publicly correcting the professors under whom they have suffered.

The last chapter represents my views on the relationship to the history of the European Community of the theories and explanations of 'integration' which were then current. I prefer to let it stand unaltered, although it no longer represents my views. When it appeared it was criticized by federalists as a denial of the role of idealism and an exaggeration of the role of national materialism in the making of post-war Europe. I am only the more convinced that it was necessary to allow the historical evidence to destroy what that evidence itself revealed as an inadequate foundation of belief and theory on which to build or explain the new European order. But four more years of research have convinced me that the historical evidence from the 1950s demonstrates that there was indeed an imperative towards wholly new forms of interdependence and to the transfer of national 'sovereignty' to non-national institutions, which the nation-state had to follow to make itself once more an accepted and strong unit of organization. It would now be possible to replace the theories rejected in the last chapter and formulate a historically-convincing intellectual foundation for the process of European 'integration', although it would be equally disappointing to federalists and their associates. I have left this to another book now in preparation and let the last chapter of this one stand as a record of what it was necessary to argue in 1984 if the population of Western Europe was eventually to be given an explanation of the European Community convincing enough to justify allegiance to it. I am profoundly grateful to the Community and to the President of the European University Institute, Herr Werner Maihofer, for supporting so enthusiastically research which must have appeared at first to be coming to wholly unwanted conclusions. To how many national governments could a similar tribute be paid?

Florence, 1986

ABBREVIATIONS AND CONVENTIONS

BIS	Bank for International Settlements
BOT	Board of Trade
CAB	Cabinet Papers
CEEC	Committee for European Economic Co-operation
ECA	Economic Co-operation Administration
ECO	European Coal Organization
EPU	European Payments Union
ERP	European Recovery Programme
FAO	Food and Agriculture Organization of the United Nations
FJM	Fondation Jean Monnet
FO	Foreign Office
FRUS	Foreign Relations of the United States
GARIOA	Government Aid and Relief in Occupied Areas
GATT	General Agreement on Trade and Tariffs
GDP	Gross Domestic Product
GNP	Gross National Product
IMF	International Monetary Fund
ITO	International Trade Organization
JEIA	Joint Export Import Agency
MBZ	Ministerie voor Buitenlandse Zaken
NA	National Archives of the United States
NAC	National Advisory Council on International Monetary and Financial Problems
NU	Det Norske Utenriksdepartement
OEEC	Organization for European Economic Co-operation
OMGUS	Office of the Military Governor, United States
SD	State Department
T	Treasury

UN	United Nations
UNRRA	United Nations Relief and Recovery Agency
Y	Ministère des Affaires Etrangères, Série Y
Z	Ministère des Affaires Etrangères, Série Z

Throughout the book 'western Europe' refers to those countries which did not become part of the communist bloc and 'Western Europe' refers to those countries except Greece and Turkey who participated in the ERP and became members of the OEEC. This convention applies also to statistical tables unless some further qualification is imposed or the countries included are specified. The phrase 'western Germany' is used to mean those parts of Germany not under Soviet occupation and 'West Germany' is used to mean the German Federal Republic. In statistical tables (..) means not available or not pertinent, (–) means negligible.

I

THE CRISIS OF 1947

Why begin a book about the reconstruction of western Europe in 1947? Because the political and economic events of that year are decisive for interpreting the past and understanding what was to come. The year of Marshall Aid, of what has been interpreted as a profound economic, political and spiritual crisis in Europe, the year when both economic recovery and reconstruction seemed to have foundered in the failure to produce a peace treaty with Germany and the inability of western European economies to function any longer without American aid, the year when Europe was divided; few years in history have been so often singled out as a political and economic turning-point. That it was a year of extraordinarily dramatic political events can readily be agreed. But it is the first contention of this book that the economic events of 1947 have usually been seriously misinterpreted and as a consequence so have the years before and after. The purpose, therefore, of beginning with an analysis of the economic crisis of 1947 is to explain the nature of European recovery and reconstruction since 1945 as well as in the years after 1947.

Some sort of economic collapse in 1947 had in fact been widely predicted. From 1940 onwards it had been repeatedly asserted that a vigorous but temporary boom caused by the rebuilding of inventories would be the immediate aftermath of the war, as in 1919, followed by a depression as the process of restocking came to an end, as in 1920. There was certainly very little evidence in 1946 that it would be otherwise, the high levels of demand in that year were attributable to government restoration of war damage, to inventory rebuilding and in some countries to the liberation of purchasing power pent up during the war. Why was this post-war boom not followed by the sort of fall in prices and output which had occurred in 1920? It might of course be argued that the length of such restocking booms is a function of the size of what has to be replaced and that the damage done during the Second World War was so much greater than during the First that the higher levels of investment needed to restore it would not have ended in 1947 but carried on well into 1948. And it is obvious from the choice of economic policies within many western European countries that the inflationary tendencies accompanying these investment programmes would not have deterred governments from allowing these conditions to prevail beyond the end of 1947. But it is by no means certain that the capital loss caused by the Second World War was so much greater than that caused by the First, and in any case high levels of output and employment continued in most European countries throughout 1948 more convincingly than in 1947 and no one has wished to attribute this to a restocking boom still governing those economies by the end of 1948. The expected brief post-war boom turned into a general trend of growth and prosperity which, in spite of the volatile economic movements underlying it, predominated until 1967, instead of into the low levels of growth of output and income which prevailed after 1920.

Yet the year 1947 is most frequently portrayed as a year of acute economic crisis in Europe of which the alarming political events were in some way a reflection and from which western Europe was 'saved' by Marshall Aid.[1] Even those historians who see the Marshall Plan as the product of an aggressive American foreign policy designed to impose America's will on Europe and the Soviet Union have accepted the impression, conveyed by the State Department to Congress and the American people, of a European continent on the verge of total collapse, from which it had to be rescued by American aid. This was the way in which European economy and society were portrayed by William L. Clayton, the United States Assistant Secretary of State for Economic Affairs, in the famous memorandum written in May on his return from Europe, which most scholars have seen as the starting point of the European Recovery Programme, the Marshall Plan as it has more usually been called.[2]

> Europe is steadily deteriorating. The political position reflects the economic. One political crisis after another merely denotes the existence of grave economic distress. Millions of people in the cities are slowly starving. ... The modern system of division of labor has almost broken down in Europe.[3]

George Marshall himself incorporated these ideas and even some of the wording into his famous speech at Harvard in June, where he offered American

---

[1] 'With food and raw materials, it saved Europeans from imminent economic ruin.' R. Mayne, *The Recovery of Europe* (London, 1970), p. 107.

[2] William Lockhart Clayton, 1880–1966, a millionaire director of a firm of Texas cotton brokers. Served in War Industries Board in First World War. Director and Vice President of Export-Import Bank 1940. Deputy Federal Loan Administrator 1940–2, Assistant Secretary for Commerce 1942–4. Surplus War Property Administrator 1944. Assistant Secretary of State for Economic Affairs 1944–6. Under-Secretary of State for Economic Affairs 1946–7. A militant free-trader who became an author of political tracts in his seventies. Dalton called him 'ideological Willie'.

[3] FRUS, 1947, vol. III, p. 230, Memorandum by Clayton, 'The European crisis', 27 May 1947.

aid to Europe.[4] Paul Hoffman, who was to become the first administrator of
the European Recovery Programme, remembered the European economy as
being in desperate straits even in 1948.

> Fifth columnists were hard at work in France, Italy and Germany. In all
> these countries the Communists were getting to be perilously strong. They
> were busy exploiting the hunger and the hopelessness and the lack of jobs
> among tens of thousands of people. Broken factories were operating
> fitfully and often slowed to a halt for lack of raw materials and repair parts
> for equipment. Farmers raised little more than enough to feed themselves.
> The transport system was in too bad a state of disrepair to carry even the
> slight food surpluses to undernourished city dwellers.[5]

Lord Franks, who was the chairman of the Committee of European Economic Co-operation set up in response to Marshall's speech, later considered
that, 'in the spring of 1947 the economic and social state of Western Europe
was far graver than in the thirties'.[6] Yet as Marshall was taking his words from
Clayton most European countries were still in a period of rising output and
expanding foreign trade. It could not be shown that any population outside
Germany was in danger of starving and even there diet was slightly improved
over the previous year. There were no bank crashes and few bankruptcies.
Profits and investment were high and so in most countries was the level of
employment. How should we categorize the European economic crisis of
1947 when virtually none of the symptoms of earlier economic crises can be
observed? How did Clayton, Marshall, Hoffman, and many Europeans too,
come to believe that by summer 1947 there was an impending collapse of
European capitalism?[7] How may such high drama be reconciled with so little
evidence of economic disturbance?

Only one phenomenon associated with previous economic crises occurred,
a severe fall in gold and foreign exchange reserves in some countries associated
with acute balance of payments difficulties. Yet this was sufficient to bring
crashing down one of the pillars on which the post-war capitalist world was
intended to be based, the free convertibility of sterling into dollars. The one
observable symptom of economic crisis thus had more in common with those
post-war European economic crises still to come which were confined largely

---

[4] Something of the document's origins is told in E.C. Garwood, 'Will Clayton. A short
biography', *Texas Quarterly* 1 (4), 1958. The strongest case for its great influence is made by J.M.
Jones, *The Fifteen Weeks: An Inside Account of the Genesis of the Marshall Plan* (New York,
1955) and the strongest case against it by J. Gimbel, *The Origins of the Marshall Plan* (Stanford,
1976).

[5] P.G. Hoffman, *Peace Can Be Won* (London, 1951), p. 28.

[6] Lord Franks, 'Lessons of the Marshall Plan experience', in OECD, *From Marshall Plan to
Global Interdependence* (Paris, 1978), p. 18.

[7] W.A. Brown and R. Opie, *American Foreign Assistance* (Washington DC, The Brookings
Institution, 1953), p. 125, in one of the more measured works on the subject attribute Marshall
Aid to 'the steady economic deterioration throughout Western Europe'.

to the area of international financial transactions and were more associated with problems of adjustment to high output and employment than with weaknesses in the essential fabric of production and investment. In those crises of the 1950s the greater quantity of money, of several kinds, in relation to national incomes, engendered in part by post-war government economic policies, enormously increased the stock of transferable liquid assets in private and corporate hands. The growing familiarity with foreign exchange as a valuable asset of this kind, providing the holder was ready and able to anticipate its volatile changes of value by switching from one foreign currency to another, was to become a persistent aspect of the international financial history of the post-war years. This tendency had already been clearly observable in Europe in the period of wildly fluctuating exchange rates which followed the First World War and there was nothing in the Bretton Woods agreements designed to curb it. Had the British economy in the 1930s operated at higher levels of employment the increased demand for imports might have made the balance of payments so weak as to have made it difficult to maintain confidence in the sterling exchange rate. In that sense the higher employment and imports of the post-war period were always likely to produce a loss of confidence and a speculative movement against sterling. The limited convertibility of sterling into dollars, imposed by the terms of the Anglo-American Financial Agreements which had ratified the post-war dollar loan to Britain, was in fact brought to an end in August after only six weeks, when holders of sterling, suspecting that its value in terms of dollars would fall steeply, began to disembarrass themselves of it at an increasing rate. The sums involved were trivial compared to the amounts involved in similar anticipatory movements over the next twenty-five years, but the crisis nevertheless might be seen as the harbinger of those later more massive movements which at times forced violent switches of economic policy on economies which, from all the evidence of their internal production figures, were flourishing. What was the case in 1947? Was western Europe on the brink of economic collapse or was it merely having to come to terms with the new and still puzzling phenomena of relative differences in the level of prosperity?

The demands for reconstruction loans and trade credits made in increasingly urgent terms from western Europe were often backed, in the hope of success, by painting an image of a continent where economic and social discontent were mounting to levels so dangerous as to call into serious question the future of capitalism there. It was hardly to be expected that requests for aid from France and Italy, where the communist parties held a powerful electoral position, would not be accompanied by claims that since the ruling governments could only prevent this serious situation through speedy economic success in recovery they were thus entitled to more aid. But the military administration in Germany had also begun to feel itself involved in a competition with the Soviets for the political allegiance of the German population. As the Department of State increasingly moved towards the formulation of a policy of active intervention in western Europe in order to preserve what it saw as America's vital strategic interests there, the idea that were America not to intervene there would be economic collapse in western Europe proved a most useful concept in mobilizing public and political support behind a policy that broke so sharply with hopes of a speedy return to isolationism. The usual defence of Marshall Aid before Congress was that it was 'saving Europe' and in so doing making safer the future of American society. In this way the propaganda in favour of Marshall Aid on both sides of the Atlantic strengthened the inherent fears and hopes of those circles in the American administration which first conceived the programme and confirmed their belief in its fundamental social, economic and political importance. The spiteful Soviet response and the onset of an avalanche of Cold War propaganda on each side then drove out for some time any further questioning of this aspect of the Marshall Plan.

The Marshall Plan was predominantly designed for political objectives. Conceived and pushed through by the Department of State itself, it represented a return to a position of pre-eminence in the making of national policy by that department.[8] Any more realistic, purely economic view of the situation, such as that taken on occasions by the United States Treasury, tended to be judged as of lesser importance because it was making only a limited judgement about issues of lesser importance than the grand design as a whole. In that sense the ultimate purposes of the Marshall Plan were almost entirely political albeit that its mechanisms were almost entirely economic.

In a year of such dramatic political events it would be absurd to suppose that urgent political fears and hopes did not have a powerful impact on economic events. But the task is to examine the economic nature of the crisis. Was western Europe in fact threatened by an economic crisis at all? If it was, what was the nature and cause of the crisis? How appropriate was Marshall Aid to meeting it? Only when these questions have received some answers can we understand the intricately interwoven pattern of political and economic events over the following three years which created post-war western Europe out of the ruins of the 1930s.

THE NATURE OF THE ECONOMIC CRISIS

The argument was cogently expressed at the time that the growth of European industrial production and the pace of European recovery had in fact slowed

---

[8] This process has been most thoroughly described. The work of Jones, *The Fifteen Weeks*, is a panegyric of the State Department's role. Dean Acheson, who became Marshall's Under-Secretary and later Secretary of State himself, has amply described the earlier disillusionment with the State Department's ineffective policies under Secretary-of-State Hull in several works of which D. Acheson, *Present at the Creation* (New York, 1970) is the most telling. The best and most just assessment is that of H. Arkes, *Bureaucracy, the Marshall Plan and the National Interest* (Princeton, 1972).

down in 1947 or even halted as had been expected.[9] This had the effect, it was argued, of reducing the flow of exports, increasing the flow of imports and turning the difficult European international trade and payments position of 1946 into an impossible one. The harsh winter of 1946/7 was said to have impeded recovery by disrupting production and causing an acute fuel shortage. The generally low level of agricultural output and the bad harvests of 1947 were said to have increased the need for food imports. The low level of food supply was said to have either prevented the necessary increases in, or reduced the level of, labour productivity and also to have caused a general crisis in morale.

There were in addition specific extra-European developments which were also held at the time to have been responsible either as contributory to the decline in European output or as independent causes of the trade imbalance. The emphasis given to such causes varied greatly but was usually combined with the hypothesis that the crisis was also the result of structural changes in the international economy brought about by the war itself. Whether these structural changes were permanent or merely the temporary after-effects of the war was, and indeed still is, a matter of much dispute. The more such structural changes were seen as fundamental and long-lasting, the less importance in the crisis was attributed to the specific events of 1947 and the more was it seen as the inevitable outcome of the failure of the post-war peace settlements and the Bretton Woods agreements to tackle adequately the problem of reconstruction. Contrariwise, the more such structural changes were seen as merely a temporary phase of disequilibrium in world trade and payments out of which a new equilibrium would automatically emerge, the more weight was attached to the specific events of 1947 itself in impeding the arrival of that new equilibrium. The more explanations tended in the first direction and assumed a fundamental structural imbalance in world trade and payments, the more was the blame for the crisis laid at the door of the United States, because it was the only country which could put right these imbalances by positive international actions to make a new equilibrium possible. The more explanations tended in the second direction and assumed there to be no barriers to the automatic return of international equilibrium other than those erected by governments themselves, the more was there a tendency to lay the blame for the crisis on the policies pursued by the European governments, who, by their ready spending on reconstruction and inflationary policies, encouraged imports, raised domestic demand at the expense of exports, and postponed the moment of attainment of a new

---

[9] This argument was developed most fully in UN, Dept. of Economic Affairs, Economic and Social Council for Europe, *Economic Survey of Europe in 1948* (Geneva, 1949). T. Balogh, *The Dollar Crisis* (Oxford, 1949), p. 216, claimed that 'European production, after a vigorous recovery immediately after the war, showed signs of flagging in the first half of 1947'.

equilibrium.[10] These differences of opinion have not been laid to rest by time.

Thus it is frequently asserted either that there was a reduction in the outflow of United States aid to the rest of the world in 1947, which, by reducing the general level of world availability of dollars, made it increasingly difficult for western Europe to obtain those imports from the United States on which reconstruction depended, or that the changes in the geographical pattern of world trade during the war by which America obtained a much greater share of its primary imports from nearby countries, the Caribbean basin in particular, brought about a long-run change in world trade which made it more difficult for European countries to earn dollars from exports to third markets. Or it is argued that the war had so increased the level of self-sufficiency of the United States that it had made it impossible for any world trade and payments equilibrium to appear unless the United States committed itself to a long-run programme of foreign investment combined with any other means of financing its export surpluses.

Reducing these broad economic positions to political positions the issues tended to be seen more simply. If there was an economic crisis in 1947, was it because the dislocation caused by the war was greater than the United States had assumed in demanding allegiance to the multilateral trade and payments system, which it sought as the basis of the post-war settlement? Or was it because European countries had entirely refused to acknowledge the harsh economic realities of the post-war world and embarked on ambitious policies of national reconstruction sustained by economic controls and other devices which only made the situation worse? Did the dollars eventually made available under the European Recovery Programme simply accelerate the process (which would in any case have taken place) by which international trade and payments returned to equilibrium? Or did the European Recovery Programme and the policies associated with it themselves provide the necessary restructuring of the pattern and mechanisms of payments and trade which alone could make the Bretton Woods agreements operable?

DOMESTIC ECONOMIC CRISES

The evidence for stagnation or even for a slowing down in the growth of industrial production in western Europe in 1947 is, in fact, most unconvincing.

---

[10] This was in essence the view of G. Haberler, 'The foreign economic policy of the United States', in S.E. Harris, *The European Recovery Program* (Cambridge, Mass., 1948) or of R. Harrod, *Are These Hardships Necessary?* (London, 1947). By contrast the dollar shortage was seen as so persistent as to represent a 'structural' problem in world payments by, for example, T. Balogh, *The Dollar Crisis*, C.P. Kindleberger, 'Balance-of-payments symmetry and the dollar' in T. Balogh, *Europe and the Dollar* (Cambridge, Mass., 1966), and R.F. Mikesell, 'Regional multilateral payments arrangements', *Quarterly Journal of Economics*, 62, 1948.

It has essentially been based on the United Nations data which aggregated national industrial production indexes into a quarterly index for the whole of Europe. This gives the result shown in table 1. What concerns us here,

Table 1   An index of the level of industrial production in Europe (1938 = 100)

	1946				1947		
	1st quarter	2nd quarter	3rd quarter	4th quarter	1st quarter	2nd quarter	3rd quarter
Including Germany	68	74	76	83	78	85	86
Excluding Germany	80	87	88	98	93	100	99

Source: UN, *Economic Survey of Europe in 1948* (Geneva, 1949), table 1.

however, is the movement of industrial output, not in Europe as a whole, but in those countries which subsequently formed the Organization for European Economic Co-operation (OEEC), 'Western Europe' as they are called in this book, and not aggregated in this way but disaggregated into monthly movements. Monthly movements for those countries which are sometimes said to have shown a faltering in the growth of output are shown in figures 1 and 2. The fall in the quarterly production figures in the first quarter of 1947 was mainly attributable to the fall in output in one month only, February, in the United Kingdom. This had a specific cause, the low level of availability of coal aggravated by the harsh weather that prevented its movement to power stations and factories. This was the month in which coal supply to British factories had to be rationed and the labour force had to be used to combat the effects of the exceptionally severe and prolonged winter on a railway system starved of investment during the war. But this one grim month did not cause any break in the general upward trend of output, which was resumed very powerfully in March. The argument that the coal crisis in February 1947 revealed the fundamental economic weakness of Britain, an argument still frequently cited, is quite invalid and was largely made at the time for political purposes.

In the Netherlands the vigorous upward movement of output stopped in October 1946 but in May 1947 there began another upward surge which lasted until September, continuing thus right through the period when the growth of European output as a whole slowed down. Denmark experienced a short setback in March 1947 but by midsummer output had climbed above the level of the start of the year again. In Norway a stagnation set in in June 1947 which persisted until December. In all three the blame was placed on Allied refusals to purchase food and raw material surpluses there for Germany. It is not easy, however, to see how a marginally higher level of demand from

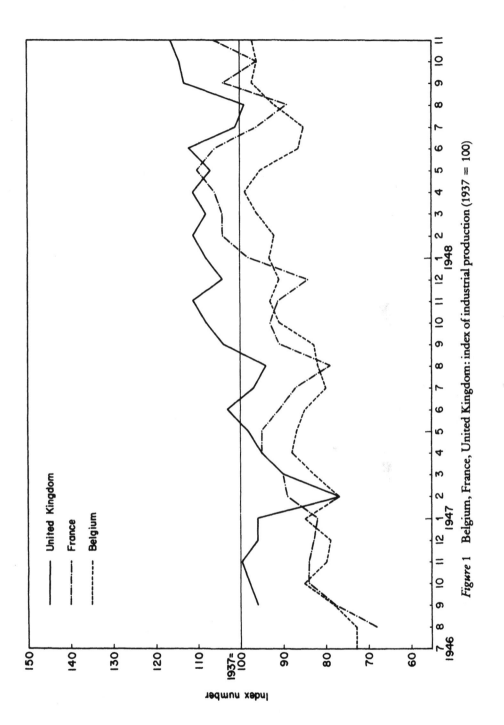

Figure 1 Belgium, France, United Kingdom: index of industrial production (1937 = 100)

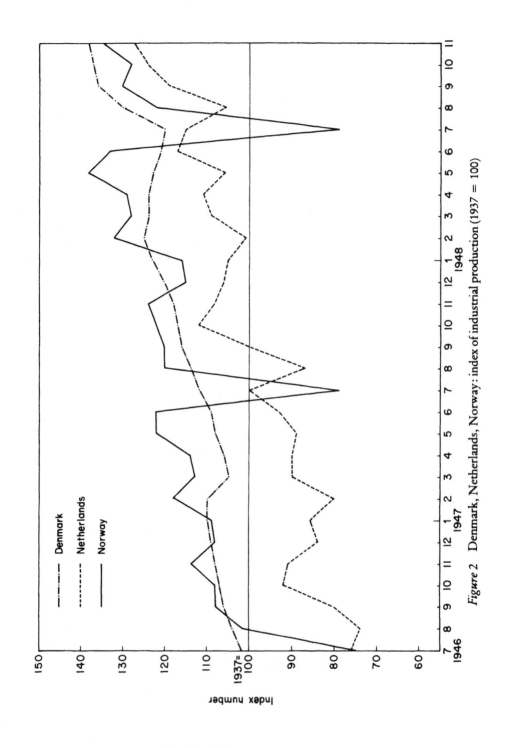

Figure 2 Denmark, Netherlands, Norway: index of industrial production (1937 = 100)

Germany for foodstuffs and raw material exports would have significantly affected these trends and, indeed, a more plausible explanation of the problems of these peripheral countries would be that they were beginning to suffer from a lack of German supply. Whatever the case there was no similar weakening of the upward trend of output in the larger producers until June. By that time a resumption of growth in Denmark and the Netherlands was under way.

It was the slackening of growth of industrial output which began in June in Belgium and France and in July in Italy which was mainly responsible for the failure of Europe's industrial production in the third quarter of 1947 to show any increase over the second quarter. A strong return to the upward trend, however, began in France in September. It was interrupted by the wave of industrial strikes unleashed by the Communist Party in November and December but was still persistent enough to make the last quarter of the year a period of clear recovery. The dip in output in June in France was mainly due to the strike wave of that month followed by the holiday period. If the trend of industrial production in France over the whole period is considered it is apparent that in spite of the fluctuations caused by labour disputes the whole period, from the start of 1946 to the end of 1948, was one of vigorous growth.[11] Belgian output began to increase vigorously once more in October after peaking in April. As will become apparent later in the book, the movements of Belgian output were much more dependent on the curious and rapidly changing circumstances governing intra-European trade, and especially on conditions governing steel exports in 1947, than were changes in industrial output elsewhere. In Italy the story was quite different. Specific deflationary measures which began in June, the freezing of bank deposits and the enforcement on the banks of a much stricter policy on reserve holdings prevented any further upward movement in industrial output in the second half of the year. Industrial output passed its pre-war level in July 1947 for one month only and did not reach that level again until September 1948 (figure 3).

The slowing down of the growth of industrial output in Europe after May was therefore by no means general in western Europe and was due to a wide variety of separate economic causes operating in separate economies. One of its components, a more marked falling away in output over the holiday period than in the pre-war period, was just as observable in subsequent years. At higher levels of employment and with holiday provision in some cases more generous than before the war a new seasonal rhythm became established. Trends of industrial output in the separate countries did not show any other obvious synchronization apart from the presence of a general, underlying rising trend in all but one of them, Italy, where it was decisively interrupted. It may well be that the sudden brief interruptions of trend at different times in different countries were caused by bottlenecks in the supply of particular raw

---

[11] M. Catinat, 'La production industrielle sous la IVe république', *Economie et statistique*, no. 129, Jan. 1981.

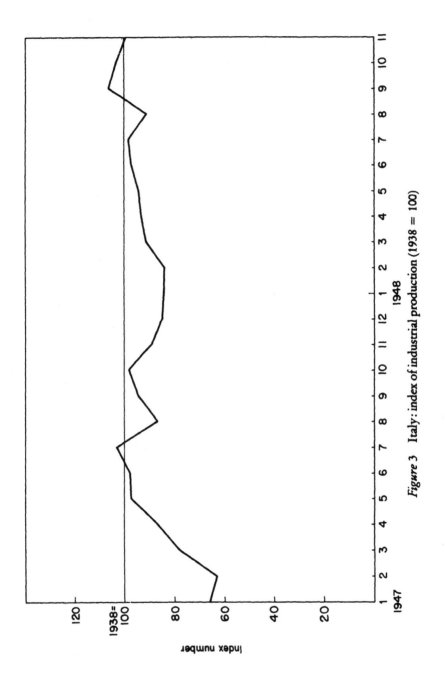

Figure 3 Italy: index of industrial production (1938 = 100)

materials or semi-manufactures and that the impact on Britain of the February coal shortage was but one instance of a series of such difficulties in Europe. In short, the occasional brief falterings in the growth of national output may have been more the result of the rapidity with which output was still expanding and the inability of supply to keep pace.

This is the most probable explanation of the marked fluctuations in output around a strong, persistently rising trend observed in the occupation zones of western Germany. There the process of economic recovery was taking place at much lower levels of output; in spring 1947 output in the Bizone was still only about a third of its 1938 level. Even at those low levels and with so many unutilized resources the upward curve of production repeatedly ran into severe bottlenecks, such as the inadequate transport and distribution systems and the shortage of coal, which caused it for short periods to flatten out or even fall.[12] The physical damage done to the infrastructure of the German economy was much worse than elsewhere in western Europe, but the differences were of scale not kind. Of course, with German output at such low levels there were finite limits to the degree of recovery in western Europe as a whole, for Germany had been not only the major supplier of capital goods to western European markets since 1890 but an extremely important export market too. The virtual absence of Germany from world trade in 1947 was, in fact, as we shall see, a major cause of the economic difficulties of that year.

As for the main emphasis of Clayton's argument, the 'existence of grave economic distress', the evidence, outside Germany, is far from convincing. In most western European countries living conditions were improving and in certain respects the standard of living was better than before the war. It must be admitted, however, that the evidence about this is more ambiguous than the clear evidence of persistently rising output.

If we plot the movement of money wages against time over the recovery period against the movement of the cost of living index or of retail prices and give both lines a common base in 1938, there is no evidence at all of a general deterioration in the standard of living in 1947 as compared to 1946, in fact the contrary is the case. The results are different from country to country, which is exactly what would be expected given the wide variety of national economic policies pursued from the end of the war. But on the whole, over most of western Europe, conditions, measured in this crude way, were distinctly better in 1947 than in 1946. The deficiencies of this procedure as a way of saying anything worthwhile about any particular country are naturally very great. In some countries wage rates were controlled; in others retail prices

[12] W. Abelshauser, *Wirtschaft in Westdeutschland 1945–1948. Rekonstruktion und Wachstumsbedingungen in der amerikanischen und britischen Zone* (Stuttgart, 1975). M. Manz, 'Stagnation und Aufschwung in der französischen Zone von 1945–1948' (Dissertation, University of Mannheim, 1968).

were controlled; and in most the cost of living index was largely composed of those items whose prices the governments kept down more than other items. In some countries physical controls over goods mattered to the consumer more than their price. But since what is at stake is the existence or otherwise of a general western European trend these defects matter much less and a general picture does emerge from such an exercise.

In Denmark, Norway, Sweden, Switzerland and the United Kingdom the relationship of wages to the cost of living in 1947 was distinctly more favourable than before the war and than in 1946. In Ireland it seems to have become so in the course of the year. In the Netherlands the cost of living was consistently higher than wage rates when compared to 1938, but not so much higher in 1947 as in 1946.

For Italy the evidence is ambiguous. The rapid inflation there was probably of more importance in determining the pattern of economic welfare during the year, by the way it redistributed access to goods amongst different categories of consumers, than was the general trend of wages and prices. None the less the gap between the cost of living and wage rates in Italy widened in August and September 1947 so that it was greater than at any time since the end of the war. At the time Marshall made his offer of aid living conditions in Italy measured in this crude way were beginning to deteriorate markedly and rapidly. It must also be borne in mind that the average level of calorific consumption, based on the official ration, was so low (table 2) that any sudden reduction in the purchasing power available to buy food would have had drastic consequences for a large number of families. When the prevalence of black market food prices rather than official food prices is taken into account, it is likely that the situation could have been even more threatening

Table 2   Estimated calorific value of daily *per capita* food consumption in Western Europe

	Crop Year 1945–6	Crop Year 1946–7
Austria	1700	2000
Belgium	2200	2400
Denmark	2900	3100
France	2300	2600
Germany	1600	1800
Italy	1850	2000
Netherlands	2300	2600
Norway	2500	2600
Sweden	2800	2800
Switzerland	..	2900
United Kingdom	2800	2900

Source: UNRRA, *Operational Analysis Paper No. 41*, April 1947; United Nations, *Salient Features of the World Economic Situation 1945–47* (Lake Success, 1948), p. 154.

for large numbers of wage earners. On the other hand, the general official availability of food, even if very low, improved in 1947 over 1946. And after September came a sharp reversal in the trends of wage rates and the cost of living index so that for those in employment there was a distinct improvement in the material standard of living. This was achieved, however, only at the cost of a decisive upward movement in the numbers registered as unemployed, 1,870,000 in September 1947 compared to a monthly average of 1,655,000 in 1946.

The only countries where these trends seem to have moved unambiguously against the wage earner in 1947 as compared to 1946 were Belgium and France, where in the course of 1947 the rise in wage rates fell below the rise in retail prices. Belgium also had a noticeably less tight labour market in the second half of 1947 than all the other western European countries except the defeated Axis powers. No one, however, has made or is likely to make the argument that Belgium was in danger of 'going communist' or that it was even suffering economic distress. The question is a more serious one for France where the evidence points to sudden and exaggerated changes in the material standard of living of the majority of the population from the end of the war to the end of 1947. Even here it would be wrong to be too categorical, for the information on price movements and on the cost of living is far from comprehensive and reveals wide differences between Paris and provincial France. Nor is the French data such that an overall comparison can reasonably be made with the calculations for other countries. Even if the very large money wage increases awarded in 1946 were mopped up by inflation and the removal of food subsidies in 1947 there was sufficient delay to allow them to contribute to an improvement in material standards in 1946. If the course of wages and salaries and an index of retail prices are plotted against time over the recovery period the result indicates, however, that in 1947 the rise in retail prices was almost twice as great as that in wages and salaries both in Paris and the provinces. The indications are also that this gap began to open up rapidly after March. As in Italy the prevalence of black market prices, especially in towns, must be allowed for, although their level probably fell between 1946 and 1947. Making this same assumption Lehoulier estimated that the real wage of an unmarried trained worker would have declined by ten percentage points between October 1946 and October 1947.[13] The money wages of industrial workers in Paris stayed well in advance of prices of essential foodstuffs until the third quarter of 1946 when prices overtook wages. In the first two quarters of 1947 there were corrective trends when bread and milk prices were held below the upward movement of wages, but from June onwards the trend was wholly adverse to the wage earner.[14]

[13] J. Lehoulier, 'L'évolution des salaires', *Revue d'économie politique*, novembre-décembre, 1948, numéro spécial, *La France économique et financière en 1947*, p. 191.
[14] J.-L. Guglielmi and M. Perrot, *Salaires et revendications sociales en France 1944–1952* (Paris, 1953), pp. 184–5.

This was the background to the wave of strikes which began in April with the strike at the Renault works. The strike movement took the trade unions and the Communist Party by surprise and placed the latter in an extremely awkward position inside the government. It may be that after May the political tensions consequent on the break-up of the coalition government and the departure of the communists gave an extra impetus to this activity, but it is not until November, when the strike movement reached a further peak, that it was actively supported by the Communist Party. Even then the deterioration in the workers' standard of living was still fuelling the political discontent.

What the trends of money wages and cost of living indices indicate, if we plot them in this way, are abstract, partial, and in many cases probably not very accurate approximations to what the historian would actually wish to measure and assess. The sources of the wage data are incomplete and unrepresentative when compared to the sweeping nature of the question posed. The official cost of living indices have the grave defects already commented on. Gross measurements of consumption as a part of gross national product do not bring us any nearer the historical reality of 1947. For most countries in western Europe the proportion of GNP going to private consumption was lower than in 1938 and this reflected mainly the higher proportion of GNP going towards investment under the various public and private efforts towards reconstruction. Only in Portugal, which had pursued a beneficial neutrality in the war, was there a tendency in the other direction. On the other hand, some of the smaller proportion going to private consumption was accounted for by a larger share going to public consumption and this was especially the case in countries like Norway and Britain where the access of most of the population to public goods greatly improved after 1945.[15] More extensive social insurance and welfare schemes, of which the British National Health Service was the most remarkable example, were an immediate response by many governments to the war and the unpleasant social and economic experiences of the inter-war years. In the three countries that mainly worried the American administration, however, Germany, France and Italy, this compensatory movement towards more public consumption does not yet appear. The high level of net investment rates in France during the period was accompanied by a very low comparative level of investment in housing and certain other public services.

In short, the statistical evidence can give only a very impressionistic and superficial answer to the question whether social conditions were deteriorating to the point where electors in France and Italy might vote into power a communist-led government. In any case, such a method of analysis is open to precisely the same reproach as the basic assumption in Washington that communist votes were generated by hunger and discontent; it is too simple.

[15] The share of public consumption in GNP at 1938 prices in Norway was 7 per cent in 1938 and 10 per cent in 1947. A. Bourneuf, *Norway. The Planned Revival* (Cambridge, Mass., 1958).

All the statistical evidence shows is, firstly, that it is most improbable, except in the cases of Belgium, Italy and France, that social conditions were worse in summer 1947 than in 1946, that for those in work in Italy they were very soon to improve, and that in comparison with the pre-war years, they varied very widely from country to country. These variations were to be more important in shaping the pattern of European history in the reconstruction period than the similarities. They represented very significant differences in the experience of the war and the choice of economic policy. The persistent lag of wage rates behind the cost of living in the Netherlands, for example, represents a lower level of private consumption than in the 1930s, while the temporary movement of retail prices above wage rates in Belgium in 1947 has to be seen in the context of a generally higher level of availability of employment and real earnings than before the war, as well as a greater degree of availability of consumer goods than in other countries.

What most concerned the population of western Europe on a daily material level was food. Industrial output in western Europe made an impressive recovery from the war, faster than after 1918. By summer 1947 it was below the 1938 level only in Belgium, France, Germany, Italy and the Netherlands. Agricultural output recovered much more slowly. Only the United Kingdom, Sweden and Switzerland had emerged in 1945 with a higher level of agricultural output than before the war. Even in the crop year 1948/9 the level of agricultural production in western Europe was still only about 91 per cent of its average levels in the period 1934–8 and by then only one further country, Denmark, had regained its pre-war levels of output.[16] In a period when controls on consumption were widespread and there was a prevailing world food shortage the extent to which the wage packet could command a supply of food was probably a more sensitive indicator of economic distress than a hypothetical real wage calculation.

Unfortunately, the food consumption figures which exist, although they take us a step further into the discussion, are themselves not so convincing as to lead to a categorical historical judgement. The data set out in table 2 show a general improvement in food availability in 1947 compared to 1946, but rationing systems were so various that there may well have been a great difference between theoretical and actual availability of food. Where rationing had proceeded undisturbed by enemy occupiers, invading allies and total changes of government, as it had in Britain, the data are obviously more meaningful than elsewhere. The International Emergency Food Organization of the Food and Agriculture Organization estimated there to be four countries, Denmark, France, Sweden and Britain, where food consumption was lower in spring 1947 than in spring 1946.[17] But in fact the only major category of

[16] UN, *Economic Survey of Europe in 1948*, p. 17.
[17] UN, Department of Economic Affairs, *Post-War Shortages of Food and Coal* (Geneva, 1948), p. 15.

food whose consumption dropped in Britain in 1947 was meat, whereas that of all other categories increased slightly.[18] In Denmark there were falls in consumption of all major categories of foodstuffs except sugar.[19] But the level of calorific consumption was higher in Denmark in 1946 than in any other European country and the deliberate reduction in food imports to provide more fodder imports did not impose any great strain on the country's social fabric. In the Netherlands, where of all the western European countries real incomes were furthest below their pre-war level, there was a general improvement in average levels of food consumption in 1947 over 1946.[20] In the worst-fed countries there was an improvement in total food availability, although in Austria, Germany and Italy the level of calorific intake was still too low to sustain a proper level of health for long. For France the information is too sketchy to permit generalization. There were difficulties in obtaining sufficient wheat from farmers throughout the summer and from August bread in Paris was made out of a mixture with maize. But these problems were related to errors in pricing policy as much as to the catastrophic harvest, whose baleful influence was felt mainly in 1948.

One possible check on these rather fragmentary evidences is the movement of infant mortality. It showed a steady improvement from the end of the war everywhere and there was no increase in infant mortality rates in 1947. In fact in that year infant mortality rates in Austria and the Netherlands returned to pre-war levels leaving only France and Germany with figures worse than pre-war.

The evidence, therefore, is as much against the proposition that standards of living were dropping generally in western Europe in 1947 as it is against the proposition that millions of people were slowly starving, as it is against the proposition that the rate of growth of output was falling. Rather the evidence is of an uneven but unmistakable improvement, sometimes mitigated by growing inadequacies or injustices in the rationing system, sometimes overshadowed by the sudden redistribution of welfare which could come from the abandonment of controls, or from rapid inflation, but real enough to sustain hope.

It was from deeper wells than hunger or material distress that any crisis in economic and social morale among western Europe's population would have been drawn. What was more at stake than the precise question of whether conditions in 1947 were better than in 1946 was the amount of hope for the future. Judgements on the standard of living in 1947 were everywhere made not with 1946 only in mind but in comparison with the 1930s. The purpose of the horror and misery of 1939–45 had come almost everywhere to be seen as

---

[18] UK, Central Statistical Office, *Annual Abstract of Statistics*, 86, 1938–48 (London, 1949).

[19] Denmark, Statistiske Department, *Statistisk Arbog*, 1950.

[20] Netherlands, Centraal Bureau voor de Statistiek, *Jaarcijfers voor Nederland 1947–50* (Utrecht, 1951), pp. 276–7.

the creation of a 'better' society and for that high purpose hardships could be politically justified. The scope of political opportunity for governments was wider in that respect than before or later. The massive consumer pressures on them, which were to dominate the next two decades, had not begun and even where government policy, as in Britain or France, deliberately sought to restrict consumption, it could still retain a sufficient body of allegiance to the pursuit of higher national goals. The waves of strikes in 1947 in France and the high communist vote there and in Italy were the product of a complicated interplay of political aspirations, of the defeat of hopes for more radical social and economic change, of the fear that such change might not be prevented by the traditional parliamentary, democratic mechanisms, of the realization that the decisions on the post-war nature of the country could no longer be postponed. Because these political tensions existed against a background of booming business conditions and falling real wages, they were given a greater immediacy and acuteness in France and expressed in a more urgent and vociferous clamour of political argument. Yet the capacity of French governments to find a consensus on their plans for internal and external reconstruction in the next three and a half years emerges time and again from this book. It was more difficult once the Communist Party had gone from office, but the consensus was there and its basis was the hope of change from the stagnation and menace of the 1930s.

THE INTERNATIONAL ECONOMIC CRISIS

If there was no weakening in the rate of growth of output, a tendency for income and social conditions to improve, no collapse of morale, to what may the balance of payments problems which resulted in the end of sterling–dollar convertibility and in the Marshall Plan be attributed? Given the uninterruptedly rising trend of output, imports were crucial, and as western European production climbed rapidly towards and in many cases above pre-war levels the volume of imports necessary to sustain it seems on all the evidence to have been greater per unit of output relative to pre-war. The value of imports was much higher in most countries than the value of exports. This repeated the experience of 1919 and 1920 and had been not only anticipated but assumed to be an inevitable short-term consequence of the end of the war and the urgent tasks of economic reconstruction. All western European governments, according to the size of their reserves, their access to aid, and their policy predilections, had some time horizon in mind by which the balance of payments would have moved into equilibrium or surplus. All were assuming large balance of payments deficits in 1946 which would begin to diminish in 1947.

But what happened instead was that for some European countries the deficit in merchandise trade, the gap between imports for domestic consumption and exports of domestically produced goods, which had indeed in most cases begun to narrow during the winter of 1946/7, began to widen again in 1947. The most striking examples are those of the United Kingdom (figure 4) and Italy (figure 5). The closing of the gap again in Italy later in the year represents the drastic change in economic policy during that year, from the readiness with which bank capital was made available in the first half of the year to the restrictions imposed from July onwards.

In six western European countries in all, Denmark, Ireland, Italy, the Netherlands, Portugal and the United Kingdom, the gap between imports and exports widened once more in the first seven months of 1947. In France and Norway the gap failed to close further. This widening in no way corresponded to an equivalent improvement in invisible earnings or in foreign exchange and gold holdings. Indeed, it corresponded with the increasingly firm public declarations of the intention of the United States to cut back on the international post-war relief programmes which recycled dollars into the international economy. The great difference in size of total imports between these countries was such that, seen statistically, most of western Europe's deficit on trade with the United States could be attributed to three countries, Britain, France and Italy, and most of the increase in the deficit to Britain, Italy and the Netherlands. In March and May for example the first three accounted for 63 per cent of western Europe's deficit on merchandise trade with the United States and these proportions did not fall significantly. But Italy's share of the total deficit fell steeply after the deflationary policies introduced in the summer. Britain's share thus automatically increased by virtue of the fact that her total imports from all sources were about one-third of the west European total. If we measure the *increase* in the size of western Europe's deficit over the first six months of 1947, the Netherlands appears as an important contributor and France does not significantly contribute. On the other hand, the value of French imports was so high that it was a matter of no small anxiety that the trade gap there failed to close. But what is more interesting historically is that the same phenomenon appeared in so many countries, even if their imports were relatively unimportant as a part of western Europe's total.

The reasons were much debated at the time. The one that found most favour in the United States was that unchecked inflation in Europe combined with over-valued exchange rates stimulated European imports and weakened exports. In most countries there were pervasive controls, in all areas of the economy, designed to prevent the excess liquidity left over from the war years or still being created by the reconstruction from being absorbed by an increase in imports. Whether these were fully effective in the conditions prevailing in spring and summer 1947 is an interesting question.[21] But there are many

[21] R. Triffin, *Europe and the Money Muddle* (New Haven, 1957) argues that they could not have been because had they effectively prevented foreign supply from mopping up excess liquidity, that liquidity would then have been mopped up in the diversion of resources and goods

reasons other than excess liquidity left over by wartime financing which account for the relentless growth of imports. In what were in most countries general boom conditions, encouraged by government, supply had become a crucial factor and the evidence shows that if the ratio of imports to exports increased this was because countries wanted it to do so, or at least were not prepared to stop it by applying existing controls more effectively.

The days had long gone in most European countries when a diminution of the foreign exchange and gold reserves to finance a large and growing trade deficit would have been an immediate indicator to the government to change its domestic economic course. For many of them the last sixteen years had been filled with experiments whose aim was to make the level of employment and welfare within the country less dependent on its external balances. Certain countries had embarked on reconstruction with the intention of using their gold and foreign exchange reserves for a time as a source of investment, in the sense that these were the only foreseeable means for the purchase of imports of investment goods above the income to be derived from the probable post-war level of exports. This was the intention, for example, in both France and Norway. In Britain domestic economic policy too was aimed at acquiring a certain independence from reserve movements even though the Anglo-American financial agreements had stipulated the limited free convertibility of sterling into dollars for current account transactions. At the start of July, however, the 'due date' for the official declaration of convertibility, the British trade balance was far worse than at any time since mid-1946 and was deteriorating rapidly.

The means used to finance these growing trade deficits were very variable both because the policies of different countries varied so much in this respect and because the experience of the 1930s and the war had created such big differences in the size of national gold and foreign exchange reserves. None the less, that these trade gaps were allowed to grow (table 3) when there was no visible sign that the United States would be prepared to finance them poses a searching question about the intentions of western European governments and it does so the more because of the greatly increased importance of imports from the United States and the much greater trade and payments deficits with that country than had existed before the war. Within the general and growing deficit of western Europe's trade was embedded a much larger deficit with the United States.

Opinion at the time was sharply divided about whether this was a long-run structural problem of the world economy or a temporary problem of the aftermath of the war. The great richness in resources of the United States, the highly protectionist policies pursued there in the inter-war period and specific

from exports, and it is very difficult to find any evidence of a weakening of Europe's export position in 1947. But Britain, whose exports grew very rapidly and where the rate of inflation was comparatively low, generated the largest absolute increase in the commercial deficit and this could plausibly be attributed to structural problems in the British economy.

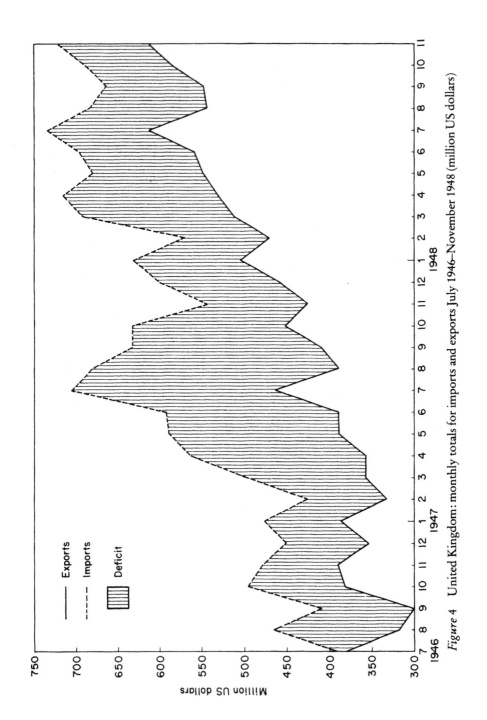

Figure 4 United Kingdom: monthly totals for imports and exports July 1946–November 1948 (million US dollars)

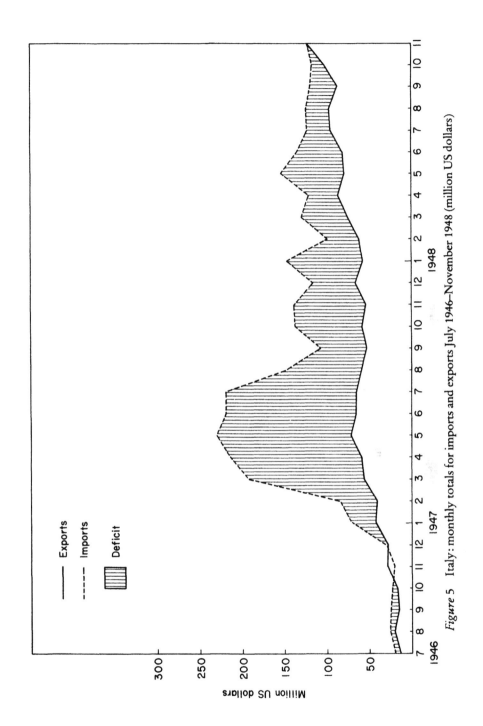

Figure 5 Italy: monthly totals for imports and exports July 1946–November 1948 (million US dollars)

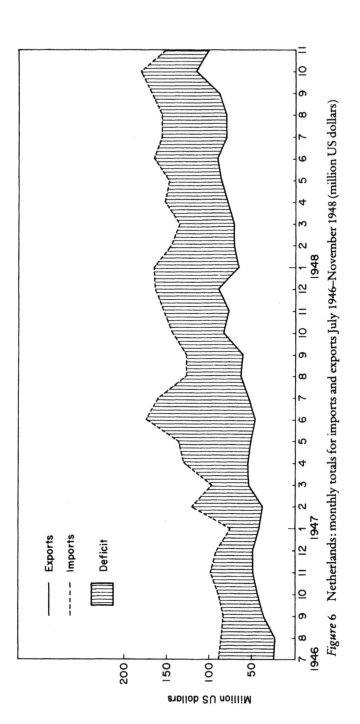

Figure 6 Netherlands: monthly totals for imports and exports July 1946–November 1948 (million US dollars)

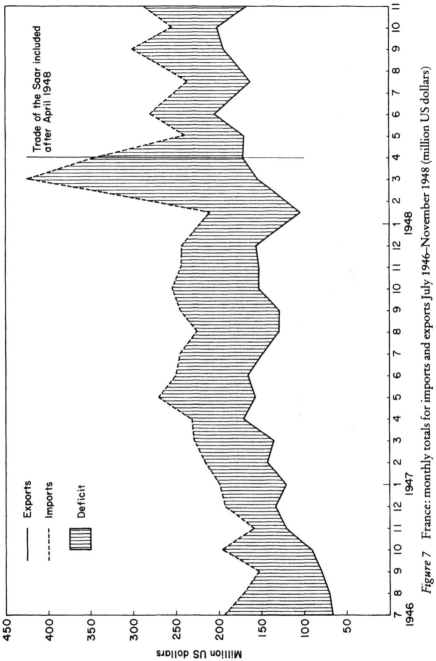

Figure 7 France: monthly totals for imports and exports July 1946–November 1948 (million US dollars)

Table 3   Deficits on merchandise trade with the United States (million current dollars)

	1946	1947
Austria	(+)0.56	(+)0.38
Belgium/Luxembourg	192.07	457.38
Denmark	42.38	104.96
France	649.13	956.19
Ireland	31.84	116.75
Italy	112.19	350.06
Netherlands	187.13	431.13
Norway	83.28	173.43
Portugal	41.28	99.89
Sweden	156.02	358.63
Switzerland	21.99	148.22
United Kingdom	764.07	950.08

Source: OEEC, *Statistical Bulletins of Foreign Trade*.

economic developments during the war had all meant that the growth of American imports had not kept pace with the growth of national income. Although the level of output of manufactures there was 70 per cent higher than in 1937, the best year in the 1930s, the quantum of imports was below the 1937 level and this was representative of what had been a continuing long-term trend. Furthermore the principal category of western European exports, finished manufactured goods, as a proportion of American imports, had in fact fallen during the war from 21.4 per cent to 17.5 per cent. What was more the proportion of those manufactures being supplied from Europe had fallen even more steeply from just under a half to less than a third (table 4). The insecure hold which European exporters of manufactures had had on the difficult American market in the 1930s had been broken by the war, because

Table 4   Composition of United States imports (million current dollars)

	From the World				From Europe	
	1938	1946	1936–40 average	% of total import trade	1946	% of total import trade
Crude materials	576	1726	109.2	(13.5)	177.4	(10.3)
Crude foodstuffs	260	814	11.2	(3.5)	15.4	(1.9)
Manufactured foodstuffs	312	503	107.0	(31.0)	99.8	(19.8)
Semi-manufactures	386	929	179.6	(35.1)	193.3	(20.8)
Finished manufactures	418	845	212.3	(46.6)	268.3	(31.7)

Source: *Statistical Abstract of the United States*.

except from the neutral countries exports had been either severely restricted to divert goods to the war effort or had been commercially impossible.

Western Europe had throughout the inter-war period and particularly in the 1930s run substantial deficits on trade with the United States. These deficits had been financed by invisible earnings in dollars and by export surpluses to other areas of the world. This pattern was not to prove a very good basis for the post-war world. The great expansion of world trade since 1945 has been driven forward by the growing tendency of the developed economies to exchange manufactured products. The United States itself was eventually caught up in the same tendency so that politicians there now look back nostalgically to a period when imports were so much smaller a part of America's total resources. That Europe should have balanced its accounts with the United States to such an extent through dollar earnings in third markets, while it might be construed as an example of the tendency to reach equilibrium in trade and payments, was not a good omen for the future of that equilibrium. The immediate possibilities of increasing European exports to America in the post-war world however were very limited in spite of the great increases in consumer purchasing power which the war brought there. Meanwhile America had become the chief, in some cases the only, source of the imports needed for reconstruction purposes. The increased dependence on imports from the United States and the fact that this was not compensated for by an increase in exports there emerges clearly from table 5. The overall deficit of western Europe on visible trade with America in 1946 was overwhelmingly made up of the deficits of the largest traders, 60 per cent of it by British and French import surpluses. But by 1947 the medium-sized European traders, Belgium, the Netherlands, Italy and Sweden also had large deficits in their trade with America.

If the relationship of the largest of the European exporters, Britain, to the composition of United States imports is considered, not only the immediate

Table 5 Balance of trade of Western Europe with the United States (million current dollars)

1937	–	−655.57
1938	–	−898.66
1946	–	−2356.11
1947	–	−4742.14
1948	–	−3345.47
1949	–	−3491.59
1950	–	−1755.92
1951	–	−2510.71

Source: National Trade Returns; OEEC, *Statistical Bulletin of Foreign Trade*.

difficulties of increasing exports to the United States become apparent, but also the fact that an increase over a longer period of time required either a great readjustment of manufacturing industry in Britain or sweeping changes in United States trade policy and consumer preferences. The principal commodities in the British export trade to the United States in 1946 and 1947 were pottery, whisky, cotton yarn and cloth, linoleum, woollen waste and rags, wool yarn, woollen and worsted manufactures, knitted goods, rayon goods and books. Exports to the United States represented 7 per cent of British exports in 1937, only 5 per cent in 1947, and not a single one of these leading commodities was among the twenty most valuable categories of United States imports. The situation for other western European exporters was the same, except for Norway and Sweden whose exports of wood pulp and paper fed one of the staple United States import trades. With this exception European exports to America consisted mainly of expensive consumer goods.

From an American viewpoint it was easy to assume that European manufactures did not sell sufficiently well in the United States to reduce this trade deficit because the lower level of productivity in European manufacturing industry and the overvaluation of European currencies made their prices too high. The wide gap between productivity levels in America and Europe was the outcome of the great gains in productivity in American manufacturing industry which technological innovation had brought during the labour shortage caused by the war, gains which it had been impossible and pointless to emulate in most continental European countries. There, the response to occupation had often been deliberately to employ labour at low levels of productivity and in any case the manufacturing industries of many continental European countries had suffered at least four years of disinvestment and depreciation of the capital stock. It was even argued at the time that the gap in productivity would prove a long-run structural change which would make the return to international economic equilibrium more difficult.[22] In fact all that was needed was for Europe to copy and apply the innovations in wartime America to make substantial productivity gains, a process of course much furthered by the tight labour markets which policy in many countries sought to induce. That higher manufacturing costs could coexist in 1947 with an overvalued exchange rate was certainly an indicator of how acute was the shortage of certain products. Belgian steel exports to other western European economies sold at twice the price of United States steel delivered in Europe. But so long as European sales stayed high there seemed no point in devaluing, for it would merely decrease the price of exports, put up the price of imports and possibly make the trade deficits worse.

The very large general American advantage over western Europe in terms of productivity, measured in terms of output per man hour, in manufacturing

[22] The argument recurs several times in J.H. Williams, *Economic Stability in a Changing World* (New York, 1953).

industry was mitigated by lower labour costs in western Europe. When the differences in the 'productivity gap' between one industry and another (for they were much less in some than others) are put into the balance with the lower wage levels in western Europe it appears that, discounting the effects of tariffs or artificially maintained exchange rates, western European exports would already have had a comparative advantage in certain lines of manufactures over American.[23] A devaluation of European currencies against the dollar might well have cancelled out many of America's comparative advantages in international trade, but in realistic terms if a payments equilibrium were to be re-established by the growth of European exports, whether through a rapid improvement in levels of productivity in European industry or through a devaluation, it would have to be after the war as it had been before, either through European dollar earnings in third markets or through invisible dollar earnings.

At the time the argument was made that the war had so changed the pattern of American production and trade as radically to impede the long-run capacity of underdeveloped economies outside Europe to earn dollars.[24] There is very little evidence to support such an analysis and much more to support the view that in this case all that was at stake was a very brief distortion in trade, the direct outcome of strategic pressures in wartime, which was already being corrected as Europe's dollar deficits grew. Although the geographical area from which America's main raw material imports came had been very much circumscribed during the war, by the activities of the enemy and by the need for the speediest possible turn-round of ships, the growth of output and consumption soon spread the demand for primary products away once more from the confines of the dollar area and back to more traditional areas of supply. The pattern was complicated and the process of import-substitution developed in the United States during the war did make a difference in the post-war world. But with such a high level of demand emanating from America, the physical damage done to underdeveloped economies by occupying forces (both friends and enemies) was probably a greater restriction on their level of exports to the United States in 1947 than any longer-run changes in the pattern of American demand.

This may be seen from the example of the biggest pre-war dollar earner among the underdeveloped countries, Malaya, which had been the major source of sterling area dollar earnings. Malaya's dollar surplus came almost entirely from exports of rubber and tin. The occupation damaged both mines

---

[23] For the United Kingdom, Sir D. McDougall, 'British and American exports: a study suggested by the theory of comparative costs', in *ibid. Studies in Political Economy*, vol. 2 (London, 1975) was able to show that, theoretically, these might include several major British manufacturing sectors.

[24] It appears, for example, in UN, *Economic Survey 1948*, as an argument to suggest that only long-run corrective action by the United States to re-cycle dollars to such countries could restore an equilibrium.

and smelters and the output of ore did not return to its 1937–9 average until 1950. Meanwhile, in the United States during the war the government had financed the construction of a new smelter designed to use concentrates which originated mainly in Bolivia and Indonesia. The pre-war import pattern of tin metal imports was that 70 per cent had come from Malaya. This proportion still held good in 1947 and 1948 but imports of ore and concentrates were now 70 per cent as high as those of metal. The war had in fact created a new trade in which Malaya did not participate. But her share in the older trade was not diminished and the new trade meant substantial dollar gains for Indonesia, like Malaya a crucial area for balancing European–American settlements. Natural rubber was a more important dollar earner than tin. Although the United States developed a large synthetic rubber industry during the war this did not reduce the post-war demand for natural rubber. Its output in Malaya in 1947 was already 58 per cent higher than in the period 1937–9.[25] Net exports in 1947, at 58,000 tonnes, were well above the level of 1938, 31,000 tonnes, admittedly a year of abnormally low United States demand. Total sales to America were slightly higher in value in 1947 than the average for the period 1934–8 and in 1948 were almost twice as high.[26]

If the overall pattern of United States raw material imports is considered, the only reasonable conclusion would be that the war changed the overall relationship of the various staple import trades to each other but, by 1947, had certainly not resulted in a lower level of demand for primary products. Thus imports of fats, oils and vegetable sources of fats and oils in 1947 were only between 60 and 65 per cent of their pre-war level and subsequently diminished. By contrast imports of crude petroleum were more than three times greater than in the 1930s, a sign of troubles to come. The increase in the volume of rubber imports over the same period was 45 per cent and for sugar, softwoods and petroleum products there were also very large increases.[27]

If the third markets in which European exporters had previously earned dollars could no longer finance so large a part of western Europe's trade deficits with the United States that was not because they were now unable to earn dollars to the same extent. It was because those European deficits were much greater and because the demand for dollar imports in the underdeveloped world was also much greater. A higher share of the dollar earnings of third markets went in fact to finance imports from the dollar zone into those markets. In that respect the underdeveloped world was facing the same temporary reconstruction problems as Europe, a desperate need for imports which, in far greater proportion than before the war, had to be purchased in

---

[25] USA, ECA, *The Sterling Area* (London, 1951), p. 373.
[26] Value of crude rubber exports from Malaya to the United States,
       1934–8   annual average $101.4 million
       1948 $194.2 million
   USA, *Foreign Commerce and Navigation of the United States*.
[27] USA, ECA, *The Sterling Area*, statistical appendix B.

dollars. The central problems, therefore, in correcting the balance of visible trade between western Europe and the dollar zone were two, one a purely temporary one, the aftermath of the war, and the other a longer-term one which might not unfairly be termed structural.

The first was that the high demand for imports, all over the world, focused on the United States as the one overwhelmingly predominant supplier. This applied as much outside Europe as to western Europe itself and in so doing weakened one of western Europe's established methods of financing its habitual dollar deficits. In the first half of 1947 United States exports were roughly a third of total world exports. Fundamentally this was a reflection of the fact that the United States had emerged from the war with much higher levels of output and productivity than in the pre-war period, while all other major industrial producers had either had exactly the opposite experience or, as in the case of Britain, had drastically reduced their exports in order to direct materials into war production. This dependence on the United States meant that the composition of United States exports to western Europe showed striking temporary differences from the established long-run pattern. This was especially noticeable in the high level of exports of food and coal.

The war marked a clear divide in the pattern of western Europe's food imports. Shortages of fertilizer, manpower, fodder, horses and machines became endemic in the agricultural surplus countries of central and eastern Europe during the war. Their agriculture suffered a far more severe drop in productivity and output than the agriculture of the more capitalized and resilient food-importing countries of western Europe, which itself recovered much more slowly than manufacturing industry. The consequence was that the large food surpluses which had been traded from central and eastern Europe to the western European countries disappeared during the war. They did not reappear afterwards. At the same time many Asian food surplus countries also ceased to provide the same surpluses to the international food trade. By the damage which it did to agriculture the war left the United States, where strenuous if not always successful efforts had been made to expand agricultural output during the war, as the obvious alternative source. Agricultural exports from the United States rose in constant (1913) dollars by 57 per cent between 1938 and 1947.[28]

It is generally implied that western Europe, because it had to find its food imports in the United States rather than elsewhere, was placed in a more difficult situation after 1945. Most accounts make much of the remarkably poor European harvest in 1947, the worst of the century, and the consequent need for an increase in food imports from the United States and Canada as a cause of Europe's payments crisis in 1947. That the weather was curious and the harvest very poor is indisputable. The exceptionally harsh winter in

[28] R.E. Lipsey, *Price and Quantity Trends in the Foreign Trade of the United States*, National Bureau of Economic Research (Princeton, 1963), table A-7.

north-western Europe followed by a summer drought resulted in crop yields which in some countries were extraordinarily low. The number of days of frost in the midlands and south of England was about 75 per cent above the average for the period 1914–40 and the mean daily temperatures in February 1947 10° Fahrenheit below average.[29] Over northern France and the Low Countries the same sharp variations from the norm can be observed. This was followed over the whole of the wheat and barley-growing areas of northern France as far south as the Loire valley by a summer where rainfall between April and October was just above half the normal quantity and the number of days with temperatures above 30° centigrade four times as great.[30] The Mediterranean zone was spared these abnormal conditions but over almost the whole of western Europe's main grain-growing areas yields and harvests were far worse than in 1946, whereas it might otherwise have been hoped that they would show a substantial recovery. The production of every major arable crop except potatoes fell.

That all these events were responsible for the increase in western Europe's imports from America in 1947 over 1938 is, however, an almost entirely unjustified assumption. The effects of the 1947 harvest on foreign trade would not in any case be fully felt until 1948, although there was an increase in food imports in the second half of 1947. It is, furthermore, only true that the disappearance of food surpluses in central and eastern Europe increased western Europe's dependence on the United States in the sense that the proportion of western Europe's food imports originating in the United States increased (table 6). The absolute level of food and fodder imports into western

Table 6   Proportion of Western Europe's* food imports originating in the dollar zone

	1934–8	1949–51
	%	%
Wheat	39.2	81.7
Maize and barley	11.8	47.1
Cane sugar	42.6	64.9
Fats and oils	5.1†	16.8
Meat	7.1	8.8
Crude tobacco	54.2	63.5

Source: UN, *Economic Survey of Europe Since the War* (Geneva, 1953), pp. 284 ff.

* The six major food importers, Belgium/Luxembourg, France, Germany (1934–8 all Germany, 1949–51 western zones), Italy, the Netherlands and the United Kingdom.
† 1938 only.

[29] UK, *Annual Abstract of Statistics*, pp. 2–5.
[30] J. Sanson, 'Les principales anomalies météorologiques de l'année 1947 en France', *Annales de Géographie*, lvii, 1948.

Europe from the United States was only a little higher in 1947 than 1938. Both the level and variety of food consumption in Europe were depressed by rationing and related controls so that few foodstuffs were imported in significantly greater quantity than before the war. Wheat and flour were the two most striking, but the United States was also able to develop new food trades to western Europe. In 1947 there were significant imports of American dairy products into western Europe, a trade which had scarcely existed in 1938 (table 7).

But, as table 8 shows, the contribution of the increased imports of food, fodder and drink to the total increase in western Europe's imports from the United States in 1947 as compared to 1938 was insignificant, relatively unimportant in relation to other categories of imports, except in Britain and the two neutral countries which had accumulated enough gold and hard currency reserves during the war to sate their post-war hunger and slake their post-war thirst on American surpluses. The information in table 8 does not, however, include Germany or Italy because of the absence of data accurate enough to use as a basis for the calculations, and both of these countries were much more dependent on American food imports than before the war. The level of food consumption there, however, was lower than anywhere else in western Europe. Foodstuffs were only a third of all Italian imports in 1947 so that even if the whole lot came from the United States the impression conveyed by table 8 would not be greatly affected. Of the countries for which data are available the average national increase in food and drink imports from the United States in 1947 over 1938 was only 16.9 per cent, and over 1946 even less, 12.4 per cent, and this figure is greatly swollen by the propensity of Portugal and Switzerland, whose food imports were very small in absolute terms, to import American food. If the total sum of 'extra' American food imports by all these countries is measured against their total of 'extra' American imports of all kinds it amounts to no more than about 3 per cent. For the cause of western Europe's increasing trade and dollar deficit we must therefore look elsewhere.

Table 7 American food exports to Western Europe*
(million 1947 dollars, fob)

	1938	1947	1948
Grain and cereals	458	869	883
Fruit and nuts	167	98	101
Meat and meat products	53	99	20
Dairy products	1	148	61
Fats, oils and oilseeds	49	77	79
Tobacco and manufactures	193	178	184
Total of these categories	921	1469	1328

Source: UN, *Economic Survey of Europe in 1948*, p. 128.

* Excludes Italy and Portugal.
  Includes Germany, Finland and Iceland.

Table 8   Increases in imports from the United States in 1947 accounted for by different types of commodity

	Category 'A' % increase in imports of capital goods and metals		Category 'B' % increase in imports of coal and coke		Category 'C' % increase in imports of food, fodder and drink*		Category 'A' imports as % of all imports from USA by the group	Category 'B' imports as % of all imports from USA by the group	Category 'C' imports as % of all imports from USA by the group
	1947/1938	1947/1946	1947/1938	1947/1946	1947/1938	1947/1946	1947	1947	1947
Denmark	29.8	29.3	45.4	39.2	-4.4	12.2	1.1	0.3	0.6
France	29.9	54.8	27.3	56.1	15.0	-10.7	9.9	7.6	0.5
Ireland	17.3	15.6	29.5	34.8	9.8	17.5	0.6	0.8	0.6
Netherlands	32.0	51.8	10.1	11.4	16.1	0.4	4.1	1.3	2.0
Norway	59.1	72.5	9.9	-10.6	6.1	-1.4	3.1	0.5	0.4
Portugal	37.3	46.3	15.5	32.6	26.5	22.3	1.2	0.5	0.8
Switzerland	27.8	28.1	8.4	8.8	31.1	40.3	1.7	0.5	2.0
United Kingdom	26.3	37.7	3.4	4.4	35.2	18.3	6.1	0.4	4.0
							27.8	11.9	10.9

Sources: Denmark, *Vareomsaetningen med Udlandet*; France. *Tableau général du commerce extérieur*; Ireland, *Trade and Shipping Statistics*; Netherlands, *Maandstatistiek van den In-Uit en Doorvoer van Nederland*; Norway, *Norges Handel*; Portugal, *Comércio Externo*; Switzerland, *Jahresstatistik des Aussenhandels der Schweiz*; United Kingdom, *Accounts Relating to the Trade and Navigation of the United Kingdom, Annual Statement of the United Kingdom*.

* Includes live animals and oils and fats for food and fodder.

American dairy products were not the only unusual American export to find their way onto European markets after the war; 1947 was also a year of costly imports of American coal. Like the increase in imports of food this could also be directly attributed to the war. It was a universal experience in European coal-mines during the war, in spite of the great demand for coal, that productivity and output declined. As in the agricultural sector this was the direct outcome of shortages of labour, capital and technological inputs. Most mines were already facing a tendency for productivity to decline and the war accelerated this. Coal output in 1947 in Western Europe was about 97 million tonnes less than the average for 1934–8 (table 10). The shortfall was partly made up by imports from America, amounting to 34 million tonnes in 1947.

No American coal had been exported to Europe in 1938 and the dollar burden of these new imports was more significant as a part of the increase in the deficit with the United States than was the increase in food imports. As table 8 shows this was particularly the case for three countries, Denmark, Ireland and France, and the volume of French coal imports from the United States made a significant increase in western Europe's total deficit. None the less coal accounted for only 3.4 per cent of the United Kingdom's increased imports from the United States and since British imports were one-third of Western Europe's, and the increase in British imports as a part of the increase in Western Europe's even larger, the relatively small contribution which the increase in American coal imports made to Western Europe's trade problems can be easily seen. Their contribution to the average increase in imports of western European countries from America in 1947 over 1938 was 18.7 per cent, and over 1946 22.1 per cent.

What did cause the increase in the trade deficit? It was neither a failure of

Table 9   Coal output in Western Europe (million tonnes)

	1934–8 (annual av.)	1946	1947
United Kingdom	230	193	204
Germany	159	66*	86*
France	46	47	45
Belgium	28	23	24
Netherlands	13	8	10
Total	476	337	369

Source: Belgium, *Annuaire Statistique de la Belgique*; France, *Annuaire Statistique*; Germany, *Wirtschaftsstatistik der deutschen Besatzungszonen*; Netherlands, *Zeventig Jaar Statistiek in Tydreksen*; UK, *Annual Abstract of Statistics*.

* Fontiers after Potsdam.

Table 10   Investment ratios in western Europe, 1938 and 1947

	Gross domestic capital formation as a % of national income at factor cost		Net domestic capital formation as a % of national income at factor cost		Net investment in fixed capital as a % of national income in 1938 dollar prices	
	1938	1947	1938	1947	1938	1947
Denmark	22	23	9	9	8	11
France	17	22	3	9	2	8
Italy	19	23	9	13	10	9
Netherlands	22	35	12	20	10	12
Norway	46*	48	15*	25	15	24
Sweden	31†	36	11†	17	9	13
United Kingdom	17	21	7	9	8	9

Source: UN, *Economic Survey of Europe in 1948*, pp. 45, 47.

* 1939.   † 1938–9.

output in western Europe nor the inability of western Europe to supply itself with food, but the consistent, very large increases in imports of capital goods and metals attributable to the vigour and success of Europe's industrial recovery. Of the eight countries included in table 8 these commodities account on average for 42.1 per cent of the increase in American imports over 1946 and they make the biggest contribution to the increase for every country except Denmark and Ireland, both of which had no coal and so were heavily dependent in that year on American coal shipments.

Capital goods, metals, vehicles, ships and planes were responsible for more than half the increase in imports in the three planned economies, France, the Netherlands and Norway. In France and Norway this was accompanied by a fall in imports of American food and fodder. Even in the United Kingdom the same commodities made a much bigger contribution to the *increase* in American imports in 1947 than did farm produce. The only country where imports of American food were the main cause of the increase in dollar imports was Switzerland. The deterioration in western Europe's balance of trade with the United States was largely caused by the very high and increasing level of imports of machinery, steel, and transport equipment.

The restocking boom, just as it had after 1918, gave rise to a high level of demand for machinery imports. With the elimination of Germany, which had become almost entirely a raw material exporter, the demand for machinery, machine-tools, vehicles, construction equipment and steel products could focus only on the United States. If we consider the most important of the western European importers, Britain, the importance of this switch becomes evident. In 1938 44 per cent of British imports of machinery by value came from the United States, 25 per cent from Germany. In 1947 65 per cent came from the United States and 3 per cent from Germany. To western Europe as a whole the increase in exports of capital goods and steel from the United States in 1947 over 1938 accounted for 61 per cent of the total increase in exports. The main contribution to the increase in dollar imports arose directly from the vigour of the European economic recovery. It arose not from any slackening off in that recovery in 1947 but from the increased level of investment in that year in plant, machinery and vehicles.

With interest rates held at remarkably low levels, with government funds earmarked for reconstruction purposes, and with several governments specifically favouring through trade controls the import of capital goods, it is easily understandable that increased dollar imports were concentrated in this area. The expansion of output in iron and steel, engineering, electricity, gas and building was faster than that of industrial production as a whole. But what provoked the payments crisis was the persistence of so many western European governments in that course as the available sources of finance for such imports dried up. They rushed towards the precipice of international bankruptcy with increasing speed and some overmastering force induced them to ignore all those warning signs which in the past, as in 1920, had been signals for a change of economic policy. The shift of emphasis towards investment, growth and high employment as prime objectives of policy became more marked as the immediate post-war upswing pursued its course, boosting what was already a high level of demand, and only Italy and Belgium proved willing in 1947 to allow that demand to sink back to a lower level. As resource utilization in many countries reached high levels in 1947 and absorbed the idle capacity present at the end of the war, new concepts of economic policy continued to promote high levels of capital formation and these in turn were reflected in the high and increasing level of imports of capital goods from the United States.

In the United Kingdom, for example, gross capital formation was about 21 per cent of national income, 4 per cent more than in 1938, a year of intensive rearmament. In Norway net domestic capital formation was about one-quarter of national income (table 10). In almost every western European country, with Germany as the one glaring exception, both gross and net capital formation were higher in 1947 than in 1938, in most cases much higher, and yet 1938 was for the continent as a whole and for the inter-war period a year of high investment levels (table 10).

It might be argued that these high levels of investment merely reflected very high levels of activity in construction because of the repair work which was the basis of physical reconstruction. It is possible to separate investment in the construction of dwellings from investment in other industries for some of the countries, however, and the figures show that it was only in the United Kingdom that investment in housing played a large part in the high investment ratios (table 11). In two of the planned economies, France and the Netherlands, there was a firm diversion of investment away from housing, which was

Table 11   Proportionate distribution (%) of total net fixed capital investment, 1947

	Private manu- facturing industry	Transport and com- munications	Housing
Belgium	13.9	34.7	11.8
Italy	8.0	66.8	2.9
Netherlands	30.9	41.3	−6.8
Norway	25.3	45.7	12.3
United Kingdom	20.2	21.1	31.6

Source: UN, *Economic Survey of Europe in 1949*, p. 41.

sacrificed to what were thought of as more urgent economic needs. In France only 25,000 dwellings were completed in 1946 and 38,000 in 1947, compared to 67,000 in 1938. In the Netherlands only 1600 were completed in 1946 and 9200 in 1947, compared to 39,400 in 1938.[31] Even in the United Kingdom, where the proportion of investment in housing was the highest of the countries in table 11, the total number of new dwellings completed in 1946 and 1947 (196,900) was only just over half the average annual total for the period 1935–8. What does appear from table 11, though, is the high proportion of investment in the transport and communications sector. Given the prevailing shortage of foreign earnings and the high dollar cost of using American bottoms new shipbuilding was a top priority everywhere in Europe. As table 12 shows, if Germany, where there were punitively strict controls on ship-building, is excluded, western European merchant fleets had virtually been restored to their pre-war size. The other major component of investment in this sector was infrastructural investment in railway and public transport systems.

Table 12   Size of Western European merchant fleets (thousand gross registered tons)

	1939	1947	1948	1949	1950
Denmark	1,175	1,025	1,123	1,170	1,269
France	2,934	2,327	2,786	3,070	3,207
Germany*	4,483	598	428	300	460
Italy	3,425	1,317	2,100	2,443	2,580
Netherlands	2,970	2,441	2,737	2,990	3,109
Norway	4,834	3,762	4,261	4,916	5,456
Sweden	1,577	1,830	1,973	2,048	2,048
United Kingdom	17,891	16,221	18,025	18,093	18,219

Source: *Lloyd's Register of Shipping*.

* 1939 = Grossdeutschland, 1947 onwards = western zones.

[31] OEEC, *Industrial Statistics 1900–1955* (Paris, 1955), p. 143.

The impact which high investment ratios had on western Europe's import trade in the circumstances of the post-war world can be seen from the example of France. The French government twice drew up import projections in 1946 to cover the period to the end of 1950 and did so in the full knowledge that the import programmes would present difficult payments problems. They nevertheless still estimated, in each case, the proportion of capital goods in total imports at between 22 and 23 per cent. This implied a far higher proportion of capital goods as a proportion of total imports from the United States than before the war. In spring 1946 it was estimated that for the period 1946–9 they might constitute 33.8 per cent of all imports from the United States.[32] In the event in 1947 capital goods and metals accounted for 29.5 per cent of all French imports from the United States, as opposed to 18.7 per cent in 1938. Imports of the same commodities as a proportion of total imports were 14.8 per cent in 1947 as opposed to 9.1 per cent in 1938. Almost 60.0 per cent of all capital goods and metals imported into France in 1947 came from America.[33] Imports of machinery and transport equipment into the Netherlands, as a proportion of all imports by value, averaged 10.6 per cent in 1937/8; they were 13.6 per cent in 1946 and 17.6 per cent in 1947.[34]

To put the matter in a different focus, it is only necessary to consider that in 1947 2.2 million gross tons of new shipping were being built in Europe, that the maximum permitted output of the German steel industry was 5.8 million tonnes of crude steel a year, and that the actual production of crude steel in the three western occupation zones was less than half that quantity. In 1937, when there had been a roughly comparable level of new shipping construction in Europe, the German steel industry had produced 15.96 million tonnes of crude steel. In that same year, when capital investment had been a smaller proportion of national income, almost everywhere the German machine building and machine-tool industry had been the second largest in the world with the second highest level of exports; in 1947 it scarcely existed. Even when the Nazi government had passed the bounds of all toleration and most European countries were committed to high levels of machine-tool imports to rearm against it, imports of capital goods by Western European countries from Germany were still more than those from America and Britain combined. They amounted to $939 million, whereas the total value from the United States was only $497 million. It was not that America's financial provision for European recovery after 1945 was inadequate. It was inadequate for the policies which western European countries pursued. And these were startlingly different from those of 1920, and in less propitious circumstances.

Western Europe's payments difficulties and its inability any longer to

[32] F.M.B. Lynch, 'The political and economic reconstruction of France 1944–47: in the international context' (PhD thesis, University of Manchester, 1981), p. 42.

[33] France, *Statistique Mensuelle du commerce extérieur de la France*.

[34] Netherlands, *Maandstatistiek van den In-Uit en Doorvoer van Nederland*.

finance its trade deficit had a further component. This was the reduced capacity of western European economies to finance their trade deficits with the United States through a high level of invisible earnings. These had in the past come chiefly from the interest on foreign investments, often in the United States, from the activities of European companies operating outside Europe, from the foreign earnings of the large European merchant fleets and from the expenditure of foreign, especially American, tourists in Europe. The inflow of these invisibles had sustained the large deficits on commodity trade with America in the 1930s. The war was to prove this to have been a precarious situation, but as with commodity trade the same argument took place as to whether Europe's decline in invisible earnings was a temporary effect of the war or representative of a more permanent shift in the pattern of world payments.

The sudden need for imports of machine tools and capital equipment from America, occasioned by rearmament in both Britain and France, had led very quickly to the forced sale of many investments in the United States in 1940 as the only means, when the further growth of exports was impossible because of the war, to pay for the additional American supply. Only with Lend-Lease could any further imports from the United States be obtained and one condition of Lend-Lease was the continued sale of British and French foreign investments. At the same time, in France the Vichy government paid part of the occupation costs imposed by the Reich through the transfer to Germany of investments in eastern and south-eastern Europe. Any precise measurement of the extent of this depletion of foreign investment is impossible. At the time of the Anglo-American financial negotiations the British government officially estimated that it had realized during the war about a fifth of its pre-war foreign investments, but the proportion of dollar foreign investments sold may have been very much higher.[35] Otherwise the extent of the change can only be measured through the changes in the balance of payments itself. In many ways this is the most realistic calculation because the real value of these old-established foreign investments in the post-war world was the volume of imported goods which the interest on them could command. The estimates of the total of French pre-war foreign investment vary by as much as 60 per cent but if we take an estimate lying in the middle range of this variation the interest on capital in the 1947 balance of payments would suggest that as much as 35 per cent of the total investment may have been lost during the war. What this meant financially in terms of the capacity to purchase imports is uncertain, but it is clear that the war had in this respect done no good to the fragile pre-war payments equilibrium. The total fall in investment earnings by Europe, of which virtually the whole would have accrued to western Europe, was estimated by the IMF at about $600 million between 1938 and 1947. If this

[35] UK, *Statistical Material Presented During the Washington Negotiations*, Cmd. 6707 (London, 1945).

figure is approximately correct, even had the whole sum been in dollar earnings it would not have gone far to remedy the deficits on commodity trade with the dollar zone. The actual loss of investment may have been less important than was usually suggested at the time and the loss due to temporary unprofitability or low interest rates more important. Much depends on how much of the interest accrued in currencies which could have been used to reduce the dollar gap.

The loss of shipping earnings due to the sinkings of merchant ships during the war was temporarily very severe. In addition the use of American ships to bring cargoes to Europe increased the outflow of dollars for freight charges. The United States merchant marine made up 52 per cent of the world's merchant tonnage in 1947 compared to 17 per cent in 1939. The western European merchant fleet was reconstituted with remarkable speed. The British mercantile marine, by far the biggest of the European fleets and comprising about 40 per cent of western Europe's pre-war shipping capacity, had almost regained its pre-war size by the end of 1947 and had a larger proportion of new and recently built ships. By the end of 1949 most western European countries had a larger fleet than before the war. As western Europe rebuilt its ships the wartime additions to the American fleet were laid up in large numbers. But the restriction of the German merchant navy to small coastal craft, together with the slowness with which the Italian fleet was rebuilt, meant that the total available quantity of Western European shipping remained less than in the 1930s even by the close of 1949, in spite of the increase in the volume of international trade. In 1947 western Europe had a deficit on shipping of $333 million and in 1948 the surplus was only $300 million.[36]

About the many other sources of invisible earnings it is even more difficult to be precise. In so far as they were reduced this was also, as it was with shipping and investment income, only a temporary outcome of the war. Tourist earnings for example were very low indeed in 1947 compared to pre-war years, but were soon to be higher. The flow of foreign investment from Europe was already building up again in 1946 and 1947. But against this was to be set the inescapable political consequences of the war which for several countries meant a much higher level of foreign expenditure. British expenditures in Germany were the most obvious example. Over the period 1934–8 the annual average expenditure abroad of the British government for all military, administrative and diplomatic purposes had been about £6 million ($25.8 million). In 1947 military expenditure alone was £209 million ($898.7 million). This increase itself more than consumed the total sum earned in foreign dividends, interests and profits in the same year. There were, however, other examples of which the high military expenditure of the Netherlands abroad and to a lesser extent of France, compared to pre-war, were notable.

The International Monetary Fund (IMF) estimates of Western Europe's

[36] UN, *Economic Survey 1948*, p. 114.

invisible balance on current account in 1947 suggest that it was zero whereas the later figures produced by the Committee of European Economic Co-operation (CEEC) record a deficit of $750 million.[37] The latter organization had no reason to paint a healthy picture so their figure may be exaggerated. The same countries in 1938 had recorded a surplus on invisibles of some $2000 million, an income equivalent to about a third of their volume of exports. Their overall balance of payments deficit on current account in 1947 amounted to $7150 million, so the deterioration in invisible earnings could be estimated as accounting for between a quarter and a third of the overall deterioration in their balance of payments between 1938 and 1947. The decline in investment earnings and in shipping earnings played roughly equal parts in this but the shipping loss was the more important in that it meant an increase in dollar freight charges. The decline in the inward flow of invisibles was less important and more easily recouped therefore than the increase in the deficit on commodity trade.

In order for the pre-war level of invisible earnings, once attained, to finance the visible trade deficit a contemporaneous reduction in that deficit was required and therefore it was at this point that the trade difficulties no longer appeared as a temporary consequence of the war, that the automatic nature of the mechanism of return to equilibrium no longer looked convincing and that the international crisis could fairly be called structural. Western Europe's trade pattern in the inter-war years, its dependence on relatively cheap non-dollar zone food imports (whose ready availability and cheapness was itself in part a function of the low levels of activity in the developed world) and on a high level of invisible earnings to sustain a growing deficit on trade in manufactures with the United States, did not look very appropriate to the post-war world. Although the causes of the shortfall in invisible earnings, like most of the causes of the trade deficit, were related to the war and were short-term in nature, the trade crisis of 1947 none the less did have serious implications for the nature of the trade and payments structure which had developed in the inter-war period.

If the United States were to act to permit Western Europe to continue importing American goods to sustain such high levels of capital investment in spite of the payments difficulties, this would still not remove the underlying causes of the payments crisis; nor might these causes be any more remediable within the framework of the inherited trade and payments system than they were within that of the Bretton Woods agreements, which had been designed to replace them. Very few had regarded the shifting trade and payments arrangements of the 1930s with satisfaction. The smaller trade-dependent economies, Belgium in particular, had struggled manfully to create an alternative, and even France had persisted as long as possible with the vestiges of

[37] IMF, *Balance of Payments Yearbook*; OEEC, *Interim Report on the European Recovery Programme*, vol. 1 (Paris, 1948).

the gold exchange standard. Foreign trade had grown more slowly than output and the pattern of international payments had not been such as to instill any confidence that it could be long sustained without a serious adjustment. If western European states were to continue to provide a better life for their populations, and that had been one objective of the long struggle against Nazi Germany, the international framework within which their economies functioned had to be changed. This could be seen beneath the rising output and high employment of 1947. The growing difficulties in international trade and payments were a much more serious threat to the future of western European capitalism in 1947 than the poor diet, the production bottlenecks and the political activities of the French and Italian communist parties.

The separate reconstruction objectives of each western European nation-state showed that they were by no means unaware of the depth of the problem and the seriousness of its implications, even though the analysis of its nature was often erroneous. Almost all these states proceeded from the assumption that the international framework of the 1930s would not, if continued, permit the achievement of their domestic economic objectives. Much political debate was in fact about whether capitalism was or could be an appropriate form of organization for achieving post-war national, social and economic objectives. Even if the radical nature of the arguments used was not matched by an equally radical understanding of the problems involved, the possibilities of fundamental economic and social change were frequently and energetically canvassed in the immediate aftermath of the war. Irrespective of the support which a fundamental change in the economic system continued to attract because of its desirability, might not such a change be the only way of successfully achieving such economic objectives as full employment or a sustained increase in output? However, the alternatives on offer from the 1930s had not only failed to integrate domestic, economic and social change with the pattern of international economic activity but had brought about severe problems through their failure to do so.

The only *international* plans and proposals for dealing with this problem were those which had emerged from the United Nations Conference at Bretton Woods in July 1944. What transpired in that otherwise obscure New Hampshire spa has had a most extraordinary hold over the way post-war history has been written. The loose agreements on the functioning of a future international economy arrived at there have been enthroned as something called 'the Bretton Woods system'. This system began to operate, however imperfectly, after 1945 and in spite of several setbacks reached its apogee in 1958, finally to collapse in 1971 when the automatic convertibility of the dollar into gold at a fixed price was ended, thus removing the main prop of the guaranteed, fixed international exchange rates on which the 'system' had depended. Histories of the post-war international economy conventionally divide their topic into two periods, the period of 'the Bretton Woods system' and that of floating exchange rates which has followed it. In fact the Bretton Woods agreements proved so unsatisfactory an international basis for reconstruction that they had little force or influence on European reconstruction once the international payments crisis in summer 1947 made their inadequacy evident. If 'the Bretton Woods system', as conceived in 1944, ever existed it ended for European countries in 1947. What later emerged in 1958, when Western European currencies became more or less fully convertible, was certainly based on very similar economic ideas, but was, none the less, something different. It would have been inconceivable had not the West European countries themselves devised between 1947 and 1951 a form of international economic co-operation more appropriate to their domestic economic objectives than the combination of sweeping, but vague, agreements in principle and precisely defined, but inadequate, international institutions which Bretton Woods produced.

The Bretton Woods agreements had assumed a world in which most of the post-war difficulties of international trade and payments would prove temporary, would be abated by relief programmes financed in dollars (such as UNRRA), and by 1947 would be no longer significant. Sterling–dollar convertibility would then break the mould of the 1930s and usher in a world-wide progress towards multilateral trade and payments based on a system of registered, fixed exchange rates, of which the international institutions created by the conference, and in particular the IMF would be the guarantor, together with the General Agreement on Trade and Tariffs (GATT). Acceptance of the agreements was the price of the post-war dollar credits to Britain and France. Clear indication that things were not so simple came with the mounting realization in 1947 that the resources to purchase dollar imports were running out. The British exchange crisis in August and the ending of sterling–dollar convertibility was only one symptom, although to have been approaching the exhaustion in so short a time of a credit of $3750 million was certainly a severe enough symptom to emphasize the gravity of the malady. Through the loopholes in the sterling transferable account system, as well as through inadequate exchange control systems elsewhere, there began a movement of capital out of Europe well above the outward official flow on capital account to finance the balance of payments deficits.[38] There was a sudden awareness in the United States that western Europe's fragile external economic position threatened its reconstruction programmes. They might be sustained, unless

[38] Britain's deficit on current account can explain only about three-fifths of the total loss of gold and dollars of £1250 million in 1946 and 1947 and only about one-fifth of the deterioration in 1947. J.C.R. Dow, *The Management of the British Economy 1945–1960* (Cambridge, 1960), p. 24.

the United States were to intervene to support them, either with long years of public economies, meaning strict controls which might prevent the return of many pleasures of pre-war life, a lower level of supply and a lower standard of living for all than before the war, or, worse still from the point of view of American post-war policy, with a persistence in the internationally destructive autarchy which had characterized the 1930s. At the same time the two snarling, acrimonious great powers faced each other across the moribund body of what had been by far Europe's most important industrial power, while on all sides threatened a war which western Europe might no longer have the resources or the will to fight. The postponement, even the defeat, of American post-war objectives seemed imminent.

In the period 1914–41 the United States had a surplus on current account of about $18,000 million. About two-thirds of this was financed by the inward movement of gold and about 90 per cent of that movement took place over the period 1934–9. This movement began to be reversed in 1941 with the coming of Lend-Lease and the stationing of American armies abroad. In spite of reconstruction aid and loans provided from the United States after the war, however, the flow was again reversed after 1945 so that the effects of the outward movement of gold from America during the war had been completely annulled by the end of 1947. It is estimated that some $5300 million in gold and banking funds flowed back into the United States in 1946 and 1947.[39] Western Europe lost about $2500 million in gold and dollar holdings in 1947 alone, about a third of its total holdings at the start of the year.[40] At the end of the year the gold and dollar holdings of the United Kingdom, which were also those of the whole sterling area, were only about half the size of the total drain during the year, those of France and the Netherlands about a third and those of Italy about a tenth.[41]

To a certain degree this situation had been forecast by Keynes and others who had urged the United States at Bretton Woods to sustain the outward flow of gold and dollars at a higher level during the recovery period. The immediate post-war outflow from the United States, reflecting the world-wide nature of the Second World War, was in fact well above anything that could have been envisaged in the 1930s. It embraced government loans, of which the single loan to Britain in 1945 made up about 40 per cent, dollar credits to purchase American government property left behind all over the world, special government relief programmes for occupied areas, as well as the generous funding of UNRRA, 74 per cent of whose income came from the United States.[42] The total of all such disbursements in Western Europe from the start of July 1945 to the end of June 1947 was $10,098 million (table 13).

[39] BIS, *18th Annual Report* (Basle, 1948), p. 115.
[40] Triffin, *Europe and the Money Muddle*, p. 31.
[41] UN, *Economic Survey 1948*, p. 120.
[42] N. Brodsky, 'Some aspects of international relief', *Quarterly Journal of Economics*, 62, 1947/8.

Table 13 United States loans, property credits, grants and relief, 1 July 1945 to 30 June 1947 and amount unutilized on 30 June 1947 (million dollars)

	Loans	Amount unutilized	Property credits	Amount unutilized	Grants and relief (UNNRA, GARIOA, etc.)	Amount unutilized	Total	Amount unutilized
OEEC countries (except Germany)	5,544	855	1,845	120	1,943	529	9,331	1,503
Germany	0	0	0	0	767	230	767	230
Rest of Europe	149	62	397	147	992	0	1,538	209
Europe, unallocable	41	41	0	0	481	274	522	315
Rest of world	692	415	461	178	2,991	875	4,144	1,470
Total for all areas	6,426	1,373	2,703	445	7,174	1,908	16,302	3,727

Source: US, 80th Congress, Senate, Report of the Committee on Foreign Relations on S. 2202, Calendar No. 978 (February, 1948), pp. 10–12.

Whereas it has been a matter of general agreement that American aid was generous the argument was and is frequently made that it was inadequate to cope with the problem because it was conceived as relief, was not long-term enough for the purpose of recovery, and was already being run down in 1947. Expenditure, although high, was temporary, and much of it was due to come to an end at the end of 1947 when UNRRA was due to be wound up. The reduction in the outflow of dollars under American aid schemes is held to have been a contributory cause of the payments crisis. It was certainly true that all branches of the American government were united on bringing UNRRA to an end at the close of 1947, that the enormous credit offered to Britain was not a pattern for credits to other European countries, that there were no other schemes for re-cycling dollars to enable the stream of American imports into Europe to continue, and that all these things combined to make the future, in the light of the trends of spring and summer 1947, look dangerous and obscure. But that the outflow of dollars was less as summer 1947 approached was clearly true only for the world as a whole, for Western Europe it is a statement that needs heavy qualification. The sum of dollars made directly available to Western Europe in 1947 was greater than in 1946, even if Interim Aid which began at the end of the year is discounted (table 14). This was mainly so, however, because of the much greater extent to which Britain drew on its American credit, more than three times as much in 1947 as in the preceding period. British drawings on the line of credit were 67 per cent of the total American loans and grants to Western Europe in 1947. They were only 23 per cent of them in the preceding period. To a large extent therefore the recycling of dollars into Western Europe was financing in 1947 the British import deficit, in absolute terms by far the largest in Western

Table 14   Net United States foreign loans and grants, 1945–7** (million dollars)

	July 1945–December 1946	1947
Net loans and grants to whole world	7444	5681
of which: grants	3611	1859
loans	3833	3822
Net loans and grants to* † western Europe	3426	3963.75

Sources: USA, *Statistical Abstract of the United States*, pp. 830–4; USA, 80th Congress, Senate, *Report on the European Interim Aid Act of 1947*, November, 1947, Calendar No. 825.

** Repayments on earlier credits as well as reverse Lend-Lease and returns of property deducted from the gross outflow.

* Includes dependencies of the United Kingdom and France.

† Interim Aid to Austria, France and Italy began on 1 December 1947 and has been discounted by deducting its monthly average total during the programme.

Europe,[43] and also the loss of dollars through the laxly supervised arrangements for sterling convertibility. The flow of American private capital, although very small, did not diminish in 1947.[44] The timing of the trade and exchange crisis is not attributable to the shrinking of the dollar outflow from America, but to the increasing demand by Western Europe on a relatively constant supply of dollars and the high rate of flow of gold back into the United States.

Freer trade and multilateral settlement mechanisms, the solution proposed by the United States during the war and enshrined in the Bretton Woods agreements, were not immediately effective solutions, because Bretton Woods made no provision for getting from the pattern of the 1930s to the desired pattern of a post-war world in which a multilateral equilibrium did not impose impossible strains on economies determined to maintain rising output and employment. The timing of the dollar shortage in international payments in summer 1947 could be blamed, with several good reasons, by Washington on accident and on government inadequacies in Europe. But had these been avoided it would still have arrived later with the planned reductions in dollar outflows from America. There were no plans in Washington to deal with what would then have been the wreck of the post-war economic settlement, unless Bretton Woods were to be saved, merely as a mechanism, by European deflations. The fact that there were no such plans or public pronouncements reflecting a true understanding of the eventual situation meant that the trade problems in summer produced even more general tension. Small wonder that a major diplomatic conference involving the three greatest European powers took only three weeks to come together after Marshall made his offer of aid and that an even more complicated conference of sixteen European countries could be called together within six weeks of the speech! European policies and ambitions were not compatible with the Bretton Woods settlement.

The speed at which these political events moved is even less surprising if we ask what plans the western European countries had to meet the crisis. Even under the new course of 'austerity', introduced as the dollar loss accelerated, the political and economic programmes of the British government depended for their implementation on the United States making *more* dollars available. All that had happened was that a few cuts had been imposed on private, not public, investment. French governments likewise assumed in all the versions of the Modernization and Re-equipment Plan which guided reconstruction that American loans would be available, for without them the Plan was not feasible, and its estimates of the likely extent of American aid were not

[43] The United Kingdom net deficit on trade for the first six months of 1947 was $1228 million, that of the rest of Western Europe $2783 million.

[44] US, ECA, *The Sterling Area*, pp. 128–9. The outflow of private US investment was no higher than in the 1930s and mainly due to the activities of a few major firms in petroleum manufacturing and distribution. Ten American companies with foreign branches were responsible for about 75 per cent of the net outflow in 1947. OEEC, *Report on International Investment* (Paris, 1950), pp. 22–3.

consistently modified downwards in 1947. The Italian economy, in spite of the drastic reductions in imports and the deliberately induced deflation of 1947, would still only be viable afterwards with dollar aid. In the absence of any definitive action on the part of the United States to provide reconstruction aid, it might be thought that European countries would have formulated positive alternative strategies to span the time until a multilateral equilibrium could be reached. But there is practically no evidence of any such policies. Contingency plans, as in France or Britain, to reduce, were it necessary, imports from the dollar zone to the essentials for reconstruction in no way measured up to the scale of the problem, for it would have affected the long-term future of the whole continent. Western European governments rushed like lemmings to and over the edge of the international framework created by Bretton Woods. Their motivation was equally compulsive. For many of them no other course of economic action was politically feasible.

It had been the main worry of the British government in the Anglo-American financial negotiations and at Bretton Woods that a more open economy would mean that a post-war recession in America would prevent Britain from maintaining full employment. Depression and unemployment were seen as originating from that huge economy on the other side of the Atlantic regularly spinning out of control with catastrophic effects on Europe. Treasury policy documents continued vaguely to imply that within a space of four or five years trade controls could be taken away and multilateral clearing and free mutual currency convertibility be established not only with the dollar but under a British lead between the pound and the European currencies. But this was more hope than practical policy. There was no British policy to help other European countries attain their recovery goals, only the extension of sterling credits to permit the purchase of more British exports. There were no other plans for easing Europe's general problem of a deficit in dollar trade, indeed no suggestion that it was a problem common to the whole area. All suggestions for joint planning for British and French recovery, or even for a greater degree of co-ordination of the process of recovery in the two countries, were turned down in London. In effect British policy amounted to no more than a belief that multilateralism in world trade was ultimately beneficial to the United Kingdom, once it was safe. Meanwhile the British trade deficit, fed by an easier access to dollars than other European countries, grew to the point where the equilibrium that would sustain a multilateral system was fast receding. Even on the national level there seems to have been no proper prediction of the changing effects of the government's social and economic policies on the future course of the balance of payments. In October 1946 a surplus of imports amounting to about £200 million had been forecast for 1947. At the start of the new year this was revised upwards to about £350 million and in May the Chancellor told the cabinet it might be as much as £700 million.[45] Only then was real consideration given to a change in policy. Before that there were only revised calculations of the increase in exports necessary to maintain a balance of payments akin to that of the 1930s in the face of the loss of invisibles and an unfavourable shift in the terms of trade.[46]

French import programmes were determined by the Modernization and Re-equipment Plan, the Monnet Plan, adopted in March 1946 as a medium-term plan for national reconstruction and modernization of the 'basic' sectors of the economy. The original intention was to steer capital investment into six of these 'basic' sectors, coal-mining, electricity, steel, cement, agricultural machinery, and transport. Later, oil, chemicals, fertilizers, synthetic fertilizers, synthetic fibres and shipbuilding were all added. One objective was to regain the peak level of output in the inter-war period, that of 1929, by 1948 and by 1950 to exceed it by a quarter. This was to be done by rapid improvements in technology and productivity so that French manufacturing industry would be more competitive and able to take a more prominent place in European markets. The ultimate intention was to modernize not only certain sectors of manufacturing industry but the whole country by transforming attitudes of mind. The Monnet Plan had important implications for future national security, not just in the sense that it intended to increase the weight of France's industrial output in western Europe and revivify the country at the same time, but also because it became the guide to foreign policy questions concerning future national security against Germany.[47] But although French import programmes were incorporated in the context of a medium-term economic plan they were not any more realistic than those of Britain. Yet any cancellation or postponement of them would have been a cancellation or postponement of the objectives of national reconstruction and security on which a political consensus had been formed.

In both Britain and France policy seems to have gone ahead fatalistically based on an unspoken, perhaps unutterable assumption that the United States would eventually have to act, that both out of its own strategic interest and as a world banker of last resort it would have to preserve in power the existing western European governments and would have to lend or give the necessary

[45] CAB 129 19, CP (47) 167, Import programme, 28 May 1947.

[46] This last phenomenon was purely a British problem. The rise in demand for primary goods, which began in 1939 and showed no weakening in 1947, would normally have meant that western Europe's terms of trade would have worsened from their unusually favourable position in the 1930s. But the post-war surge of demand for manufactures and the very high prices of western European goods meant that for most countries the rise in the unit values of their exports relative to the 1930s was even greater than the rise in the unit value of their imports. By the first half of 1947 the cost of British imports in terms of exports had risen by 17 per cent compared to 1938; that of the other important western European importers had fallen by 9.5 per cent on average. The total value of British imports in 1947, however, was just over half that of all Western Europe, so that in spite of a generally favourable, albeit temporary, shift in the terms of trade to the benefit of most western European countries, the payments deficit of the area as a whole in 1947 was made worse by virtue of Britain's dominating position in its international trade and the deterioration of Britain's terms of trade.   [47] See chapter 4.

sums of hard currency to make their post-war economic policies feasible. The Marshall Plan might be said to have ultimately justified this assumption, but that would be a glib judgement indeed. The decision in America that this was the correct way forward was a very hard-fought one. No one who has read through the State Department files on the European Recovery Programme (ERP) could fail to be impressed by the enormous effort in time, money and energy spent to convince Congress and the nation that this was the proper policy. It would have been unthinkable that any western European foreign ministry should have embarked at the time on so massive a programme of public education and propaganda in favour of its own policies. It took more than ten months before ERP became law, ten months filled with congressional enquiries, the tireless lobbying of senators and congressmen, the organization of provincial committees in favour of the ERP and of numerous speaking tours in distant areas by important and busy civil servants. And at the end the legislation was seriously amended by Congress and passed only with a substantial vote against it. Furthermore, the dollars were not made available on terms that were always acceptable to the Europeans and were so only at the cost of substantial modifications in their foreign policies. They *might* have been made available at the cost of substantial modifications in their domestic economic policies.

This was what the British government feared in particular. It had been elected by an overwhelming popular majority with a clear mandate to sustain full employment and a higher level of social welfare. Seen from the viewpoint of 1945 the economic and social conditions of the 1930s had been made utterly unacceptable by the war. Any economic policy which did not seem to offer the possibility of permanent escape from those conditions was also unacceptable. In recent years there has been a tendency to see the performance of the British economy and the condition of the majority of the British population during the 1930s in a more favourable light. But that is hardly the point; a mass of social and economic criticism before the war, followed by the powerfully forged sense of positive national purpose during the war, meant that the 1930s were now seen as wasted years. To ensure that there should be no further wasted years had become a historical imperative brooking no question, a first, necessary, inflexible priority of all economic policy.

If full employment and the welfare state were historical imperatives in British reconstruction the same could be said for the Modernization Plan in France. There, the waste of the 1930s was not symbolized by unemployment so much as by the lack of production. The revival of the German economy had been accompanied in France by economic stagnation at a low level of output, as well as by bitter quarrels over the distribution of the national product. Avoiding a repetition of this pattern was as much a political imperative in France as full employment in Britain. As in Britain the policies of the reconstruction period had evolved during the 1930s out of a critique of government policy which had become an integral part of popular thought. The war seemed to have demonstrated its rightness and the peace brought the opportunity to implement it. It was not merely from the Second World War that Europe was reconstructing but from the depression of 1929 and the human and national experience which followed.

In the other European countries reconstruction policies were very varied but most also drew their inspiration in some way from critiques of the policies pursued in the inter-war period. The Norwegian Labour Party returned with a programme of planned investment in capital goods industries over the medium term and more welfare, combining the essential elements of both British and French policies. Their calculations, expressed in the series of National Budgets, suggested that by depleting their reserves to a low point in 1947 they would be able to maintain their programme without recourse to American aid and that by 1948 shipping earnings would again be large enough to close the payments gap. About half the deficit in the balance of payments in 1947 was attributable to imports of ships. This was as falsely optimistic a view as in France and Britain. The National Budget for 1947 was framed in such a way that almost a half of net capital formation would be financed out of the expected deficit in the balance of payments.[48] Norway was not so affected by the rise in imports relative to exports in 1947 as most other European countries and from a strictly Norwegian viewpoint it could be argued that the government had got its predictions right and that it was essentially the insouciance of the British government towards its own international position at that time which knocked the Norwegian National Budget for 1947 briefly off course by generating a run on the reserves. But the reality, which should have been taken into account, was that no matter how accurately judged the forward planning, Norway's economy was only a small part of that of western Europe and could not escape the economic consequences of policy decisions in the major western European economies.

Much the same point may be made about Denmark which, although it too experienced a widening of the gap between imports and exports in summer 1947, nevertheless managed to avoid a foreign exchange crisis. At the time the judgement was sometimes made in Denmark as in Norway that there had been no error of judgement of economic policy but that changes in policy by the larger economies had endangered Denmark's position. But Denmark's foreign exchange crisis would have come later. After the war the fodder imports on which Danish agricultural exports so largely depended had to come mainly from the United States, and in fact by summer 1948 Danish reserves were half their level at the end of 1947 and even dropped below the level required for normal working balances. Although the events of 1947 passed rather quietly over Denmark, the true nature of the economic crisis of that year was nevertheless made starkly clear there even if with a delay of some

[48] Bourneuf, *Norway*, pp. 148–54.

months. The Danish government later accurately summarized the position in the following terms. 'The increasing shortage of foreign exchange, however, meant that prospects were dark for a continued reconstruction. Without the European Recovery Programme the most serious consequences for the economic life of Denmark might have materialized during the following period.'[49]

All the other smaller economies had also in common the central importance of an expansion of international trade to their national economic recovery. Belgium's concentration on reaping the rewards of its favourable position as an exporter was unique in its extent in the first half of 1947 but not even this could hope to escape the consequences of policies elsewhere. A failure of international trade to continue to expand because of a breakdown in the payments mechanism would have made Belgium's situation relatively worse than that of Britain and France. This was clear enough in Brussels where, to judge from its actions after the offer of Marshall Aid, the government had decided that something more positive than the mere injection of more dollars into the world economy was immediately necessary to guarantee recovery to a country so heavily committed to international trade and that there should be an immediate return to a multilateral payments mechanism as extensive as that before 1929.

Although all must suffer from another drop in the level of international trade, the degree of openness in the economy at which reconstruction plans aimed varied greatly. Some, like Norway, shared the view of the British that too early a move towards convertibility had been enforced and that the removal of currency and trade controls would endanger full employment and the gains which had been made in welfare. Others, like Belgium, wanted the moves in that direction to be faster and more complete. The situation was, therefore, a curious one; there was very little disagreement in principle, as at Bretton Woods, with America's plans for a post-war economic settlement based on multilateralism, but very deep disagreement over the timing of moves in that direction. In any case either the Bretton Woods agreements would not work or European domestic reconstruction policies were not feasible unless a different international economic framework were devised. The first post-war economic peace settlement had proved inadequate and the political peace settlement had failed over the question of Germany, which was a fundamental question for European economic reconstruction as well.

For the United States the problem, as it crystallized in 1947, was thus to find a policy which would meet four objectives. It would have to further America's altered view of its own national strategic and diplomatic self-interest, in particular the threat which the Soviet Union was perceived as making to America's strategic interests in Europe; it would have to prevent the impending breakdown in international trade and payments, and it would

[49] UD, 44.2/26, XIV, 'Danish report covering the period 3 April–30 September 1948', 30 November 1948.

have to do so while adhering to the main and still unchanged ultimate objectives of the economic settlement negotiated at Bretton Woods and in the Anglo-American financial agreements; and, partly, it would have to solve the problems in Germany. Even without considering the extreme importance of the future of Germany to European recovery and the international economy the diplomatic problems between Washington and Moscow and America's own internal bureaucratic policy disputes between State Department and army had both reached the point where some positive political and economic action in Germany was urgently required. None of the necessary objectives of any new policy could be met unless Germany were included in it. To attempt a reconstruction of Germany was, however, to raise the wider issue of the reconstruction of Europe. To approach the reconstruction of Europe was to tackle the problem of western Europe's position in world trade and payments. Out of this necessity to act on a world scale while concentrating on western Europe came the European Recovery Programme.

Because it was the solution to these major political objectives, as well as a response to the immediate economic problem, it was essential that the new policy should support the historical imperatives which underlay national reconstruction policies in Europe, rather than seek to recreate an international equilibrium in trade and payments at the earliest possible moment. When by late summer 1947 the Marshall Plan began to have some of the elements of a real plan it proceeded on the assumption that such an equilibrium might still not be attained even by 1951 when the ERP would have run its course. When it was attained, it would be at the much higher levels of output and employment, compared to the 1930s, which the Western European countries sought. If the great stir of public opinion in the United States against nationalization or against the restrictions on 'free enterprise' or against planning were not translated into political action by Congress this was not just because of a sensible and accurate understanding of these policies within the American government, although such an understanding was very often there, it was because the immediate problem was not seen merely as a crisis of the world payments system but as the need to prop up in America's strategic interests all forms of Western European capitalism and democratic governments, even socialists and planners, against communists and the Soviet Union. These strategic necessities meant that what the government of the United States actually paid for with Marshall Aid was not to increase the rate of recovery in European economics and to prevent Europeans in dislocated and deteriorating economies from starving, but to sustain ambitious, new, expansionary economic and social policies in Western European countries which were mostly already in full boom conditions. Those countries, driven in many cases by overwhelming historical forces to run a risk which was economically wholly unjustified, found their gambler's throw made successful by the changed circumstances of great power politics.

Thus, although there were very few indicators of an economic crisis in Europe in 1947, although the immediate difficulties of summer 1947 were no more than technical difficulties in making international payments, although the timing of these difficulties was attributable overwhelmingly to the domestic economic policies of European governments and the difficulties could theoretically have been either postponed or avoided, although most of the structural changes in the international economy which were thought of as severe problems were only short-lived consequences of the war, and although in most European countries boom conditions with rising output, rising trade and rising employment prevailed throughout the crisis, nevertheless the economic and political events of 1947 did constitute a crisis with the most profound implications. It showed that the international framework in which western European capitalism had operated could no longer sustain it and that what had been devised at Bretton Woods was no substitute. It showed that policy in occupied Germany had reached a dead-end. It showed that powerful, new, domestic, political, social and economic pressures in European countries had changed the bases of economic policy and must now be taken into account. It showed that America's changed international strategic position demanded close economic co-operation with Western Europe and with these new forces.

All economic crises seem to embody an element of illusory confidence which the crisis itself eliminates. In 1947 the unreality was as much political as economic. Its origins were in the wave of hope for a better world and a changed future for the human race which had swept across Europe and America during the defeat of the atrocious Nazi regime. If now Roosevelt's global aspirations at Teheran or Yalta seem hard to credit, if the extraordinary wave of enthusiasm for European federation in 1947 seems to have had no contact with political realities in Europe, if ambitious plans for domestic reconstruction seem to have been conceived in a sort of dream world where international economic difficulties were largely ignored, this is because our judgements are made after the disillusionment which the 1947 crisis brought. Like earlier economic crises it purged the prevalent economic unrealities. All that was immediately at stake was a malfunction of international trade and payments, itself partly due to the very success of economic recovery. But beyond that was glimpsed not just the likely end of the post-war boom but the likely end of the better world for which all had fought and towards whose creation the policies of national governments had, no matter how cautiously, been influenced. There was a common European-American interest in avoiding the circumstances of 1920 and a real American interest in backing the European governments' determination to do so. But on the details of how this could be done there were deep disagreements, and the will to do it did not imply the ability.

II

THE COMMITTEE OF
EUROPEAN ECONOMIC
CO-OPERATION

When General Marshall chose to announce on Commencement Day at Harvard University in June 1947 the readiness of the United States to provide further aid to European economies he appeared to impose only one condition.[1] This was that the aid should be used by the European countries in a co-ordinated way rather than be allocated individually to specific countries for specific purposes. There was, as all historians of the subject have shown, no Marshall Plan before Marshall spoke, only the decision that a systematic programme of aid for western Europe was in America's real interest. There was also, and on this historians have been altogether more reticent, a firm resolve that American aid should achieve a political as well as an economic purpose, that it should serve to 'integrate' western Europe, making it into a more closely united area over which certain common forms of economic, social and political existence proper to democracy and the 'free' world would prevail. No matter how nebulous the ideas when Marshall spoke the political and economic intentions behind the decision to announce the provision of aid were extraordinarily far-reaching and ambitious. The United States did not only intend to reconstruct western Europe economically, but also politically.

The intention was to undertake the task left unachieved by all after 1918. The inadequacy of the post-Versailles settlement was blamed for the economic

[1] George Catlett Marshall, 1880–1959. Army officer. Served in France 1917–19, a.d.c. to General Pershing 1919–24. Served in China 1924–7. Chief of War Plans Division of General Staff 1938. Deputy Chief of Staff 1938–9. General 1939. Chief of Staff 1939–45. Special Representative of President in China 1945. Secretary of State 1947–9. Secretary of Defense 1950–1. A national hero, as yet unsullied. A man of remarkably few words, for so exceptionally long a life of public service.

collapse of 1929, for the National Socialist Party and for the Second World War. The failure to achieve a sound and lasting reconstruction of the continent had eventually brought the United States into serious danger, and with a hostile great power on the banks of the Elbe it had become obvious that the danger had not gone away. After the Republican Party's success in the mid-term elections of 1947 an important wing of that Party, associated with Senators Tom Connally and Arthur H. Vandenberg and with the future Secretary of State, John F. Dulles, came also to support the decision to undertake the reconstruction of Europe. For many of them this was not a permanent abandonment of isolationism, rather a decision that the creation of a western Europe independent of American aid was an essential pre-requisite of any future withdrawal from Europe in safety.

If the political motives underlying the Marshall Plan were varied, much the same could be said about the economic ideas which informed it. Because the chosen instrument of reconstruction was an economic one, there had to be some intellectual harmony between the apparent economic necessity of sustaining the domestic economic and social ambitions of western European governments, by enabling them to purchase more American exports, and the political desire to produce a united strategic bloc in western Europe with close affinities to America on which the United States could depend. Like the political support for Marshall Aid the economic rationale was imprecisely formulated and held to with varying degrees of conviction by different groups. It did, nevertheless, rapidly come to have certain elements of a political ideology expressed in economic terms at a time when the United States acutely felt the need of one. It is not the intention here to analyse the way in which the detailed policy formulations of the ERP emerged from these important shifts of opinion in the United States. On the political side this has in any case already been done.[2] Here we are concerned with the reaction within Europe to certain specific American policy objectives once they were formulated. Nevertheless, it is important briefly to consider the mixture of national interest, prejudice, goodwill and misinterpretation of history which were the wellsprings of the Marshall Plan, for had it not been able to draw from such deep sources so ambitious a programme of action could not have been pursued.

There was a body of economic theory, much in vogue at the time, which supported the view that the integration of separate states, because it was a

---

[2] The political motivations in the United States for Marshall Aid are the only part of the history of reconstruction to have been adequately dealt with by historians. J.M. Jones, *The Fifteen Weeks: An Inside Account of the Genesis of the Marshall Plan* (New York, 1955) and H.B. Price, *The Marshall Plan and Its Meaning* (Ithaca, 1955) are both produced very much from the point of view of the Department of State. J. Gimbel, *The Origins of the Marshall Plan* (Stanford, 1976) is a more scholarly work giving a quite different perspective. H. Arkes, *Bureaucracy, the Marshall Plan and the National Interest* (Princeton, 1972) is a more balanced account concerned with the Marshall Plan as an event in American domestic politics and administration.

form of market expansion, would increase both output and productivity beyond the levels reached in the previously unintegrated areas. Specifically, it took the form of a proposition of customs union theory, that if all restrictions on the movement of factors of production were removed from a particular area this would maximize the efficiency with which those factors were used and thus maximize output, income and wealth over the same area to the point where the benefits to each part would be greater than if that part had remained outside the union. Over time, so ran the theory initially, although doubts were quickly cast on this extension of it, discrepancies in wealth and income between the constituent parts of the union would also diminish as each part was able to maximize its own particular comparative advantage. If customs union theory were correct there would be no economic sacrifice, except in the very short run, involved in the process of economic integration.

It is not a theory which has stood up well to the test either of further economic analysis or of historical practice. The history of the Common Market has been more one of economic divergence than harmonization, although much of this might certainly be fairly attributed to persistent and even increasing differences in national economic policy. But the more general idea that market expansion, of which political integration or customs unions could be considered specific forms, is inherent to the whole process of long-run economic development and thus that some form of integration might be an ineluctable, inescapable consequence of economic development has survived better. The increasing importance of foreign trade as a proportion of GNP, the growth of foreign investment, the development of the technologies of transport and production, all, it is argued, encourage specialization and raise the minimum efficient size of the productive unit so that ever larger markets become a necessity for efficient production. Trade links and the interdependence of factors of production will, unless they are impeded, grow faster than output itself, stimulated by the maximization of factor utilization, by technology, and by the growing internationalization of taste and preference. There was certainly much in the history of nineteenth-century Europe which could be adduced in support of these more general ideas.

American advocates of European integration naturally justified them more from conclusions drawn from their own history. Productivity, it was argued, had in the twentieth century risen to higher levels than in Europe because the market for which goods were produced was larger and more standardized. The level of *per capita* national income was higher because this vast market was a customs union and derived all the economic benefits from that. European markets, by contrast, were limited and the total stock of resources on which any European producer could draw without encountering severe international barriers to their flow was much smaller. The potential for Europe to reach similar levels of productivity and prosperity to the United States was therefore limited by the fact that it was not so possible to achieve economies of scale in manufacturing and distribution. European integration would so increase productivity in western Europe by permitting these scale effects that the trade gap with the dollar zone would be closed as European goods became once more competitive with American goods. By creating a United States of Europe America could restore the equilibrium in world trade missing since 1914. Without that equilibrium, as 1947 had shown, the multilateral world of trade and payments at which American policy had aimed was impossible. By promoting European recovery Marshall Aid was bringing nearer, it was argued, the possibility of a world-wide equilibrium and a genuinely multilateral system. Thus European integration, no matter how political the immediate motives for seeking to promote it, was intellectually assimilated into the mainstream of earlier American foreign policy and there briefly reigned a happy harmony between the political desirability and the alleged economic advantages of integration.

The trouble with this assimilation was that it could be much more plausibly argued that before 1945 the existence of a multilateral system of trade and payments had depended on the disequilibria in trade and payments between Europe and the United States rather than on an equilibrium between the two continents. The payments deficits of the United States to western Europe before 1914 and its trade and investment surpluses with Europe after 1918 had both been compensated through a complex network of world trade and investment and might be argued to have been themselves a motor in the growth of the international economy and the extension of the concept of division of labour and specialization to the rest of the world. It was hard to see how an equilibrium in payments between the two areas would be achieved without eliminating from the benefits of the international payments system most of the third markets through which western Europe and the United States had previously balanced their accounts. If the purpose of European integration was to produce as quickly as possible a western European economy which did not require aid to purchase American exports – 'viability' as this goal came to be called in Washington – this might well have the result of reducing world trade as well as the need by third countries for a multilateral system.

It was not in fact at all clear that European integration was a step towards a world-wide multilateral system.[3] Like all simplifications of economic ideas for political purposes the economic justification for the political aim of European integration was not very impressive intellectually. It held its ground in the United States and among many circles in Europe, not just because of its political usefulness at the time, but because of the new and increasing interest in the process of economic growth as an instrument for forging a political

---

[3] Note the critical analysis of the policy on these grounds by C.P. Kindleberger, 'European Economic Integration', in *Essays in Honor of John Henry Williams* (New York, 1951). He had only recently himself been in the State Department.

consensus. If communism was a creed of the poor and discontented, the disinherited of the earth, the steady increase in *per capita* national income which the process of economic growth implied also had political connotations. It should lead at a certain point to pluralist democracy. At a certain level of *per capita* national income a set of political and social values would emerge akin to those in the United States and, in a world made safe for democracy, communism would appear as a political and intellectual anachronism. Furthermore the growth of the national income would still those bitter quarrels over its distribution which had been part of the fabric of European political life and unite large areas of political opinion in one common political and economic goal, an increase in national income *per capita*. Once the economic task of government was to produce such an increase economic decisions became more expert and technocratic, more divorced from the distressing world of political squabbles and if all that was sought was the best way of achieving this goal a new and more cohesive coalition of political interests could be formed. If this happy outcome depended on economic growth and growth on investment and investment on markets there was a clear link between the integration of western Europe into one larger market and the achievement of a stable, loyal, political bloc. Given the capacity to manage the economy through the manipulation of demand, sustained economic growth should be achievable and, somewhere along the path, a world without poverty, extremists or countries endangering the United States.

Where could the task be easier than in western Europe? What chance was there that the United States should seriously even consider the alternative of defending its real interest in a similar way in China in the same year? With one short vigorous push of American aid western Europe would reach the desired goal. Integration would soon appear to Europeans as a logical next step towards achieving a higher rate of growth of *per capita* income, so that sustained economic growth, prosperity, pluralist democracy and a politically united western Europe would be one common goal, a heaven to which the earth-bound sufferers of 1947 could aspire, helped by glossy images of its representation in the United States.

The extent to which these ideas were held in the population, legislature and administration was very variable. For those who believed in them all they provided an unshakeable missionary faith by which the New World could not fail to reform the Old. Paul Hoffman, who was to become the first head of the ECA, brought to it a complete adherence to the supposed economic advantages of integration and larger markets.[4] He had been the chief executive of a major

[4] Paul Hoffman, 1891–1974. A car salesman who became a millionaire by the age of thirty-five. President of Studebaker car corporation 1935–48. Administrator of the ERP 1948–50. President of Ford Foundation 1950–3. Chairman of Studebaker 1953–6. Head of UN Special Fund 1959–65 and then Administrator of UN Development Programme. Prominent in the Republican Party, he played a part in persuading Eisenhower to run for the presidency. An energetic man, he had seven children and married again at the age of seventy.

American car corporation. 'Obviously', he was to write, 'the greatest single contribution the ECA could make to Europe's enduring prosperity was to help it toward economic integration'.[5] John F. Dulles, the future Secretary of State, who was another ardent Republican supporter of a united western Europe, would have put the political rationale for integration first, but had no less a messianic commitment to its economic justification. In Congress and Senate there was plenty of support for men like Senator Fulbright who wanted to make European political unification a condition of the provision of American aid.

As for those in the civil service who were more constantly and directly concerned with detailed policy formulation towards western Europe, the extent to which they accepted these ideas will partly emerge in the course of the book. They covered the whole possible spectrum from missionary belief to scepticism and the believers were divided between realists who wished to advance the cause slowly and ardent advocates of faith in action. None the less this set of nebulous, imprecise ideas did provide a prop of belief in a time of need as well as suggesting a rationale other than the merely technical or strategic for a large programme of aid to western Europe. From Marshall's speech to the first clear definitions of the policy objectives the ERP took about two and a half months of intense discussion in Washington. Over the same time the European countries were constructing a 'European organization' as Marshall and the Department of State had requested. It was designed to resist the impact of all such ideas.

CREATING THE EUROPEAN ORGANIZATION

The British ambassador in Washington was forewarned of Marshall's speech at Harvard and given relatively specific hints that the United States would like to see as an immediate response the formation of some sort of common European organization which would co-operate in administering a programme of aid with whatever American organization would be given the same task.[6] Immediately after Marshall's speech William L. Clayton was sent to explain the new course of American foreign policy in London and Paris. He was not the wisest choice because he was already known for his extreme free-trade views, which had aroused stiff suspicions in international economic negotiations after 1945 and particularly in Britain during the negotiations for the Anglo-American financial agreement.[7] In the event most of his conversations

---

[5] P. Hoffman, *Peace Can Be Won* (London, 1951), p. 109. The ultimate purpose was to preserve the world from 'the gang in the Politburo' who were trying to take it over, compared to whom 'Hitler was a baby'. Speech by Hoffman to the Chamber of Commerce of the State of New York, 6 January 1949, *New York Times*, 7 January 1949.

[6] T 236/782, Washington embassy to London, 2 June 1947. The story that Bevin when woken with news of Marshall's speech instantly decided to launch a European initiative to take advantage of it would be an agreeable myth did it not overrate the British contribution. It is told by, amongst others, R. Mayne, *The Recovery of Europe* (London, 1970), pp. 104–5.

[7] Although they were wholly appropriate for a Houston cotton-broker.

in Paris took the form of listening to storms of protest about suspected British-American agreement over some degree of industrial revival in Germany, and in London his visit did more to stimulate British opposition than support.

The abrupt ending of Lend-Lease in 1945 had been understood in London as a direct attempt by the United States to assert its power over Britain. Making support for America's multilateral trade policy the price of the dollar loan had led to further resentments and fears for the success of British full employment policy. These had been assuaged by the eventual recognition of Britain's importance to European and world recovery embodied in the acknowledgement of sterling's international status in the Anglo-American Financial Agreements. Washington's new policy now seemed to be denying Britain's world role and the role of the sterling area, and Clayton's overenthusiastic talk of European integration, coming as it did from a free-trader of nineteenth-century stamp, was seen also as a serious threat to the domestic economic objectives of the Labour government. At the same time at the trade negotiations at Geneva, where Clayton was the chief American negotiator, the United States was pursuing its frontal attack against trade 'discrimination', of which British imperial preferences appeared to be the most disapproved form.[8] The American administration had in fact only succeeded in getting Congress to accept the possibility of lower American tariffs against the pledge that British imperial preferences would also go.

In London, Ernest Bevin, the Foreign Secretary, protested to Clayton that the new policy of providing aid to western Europe as an integrated bloc rather than individual countries would mean that Britain would now be 'just another European country'.[9] As such it would have no protection from the next United States slump. The United States might then change policy again and leave Britain helpless. Bevin's policy was to get the United States to accept that the United Kingdom should have a special interim position for some years rather than have to seek its dollars from the same common pool as its European neighbours. As the exchange crisis worsened Bevin later privately indicated to the American ambassador, Douglas, his unwillingness that Britain should have to seek financial support on the same terms as other European countries. Douglas reported that,

> He suggests personally and informally the possibility that the International Bank might be able to provide this relief to the tune of a billion dollars which, he believes, will be sufficient to carry them over the hump by the

[8] Britain had agreed to participate in the negotiations, which led eventually to the General Agreement on Trade and Tariffs (GATT), as a condition of the dollar loan.

[9] FRUS, 1947, III, p. 271, Meeting of Clayton with members of the British cabinet, 24 June 1947. Ernest Bevin, 1881–1951. Illegitimate child of a domestic servant. Began a lifetime of work at thirteen as a van boy. National organizer of the Dockers' Union 1910–20. Creator of the Transport and General Workers' Union, the world's largest, and General Secretary of it 1921–40. Minister of Labour and National Service 1940–5. Foreign Secretary 1945–51. Formidable, relentless, very able.

middle of next year, and which, he believes, will place Britain in a position where she can provide assistance to France and play her role in Germany.[10]

To participate on equal terms, Bevin feared, in a common European recovery programme would be against British economic and political interests. Rather it was Britain who should take the lead in promoting the recovery of western Europe. This would not be through any programme of political integration, he suggested, but through limited measures of economic co-operation such as the sectoral industrial agreements being discussed between Britain and France.[11] 'The British', Bevin said, 'did not want to go into the programme and not do anything. ... This would sacrifice the "little bit of dignity we have left".'[12]

The concept of western European economic integration in however limited a form did not offer any immediate prospect of relief of Britain's economic difficulties and it raised all manner of complicated issues about British relationships with the Empire and Commonwealth as well as for the world-wide nature of British trade. The inter-ministerial committee which was subsequently set up to deal with all issues relating to the ERP, the so-called 'London Committee', put the matter succinctly.

> This is an artificial means of getting assistance for UK. We are not economically a part of Europe (less than twenty-five per cent of our trade is with Europe); the recovery of continental Europe would not itself solve our problem; we depend upon the rest of the world getting dollars (UK and Europe's deficits with USA are only half the world dollar shortage).[13]

This was in line with the Treasury's analysis of Marshall's proposals, wherein the likely failure of any European recovery programme to remedy the shortage of gold and dollars in third markets was seen as the first weakness. The second was that any such proposals would be slow to come into operation, and the third that they were explicitly anti-Soviet and as such might not be greeted with overwhelming enthusiasm by all western European countries.[14] The Foreign Office did not think the United States would so quickly be able to by-pass its own brainchild, the United Nations, and events were to prove this view not without foundation.[15]

The logical response was Anglo-French co-operation especially as the State Department wanted a European initiative in response to Marshall's speech

[10] SD 841.51, 5837, Douglas to Washington, 25 July 1947. There would not have been the slightest chance of getting such a proposal through the American administration, let alone Congress, and the size of the proposed loan would certainly not have allowed the United Kingdom to 'provide assistance to France'. It was, furthermore, twice the balance of dollars still available to the International Bank for lending at that date (US, Senate Papers, 80th Congress, 2nd Session, *European Recovery Program, Report of the Committee on Foreign Relations on S.2202*, 26 February 1948).   [11] These were of virtually no importance.
[12] FRUS, 1947, III, p. 281, Second meeting of Clayton with British cabinet ministers, 25 June 1947.   [13] FO 371/62579, Memorandum for the Paris delegation, 15 July 1947.
[14] T 236/782, Programme of European reconstruction, 6 June 1947.
[15] ibid., Brief for Mr Bevin for his discussions with M. Bidault, n.d.

and the creation of a 'European organization'. Both in London and Paris it seemed essential to take joint control over that organization from the start with the intention of blunting the force of American policy and turning the 'European organization' into something less threatening to both British and French aims in Europe.[16]

When Bevin travelled to Paris to meet Georges Bidault, the French Foreign Minister, immediately after Marshall's speech this was therefore not merely to consider the terms of the invitation to the Soviet Union.[17] The State Department's own decisions had already meant that it was not itself prepared to be seen to be excluding the Soviet Union from the offer of aid, but the insistence on a co-ordinated response and on the treatment of Europe as one common economic area meant that the terms could not possibly be acceptable to Moscow.[18] In any case like Marshall, neither Bevin nor Bidault wanted Soviet participation in the programme, unless it were entirely on western terms, and neither expected it. It was in this meeting at Paris that the basic structure of the common European organization was first discussed. The preliminary ideas and decisions which emerged there were to determine not only the nature of a grand European conference to be held in Paris, but also much of what was subsequently to be the structure of the Organization for European Economic Cooperation (OEEC) which, almost one year later, was to emerge from the conference.

Both parties agreed that the detailed work of any such conference should be done by a series of technical committees whose functions would be limited to working out the details of Europe's dollar deficit and of possible areas of economic co-operation which would be limited and non-committal. Originally, technical committees were proposed to deal with transportation, energy, food and agriculture, and iron and steel.[19] When the conference met, further committees were formed to deal with timber and with manpower, and the detailed components of the dollar deficit were put together by yet further committees. These decisions on the structure of the European conference

[16] 'Had Mr Bevin travelled to Paris with a staff of experts to talk with M. Bidault for two days so that they could send an invitation to Mr Molotov to join them?', D. Wightman, *Economic Co-operation in Europe* (London, 1956), p. 34.
[17] Georges Bidault, 1899–1983. A history teacher and journalist. Became the second head of the National Resistance Council in 1943. Minister of Foreign Affairs 1944–8, 1953–4. President of the Provisional Government May 1946. President of the Council October 1949 – June 1950. President of the Mouvement Républicain Populaire 1949. In 1959 became the head of the Rassemblement pour l'Algérie française. Prosecuted for treason 1962 and fled to Brazil for four years after a period in hiding. His hobby was looking for mushrooms.
[18] A surprising number of historians are reluctant to admit that Marshall and the State Department wished to exclude the Soviet Union rather than merely wishing not to be seen to have excluded it. Lundestad gives the impression that the United States did not positively want to exclude the Soviet Union, a view which he supports from the evidence of later interviews with those involved. G. Lundestad, *The American Non-Policy Towards Eastern Europe 1943–1947: Universalism In An Area Not of Essential Interest to the United States* (Oslo, 1978), p. 402.
[19] France, Ministère des Affaires Etrangères, *Conférence des Ministres Etrangères de la France, du Royaume-Uni, de l'URSS* (Paris, 1947), pp. 10–12, Bidault to Bonnet, 10 June 1947.

were still therefore fluid, able to be modified in detail as American ideas emerged more clearly and to meet the as yet unknown wishes of the other countries who would attend. The principle, however, that the work would be done in separate committees which would be empowered to handle no more than technical detail was firmly decided and that was the important issue. Wider questions of European integration would be entirely out of place at such a level.

The second principle which was also determined by Bevin and Bidault at Paris was that these committees should be supervised by a much smaller 'executive committee' of no more than five countries which would draw up the specific proposals to be presented to the conference and liaise with the Americans. This committee, which when the conference met was to become formally the Executive Committee of the CEEC, was designed as the main instrument for Anglo-French domination of the proceedings. The arrangement was grudgingly sanctioned by Clayton on condition that Italy, which was likely to sympathize more closely with American policies, would also be a member.[20] The appointment of the other two members was left to the British and French but one place had obviously to be filled from Benelux. Britain insisted that any Benelux representative be Dutch.[21] In fact by previous arrangement the Benelux countries had agreed amongst themselves to support their attempt at complete union by sending a joint delegation to the conference, so that the Dutch representative on the Executive Committee, H.M. Hirschfeld, served as representative of all three.[22] The last place, after much argument, went to Scandinavia as a bait to induce the Scandinavian countries to participate fully. The choice eventually fell on Norway, because it was by no means certain that Sweden would need, request, or even accept dollar aid. This was a decision of much importance, for Norway was to be thrust into playing a crucial role in the first months of the attempt at a European organization, precisely at the time when the internal debate over whether the country should be neutral or allied with the western powers was at its most intense. In the later history of the OEEC the composition and title of the Executive Committee was to be slightly widened to cope with changed political realities but it remained an instrument to guarantee the control of the two larger European powers.

It may well be true, as van der Beugel recounts, that many of the participants

[20] FRUS, 1947, III, p. 292, Meeting with Clayton of members of the British cabinet, 26 June 1947. The idea of such an executive committee came originally from the French, FO 371/62568, Conversation between Sir O. Franks and Alphand.

[21] MBZ, 610.302, Foreign Ministry to Ministry for Economic Affairs, 3 July 1947.

[22] Hans Hirschfeld, 1899–1961. Born in Hamburg, the son of a Russian-Jewish father, he was responsible as Secretary-General of the Ministry of Economics after 1931 for the bilateral trade agreements with Germany. In the same position and as Director-General of Commerce and Industry, 1947–52, a figure of central importance both in the formulation of reconstruction policy in the Netherlands and in the history of the Benelux union. Chairman and director of many companies.

in the technical committees, by being brought together in this common enterprise, acquired a wider comprehension of the common nature of European economic problems and even developed not only a certain feeling of affinity with each other but of solidarity against their own national governments at moments when these governments did not show the same comprehension.[23] But there was little direct influence which they would be able to exercise on their governments. Only Italy was to choose a representative of ministerial status as head of its delegation and representative on the Executive Committee.[24] The others chose senior civil servants who were already closely involved in the formulation of national reconstruction policy but who remained only the executants and advisers of their ministers. Thus before the conference began the stage was set for a fundamental opposition between the far-reaching hopes and ambitions of the United States and the machinery of the conference, which had been designed to thwart any such ambitions. This opposition was to persist throughout the conference and throughout the first years of the OEEC. There were to be occasional American victories over these organizational barriers, but only small ones and eventually Washington began to pursue the grail of European integration by other routes.

This Anglo-French collaboration was not based on any general agreement about the future nature of Europe other than on the fact that it should lie in the hands of what were now its two most powerful nation states. It was not even based on any agreement about the future role of Germany. But it was not only against the United States that this common front would have to be maintained but also against all the smaller western European countries. For the first time questions about the reconstruction of Europe were to be handled outside the framework of the great power conferences. What would be the attitude of the smaller powers?

The exclusion from all decision-making about Germany had been particularly resented in Brussels and The Hague. There, anxious eyes were turned on the crippled German economy and angry protests beginning about Allied policy. The coming conference was seen as a chance to bring pressure to bear on the greater powers over the German question. The Anglo-French attempt to dominate the procedure and structure of the conference only stoked the fires of resentment the more and these circumstances no doubt made the task of formulating a common Benelux policy easier. The first element of this common policy was that the growth of European and therefore German output must be as rapid as possible. Translated into action this meant that

[23] E.H. van der Beugel, *From Marshall Aid to Atlantic Partnership* (Amsterdam, 1966), pp. 71–2. The author was himself one of the Netherlands' delegates to the Paris conference.

[24] Pietro Campilli, 1891– . Served in a wide range of ministerial and governmental positions from 1947 onwards. He was eventually to become president of the European Investment Bank. A banker and bank administrator, he retired from public life on the fascist seizure of power although this did not prevent his making a highly successful private business career. He was a friend of de Gasperi and closely shared his political views.

United States aid should not be used to subsidize long-term capital investment plans such as the Monnet Plan, whose purpose was to create over a four- to five-year period new comparative advantages for the French economy at the expense of countries, like Belgium, seeking to maximize output as quickly as possible. Dollars should be made available as soon as possible but only for the immediate short-term utilization and maximization of existing European productive resources. This would effectively maintain Belgium's lead in the recovery process and prevent her capital goods export markets from being eventually captured by the output from modernized French plant, while she was herself persisting with older plant. Secondly, in the Belgian view, dollar aid must be secured to back a plan to introduce currency convertibility and multilateral trade in western Europe as quickly as possible. For the Benelux countries intra-European trade was fundamental to their economies and already Belgium was running into export difficulties because of her surpluses with virtually all European countries. This was the origin of the Belgian payments proposals to the European conference which, after long argument and much alteration, eventually were to be transmuted into the first post-war European payments agreement. Thirdly, the greater powers must be forced to put the German question on the agenda of the conference. Ruhr coal output must be increased and once the overall level of industrial output had reached the level foreseen in the levels of industry agreement drawn up after Potsdam Benelux must at once press for higher levels. Internal economic policy in Germany must be governed by these 'European' principles and taken out of the hands of the occupying powers.[25] All this meant that the proposed structure of the conference would also have to be changed so that all countries attending should be present on all the committees.[26]

The attitude of the neutral powers was even more sceptical about French, British and American policy. By virtue of the position it was given on the Executive Committee, once the conference met Norway was forced into being their spokesman. The Norwegian Foreign Minister, Halvard Lange, told the cabinet on 17 June that it would be better not to participate in the American programme if this were economically feasible.[27] Until the end of May Norway's foreign exchange reserves had been increasing. The anticipation was that they would decline in 1948 because of the increasing demands made by imports and shipping charges but that as the Norwegian merchant marine was restored to its very large pre-war size the flow of invisible earnings would

[25] MBZ, 601.302, Ontwerp-Memorandum betreffende het standpunt van Belgie, Luxemburg en Nederland in te nemen op de Conferentie in Parijs ... , 10 July 1947.

[26] MBZ, 601.302, Netherlands embassy in London to Foreign Ministry, 10 July 1947.

[27] H. Pharo, 'Bridgebuilding and reconstruction, Norway faces the Marshall Plan', *Scandinavian Journal of History*, 1.2, 1976, p. 134.

Halvard Lange, 1902–70. Son of a pacifist historian. Studied in Italy and London. Journalist. Joined resistance movement, captured, tortured, and interned in Sachsenhausen concentration camp. Foreign Minister, 1946–65. In his last years he campaigned for Norway's entry into the EEC.

enable Norway to reach the safety of independence by 1949. The planned rate of improvement in the standard of consumption was in any case lower from 1948 onwards. The certainty that this medium-term forecast would not go awry and leave Norway dependent on dollar aid has to be seen in the context of the general fervour and exaggerated confidence which pervaded the small group of Keynesian economists and statisticians who had devised the first Norwegian national budget. They were convinced that national income accounting and improved knowledge of the economy would enable the Norwegian Labour Party to pursue a radically different set of reconstruction policies, in which full employment would be a first objective and some measure of gross overall planning of resources and rewards a second. Their own remarkable abilities probably blinded them to the coming international threats to the exchange reserves, on which in the initial stage a very high proportion of capital investment depended.[28]

The issue was confused by uncertainties about the east-west split. Norway had thrown its support energetically behind the United Nations and hoped to find its security there rather than in full allegiance to an American power bloc. Common sense suggested it was better, given the economic assessment, to assume a non-committal attitude to the Paris proceedings. Norway and Sweden therefore championed the cause of the United Nations Economic and Social Commission for Europe, which already represented all European countries, as the European organization to handle Marshall Aid. At the start of the Paris conference they pressed this point vigorously; at the end of the conference they objected to a new permanent European organization because there already was one. It was entirely unacceptable to the United States to use the Economic and Social Commission for Europe in such a way; that would have been to repeat the difficult political experience with UNRRA. If there were to be any eastern bloc countries in the new organization they would have to be defectors from that bloc.[29]

American and western European relationships in the coming conference were further confused by the fact that two of the countries which attended, Greece and Turkey, were not only not in western Europe but were already receiving military aid under separate legislation from the United States. Both strongly resented being incorporated into a more general aid programme and did strikingly little to help in the formulation of that programme. The issues of western European integration discussed there had virtually nothing to do with them, yet the pretence, and sometimes the actuality, was that their aid depended on the resolution of such issues. Both became members of the ERP and it would be fair to say that for most of the other members they were a

[28] Bourneuf, *Norway*. The author was herself a member of the Economic Co-operation Administration mission in Norway.

[29] Five of the sixteen countries which subsequently came to the conference were not in fact as yet members of the UN.

thorough nuisance throughout. Their delegations were a source of constant complaint from the other delegations, because they could scarcely be bothered to provide the statistical information required by the ERP with any more than a flimsy pretence of subscribing to its operations. Their governments persisted in making direct representations about aid to Washington. There was already a separate American aid agency in Greece, the United States Economic Mission to Greece. On a *per capita* basis Greece had already received more dollar aid even than the United Kingdom since the end of the war and the 'European organization' could only appear in Athens as a threat to this situation.[30] The separate problems of Greece and Turkey lie outside the scope of this book but it is worth emphasizing at this point that they often intruded in a most disruptive way into the economic arguments over western Europe because of their unwilling inclusion in a common framework of American aid.

After the angry departure of the Soviet Foreign Minister, Vyacheslav Molotov, from the Paris meeting with Bevin and Bidault, Czechoslovakia and Hungary were prevented from attending the grand European conference by the Soviet Union and Poland's interest in the proceedings died an understandable death. The sixteen countries which sent delegations to Paris on 12 July contained the whole of the western democratic bloc for which the United States was looking, with the addition of Greece and Turkey and also of Portugal, which was no democracy. But the Spanish dictatorship was too foul-tasting to be swallowed by left-wing parties in western Europe which had spent so long denouncing it and its inclusion would not exactly have made the new policy easier to sell inside the United States. Had Spain been included its economic isolation from western Europe might have ended in 1947 and not almost a decade later, but we do not know what the opinion of the Spanish government really was nor how ready they would themselves have been to co-operate. As though to proclaim a renunciation of the failures of the inter-war period the conference at the outset took the name Committee of European Economic Co-operation (CEEC).

THE COMMITTEE OF EUROPEAN ECONOMIC CO-OPERATION

The more enthusiastic advocates of a united Europe have seen the CEEC as the first solid, political step towards that goal, evidence that Western Europe could work and plan in harmony even if only on an inter-governmental base. This interpretation is sustained by the one account of the CEEC which exists, that of van der Beugel.[31] Furthermore, van der Beugel is at pains to depict the

---

[30] Over the period 1 July 1945–30 June 1947 Greece had received $99.3 per inhabitant in grants and loans, the United Kingdom $94.8. The Greek receipts were mostly grants, those of the United Kingdom loans. (US, Senate Papers, 80th Congress, 2nd Session, *Report of the Committee on Foreign Relations on S.2202*, 26 February 1948.) In addition Greece had received about £29 million in military aid from Britain and had had about £40 million of sterling debt cancelled.

[31] Van der Beugel, *From Marshall Aid*.

history of the CEEC not only as a positive step towards European economic integration but also towards a closer harmony of purpose between western Europe and the United States. Neither of these interpretations is justified by the historical record. The CEEC did more to emphasize the lack of co-operation between European economies than their willingness to plan in harmony, and far from bringing western Europe and the United States to a closer economic understanding it only served to emphasize how far apart they were.

There were sixteen countries represented in the CEEC, which met in Paris on 12 July.[32] Five had colonial empires, two had less than one million inhabitants. Two were important powers with large armed forces, one was occupied by two of the others and two had been neutral powers for more than a century. Two had *per capita* national incomes clearly exceeded only by that of the United States, four were still underdeveloped economies. Some had based their recovery on planning and stringent controls, others had been ardent advocates of decontrol and a *laissez-faire* economy. Some had a world-wide pattern of trade and investment, for others their international economic connections were overwhelmingly with the European continent. The one country whose affairs more than any other had been responsible for the conference and which was the most important Western European economy was not represented there at all.

There were as yet no German organs of government which the Americans could reasonably expect to provide German representatives at Paris. The possibility was there that the Bizone and the French zone of occupation might be represented by the occupying forces. The Benelux countries would have welcomed some form of representation of Germany as a way to initiate discussion on Allied economic policy there.[33] But the most that was acceptable was that the Military Governments in the occupation zones should be requested to provide the necessary statistical information on the same terms as the national governments officially represented.

During the course of the Paris conference American policy on the objectives of Marshall Aid and on the methods of its administration were also being defined in detail in Washington. The concept of a 'European organization' came to be defined in such a way that the CEEC was firmly expected to be an extremely important step forwards towards Western European economic and political integration, a Western European government in embryo. The State Department wanted the European conference to give birth to a permanent European organization which would bring together the Western European countries into a close economic association and it wanted that association to be a stepping-stone towards some form of political integration. The CEEC

[32] Austria, Belgium, Denmark, France, Greece, Iceland, Ireland, Italy, Luxembourg, the Netherlands, Norway, Portugal, Sweden, Switzerland, Turkey and the United Kingdom.
[33] MBZ, 610.302, Laatste ontwikkeling van de conferentie te Parijs, 12 September 1947.

had quite other, and much less far-reaching, plans for European reconstruction, most of which were based on the idea that even economic co-operation between nation states could be expected to be no more than temporary and only to be attained in the event of real immediate gains by all those co-operating and only the smallest of sacrifices. The gain the members of the CEEC were looking for was dollar aid. What was not yet clear was what sacrifices they would make to get it. Once American policy was formulated they were to be faced with an apparently firm and unacceptable price for that aid.

Before that moment arrived the deep internal dissensions between the European countries themselves had come into the open over three separate issues. The first and by far the most important was the problem of Germany. The second was that of the mechanism by which international trade was to be conducted within Europe. The third was the particular economic problems of Italy. All were brought to the forefront by the American insistence that the CEEC should make a set of recommendations about the size and nature of dollar aid to Western Europe which the Department of State would present in the form of an official report to Congress. This, it was argued, would convince Congress that a real political change was on the way and that the money was not being provided to re-create the old European system. The task of the CEEC was thus to write a common report of this kind explaining what the aid would be used for across the member countries as a whole. But on all these three issues it proved impossible to get a sufficient measure of agreement for them to be touched on in such a report in any fashion other than a blatantly elusive one.

Since April the British and Americans had been discussing an increase in those levels of industrial output in specific sectors of industry in the Bizone permitted by the Potsdam agreements. This took place against a background of total opposition to any such proposals in France. There was, however, no forum of any kind in which France could make this opposition tell. France had not been a party to the Potsdam agreements and French foreign policy was to demand a partition of Germany into smaller states, the annexation of the Saarland and the 'internationalization' of the Ruhr, before any plans for German economic recovery were formulated. The day on which General Lucius Clay, the American Military Governor in Germany, officially informed Washington that final agreement on a revision of the permitted levels of industry in the Bizone had been reached, 12 July, was the same day that the official opening ceremonies of the Paris conference were performed.[34] Clayton

[34] Lucius DuBignon Clay, 1897–1978. Son of a Senator. Graduated from West Point into the Corps of Engineers. Responsible for the design and construction of the Red River Dam 1938. Assistant to the Administrator of Civil Aeronautics 1940, where his task was to set up a national system of airfields. Assistant Chief of Staff for Materiel 1942, then Director of Materiel. Served in France 1944 and then under Byrnes as Deputy Director of War Mobilization and Reconversion. Deputy Military Governor of Germany 1945. Commander-in-Chief, European Command, and

had already received the full force of French objections to these negotiations; during his talks in Paris, Georges Bidault's view was that if the new figures for German industry were publicly announced the sixteen-nation conference in Paris would be doomed to failure and 'there would be no Europe'.[35] To come to any agreement about Germany before the Paris conference had itself resulted in decisions would 'be to give priority to the reconstruction of Germany over the reconstruction of France'.[36] A successful outcome of the European conference had been put into jeopardy before it had even begun.

When it began the situation was made even more tense because it offered not only to France but also to the smaller Western European countries their first opportunity to participate in any international decisions about the fate of Germany. For the most part the economic logic meant that the smaller countries would espouse a speedier reconstruction of Germany than even that which Britain and the United States had tentatively agreed on. At the plenary session of the conference on 17 July the Benelux delegation put their brief into practice and demanded that the level of economic recovery in Germany be considered by the conference as an inescapable part of the European recovery plan and in the Executive Committee, the Benelux delegate, Hirschfeld, insisted even more strongly on these points. For Benelux, he complained, the 'currency curtain' in Germany (the refusal of the Joint Export-Import Agency which controlled the Bizone's external trade to increase its volume of intra-European trade for fear it would accumulate soft currencies instead of dollars) was as bad a problem as the iron curtain and he described Allied policy in the Bizone as 'totalitarian'.[37] Although the British and French representatives insisted this was not the business of the conference, the Italian delegate supported the Benelux position on the grounds that Germany was the major market for Italian as for Benelux exports. Even the Norwegian representative, while insisting on restrictions being maintained on those areas which competed directly with Norwegian interests, fishing, whaling, shipping and shipbuilding, spoke in favour of an accelerated German recovery and for much wider consultations with the smaller powers about policy in Germany. The French took the same attitude to this as they had to American policy. If the conference proposed increasing German output beyond the 'level of security' France,

---

Military Governor 1947. Chairman of Continental Can Corporation 1949. President's Personal Representative and ambassador in Berlin 1961–2. Merchant banker 1962 onwards. An autocratic liberal, prejudiced, irascible, hard-working, honest and very able. His career shows that those who persistently get a poor record for tact, judgement and common sense from their superiors in peace time, as he did, may rise very far in different circumstances. He claimed to be the only man on Wall Street to have established a government.

[35] FRUS, 1947, II, p. 983, Caffery to Marshall, 11 July 1947.
[36] FRUS, 1947, II, p. 992, Communication from M. Bidault, 17 July 1947.
[37] MBZ, 610.302, Verslag van der Vergadering van het Comité Executif dd. 15 Augustus 1947, 15 August 1947.

Hervé Alphand, the head of the French delegation, declared, would take 'an entirely negative position'.[38]

The British, who had been the first and most ardent in their desire to increase the permitted German level of industry, now began to retreat and to persuade the Americans to do likewise. The problem in Washington, however, was that although the State Department was at least prepared to consider such a move in order to save its new European policy, the army was not, for it was purely concerned with Germany. Marshall managed to persuade the new Secretary for the army, Kenneth C. Royall, to sign an agreement postponing publication of the revised figures until 1 September, so that the French could make representations in Washington.[39] But the French government got wind of the revised figures through some rash army publicity in Germany and redoubled their protests. Bidault threatened to resign if there were no change of policy.[40] Although the Marshall-Royall agreement had stipulated that no other power be consulted on the new level of industry agreement, the State Department had nevertheless to ask that this deal be modified so that there could be tripartite talks in London with the French. In the conference in Paris the technical committees which were compiling the statistical information on Western Europe's economic situation and needs had come to a standstill, because the French delegates were not prepared to consider the effects of any programmes for coal, coke or steel production which were incompatible with the original agreements on the level of industry in Germany.

Any effective progress at the Paris conference, and in particular the publication of a joint report to Congress, had now also to depend on the discussions about Germany which would take place quite separately. The Paris conference had scarcely been set in motion before it had stuck fast on the obvious, dangerous and unavoidable reef which lay across its route. Thenceforward any settlement in Germany had to be by agreement with France and any progress towards a joint European agreement on the use of American aid in reconstruction had to depend on the settlement in Germany. When the Benelux delegation was preparing its proposals for an intra-European payments system to be submitted to the Paris conference, Hirschfeld asked Clayton if such proposals should be based on the existing permitted Bizone levels of industry and received an answer which was 'exceptionally vague'.[41] The Franco-German problem had at last occupied the centre of the stage; European

[38] FO 371/62568, Draft record of second meeting of CEEC, 17 July 1947.

Hervé Jean-Charles Alphand, 1907–   . Son of an ambassador. In charge of negotiating French commercial agreements in the Ministry of Finance from 1937. In charge of economic affairs in the National Liberation Committee in 1941 and appointed head of the Economic Section of the Ministry of Foreign Affairs in 1944. Ambassador in Washington, 1956–65. Then Secretary-General of the Foreign Ministry until 1972. Almost a friend of General de Gaulle and heartily disliked in the Department of State.

[39] Gimbel, *Origins*, pp. 236 ff.

[40] General Clay threatened to resign if there was a change of policy.

[41] MBZ, 610.302, Besprekingen met de Undersecretary of State Clayton op 31 July 1947.

integration would only become a part of the play in so far as it was related to solving the dilemma of the main actors and the main plot.

The delegations of the sixteen nations busied themselves with organizing the completion of a set of statistical questionnaires prepared by the French while they awaited the outcome of the Franco-British-American talks. Before the talks began the French seem to have decided that the separation of the Ruhr from Germany was no longer attainable, and that in the context of America's new European policy the essential aim was to make sure that through the 'internationalization' of the Ruhr they would still have access to its resources and control over the future development of the German economy.[42] As they had done over the question of the level of industry, the British government now tried to mediate. Bevin was not averse to the idea of an internationalization of the Ruhr providing the Soviet Union had no part in it, although he was certainly not prepared to allow it to mean French contol over Ruhr industries, which was the French objective. He was prepared to urge the United States to accept some form of internationalization as a way of allowing the CEEC to proceed and to present its report, otherwise there would be no ERP.[43] The United States had little choice but to concede something to the French, otherwise its new policy was lost at the outset; without France an 'integrated' western Europe had no meaning.

The concession was made at a meeting on 14 August by Clayton, accompanied by the ambassadors in London and Paris. Although the agreement that was reached there was only provisional in so far as it had to be accepted by the superiors of both sets of negotiators it was an important turning-point in the history of European reconstruction, for it not only allowed the CEEC to proceed towards submitting its report to Congress but also finally brought the Americans and the French to the negotiating table over the future of Germany with specific commitments on each side. The United States agreed that it would

> join in support of inclusion in a binding international agreement in connection with the peace settlement with Germany (presumably the Peace Treaty or the Disarmament and Demilitarization Treaty) of articles providing for the establishment of an International Board composed of representatives of UK, US, France, Benelux and Germany with power to allocate Ruhr output of coal, coke and steel between German internal consumption and exports...[44]

The internationalization of the Ruhr in some shape or form had become the price which the United States would have to pay for the ERP. The American negotiators agreed that 'a broadly phrased public statement incorporating the

[42] See below, pp. 141-3.
[43] FO 371/65399, Meeting in the Secretary of State's room, 8 August 1947.
[44] Y 62.3, Texte établi à la réunion du 14 août 1947.

substance' of the secret agreement would be issued. It could be no more specific, because the official position was that no decisions would be taken about the future of Germany outside the context of the Council of Foreign Ministers, next due to meet in London in three months' time. In effect France had thrown over the Soviet Union by excluding it from all future part in the management of the Ruhr in return for a firm American commitment, to give, as Caffery, the ambassador in Paris, phrased it to Marshall, 'sympathetic consideration' to an international authority to allocate the Ruhr's resources.[45]

It was a price paid with ill grace on the American side and the French could well be forgiven for thinking that the American commitment was firmer than the actions of the American government subsequently suggested. When Bevin half-heartedly asked the United States for a more overt recognition of the change of policy which had been forced on them he was sharply told by Douglas that the American government 'felt that no further price should be paid to France in this matter'.[46] On their part, the French, too, had paid a high price. They agreed, firstly, not to object to the revised level of industry agreement when it was published. Secondly, they agreed to start negotiations for the fusion of their occupation zone with the Bizone at the conclusion of the November Council of Foreign Ministers, except in the extremely unlikely event of the Foreign Ministers agreeing to the quadripartite unification of Germany.

This August agreement was to be the basis of all future French policy towards Germany and towards the joint problem of French and German reconstruction, leading through a long struggle over the form and shape of an international authority for the Ruhr eventually to the Schuman Plan. But the precise nature of any American support for the internationalization of the Ruhr had not been decided. Obviously everything must officially wait until the London Council of Foreign Ministers had indeed failed. But what would happen after that? The agreement allowed the CEEC to proceed, but uneasily. France signed the public statement on the tripartite talks 'with serious hesitation'.[47] Nor did the French delegation to the CEEC cease to criticize the level of industry proposals for the Bizone and their implications for Western Europe as a whole. The first submission of the Bizone programme to the CEEC had implied a level of iron output which, assuming the Bizone could meet all its own needs for coke, would have meant that there would be a coke deficit of 12 million tonnes in 1951 from which the French iron and steel industry's programmes would be the main sufferer. These figures were subsequently modified in the technical committee, but maintaining the revised level of industry programme for the Bizone meant that the import needs of the French iron and steel industry looked at severe risk. On the figures which the

[45] FRUS, 1947, II, pp. 1041–2, Caffery to Marshall, 19 August 1947.
[46] FO 371/65201, Conversation between Bevin and Douglas, 18 August 1947.
[47] ibid., Minutes of the 4th meeting of the tripartite talks, 27 August 1947.

technical committees eventually used after the August agreement the projected output of 12 million tonnes of steel in France in 1951 appeared likely to be between 2 and 3 million tonnes more than would actually be feasible. It was therefore understandable that the French attitude should be to make no further concessions, other than those necessary to allow the CEEC to terminate its work, until the promised talks were held and the scope and powers of an international authority for the Ruhr defined. On this, as on Germany as a whole, the Benelux delegation formed the opinion that the Americans and British 'did not yet know what they wanted'.[48]

The American government had originally set a deadline of 1 September for the successful conclusion of the Paris conference and the issuing of the report. This was why the agreement between Marshall and Royall not to publish the details of the revised level of industry agreement for the Bizone had been arranged to expire at that time. But in large part because of the central importance of what was to happen in Germany this deadline could not be met. As it approached, however, it became increasingly clear that French policy towards Germany was not the only obstacle towards an effective conclusion to the Paris conference. As far as Germany was concerned the best Washington could hope for by that date from the Paris conference was that it would not publicly flaunt its disagreements over Germany before Congress nor, which might be worse, publish a report which simply omitted all mention of German recovery.

But it also became clear that what was likely to emerge from the Paris meeting would be far short in other ways of the sort of document which the American administration hoped to see as backing before Congress. In two other areas irreconcilable differences of opinion also appeared at once. One was in the discussions on creating a more flexible system of intra-Western European trade, the other over the question of the freedom of movement of labour. The first was an issue pushed hard by Belgium with some support from the Netherlands but opposition from everyone else, the second by Italy with opposition from all sides.

No countries in the world were more dependent on foreign trade than Benelux. Belgium was in a more favourable situation in 1947 with respect to commodity trade than almost any other CEEC country. Its overall surplus on intra-Western European trade was not much more than a quarter of its deficit on dollar trade in the same year. But output had recovered so much more rapidly there than elsewhere that it could not unreasonably be claimed that the existing methods of bilateral trade were reducing the size of Belgian surpluses in intra-Western European trade by restricting the capacity of other Western European countries to take Belgian exports. Most intra-Western European trade was conducted through bilateral trade agreements, usually of annual duration, which aimed at a near equilibrium in payments between the countries

<hr />

[48]   MBZ, 610.302, Bespreking met Sir Oliver Franks, 31 August 1947.

in question over the year. Once the margin of permissible debt was reached by any importer from Belgium all further imports would have to be paid for in gold or hard currency. It was therefore very much in Belgium's immediate interest that the proffered American dollars should be used to provide extra backing for intra-Western European trade.

One of the Belgian delegation to the CEEC, Hubert Ansiaux, proposed at once to the committee of financial experts that they should recommend a scheme based on the multilateral use of the existing small credit margins, which the bilateral agreements usually contained, with the credit margins being specifically backed by dollar aid. Ansiaux discussed his proposals in London on 23 July and with Dutch and French experts who visited London a few days later. Neither the Bank of England nor the Treasury thought they would work nor that they would be acceptable in Washington.[49] Their view, which was, it was soon to be shown, shared by the Americans, was that the inflationary policies of the French government would in any case make any such scheme out of the question, since it would mean extra dollar aid for France's intra-European trade deficits. But in reality the British government was no more willing than France to place restrictions on domestic economic policy in the interests of easing intra-European trade, especially, it might be added, to further a plan which would obviously ease Belgium's trade and payments problems first and foremost.

It was agreed that Ansiaux's proposals should go forward to the Executive Committee at the end of July in substantially different form. The implication that the credit margins in the trade agreements should effectively become convertible was dropped and the request for specific American funds to back up the scheme not mentioned. This was now little more than an open invitation to all the countries to discuss alternative schemes. Even so it did not meet with an enthusiastic reception. 'The Norwegians said that the Benelux proposal is all rubbish because it could take many years before most European currencies can become convertible'.[50] The outcome of the discussion, none the less, was that CEEC set up a committee on payments agreements to take over the work so far done by the 'financial experts committee' to try to produce a workable scheme.

The committee on payments could not be faced with the same deadline as the CEEC and indeed there would have been no point since the assumption now was that dollar aid would not be specifically provided for a payments scheme. The American government had decided that aid for such a purpose would constitute an admission to Congress that the IMF had failed as an instrument of international reconstruction.[51]

---

[49] Congress was not likely, the Bank of England thought, to put up money for 'a second Marshall Plan', T 236/794, Bank of England to Treasury, 22 July 1947.

[50] T 236/794, Memorandum by Sir D. Waley, 29 July 1947.

[51] Truman Library, President's Committee on Foreign Aid, Box 11, Second memorandum concerning the financial program to be elaborated by the European Economic Co-operation Committee, 26 July 1947.

It was understandable that in the technical committee on manpower the discussions should have been dominated by Italian problems. In opting for deflation the Italian government had, at least in the short run, made Italy's long-run problem of low earnings and massive regional underemployment even worse. The solution was sought, as it had been before 1921, outside Italy. Since, however, there was no longer the freedom of international labour migration which had characterized the years before 1914 this solution meant formal European or international agreements permitting and controlling Italian emigration. This was a major interest of the Italian government in European economic co-operation.

Italian pressure produced disagreements in the manpower committee which are clear from its contribution to the CEEC report.[52] It recommended policies of full employment and at the same time that immigration agreements should be signed with countries with labour surpluses. This could hardly have meant Germany; the political difficulties would have been too great on both sides. In reality the only such agreement that did exist was one between France and Italy. In France the Modernization Plan was predicated on a high level of labour inputs into French industry and it was at first supposed that this could only be achieved by massive immigration.[53] Two agreements were signed with Italy, in March and November 1946, of which the second foresaw the immigration of 200,000 Italians into France in 1947. In fact only about 50,000 arrived, but this did not slow down the achievement of the Plan's labour targets. Already it was becoming evident that the need to import labour was smaller than had been thought, because of the rapidity with which it moved from less productive sectors. In any case, of the 479,000 foreign workers, other than seasonal agricultural workers, who migrated into France over the years 1946–9, over half were Algerian.[54] Algerian immigration was not subject to the same rigorous official controls as that from Italy and Algerian workers received lower wages. France in fact had already come to appreciate by the time of the CEEC conference that it had little to gain from the free movement of labour between itself and Italy. There were, it seems, also strong reservations in the French government about the political persuasions of the Italian workers selected for France. As Alberto Tarchiani, the Italian ambassador in Washington, 'laughingly' told the State Department, 'It might be good for his country if it could ship its Communists to France.'[55]

The Italian representatives could get no further on the labour committee of the CEEC than an agreed statement of general health and social security provisions to be applied to the recruitment of foreign workers. As compensation

[52] CEEC, *Technical Reports*, vol. II (Paris, 1947), p. 437 ff.

[53] The plans and figures are discussed in G. Tapinos, *L'immigration étrangère en France*, Institut national d'études démographiques, Travaux et Documents, Cahier No. 71 (Paris, 1975), pp. 1–46.   [54] ibid., p. 29.

[55] Truman Library, Clayton Office Files, Memorandum of conversations, visit of Tarchiani to Matthews, 1 July 1947.

it was agreed by CEEC that the countries should attend a special international conference, to be called by the Italian government in Rome in January 1948, where the issues would be reconsidered. This conference was intended to give particular consideration to the transfer of miners and agricultural workers. Here was another pointer to the failure of co-operation in this direction. Italy wished to export unskilled labour; the demand in Europe was largely and increasingly for skilled labour.

When the manpower conference met in Rome the tide had set even more strongly against Italy's hopes. The CEEC had estimated that the immediate labour need in Western Europe (omitting Germany) was about 700,000 workers. The estimates of need presented at Rome in January were for only 380,000.[56] There was free movement of labour between most European colonies and the mother territories as there was between Ireland and the United Kingdom and this, together with the already rapidly developing attraction of labour from the agricultural sector in all European economies, had led to a very active period of labour movement which had made little impression on Italy's labour surplus. The Italian government estimated that it had 1.7 million workers 'available' for emigration.[57] The British delegates were extremely unwilling to countenance any genuine relaxation of restrictions of manpower movements in Western Europe. Their attitude to the Italian proposals for a large international organization to deal with European labour transfers was frankly hostile and that of the other countries scarcely more welcoming. The Rome manpower conference rejected the Italian proposals and, had it not been for a late concession by France, the conference would have been a complete failure. The French delegates proposed that a special committee be formed solely for the purpose of day-to-day administration of Italian labour migration to France. This solution included an agreement that the French government might consider in future allowing the committee to administer Belgian and Portuguese migration to France. As the United States observer commented to his government the conference *had* to produce something and that was probably why Britain agreed to this feeble change on condition that the committee remained part of the CEEC and had no independent life.[58] In return Britain won the establishment of a parallel committee to deal with displaced persons, the great majority by now Poles in camps in the Bizone and Britain. Even this innocuous agreement, an utter failure from

[56] SD, 840.50, 5648, Manpower conference, provisional general report.

[57] Until the currency reform in June 1948 unemployment was a relatively meaningless concept in West Germany. Once the reform had introduced money wages as the norm numbers in registered employment fell steeply so that at the end of June 1949 there were 1,237,712 officially unemployed in the Bizone (OMGUS, Dk. 113.001, 'Unemployment and underemployment in the Bizonal area of Germany'). There were about 300,000 'displaced persons' still in camps in Europe at the time of the manpower conference. Such figures put Italy's problems as well as the extent of European co-operation on economic policy in these years in perspective.

[58] SD 840.50, 5650, Confidential report on international manpower conference, n.d.

the Italian point of view, was accepted with even more reluctance by Sweden and Switzerland than by the United Kingdom.

The experience of the manpower committee was only distinguished from that of the other technical committees by the fact that it gave rise to an international conference, however abortive. As soon as any issue involving co-operation at a level of significant importance arose, where government might be involved, the issue was quickly avoided. The technical committees of the CEEC were the precursor of the subsequent fact-gathering and analysing activities of the OEEC. They were a useful innovation in the European economy but they could not function on any higher level. Their task was to prepare the basic information for the separate chapters in the report to be submitted to Congress, no more, and only the manpower committee briefly and ineffectively broke these bounds.

The delegations to Paris themselves had to wait for the outcome of the more important discussions about Germany elsewhere and were unable to incorporate any clear statement about German recovery in the report because there was no political agreement about it at a higher level. The attempts at raising economic problems common to the whole of Western Europe within the framework of the CEEC had only emphasized, as in the case of payments or manpower, the profound disagreements between European countries. The report therefore began to take the shape which would be least acceptable in Washington, a set of sixteen separate requests for aid, thinly and inadequately disguised as a common European programme and embellished with plentiful but singularly unhelpful statistics. Meanwhile the ERP was emerging in Washington as a coherent plan rather than a nebulous idea. As it did so, and as the deadline for submitting the CEEC report approached, the State Department officials mainly concerned with it began to realize its true nature.

In August the Americans let it be known that they were envisaging aid over a period of four to five years and that the aid would be roughly the sum necessary for Western Europe to achieve a trade and payments equilibrium with North America by the end of that time. Compiling the total requests into one European report, however, produced a sum of $29,200 million over a four-year period. That was more than twice the total sum disbursed everywhere in both grants and loans by all United States sources, including UNRRA relief funds and 'relief' disbursements by the occupation forces, between the end of the war and Marshall's speech. It was much more than Washington had been envisaging. The draft report was unable to demonstrate any real steps towards a rationalized integration of the separate economies and it was considered in the State Department, and would certainly be considered in Congress, that that was one reason why the bill was too high. The costs of capital equipment imports for reconstruction in each country had, for example, been accepted without any investigation into how far the imports were competitive or complementary. There was no specific provision anywhere in the draft report for any form of common allocation of resources or common recovery planning. Each country's recovery plans over the four-year period and the role of dollar imports in those plans had been considered as sacrosanct.

Worst of all from the American viewpoint the draft report apparently contained no provision whatsoever for a continuing 'European organization' after the conference had ended. The Scandinavian countries, although accepting under protest that the aid requests should be drawn up in Paris and not by the United Nations Economic and Social Commission for Europe, were opposed to creating any permanent rival to the United Nations body. More important, the conclusions reached by the tripartite talks on Germany were not such as to obtain as yet a French agreement on the future 'European organization'.

On 22 August the internal committee in the State Department which had been formed to supervise progress on the Marshall Plan recommended that the CEEC report, of which it had received advance news, should be jointly screened by all the participating countries to reduce the sum of aid likely to be requested. This meant that the deadline for the publication of the report, 1 September, could not be met.[59] Two days later Under-Secretary Robert Lovett told Marshall that 'Progress so far is disappointing in that all that has come out so far is sixteen shopping lists which may be dressed up by some large-scale but very long-term projects such as Alpine power, etc.'[60] The official phrase for the American attitude towards the conference's proceedings had been 'friendly aid'. The reality behind this phrase now appeared. From Lovett's rejection of the draft report to the final disorderly breaking up of the conference direct American pressure on the European countries became intense. Two State Department officials, Charles Bonesteel and George Kennan, were sent to Paris to reinforce the efforts of the ambassadors in Paris and London and Clayton came from Geneva to Paris to help the offensive. The complaints which this group formulated were specific. Firstly, the sum requested in aid was too large, because there had been no rational co-operative exercise which might reduce it. Secondly, even this sum would not produce equilibrium between Western Europe and North America at the end of four years, again because no proper co-operative effort had been made to do so. Thirdly, some of the commodity estimates were considered to be based on excessively optimistic assumptions. There would not, for example, it was argued, be any possibility of Europe finding in the prevailing world shortage the quantities of steel scrap and even finished steel which were claimed as essential imports in the draft report. This point was already being particularly

[59] FRUS, 1947, III, p. 369, Minutes of meeting on Marshall Plan, 22 August 1947.

[60] FRUS, 1947, III, p. 372, Lovett to Marshall, 24 August 1947. Robert Abercrombie Lovett, 1895– . Decorated as a pilot after the First World War. Educated at Yale, Harvard and the merchant bankers, Brown Bros., Harriman. Became special assistant to Henry J. Stimson in 1940. Assistant Secretary of War for Air 1941 to 1945. Appointed Under-Secretary in the State Department July 1947. Secretary for Defense, 1951–3. It would be impossible to have a better claim to the American establishment.

emphasized by the so-called Harriman Committee which had been set up to consider the impact of a European aid programme on the American economy and it has to be remembered that there were still controls on steel allocation within the United States in 1947. Fourthly, there had been no proper consideration of the role of each country's longer-term, national capital investment programmes as a part of European recovery as a whole. Some of them, it was thought, did not belong. Fifthly, there was nothing in the report about measures to promote internal financial stability in the European economies. It was clear to all that inflation added to imports but of course some countries, France in particular, had deliberately chosen such a path to recovery. To demand that all countries pursue roughly similar monetary policies in order to reduce the estimated total of dollar aid to support imports, and no doubt to make integration easier, was to tread very dangerous political ground and showed how far-reaching American aims were. Sixthly, there was no specific provision in the draft report for any multilateral trade and payments system between the European economies. Lastly, the report remained silent on the institution of a continuing European organization to oversee the recovery programme.[61]

These points when formulated were put directly to the Executive Committee which met with the five Americans. There was one point on which it hardly seemed possible for any concessions to be made to the Americans no matter how strong the pressure. The British and French members of the Executive Committee, Franks and Alphand, both believed that, even outside the political pressures which had to be resisted, it was economically impossible and pointless for the report to produce a figure for aid which would ensure equilibrium between western Europe and North America in 1952, because that equilibrium had to be reached through a world-wide network of settlements.[62] The Executive Committee agreed to reconsider the report and to prolong the conference past the deadline of 1 September. But on one issue the Norwegian member, Ole Colbjørnsen, dissented from the Americans and his colleagues.[63] The other members of the Executive Committee gave their purely personal opinion that it would now be necessary to provide for 'a continuing organization', but Colbjørnsen on behalf of his own country and Sweden expressed 'full reservations'.[64]

[61]   FRUS, 1947, III, p. 391. Paris embassy to Washington, 31 August 1947.

[62]   Sir Oliver Franks, 1905– , later Lord Franks. A professor of philosophy in Glasgow University who had had a meteoric rise within the civil service during the war. Permanent Secretary in the Ministry of Supply 1945–6. Head of the British delegation to the CEEC, 1947–8. Ambassador to the United States 1948–52. Later a bank director and Provost of Worcester College, Oxford. Author of a book on the mixed economy, which like many people in post-war Britain he confused with planning. He was well-liked in the State Department.

[63]   Ole Colbjørnsen, 1897–1973. Employed in Norwegian trade mission to the Soviet Union 1922–8. Executive of a shipping company in London 1929–31. Economic journalist on *Arbeiderbladet* 1932–40. First Labour member of parliament for Oslo 1937. Financial, then commercial counsellor in Washington embassy 1940–8. Head of Directorate for Economic Defence Preparations 1949–67. Author in the 1930s of several works on economic planning. Known as well for his voluble enterprise as for the quieter aspects of a civil servant's life.

[64]   FRUS, 1947, III, p. 391. Paris embassy to Washington, 31 August 1947.

Through the first week in September each country separately deleted certain requests for aid which had been intended to cover capital goods imports, but this process was no nearer an approach to a common plan than the one which had included them in the first place. In any case even when it was complete the draft report still contained a larger sum for capital goods imports than the Americans thought appropriate. At the same time a fixed percentage cut was made on the total of each country's aid requests, a process which deliberately avoided what the Americans had wanted, the mutual screening of each country's requests by all the others. The American contingent in Paris gave stern advice to Washington that the State Department should stop the submission of the report in the form in which it was likely to emerge and should require the national governments to give fresh instructions to their Paris delegations.[65] Lovett accepted this drastic policy and recommended 'that the work to date not be considered as constituting a program'.[66] A mighty and urgent effort was now made to bring pressure to bear on all the European capitals. The public stance that the Europeans were to be left free to formulate their own aid requests was exchanged for the reality of strong political pressure. The CEEC report to Congress would have to be shaped by the Americans as much as or more than by the European countries. In the context of these events of the end of August and early September the claim, still often made, that the Soviet Union could also have participated in Marshall Aid, can be seen as the nonsense that it is.

It is impossible to read through the State Department committee papers without being impressed by the immensity of the effort of public persuasion which the administration felt it had to undertake to ensure that the ERP would pass Congress. After the long eclipse of the State Department's influence under Roosevelt, its resurgence was inseparably linked to the new European policy and this was doubtless a good incentive to tackle seriously the business of making sure that things did not go wrong once the legislation reached Congress, and that in itself was a powerful motive for forcing a report which would do more to persuade Congress of the definitive nature of the ERP. The gap between Congress's expectations of European integration and the more realistic ones of the State Department was a wide one. Nor were the State Department's own expectations noticeably realistic in the first place. The outcome of such pressures on the European countries was always likely, therefore, to be that they would subscribe to forms of words which, not being followed by the action they seemed to promise, would only lead to greater disillusionment in both Congress and administration afterwards. The one commitment now asked for which could not be covered by words without ensuing action was the one to form a 'continuing organization' and insistence on this by the United States, an insistence which was not in the circumstances avoidable, made a collision certain.

[65] FRUS, 1947, III, p. 405, Paris embassy to Washington, 5 September 1947.
[66] SD, RG 353, 27, Remarks by Lovett to Interdepartmental Committee on the Marshall Plan, 9 September 1947.

The United Kingdom was still officially supporting a position where the technical committees of the CEEC would be discontinued and their work transferred to the United Nations Economic and Social Commission for Europe.[67] Such a decision would leave the possibility that the other committees could be recalled or revived if the other governments eventually decided this to be practical.[68] Norway supported this position. France and Italy were in favour of agreeing to reconvene the CEEC once Congress had passed the aid bill. That would give time for the promised talks on Germany to be held and would permit France to keep the German settlement as the precondition of common European action. Benelux was more cautious but eventually supported the Franco-Italian position.[69]

All delegations were agreed that the CEEC could not continue to meet for a much longer time and draw up a new report. The divisions of opinion had therefore to be patched over in one way or other in a very short time and under constant American pressure, which went as far as requesting the British government to join with Washington in a joint statement condemning the report.[70] The 'London Committee', now in a weak position, instructed the British delegation to concede that both the plenary conference (CEEC) and the Executive Committee be 'temporarily' maintained, in an inactive state, until Congress had concluded its debates on Marshall Aid.[71] On 7 September the Norwegian delegation heard that the British had changed their mind.[72] It was now useless to cling to the idea that a recovery programme would be operated through the United Nations. Norway had to make a crucial choice. The nature of that choice has given rise to a debate in Norway as to whether it was made on political or economic grounds. The harsh truth beginning to be realized was that the foreign exchange reserves were no longer sufficient, after the exchange crisis of August, to enable Norway to continue with her reconstruction programme without dollar aid.[73] To plan that almost one half of net

[67] FO 371/62580, UK delegation to London, 5 September 1947. CEEC had collated information which governments had not provided to the Economic and Social Commission. But when the Commission's first comprehensive survey of the European economy was published by the United Nations, *A Survey of the Economic Situation and Prospects of Europe* (Geneva, 1948), supervised by Gunnar Myrdal, it was far more professional than the two volume report of the CEEC. Its appearance created a minor alarm in Washington because it also constituted a scholarly critique of the bases of American economic policy in Europe. The State Department commissioned in turn a critique of the UN report from the International Bank (K. Varvaressos and R. Zafiriou, *The Report of the Economic Commission for Europe 'Economic Survey for 1948', A Summary and Contents* (Washington, May 1949)) which was intended to be used to counter the influence of the UN report on members of Congress. It was never officially published, wisely, for it is not as comprehensive nor a very convincing refutation.
[68] FO 371/62565, Minute by UK delegation, 31 August 1947.
[69] FO 371/62580, UK delegation to London, 6 September 1947.
[70] ibid., FO to UK delegation, 8 September, 1947.
[71] ibid., FO to UK delegation, 8 September 1947.
[72] UD, 44.2/26, V, Colbjørnsen to Sunnanå, 7 September 1947.
[73] Pharo, 'Bridgebuilding', p. 140, indicates that on 7 September the Norwegian delegation received an estimate revising Norway's estimated future foreign exchange reserve needs upwards by about 70 per cent.

capital formation in 1947 would come from the balance of payments deficit, as the National Budget for that year had done, had been to give hostages to fortune in a year of such severe international disequilibrium. The moment of decision came when Britain finally accepted a purely Western European organization, instead of the United Nations organization which she had originally supported, and in that sense it is true that the decision was a political one. It is not necessarily true, however, that, had it not been for Britain's change of position, Norwegian domestic economic policy would have enabled Norway to remain independent of dollar aid; indeed the evidence is more to the contrary.[74]

Clayton and Lewis Douglas, the American ambassador in London, attended the meeting of the Executive Committee on 10 September where Clayton insisted that the CEEC meet for a further month and produce another report.[75] The Executive Committee unanimously refused. The discussion was 'extremely confused' and its only result was that Clayton suddenly jumped to his feet and stormed out of the meeting. 'It was really a very strange perform-ance' as Hirschfeld reported.[76] Bidault's reaction was that it was 'quite intoler-able' and that 'he would not yield to pressure of this nature'.[77] Alphand told the chief Swedish delegate to the CEEC, Hammarskjöld, that it was impossible for the French government to accept all the American demands because of the internal political situation in France.[78] The Norwegian delegation reported to Oslo that, 'The American demand means we should write a new report at American dictation.'[79]

In spite of the evident need for dollar aid in most countries American demands had brought the conference to deadlock. In retrospect it can be seen

[74] This, however, was not the view of the Minister of Commerce at the time, Erik Brofoss, who continued to maintain that it was only Britain's change of political position under American pressure which forced Norway to change its position. (E. Brofoss, 'The Marshall Plan and Norway's hesitation', *Scandinavian Journal of History*, 2 (3), 1977.)
Erik Brofoss, 1908–79. Accountant and economist. Employed in government insurance office, 1935, and Oslo tax bureau 1937. Secretary to Norwegian Refugee Administration in Stockholm, 1942, then in the Financial Department of the Government in Exile in London, where he was concerned with preparing post-war economic and financial plans. Minister of Finance 1945. Minister of Commerce 1947–54. Director of the Bank of Norway 1954–70. Governor of the IMF 1970–3. A leading figure in the history of post-war planning.
[75] Lewis Douglas, 1895–1974. His father owned a copper mine in Arizona. Taught history at Amherst College and then followed the family business until becoming a congressman in 1927. Director of the Budget under Roosevelt in 1933 but resigned eighteen months later. Became Principal and Vice-Chancellor of McGill University and then President of the Mutual Life Insurance Company. Ambassador in London 1947–50. More intelligent than many people in this book.
[76] MBZ, 610.302, Laatste ontwikkeling van de conferentie te Parijs, 12 September 1947.
[77] FO 371/62582, UK delegation to London, 11 September 1947.
[78] UD 44.2/26, Henvendelsen fra amerikanerne, 12 September 1947.
Dag Hammarskjöld, 1905–61. Son of a judge. Served in the Riksbank 1936–45 whereafter 1940 he was Director of the Office of Foreign Exchange. Appointed Head of Swedish delegation to CEEC 1947. Eventually chosen as second Secretary-General of the United Nations on whose behalf he died in a plane crash in Zaire.
[79] UD 44.2/26, Norwegian delegation to Oslo, 12 September 1947.

that the American position, although very strong, was not so strong as the more determined integrationists in Washington had assumed. Mainly this was because of the great press of different problems to which Marshall Aid was now seen as the answer. The spiteful Soviet reaction to the CEEC conference, the attempt to mobilize trade union opposition to Marshall Aid in France and Italy and its implications, had greatly increased American nervousness about 'red' governments in Paris and Rome. After the first flush of enthusiasm of Marshall's speech and the calling of the Paris conference the size and complexity of what was at stake in the new policy now became alarmingly apparent.

On the most optimistic calculations Marshall Aid was not now likely to flow to Europe until early summer 1948, because Congress itself would need to see that some of the problems which had arisen were on their way to being resolved before it would vote such large sums and sanction the new direction of foreign policy. Meanwhile UNRRA aid would be virtually coming to an end at the close of 1947. Once the decision had been made in Washington to launch the American diplomatic offensive against the recalcitrant CEEC the State Department's original timetable was already in tatters. On 6 September the State Department therefore recommended to Truman that urgent aid should be given to some European countries before the details of 'the long-term programme' had been worked out and this statement was released four days later to the press, two days before the breakdown of the Paris conference.[80] The countries chosen for 'interim aid' were France, Italy and Austria and the aid was intended to bridge the gap before Congress sanctioned the ERP. Interim Aid was free of all the conditions and negotiations on which Marshall Aid was dependent and the task of convincing Congress to provide it was undertaken by Truman himself on 17 November. Interim Aid was presented by Marshall to the joint session of the Senate Foreign Relations Committee and the House Committee on Foreign Affairs as an aspect of 'the long-range program', but even so 'essentially a relief program' and not a little Marshall Plan.[81] None the less the need for Interim Aid to support what Washington considered the three governments most threatened by Soviet tactics showed quite clearly that the Western European countries still had bargaining power.

The two days after Clayton departed so brusquely from the discussions with the Executive Committee were filled with a flurry of telegrams and confused private meetings whose main purpose was to persuade both Clayton and Bidault to take less extreme positions.[82] Monnet apparently persuaded Bidault and Douglas Clayton.[83] Eventually the Americans enumerated six

[80]   FRUS, 1947, III, p. 410, Lovett to Truman, 6 September 1947.

[81]   US, Senate Papers, 80th Congress, 1st session, Report No. 771, Calendar No. 825, *European Interim Aid Act of 1947*, 21 November 1947, p. 9.

[82]   These events are glossed over by van der Beugel, *From Marshall Aid*, p. 81, in a half-page of hurried, misleading discretion. They conflict with his general theme that European integration arose from American-European harmony, an idea quaintly sanctioned by Henry Kissinger in the introduction.

[83]   FO 371/62582, UK delegation to London, 11 September 1947. On the American side the negotiations are covered in FRUS, 1947, III, pp. 391–446.

points which, while still leaving a report which 'fell far short' of being acceptable to 'the American people' would, if the Europeans agreed to them, allow matters to proceed without CEEC meeting for a further month and writing a new report.[84] The six points were much less of a commitment to integration than the earlier American demands. The countries were to obligate themselves to the group as a whole to attain the production targets for certain commodities covered in the report. The financial section of the report was to be rewritten to avoid all suggestion that financial 'stabilization' might be postponed until aid had been received and output had increased. The report was to lay greater emphasis on the elimination of barriers to intra-European trade. The requests for items of capital equipment were to be carefully separated from other forms of requests for aid. The conference was not to be 'adjourned', but only 'recessed'. Once the Marshall Aid bill had passed Congress the European countries were to undertake to form a permanent 'European organization'.[85]

When these six points were presented to the Executive Committee they agreed that the CEEC meet for one more week at the end of which the report would be published as a 'first' report, but not, as the Americans tried to insist, as a 'temporary' report.[86] Most of the points were met by blurring the issues in the text of the report. The second point was directed chiefly at France, but, although the fourth chapter of the report stated that no country could expect aid without 'stabilizing' the economy, French internal domestic policy showed little change. This sort of cosmetic operation could not cover properly the last two points, which required a specific commitment. Norway had decided to abandon its opposition to a 'continuing organization', and the reality of the British position was that it would accept such an organization if France would, and the French acceptance was dependent on what happened about Germany. On 17 September the Swedish delegation returned from Stockholm prepared to accept a weakened version of the sixth point, which was accepted by the Americans.[87] The report was publicly accepted in a brief ceremony on 22 September by the ministers who had formally opened the conference. Norway stipulated that the report be submitted to the Storting before its acceptance became official.

Although circulated with fanfares of publicity as a great step forward in European co-operation, the report was a long way from what the Americans had desired. The commitment of the European countries to common action, furthermore, was obviously even less than the wording of the report vaguely implied it to be. The report dwelt on examples of intra-European co-operation, such as the Scandinavian customs union discussions, which were certain to be amongst the most fruitless of all possible diplomatic negotiations, the Franco-

---

[84] FRUS, 1947, III, Paris embassy to Washington, 12 September 1947.　　　[85] ibid.

[86] The Foreign Office however objected to the use of 'first' and the report was eventually published as Committee of European Economic Co-operation, vol. 1, *General Report*, vol. II, *Technical Reports*, in each country.

[87] FRUS, 1947, III, pp. 435–6.

Italian customs union discussions which, as we shall see, were in fact directed towards a quite different kind of European integration from that desired in Washington, and on a variety of trivial schemes for industrial and transport co-ordination. It did incorporate the revised level of industry figures for the Bizone in the general commodity analyses. On the overall problem of Germany, however, it offered only a two and a half page 'Appendix' accurately pointing out that

> The incorporation of the Western Zones of Germany into the plans elaborated by the Conference, while essential for practical economic reasons, inevitably created considerable difficulty, because a number of fundamental policy decisions with regard to the German economy, which lie beyond the scope and competence of this Conference, have not yet been taken.[88]

Otherwise the Appendix was a splendid compilation of all possible conflicting views, sometimes represented in the same sentences. The output of the Ruhr coalfield was to be used to contribute both to European and German recovery but 'the German economy must not be allowed to develop to the detriment of other European countries as it has in the past'.[89] Any arrangements affecting Germany's international trade were to be incorporated into the ERP and the German tariff was to be liberalized to conform to the principles of the International Trade Organization proposed at Bretton Woods.

Throughout the disputes over the report the American team in Paris had pushed the idea that a CEEC mission should come to Washington to help in the presentation of the report to Congress, a visible and audible demonstration of the new spirit in Europe. The Norwegian delegation had rejected the idea as 'dangerous and unnecessary'.[90] The matter was now settled by the United States agreeing that the discussions in Washington would be 'technical' and the CEEC members be there as technical experts. The CEEC representatives who took part in the Washington conversations which began on 9 October need not have been too apprehensive. Most of the meetings were specialized discussions on such issues as productivity, capital investment projects, balance of payments problems and so on and were all carefully structured beforehand to prevent any issues arising on which such relatively low-level delegates would have not been empowered to speak.[91] At the outset the delegates were addressed in a somewhat lordly way by Lovett who made clear how much was still undecided in planning the ERP. As a public relations exercise it probably did very little to convince Congress and its main use was in bringing home to the members of the Interdepartmental Committee on the Marshall Plan certain economic weaknesses in the State Department's ideas. On the issue of European integration virtually nothing was said.

[88] CEEC, vol. 1, *General Report* (Paris, 1947), p. 69.   [89] ibid.
[90] FO 371/62580, UK delegation to London, 6 September 1947.
[91] There are complete records in FO 371/62671–5 and in Truman Library, Papers of the President's Committee on Foreign Aid.

There could in reality be no further pressure on the European countries in that direction until the American government had decided the extent and form of Marshall Aid, until Congress had provided it, and until the conference on Germany, to which France had now brought the United States, had taken place. Even the existence of the 'continuing organization' depended on some measure of agreement on the German question. In spite of the large number of countries which participated in it and the length of time it lasted, the CEEC had proved an indecisive event. It had done more to reveal the economic and political differences of opinion between Western Europe and the United States and between the Western European countries themselves than to create the strategic bloc which Marshall Aid was intended to produce. For such a great effort it did virtually nothing to promote either reconstruction or integration in Western Europe. There could be no effective steps in either direction until, firstly, the size, conditions and objectives of Marshall Aid were more clearly determined and, secondly, the question of what was to be done in Germany was answered.

III

THE EUROPEAN
RECOVERY PROGRAMME

The aspect of the economic reconstruction of Europe to which most energy and attention has been given and the one which still seems to awaken the most interest is that of the impact of the ERP on European economic and political life. To what extent is modern Western Europe the creation of the Marshall Plan? Could it have been otherwise? These are questions repeatedly mulled over in conferences and newspapers. At the height of the Cold War American scholars sought to demonstrate that the Marshall Plan was the cause of Western Europe's remarkable economic performance and that it had 'saved' western Europe for democracy.[1] International economists in the United States, whose subject the Marshall Plan had made important to American government policies, wrote more guardedly in much the same vein.[2]

When in reaction a 'revisionist' school of historians appeared in the United States, attributing the Cold War as much to American policies as to those of the Soviet Union, the Marshall Plan came to be seen in an opposite light, as an act of imperialistic foreign policy by the United States.[3] In extending its great power interests to the river Elbe, and even beyond, the United States narrowed the range of economic and political choice for European societies, it was argued, and tried to turn them into political and economic satellites. Marshall Aid was interpreted as a device for furthering American exports and capital investment. Although they might have revised everything else, however, the 'revisionist' historians in no way revised the earlier views of the economic effectiveness and importance of the Marshall Plan. They were simply less pleased by its results.

Until very recently few doubts have been expressed about the overall

[1] The most typical of the genre is H.B. Price, *The Marshall Plan and Its Meaning* (Ithaca, 1955).
[2] H.S. Ellis, *The Economics of Freedom* (New York, 1950) could serve as an example.
[3] J. and G. Kolko, *The Limits of Power. The World and United States Foreign Policy 1945–54* (New York, 1972) has proved the most interesting and the most discussed.

importance and effectiveness of Marshall Aid in promoting European recovery. In general it has been seen as the indispensable starting-point of Western Europe's remarkable subsequent prosperity.[4] But with the beginnings of a more methodical history of the period the focus of the debate has changed, so that the question now posed is whether Marshall Aid was as important in contributing to the post-war settlement as everyone, Cold War historians and 'revisionists' alike, had assumed.[5] The length of time needed before this debate could be seriously begun is in itself an interesting phenomenon because the earlier works which argued for the central importance of the Marshall Plan certainly did not do so from any profound analysis of the Western European economies at the time, but more from a set of rather glib political and economic assumptions. The main reason for the scepticism about the overall importance of the ERP has been that quantitative measures of its impact on the European economies suggest that its contribution to them was greatly exaggerated by Cold War historians and that it also brought few, if any, of the economic advantages to America which 'revisionist' historians suggested. As a total sum Marshall Aid does not look large in terms of Western Europe's total foreign trade or investment. American exports to Europe did not increase but fell during the European Recovery Programme and American capital exports to Western Europe were at one of their lowest ebbs.

Similarly, many of the dramatic political changes in Western Europe which were once ascribed to American interference and alleged to be the price of Marshall Aid, the departure of the Communist Party from the French government in 1947, for example, or the defeat of the more radical aspirations for economic and social change which were noticeable in Western Europe between 1945 and 1947, have been shown to be part of the course of internal political development in the European countries concerned, rather than the result of American intervention. The ERP and its ideas appealed to powerful sections of political opinion in every Western European country and their influence was much stronger than anything brought to bear from outside. The political and economic influence of the Marshall Plan must in any case be seen as parts of a whole and if it is indeed true that, economically, Marshall Aid was not of major importance to Western European economic recovery, then it must follow that its influence on Western Europe's internal political choices would also be small.

The scope of the ERP was so large that these sweeping considerations are not unreasonable, although from a purely national standpoint the importance of Marshall Aid would seem entirely different from one European country to

[4] 'At the vantage point of twenty years' distance it seems fair to say that the Marshall Plan was Europe's "great leap forward", ... With investment aid, fertilizers, machines and machine-tools, productivity programmes and planned growth, it laid the foundations of later prosperity.' R. Mayne, *The Recovery of Europe* (London, 1970), p. 107.

[5] C. Maier, 'The two postwar eras and the conditions for stability', *American Historical Review*, 96 (2), 1981; S. Schuker, *ibid*.

another. At one extreme of the spectrum might be set Austria or the German Federal Republic, where the assumption must be that Marshall Aid made so great a contribution to economic recovery as to make the question at the very least well worth debating, and at the other end Belgium, where Marshall Aid was so small in terms of the Belgian economy that the question hardly seems worth debating at all. The precise effects of the ERP on each Western European economy, how it was used, and the contribution it made, can only be the concern of this book in a very superficial way because what is under discussion here is the impact of the ERP on the reconstruction of Western Europe as a whole. Belgium's recovery and reconstruction depended on that of Western Europe and thus the contribution of Marshall Aid to economies other than Belgium is of serious importance in estimating its importance for Belgium's own economic and political life. With less force a similar statement could be made about the larger economies and this was one basic tenet of the whole programme of action. But that still leaves plenty of scope for debate on a purely national level which can hardly be resolved here and which is likely to continue.

The implication of the book as a whole is that the debate about the economic effectiveness of Marshall Aid at the moment focuses on questions which are too narrow and in certain respects sterile and unanswerable. Marshall Aid's prime importance was that it was one of several contemporary attempts to reconstruct Western Europe's economic and political framework. They were all related to the existence of the ERP, which served as the impulse to them, but their relationship to its economic effectiveness was an extremely complicated one. Most of them, indeed, were intended in one way or another to thwart its economic or political objectives. Historical judgements about the Marshall Plan's effectiveness must be at least as much about its immediate impact on these alternative attempts at economic reconstruction as on the effectiveness of the ERP itself. If the quantitative questions about the ERP's economic importance could be definitively settled, all the further questions about Europe's reconstruction which scholars have ignored in their concentration on Marshall Aid would still remain. Nevertheless, an assessment of the scope of the ERP in quantitative terms must be the starting-point for any attempt at assessing its impact.

THE ECONOMIC EFFECTS OF MARSHALL AID

It cannot be argued, except in retrospect, that the Marshall Plan marked an acceptance by the United States that, because its real interests lay in the creation of a multilateral world trading system, it must act consistently as a creditor country and recycle dollars or gold into the international economy. At the time of its inception the ERP was no more than a tardy acceptance of the argument made in 1945 by Europeans that there was a large task of economic reconstruction to be undertaken in Europe which would require extensive American credits before the international economic relationships envisaged by the Bretton Woods agreements could become effectively operational. It replaced a short-term outflow of dollars for relief by a medium-term outflow of dollars for reconstruction. The difference with the period after the First World War was that it did so much earlier, on a more generous scale, but, above all, with the direct commitment of the United States government within a comprehensive plan with specific political and economic objectives.

There was in fact no alternative to direct government involvement even if only the economic objectives are taken into consideration, although these by themselves would not have been enough to commit the United States to such a course of action in 1947. Between 1870 and 1914, when the United Kingdom had functioned as a creditor economy in the international economic system, the average rate of net foreign investment was 5.2 per cent of GNP and, in addition, in almost every year the United Kingdom ran a balance of trade deficit. The United States, by contrast, after 1945 had an outflow of foreign investment which, measured against GNP, was less than half of that proportion and a very large balance of trade surplus. This outflow of sterling, backed up by an outflow of francs which was roughly similar as a proportion of French GNP, had financed the expanding pattern of multilateral trade before 1914. As far as the United Kingdom was concerned almost the whole of this outflow of sterling was private investment. After 1945, however, when the United States economy was booming and the demand for capital there high, and when American investors did not regard investments in western Europe as offering either security or profitability, American private foreign investment was very small, far too small to offset trade surpluses. It mainly consisted of direct investment by United States corporations out of undistributed profits, of which the most noticeable was the reinvestment by oil companies in petrol refining.

Over the period 1946–8 government long- and short-term loans financed 19 per cent of United States exports of goods and services.[6] The most important element in this outflow was the line of credit to Britain, followed by Export-Import Bank loans and property credits for war surplus equipment. To this should be added the outflow of interest-free dollars, chiefly through UNRRA and the GARIOA programme. The United States contribution to the UNRRA programme itself came to $2817 million by the end of 1947, more than the British drawings on the line of credit by that date and more than the total of Export-Import Bank loans. By the end of 1948 $1929 million had been expended under the GARIOA programme. Therefore grants and credits

[6] G. Patterson, *Survey of United States International Finance, 1949* (Princeton, 1950), p. 65. Over the period 1906–13, when net foreign investment averaged about 8.5 per cent of GNP, it would have amounted to a total sufficient to finance 43.4 per cent of Britain's total export trade. (Data on net foreign investment from C. Feinstein, *National Income, Expenditure and Output of the United Kingdom 1855–1965* (Cambridge, 1972).)

together over the same period would have financed about 34 per cent of the export of American goods and services.

If all other forms of dollar provision are counted, Interim Aid, military aid to Greece and Turkey, aid to China, the special programme for the Philippines and so on, the net outflow of foreign aid, both loans and grants, from July 1945 to the end of 1946 was $7444 million, in 1947 $5681 million, and in both those periods higher than in any calendar year under the Marshall Plan.[7] On the other hand the proportion of ERP aid provided as grants was very high, 92 per cent in 1949, and the loans were on favourable terms, for thirty-five years at 2.5 per cent interest rate and repayments not having to start until 1952. Marshall Aid systematized the outflow of dollars, reduced the cost to the recipients and concentrated the dollar outflow geographically on Western Europe, but it did not increase the relative size of the dollar outflow compared to the earlier years when the theme was relief rather than recovery.

The outflow of dollars under Marshall Aid represented 2.1 per cent of United States GNP in 1948, rising to 2.4 per cent in 1949 and then falling away to 1.5 per cent. The GNP was much larger than that of the United Kingdom before 1914 and the ratio of American foreign trade to it much smaller.[8] Unilateral transfers, of which the ERP grants were by far the largest part, financed about 32 per cent of the exports of American goods and services in 1949, the peak year of ERP. Loans in that year were only $452 million compared to a total for all unilateral transfers of $5211 million, so that the proportion of the export of goods and services financed was about what it had been before Marshall Aid started. There were no signs before 1950 of an end to international dollar scarcity nor of a return to an equilibrium in international payments sufficient to enable Western European economies to sustain imports from the United States without aid. The vigorous progress made in that direction in that year was at once cancelled by the effects of the Korean war. An equilibrium in world payments and 'viability' between Western Europe and America after the end of Marshall Aid still depended on the United States running a large balance of payments deficit.

At no time was the ERP the sole source of American grants and loans. It overlapped at the beginning of the programme with existing programmes and from summer 1951 became confused with aid for military purposes under the Mutual Defence Assistance Programme. The funds for the ERP were first made available by Congress on 3 April 1948, although they were to be voted, contrary to the administration's wishes, for only one year at a time. From then until 30 June 1951, when what was left of the ERP was merged with the defence programme, the total sum made available for the ERP (including the separate loan programme for Spain) was $12,534.9 million, of which about $12,200 million had been committed by the end of June. It was committed in

---

[7] US, *Statistical Abstract of the United States, 1952*, pp. 830 ff.

[8] Gross exports were 5.3 per cent of GNP in 1948.

three principal ways, as grants, loans, and 'conditional' aid. 'Conditional' aid was aid awarded as backing to the intra-Western European payments agreement of 1948 and subsequently extended to further agreements, aid which although provided from the United States in fact financed trade between two Western European countries and so was transferable.[9] Grants accounted for $9199.4 million, loans for $1139.7 million and 'conditional' aid for $1542.9 million.

The existence of the 'conditional' aid scheme in itself raises serious methodological issues in apportioning the total of ERP aid received by different countries. In terms of the country to which aid was originally allocated the United Kingdom received 23 per cent of the total and France 20.6 per cent. The detailed way in which the allocation of the sums was finally decided will not be known without a full history of the operations of the Economic Co-operation Agency (ECA), but it is not important here because the nature of the crisis which produced Marshall Aid meant that one principle of allocation overrode all others. The gross dimensions of aid allocations to each country were determined by its dollar balance of payments deficits. The European countries were required, first in the CEEC and then in the OEEC, to draw up in one comprehensive programme a statement of their annual requirements in dollar imports and it was against this programme that aid was awarded to cover the imports. The bigger the dollar deficit on foreign trade the larger the share of Marshall Aid. If there was occasional adjustment by ECA according to other principles, in favour perhaps of poorer economies, it must have been very slight. There was more scope for such adjustment in the first round of allocations because that was announced before the OEEC had begun to function as the forum where dollar import needs were first decided and well after the CEEC had broken up, although the report of the CEEC to Congress existed as a public guideline to dollar import needs.

Aid was not therefore allocated in any fixed proportion to national income and in so far as it was correlated in size with any particular indicator it was so, although only very loosely, with the volume of foreign trade. Its impact on national income was thus an indirect one through the foreign trade sector. After the 1948 Agreement for Intra-European Payments and Compensations a certain amount of aid was in fact used directly to finance deficits in intra-European trade rather than dollar deficits only. An attempt at measuring the ratio of aid to national income after it had been redistributed through this intra-European payments mechanism was made by the Bank of International Settlements and the results are shown in table 15. Measured in this way it could hardly be argued that in the first year of the ERP it did not make a significant contribution to the growth in that short period of six countries in particular, Austria, where it contributed an extra 14 per cent to the national income, the Netherlands, where its contribution was 10.8 per cent, Ireland, where the figure was 7.8 per cent, France, where it was 6.5 per cent, Norway,

[9] For a fuller description see pp. 271–8.

Table 15   Percentage of national income represented
by net ERP aid after operation of drawing
rights, 1 July 1948 to 30 June 1949

Austria	14.0
Belgium/Luxembourg*	0.6
Denmark	3.3
France*	6.5
Western Germany (Trizone)	2.9
Iceland	5.0
Ireland	7.8
Italy	5.3
Netherlands*	10.8
Norway	5.8
Sweden	0.3
United Kingdom	2.4

Source: BIS, *19th Annual Report* (Basle, 1949), p. 20.

* Including aid to overseas territories.

5.8 per cent and Italy, 5.3 per cent. These are no small sums, and even 2.4 per cent of the British national income, although only at the time about one year's growth of national income, represents a very substantial transfer. Accepting, therefore, that over the period of the ERP as a whole the transfers were by no means so abnormally large in historical perspective as to cause Marshall Aid to be singled out as an exceptional economic phenomenon in the way it was at the time and for twenty years afterwards, an added precision is needed in such a judgement. Over the first year of the programme, from summer 1948 to summer 1949, it was an important addition to national income in all the recipient countries except Belgium and Sweden, which effectively received only 'conditional' aid.

On the other hand, when we ask 'how important?' judgement must ultimately be subjective. The rates of growth of national income in Western Europe after 1945 were much higher than in the inter-war period. They averaged, over the period 1945–60, almost 5 per cent in the Netherlands and 4.4 per cent in France. The contribution of the ERP at its peak therefore (when outflows of dollars were at their highest and European national incomes at their lowest), was equivalent to about two years' 'normal' growth of national income in the Netherlands and about one and a half year's 'normal' growth in France. There is only one of the receiving economies, however, namely Belgium, where a case could be made that the rate of growth of national income was showing a tendency to fall in summer 1948, when this sudden accretion to national income became available, and it did not become available in any significant size to Belgium. One result of Marshall Aid was thus to give a further sharp upward thrust from summer 1948 for one year to growth rates which were already high.

Over the whole period of the ERP its addition to European national incomes was, of course, less significant. Table 16 pursues the same type of analysis, for the main beneficiaries of Marshall Aid, as that attempted by the Bank of International Settlements. It should, however, be noted that before the general European devaluations against the dollar in 1949, the variations in exchange rates for some countries are such as to make such calculations only valuable as gross orders of magnitude. In fact the complexities of Austrian exchange rates were such as to make the calculation so hypothetical as to be meaningless and it has accordingly been omitted. In this respect it should also be noted that the precise basis on which the Bank of International Settlements' calculations are made is not specified; however the results in tables 15 and 16 are not in disaccord.

Table 16   Total net ERP aid after utilization of drawing rights as a percentage of 1949 GNP

	(A) *At pre-September 1949* *exchange rates*	*(B)* *At post-September 1949* *exchange rates*
France	9.9	11.5
Italy	8.8	9.6
Netherlands	16.1	23.1
United Kingdom*	5.2	7.5
West Germany†	4.7	5.9

Source: Values of ERP aid calculated to include total allotments to countries in question by 30 June 1951 plus 'defence support' aid from then to 30 December 1951. Data from US, *Statistical Abstract of the United States*, 1954 and W.L. Brown Jnr and R. Opie, *American Foreign Assistance* (Washington DC, 1953), pp. 222, 246 ff. Effect of drawing rights calculated from W. Diebold Jnr, *Trade and Payments in Western Europe* (New York, 1952), pp. 40, 45. The exchange rates used in column (A) for France and Italy are, for France the average of the registered exchange rate in 1948 and the median import exchange rate for the first three quarters of 1949, for Italy the IMF par rate (which was not officially altered).

* GDP   † 1950

The Netherlands, and presumably Austria, must be singled out by this method as benefiting from the ERP on a different scale from the others. The total monetized contribution of ERP to the Netherlands economy was between three and a half and four and a half years of prevailing rates of growth of total output of the economy. For France it represents between two and two and a half years' growth, for Italy and the United Kingdom approximately two and for West Germany about half a year. But the growth of GNP is not a function of simple monetary transfers but of how the national product is used. It would therefore be more correct to say that what was transferred to the Netherlands by the ERP was the potential to increase the growth of its GNP by the equivalent of roughly four years of the prevailing rate of growth. Accepting therefore that Marshall Aid had only a marginal effect on the potential for growth of total economic output in Belgium, Denmark, Sweden and West Germany, the question must be how well did the other economies utilize the much greater potential which it gave them?

To answer this question we must confront the first economic purposes of the ERP in 1947. The value of Marshall Aid to Western European countries primarily consisted in the fact that it allowed them to continue to maintain a high level of investment and imports and avoid the deflations or the further increase in trade controls which were the only other possible responses to the crisis of 1947, and in particular it permitted them to maintain a flow of dollar imports. These purposes became less clear-cut after 1948. That was a year of social stability and undisputed economic advance in Western Europe and as American political anxieties were allayed the longer-term goal of Marshall Aid, to enable western Europe to eliminate its payments deficit with the United States by 1952, came into the forefront. With it came the idea, pushed into the background in 1947, that over-investment and inflation were the main barriers to reaching this goal. Inflation could also be presented as inimical to social and political stability. It is often suggested that through Marshall Aid the United States exercised a malign influence on European recovery by demanding less inflationary policies and by insisting on reductions in the levels of income and consumption at which governments were aiming.[10]

It is certainly true that reducing the rate of inflation did become a priority of American policy in 1948 and remained so. In this it was supported by the pressures of several Western European governments in OEEC. The 'Interim Report' of OEEC at the end of 1948 insisted on balanced budgets as a condition of the European Recovery Programme.[11] But the Interim Report was a last-minute, face-saving substitute for the coherent, long-term West European common programme which OEEC had been unable to produce and thus, as far as European governments were concerned, was simply an agreement to disagree and had no policy-making force. The pressures exerted were mainly against France and by the end of 1948 the French government itself had become concerned to slow down the rate of inflation there too. At no time was it an objective of ECA policy to produce deflationary policies in Europe. The country most severely criticized publicly by ECA was Italy, precisely because of its deflationary policies, whereas for all the attempts to persuade the French government to reduce inflation ECA gave almost un-questioning backing to the high level of investment in the French economy. Objectives did become more complex after 1947 but the central objective of that year remained central. In 1949 the United States government based its

[10] 'The ECA, in its general financial policy, introduced strict bankers' criteria of balanced budgets, stable currencies, high profits to entice investment, and low wages to discourage consumption.' J. and G. Kolko, *Limits of Power*, p. 429.
[11] OEEC, *Interim Report on the European Recovery Programme* (Paris, December 1948), vol. 1.

requests to Congress for ERP funds on the assumption that levels of capital formation in Western Europe should still be at about 20 per cent of GNP. Marshall Aid remained throughout a device to permit expansion in Western Europe. The most tangible expression of this was the imports which it was not necessary to forego.

The most striking example of the overall contribution of American aid to imports was that of West Germany, although in that case ERP was only a contributory factor. Between 1945 and 1948 about two-thirds of all imports into the western occupation zones of Germany were financed by American aid. In 1949 the proportion was about 39 per cent, about 22 per cent financed under the GARIOA programme. So low was the level of food supply in West Germany and the population so much more rapidly increasing than elsewhere in Western Europe that it is obvious that the main contribution of Marshall Aid in this case was in helping the other aid programmes to provide the necessary imports to keep the population alive and able to work. In that sense Marshall Aid was for its first two years in Germany primarily a supplementation of relief in spite of its more far-reaching objectives. By the end of 1949 procurement authorizations for commodity shipments to Germany under the ERP programme amounted to $723.3 million of which as much as $569.3 million was food and agricultural commodities.[12] This was a special case, not fairly representing the overall objectives of ERP before the end of 1949, and, as Gimbel argues, some action of this kind would have been unavoidable in Germany even had there been no Marshall Plan.[13] Harris's calculations, derived from those of the State Department, suggest that the dollar earnings of the Bizone over the first fifteen months of ERP were not thought likely to be more than 10 per cent of its dollar receipts.[14]

Those of France were estimated to be no more than 19 per cent of its likely dollar receipts over the same period, but France, nevertheless, serves as a more central case, because, in spite of its propensity to run large balance of trade deficits and soak up Marshall Aid to pay for them, the imports were much more geared to reconstruction than relief. Imports covered by Marshall Aid payments amounted to 20.6 per cent of all imports in 1949 and in 1950 to 14.8 per cent. The Modernization Plan had been based from its beginnings on the assumption that American aid was indispensable if planning targets were to be achieved and in fact it had begun its life as a one-year import programme from the United States.[15] To retreat into a closed economy would have been to throw over the very intentions of the Plan by abandoning its central concept of modernization of capital equipment and as long as the Modernization Plan was the basis of French reconstruction a high level of imports from the United

[12] US, Dept. of Commerce, *Statistical Abstract of the United States, 1950*, p. 836.
[13] J. Gimbel, *The Origins of the Marshall Plan* (New York, 1955).
[14] S.E. Harris, *The European Recovery Program* (Cambridge, Mass., 1948), p. 169.
[15] F.M.B. Lynch, 'The political and economic reconstruction of France 1944–1947: in the international context' (PhD thesis, University of Manchester, 1981), pp. 276 ff.

States was inevitable. But that, of course, is not to argue that recovery and reconstruction in France were impossible through any other policy, although they would have been very difficult, nor that a sufficient level of imports from America would have been unattainable without Marshall Aid.

It was in the United Kingdom, rather than in France, that the threat of an almost total independence from dollar trade as a policy choice was more frequently allowed to surface. If the fears in the United States that this would happen were greater than the force behind the threat, the existence of the sterling area certainly gave the threat more force than any similar threat France could have made. Imports funded by Marshall Aid were only 11.3 per cent of British imports in 1949 and 7.5 per cent in 1950. The quantity of imports provided by ERP aid was obviously not indispensable to reconstruction in the United Kingdom, although that is not to argue that it was not important to achieving reconstruction along the lines that the majority of the British government wished. A major shift in the British import programme away from the dollar zone in 1947 would have meant cuts in the food rations to a level lower than that during the Second World War, a grim political prospect even for a government with so large a majority.

Treasury calculations were that, if aid was refused and the likely import surplus over the financial year 1948/9 financed out of the reserves, there would still be reserves of about £270 million at the end of the year. This would be less than half the level they had fallen to during the convertibility crisis in August 1947. The Treasury view was that the lowest level of safety was £500 million. Preventing the reserves falling below that level and doing without dollar aid was possible, but only by the most drastic import restrictions. These would mean no more imports of food and tobacco from the dollar zone, except for Canadian wheat, a sharp reduction in oil imports and a general cut of 12 per cent in the level of raw material imports. This would in turn mean a reduction in the basic rations of tea, sugar, butter, bacon and cheese and a level of calorific intake for the population about 10 per cent below the average of the pre-war period. There would have to be further widespread restrictions on consumer goods and there would be as many as one and a half million unemployed. The Chancellor reported to the cabinet:

> These readjustments to the balance of payments would administer a number of violent shocks to the home economy at a number of separate points. The results to the structure of output, exports, investment, consumption and employment are extremely difficult to assess. We should be faced with an abrupt transition from a partially suppressed inflation to something not unlike a slump.[16]

[16] CAB 129/28, CP (48) 161, Economic consequences of receiving no European recovery aid, 23 June 1948.

Two days after hearing that forecast the cabinet decided to sign the Marshall Aid agreement.

The issue is not resolved by estimating the value of ERP-financed imports as a proportion of total imports. It is necessary to ask what the commodities imported under ERP were, for they might well have had a greater importance to the importing economy than their overall statistical contribution to total imports might suggest. Over the programme as a whole almost a third of ERP imports consisted of agricultural products which, except in the case of Denmark, were made up almost entirely of food. Of the raw material imports one, cotton, was responsible for 14 per cent of the value of all shipments. Nevertheless it also appears that capital goods continued to play an unusually important role in imports from the United States. There were exceptions to this. One was those countries where food was in shortest supply, Austria and Germany (table 17). The other was the United Kingdom and Ireland. In the United Kingdom food imports were 40 per cent of all imports, and machinery,

Table 17   Value and composition of all ERP-financed shipments
3 April 1948 to 31 December 1951 (million dollars)

	Total value	% of total
Food, feed, fertilizer	3,209.5	32.1
Fuel	1,552.4	15.5
Cotton	1,397.8	14.0
Other raw materials and semi-finished products	1,883.1	18.8
Tobacco	444.5	4.4
Machinery and vehicles	1,428.1	14.3
Other	88.9	
Total	10,004.3	

Source: US, *Statistical Abstract of the United States, 1952*, pp. 836–7.

steel and vehicle imports in general a very small proportion of the total. So large a proportion of total ERP-financed imports went to Britain, however (about 23 per cent), that the British propensity to import food and raw materials causes the general breakdown of ERP-financed imports in table 17 to be seriously misleading, especially when it is also taken into account that ERP-financed shipments to Germany were essentially for relief. As table 18 shows, imports of machinery, vehicles, iron and steel, and iron and steel products were more than 20 per cent of all Marshall Aid imports in Belgium, France, Italy, the Netherlands, Norway, Portugal and Sweden.[17] If these

[17] Only in the case of Belgium/Luxembourg were cars a significant item in vehicle imports from the United States. Otherwise it refers to lorries, buses and other items of public transport equipment.

Table 18   Imports of machinery, vehicles, iron and steel, and iron and steel products* as a proportion (%) of all ERP-financed shipments

Austria	11.3
Belgium/Luxembourg	36.8
Denmark	19.8
France	23.4
Iceland	41.8
Ireland	8.9
Italy	20.6
Netherlands	24.2
Norway	25.7
Portugal	22.2
Sweden	25.5
United Kingdom	8.8
West Germany	3.3

Source: US, *Statistical Abstract of the United States, 1952*, pp. 836–7.

* Includes ferro-alloys.

proportions are compared to the proportion of the same commodities in all imports (table 19), it can be seen that over Western Europe as a whole the Marshall Plan continued to finance that increase in capital goods imports from the United States which had provoked the payments crisis of 1947, and so enabled Western European countries to continue those policies while preserving some elements of a co-operative international payments system.

The clearest demonstration of this is the case of France, the second biggest importer of Marshall Aid commodities, where (table 19) the proportion of these commodities represented by foodstuffs was very much lower than the proportion of food in all imports. Conversely the proportion of machinery and vehicles in Marshall Aid imports was very much higher than in all imports; it accounted for 38.8 per cent of Marshall Aid imports in 1950 but only 10.5 per cent of imports in general. By the time Marshall Aid began to flow the proportion of state investment specifically directed towards the tasks identified in the Monnet Plan as 'equipment and modernization' was higher than that for repair of war damage and the restoration of public services, in 1949 more than a half of total state investment.[18] Marshall Aid was of very much greater significance in maintaining the flow of capital goods imports which sustained the Modernization Plan than it was as a contribution to French imports in general.

Although this pattern is seen most strikingly in the case of France table 19 also indicates that in all the countries which would come into consideration in this respect, except Norway, machinery and vehicles were a much higher

[18] INSEE, *Mouvement économique en France de 1944 à 1957* (Paris, 1958), p. 90.

Table 19   Composition of shipments under the European Recovery Programme compared to all imports, 1949 and 1950

	As a % of 1949 ERP shipments	*As a % of all 1949 imports*	*As a % of 1950 ERP shipments*	*As a % of all 1950 imports*
Austria				
Food	77.7	26.2	42.9	21.9
Coal and related fuels	4.5	14.4	0	15.6
Machinery and vehicles	11.9	6.8	21.0	10.5
Denmark				
Food	16.7	8.6	13.0	8.5
Coal and related fuels	0.3	10.1	0	10.0
Machinery and vehicles	21.9	12.9	20.1	11.2
France				
Food	12.5	24.0	0.3	24.6
Coal and related fuels	8.8	10.1	0.4	5.0
Machinery and vehicles	21.1	9.1	38.8	10.5
Italy				
Food	35.2	27.0	8.8	17.4
Coal and related fuels	10.5	11.5	0.1	8.8
Machinery and vehicles	6.9	1.1	29.7	3.1
Netherlands				
Food	23.1	15.2	36.6	15.8
Coal and related fuels	1.8	3.6	0.4	3.0
Machinery and vehicles	22.5	11.5	26.8	9.3

(Table 19 *contd.*)

	As a % of 1949 ERP shipments	As a % of all 1949 imports	As a % of 1950 ERP shipments	As a % of all 1950 imports
Norway				
Food	18.8	10.3	48.2	13.1
Coal and related fuels	0	3.9	0	3.8
Machinery and vehicles	6.0	36.4	22.0	33.1
United Kingdom				
Food	32.5	42.7	34.0	37.9
Machinery and vehicles	8.3	0.4	12.2	0.3
West Germany				
Food	48.6	43.6	34.5	40.1
Machinery and vehicles	3.5	1.6	4.2	2.6

Source: UN, *Yearbook of International Trade Statistics*; US, *Statistical Abstract of the United States, 1950, 1951.*

proportion of ERP-financed imports than they were of all imports. In a general sense it is true that the United Kingdom used its Marshall Aid for food imports, these being much the largest single category of ERP-financed imports. But even in Britain they were a significantly smaller proportion of Marshall Aid imports than of all imports, whereas a much greater proportion of Marshall Aid imports than of all imports consisted of machinery and vehicles. Furthermore table 19 also shows a decisive swing in Western Europe from importing food with Marshall Aid in 1949 to importing capital goods in 1950. Italy, for example, received 6.9 per cent of its ERP shipments as machinery and vehicles in 1949 and almost 30 per cent in 1950. Both there and in Austria, as the worst of the food shortages were relieved, the dollars were used, as they were already being used elsewhere in Western Europe, to sustain the capital goods imports from the United States on which the high levels of domestic capital formation depended.

But, accepting that once ERP imports are disaggregated in this way, their importance to the reconstruction of Western European economies appears much greater than when they are grossed as a part of all imports, was the process of reconstruction actually dependent on them? A definitive answer to this question is impossible without a series of detailed national studies of how gold and dollars were allocated to imports from hard currency areas. When the ECA authorized imports under the ERP it effectively extended the quantity of dollars which could be nationally allocated, by whatever system prevailed, for imports from the dollar zone. Had no ERP dollars been available for imports in 1949 and 1950, what would have been the consequence?

Food was the principal category of imports from the United States for Western Europe as a whole under Marshall Aid. Let us assume as a working hypothesis that if there had been no ERP European importers would have still had enough hard currency to obtain half the value of the food imports from the dollar zone which they actually obtained in 1949 as Marshall Aid shipments. They would then, had they wished as a group to maintain the same overall level of food imports, have had to obtain from the non-dollar zone a value of imports 12 per cent greater than their actual non-dollar zone food imports in that year. The assumption in this hypothesis is that the food supply would have been equitably distributed between the Western European nations. It would have been extremely difficult to have achieved such an increase in non-dollar zone food exports in 1949, it may have been difficult to pay for them, and, even had it been achieved it would have meant major shifts in the pattern of food consumption in Western Europe.

But would it have been necessary to maintain the same overall level of food imports had there been no Marshall Aid? The increase in the estimated calorific value of daily *per capita* food consumption in Western Europe between crop year 1946/7 and crop year 1948/9 was 20.5 per cent.[19] Assuming the calorific value of equal proportions of imports, however constituted, to be equal, the reduction in calorific intake in 1949 caused by forfeiting half of the food imports obtained through ERP would have been roughly 10 per cent. The population would therefore still have been 10 per cent better fed in 1949 than in 1947. By keeping the level of food supply to the Western European population at the level of calorific intake of 1947 there would theoretically have been no need to expend Marshall Aid or other dollars on food imports.

Would European countries in that case have had enough dollars to maintain the same level of capital goods imports from the United States as they maintained under the ERP? If we look at the value of capital goods imports under ERP authorizations in the six leading Western European importers of capital goods[20] in 1949 we find that in four cases the value could have been covered by the value of exports to the United States and Canada in that year, but that in two others, France and the Netherlands, it could not have been. The shortfall in the case of France is especially notable. Capital goods imports

[19] UNRRA, Operational Analysis Paper No. 41, April 1947; UN, FAO, *Yearbook of Food and Agricultural Statistics, Production*, 1952, p. 175.
[20] Belgium/Luxembourg, France, Italy, the Netherlands, the United Kingdom, and West Germany.

into France under the ERP were more than twice the value of exports to the United States and Canada. In 1950 they could have been covered in five cases, although only very narrowly in the Italian case, and once again French imports could not have been covered. Had the six major Western European importers of capital goods had no dollars other than those earned by exports, only the two with the most ambitious reconstruction plans, France and the Netherlands, would have had to reduce capital goods imports from the dollar zone, providing all were prepared to maintain the same level of food consumption as in 1947.

This, however, is to make so low an estimate of the availability of dollars had there been no ERP aid as to be unrealistic. Let us therefore revert once more to the first working hypothesis, that had there been no Marshall Aid European countries would have been able to obtain only half the value of dollar imports that they actually did obtain under the ERP. Using this hypothesis shows how much more dependent Western Europe was on Marshall Aid for capital goods than for food. In the case of machinery and vehicles, confining ourselves again to the six leading importers, this would still have meant a fall in machinery and vehicle imports from the dollar zone in 1949 equivalent to a 34 per cent increase in the total of imports of those commodities from other sources in the same year. For 1950 the percentage increase in imports from other sources would have had to be 30 per cent. In this case, unlike the case of food, 'other sources' would have had to be the Western European countries themselves, so this would have meant in 1949 an increase of more than a third in Western European exports of machinery and vehicles. This was clearly not possible, especially as any attempt to achieve it would have increased the demand for other categories of imports, of which a large proportion were actually obtained under ERP financing. Precisely the same objection would apply to the alternative solution, an equivalent increase of domestic output of machinery and vehicles in each of the countries concerned.

But it is clear from the preceding calculations based purely on the capacity of dollar earnings to purchase the same imports of capital goods as those obtained under the ERP that the inability of Western European capital goods suppliers to increase their exports to western Europe by the requisite third would have penalized two countries, France and the Netherlands. The question therefore is whether France and the Netherlands would have been able to maintain the same inputs of capital goods even under this more favourable hypothesis. The value of French and Dutch capital goods imports from the United States and Canada above the level of their exports to the same countries in 1949 was $104.1 million. To have obtained this value of capital goods imports in intra-Western European trade would still have required an increase of 11 per cent in the value of that trade in that year. It does not seem possible therefore that France and the Netherlands could have acquired the same level of capital goods either from increased domestic output or from shifts in the pattern of foreign trade. For them the absence of a European recovery programme would have altered the speed and rhythm of reconstruction. The mechanism by which it would have done so would have been by preventing them obtaining the level of capital goods necessary to sustain the French Modernization Plan and the Dutch Industrialization Plan.

If Western European countries, therefore, were to eat as well as they did in 1949 they would not have been able to maintain the same level of capital goods imports as they did, had there been no Marshall Aid. The rate of increase of output would have slowed down and so would the rate of increase of productivity. This in turn might have slowed the growth in real income, and the rhythm of expanding output, increasing productivity and increasing incomes which spanned the transition from reconstruction to the consumer boom of the 1950s might not have been high enough to effect the transition. On the other hand, had they eaten at the level of 1947 they could all have avoided these consequences except France and the Netherlands. Norway could have got by, but of the three countries with the most ambitious domestic plans for reconstruction two would not have been able to achieve them at the rate they did without Marshall Aid. This conclusion rests on a number of hypotheses which may be unacceptable. But even to those who find them so it has a heuristic value, it illustrates once more that Marshall Aid was designed to permit domestic economic policies far more ambitious than those of the inter-war period to continue in Western Europe.

Because capital formation was so high after 1947, even if we assume that the whole of Marshall Aid went into capital formation it would represent in most countries only a small part of the total. In 1949 it would have theoretically amounted to about a third of gross domestic capital formation in Italy, about a fifth in West Germany, and a little more than a tenth in the United Kingdom and France.[21] What proportion of Marshall Aid funds did actually contribute to capital formation cannot be determined, because all of them could theoretically have had the effect, no matter how it was deployed within the economy, of releasing other funds for investment.

Nevertheless there was one device of particular relevance incorporated into the programme, the counterpart funds. The equivalent in national currency of the value of imports financed under ERP grants was deposited in special accounts in the importing country. The use of these funds was dependent on ECA approval, but, providing governments were prepared to get American approval for each project, counterpart funds could be used to supplement domestic sources of capital. The minimum contribution to gross domestic capital formation of ERP funds could thus be set as the proportion used to finance imports of capital goods plus the total of counterpart funds used for investment purposes. Above that it is only possible to guess at the other parameter by, for example, in the case of the United Kingdom assuming what

[21] Maier, 'The two postwar eras'.

contribution the use of dollar aid to reduce government debt made to the availability of funds for internal investment. Wherever the second parameter is set, the overall proportional contribution of Marshall Aid to capital formation outside Italy and West Germany must have been small.

In fact only France, Germany and Italy used their counterpart funds almost exclusively for investment purposes. Austria utilized about half of its counterpart in this way, the Netherlands 38 per cent and Denmark 17 per cent. Elsewhere it was either left unused or used for other purposes of which the main one was debt retirement. The United Kingdom and Norway chose to utilize the whole of their counterpart for debt retirement. Neither, perhaps, was prepared to accept any degree of American responsibility in the selection of investment projects, or they conceived it as an anti-inflationary device.

But this judgement is to assume a state of perfection in national capital markets which was far from being the case after 1945. If we look at the extreme example of this, the German Federal Republic, self-finance (the reinvestment of profits) and short-term bank credits were the sources of three-quarters of all investment from June 1948 to 1949, of 65 per cent in the second half of 1949 and 53 per cent in 1950. The capital market and government together were responsible in the first year after the currency reform in June 1948 for only 21 per cent of investment and even in 1950 for only 34 per cent.[22] Over the period 1948-52 in the Netherlands self-finance accounted for two-thirds of total investment.[23] In the first place this meant that the counterpart funds available for investment were, in one year, 1950, as much as a third of the total of long-term investment finance available in Germany from government sources, although after that their significance dropped away. More importantly, in the second place, it meant that Marshall Aid was directly of much more value to certain basic industries which were unable to attract private long-term capital investment for reconstruction or to finance their own investment. This was especially the case in infrastructural development, such as electricity, gas and transport, in coal-mining and in the steel industry.

The area of investment which attracted the largest sum in direct counterpart fund investment in Western Europe was electricity, gas and power supply, followed by transport and communications, including shipping. Mining, however, principally coal-mining, received $449.9 million of counterpart fund investment over the whole ERP programme. The pattern of counterpart fund investment reflects the pattern of government investment before the Marshall Plan. It supported the last surge of government investment in immediate reconstruction tasks, rebuilding the railways and transport systems and repairing and modernizing the public utilities, and then moved on either to financing the expansion of capacity in what were called, in the terminology

[22] Bundesverband der Deutschen Industrie, *Geschäftsbericht 1950* (Cologne, 1951).
[23] W. Brakel, *De Industrialisatie in Nederland gedurende de periode der Marshall-Hulp* (Leiden, 1954), p. 92.

Table 20   Investment of ERP counterpart funds by sector (million dollars)

Sector	Total*	Austria	France	Germany	Italy and Trieste	Nether-lands
Electricity, gas and power	956.0	50.6	724.5	166.6	0	0
Transport, communications, shipping	781.3	96.9	281.3	56.1	269.9	13.7
Agriculture	623.9	44.1	203.9	70.5	99.5	138.9
Coal mining, mining and quarrying	452.4	17.3	340.2	82.4	0	0
Primary metals, chemicals, strategic materials	332.8	38.4	105.1	52.6	20.6	21.9
Machinery	164.2	9.4	10.4	61.0	83.2	0
Light industry	64.7	28.7	10.8	24.0	0	0
Petroleum and coal products	22.0	0	11.7	10.3	0	0
Technical assistance	20.3	0.5	0	4.6	5.6	0.1
Other and undistributed	452.1	14.9	157.4	101.3	113.1	5.9
Total	3869.7	300.8	1845.3	629.4	591.9	180.5

Source: W.A. Brown Jnr and R. Opie, *American Foreign Assistance* (Washington DC, Brookings Institution, 1953), p. 237.

* Including Greece and Turkey.

of the Monnet Plan, the 'basic' sectors, those which needed to expand before the rest of the economy could (as in France, Germany or Austria), a mixture of these and agriculture (as in Italy), or the agricultural sector itself (as in the Netherlands).[24]

Roughly half of the total counterpart fund investment in Western Europe was in France. The deployment of these funds was the subject of a tense struggle within the French government. The private capital market was unable to respond to the demands of the Modernization Plan and the hold of the Planning Commissariat on public funds was very tenuous, even the publicly controlled banks were unwilling to provide investment finance to the basic sectors chosen by the Modernization Plan.[25] The creation of the Fonds de Modernisation et d'Equipement in January 1948 as a separate Treasury account for the Modernization Plan would not by itself have solved this problem had not the government allowed the counterpart funds to be part of this account and in so doing allowed that part to escape from the incessant,

[24] The Monnet Plan had singled out agriculture as a 'basic' sector for investment.
[25] R.F. Kuisel, *Capitalism and the State in Modern France* (Cambridge, 1981), p. 240. The Crédit Lyonnais refused in 1948 to finance one of the two major investment projects in the steel industry, the continuous strip mill at Sérémange.

variable, short-term, political pressures, as well as the delays, of budgetary control by parliament. Not only therefore did the counterpart funds represent a greater proportion of the investment in the sectors singled out by the Modernization Plan than in the rest of the economy, but they also made the Modernization Plan politically easier to achieve provided the Planning Commissariat and the Ministry of Finance remained in agreement. The counterpart funds amounted to a third of the total investment undertaken by the Fonds de Modernisation et d'Equipement in 1948, a half in 1949 and 30 per cent in 1950.[26]

In the Federal Republic the counterpart was deployed through a special bank, the Kreditanstalt für Wiederaufbau, which had already been created to use aid for reconstruction in the Bizone. Its constitution, finally agreed in summer 1948 after much argument, only allowed it to supplement investment from other private banks. The Kreditanstalt could also use GARIOA funds and was linked by a Joint Secretariat to the Staatliche Erfassungsstelle für öffentliche Güter (StEG) which handled the proceeds from the sale of army surplus stores.[27] The investment projects which it undertook were selected by an inter-ministerial committee. The first of them were credits to the basic industries in the public sector which were governed by price controls and had little possibility of self-finance. By February, when the Allies agreed to its 'Sofortprogramm', a plan of public investment had emerged which, although on a much more modest scale, had some resemblances to the Monnet Plan in its priorities, the main differences being the inclusion of housing as one of the priority sectors and, for obvious reasons of political uncertainty, the omission of steel. The other sectors chosen were electricity, coal-mining, transport, 'other industries', projects in west Berlin, and agriculture.[28] These priorities did not greatly change as the ERP funds flowed in, except that specific allocations were made to smaller firms and the preponderance of energy and coal-mining grew, rather at the expense of other targets.

If a detailed breakdown of the investment of counterpart funds in the Federal Republic is made, the importance of investment in coal-mining appears yet more clearly. Over the Marshall Plan period as a whole, to the end of 1952, the electricity industry received DM967.3 million out of counterpart funds and coal-mining appears as the second most important investment target with DM581 million.[29] In the two years 1949 and 1950 ERP funds accounted for 43.5 per cent of the total investment in coal-mining, a far higher proportion than in any other sector. Although, for example, the electricity

---

[26] Commissariat au Plan, *Rapport Annuel, 1952* (Paris, 1953), pp. 78, 84.

[27] K. Magnus, *Eine Million Tonnen Kriegsmaterial für den Frieden. Die Geschichte der StEG* (Munich, 1954).

[28] M. Pohl, *Wiederaufbau, Kunst und Technik der Finanzierung 1947–1953. Die ersten Jahre der Kreditanstalt für Wiederaufbau* (Frankfurt-a-M, 1973), pp. 48 ff.

[29] There are more detailed quantitative breakdowns in W.W. Kretzschmar, *Auslandshilfe als Mittel der Aussenwirtschafts- und Aussenpolitik* (Munich, 1964).

industry was the biggest recipient of counterpart funds, ERP funds over the same period represented only 29 per cent of the total investment in that sector. Beyond these two sectors the biggest proportional contribution was made to the iron and steel industry where counterpart funds represented 16 per cent of total investment over the years 1950 and 1951.[30]

This high proportion of counterpart fund investment in coal-mining must, furthermore, be seen in the context that Marshall Aid was not the most important source of American aid to the Federal Republic. From the start of 1948 to the end of 1951 ERP aid to the Federal Republic amounted to $1317 million, $1382 including drawing right gains; aid from other sources to about $1500 million. Of these the most important by far was the GARIOA fund whose deployment was linked through the inter-ministerial committee and the same liaison channel with the American government to the activities of the Kreditanstalt für Wiederaufbau. The renewed shortage of coal, coke and steel in the last two months of 1950 showed the deficiencies of self-finance and of the private capital market. The outcome, after a tense political struggle over the way to finance such a programme, was another special programme of investment for coal-mining, steel, electricity and gas.[31] This programme was run through a special account in the Industriekreditbank, but the Kreditanstalt was again involved in all those areas where it was already providing finance.

Public enterprise and coal-mining in West Germany thus depended heavily on investment from ERP funds. That these sectors were a bottleneck to increasing production was amply demonstrated by the way the great surge of output in the German economy in 1950 produced energy blackouts and coal shortages in winter 1950/1 reminiscent of 1948. Yet it cannot be argued that American aid was indispensable to the breaking of this bottleneck, because there was always the possibility, even after the currency reform, of pursuing policies less favourable to self-finance and more favourable to public invest-ment. What Marshall Aid did do, just as in France, was to permit the continuation of the existing economic policies, albeit in a more ironical way. It provided a cushion of funds for public investment whose deployment allowed the Federal government to persist in fiscal policies and income distribution policies designed to put the utmost possible emphasis on private investment.

Investment of the counterpart of ERP aid was manifestly not as important to European reconstruction as the flow of imports. But the aid, just as in the case of imports, was of relatively greater importance to those sectors which bore the main weight of reconstruction in both France and Germany. This does not mean, however, that these were the sectors whose output increased

[30] E. Baumgart, *Investition und ERP-Finanzierung* (DIW Sonderhefte, N.F. 56, Berlin, 1961), p. 122 ff.
[31] H.R. Adamsen, *Investitionshilfe für die Ruhr. Wiederaufbau, Verbände und Soziale Marktwirtschaft 1948–1952* (Wuppertal, 1981).

the most even though there was a marked shift in the pattern of Western Europe's industrial output over the period 1945–51, compared to pre-war, in favour of capital goods and the infrastructural public service industries. In France and Germany Marshall Aid was used to circumvent the weaknesses of the private capital market and the difficulties posed by controls over government finance to help to break what governments perceived as bottlenecks in the recovery process. There are indications that policy was the same in Italy and Austria. In Austria, for example, there was a major shift in the allocation of counterpart funds from the transport sector to the basic industries at the end of 1949.[32] A similar shift can be observed in the general pattern of government investment for reconstruction throughout Western Europe at an earlier date. Counterpart funds were thus a useful, but by no means indispensable, aid to government recovery policies and one whose use, far from distorting those policies allowed them to be continued. This was as true for the planned economy of France as for the 'social market economy' in the Federal Republic. In either case Marshall Aid made easier policies which would otherwise have run into severe difficulties and had to be modified, it served to defend both governments, in spite of the differences between them from the standpoint of economic policy, against domestic political pressures.

The first obvious conclusion to draw is that it would be entirely wrong to consider that there was any equality in the effects of the ERP on the separate nation states. But that viewpoint was expressly rejected by the American administration which proceeded from the assumption that Western Europe's economic problem was common, and that therefore the entirely marginal impact of Marshall Aid on the Belgian or Danish economies was as important for Europe, and therefore for Belgium and Denmark, as the important role played by the ERP in the development of the Austrian, Dutch or French economies in the same years. If we express the value of Marshall Aid as a financial transfer to the national product of the receiving countries it becomes clear that the current trend to play down its importance should not be taken too far. In the first year of its operation the ERP meant a large increase in national income for the majority of the recipients, especially for Austria and the Netherlands. Over the whole course of the ERP the principal gainers, by the same measurement, were the Netherlands, France, Italy and, although the calculation has not been made, presumably Austria. Marshall Aid permitted a level of imports from the United States of investment goods appreciably higher than could otherwise have been the case. If we ask whether the same level of imports could have been achieved without the existence of the ERP, we must conclude that in the case of two economies, France and the Netherlands, it could not. Whether the American administration was correct in

---

[32] Austria, Bundeskanzleramt, Sektion für wirtschaftliche Koordination, *Zehn Jahre ERP in Österreich 1948/58, Wirtschaftshilfe im Dienste der Völkerverständigung* (Vienna, 1959), pp. 72/3.

choosing to judge the need for and success of the ERP in a global context, rather than by its purely national impact, depends on the extent to which the continued vigorous growth of the western European economies in this period would have been slowed down by a slower rate of growth of output in those two countries. Although the impact of Marshall Aid on levels of investment and capital formation in Western Europe cannot be finally measured there is no reason to suppose that it was of sufficient importance to modify these conclusions. It did, however, help the governments to widen bottlenecks in the recovery process, where this was dependent on public investment or might otherwise have suffered from the imperfections of post-war capital markets.

MARSHALL AID AS POLITICAL LEVERAGE

An alternative approach to the question of the importance of Marshall Aid is to ask how much economic and political leverage it gave to the United States over Western Europe. Was the economic and political need for aid so great that in order to obtain it Western European countries had to concede to their own detriment particular points of policy or economic advantage to the United States? It was a very strong fear in Western Europe that the price of aid would be an unacceptable loss of independence of policy and action and it is part of the argument of the 'revisionist' historians that this proved in fact to be the case.

The enormous political ambitions of the ERP were based on the exaggerated impression in the United States of the severity of Western Europe's economic position in 1947. On the other hand, since Western European countries would have rejected out of hand as the price of Marshall Aid the ultimate political aims of the ERP a measure of the extent of the difficulties in which they found themselves is what concessions in this respect they felt obliged to make as those aims became clear. This had already received a preliminary test in the CEEC, but the test was of an indirect nature because Congress had not yet sanctioned the aid programme. A more direct test came in the bilateral treaties which each country was obliged to sign with the United States in order to obtain ERP aid. Drafts of the bilateral treaties were made available at the start of May 1948. Because the diplomatic negotiations on the texts of these agreements were subject to the scrutiny and final approval of democratic assemblies they tended to be the most publicly discussed aspect of the inauguration of the ERP. Ratification of the bilateral agreements provided a focal point for fears of loss of independence to express themselves and there was no country in Western Europe where the charge was not levelled at the government that it was selling vital national interests for dollars.

In retrospect the bilateral negotiations were much less crucial than contemporary opinion supposed; the political struggle over the nature of the 'continuing organization', the OEEC, about which the public was informed only by occasional press leaks and some shrewd newspaper guesswork, was of more importance. Although at first the draft texts of the agreements produced angry reactions, much of that was due to their legal language, which was soon modified to meet with European usage, and the negotiations did not prove particularly difficult, because the American conditions, with a few exceptions, were in fact considerably more lenient than the Europeans had feared they might be.

Nevertheless, the bilateral agreements were a systematic attempt by the United States to determine how far it should and could exact political and economic concessions in return for foreign aid and as such were an early determinant of a vital aspect of American foreign economic policy for the next thirty years. They could be sifted by critics of American capitalism, nationalism or imperialism for clues and pointers as to what the United States would insist to be its vital political and economic interests even when dealing with rich and relatively powerful countries. What emerges is a curious mixture of large and small issues which seems faithfully to reflect the pressures of the American political system on diplomacy.

Taking three of the larger issues first shows the limits of power conferred by the ERP. One was the American wish to embody in the agreements a clause forcing the European countries to offer most-favoured-nation treatment to German trade. The second was the demand in the draft treaties that the signatories must register and discuss any projected changes in the exchange rate of their currency with the IMF before they made the change. The third was the refusal of Switzerland to sign a treaty which would mean the same formal links with the 'continuing organization' of Western Europe as the other members of the OEEC accepted.

The British government was first informed on 4 May that the bilateral agreement might include a promise of most-favoured-nation treatment for the exports of both Germany and Japan.[33] Objections were formulated almost immediately. The threat could not have been unexpected. The United States had tried, but failed, to obtain most-favoured-nation status for Germany at the Geneva trade conference and again later at Havana. On the second occasion it had been supported by Benelux and by the Scandinavian countries. The proposal was also made at the London tripartite talks on Germany. The cost of the occupations of Germany and Japan had made the exports of these countries seem almost more precious to America than her own and the proposals emanated and received their strongest support from the Department of the Army. But there were deeper implications in the American proposal. If trade were a force for integration, it was vital to stop the sort of discrimination against German exports which had been practised in the 1920s. British opposition to the proposal took account of its obvious political repercussions

[33] T 236/810, London to UK delegation, 4 May 1948.

in France but was also based on the reasonable argument that there would be no reciprocal treatment by the occupying authorities in Germany, because existing German tariffs were not in operation and were useless.[34] French opposition needed to go no further than the argument that the proposal would be a godsend both to the French Communist Party and to de Gaulle's new movement. Both Britain and France attempted to bring Italy into a common front on the issue on the ground that what was grist to the French Communist Party would be just as welcome to the Italian communists. On 20 June, however, Italy accepted the bilateral with the most-favoured-nation clause still in it leaving Britain and France in joint isolation.[35]

Because America was paying most of the costs of the Bizone it had to be admitted that an attempt to promote its exports was difficult to oppose in London! Britain and France suggested that the clause might be negotiated in a separate protocol, less in the glare of parliamentary enquiry. Any such protocol could, through being ratified by all the signatories to GATT, ensure that when a German government was formed it would be obliged itself to offer the same commercial terms. Such a procedure would have been too long-winded, so the United States suggested the clause in the bilateral be limited in its effect to two years after which any German government would presumably have to bargain for itself. But the United States also insisted that Japan be included in the same clause or in the protocol. The agitation of the British textile industries was loud and strenuous against this and was accompanied by an outburst of public and parliamentary opinion which set the government adamantly against any concessions to Japan whatever might be done to acknowledge America's interests in Germany. The position was summed up by Sir Stafford Cripps, the Chancellor, to his cabinet colleagues on 21 June, showing precisely what concessions he was constrained to make.[36]

> He said that he was not prepared to agree that the most-favoured-nation protocol should extend to Japan. It was only after some hesitation that he had come to the conclusion that we could properly accept its application to Germany. He had been influenced by the considerations that it was in our own interests to rebuild the German economy, that the validity of the

[34] ibid., Meeting of London Committee, 6 May 1948.
[35] Norway tried to bargain for the use of more of her shipping in the carriage of Marshall Aid goods if she accepted the clause, but failed.
[36] Sir Richard Stafford Cripps. 1889–1952. Son of a peer and a nephew of Sidney Webb. Achieved some early academic success as a chemist before becoming a successful and wealthy barrister. Joined Labour Party 1929 and became Solicitor-General 1930–1. A severe critic of parliament and the monarchy in the 1930s. Expelled from the Party, 1938, for his strenuous advocacy of a popular front. Ambassador to the Soviet Union 1940–2. Leader of House of Commons and member of war cabinet 1942. Minister of Aircraft Production, not in the war cabinet, 1942–5. President of Board of Trade 1945. Minister for Economic Affairs 1947. Chancellor of the Exchequer 1947–50. Author of books about God, democracy and socialism.

protocol would not extend beyond two years, and that it was unlikely in that time that German industries would be able to compete with our own in overseas markets.[37]

Four days later Douglas saw Bevin and Cripps together and came to a possible compromise with them. The United States would drop its insistence on a most-favoured-nation clause for Japan in return for an assurance that Britain would subsequently undertake an independent negotiation with Japan, and in return also for an extension of the time limit of the German clause to two and a half years.[38] The period for negotiating the bilaterals expired on 3 July. They had to be signed before the OEEC could begin. It was essential to come to terms with Britain and France if anything was to be hoped for from the 'continuing organization'. Kenneth Royall, the Army Secretary, wanted to threaten to withhold assistance if the American terms were not met, but when the decision reached Truman he decided against such a course. The record of the Havana conference was searched and an effort was even made to find Clayton, who was touring in Canada, in the hope of discovering some past inconsistency in the British position which might be used at the last moment, but to no avail.[39] From Paris the American ambassador, Jefferson Caffery, had made his habitual prediction that the French government would fall were the text not altered.[40] There was nothing to do but concede the point to London and Paris. After two rather hopeless days of resistance the most-favoured-nation clause for Japan was also removed from the agreement with the Netherlands.

The articles and phrases in the draft bilateral agreements which related to exchange rates, especially Article X, met with more extensive opposition. Their wording seemed to imply that the United States could require the European countries to consult with the IMF about alterations in the exchange rate of their currencies whenever the IMF felt this necessary. All felt this to be an infringement of their national sovereignty. In the first place it appeared to give America an extra weapon in forcing a future devaluation of European currencies against the dollar. That many currencies were overvalued was a common assumption, but not all European governments shared the growing American view that a general readjustment would promote more European exports and narrow the payments gap. All were determined, in any case, to keep the timing of such decisions a matter of purely national policy. The rules of the IMF required them merely to 'notify' the Fund of changes and those rules had already become more honoured in the breach than the observance. In spite of IMF protests France had operated multiple exchange rates, which were by any reasonable definition discriminatory and thus in breach of IMF

---

[37] T 236/812, Meeting of cabinet Economic Policy Committee, 21 June 1948.
[38] SD 840.50, 5668, Telephone conversation Douglas–Thorp, 25 June 1948. Perhaps this indicated an increasingly pessimistic view of the time needed to set up a German government.
[39] ibid., passim.   [40] ibid., Paris embassy to Washington, 21 June 1948.

rules, since January. The British decision in August 1947 to end sterling convertibility against the dollar had been a purely national one. Consequently Article X was seen, not unreasonably, as an attempt by the United States to bend the IMF more completely to its own purposes and to use it to intervene in crucial areas of national economic policy-making.

It was this clause above all which left Bidault 'strongly disturbed' about the bilateral and led the former Prime Minister, Paul Reynaud, to tell the American ambassador that were it his government he would never present the draft agreement to the Chamber.[41] Hirschfeld felt that many members of the Dutch parliament would similarly feel that their sovereign rights were seriously restricted.[42] The text caused the Swedish government 'seriously to question whether it is advisable to tie itself inextricably in such commitments especially since OEEC may have progressively greater political implications.'[43] The British view was that Article X could only increase the pressures for devaluation on European currencies, that it had nothing to do with the European Co-operation Act and that it was 'unacceptable'.[44]

The origins of Article X, were they traced back in detail, would surely reveal much of the complexity of the process of American policy-making. When the French government had introduced multiple exchange rates the IMF had asked the National Advisory Council on International Monetary and Financial Problems to condemn them and had received much support there. The State Department had had to fight hard on behalf of the French action, backed as usual by Caffery's insistence that the French government's life was at stake, and this fight only exacerbated the conflicts between the IMF, which still represented the Bretton Woods settlement and the American economic interests of 1945, and the State Department, which saw the immediate political and economic objectives of the ERP as now overriding the more general considerations of Bretton Woods. The language of the draft bilateral agreement was in certain aspects a rather despairing attempt to gloss over these differences. Article X was, in short, a weak position to defend. On 16 June the National Advisory Council decided to drop it on the advice of the State Department and the ECA. Speaking for the State Department Willard Thorp put the matter in perspective.

The United States had tremendous leverage and could impose on these countries many things to which they would object. It was difficult to say just when foreign countries would refuse to co-operate in the program. It was important that there not be agreements which would lead to charges of American invasion of sovereignty. There might be some countries which

[41] SD 840.50, 534, Paris embassy to Washington, 19 June 1948.
[42] SD 840.50, 5663, Hague embassy to Washington, 26 May 1948.
[43] ibid., Stockholm embassy to Washington, 14 June 1948.
[44] T 236/810, London Committee, Working Party on the Draft Bilateral Agreement, 25 May 1948.

would consider this article as being more than they could take. Those in the worst situations would have to take whatever they were told but with respect to the latter countries it would not matter too much what was put into the agreements since the United States would in any event be in a position to insist that appropriate measures be taken.[45]

The decision was taken not to drop the offending article immediately, but to drop it as a last major concession in the negotiations. Thorp's distinction between those countries 'that would have to take whatever they were told' and the others defined one parameter of the exercise of American power. Neither Britain nor France was in that category and if the bilaterals were to be more or less standardized they had to be accommodated to the realities of these differences in power.[46] There were other levers to use on the less powerful. The reasons for taking this decision in the National Advisory Council reveal, however, what proved to be an over-optimistic appraisal of the strength which Marshall Aid conferred. It was the opinion of the Council's staff committee that phrases in other articles of the agreement gave more or less the same range of powers to the United States. If the United States did want to bring pressure to revise exchange rates it would still have powers to ask for a review and this would naturally mean doing so through the IMF. This, when done, did not get America very far in 1949.[47]

Another perspective on these parameters of power is provided by the American negotiations with Switzerland. The Swiss government did not wish to sign a bilateral agreement or the OEEC convention, although its intention was to be a member in all other ways. Foreign trade was a major component of Swiss national income. In 1948 Swiss exports to Western European markets accounted for 50 per cent of total export trade and imports from Western Europe for 46.9 per cent of the total import trade.[48] The United States, however, was the single largest Swiss export market and had been so since the war as the release of pent-up consumer demand there had attracted imports of natural and artificial silks, high-quality cotton textiles and embroideries and, above all, watches. The level of Swiss watch exports to the United States in 1947 and 1948 was, for example, six times in current values its level of 1938.[49] These exports still only covered half of Switzerland's imports from the United States and the overall Swiss trade balance stood in deficit at about $360 million in 1948, a sum roughly comparable to the record deficit of 1947. Within Western Europe, however, Switzerland was on balance a creditor. Its earnings from invisibles combined with its reserves meant that the deficit with the

---

[45] SD, NAC, Meeting of 16 June 1948.
[46] This was the attitude of the British government to the original text of the bilateral which 'puts us on the same footing as countries like Greece and Italy'. T 236/811, London to UK delegation, 2 June 1948.   [47] See below p. 289.
[48] Switzerland, *Statistisches Jahrbuch der Schweiz*, 1948, pp. 276, 286–7, 300–1.
[49] ibid., p. 305.

United States could be financed without recourse to dollar aid. At least three-quarters of the total trade deficit was probably covered by invisible earnings.[50] In the previous year the reserves had fallen only slightly. Part of this fall may well have been to cope with the record import surplus, but if this was so it was amply covered by the movement of foreign funds into Switzerland in autumn 1947. In 1948 the total reserves increased, in spite of the persistence of the large trade deficit. Switzerland could not therefore afford to be excluded from Western European markets nor from any Western European payments system, but the extent of American economic leverage over it was not necessarily such as to justify risking its neutrality. Because the European countries did not insist on any such infringement but were solely interested in reaching a working arrangement which would establish Switzerland as a functioning member of the OEEC, the United States was from the outset in a weak bargaining position against a tiny country.

It was true that if ERP aid were used to back a European payments agreement this would ease Switzerland's trading difficulties. It was also true that the ECA could make it more difficult for her to obtain supplies by giving preference to the other Western European countries for dollars for commodities in high demand and could even bring pressures to impose physical controls on the destination of the commodities themselves. At the end of April the United States deployed all those threats.[51] By June, however, America was ready to seek a possible way out in an exchange of notes which would cover Switzerland's adherence to the common programme while permitting her not to sign a bilateral treaty. What the notes would say was still far from settled.

The issues became more sharply defined when the OEEC itself began to undertake the allocation of aid. Switzerland refused to submit its import requirements to the OEEC for screening by the other members and because it was not bound by any treaty it was, legally, on good ground. At this point the American government threatened more firmly to withhold import licences for Swiss orders unless Switzerland co-operated on equal terms with the full members.[52] This proved the start of reaching an agreement, because it forced an accurate appraisal in the State Department of where American priorities lay. They lay in the full submission of Swiss imports to OEEC scrutiny and in Swiss co-operation with the United States in control of 'strategic' trade. The first could definitely be obtained and the second might be obtained with the sacrifice of the bilateral agreement. The mounting tide of public opposition in Switzerland to the bilateral agreement eventually clinched the matter. Already in January the Social Democratic Party had published its 'theses' on the Marshall Plan, accepting it only on the grounds that Switzerland would reject

[50] The only estimates are those in BIS, *18th Annual Report*, pp. 78/9, *19th Annual Report*, p. 82.
[51] SD 840.50, 5659, Visit of Swiss minister in United States to State Department, 29 April 1948.   [52] SD 840.50, 534, Washington to Bern, 28 July 1948.

all political conditions which might be imposed. This attitude was restated more firmly in October and at the start of November a full-scale debate in the Swiss parliament made it obvious that the treaty had little chance of acceptance there. At that point the United States government finally informed Switzerland that it would not insist on the signing of a bilateral agreement.[53]

In all these three instances it had already become evident that the leverage afforded by Marshall Aid was insufficient for the United States to force through its own policies. Each, however, concerned a vital area of European interest, for France and Britain the resurgence of Germany, for Switzerland neutrality, and for all Western European countries control over their own exchange rates. When smaller issues were at stake the United States was able to gain points of policy even against the more powerful.

One of these was the stipulation that European countries should provide guarantees that private American investments in Europe under the Economic Co-operation Act could be converted back into dollars for repatriation and offset against ERP grants. In 1949 this was extended to cover profits from investment. Before 1949 the nature of the guarantee was very limited and there was in any case very little private American investment under its terms. By the end of 1949 a mere $3.9 million had been so guaranteed, $3.5 million of it in the United Kingdom.

The bilaterals also included a clause which allowed the ECA to set aside up to 5 per cent of the total appropriation for each country to allow the purchase of strategic materials for the American economy. Congress was keen on this policy and pressed the ECA to use its bargaining powers in this respect to the full extent and there were fears in Europe about an invasion of colonies by American investment. But the operations under this clause were very limited and by 1949 the emphasis in Western Europe had swung towards encouraging American investment in and purchases from colonies as a way of furthering their development. By June 1951 about $100 million of ERP funds had been used to get strategic materials.

Approval for use of the counterpart funds had to be obtained from the United States government. In West Germany the Americans did raise serious objections to the counterpart fund investment programme in 1950. The ECA attempted to restrict it more to certain 'critical sectors', steel and coal which were in short supply, and differentiate it from the general pattern of investment which favoured consumer goods industries more.[54] But pressures of this kind were not very forceful when investment of counterpart funds was so small a part of total investment. Face to face with an American objection it was always open to a European country to switch the sources of investment capital and transfer an alternative investment to funding from the counterpart funds. The Monnet Plan in France was by far the biggest user of counterpart fund

[53] SD 840.50, 535, Washington to Bern, 4 November 1948.
[54] Pohl, *Wiederaufbau*, pp. 85–93.

investment and its projects appear to have met with no serious American objections throughout.

What were more trying for the European countries than these slight encroachments on their independence of action were the changes written into the Economic Co-operation Act by Congress to satisfy economic interest groups in the United States. That these had to be accepted under protest is a better definition of the strength of American leverage than the concessions eventually made by the European countries in the bilateral agreements.

Congress placed into the Act a clause requiring 50 per cent of the goods shipped under the ERP to be carried in American bottoms at American freight rates. This was much against the wishes of the ECA, for it meant using the ERP appropriations for charging the European recipients high freight rates in dollars. In 1949 Congress increased the force of the restriction by requesting the ECA to make the 50 per cent figure apply as nearly as possible to each country and also separately to bulk, liner and tanker vessels. Congressional sentiments were perfectly understandable when kilometres of American merchant ships were being laid up in San Pablo Bay while the European shipbuilding industry had order books full to the end of the projected period for Marshall Aid, but the restriction was a costly subsidy to an uncompetitive American mercantile marine. Similarly, Congress specified that a quarter of all wheat exports financed by the ERP should be exported as flour milled in the United States. In 1949 the proportion was reduced to 12.5 per cent.

There were also restrictions placed in the Act to protect American farmers. Whenever the Secretary of Agriculture determined an agricultural commodity to be in surplus relative to the needs of the domestic economy, the ECA would only be able to purchase the commodity from United States sources. In this case the Department of Agriculture could also subsidize such purchases by as much as 50 per cent of the market cost. This was in fact done during the ERP for eggs, peanuts, fruits and tobacco. Of the food and other agricultural goods shipped under the ERP authorizations in 1948 61 per cent was purchased in the United States and in 1949 78 per cent. It was theoretically always open to European countries not to use their Marshall Aid for food imports, but outside the United States food surpluses were not always easy to find. Because when the import programmes were drawn up it was in the context of a general European agreement in the OEEC subsequently renegotiated with the Americans, the burden of dollar food imports had to be more evenly distributed than it might otherwise have been. It is very likely that the ERP induced a higher level of United States food exports to Western Europe than would otherwise have been the case.

Lastly, and much more difficult to establish, is the question of the extent of American pressure on east-west trade in Europe. The State Department manoeuvred to keep this issue as far as possible out of the bilateral negotiations precisely because it was aware that it would be construed for what it was, a more serious attempt than these other issues to infringe the independence of action of Western European countries in return for dollar aid. But there was at that time no publicly declared intention of limiting Western European exports to eastern Europe other than of goods produced with Marshall Aid supplies or components and which might further 'Soviet war potential'.[55] The ECA wished to impose a more restrictive policy from the start and accused the State Department of actually promoting east-west trade as a means of re-establishing Western Europe's geographical pattern of raw material imports.[56] In reply they were assured that the publicly favourable view of east-west trade was essentially a counter-propaganda device.[57] When the lists of strategic materials on which the United States wanted trade restrictions imposed were eventually drawn up they went a long way to confirm this. Two lists were drawn up of which the first (List 1A) contained a short list of items most of which very few of the Western European countries would have considered exporting eastwards in the political circumstances of autumn 1948. The second (List 1B) was longer and much more all-embracing. It ran into strong objections in Paris and London and, as was inevitable, in Bern and Stockholm where it was seen as another direct threat to the policy of neutrality. The subsequent long negotiations through which the United States mostly obtained its own way on this issue need a study entirely to themselves before any convincing judgement could be made about the value of Marshall Aid as a lever in this case.[58] What may be noted here is that the United States was on the one hand deeply worried by the impact of such a policy on European political and public opinion and, on the other hand, keen to present a united front against the eastern bloc, and these two fears and aspirations were present at every aspect of the bilateral negotiations on the Marshall Plan. They functioned as two further limitations on the extent to which economic bargaining power could be translated into political power. As the State Department explained in this particular case, 'While OEEC countries cannot give effect desired restrictions without some public action, such as increased export controls, our objective is have such action explained as unilateral decision unrelated US policy.'[59]

In the whole context of the ERP, however, it is only the limitations placed on trade between Western and eastern Europe and the extent of the power which Marshall Aid may have given to get the limitations initially established which seems worth citing as an instance of American 'imperialism'. All the

---

[55] SD 840.50, 534, Washington to London embassy, 16 July 1948.
[56] SD 840.50, 535, Harriman to Washington, 13 September 1948.
[57] ibid., Washington to Harriman, 13 September 1948.
[58] They also deserve a study in themselves for their importance in the post-war world for they have lasted in one form or another until the writing of this present book. There is one comprehensive study based on the economic data alone, G. Adler-Karlsson, *Western Economic Warfare 1947–1967, A Case Study in Foreign Economic Warfare* (Uppsala, 1968).
[59] SD 840.50, 535, Washington to Paris embassy, 26 November 1948.

others are too unimportant economically by the side of the enormous political ambitions of the ERP for European reconstruction. On the level of high policy the chief string attached to Marshall Aid was that economic and political integration would be the basis of Europe's reconstruction. Beside so huge an objective the successful manoeuvrings of the American farm and shipping lobbies pale into insignificance. They were regarded as minor irritants by European countries girding themselves to resist a much more comprehensive threat to their national economic and political existence.

The purpose of Marshall Aid was, through furthering the process of economic recovery in Western Europe, to develop a bloc of states which would share similar political, social, economic and cultural values to those which the United States itself publicly valued and claimed to uphold. Any exact enquiry into what these values might be and into the degree of similarity that might have been acceptable, while it would provide ample scope for cynicism, would be beside the point, firstly, because for the strategic purpose the definition 'sufficiently similar to be an ally of the United States' was workable, and secondly, because the question of what values the ERP should propagate was answered as much by the fashions of the time in the United States as by deeper and longer-run traditions. Thus the ECA propagated energetically, and from 1950 by a special programme financed from ERP funds, the values of so-called 'free enterprise', of entrepreneurship, of efficiency, of technical expertise, and of competition. These were all brought together in the concept of productivity. Increasing the productivity of European labour and capital to the levels which the United States had attained in the Second World War could be presented as not merely economically desirable, in the sense that by increasing Europe's exports it would diminish the dollar gap, but also as politically neutral. It was of course no such thing, for it involved trying to impose a set of particular human and economic values on the societies in question. When parties of British industrialists were taken around marginally more productive American factories this was a useful and sensible technical exercise whose political and social implications were at a very low level. When the ECA subsidized the productivity train to tour southern Italy with a barrage of propaganda about the advantages of the American economic system, the political intent was overwhelming, even if the means of achieving it were rather ludicrous.

The intention was that values would follow aid, rather as in previous centuries trade had been thought to follow the flag, and that these values would deeply influence the political development of the European countries in a favourable direction. Improvements in productivity would bring a higher level of wealth and income, and thus weaken and eventually eliminate the social and political tensions which had been so obvious in 1946 and 1947 and on which communism in particular was thought to thrive. In so far as consistently high rates of growth of national product in Western European countries after the war did eventually reduce in most countries the tensions of political argument, or at least reduce those arguments to a narrower range for most participants, this idea proved to have a certain rough and ready force. The question of the way in which these higher rates of growth were attributable to improvements in productivity is a much more controversial one. The even more searching questions, whether such a process would permanently still the disputes over the grossly unequal distribution of the increasing wealth and how long high rates of growth of GNP in the western world could last, were not only scarcely heard but they were not to be loudly voiced for another twenty years. The set of political values which became associated with the concept of productivity received, therefore, a less questioning acceptance then than it would do now and could thus be taken up by a relatively wide range of political opinion. This was essential, for if productivity were the key to growth and growth the key to political stability, investment was the key to productivity (or so it was thought), and if investors were to feel sufficient confidence in the Western European future to invest, they must be faced with political systems sufficiently broadly based to guarantee the future security and value of their investments. Around the concepts of productivity and growth coagulated a possible political and economic programme for politicians of several different persuasions whose political aims and values coincided with those of the ECA. Marshall Aid became their support and through its technical operations the ECA was in fact pursuing complex political and social goals in European countries.

On the other hand the forces within those countries pursuing the same goals were usually much stronger and had much more effective weapons to hand than the ECA. The 'politics of productivity', to use Maier's phrase,[60] were every bit as useful to European politicians hoping to back a central political position with a suitable economic programme which could be presented as quite neutral. One reason why the idea of European integration, for instance, had been taken up in the United States so avidly was because it seemed to fit so well into this set of values. If the argument were accepted that a larger market brought automatic gains in productivity, or indeed that Europe could not achieve these productivity gains without creating a larger integrated market, European integration appeared as no more than following through the inherent economic logic of Europe's economic development. But it was also thought of in exactly the same way by various groups of opinion in Western Europe, as indeed it still is, and they were eager to use American foreign economic policy as a lever to achieve their own ultimate objectives. To them it seemed at times that they were the just men long oppressed into the hands of whose deliverer God had put invincible might. In the event this

---

[60] C. Maier, 'The politics of productivity: foundations of American international economic policy after World War II', in P. Katzenstein (ed.) *Between Power and Plenty: The Foreign Economic Policies of Advanced Industrial States* (Madison, 1978).

proved not to be the case and the distance from the centres of power at which many of the most ardent European integrationists were held showed that the leverage which Marshall Aid gave to the United States in matters of grand policy was small unless it were coupled to genuinely powerful political forces in Europe.

About so complex and varied a set of politico-economic relationships it seems vain to generalize. Yet it can certainly be said that the idea that the United States sought no extra political or economic gain in return for Marshall Aid is nonsense, that the idea that the gains achieved were so large as to have shaped the politico-economic future of Western Europe is nonsense also, that the gains made by the United States can only be judged in relation to specific issues and specific countries, and that the limitations to the exercise of American power and influence through the ERP were subtle, complicated, but always present and often narrow. In the end it is, at least as far as Western Europe is concerned, for the story might be very different in Greece, those limitations that are the most striking aspect of the story. They emerge as the story is told.

IV

FRANCE AND THE
CONTROL OF
GERMAN RESOURCES

THE MONNET PLAN AND FRENCH AND GERMAN RECONSTRUCTION

In writing his denunciation of the Treaty of Versailles Keynes achieved one of his finest, most comprehensive judgements. 'Round Germany', he wrote, 'as a central support the rest of the European economic system grouped itself, and on the prosperity and enterprise of Germany the prosperity of the rest of the Continent mainly depended.'[1] For a man born and brought up at the height of Britain's imperial power it was a percipient remark whose accuracy has been amply borne out by all subsequent research. From the 1880s onwards Germany was the pivot of the continent's international trade and payments and the driving force in its technological advance. Production costs, prices, wages and social conditions there were becoming determinants of those elsewhere. The failure of the Treaty of Versailles to come to terms with these facts soon gave rise to a proliferation of alternative schemes involving attempts to link French and German industry by government agreements, to encourage French investment in German reconstruction in return for some French control over German output, or, alternatively, by a more extensive framework of private cartelization.[2] These ideas were only interrupted by the French occupation of the Ruhr, which could neither achieve the enforcement of the Versailles treaty nor harmonize French and German economic interests. Until 1924 no framework which offered any hope of such a harmonization could be found. The fragile framework then provided by the Dawes plan

[1] J.M. Keynes, *The Economic Consequences of the Peace* (London, 1919), p. 14.
[2] There are numerous accounts of these plans: J. Bariéty, *Les Relations franco-allemandes après la première guerre mondiale* (Paris, 1977); S.A. Schaker, *The End of French Predominance in Europe: The Financial Crisis of 1924 and the Adoption of the Dawes Plan* (Chapel Hill, 1976); M. Trachtenberg, *Reparation in World Politics. France and European Economic Diplomacy, 1916–1923* (New York, 1980).

survived only until the first major cyclical downturn and the history of the continent was subsequently dominated first by the catastrophic depression and afterwards by the attempts of the Nazi government to reaffirm the realities of Germany's position in Europe by refashioning the society and economy of the continent to conform to their own views.

The success of their efforts in 1940 showed how useless all French policies after 1918 had been in providing any reasonable form of national security. The unconditional surrender of Germany in 1945 was seen therefore as an opportunity which must not be missed. Germany was to be permanently weakened by being turned once more into a weak confederation of states with no central institutions. One of these states, which would embrace the Ruhr area, would have a different status; it would be 'internationalized' so that its resources were at the disposal of other European economies as well as Germany.

Although these plans already formed the basis of foreign policy towards Germany under the provisional government they found no hearing at Potsdam where France took no part in the formulation of the first basic decisions between the occupying powers on the future of Germany. In one sense the decisions taken there did not seem too far removed from French wishes, especially the agreement to enforce very low levels of output on the German economy, to extract reparations, and to restrict the German standard of living so as to use Germany's resources for the reconstruction of Europe's other economies. The consequences for the German economy and population were in fact even more severe than intended, partly because of the ruthless seizure of resources by the occupying powers and partly because of the failure to implement properly the corollary of these agreements, that Germany should be treated as one economy. In effect, the four occupation zones were run from the outset like separate independent economies and one consequence was that before 1948 neither output nor the standard of living in Germany had even attained the harsh upper limits set for them. In another sense, however, the Potsdam agreements ran directly counter to French wishes. Whatever happened in practice, the principle had been established there that Germany was to be treated and governed as an economic entity. The reparations which were to be paid to the Soviet Union, for example, were to be provided not merely from the Soviet zone of occupation but from the western zones as well. The American wish to proceed to a comprehensive settlement with the Soviet Union, starting from the basis of the Potsdam agreements and the Russian wish to maintain the authority of the Allied Control Council as, at least, the guarantee of future reparations payments, were likely to be formidable barriers to any further infringements of German territorial integrity. As for the Ruhr itself, it had passed under British occupation and there seemed no good reason why the British should give up to international control the most important part of their occupation zone.

The full range of French proposals for the future of the Ruhr was first placed before the British in October 1945. The area, vaguely defined but embracing the whole coalfield east of the Rhine, was to be turned into an international state with its own independent government supervised by an international authority made up of French, British and Benelux representatives and guaranteed as a neutral and independent state by the United States and the Soviet Union. It would have its own customs barriers and its own currency. The political regime there would be more favourable for the inhabitants than elsewhere in Germany, because with the formation of the government the role of the occupying forces would be substantially weakened and the authority of the Allied Control Council curbed. It was assumed that the Ruhr would have a substantial trade surplus. The disposal of this surplus would be under international control to some extent. The Ruhr's share of reparations obligations would have to be met and the provisional arrangements made for using Ruhr coal surpluses to assist European recovery generally would have to be honoured. The disposal of any additional trade surplus would be left to the negotiation of trade agreements between the government of the Ruhr and any other German government or governments.[3]

For all this the British showed absolutely no enthusiasm. If the Ruhr did have a regional trade surplus, of which the British were by no means convinced, it would serve to reduce the costs of occupation of the British zone as a whole. To subtract the Ruhr from Germany would permanently weaken the German economy to the point of danger; not only would it repeat the errors of Versailles but it would strengthen the Russian position by perpetuating a poverty-stricken Germany. Juridically, it might give the Soviet Union more rights in the western zone than they now had, while it was clear that in their own zone they were ignoring the Potsdam agreements if they proved inconvenient.

The same objections were made by the Americans when the proposals were put to them a month later. It was still the intention of Secretary of State Byrnes to make the Potsdam agreements work. If the French refused to agree in the Allied Control Council to any central German organizations the French zone of occupation would simply be left out of all arrangements which were to be made. In Moscow in December the French received no more encouragement. Their negotiators were left with the distinct impression that the Soviet Union regarded the internationalization of the Ruhr as a device to guarantee the resources of the area to a western power bloc and to limit the flow of reparations eastwards. Molotov would not be moved, even by the French description of the Ruhr factories as 'international public utilities'.[4]

The economic purpose of the French proposals was straightforward. As Maurice Couve de Murville, at that time a career diplomat in the European

    [3] Y.62.3, Conversations franco-britanniques sur la Ruhr et la Rhénanie, 12–26 October 1945.
    [4] ibid., Compte-Rendu des entretiens franco-soviétiques relatifs au régime futur de la Ruhr et de la Rhénanie, 12–21 December 1945.

section of the Quai d'Orsay, put it to the Americans, 'With the aim of military security we prefer to increase French steel production and output to the detriment of the Ruhr.'[5] Early attempts under the provisional government at formulating a national economic plan for recovery and reconstruction had been based on the idea that France would become Europe's largest steel producer.[6] Although Pierre Mendès-France had not been able to get these plans accepted as official policy, from March 1946 the Modernization and Re-equipment Plan did become the central guide to reconstruction planning under Jean Monnet, its first head and chief advocate.[7] The Monnet Plan had important international as well as domestic intentions. One aim of modernization was to make the French economy more internationally competitive in the future, particularly against German competition. But the Monnet Plan went further than this. The projected increases in the output of steel, for example, only made economic sense if it was assumed that French steel exports would replace former German steel exports. Furthermore, these output increases could only be achieved by increasing the inputs of German coal and coke into the French economy. It has often been observed that the Monnet Plan was drawn up on the assumption that it could only be achieved with loans to acquire American imports. But the United States was not the only part of the international economic environment which the Monnet Plan had to try to regulate. The supply of coal and coke from Germany was just as essential. The Monnet Plan therefore from the outset had important implications for foreign policy as well as for domestic economic policy. It tied the economic reconstruction of Germany inextricably to the reconstruction of France and, as the hopes of implementing the earlier and more drastic policies towards Germany faded, it offered an alternative programme for attempting to provide for future national security against Germany.

The immediate proposed increase in steel production in the Monnet Plan was not, it is true, very much greater than the level of steel output attained in 1929, the peak year of the inter-war period. The more distant target, however, was for an output of 15 million tonnes of steel, far beyond the 1929 level. Although the quantities of coal and coke needed to achieve this were not so

[5] ibid., Conversation franco-américaine au sujet de la Ruhr, le 15 novembre dans le bureau de M. Alphand.

[6] P. Mioche, 'Aux origines du Plan Monnet, 1942–47', *Revue Historique*, no. 538, 1981.

[7] Jean Omer Marie Gabriel Monnet, 1888–1979. Inheritor of a brandy business. Civil servant in the French Civil Supplies Service in London, 1914, where he was taken up by Clémentel and became in 1917 head of the London Mission of the Ministry of Commerce, and, 1918, a member of the Allied Maritime Transport Committee. 1919–21, Deputy to the Secretary-General of the League of Nations. 1926, vice-president of the French branch of an American merchant bank and subsequently in charge of its financial operations in San Francisco, then Stockholm, then China. 1940, exile in London, then member of the British Supply Council in Washington and head of supply, armaments and reconstruction in the National Liberation Council. 1946–52, High Commissioner of the Plan for Modernization and Re-equipment. 1952–5, President of the High Authority of the European Coal and Steel Community. 1956, founded Action Committee for the United States of Europe. An assiduous self-publicist and a remarkable collector of disciples.

large in terms of total world trade and output of either commodity, the fact that the necessary resources were German made their acquisition into something of deeper significance, it made them the decisive test of whether France could redeem anything from the opportunity presented when the Third Reich signed the unconditional surrender.

The dependence of the French iron and steel industry on German coal and coke supplies dated from the development after 1890 in Lorraine of a large basic steel industry using the local minette ores. After the First World War, when France regained the part of Lorraine which she had lost in the Franco-Prussian War, the French steel industry, at least in terms of capacity, was a major international force, but its theoretical dependence on German inputs was even higher. Although mineral fuel was used for a wide variety of purposes in the iron and steel industry, so much so indeed that the industry normally consumed more than a fifth of the total availability of coal and coke on French markets, the greatest single need, and one that was unavoidable, was in the smelting process. Minette ore was successfully smelted only with a large input of suitable metallurgical coke. This came either in the form of German coke made from Ruhr coal or of suitable grades of Ruhr coking coals for transformation into coke in France. The domestic output of coking coal in France itself was too small to provide for much more than the needs of the steel industry in the northern departments, with the result that the eastern steel industry was unable to emancipate itself from this import dependence in the inter-war period. Of course, the degree of dependence was a function of the level of capacity utilization, and in the 1930s capacity was used at very low levels. The intended full utilization of capacity after 1945 would have increased the need for imports markedly over their level of the 1930s without the further ambitious targets of the Monnet Plan for increases in steel-making capacity.

What is so curious is that in spite of the long and bitter quarrels after the First World War over the size of German coal and coke reparations deliveries to France and the French determination to resolve this problem by establishing a direct lien on Ruhr resources after the Second World War, the precise extent of France's import needs from Germany in any combination of circumstances never seems to have been accurately determined. The whole issue seems to have become so entangled in the intricacies of international power politics as to have left behind cooler considerations of economic rationality, and the Monnet Plan does not seem to have done anything to change this situation.

In 1928, when the total make of French pig-iron was 10.1 million tonnes, the iron and steel industry consumed for all purposes 11.0 million tonnes of coke, of which 3.9 million tonnes were imported from Germany.[8] At the lower level of pig-iron output in 1936–8, 6.7 million tonnes annually, only 1.7

[8] Figures for metal production throughout from France, *Annuaire de statistique industrielle*, for fuel production and consumption from France, *Statistique de l'industrie minérale* and *Annales des mines*.

million tonnes of German coke were imported. In the inter-war period there was, at least in theory, an alternative supplier, the United Kingdom. But the Lorraine blast-furnaces were geared to German coke, and British coking coal surpluses went mainly to Scandinavia. After 1945 this alternative source of supply no longer existed, the decline in British coal output meant that Britain no longer had an exportable surplus. It was not in fact until 1952 that French pig-iron production again reached the approximate levels of 1928 but as it climbed, albeit somewhat falteringly, back towards that target the dependence on German resources seemed even more inescapable than after 1918.

In 1950, at a level of pig-iron output of 7.76 million tonnes the total consumption of coke for all purposes by the French steel industry was 8.14 million tonnes. Of this, 4.66 million tonnes were domestically produced and 3.48 million came from imports. By 1952 pig-iron output had reached 9.77 million tonnes. At that level total coke consumption by the industry had risen to 9.35 million tonnes, of which 5.50 million tonnes was domestically produced and 3.85 million came from imports. As in the aftermath of the First World War the situation was eased by France's access to the coking coal and coke of the Saarland. Although some imported coke came from the Netherlands and Belgium for the neighbouring northern French steel industry, coke imports were largely made up of coke from the Saarland and the Ruhr. In 1950 the Saarland's contribution to the total imports was 1.19 million tonnes, that of the Ruhr 1.94 million tonnes. In 1952 the Saarland supplied 0.8 million tonnes and the Ruhr 3.42 million. Steel production ran consistently at about a million tonnes a year above the output of pig-iron, so that we may hypothesize that, in the absence of any radical change in the pattern of French international trade in the intermediate products of the industry (and no such change seems ever to have been envisaged), at a projected level of 15 million tonnes steel output a year, as ultimately envisaged by the Modernization Plan, French pig-iron output would have had to reach 14 million tonnes a year. This would have necessitated a volume of coke inputs into the industry of at least 13 million tonnes.

This was 7.5 million tonnes more than the quantity of domestic coke used by the industry in 1952. The possibility of obtaining such an increase from domestic resources was extremely remote. Thanks to an exceptionally high level of demand and great efforts on all sides French coal output had increased by 8.1 million tonnes from 1947 to 1952. In 1947, out of a total output of French coal of 47.3 million tonnes, only 5.9 million tonnes could be processed into coke; in 1952 from an output of 55.4 million tonnes 7.8 million tonnes had been processed into coke.[9] The main problem was geological, the lack of suitable coking coals in France's total coal resources. Not all the increase in the quantity of domestic coal processed into coke went into the production of metallurgical coke, about 250,000 tonnes went into the production of coke for

[9] Including semi-coke.

heating, and only an insignificant part of this could have contributed to the increase in consumption by the iron and steel industry. From where, it may well be asked, did the Commissariat au Plan expect to find the increased supply, even if it proved possible to obtain once more the 1928 level of supply from Germany?

Determined research efforts were made to produce a satisfactory coke from mixtures of French and German coals, but they were not crowned with any convincing success until later in the 1950s. Part of the gap had always been made up by imports of coking coal. In general the French economy had been highly dependent on coal imports since the early nineteenth century and in the inter-war period France was the world's most active coal market. In this respect the iron and steel industry was only following the pattern of numerous other major French industries, except that its import needs were much more heavily concentrated on imports from Germany. In fact, in 1928 coal imports from Germany were only a little more than a quarter of total French coal imports, but more than half their quantity was consumed as coal by the iron and steel industry and most of the rest was coked in France for use in French blast furnaces.

With the low levels of coal output in the Ruhr after 1945 the French iron and steel industry found itself faced with an acute production crisis in winter 1946/7. The French negotiations for a dollar loan in spring 1946 had been supported by a hastily prepared import plan. This seems to be the first public appearance of the Modernization and Re-equipment Plan and the suggestion that it should be expressed as a medium-term programme covering a five-year period, rather than as an emergency programme for one year only, seems to have come, not from Monnet and the planners, but from the Economic Section of the Ministry of Foreign Affairs.[10] An interesting aspect of this first version of the Plan is that the dollar sum allocated to coal imports was so low as to make it obvious that the intention was to acquire the necessary coal from Germany, in accordance, presumably, with the policy objectives of the Ministry of Foreign Affairs. When the Modernization Plan was formally accepted by the government in March the Prime Minister, Félix Gouin, explained that, even though the targets meant that French coal output would increase to 65 million tonnes in 1950, there would still be a shortfall of between 20 and 30 million tonnes a year if planning targets in the 'basic' sectors were to be met. This was intended to be partly met by an Allied allocation of 1 million tonnes of Ruhr coal a month to France.[11] This was by itself more than 4 million tonnes above the combined weight of coal and coke imports from Germany in 1928, leaving the question of how large a fuel surplus France obtained from the Saarland entirely out of the question.

[10] F.M.B. Lynch, 'The political and economic reconstruction of France 1944–1947: in the international context' (PhD thesis, University of Manchester, 1981), pp. 276 ff.

[11] ibid., p. 163.

In reality in the first six months of 1946 the situation was that half French coal imports came from the United States and less than a seventh from the Ruhr. Yet coal deliveries from the Bizone to France were not again to reach their level of the first half of 1946 until 1948. How seriously they fell, and how very far short of the wildly optimistic hopes of Monnet and Gouin, is apparent from the figures in table 21. To a small extent this was alleviated by a marked increase in coal production in the French zone of Germany and a rather less pronounced increase in the Saarland. Although these increases placed French diplomats in a strong position to argue in common with the Americans that the British were not doing an efficient job in getting coal out of the Ruhr pits and into European factories, they could not make much difference to France's economic situation. As table 22 shows the British zone was throughout the whole period responsible for more than 80 per cent of German coal output, and in 1947 output there was still only 64 per cent of its 1936 level. It was this which at once made nonsense of a plan which in any case was based on the economic irrationality of restricting German industrial output to so low a level as to erect insuperable barriers to the economic recovery of the other European economies. As the analysis of the payments crisis in summer 1947 in chapter 1 showed, for France an important element in the failure to continue to close the gap between exports and imports was the increase in imports of American coal in 1947 over 1946. They amounted in 1947 to 12 million tonnes, whereas in 1946 they had been only 5.2 million tonnes.

Of the total quantity of coal processed into coke in France in 1947, 8.1 million tonnes, only 0.7 million tonnes was 'German' coal, while an equivalent quantity was made from American imports. It may well be, however, that about the same quantity was coked in France from Saarland coals, not

Table 21   Hard fuel deliveries from the Bizone to France and Benelux (thousand tonnes)

	France*	Luxembourg	Belgium	Netherlands
1946				
1st quarter	703	333	636	421
2nd quarter	491	280	457	450
3rd quarter	563	416	309	426
4th quarter	310	328	211	329
1947				
1st quarter	326	278	172	210
2nd quarter	467	357	206	286
3rd quarter	525	398	272	349
4th quarter	609	422	291	386

Source: OMGUS, *Wirtschaftsstatistik der deutschen Besatzungszonen.*

* Including north Africa.

Table 22   Net colliery output of hard coal in Germany (thousand tonnes, monthly average)

	Total	British zone	French zone	American zone	Soviet zone
1945					
3rd quarter	3,030	2,479	326	88	146
4th quarter	4,832	4,031	503	111	187
1946					
1st quarter	5,288	4,388	586	114	200
2nd quarter	4,948	4,059	585	100	204
3rd quarter	5,702	4,699	682	106	215
4th quarter	5,957	4,844	776	117	220
1947					
1st quarter	6,859	5,677	841	118	223
2nd quarter	6,359	5,225	802	110	222
3rd quarter	7,446	6,162	924	121	239
4th quarter	7,922	6,641	1,227	119	234
Comparable annual figure for 1936	11,126	9,746	967	120	293

Source: OMGUS, *Wirtschaftsstatistik der deutschen Besatzungszonen.*

officially classified as imports. By 1950, when 9.6 million tonnes of coal were coked in France, the contribution of German coking coals was 1.9 million tonnes plus 0.9 million tonnes from the Saarland. This was still a long way from what was needed to make the Modernization Plan's targets ultimately realizable. When by 1952 the output of pig-iron had reached approximately the 1928 level, still, that is to say, more than 3 million tonnes below the hypothetical level to which it would have to rise to reach the Modernization Plan's targets, the contribution of German coking coals to French supply had not increased. In that year 1.8 million tonnes of imported German coals were coked in France and 0.7 million tonnes of Saarland coal. The proportionate contribution of all German coals to French coke output had therefore fallen from 28.5 per cent in 1950 to 20 per cent. The reason was the very high level of demand for steel and therefore for coking coal in Germany and throughout the world in that year.

But in what conditions other than a high level of world demand could France hope to sustain a level of output of 15 million tonnes of steel a year? When such conditions prevailed, even at an output level of 10.8 million tonnes a year in 1952, it was necessary to import 1.9 million tonnes of coking coal from the United States. And yet it was not only in France that post-war national reconstruction plans envisaged large increases in steel production. British investment plans implied a total crude steel output of about 17.4

million tonnes in 1953, 4 million tonnes more than in the best year in the
inter-war period. Italy, Sweden and Belgium all also forecast for that year a
level of output higher than before, even if their plans were less grandiose
than those of either France or Britain.[12] German steel production was to be
limited under the Potsdam agreements to 5.8 million tonnes annually, a
figure later increased with French agreement in the tripartite negotiations
during the CEEC which promised negotiations on the internationalization
of the Ruhr to 10.7 million tonnes.[13] This was 8 million tonnes less than
output in 1936 and would have left a theoretically available export surplus of
coke-oven coke from Germany sufficient to provide for the increased needs
of France and the other European states, assuming that output and processing
of coking coal and coke were also at the same level as in 1936 and that
Germany could return to using Swedish iron ore.

Table 23   Output of coke-oven coke in West Germany (million tonnes)

1936–8*	34.9
1946	9.6
1947	14.0
1948	20.3
1949	25.1
1950	27.3
1951	33.6
1952	37.3

Source : Statistisches Jahrbuch für das Deutsche Reich ; OEEC, *Industrial Statistics.*
* Annual average for territorial area of Federal Republic.

In practice, however, the post-war world was faced with an acute coal
shortage caused by the decline in coal output in many important areas during
the war, a decline which in some cases took place from relatively low levels
of output, and by the rapid increase in industrial output during the reconstruction boom. Coal still dominated the energy inputs of all the major
Western European industrial producers. In 1937 more than 90 per cent of
total energy consumption in France, Germany, Britain and Benelux had
come from solid mineral fuel.[14] Although national recovery plans all foresaw
a marked increase in oil imports this could only have a marginal effect on the
situation before 1952 and, in any case, presented foreign trading problems of

[12] The British plans are thoroughly analysed in D. Burn, *The Steel Industry 1939–1959.
A Study in Competition and Planning* (Cambridge, 1961); Belgian investment in C. Reuss,
E. Koutny and L. Tychon, *Le Progrès économique en sidérurgie. Belgique, Luxembourg,
Pays-Bas 1830–1955* (Louvain, 1960), pp. 280 ff.
[13] France had been at the time of the Potsdam agreements prepared to consider a level of 8
million tonnes over the reconstruction period, subsequently to be reduced to 6 million. Y.62.3,
Compte-rendu d'une réunion qui s'est tenue le 19 octobre (1945) à la Trésorerie.
[14] UN, Statistical Papers, Series J, no. 1, *World Energy Supply in Selected Years*, 1954,
pp. 276–8.

increasing complexity. In most countries the quantity of solid fuel hypo-thetically required to sustain the level of industrial output, if solid fuel consumption ratios had been what they were in 1937, was considerably above the actual level of fuel consumption (table 24). The gap was partly covered by a marginal increase in the use of other types of fuel, but more significant than the increased use of other fuels were shifts in the production

Table 24   Solid fuel shortages in post-war Europe

	Index of solid fuel consumption (1937 = 100)		Ratio of domestic output of solid fuel to total consumption		Index of hypothetical solid fuel require-ments* (1937 = 100)	
	1946	1947	1946	1947	1946	1947
			%	%		
Belgium	83	93	91	87	79	90
France	79	85	83	75	84	95
Germany	53†	64†	111	107	..	..
Netherlands	67	81	75	75	85	98
United Kingdom	94	101	103	101	102	110

Source: UN, Department of Economic Affairs, *Post-War Shortages of Food and Coal* (New York, 1948), pp. 21, 22, 37.

* Assuming hypothetical solid fuel requirement in industry to be proportional to the index of industrial production.
† 1937 figure relates to pre-war territory, 1946 and 1947 to post-war.

process to economize on solid fuel. One of these shifts took place in Belgium where Belgian iron and steel producers used more high-grade Swedish ores than in the pre-war period in order to economize on solid fuel inputs into the blast-furnace. The sufferer was France. The post-war years were difficult ones for the export of low-grade French iron ores which before the war had been a major export. Meanwhile in Germany most of the steel works, in order to save foreign exchange, were forced by the occupying authorities to use low-grade native German ores, which meant an input of about 5 tonnes of coal equivalent to 1 tonne of pig-iron compared to the average pre-war ratio of about 2 to 1. The ratio of coke requirements to steel output in occupied Germany was estimated to be about twice its pre-war level.[15] Even the assumptions derived from supposing that the revised levels of permitted steel output in Germany after autumn 1947 could be made to stick had therefore little validity as a rational basis for the Modernization Plan.

Much the same could be said of the glib assumptions about the theoretical size of German coal surpluses in general after Potsdam. The consumption of

[15] N. Balabkins, *Germany Under Direct Controls: Economic Aspects of Industrial Disarmament 1945–1948* (New Brunswick, 1964), p. 130.

coal by the French iron and steel industry, as opposed to coke, was 1.8 million tonnes in 1950 and 2.1 million tonnes in 1952. As in the inter-war period this was mainly German coal, but in this case there was no bottleneck, for the demand was easily met by the combined total of imports from Germany and the available surplus from the Saar, 5.6 million tonnes in the former year and 6.5 million tonnes in the latter. For the rest of the economy, however, coal remained scarce. Domestic output plus imports in 1952 amounted to 64.6 million tonnes, about the level that Gouin had said domestic output itself would have to reach to make the Monnet Plan feasible.

In the light of these considerations it has to be asked, in what direction the Monnet Plan and French diplomacy were marching? The answer is, if the Monnet Plan was to be fully realizable, towards permanently maintaining the German economy at so low a level of industrial output as to guarantee the availability for the future, not just of the 3 million tonnes of coke and 1.8 million tonnes of coking coal on which the French steel industry had depended before the war, but of at least twice those quantities. Far from being based on a liberal internationalism, the Monnet Plan was based on the crudest possible expression of mercantilist principles. It was aimed at seizing German resources in order to capture German markets.

Since the pursuit of domestic economic recovery objectives now seemed dependent on the successful pursuit of foreign policy objectives in Germany French governments did not abandon hope of modifying the Potsdam decision that Germany would be treated as an entity. They took their case to the meetings of the Council of Foreign Ministers. This persistence brought a certain modification of the British attitude. Although Bevin was still absolutely unwilling to countenance a separation of the Ruhr from Germany, he was prepared to try to resolve the problem of the future ownership of Ruhr resources within an international context. The Foreign Office was prepared to consider transferring the share capital of the sequestrated Ruhr firms to an international holding company in which the Soviet Union would be given some shares so that they did not regard Ruhr output as a monopoly of the west.[16] These ideas came nowhere near meeting French wishes and the disaccord between the two countries was irreconcilable by spring 1946. In March when Pierre de Leusse of the Commissariat General for German Affairs visited Berlin to discuss the issue with the political advisers of the American and British Commanders-in-Chief he could scarcely have received a worse reception. Both told him that continued French opposition in Berlin to the creation of any central German administrative or governmental organizations was playing directly into the Russian hands and would no longer be tolerated by France's western allies, who would act independently of the French position.[17]

[16]   Y.62.3, Telegram Massigli to Paris, 3 January 1946.
[17]   ibid., Direction d'Europe, Conversations sur les problèmes allemands, 14 March 1946.

On the American and British side the idea that predominated was the conviction that the Potsdam agreements had become for the Soviet Union a device to keep the German economy at a level of output so low as to produce a social and political vacuum in the heart of Europe which the Soviet Union itself could eventually hope to fill. In the meanwhile the Soviet Union would continue to draw reparations from Germany, which to American eyes were being financed by American expenditures there, rather as German reparation payments between 1924 and 1929 had been financed by the inflow of American capital investment. Even in the first two years after the German surrender, when the United States was committed to a policy of extracting reparations from Germany, it was not prepared to see these reparations extracted from the current production of an economy at so low a level of output that the population would have to be sustained by American aid and supply while reparations were being paid.[18]

As long as there were no definite plans to reconstruct the German economy and as long as the emphasis was still on reaching a general agreement about the future level of reparations from Germany, French economic objectives were still not definitely out of reach, although the possibility of achieving them by the drastic peace treaty envisaged was only slight. The British plans for the Ruhr, which were revealed in April, made few concessions. The pre-war political divisions of the Ruhr area would be eliminated by the creation of a new Land, North Rhine-Westphalia. It would include parts of the state of 'Rhenania', which the French had wished to separate, as well as the whole of the Ruhr, which would be linked indissolubly to its surrounding area. The government of the new Land would pass an act 'socializing' the coal, steel, and engineering firms by the creation of public corporations. Once a peace treaty had been signed there could be some international control over these corporations and the British government was prepared to countenance a situation in which, for example, part of their export earnings might be paid into a special external account for use in European reconstruction generally. But there appeared to be no barriers to the subsequent transfer of these public corporations from the ownership of the Land government of North Rhine-Westphalia to a central national government. At the same time as the British began to implement their policy, General Clay announced the suspension of further reparations deliveries from the western zones to the east in order to compel the Soviet Union and France to form a central governmental organization in Berlin, and the British supported him. A more positive, concerted reconstruction of the economy in their own zones by the British and the Americans was an obvious response if the move failed.

[18] There are numerous analyses of the failure of the Potsdam agreements. J.H. Backer, *The Decision to Divide Germany* (Durham, N.C., 1978); J. Gimbel, *The American Occupation of Germany: Politics and the Military, 1945–1949* (Stanford, 1968); and M. Gottlieb, *The German Peace Settlement and the Berlin Crisis* (New York, 1960), are the best.

The allocation of coal surpluses from Germany was in principle delegated to a United Nations body, the European Coal Organization (ECO), but most of the coal itself was under the control of the British military administration. In June 1945 the British had created the North German Coal Control to supervise all coal-mining in their zone and in December had expropriated all collieries. In September the former Rheinisches-Westfälisches Kohlensyndikat, which had been responsible for marketing most of the Ruhr coal, had been replaced by the North German Coal Distribution Office, which depended on the British Military Governor. In the iron and steel industry German administration remained longer, but the German administrative body, the Verwaltungsamt für Stahl und Eisen, was entirely subordinated to the British administration, until in August 1946 all iron and steel works were also seized from their former owners and put under a British body, the North German Iron and Steel Control. The increasing cost of the occupation was a serious drain on the British economy and it was this which had first motivated the British government to press for less drastic restrictions on the level of German steel output. However, from the outset the British appear to have been extremely sceptical that Germany ever would in fact be treated as an economic whole.[19] The emphasis on transferring economic responsibility, even for policy formulation, to Germany became a more marked aspect of British administration. That, of course, was only for policies which the British government wished to favour, but it made the situation no less threatening to France. This was not only the case with the policy of 'socializing' Ruhr industry, but also with land reform, or with creating a national, democratic trade union organization, for all these implied the eventual creation of a centralized German state.[20] The trend of British policy, the general agreement between Britain and the United States that the great danger of the situation in Germany was the Soviet Union and that some larger organs of government must be created there in spite of Russian tergiversation and French opposition, the mounting cost of the occupation on Britain's strained dollar resources, all made it impossible for the existing state of affairs to be tolerated any longer in London. As the coal crisis became more acute, Britain and the United States eventually did act politically in Germany without France, as they had threatened, and merged their zones from the start of 1947 into the Bizone.

Even then the hopes for an internationalization of the Ruhr in some form were not lost. When Marshall became Secretary of State, Henri Bonnet, the French ambassador, was given a comprehensive statement of American thinking on the issue. If the Soviet Union accepted the proposals for a long-term security treaty against Germany which Secretary of State James F. Byrnes had

[19] D.C. Watt, *Britain Looks to Germany* (London, 1965), pp. 48–9.
[20] G.J. Trittel, 'Von der "Verwal tung des Mangels" zur "Verhinderung der Neuordnung". Ein Überblick über die Hauptprobleme der Wirtschaftspolitik in der Britischen Zone', in C. Scharf and H.-J. Schröder (eds) *Die Deutschlandpolitik Großbritanniens und die Britische Zone 1945–1949* (Wiesbaden, 1979).

offered, the United States was in principle in favour of the idea that the Ruhr industries, including the chemical industries, should be at the disposal of the whole of Europe and contribute to the whole continent's recovery. As to how this might be achieved and what internationalization would look like in practice the American government was at that stage, February 1947, unclear.[21] For France the matter was more urgent than this. Marshall was told that the problem was coal and that France must have half a million tonnes monthly from the Ruhr in 1947 and 1 million tonnes monthly in 1948. The French wanted their own technicians and managers in the Ruhr to make sure these quantities were forthcoming. Pierre-Henri Teitgen, who was interim Foreign Minister, indicated that 'this question of French reconstruction and German reconstruction dominates the political structure. If we had precise guarantees in the area of coal the political problems themselves would perhaps appear simpler to us'.[22]

The failure of the Moscow Council of Foreign Ministers in summer 1947 to agree on any solution for Germany probably made agreement between the western powers on German coal easier. It no longer seemed in American eyes worthwhile to pursue in the short term a solution on the basis of the Potsdam agreements and France's position was marginally strengthened. It was agreed in the corridors of the Moscow conference that after 1 July 1947 France's access to German coal resources would be regulated by the so-called 'Moscow sliding-scales'. The scales were to operate in the following manner. When German coal output reached 280,000 tonnes a day the export surplus would be deemed to be 21 per cent of the output, of which France would be entitled to a 28 per cent share. Thence through a sliding-scale the export surplus would increase to 25 per cent of output when output reached 370,000 tonnes a day. These figures would include, however, the output of the Saarland of which the Allies had in the interim handed over the use to France. For France the value of the agreement was that it did give her, henceforward, a fixed entitlement to German coal accepted by the other western occupying powers. But how much coal that was likely to mean was not easily to be forecast.[23] Apart from establishing a lien on part of Germany's coal 'surplus' France had made no progress before Marshall's speech at Harvard either in breaking the immediate bottleneck which was holding back steel production or in solving the longer-term coke problems of the French steel industry. French policy had, in fact, been fundamentally impractical. The idea of a political separation of the Ruhr from Germany simply never looked feasible as a piece of power politics.

[21] Z.17.5, Bonnet to Bidault, 19 February 1947.

[22] Y.62.3, Entretien entre le Président de la République et le Général Marshall, 6 March 1947.

[23] The assumption of the Potsdam agreements had been that Germany would have an export surplus of 45 million tonnes of coal yearly. On the basis of this highly abstract reckoning the Moscow sliding-scales would eventually have provided France with about 12.6 million tonnes a year of German coal. But there is no reason to suppose that these calculations used at Potsdam were regarded any longer as valid or realistic at Moscow.

The argument was better couched in terms of coal and coke, because in those terms it did reveal the extremely serious nature of the problems facing European reconstruction as a whole. But it was only when the coal shortage in France became acute in 1947 that it was couched in those terms and directed towards achieving some immediately practical results. How small those results were is a measure of the inadequacy of the policies pursued. Shortly after the Moscow sliding-scales were established Marshall offered the general programme of American aid. It was obvious that one of its central purposes was the reconstruction of the German economy. The idea of a separation of the Ruhr's resources from those of Germany had passed from improbability into fantasy.

THE FRENCH AND GERMAN ECONOMIES IN THE LONDON CONFERENCE

As things stood in June 1947 the situation for France was a very dangerous one. An urgent American drive to integrate western Europe, including western Germany, into a united economic area with few or no barriers to the movement of factors would leave France unprotected and face to face once more, while her own economic reconstruction was only just beginning, with a West German economy reinvigorated by dollar aid and with an ample supply of resources and cheap labour. How, from the danger of summer 1947, a weak and isolated France plucked the foundations of safety and prosperity is one of the most remarkable aspects of our story. The outcome probably suggests that France's position was not in reality so weak in 1947 as it seemed to be, in the sense that without France no integrated western Europe was possible in any form. But both by luck and by design the harmony between French domestic economic policy and French foreign policy after 1947, in Europe if not elsewhere, was remarkably close. It may be true that when a man is about to be hanged it concentrates his mind wonderfully and the contrast is nowhere more striking than with the dissipation of British policies and the startling gap between domestic economic realities and foreign ambitions there. Even so, there was also much courage, imagination and determination needed in Paris to pursue consistent goals through the rapidly changing circumstances after June 1947 and by rapidly changing policies. It is difficult to resist the conclusion that such adaptability came more easily to those who in a recent and short space of time had seen most of what they had held valuable and secure destroyed or perverted and who to that extent were more open to change and improvisation. The rewards proved to be very great.

From the menacing situation of summer 1947 France gradually rescued itself by putting together a quite different basis for Western European reconstruction from the one which America offered. It was one which in the event proved, at least to the countries concerned, more feasible, acceptable and realistic. It was to lay one of the foundation stones of three decades of peace and prosperity in Western Europe. The internal evolution of these policies within French political life itself, within the parties, within the Assembly and in public opinion is not the theme here; the argument is concerned with the practical expression of these changes in international political and economic events. This is not to put the cart before the horse. French political and public opinion on the German question evolved in the way it did because it had to come to terms after June 1947 with harsh international political and economic realities, realities which eventually brought together people and groups who had started from very different standpoints.

Ominous though the ERP seemed for French ambitions in Germany, it had at least presented France with one new opportunity. Without full French participation the ERP was meaningless. The French refusal to participate fully in the work of the CEEC until France was allowed to participate on equal terms with the western Allies in the decisions which would now have to be made about Germany had produced immediate results. If the London Council of Foreign Ministers in autumn 1947 proved as unfruitful as it threatened to be, France would be invited to settle the economic and political future of the western zones in conference with its western allies. To obtain French participation in 'the continuing organization' the United States had undertaken to support some form of international control over the allocation of Ruhr resources. Although presumably now in a much more limited form, the internationalization of the Ruhr had become the price for French participation in the Marshall Plan.

This was a price which the United States had agreed to pay only very reluctantly and from the French standpoint it was important that it should be paid before France's bargaining position weakened. In early October therefore the French government tried to press home its one advantage in two ways. Firstly, in drafting its proposals for internationalization it proposed a Ruhr Authority which would have precise powers over the economy. It should be able to plan output, investment, financial policy and the allocation of resources. Before it entered into power the Bizone Coal and Steel Control groups should be turned into an 'Inter-Allied Control Group' with the same range of powers.[24] French personnel should be helping to run the firms and determining the allocation of coal and coke before the Authority had been instituted. The American attitude was that the nature of any settlement still had to wait on the outcome of the London Council of Foreign Ministers and could then, if no progress was made there towards a quadripartite settlement, only be determined in concert by a tripartite conference to which the French proposals would have to be submitted. As for French participation in running Ruhr industries and determining their future ownership, it was entirely unreasonable to expect it while the French zone of occupation remained separate.

[24] Y.62.3, Contrôle et gestion des mines et aciéries de la Ruhr, 29 September 1947.

The problem of coal and coke supply was treated as a separate issue in Washington, not just because the internationalization of the Ruhr was still thought of as a distant issue, while the coal shortage was urgent, but because the American government, strenuously urged on by Clay, wanted to stop the British plan to 'socialize' the Ruhr industries. Taking such major industries away from private ownership was an idea to which the American Military Government was strongly opposed and it blamed the shortage of coal on what it saw as a British obsession with questions of ownership rather than production. Here, French and Americans were entirely in agreement. France opposed 'socialization' on the grounds that it was the first step towards handing major industries over to a future central West German government, as well as on the grounds that it was an obvious barrier to eventual French direction and management of the Ruhr firms. The United States had demanded a series of technical meetings on the question of coal supply for October and it was only necessary for the French to continue to complain vociferously about the shortfall in coal supply at these meetings, point to the fact that in their own zone output was higher than before the war, and wait for Clay to kill Bevin's plans. After all, the North German Coal Control was now as much American as British and America was paying fourth-fifths of the costs of the Bizone. Although it was not openly acknowledged, the October coal conferences effectively ended the British intention of transferring the coal and steel resources of the Ruhr to public ownership. The future problem of their allocation by an international body would now also have to be a problem of the relationship of such a body to private capital. On an economic level this did not necessarily make matters easier for France; it was already becoming clear that the United States would oppose any form of internationalization of the Ruhr which would mean that the international authority would be able to intervene directly in the day-to-day management of the firms or impose limitations on private business policy.

On the other hand at the same coal conferences France did gain two further concessions of undoubted value. Two important principles were established. The first was that coal consumption in each zone of Germany should be linked to the output figure so that failures of output would have a less drastic impact on the allocation of coal for export. The second was that coke also should be allocated for export as a fixed proportion of the coal allocation. These were both issues which the French had pressed unsuccessfully at Moscow in the summer when the sliding-scales were established. The other issue which they had pressed there had been the international acceptance of the complete incorporation of the resources of the Saarland into the French economy.

' The issue of the Saarland was one of relative insignificance by the side of that of the Ruhr, but France also required a definite settlement there before either the conference on Germany or the 'continuing organization' had any real chance of success. In the CEEC committees France had treated Saarland resources as part of French resources and the economic fusion of the area with France was more or less complete. Now that it behoved Britain and America to obtain a larger measure of French goodwill the Saarland issue could be settled quickly, in principle. In practice it proved more difficult, because the Saar's resources, as far as the European Coal Organization was concerned and as far, also, as the Moscow sliding-scales were concerned, were German resources and if France was to claim them in their entirety the question arose, by how much should that reduce her claim on reparations and coal deliveries from the rest of Germany? Negotiations with the Bizone officials began on 9 January and one week later the experts had submitted a plan to their governments for the withdrawal of Saarland coal from German resources.[25] The formula had been worked out in the coal conferences in Berlin in October. But the negotiations then broke down because of a large disagreement about the equivalent value of other reparations represented by industrial plant in the Saarland. The British and Americans initially valued this at about 150 million 1938 Reichsmarks, whereas the French estimate was 20 million 1938 Reichsmarks.[26] It took until 20 February to reach a compromise between these figures. The value was fixed at 46 million 1938 Reichsmarks, on the assumption that the ratio of pre-war Saarland output to German output was about 1 : 50. Only then were the decks cleared for the London Conference on Germany which was to take up the question of the whole future of West Germany including the Ruhr.

Immediately on the failure of the London Council of Foreign Ministers the Military Governors of the Bizone began to create a rudimentary higher economic and political organization to show that the Allies did intend to provide for democratic government. It was not intended to prejudge the nature of any constitution. Indeed, as it turned out, the Americans and British were far from even a basis of agreement on the nature of the constitution of any future German state. The new governmental bodies were created from the existing unelected Landtage and could claim no greater degree of representativeness.[27] They none the less called forth a series of protests from Paris that they were anticipating the outcome of the promised conference on Germany. Not unreasonably the British–American response was that they could make whatever arrangements they wanted in the Bizone until such time as there should be some general agreement covering the three zones. But the French view was, also not unreasonably, that because the 'continuing organization' now depended on prior agreement about the Ruhr, the limitations to German

[25] FRUS, 1948, III, p. 22, Murphy to Washington, 11 January 1948. ibid., p. 28, Murphy to Washington, 17 January 1948.   [26] ibid., p. 55, Murphy to Washington, 1 February 1948.
[27] The membership of the Economic Council (Wirtschaftsrat) was increased at the start of 1948 from 52 to 104 and the Executive Council (Exekutivrat) became an assembly of the separate Land assemblies. The Administrative Council (Verwaltungsrat) was newly created from the separate administrations.

sovereignty which this would necessitate should be first decided before any active national political life was permitted to restart in Germany. Robert Marjolin, who had served as Secretary-General of the CEEC, and was therefore the most likely candidate for the same post in the 'continuing organization', approached the private office of the British Prime Minister Clement Attlee to plead that Britain support French claims to control of the Ruhr firms because that, as he wrote, was now the real obstacle to implementing the ERP.[28]

Whether this really was the case was very much a matter of political judgment. France did not only wish to emerge from the conference on Germany with the Ruhr's resources safely under control. The French negotiating position was that if a West German state were to be created it should have virtually no central authority and not be a state in the sense of other western European states in the 'continuing organization'.[29] In British and American eyes this was no less an obstacle to implementing the ERP.

The London Conference on Germany began on 26 February 1948 and the first, immediate objective was to reach an agreement that the ERP and 'the continuing organization' would go ahead and that western Germany would be included in both. This achieved, the conference adjourned on 6 March. It began its work again on 20 April. This time the objectives were more diffuse, although the primary one was to make recommendations on the future political organization of Germany. At the same time the conference drew up recommendations for the future control of the Ruhr and for future guarantees of security against Germany. It then adjourned once more on 1 June. These recommendations only narrowly passed the French Assembly, so narrowly that the French government announced its intention to seek their modification in the next stage of the conference. The recommendations were transmitted in a set of documents to the Ministers-President of the western German Länder who then initiated the internal German constitutional discussions. The Preparatory Constitutional Committee reported back to the Ministers-President on 31 August with a draft constitution, a general commentary on it and one or two minority opinions. After considerable further argument with France the London conference was recalled once more on 11 November and remained in session over Christmas arguing over the details of the international authority which was to control Ruhr resources and its relationship to the other military and economic control bodies to be imposed on the new West German state.

[28] T236/806, Note from W. Gorell Barnes, 16 January 1948. Robert Marjolin, 1911– . An economist, educated at Yale. Worked with Monnet in the French Purchasing Mission in the United States eventually becoming its head in 1944. Director of Foreign Economic Relations in Ministry of National Economy, 1945. Deputy Commissioner-General in the Commissariat au Plan 1946–8. Secretary-General of the OEEC, 1948–55. Professor of Political Economy, University of Nancy, 1955–7 and deputy head of French negotiating team in the Common Market negotiations 1956/7. Vice-President of the Commission of the European Communities, 1958–67. Professor of Economics, University of Paris, 1967–9. Then a business and government administrator in the steel, oil and car industries.
[29] Y.54.1, Direction d'Europe, 'Note', 24 January 1948.

There were several different points at which the economic reconstruction of France and Germany became entangled in the web of international economic diplomacy. The London conference was only one of these. Economically, two separate arenas for decision-making about Germany had been created by the tripartite agreements in August 1947 which had permitted the CEEC to continue, the London conference and the 'continuing organization'. The latter could not be constituted, according to the agreement in autumn 1947, until the former had made a public statement about an international authority for the Ruhr and the French had at least agreed to begin talks on the fusion of their occupation zone. Whether the talks on the fusion of the French zone would be held entirely separately from the London conference and be yet another forum for decision-making about Germany was uncertain. This question would have to be postponed until the first session of the conference would have allowed the 'continuing organization' to be created. The complicated interactions between the OEEC and the London conference throughout 1948 were such as to create great complexities for the United States and to allow the European countries, and especially France, more scope for manoeuvre than the Americans had either foreseen or wished. At the same time the German problem undermined the very foundations of the OEEC as it had done those of the CEEC and proved a severe barrier to any effective progress toward the OEEC becoming a vehicle for integration.

Making a somewhat arbitrary division for the sake of clarifying the issues it can be said that there were five areas where the relative speed of French and German economic reconstruction might be affected by international diplomacy. Firstly, there was the question of the level of output to be permitted in West Germany. If a German economic recovery was to be promoted it might have to be in the context of a general agreement to raise once more the levels of industrial output to be permitted. Where would this leave France's ambitious claims on the Ruhr?

France wanted to impose a permanent limit on the level of West German steel production, the United States did not. What swayed American thinking very much were two related concepts. The first was the idea of the future 'viability' of Western Europe in international payments with America, that constant theme of the debates in Congress on the Marshall Plan. It might be impeded if German output were held at low levels. The second was the idea that the German steel industry was a vital element in Europe's defence. On this second point the European powers were in an awkward dilemma, rearmament might mean either that the European Allies would use German steel for that purpose or that they would increase the domestic demand for their own to such a point that they would leave the German steel industry free to capture their export markets. One of the most hard-fought battles over the constitution of the Ruhr Authority was the French attempt to give the Authority the power to allocate German pig-iron for export. Ultimately nothing was decided in 1948 about the limits set to German steel production and capacity. German steel output in 1948, at 5.8 million tonnes, was in any case only just over half the limit imposed by the revision of the Potsdam agreements. This limit remained in force until 1950 and was not formally removed until 1952. On the other hand it was also perfectly clear that the United States would not agree to carry over the restrictions on western German output, other than perhaps those relating to some of the armaments industries which were absolutely prohibited, into any future peace treaty with the constitutional West German state. Although in the London conference a direct conflict on this issue could be avoided, within the OEEC the battle was inevitable and fierce. Although it was fought there on the issue of how much Marshall Aid should be programmed for West Germany it was the same battle, because the specific items of aid allocation to which the OEEC took objection and on which the United States, in contrast, insisted in summer 1948 were those which permitted a level of imports likely to result in increases of output beyond the limits set in the revision of the Potsdam agreements.

Secondly, both Britain and France wished to continue with the dismantling and seizure of German capital equipment as reparations, while the United States, with some exceptions, did not. The British and French motivation was mainly the conviction that the equipment transferred from Germany was important to their own economic recovery, but there was also a desire to maintain what was left of Four-Power Control or at least the legal semblance of not having broken the Potsdam agreements. The United States sought from the start of the London conference an agreement to reduce the extent of dismantling in Germany and to remove some of the restrictions on German industry.[30] This issue was left in abeyance in the first two stages of the conference, but was brought to a head by the OEEC's disagreement in the summer with the Bizone administration and the ECA over the extent of aid for Germany. Before the Economic Co-operation Act had passed into law five of the government departments in Washington, State, Army, Agriculture, Commerce and Interior, had been invited to submit a report reducing the list of German plant scheduled for dismantling and reparations, where doing so could increase the world supply of commodities in excess demand. They sent a technical mission to the American zone which submitted its report in July recommending that some plant be taken off the list and concluded that dismantling did not 'most effectively serve the purposes of the European Recovery Program'.[31] The report arrived at the height of the dispute with the European countries in the OEEC and served to make it worse. Hoffman asked for the dismantling programme to be suspended until its effects could be more fully examined particularly with respect to those 163 plants due to be dismantled which the technical mission had singled out as being especially useful to the ERP.

[30] FRUS, 1948, II, Douglas to Washington, 20 February 1948.
[31] ibid., Final Report of the Cabinet Technical Mission on Reparations, p. 787.

This further examination was conducted by an ECA team led by an industrialist, George M. Humphrey, which became known as the Humphrey Committee. The British and French objected to any delay in dismantling to allow the committee to examine the situation; General Clay objected to the delay in stopping the dismantling which would be caused by the committee's appointment! From the moment the Humphrey Committee was appointed and ECA had requested a pause in the programme, dismantling became a major political issue. The report of the Humphrey Committee was finally made available on 12 January 1949, although its contents were widely known in December 1948. It recommended the removal of 167 plants from the dismantling list, including the Thyssen steel works in Hamborn. The Washington agreements of April 1949, which eventually redefined the prohibitions and restrictions on German manufacturing industry, were the outcome of the committee's report, but the committee's activities and report provoked such opposition in France and Britain as to be one of the main reasons why all the separate areas of economic dispute about Germany in 1948 had finally to be brought together in spring 1949 into one grand economic settlement. The issue, in fact, like that of the permitted levels of output, remained unresolved either in the London conference or in the OEEC throughout 1948.

Thirdly, there was the issue of the relative shares of ERP aid of Germany and France. This had already emerged as a central problem in the CEEC and would be no less so in the OEEC. The intention here is to concentrate on those Franco-German economic problems which were cause for action in the London conference; in the next chapter the problems which arose in the OEEC are analysed. Suffice it to say here that the dispute over relative aid levels erupted in the OEEC in the middle of the London conference and also that the progress of the decisions in the London conference for the first part of the year was not such as to make France any more willing to renounce in the OEEC its hypothetical share of American aid in favour of West Germany. For Britain the issue was peculiarly ambivalent; too little aid to the Bizone worsened the external economic situation, too much presumably reduced Britain's own hypothetical share.

Fourthly, there was the question of the terms on which the French occupation zone would be merged with the other zones. France hoped to postpone all action until the precise meaning of the American commitment to internationalization had been discovered in an agreement on the powers of the proposed international authority for the Ruhr. This was not to be. The matter was settled at once by a direct American threat to reduce or even end Marshall Aid to the French zone if discussions on the merger of the zones were not to accompany the conference. Douglas was empowered in a telephone conversation during the night of 1/2 March to make the threat.[32] Having been forced to enter into negotiations, however, the French could still prolong them as long

[32] SD 840.50, 532, Lovett to Douglas, 2 March 1948.

as they remained unsatisfied about all the other issues, and they did so. The negotiators had specific instructions that it would be politically 'too difficult' to present an agreement on a zonal merger until an agreement on the Ruhr had been conceded.[33]

Lastly, there was the question which, for France, was the central economic issue at the London conference, control over the Ruhr resources. Because the British Military Government had displaced the original owners of the steel works and mines, it was still possible to hope that international control of the Ruhr would mean international management of the firms, and France's intentions were to have French managers and supervisory boards controlling them directly. This issue became inextricably tangled in the political and constitutional discussions, because any such international body had to have the power to execute its decisions and it only seemed possible to exercise that power through some form of supervisory political agency. In this way the conference came ultimately to the idea of the Military Security Board, which finally emerged, and a complicated series of control boards to supervise particular sectors of the economy, which in the event did not. Control over Ruhr resources was useless without the power to allocate those resources. In the end, therefore, and most importantly, what was at stake was a mechanism by which France could obtain some say in the allocation of Ruhr coal and coke within and beyond the German frontiers.

On this issue, the control of the Ruhr firms and the allocation of the Ruhr's resources, it is necessary to consider in some detail what occurred at the London conference. This was the crux of the matter and it was in the battle to resolve it that a way forward to a more durable reconstruction of Europe than after the First World War was found. It was on these issues in particular that French policy was forced to change and in such a way as to alter the political shape of Western Europe.

Although the Landtag of North Rhine-Westphalia had been encouraged to introduce legislation to 'socialize' the coal-mines the possibility of this actually happening had receded rapidly with the formation of the Bizone, because of Clay's strong opposition to any form of public ownership, and it had finally disappeared, although the British government did not outwardly admit this, at the 'coal conferences' in September 1947. The problem of who should run the mines and factories was made more acute by this. The former owners remained dispossessed, some of them permanently discredited, some in gaol, some still the subject of denazification procedures. On 12 February 1948 the Bizone government announced its intention of placing the coal and steel industries under the day-to-day management of boards of trustees. The history of these boards of trustees, the Deutsche Kohlenbergbau Leitung and the Treuhandverwaltung für Stahl und Eisen, is an obscure and chequered one. As long as the Coal and Steel Controls, which were immediate organs of

[33] Y.62.3, Telegram, Bidault to Massigli, 4 March 1948.

the Military Government, functioned, the boards of trustees were really only holders of the capital. Their entry into office was so frequently delayed that it is probable that the British and Americans were themselves glad to defer the matter, especially as the British had not publicly abandoned their plans to 'socialize' the Ruhr coal-mining industry.

International supervision and control of the Ruhr industries as a way of getting a guaranteed supply of coal and coke was of value to France only if decisions on output and allocation could be enforced at the level of the firm. That was a reasonable historical inference to draw from the melancholy history of the German evasion between the wars of the clauses of the Treaty of Versailles limiting rearmament. The commitment extracted from the United States to support internationalization had extended to determining the proportion of German coal output to be allocated to export, but the powers of any Ruhr authority beyond the capacity to make such decisions had not been discussed. The French proposals for the London conference were the same as those which they had pressed on the Americans in October. Although the Ruhr would no longer have its own separate constitutional government, internationalization would mean a wholly separate economic regime supervised by a new body, the International Ruhr Authority. The Authority would have powers over planning and investment inside the Ruhr's economy and would be able to control the internal allocation of resources as well as their division between internal consumption and exports. It should come into existence as soon as its terms were decided and thus be at first under the powers of the Commanders-in-Chief until the end of the occupation regime. This in turn would mean that it could call on the soldiers to enforce its decisions.[34]

The commitment of France's allies to some form of internationalization, the fact that the bill to 'socialize' the Ruhr industries was even now on its way through the Landtag of North Rhine-Westphalia, the obvious American will to return the sequestrated Ruhr industries to private ownership as soon as possible, all meant that the London conference could not even formally open without all three parties coming to a preliminary understanding as to what the commitment of last August to the French had really meant. The American hope was that internationalization would prove a step towards European integration, the first stage in integrating a new West German state into one western European economy.[35] Douglas therefore proposed to implement the American promise by not confining the new international authority to the Ruhr alone, but extending its control over the whole of the neighbouring coal and steel industries in France and the Benelux too.[36] This was a quite new and threatening version of Bidault's angry remonstrance against the British a year earlier that 'The Ruhr belonged to Europe'.[37]

[34] Y.62.3, Proposition de la délégation française Ruhr, 27 February 1948.
[35] Y.54.1, Telegram, Massigli to Paris, 24 February 1948.
[36] ibid., Massigli to Bidault, 27 February 1948.
[37] R. Steininger, 'Ruhrfrage und Sozialisierung in der anglo-amerikanischen Deutschlandpolitik 1947/8', *Vierteljahrshefte für Zeitgeschichte*, 27 (2), 1979.

Furthermore, it was also obvious that within this context of European integration the Ruhr industries would be disposed of according to American wishes. As Attlee had told the British cabinet in October, it was Britain's rapidly deteriorating dollar situation in which the drain of dollars to the Bizone played an important part which had not only forced Britain to go to the coal conferences but meant that it would be necessary to abandon most of the hopes for independent action in the Ruhr.[38] In June 1947 the American administration had first formulated its alternative plans to the British intentions. This was that the boards of trustees which Britain had intended should supervise the transition to 'socialization' should be appointed for a maximum period of five years only and should hold the capital of the firms only until a democratically elected government in Germany could itself determine future policy on ownership. Although the Landtag of North Rhine-Westphalia continued to debate the 'socialization' bill through the early stages of the London conference, the question now really at issue was whether the Ruhr Authority would be able to intervene at a detailed level in the activities and recommendations of the trustees who were to be appointed.

It was made absolutely clear that no such powers would be acceptable to the Americans and that France must give up all idea of the Ruhr Authority officially obtaining legal powers over detailed day-to-day management.[39] The French team, in fact, had to concentrate all their efforts on maintaining the principle that the Ruhr Authority would be officially endowed with powers over the allocation of coal resources between domestic and external use. In these circumstances there was no question of France accepting that the Authority should extend its powers over any wider geographical area than the Ruhr.

The idea that the Ruhr Authority would be a pledge of future national security now looked much weaker than it had when France had fallen back to that position in August. However, in the hope of softening or removing what it assumed would be a punitive aspect of the settlement with Germany the United States sought instead to offer France guarantees of military, rather than economic, security. Douglas suggested that the conference go ahead on the implicit assumption that American troops would stay in Western Europe until the threat from the Soviet Union had gone. In addition he proposed that the three western Allies, together with the Benelux countries, who were to be associated with them in the next stages of the conference, should constitute a Military Security Board to enforce disarmament and demilitarization on a future West German state.[40] Instead of the International Ruhr Authority itself supervising and enforcing the Potsdam decisions forbidding certain industries in Germany, this would be done by bequeathing the powers of the Military Governments to the Military Security Board which would function as an organ of a Western European military alliance. The assurance that American

[38] ibid. [39] Y.62.3, Direction d'Europe, Note pour le Président, 8 March 1948.
[40] Y.54.1, Massigli to Bidault, 5 March 1948.

forces would remain was crucial if France was to accept that the Ruhr Authority would exclude rather than permit French direction of the Ruhr firms. But it did not necessarily make it easier for the United States to obtain French acceptance of its plans for the future ownership of these firms. To whom exactly would the Ruhr firms be returned? And would France have any say in who those persons were?

It was not until August 1948 when the Landtag of North Rhine-Westphalia called a special sitting to proceed with the third reading of their bill for 'socialization', that the hostile attitude of the Military Governors was finally made clear. The interval was filled by the tangled efforts of the London conference to come to terms with France on these two questions. By April it had been more or less accepted in London that the function of the boards of trustees would now be quite different. To appease the general opinion that big business in Germany had been an ally of German fascism, and in accord with the Potsdam decisions on the 'decartelization' of German industry, which had been based on the same loose assumption, the firms would now be broken up into smaller, less integrated units. It would be the task of the trustees to put forward a plan for doing this. The firms would subsequently be disbarred by law from reintegrating with each other. It was thought that this would go some way to meeting French wishes for security.[41]

French policy was to support the deconcentration of the firms and to try to push it further while at the same time making the appointment of the trustees and the laws governing their future form and behaviour dependent on the International Authority for the Ruhr. The strength of this body was to be determined only in the third, November, session of the conference. The day before that session began the Bizone commanders jointly issued Occupation Law No. 75 announcing their intention of implementing at once the decision to create the temporary trusteeships for the management of the coal and steel industry originally announced in February and then postponed, and thus to proceed forthwith with the transfer back to private ownership. The discontent of the French Assembly with the constitutional provisions for West Germany which had emanated from the earlier sessions of the London conference had already led the French government to announce its intention of trying to modify the guiding principles laid down in the first session of the conference for the International Ruhr Authority. The setting-up of the Federal Republic had been approved by the French Assembly on 17 June by only four votes. But there can be no doubt that Law No. 75 was promulgated on the day it was in order to slam the door on any French attempt to make this modification reach

[41] Erik Nölting, one of the SPD's spokesmen in the Landtag put the matter succinctly. 'At times', he said, 'I have the impression that the question of deconcentration is being pushed into the foreground not so much to draw the poisoned fangs of capitalism as to make socialism itself toothless.' OMGUS, H.G. Schmidt, *Reorganisation of the West German Coal, Iron and Steel Industries Under the Allied High Commission for Germany, 1949–1952*. Report of the US High Commissioner for Germany, 1953.

as far as the individual firm.[42] There were, in short, in spite of the Assembly's manifest discontent, still to be no French managers in the Ruhr.

Schuman, the French Foreign Minister, protested bitterly on the same day, the thirtieth anniversary of the armistice which had ended the First World War.[43] There would, he said, 'now be nobody inside the house at all'.[44] At a press conference six days later de Gaulle called Law No. 75 'the gravest decision yet taken in the twentieth century'.[45] Given the tiny majorities by which the different stages and clauses of the London conference's earlier decisions on Germany had passed the French Assembly, one of them by one vote only, against combined communist and Gaullist opposition, the next stage of the London conference looked as though it might never begin. It was saved by a last-minute concession by the United States which made few headlines but which was none the less crucial. Correctly appraising the situation that the true direction and control of the firms as long as the occupation regime lasted would lie with the Coal and Steel Controls, France had asked in May to be given membership of these control bodies, only to get the obvious reply that this must await the fusion of the French zone with the Bizone.[46] Marshall now flew to Paris to discuss the whole range of policy towards Germany personally with Schuman and Bevin. There he offered to allow French personnel to join the Bizone Coal and Steel Controls before any details of the merger of the French zone had been agreed.[47] French personnel now had a direct participation, not just in the management of the mines, but, even more important, in the allocation of their final output. It was still, however, only to last until these powers were transferred to a constitutional West German government, unless in the third stage of the conference France could in some way have the managerial and allocatory powers of the Controls transferred to the Ruhr Authority itself.

As for the constitution and powers of the International Authority for the Ruhr, to which the conference then proceeded, few bodies can have been argued about for so long which in the end did so little. Its historical importance

[42] The policy it promulgated was rejected by the French Assembly in a debate by more than 200 votes.

[43] Robert Schuman, 1886–1963. Born in Luxembourg and then became a German citizen and lawyer in Alsace. Fought in German army in First World War and became a French citizen for the first time in 1919, the same year in which he was elected a deputy. Voted for the transfer of power to Pétain at Vichy in 1940 but then joined resistance. Briefly imprisoned in Germany. One of the founders of the Mouvement Radical Populaire. Minister of Finance 1946. Prime Minister November 1947–July 1948. Foreign Minister almost without interruption 1948–52. A man of strong personal convictions, of marked private modesty and diffidence but great public confidence. A lifelong bachelor.

[44] FO 371/70630, Paris embassy to London, 11 November 1948.

[45] J. Touchard, *Le gaullisme 1940–1969* (Paris, 1978), p. 114.

[46] Y.54.13, Direction d'Europe, Note, 15 May 1948.

[47] FRUS, II, 1948, Minutes of a meeting of foreign ministers, 19 November 1948. Marshall said that 'the possible alternative of de Gaulle filled him with terror' (FO 371/70631, UK delegation to UN Assembly to London, 21 November 1948), and not many things did that.

lay precisely in that, because its powers were so inadequate as to be capable only of producing ill-will, it paved the way for the European Coal and Steel Community.[48]

The British had given the proposal to establish the International Authority for the Ruhr their full backing providing Benelux was also associated with it and they had also supported the parallel French demand for a long-term military occupation of Germany. Forty years was the suggested term.[49] Bidault in the French Chamber spoke of an unlimited occupation period. The Benelux countries themselves were fully in support of the Ruhr Authority.[50] The only tactic available to the United States was to try to ensure that the Ruhr Authority's powers were so weak that it would not run counter to their own plans for Germany.

The text of the original statement of principle as it had emerged in March from the London conference stipulated 'that access to the coal, coke and steel of the Ruhr should not in the future as it was in the past be subject to the exclusive control of Germany'.[51] By May this had been modified in the text of the final agreement to stipulate 'that access to the coal, coke and steel of the Ruhr, which was previously subject to the exclusive control of Germany, be in the future guaranteed without discrimination to the countries of Europe co-operating in the economic good'.[52]

Apart from this fine statement, everything important about the Ruhr Authority had been left to be decided in the next session of the conference; what its powers would be, what its composition, and the dates when it would begin and cease to function. These issues threatened to be stormy. Clay had taken 'a very tragic view' of the American acceptance of any idea of a Ruhr Authority, holding 'that it will drive the Germans into the arms of the Communists'.[53] As far as the American Military Government was concerned it would be one more device, besides the OEEC, to impede economic recovery in Germany. Its position was that there could be no question of a Ruhr Authority having any powers to allocate Ruhr resources so long as those resources were effectively under the control of the Bizonal administration.

The American team at London therefore tried to make the Ruhr Authority's powers depend on future agreements between the Commanders-in-Chief in the Bizone on the one hand and the United States government on the other relating to the ERP. The output levels to which the ERP import programmes were geared would thus take precedence over any allocation decisions by the

[48] Melandri suggests on the basis of an interview with Robert Murphy, Clay's political adviser, that Monnet spent all spring and summer 1948 trying to get the Ruhr Authority turned into a genuinely European authority, but there is no other evidence for this as yet, whatever it means. P. Melandri, *Les Etats-Unis face à l'unification de l'Europe 1945–1954* (Paris, 1980), pp. 154–5.
[49] FRUS, II, 1948, Douglas to Washington, 21 February 1948, p. 78.
[50] ibid., Douglas to Washington, 26 February 1948, p. 92.
[51] ibid., International control of the Ruhr, 5 March 1948, p. 135.
[52] ibid., International control of the Ruhr, 26 May 1948, p. 285.
[53] FO 371/70626, Robertson to Strang, 13 March 1948.

Ruhr Authority, and the decisive figure in determining the allocation of German coal resources would be the administrator of the ERP. Faced with this possibility the French threatened to break off the talks there and then.[54] However, against any suggestion that the ECA and OEEC should have decisive international economic importance the French could always rely on British support. The United Kingdom was flatly opposed to the ECA having such a say in the determination of future output levels in Germany. The State Department had no alternative but to face Clay's wrath. Although the decision had already been taken in Washington to replace the Military Governor by a civil administration, as the Berlin crisis came nearer it seemed necessary to postpone any change and to leave the soldiers in absolute charge. In any case, leaving the American army effectively in command of the Ruhr's resources for the moment suited America's book, always provided of course that Washington could enforce on its own army the policies of the ECA.

This was by no means so certain. The import programmes for the Bizone which were submitted to the OEEC were drawn up by the Joint Export–Import Agency (JEIA), whose constitution had been determined under the fusion agreements between the British and American Military Governments. Voting on the JEIA was weighted according to the value of the financial contribution of the power exercising the vote, thus giving the USA the power to override British decisions there. Clay's fury that, having obtained these powers, he should then find that, because of the ERP's insistence on European integration, the programmes were opposed by Britain and France in the 'continuing organization' was wholly understandable. So was his determination not to let anything emerge from the London conference which would make it easier for France to block German recovery. In particular, his suspicion was directed towards all French attempts there to institute a set of sectoral control boards in the Ruhr. The more the State Department appeared likely to make concessions to France, the more Clay sought to use the outcome of the London conference as a way of limiting the scope which the OEEC gave to Western Europe to delay German recovery in the name of common Western European action. Reviewing the position for its own officers before the congressional hearings on the 1949 appropriations the State Department put the matter bluntly,

> While the Army Department and Military Government in the field pay lip service to the concept of joint action for European recovery, there is little or no evidence that this policy is put into practice. The Army, with its separate responsibility in Germany and separate appropriation takes what can best be described as a highly nationalistic German view of the problem.
>
> The ECA mission to the Bizone is virtually isolated and has remarkably little to do with the German recovery program.[55]

[54] Y.62.3, Telegram Massigli to Paris, 6 May 1948.
[55] ECA, 1, State Department Briefing Papers, 4 February 1949.

If that was what the State Department felt about it, it was scarcely surprising that in the London conference one French aim was to have the American army deprived of all economic influence in West Germany, while retained there as a strategic influence.

The army's own appropriations were the GARIOA funds which they spent by making as liberal an interpretation as possible of the restrictions imposed by the governing document, JCS 1067.[56] When the London conference agreed to institute civilian High Commissioners to take over from the Military Governments the decision was made that aid from the army appropriations would be run down and channelled through similar organizations in Germany to ERP aid. With the eventual proclamation of the Occupation Statute and the end of military rule, the French zone would be merged with the Bizone and the Federal Republic would sign its own bilateral agreement with the United States and enter the OEEC as a full member. This procedure suited French objectives, rather than West Germany having two sources of aid whose disposal would be generally handled by the American Army, it would now have to fight for itself in 'the continuing organization'.

The difficulty was that the United States, ready though it was to come to this tidy solution to further the pursuit of integration, was by no means ready to concede that whatever powers were given to the Ruhr Authority would also be given to a similar body in any future peace treaty with either a West German or an all-German government. When the second session of the London conference broke up it submitted the final agreed version of the document constituting an International Authority for the Ruhr to all the governments concerned. The United States, Britain, France, Belgium, the Netherlands, Luxembourg and Germany were to have membership, with America, Britain, France and Germany each having three votes and the Benelux countries three between them. But the German representation and the German votes would for the time being still be exercised by 'those powers which share the responsibility for the economic administration of that part of Germany which includes the Ruhr'.[57]

The Authority's tasks were to divide the quantities of coal, coke and steel from the Ruhr between domestic consumption and exports, but, and this was the bitter pill for France, only in accordance with the aid programmes formulated in the OEEC. Three months later the first such programme from the OEEC was to be overturned by the American administraton because it was not favourable enough to the Bizone! The Authority's other principal function was to ensure that the German authorities did not introduce discriminatory measures on the movements of coal, iron and steel products in international trade. It could request information and it could report breaches

[56] The way in which the formula was interpreted widely is analysed in J.H. Backer, *Priming the German Economy: American Occupational Policies 1945–1948* (Durham NC, 1971).
[57] FRUS, 1948, II, International control of the Ruhr, 26 May 1948, p. 286.

of conduct to the Military Governors, its only specified executive arm. Effective day-to-day control would remain in the hands of the Military Governments and when those governments were wound up the powers which they exercised would be transferred 'to such international body as may be designated for these purposes by the Peace Settlement'.[58] That is to say there was no guarantee and a decreasing likelihood that once the Military Governors had departed the Ruhr Authority would get any of the real economic powers which Clay was so reluctant to relinquish while he was still there. For the time being by a majority vote the Authority would be able to ask the Military Governors to enforce its wishes and after the institution of civil government its powers appeared likely to be even less. 'You will', the head of the British delegation to the OEEC was informed from London, 'be quick to observe that the Ruhr document is full of sound and fury but signifying practically nothing ... one of the principal problems has been to find relatively harmless things for the "Authority" to do.'[59]

Why, then, did France accept at this stage an outcome so much less than the one thought essential to future national security? The question is the stronger because during the same stage of the London conference France also failed to achieve the political settlement on the future West German constitution which had also been regarded as essential to future security. As far as the constitution of West Germany was concerned French negotiating tactics were to ensure that there was no directly elected central national assembly, but only one chosen indirectly from the Land parliaments, with whom, because they would be chosen by universal suffrage, the main political weight and responsibility would remain. This was not what the United States meant by a federal West Germany, which was considered inconceivable in Washington without its own national democratic assembly, even though many checks and counterbalances would remain in the powers given to the Länder. By the end of May 1948 it had become certain that the second stage of the London conference would recommend a West Germany with a more unitary constitution than France considered acceptable and an International Authority for the Ruhr with neither the powers nor the duration which France considered indispensable. The inevitable moment of choice had arrived. The choice had not been imposed on France by acceptance of the Marshall Plan. Within the CEEC France had been able to rely on British support against all American attempts to force political integration on to Western Europe and even on a certain measure of British support for the idea that German economic recovery should be slower than that of the rest of Western Europe. But in the London conference there was no British support for French views on the German constitution. Indeed, it was made clear to the French that if the National Assembly rejected the proposals for the German constitution and the Ruhr

[58] ibid., p. 287.
[59] FO 371/70628, Stevens to Hall-Patch, 28 May 1948.

Authority as they had emerged from this stage of the London conference the United States and Britain would still go ahead by themselves with their own version of a future Germany.[60]

This in itself was a most powerful reason for the French to accept the terms proposed. What would they have been left with had they refused? They would have been seen as the enemies of the new German democracy as well as of a future German national state of any kind. They would have had no say whatsoever in the disposal of the Ruhr's resources. In the background lay worse fears. Suppose the United States returned to the policy of settling the fate of Germany directly with the Soviet Union and then withdrawing from Europe? A resurgent nationalism in Germany would demand unification and might find it in an alliance with the Soviet Union against France. Not to accept the agreements at the London conference would have endangered France's future national security even more than to accept them. To the threat from Germany would have been joined the threat from the Soviet Union and against that double menace the Brussels Pact was no shield. Not to accept would have been to end almost all French influence over the future Germany save that exercised in the French zone of occupation. How little that would be worth was lucidly set out by Michel Debré.

> The economic disequilibrium of our zone is such, particularly since the Saarland was joined to France, that it can no longer survive: only American credits are going to allow the French zone not to sink into destitution and unemployment. Our administrative powers will therefore lose their *raison d'être* and our possibilities of exploitation, already condemned in principle by political wisdom (but in reality continued) would come to an end.[61]

The conclusion from such an unavoidable analysis was only a short step logically; in terms of Europe's future organization it was a giant's pace. If, faced with this defeat, what France sought in Germany was influence over the future society there and access to the Ruhr resources, these could only be achieved by a closer Franco-West German political association and economic co-operation. From the time the decisions of the second stage of the London conference had to be accepted or refused there began a determined search in Paris for an entirely different solution, and now the only logical one, to the problem of Franco-German relations.

The final summary of the second stage of the London conference submitted to Schuman left no doubt that a more positive policy towards the future Germany had now to be devised.

> It is essential to conclude this summary by establishing that the French Government obtained the only possible result at the present moment if it

[60] Y.54.13, Massigli to Paris, 3 June 1948.
[61] Y.61.1, Notes by Michel Debré, 11 May 1948.

sincerely wishes the construction of a viable western Europe, that is to say one in which Germany will voluntarily take its part. ... If the conclusions of the London Conference are rejected by the Parliament, German unity will still be achieved and it will be achieved against us, either by the path of communism or by the intermediation of American imperialism. No policy of Franco-German co-operation will then be possible.[62]

But from where was such a policy of Franco-German co-operation to emerge? Even if the outcome of the second stage of the London conference was the best that could have been achieved, this was clearly not the judgment of at least half the members of the National Assembly, who were extremely dissatisfied with what had been brought back. Opinion there was so strong that before the debates in June the government twice unsuccessfully tried to persuade its allies to let them inform the Assembly that the statement of principles on the Ruhr Authority still left open the possibility of direct international management of the firms by some other route.[63]

By any standards French policy had suffered a severe setback. The imminent creation of the new West German state made the need for a radical change of policy even more pressing. This was wholly accepted in the Foreign Ministry by those responsible for policy formulation. What they began to seek from 1948, instead of the one-sided exercise of control over the Ruhr in a perpetually weak and fragmented Germany, was some form of Franco-West German agreement or even association which would still guarantee access to the Ruhr's resources and diminish the threat to national security. But the problem was to formulate a policy along these lines which would be acceptable to Schuman, and after Schuman to the other ministers, a harder task, and after them to the National Assembly and the country, perhaps a task still harder, and after that to the Federal Republic, possibly hardest of all.

To revert to the ideas of the 1920s and leave private interests on each side to work out a solution would be an even bigger setback. Too much had been invested in the attempt at the highest political levels to take away the right of either the Ruhr industrialists or a future German state to dispose at will of the Ruhr's resources. In any case, there were still no private owners in the Ruhr legally in a position to repeat the policy of the 1920s and enter into a cartel with their French counterparts. The French coal industry had passed under national control. And would a private entente of this kind, towards which several French and German industrialists were edging their way, if it did become possible, serve the purposes of the Modernization and Re-equipment Plan? It might well serve as a way of resisting the expansion of the French steel industry which was a basic requirement of that plan.

[62] Y.54.13, Direction d'Europe, Note, 3 June 1948.
[63] FRUS, 1948, II, Washington to Paris embassy, 10 June 1948, p. 326; London embassy to Washington, 16 June 1948, p. 331.

If, however, as Bidault had claimed, the Ruhr belonged to Europe, this could hardly be allowed to mean that France should abandon all special claims on Ruhr resources and allow the future levels of output in the Ruhr and the disposal of its resources to be determined by the OEEC, ECA, or a new Western European super-state in which West Germany would be on an entirely equal political status with the other members, and economically, soon perhaps more powerful. The solution which the United States had proposed at the start of the London conference was thus no solution either, not least because in the context of American plans the internationalization of the Ruhr would be the first step towards a liberal customs union in western Europe in which France would presumably be precluded from imposing any discriminatory arrangement on Germany to guarantee access to the needed resources.

There was in fact no good reason not to press ahead and try to get the powers of the Ruhr Authority extended, even though a drastic change of policy was now needed. It was not easy to see what France could offer West Germany in return for a Franco-German agreement on Ruhr resources other than the removal of the limitations which the Ruhr Authority imposed on West German sovereignty and of its powers over German resources. In that case the more powers the Authority eventually had the better. If, after the Federal Republic had come into existence, a policy which was politically acceptable to government and people looked feasible, a strong Ruhr Authority might be the lever on Germany which could make it feasible. The more West Germany had to gain, the harder the bargain France could drive.

The French intention in the third stage of the conference therefore was to persuade their allies to allow the Ruhr Authority to take over the powers and functions of the Coal and Steel Controls as they were wound up. In fact, even if only at the very end, France came out of the tortuous bargaining process which ensued with considerably more success than out of the second stage of the conference. Gradually the United States and the United Kingdom conceded the possibility that certain powers appertaining to the Military Governors and some of the activities of the Controls might be vested, if needed, in the International Authority for the Ruhr. As far as the powers passed on from the Military Governors were concerned, however, these would be confined to the supervision of the laws against excessive concentration of industry and against the return of former Nazis to ownership. In case of infringement of these laws the Ruhr Authority, under the terms of the Occupation Statute which was to define the relationships between occupiers and the West German constitutional government, would be able to request the Military Security Board to intervene and presumably in the one case annul the German law or in the other dispossess the offender once more.

The first of these powers was not without importance. More than a third of Ruhr coking coal, by some estimates as much as a half, was commercially tied to German metallurgical firms and could therefore, once the Coal Control had been disbanded and unless new control boards were given powers to prevent it, be consumed by German steel works at internal transfer prices. It might be possible under the laws on industrial deconcentration to break up some of these connections. The second concession admitted the principle that the Ruhr Authority could, if only in flagrant cases, have some say in who ran the firms. The powers transferred from the Coal and Steel Controls were limited by the Ruhr Authority's lack of its own executive powers. It would now be able to examine prices, tariffs and transport charges but it could only request changes. Its powers had therefore been considerably extended under French pressure in the last stage of the London conference, but it still lacked the immediate executive force of the Coal and Steel Controls. Its allocation of coal would still have to conform to the European-wide programmes of reconstruction which the OEEC was intended to produce, and in which the Bizone programme had by now been seen to be subject to dictation by the United States. Although regarding this third stage of the London conference as having brought, within the framework of the new policy objectives, considerable success, the French negotiators saw no reason not to pursue the matter further. Their objective was to create a series of sectoral control boards in the West German economy which would have the same executive force as the doomed Coal and Steel Controls and would be supervised by the Allies through the new governmental machinery.

The draft text of the detailed agreement on the International Authority for the Ruhr was officially released on 28 December 1948. Powers over production, investment, development and management in the Ruhr industries, currently exercised by the Coal and Steel Controls, were to be transferred at the appropriate time, and if the six powers considered necessary, 'to the Ruhr Authority or to the Military Security Board or its successor or to some other international body'.[64] This wording still left open the possibility of a less punitive Ruhr Authority on which Germany would be represented on more genuinely equal terms, an authority of the kind which America had wanted at the start of the London conference.

In fact on the last day of the negotiations, when everybody had met just to check and sign the final communiqués, the American delegation, in an astonishing manoeuvre, presented an extra minute which they insisted on including in those communiqués. The first part stipulated that the powers to be devolved on the Ruhr Authority from the Commanders-in-Chief would not be 'those which would be applicable to a detailed control of the operation and management of the industries and which would constantly interfere with the normal and regular responsibilities of management'. The second part stipulated that the powers so transferred would be 'a preliminary step towards developing a

[64] FRUS, 1948, II, Communiqué of the London Conference on the Ruhr, 28 December 1948, p. 580.

closer integration of the economies of Western Europe and that the Signatory Governments will promote that closer integration for the benefit of Europe, looking forward to the time when such powers will no longer be necessary.'[65] Not only was this sweeping addition presented at the last moment of a ten-month-long conference but it was accompanied by a threat that if the second part were not agreed the United States would itself publish it as a unilateral declaration.

Under such threat the French had to accept something, but when they accepted a weakened version the British cabinet objected to this on the grounds that it involved them in a commitment to promote European integration. In the end, and only after an all-night argument, everybody accepted a version which read

> It is further understood that any powers transferred to the Authority in this connection ... for economic as opposed to security purposes will be transferred for the purpose of contributing toward that closer association of the economies of Europe which the Six Powers have set out as one of their objectives in the preamble to the agreement and which should create conditions in which such powers will no longer be necessary.[66]

Whether this really made the agreement more acceptable to a West German government rather than to United States opinion is a moot point. In any form it was an electoral millstone around the neck of a German government and it had been made less acceptable to France.

On the other hand the fact that such a form of phraseology could be agreed at all shows how after May France had altered the intentions of its policy, even if the outward semblance and expression of that policy remained the same. By the end of November the French negotiators were persuaded that 'everything which is happening on the other side of the Rhine proves that the reconstruction of Germany has the first priority among American preoccupations'.[67] Only two choices were left. One was to withdraw entirely from the occupation of Germany in the hope that this would shock the Allies into some consciousness of how they were ignoring French needs. This was no more than a counsel of despair, the hope might be vain and all France's bargaining counters would have been surrendered. That left

> only one solution: to abandon completely and without reservation our malthusian policy with respect to Western Germany and to establish a common ground of economic and political association with that Germany inside the Western Union in the course of development. ... We must maintain our positions on the question of the internationalization, or more

[65] FO 371/76497, Stevens to Penson, 29 December 1948.   [66] ibid.
[67] Z.18.1, Direction d'Europe, Sous-direction d'Europe Centrale, Note, 24 November 1948.

exactly the 'westernization' of the Ruhr. However, here too, we must try to go beyond the issue. We must seek the internationalization of all the western mining areas.[68]

The way in which this might be done still, however, resembled in many ways the thoughts of 1945. The creation of public mixed authorities, not unlike those which the Soviet Union had established in occupied eastern Europe, which would attract private French capital into the reconstruction of the Ruhr and thus guarantee future close association between French and German firms might fill in, it was hoped, in the period of time during which the French public would have to be prepared psychologically for a more formal Franco-German economic association. How long a period of time this might be was vague, certainly longer than the time that was going to be vouchsafed! Meanwhile studies of a possible western European customs union could be undertaken. But that was a longer-term project because of the inherent dangers of economic specialization in any such union 'and it was not a question of France giving up her key industries'.[69] Politically, the way forward might be through a common charter of association between French and German political parties. Whatever route was chosen, however, now, at the end of the third stage of the London conference, positive action along these lines was imperative.

The experience of the years which followed the Treaty of Versailles can only make us sceptical about the value of these substitute guarantees. The controls can be avoided even if it is accepted that all the controlling powers are determined to apply them. The bans and limitations are only of value in so far as they are definitive and strictly enforced. One practical example illustrates this point of view: steel production in Germany had been definitively fixed in 1946 at 7.5 million tonnes. It was fixed in 1947, no less definitively, at 11 million tonnes, today it is a question even in certain allied circles of raising this ceiling and in any case of leaving in Germany a productive capacity clearly greater than the authorised level.

That is why the French government has come to the conviction that the guarantees which it is seeking will only be capable of being validly secured in a kind of association of Germany in a larger framework, that of Europe. To take again the same example as above, steel made in the Ruhr would no longer be German steel but a part of European steel. France would be associated on equal terms with Germany in the control of this steel cartel. In this way she would have her word to say, better than by way of international controls, in the question of the German steelworks.[70]

[68] Z.18.1, Direction d'Europe, Perspectives d'une politique française à l'égard de l'Allemagne, n.d.   [69] ibid.
[70] Z.17.1, Direction d'Europe, Sous-direction d'Europe Centrale, L'Allemagne et l'union européenne, 4 January 1949.

Starting the London conference with a policy based on the partition of Germany and direct French management of the Ruhr resources, within less than a year opinion in the French Foreign Ministry had moved to the idea of a solution which began to resemble the later proposals for the Coal and Steel Community. The Schuman Plan did not, as all commentators on it have so far suggested, emerge like a *deus ex machina* from the Planning Commissariat in spring 1950. It was in essence already there at the end of the London conference. All that was lacking was a precise economic formulation of such a policy which went beyond the vague ideas of an understanding between French and German industries in a wider European framework so that it was acceptable to the other Western European countries and so that it was acceptable to the United States and did not appear there as a barrier to American ideas on integration.

✳   ✳   ✳

It is not the task of this book to analyse all the political complexities surrounding the conception and birth of the German Federal Republic, a rich subject in itself. So far it has been described almost entirely from the standpoint of the internal political progress towards a democratic constitutional state in Germany.[71] The international parameters within which this internal political progress was permitted to take place have not received the same attention.[72] They were very largely economic. How false a picture of the origins of the German Federal Republic those books paint which just depict the negotiations with the Allies over the nature of its constitution! Complicated in their details though these were, there was nevertheless a large area of basic political agreement, on constitutional democracy, on the subordination of the executive to the legislative assemblies, on the incorporation into the constitution of certain basic individual human rights, on a constitutional court to uphold those rights and preserve democracy and so on. On the future of the economy no such basic area of agreement existed and the issue which proved most irreconcilable was the relationship of Germany's economic recovery to that of France. As the British cabinet had been succinctly told in 1931, 'World recovery ... depends on European recovery; European recovery on German recovery; German recovery on France's consent; France's consent on security [for all time] against attack.'[73] The situation had not changed.

[71] There are several analyses. J.F. Golay, *The Founding of the Federal Republic of Germany* (Chicago, 1958); P.H. Merkl, *The Origin of the West German Republic* (New York, 1963); and K. Niclaus, *Demokratiegründung in Westdeutschland. Die Entstehung der Bundesrepublik 1945–1949* (Munich, 1974) are reliable guides.

[72] In spite of the excellent pioneering work of H.-P. Schwarz, *Vom Reich zur Bundesrepublik. Deutschland im Widerstreit der aussenpolitischen Konzeptionen in den Jahren der Besatzungsherrschaft 1945–1949* (Neuwied, Berlin, 1966) and the useful book of essays, *Westdeutschlands Weg zur Bundesrepublik: 1945–1949, Beiträge von Mitarbeitern des Instituts für Zeitgeschichte* (Munich, 1976).

[73] CP 301 (31), Changing conditions in British foreign policy, 2 December 1931.

One important step towards a resolution of this problem had been taken, however. The Monnet Plan had become a guideline to French policy towards the reconstruction of Europe as well as to domestic reconstruction. The Ministry of Foreign Affairs had tried to make it so from the outset and to draw out its implications for French national security. The Plan's goals were only achievable given a certain measure of control over the disposition of Germany's resources. As soon as it proved that this could not be surely obtained through occupation, annexation, partition or international regulation, the inherent logic of following the Plan's guidelines meant that it would have to be sought in Franco-German association. It was therefore the existence of the Monnet Plan as the basis for French domestic reconstruction which pointed the way with increasing inexorability to a resolution of that central problem in western European reconstruction which had defeated everyone after 1918.

As soon as Marshall Aid was offered and the offer embraced the German economy as well the logic of the Monnet Plan implied that it might now only be achievable within a Franco-German association. Only two months after Marshall's speech at Harvard and only three weeks after the opening of the CEEC the French government made its first proposals to Benelux for the formation of a western European customs union.[74] But it was not until French proposals on the future West German constitution were decisively rejected in the second stage of the London conference that the French government finally had to come to terms in June 1948 with the fact that the German Federal Republic would be a unitary sovereign state and that there was not sufficient support elsewhere for France to be sure that controls over the use of German resources and the German economy would be strong enough or durable enough for the Monnet Plan to be achieved in any other way than through a Franco-German association. The extent and likely durability of the controls subsequently obtained through the International Ruhr Authority did nothing to modify this conclusion. By the start of 1949 the first proposals emerged that the way forward was through a Franco-German coal, iron and steel cartel which would be managed and controlled within the integrated European common market.

In comparison with the period 1918–24 there were two obvious advantages in pursuing this goal. There was now a public commitment by the United States to provide aid for both French and German reconstruction as well as an organization in which the other Western European states had some say in the way in which it would be done. Secondly, the Germany in question was smaller and very much weaker. The second of these advantages was a rapidly expiring one because for all the other members of the OEEC as much as for the United States it was becoming essential that West German economic recovery be accelerated and this was the main constraint on the imposition of controls over Germany's economy. French reconstruction objectives did not,

[74] See below pp. 233–5.

however, merely depend on access to certain German resources to enable the planning targets to be met and on controls over German output to make them meaningful. They depended even more on France's neighbours, Britain and West Germany above all, pursuing economic policies which did not make the Monnet Plan impossible or meaningless. No one could doubt after the experience of Nazi Germany the catastrophic immensity of the effort required to pursue high levels of output and employment in one country alone, to say nothing of their destructive repercussions on the world around it. And to these ambitions France had now added another, a high level of material welfare. Without achieving these things reconstruction would be a failure, perhaps the same kind of failure which had appeared in 1929, and not just for France but for the other Western European countries most of which had similar combinations of objectives. The extent to which control over German resources was useful and successful would be one of the degree to which the economic policies of the future West German government would be co-operative rather than disruptive. The international framework of controls as it appeared when the text of the agreement on the International Ruhr Authority was issued at the end of Christmas week 1948 was not therefore at all satisfactory from the French point of view and from the time the Federal government took office all efforts were concentrated on finding a better basis for the necessary Franco-German association without which the goals of the Monnet Plan might not be realizable.

The long history of both private and governmental attempts after 1870 to achieve an international regulation of the western European coke, ore, iron and steel markets underlay the whole problem. The relatively small number of tons of coke, coal, iron ore and steel took on an aura of political importance which seems out of all proportion to its economic significance, the same aura it had taken on after 1918 and, indeed, throughout the tangled history since 1870 of the Franco-German frontier. What is so curious is how, in spite of this tangled history and in spite of the failure of the Versailles Treaty to permit the real growth of welfare in either France or Germany, not only the economics of the relationship of coal, iron ore, coke and steel to the Franco-German dispute continued to be misunderstood, but that France's earlier post-war proposals for Germany should have come so close to repeating the economic errors of the unenforceable Versailles Treaty. France's real problem, one that should have been much earlier visible and defined in view of the much clearer formulation of national economic reconstruction objectives after 1945 than 1918, was how to create, in western Europe at least, a framework for economic expansion and growth which would permit the successful realization of the wider objectives of the Monnet Plan. It should have been earlier visible because the plan had been brought into being to remedy the economic catastrophe of the inter-war period.

Comparing the experience of western Europe after the two world wars suggests that a satisfactory economic settlement was in this respect much more important and useful than any treaty of peace. The fundamental failure of the Versailles Treaty was that it did not provide, any more than the hastily abandoned 'Morgenthau Plan' or the Potsdam agreements, for the future welfare of western Europe's inhabitants in a reasonably durable political framework. Indeed, the political framework which it provided greatly exacerbated the economic difficulties. In this light it is the economic objectives of French European policy after 1945 which were the true determinants of a more lasting western European settlement, for they would determine, just as the changing economic objectives of French policy after the signing of the Versailles Treaty did, the conjoint pattern of French and German economic recovery. It was out of this expression of French national interest that the first real steps towards 'supra-nationality' in Europe were taken.

V

THE DEPOLITICIZATION
OF THE OEEC

There is no history of the OEEC, only descriptions of its functions and juridical guides to its labyrinthine structures. This may seem entirely understandable. For what can there be to interest a historian in an international organization which annually repeated the same functions and, while on rare occasions it may have done something to influence the decisions of a particular government, for the most part existed only to record and reconcile those decisions and analyse their consequences? Its task for most of its life was merely to adjust to and then chronicle decisions made elsewhere. Yet this was not always so. It was called into being by the United States as the first stage in the political and economic integration of Western Europe, the embryonic hope for a Western European government. How, in spite of the power and influence of the United States, and of the fact that in the first five years of the OEEC's foundation there was the most rapid move towards economic integration in modern European history, OEEC ended by being no such thing, is a central theme in Europe's reconstruction.

It measured the real limits of American power in western Europe. It marked the defeat of American ambitions for the one, common, unregulated market with an uncontrolled flow of factors which the ECA wanted to see as the first step towards the United States of Europe. It demonstrated the impracticability of any form of European integration other than for specific and limited purposes. Above all it demonstrated that the shifting pattern of temporary alliances for short-term purposes was still, as it had been in the 1930s, the basis of all international economic policy-making in western Europe.

In attempting to create a quite new form of institutional expression of economic interdependence the United States only strengthened the earlier pattern based on the nation state. The OEEC simply served as a more convenient forum for making and unmaking the temporary national alliances on specific economic issues which had in the 1930s been more troublesome to make. In collecting permanent delegations of sixteen countries into one centre the organization reduced, as economists would now express it, the transaction costs of such actions. No rational participant in the process of political bargaining which centred on the OEEC during its first two years would have reasonably denied that what took place there demonstrated most forcefully that the American standpoint that there was an urgent need in Western Europe for a new institutional framework for the economic interdependence of the Western European states was correct. But the underlying theoretical assumptions on which the OEEC was based, as well as its inherent, structural political weaknesses were such as to make the *traditional* pattern of political activity which took place there a more rational response to the particular problems of the Western European economies.

The idea of a 'European organization' had been born with the idea of the ERP. The new Western Europe would have to be built by the Europeans themselves and Marshall Aid would only be the opportunity; a noble idea, but, as the analysis in chapter 1 indicated, altogether too messianic to be appropriate to the circumstances. Furthermore, it was distinctly inappropriate, too, to expect a new, integrative, political form to be created in response to an aid programme which was administered in the country of origin in the most traditional way. The corresponding American organization, the ECA, was quite indistinguishable in its form and method from any other part of the national bureaucracy of the United States. It was deliberately temporary, of course, but that is not at all uncommon in Washington and, in fact, when the idea of a 'European organization' was conceived it was assumed that the Department of State would administer the ERP. The United States acted and was represented in Paris at the OEEC as a nation state through the traditional, national, diplomatic process and pursued purely national interests there. None of the member countries of the OEEC supported the full scope of America's ambitions for it. Marshall Aid did not provide sufficient economic leverage to overcome this difficulty. The American response was to seek to form transient alliances for limited items of policy with groups of states within the organization. That these were never strong enough to be successful against the Franco-British opposition is perhaps less interesting than the immense conceptual gulf between the way the United States wished the European countries to behave in Paris and the way it behaved itself.

This gulf was a great temptation to European countries themselves to seek occasional alliances of national interest with the United States, rather than act in concert. Each European country hoped to use certain elements in the new American policy to support its own aims and ambitions in European reconstruction. The possibilities of success in this direction inevitably coincided with the extent to which national policy aims could be clothed in the shining new raiment of 'integration'. That is doubtless the normal penalty of such a wide gap in policy between aspiration and feasibility. But there were scarcely two people in Washington in 1948 who were in agreement about what 'integration' meant in practice, so there was ample scope for European countries to make its meaning foggier by dressing up their own national interests in the same language.

There were two fairly precise ways in which in 1948 American policy did try to force the OEEC to produce a measure of Western European economic integration. The first was by making it recommend the allocation of ERP aid between the different member states. The second was by making it produce a common European 'long-term' plan for economic recovery coinciding with the estimated duration of the ERP. Both these policies failed. In discovering why they did so we can identify the biggest obstacles in Western Europe to American policy. The aim is not a negative one; the nature of the opposition in the OEEC to American policies did much to shape the eventual successful reconstruction of Western Europe outside the confines of the OEEC.

Of these obstacles the most serious and pervasive was that of Germany's future. Membership of the organization gave France an important voice in all discussions about the reconstruction of the German economy, and in a forum where the United States was not a full member. The OEEC would not in fact, as we have seen, have come into existence at all had not the United States to some extent committed itself to joint agreement with France on the future political framework for Germany. The OEEC then provided France with an additional arena in which to oppose or delay unwelcome decisions made elsewhere on Germany, and one in which the interests of the smaller powers in the German question could occasionally be combined with its own to thwart American objectives.

Every bit as divisive, and just as foreseeably so, were the wide differences in domestic economic recovery policy between the Western European countries. Had the United States not intervened with Marshall Aid, pressures on the balance of payments and the reserves might have reduced the dissimilarities of economic policy in Western Europe by curbing the speed at which some of the economies could hope to fulfil their ambitions. But by allowing French and Dutch international deficits to continue relatively unabated it supported the bolder objectives of planners there while at the same time it was to prove unable to modify the contrary economic policies in Italy. When the OEEC superimposed on the problem of deciding by what principles aid should be allocated to countries pursuing such different policies the attempt to further reallocate the aid to support the rudiments of a multilateral payments system, almost every possible difference of domestic economic choice was dragged into the conflict.

Underlying these differences of choice of policy were fundamental differences of economic situation. Using aid to improve the trading network in Western Europe was of crucial importance to economies like Belgium or the Netherlands which lived from intra-European trade, but of only low priority to the United Kingdom, whose trade was mainly elsewhere. Using aid to support investment projects thought crucial to national development was considered essential in France or the Netherlands; Denmark and Belgium by contrast were more prepared to allow the direction of investment to be shaped by international patterns of comparative advantage. Italy was concerned to develop a free labour market but apprehensive about a free capital market, tendencies perfectly in line with its previous development; others, like the Netherlands, where population had increased rapidly, were concerned with getting foreign capital and keeping out foreign labour. Whatever the temporary fads of economic policy these sorts of attitudes reflected long-run differences in economic realities, and they, too, were brought into conflict at once in the OEEC.

These disputes and differences between the European nation states did not ease the path of the United States. On the contrary, by increasing the complexity of the problems which it faced they made the defeat of its sweeping plans more probable. The influence which the smaller states could bring to bear at crucial moments proved that in the interplay of real national interest within the OEEC even the smallest country, by a careful choice of objectives, could sometimes get its own way. The immediate areas of international decision-making in the OEEC were often, as has since tended to be the case in the EEC, matters of smaller importance in themselves to the larger national economies than to the smaller, however much they ultimately symbolized important policy issues. The larger economies were forced into a bargaining forum where the smaller economies had more reason to spin out the process of diplomatic argument because the potential gains and losses were greater. From the outset it was the smaller states which were the more ardent supporters of the OEEC. But their common interests were not great and when they did coincide they did not necessarily coincide with that of America. It took only two years of struggle in the ever more intricate undergrowth of OEEC politics for the United States to abandon its frontal attack on the European state system and approach its reform by a more tangential and gradual route.

While refusing, however, the redefinition of international economic interdependence proposed by the United States, the European states began at the same time to move towards their own form of it, outside the OEEC and beyond the pressures of Marshall Aid. Before Marshall Aid ended, the 'continuing organization', which had been intended eventually to assume many of the economic powers of national governments, had become merely a consultative group. Interdependence was to develop in bodies which had the advantage of growing from the roots of Europe's own history and not of being grafted on to it from a New World stock. But the need for such growth was made obvious by the experience of the first two years of the OEEC, just as that experience made obvious which forms of it were unacceptable.

The process of discussion of economic policy and the elementary forecasting of its medium-term impact on foreign trade and payments, which was unavoidable in the context of the OEEC, did bring home to the European states how far apart their economic conceptions were and from the start of the CEEC and throughout the first years of the OEEC the interest in and knowledge of what was being attempted in other countries greatly increased. This was not hard for they had both been almost entirely lacking before 1947, nor were they ever high enough afterwards. But the OEEC created a forum in which these inter-European disputes had to be faced and discussed, and always in the context of a common interest in opposing integration on American terms. It was the crucible in which the various possible amalgams of national economic and political interest were tested under the heat of American pressure. Which would prove the stronger had already become clear when American pressures changed direction and the OEEC was allowed to sink into dull but durable bureaucratic routine.

THE CONSTITUTION OF THE OEEC

The United States had not wanted the OEEC to be in Paris.[1] Neither had some of the smaller countries. The Dutch preferred London and the Danes Brussels.[2] But the CEEC had met there and the British view was that if they had the major chairmanships and the French the location as well as the office of Secretary-General a satisfactory defence would exist both against the ambitions of the United States and the importuning of the smaller powers. In fact on the eve of the first meeting of the working party which created the organization Bevin told Bidault that the pressure was such that Paris could not be the permanent seat. But as soon as Bidault 'flatly rejected'[3] this the compromise was easy. It was that Brussels should become the headquarters of the common defence organization created by the Brussels pact and Paris that of the OEEC, and this was agreed in the joint Benelux delegation to the working party on 15 March.[4] Against their wishes the Americans had to accept that Paris would be the permanent seat of the OEEC.[5] As though to flaunt Western Europe's determination to advance towards a capitalist future it was housed in a property bought from the Rothschilds.

The much more important issue of the constitution was, by contrast, resolved only with great difficulty and with no one entirely satisfied with the outcome. Nominally the CEEC had been a standing conference of ministers, but in fact they had performed only the formalities of opening and closing it

[1] SD 840.50, 532, London embassy to Washington, 3 March 1948.
[2] ibid., The Hague embassy to Washington, 20 January 1948. SD 840.50, 5648, Copenhagen embassy to Washington, 18 February 1948.
[3] SD 840.50, 532, Paris embassy to Washington, 15 March 1948.
[4] ibid., Paris embassy to Washington, 16 March 1948.
[5] FRUS, 1948, III, Caffery to Washington, 20 March 1948.

and the work had been done by their deputies, senior civil servants for the most part. The United States wanted the new organization to be a ministerial organization in reality, with frequent meetings of the supreme body, the Council, at ministerial level, although how far such an aim was thought achievable seems to have varied very widely amongst those concerned.[6] All, however, in Washington agreed that the power which Britain and France had wielded through the Executive Committee in the CEEC must be curbed by giving the Secretariat-General of the new organization important independent powers and also by imposing a strong personality, who agreed with American policy, on the organization as its chairman. On the Anglo-French side the objective was to devise a constitution which would allow Britain and France jointly to resist all unwanted pressures towards integration and also keep the smaller states in order. The Franco-British intention was to keep the small, powerful, Executive Committee as in the CEEC, dominated by them as permanent members, and a Secretary-General, chosen by them, who would be but the servant of the OEEC and have no independent powers. Marjolin had done his job well and what was more it could 'fairly be assumed that he will play in with the London views to a considerable extent'.[7] Both countries had virtually put him in place in January before they even began their round of consultations in other capitals.[8] It was as much a part of their plans as having Bevin as chairman of the whole organization so that he could exercise ultimate power at the ministerial level when it had to be exercised and also as having the head of the British delegation as Chairman of the Executive Committee to exercise effective day-to-day power in consultation with the French chief delegate. Since Franks was to be named as ambassador to the United States, to the annoyance of Washington, where it seemed to indicate that Britain was giving preference to Washington over the OEEC as a forum for Marshall Aid discussions, his deputy, Edmund Hall-Patch, would become Chairman of the Executive Committee and thus for most purposes a little-known British civil servant, already unpopular with the Americans, would be effectively the most important man in the organization.[9]

The Americans had their own favourite candidate for Chairman of the

[6] SD RG353, 34, ERP Committee, Proposed US Position on Next CEEC Meeting, 25 February 1948.

[7] FO 371/71787, Paris embassy to London, 9 April 1948.

[8] FRUS, 1948, III, Geneva consulate to Washington, 13 January 1948.

[9] Sir Edmund Hall-Patch, 1896–1975. A most interesting person. Born in Russia and brought up in Paris, a spasmodically successful musician and a failed novelist. Served with the Reparations Commission after the First World War. Became financial adviser to the government of Siam from which post he was driven by Montague Norman, the Governor of the Bank of England. Played the saxophone in New York before rejoining the Treasury in 1935, on whose behalf he served most of the time in China and Japan. Seconded to the Foreign Office in 1944. Deputy Under-Secretary of State and leader of the British delegation to the OEEC in 1948. Executive Director of the IMF 1952. A Catholic bachelor on whose imaginative advice Bevin placed much reliance: 'Send for 'All-Patch,' he would say, ''e'll make yer flesh creep.'

organization, the Belgian Prime Minister and Foreign Minister, Paul-Henri Spaak.[10] He had been an ardent, although vague, supporter of European union since 1944, and had become a prominent, if not particularly effective, international figure. His Churchillian pose, reduced to an appropriate post-war size, seems to have given him some appeal as a strong man who would shape the new organization into the desired mould. For the first year and a half of the life of the OEEC the Americans were engaged in a perpetual intrigue to get him into a position of greater power.

The Americans originally hoped that the strong Secretary-General might also be provided by Benelux, in the person of Hirschfeld.[11] He would have been unacceptable to the Scandinavians, who in general regarded British figures in the leading positions as their best defence against American pressures towards integration, and it was crucial to persuade the Scandinavians to attend. The Benelux countries themselves were determined that the OEEC should not be a repeat of the CEEC and that in the new organization the smaller countries should be able to escape from Anglo-French domination. They wanted at least one chairmanship, either of the Council or of the Executive Committee, and they wanted the secretary-generalship, for which Hirschfeld was their candidate.[12]

Not only did Benelux insist on posts being allocated to smaller countries, they also only agreed to the OEEC on condition that an intra-western European payments scheme similar to the one which they had proposed in the first CEEC conference be again considered. This was also very upsetting for British plans. After the convertibility crisis of August multilateral payments schemes were regarded very suspiciously in London and there the response was to try to confine any payments discussions to the Brussels Pact countries and avoid the further problems of a larger payments scheme covering the sixteen.[13] A payments system which backed up the Brussels Treaty might be of some practical value to Britain, a multilateral settlements scheme covering the whole of the OEEC was seen only as a threat to the sterling reserves. But Britain and France had to accept that one immediate task of the new organization would be to try to devise a better settlements mechanism for intra-European trade.

For the other smaller countries the difference in their attitude to the idea of a 'continuing organization', compared to September 1947, was a testimony to

[10] Paul-Henri Spaak, 1899–1972. Prisoner-of-war in Germany in the First World War. Lawyer and revolutionary socialist deputy in 1920s. Minister of Transport, 1935, when he became a right-wing socialist at once. Foreign Minister 1935–8, 1940, 1948–51, 1954–7, 1961–6. Prime Minister 1938 (at age 39), 1948–51. In exile in London 1940–4. 1946, President of the General Assembly of the United Nations. Secretary-General of NATO 1957–61. A voluble advocate of the unity of European peoples, he could not speak Flemish.
[11] SD RG353, 34, Proposed US position, 25 February 1948.
[12] FO 371/71786, UK delegation to London, 6 April 1948.
[13] T 236/814, Meeting of London Committee, 6 February 1948; SD 840.50, 5647, The Hague to Washington, 7 February 1948.

the growing fear of Soviet policy and to the extent to which the trade crisis of 1947 had made them aware of their dependence on a western Europe which, as a whole, could not continue to pursue the same policies without American aid. Their opposition to the principle of the organization was now only slight. But they were not prepared to accept a constitution like that of the CEEC. Speaking in a very different vein from eight months before, Halvard Lange told the Storting that without American aid economic collapse would be inevitable in several European countries. The worry now was more that the new organization would become confused with the Brussels Pact and ideas of western union and so acquire a defence and military significance. Switzerland, Norway and Turkey still wanted the constitution to say that the OEEC would be temporary, until the end of Marshall Aid that is.[14] Switzerland and Norway both were eventually swayed, however, by the idea that the focus for political integration was now more likely to be the Brussels Pact than the Paris OEEC which would be more a European instrument for resisting integration. The Swedish Foreign Minister, Östen Unden, was not so convinced of this and had to be energetically argued by the French and British into putting in the necessary personal appearance at the opening ceremony.[15]

Counsels within the State Department were divided over how much pressure to bring to bear on shaping the constitution. The main problem was to be absolutely clear about what the OEEC was supposed to do apart from helping to co-ordinate the ERP. Any other task, mutually enforcing financial stability, actually reducing barriers to trade, effectively deploying underemployed resources, would, as Marshall pointed out, be on a higher level of political difficulty.[16] It was on these issues that the previous conference had more or less broken down. Henry Labouisse, who was to be the chief American contact with the working party on the constitution nevertheless told the group that the 'American people and Congress were expecting something of a dynamic and dramatic nature from the current discussions.'[17]

He handed Franks a statement on 17 March of what sort of constitution the United States would like to see.[18] The Italian delegation was given a briefing on the same point in the American embassy before leaving for Paris.[19] The working party at first refused to have American 'observers' at its deliberations, but this was no more than a constitutional nicety for there were numerous informal meetings with Labouisse and his team and once the first drafts were completed American 'observers' not only sat in on the process but commented in great detail on and even drafted amendments to the proposals.[20] As far as

[14] FRUS, 1948, III, Caffery to Washington, 20 March 1948.
[15] SD 840.50, 532, Stockholm embassy to Washington, 5 March 1948.
[16] FRUS, 1948, III, Marshall to Caffery, 22 March 1948.
[17] ibid., Caffery to Washington, 23 March 1948.
[18] FO 371/71809, Proposed United States position paper on structure and functions of continuing CEEC organization.
[19] SD 840.50, 532, Rome embassy to Washington, 13 March 1948.
[20] FO 371/71785, London Committee, 'Report on the Working Party', 29 March 1948.

the general commitments were concerned Washington appeared reasonably satisfied.[21] The obvious exception was the lack of any firm commitment in the constitution to the elimination of trade barriers. The drafting of Article 5, which covered this, gave more trouble than any other because France and Benelux also wanted a more positive commitment to be expressed.[22] The State Department decided that it could get no further at this stage, but in fact an absolute insistence on the reduction of trade barriers was to be a pillar of American policy towards the OEEC and this decision was purely tactical.

At American insistence a general clause which would permit the exclusion of communist governments from Marshall Aid was also included. This was to cover American fear of the outcome of the forthcoming Italian general elections. The official position that Marshall Aid was for all made any direct statement to the contrary embarrassing, so that to cover the dreaded eventuality of a communist electoral victory in Italy in April the State Department intended to arrange for an influential political figure to state in public that the ECA would be justified in providing no aid in such circumstances.[23] In the event Marshall himself grasped the nettle and said as much on 19 March in a speech at the University of California when he proclaimed that a communist government in power 'could only be considered as evidence of the desire of that country to disassociate itself from the programme. This government would have to conclude that Italy had removed itself from the benefits of the ERP.'[24].

In the two crucial matters of the powers of the Executive Committee and the appointments to office America had less cause for content. These were not decided within the working party but at high governmental level. The American desire that the members of the Executive Committee should be ministers who should meet often seems to have received support from Monnet who encouraged them to try to force such a change from the original concept of the CEEC.[25] It argued a certain arrogance in Washington that busy ministers in the inner circle of government should be expected to attend a committee which, whatever its significance for the future in American eyes, would not, even if the Americans got their own way, often at first discuss matters of great importance. On the other hand the American dilemma was real. To have the ministers' deputies, as in the CEEC, deciding everything that could be decided on the spot, meant having Hall-Patch, the head of the British delegation, and Alphand as the two most important men. Douglas, however, met with Bevin's firm refusal of any change in this direction.[26] The French government, after a lot of internal argument, had also earlier decided, in spite of Monnet, that the ministers' alternates on the Executive Committee

[21] SD 840.50, 5651, Washington to Paris, 27 March 1948.
[22] FO 371/71785, 'Report on the Working Party', 29 March 1948.
[23] FO 371/71829, Washington embassy to London, 15 March 1948.
[24] ibid., Washington embassy to London, 20 March 1948.
[25] SD 840.50, 532, Paris embassy to Washington, 18 March 1948.
[26] SD 840.50, 533, London embassy to Washington, 16 April 1948.

would be civil servants as before.[27] The draft constitution had already sub-ordinated the Secretariat-General to the Executive Committee, so that the Committee's status and role were now defined. Which countries should be on it?

The general idea was that although all nations could not be represented on the Executive Committee each nation state would have another which would keep a watching brief for it. Thus either Norway or Sweden would do this for each other and for Denmark, Britain would do so for Ireland and the same arrangement would presumably apply, without much felicity, to Turkey and Greece.[28] 'Austria', as the Foreign Office suggested, 'would keep a place warm for Germany in later years'.[29] In the event this place was first offered to Switzerland in the hope of persuading that country to play a fuller role. Of the seven places which were to be allocated, Britain, France and Italy would effectively be permanent members, West Germany would ultimately become a permanent member, Benelux would always have a representative and the last two places would always go to Scandinavia and to south-eastern Europe.

Two weeks before the first full session of the working party on the constitution Spaak made a passionate plea in the Belgian parliament for linking the Brussels Pact and the OEEC, in which he lavished some rather fulsome praise on the United States. Essentially the speech was to back up the Benelux proposals for a consultative council with real economic powers as a part of the Brussels Pact. But since the United Kingdom was opposed to any such economic powers in the consultative council the speech had the secondary purpose of advocating more powers for the Council of the OEEC as against the Executive Committee and of establishing himself as the 'strong' candidate in American eyes. When the working party met, Benelux tried to break the Anglo-French monopoly of the important positions by advocating separate chairmanships of the ministerial meetings (on the rare occasions when they were likely to be held), of the full Council, and of the Executive Committee. The whole issue became entangled with the allocation of posts within the separate bodies to be created under the Brussels Pact and Benelux would have been prepared to accept the original Anglo-French proposals for the OEEC in return for greater Benelux influence over the separate defence organization in Brussels or, which was much less likely, greater economic powers for that separate organization as a whole.

In these circumstances the Foreign Office began to consider a compromise in which the chairmanship of the Executive Committee should be for a limited term only and that it should go to Benelux after Britain. There was less than perfect harmony in the Benelux delegation about Spaak's candidacy, but

[27] ibid., Paris embassy to Washington, 1 April 1948.
[28] The practical difficulty with this combination was also 'that no delegate from this area has demonstrated, either last summer or current session, that he has any grasp of "what it is all about" ' SD 840.50, 532, Paris embassy to Washington, 26 March 1948.
[29] FO 371/71787, Memorandum by Makins, 13 April 1948.

Hirschfeld, whom the Dutch would have preferred, was no more acceptable to the Scandinavians than Spaak.[30] The other possible compromise, in which Marjolin would be ditched at the last moment as Secretary-General, also began to appear therefore in London as a way of avoiding Spaak. Benelux regarded Marjolin as too close to Alphand and they did not want a Frenchman in the post. They pressed the claims both of Baron Snoy and of Paul van Zeeland.[31]

One week before the foreign ministers were due to arrive in Paris to sign the charter of the OEEC the outcome was less clear than it had been when the working party first met and it was obvious that it would have to be settled by a series of deals between the ministers themselves when they arrived. If the United States, however, had hopes that these pressures would so weaken the Franco-British position that the constitution of the OEEC would at the last moment be made more malleable to America's intentions there, they were rudely dashed by a squabble about the role of Germany in the organization in which America was publicly worsted. It was the first of a long series of proofs that the crucial question, and one so far beyond the reach and competence of the OEEC that it bade fair to destroy it from the start, was that of the future relationship of France and Germany.

The opening ceremony of the OEEC was regarded by politicians in Germany as an event full of hope for the future, a sign that for their country's future status better things would come out of the London conference than the International Authority for the Ruhr. They could see the end of reparations and of controls on the level of industrial output and they were encouraged to do so by Clay and the American administration in the Bizone, which selected three German politicians to be present with the representatives of the Military Government at the opening ceremony. No agreement had yet been reached at the London conference on the powers and the status of the Ruhr Authority and neither France nor Britain had any intention of allowing German politicians to return to the international scene as part of the initiation of the OEEC. France flatly refused to be present at the opening if any Germans appeared. 'German technical advice', Alphand told the Americans, 'was not needed and German politicians were not wanted.'[32]

[30] FO 371/71786, Paris embassy to London, 6 April 1948.
[31] Jean-Charles, Baron Snoy et d'Oppuers, 1907– . Descendant of a long and noble line. Trained as a banker and legal expert. Attaché au cabinet in the Belgian Ministry of Economic Affairs 1934–46. Head of economic negotiations 1936–8. Secretary-General of the same ministry 1939–59, except under the occupation. President of the Council of the Benelux Union 1946–59. Head of Belgian delegation to the Messina Conference. Representative of Belgium to the EEC 1958–9. Married a countess by whom he had seven children.
Paul van Zeeland, 1893–1973. Won Croix de Guerre in First World War. An economist with a postgraduate degree from Princeton who became a financier and Deputy Governor of the National Bank of Belgium. 1935–7, Prime Minister of all-party government and one of the architects of the bank reform of those years. Forced to resign in financial scandal. In exile in Britain and America from 1940. Foreign Minister 1949–54. An ardent supporter of European integration.
[32] FO 371/71789, Paris embassy to London, Meeting between Alphand and British and American representatives, 6 April 1948.

To the fury of Clay and against the advice of General Sir Brian Robertson his British counterpart, the invited German politicians had to be told to stay away. The French were not even prepared at first to have the Military Governors sign the convention on Germany's behalf, because there was nothing in it which mentioned the restrictions on German industrial activity. They insisted therefore that the Military Governors should make a statement at the signing ceremony to the effect that Germany would fulfil its obligations in this respect. This was altogether too much for Clay who refused to turn up at all. At the birth of the OEEC therefore the hopefulness of the occasion was much dimmed, for the convention was signed on behalf of the Bizone only by the British Military Governor, who accompanied his signature with a terse and frequently re-drafted statement which went some way to meet French wishes. German representation in the OEEC would be limited to its working sub-committees. At the higher levels Germany would be represented only by personnel of the Military Governments. The German advisers would in fact have to be 'infiltrated' into the organization as its meetings developed.[33]

This dispute took so much time that when the moment arrived for the Council of the OEEC to hold its inaugural meeting Benelux had still not ratified the clause in the charter stipulating Paris as the permanent seat of the OEEC, nor had they accepted Marjolin as Secretary-General. When Bevin arrived for the ceremony he instantly decided that the common constitutional front against America must be preserved. He decided not to separate the chairmanships but to persuade the other participants to offer Benelux the chairmanship at both ministerial and official levels of the meetings of the Council.[34] This was hastily discussed with Alphand. The delegations then broke off to take part in the official signing ceremony, signed the agreement, and then hastily met again in unofficial conclave to determine its meaning and implementation. It was the ominous herald of future decades of European deadlines at which complicated compromises on issues which appeared to be less than perfectly related had to be reached in frantic last-minute personal negotiations. Britain and France kept Marjolin, France kept Paris as the permanent site, and Benelux won the chairmanship, to which Spaak was then elected with 'no enthusiasm on the part of the others present'.[35]

Before the OEEC had really begun to function, therefore, the obstacles to the pursuit of America's aims were already large. In accepting a constitution substantially different from what it had wished America had been forced to accept that Marshall Aid could not so quickly lever out of place the realities of the European state system. The constitution of the OEEC was such as to impose a formidable barrier to America's longer-term political ambitions for it. This was to become yet clearer as soon as the organization began to function.

[33] T 236/807, London Committee, 'Participation of Western Germany in the CEEC', 2 March 1948.   [34] FO 371/71860, Paris embassy to London, 19 April 1948.   [35] ibid.

THE INTOLERABLE BURDEN

The last stages of the failure to provide the OEEC with a suitable constitution had been accepted relatively philosophically in Washington because it was assumed that the power to do this still lay in American hands once America began to provide the aid. Pragmatism had made it essential to have the OEEC set up, in whatever form, in conformity with the timetable and then to set to work to change it afterwards. The method for changing it and turning it into a genuine force for European economic integration had already been decided. Congress had decided that the ERP appropriations could only be annual. The first such appropriation had come so much later than originally hoped that the decisions within the ECA about the division of the appropriated sum between the separate countries had already been made and were announced as soon as Congress had voted the money. But the intention was to make the OEEC itself undertake this task of allocation. The CEEC had been asked to screen the separate national requests for aid in a process of mutual consultation, and had not really done so. The OEEC would not only have to screen the national requests for Marshall Aid but would have to fit them into a consistent medium-term plan for European recovery in which Western Europe would have to be considered as a whole and not as a collection of separate national entities. This was not a universally supported policy in the State Department, but it was supported by Averell Harriman, who had been appointed Special Ambassador with ECA, as well as by Hoffman.[36] On 5 June Harriman addressed the OEEC Council and told them of the American decision. The OEEC would itself be asked to recommend the allocation of aid to the separate European countries in the second year of the programme in accordance with the annual sum of money to be made available by Congress.

That it would stick in the throats of European governments that decisions so important to their economic welfare should have to be taken in international consultation was obvious. Harriman, however, hoped to use this as a lever to force a higher level of government representation by responsible ministers in the OEEC Council and so at the same time weaken the Executive Committee and thus bring the OEEC more into line with Washington's original wishes.[37]

[36] William Averell Harriman, 1891– . Railway company director and merchant banker. Served in Office of Production Management 1940–1. Special Representative of the President in UK 1941. Ambassador to USSR 1943–6. Ambassador for ERP 1948–50. Special Assistant to President 1950–1. Director of Mutual Security Agency 1951–2. Governor of New York 1955–8. Assistant Secretary of State 1961–3, then, 1963–5, Under-Secretary of State. Personal representative of President in Vietnam negotiations in Paris 1968–9. Although very rich, he worked very hard.

[37] Van der Beugel was told by State Department personnel that the desire to 'protect' Washington from the constant beseechings of European finance ministers on visits was a major motive, but, as he himself agrees, the decision must have been made at a very high level. (E.H. van der Beugel, *From Marshall Aid, to Atlantic Partnership* (Amsterdam, 1966), pp. 140–1.) It was also, it seems, a decision made with grave hesitations about whether the OEEC would be able to function in this way. (FJM, AMF 14/5/17, Ball to Monnet, 10 July 1948.) Monnet wanted the task done 'by a panel of distinguished Europeans with no official governmental connections'. He would no doubt himself have been the most obvious candidate.

The European governments were by no means convinced, rightly as it proved, that the American executive and Congress would, when it came to the point, so cheerfully accept decisions made in Paris about their money, even for so great a cause. But that was a more distant problem; the immediate, inescapable problem was how to agree on the distribution of aid while retaining the apolitical technical nature of OEEC.

How much aid, for example, should be allocated to the Bizone? Obviously the basis of assessment could not be changed from the first year of the ERP and would thus remain related to the size of the import deficit. But who was going not only to produce a European agreement but also one agreeable to the American government on the size of the Bizone's import surplus and the proportion of it to be funded by American aid at the expense of aid to other countries? Yet neither the British nor the French could risk having the Bizone's allocation decided outside the general European programme, otherwise the Americans might fulfil their worst fears and give priority to aid for Germany. Face to face with this problem the Economic Policy Committee of the British cabinet decided to put every pressure on Washington to make the American government continue to decide the overall allocation of Marshall Aid.[38] Three days later Cripps saw Thomas K. Finletter, the head of the ECA mission in Britain and told him the burden was 'intolerable' and must be removed. Finletter told him there was no chance of any change.[39]

It was in these circumstances that Monnet sold the idea to the French government, which in turn sold it to Whitehall, of a small committee of the major countries, in fact an even smaller and more powerful version of the Executive Committee, which would be empowered to do the job.[40] Monnet intended the group to be no larger than three, but it was approved by the Council on 13 July with four members and has gone into history as the Committee of Four. The representatives were from Britain, France, Holland and Italy.[41] Their

[38] FO 371/71826, Meeting of Economic Policy Committee of the cabinet, 22 June 1948.
[39] T 232/10, Conversation between Cripps and Finletter, 25 June 1948.
[40] T 232/10, Conversation between Makins and Hall-Patch, 5 July 1948.
[41] Eric Roll (later Baron Roll of Ipsden), 1907– . Professor of Economics and Commerce in the University of Hull 1935–46. Deputy Head of the British Food Mission to North America 1941–6. Under-Secretary to the Treasury 1948–9. Member of the delegation to the OEEC 1949. Later Deputy Leader of the delegation for negotiations with the EEC 1961–3. Then Permanent Under-Secretary in the Department of Economic Affairs. Subsequently a merchant banker, a director of *The Times* and of the Bank of England. Author of several books including a much read *History of Economic Thought*.
   Guillaume Guindey, 1909– . The son of a prefect. Director of foreign financial transactions in 1946. Subsequently a director of several government-controlled companies including the telecommunications company Finextel. Director-General of the Bank of International Settlements 1958–63.
   Dirk Pieter Spierenburg, 1909– . Director-General of Foreign Economic Affairs, 1945, and subsequently head of the Dutch delegation to the OEEC. Member of the High Authority for Coal, Iron and Steel, 1952, and subsequently Vice-President of it.
   Giovanni Malagodi, 1904– . Director of Italian Bank of Commerce 1933. Director-General of Franco-Italian Bank of Latin America 1937. Served in a variety of economic and financial advisory posts to government 1947–53. Liberal deputy for Milan from 1953. Subsequently occupied several ministerial positions and became Secretary-General of the Liberal Party. A wine grower. Author of several books on liberalism and on emigration.

conclusions were not to be binding on the full OEEC Council but merely recommendations to it. Although, therefore, the four members of the committee were not supposed to act in any way as representatives of their own nations no element of supranationality was involved because they would produce only suggestions and not decisions. The Committee of Four would obviously have to make recommendations which tallied with the annual sum to be made available. They were told in early July that this would be $4875 million, about $500 million less than had been expected. They could not produce a set of individual requests, as the CEEC had done, misleadingly termed a common programme, but must produce a set of proposals genuinely related to the area as a whole and to the sum suggested. Yet the sum total of the individual national programmes, when they received them, was bound to be far in excess of that. Furthermore, the group could not possibly make any effective recommendations unless it considered not just Europe's import balances with the United States but intra-European trade balances also and, what was worse, mechanisms for intra-European payments, because an attempt at a multilateral intra-European payments scheme had been a condition of Benelux participation in the OEEC. What assumptions should they make about the amount of dollars required by each European country to make settlements with other European countries? The Committee of Four decided, in the event, to assume that there would be an intra-European payments system soon in operation which would exclude the need for intra-European dollar payments. But at every turn they were facing similarly important issues on which, to reach any satisfactory conclusions, they would have to pronounce.

The Committee of Four spent three weeks questioning national delegations about the submissions in the separate national aid programmes and was then sent away to a secret place where it would be immune from all further influence from the OEEC or home.[42] The four were in fact virtually locked away in seclusion until they could come up with a final report. In the hope of making this bizarre procedure work the four countries most intimately concerned vaguely agreed that their governments would accept the Committee of Four's conclusions.[43]

When the Committee of Four began its work Harriman was already busy trying to change the constitution. His idea was that, to avoid the obviously valid objection that the European foreign and economics ministers were too genuinely busy to attend at all frequently, the meetings of the OEEC Council should specialize in particular problems, those ministers relevant to the

[42] It was actually in Chantilly.

[43] T 232/10, Paper of Chancellor, 15 July 1948. But as always such government agreements had an escape route. The British cabinet had also decided that if Britain emerged with less than $1271 million in total aid allocations, they would charge the other participating countries dollars for their oil imports from British companies! Although Britain and France had agreed to accept the figures emerging from the Committee of Four they had not agreed the permissible extent of France's sterling deficit in 1948, a large part of which was for oil imports.

problem under discussion should attend and that such ministerial meetings should be held frequently.[44] 'The situation', he told Marshall, 'requires a surgical operation not just palliative treatment.'[45] He and Hoffman, therefore, with Marshall's approval, decided to approach Spaak first of all and having safely recruited his support bring further pressure on London and Paris.[46] Spaak agreed with Harriman's proposed changes at once.[47] The next step was that Hoffman should come to Europe and address a meeting of the OEEC council at ministerial level and explain to them precisely what the State Department would like to present to Congress before the debate on the next round of appropriations as evidence of the progress of European integration. The alarmed Europeans, who had no idea what Hoffman might say, but who feared he might make the most impossible demands, objected strongly. In any case the time before the date of Hoffman's planned speech, 25 July, was short, and to fetch sixteen foreign ministers to Paris to hear a speech by a still unknown American political figure underlined rather firmly America's power and advantages. It took an intense diplomatic offensive by the United States, undertaken through the ambassadors in all the western European capitals, to stage the event. Sweden, alone, refused to be represented at ministerial level.

Hoffman's speech was intended to prepare the ground for the solution which he and Harriman now favoured, that there should be frequent ministerial meetings and that Spaak be endowed with much greater executive powers as 'Director-General' of the OEEC. In effect the formation of the Committee of Four had shown the political weakness of the manoeuvre of forcing the OEEC, in the form in which it had constituted itself, to recommend the division of aid. It was already clear that when the Committee of Four submitted its report the divisions between the European countries were only likely to be further emphasized and that many countries might refuse to accept recommendations made from so low a level. While the Committee of Four was at work Hoffman told Franks that in his own opinion the level at which it was happening was too low.[48] In his address Hoffman asked for a constitutional reform which would give the OEEC powers which were not at every turn dependent on the agreement of the individual countries.

The speeches of response were polite formalities apart from that of the Irish Foreign Minister, Sean MacBride. MacBride had campaigned vigorously in the first half of 1948 to persuade the ECA not to acknowledge the partition of Ireland in the allocation of aid. He had been firmly silenced by Washington lest he endanger the passing of the ERP legislation.[49] Washington in fact showed even less sympathy for the Irish position, awarding the Republic no

[44] T 236/822, UK delegation to London, 12 May 1948.
[45] SD 840.50, 534, Harriman to Marshall, 17 July 1948.
[46] ibid., Marshall to Harriman, 22 July 1948.
[47] ibid., Harriman to Washington, 25 July 1948.
[48] T 232/29, Washington to London, 20 July 1948.
[49] SD 840.50, 5655, Dublin to Washington, 23 March 1948.

grants during the first year of the programme but only loans, probably because of its neutrality during the war.[50] Nevertheless MacBride had lingering hopes that a genuinely supra-national OEEC might still work in favour of Ireland as of all smaller nations and hoped to break the domination of the British and French over the OEEC by making it more genuinely representative of all Western European countries. But Ireland's support was to be less of a help to Harriman than a nuisance to Britain.

Harriman followed up Hoffman's speech by arguing for Spaak's appointment as 'Director-General' with 'immoderate vehemence' at a dinner with Schuman and Reynaud where he threatened the French that unless something of the kind happened Congress would not next time round vote any aid for France.[51] He told the British delegation that in the near future many decisions would have to be taken in the OEEC by ministers and when the British delegation suggested that for this it would still be necessary for officials to prepare the ground his reply betrayed the same vehemence. It was 'that if ministers had to come frequently to Paris they would see to it that their bureaucrats had instructions to get on with the job'.[52] Faced with this kind of attitude Britain and France could no longer merely stonewall. On Hall-Patch's suggestion the OEEC Council agreed that from time to time there should be small meetings of the relevant ministers, not at the Council level but at the Executive Committee level, and that Spaak could occasionally call meetings of certain ministers at the Council level when he thought it useful.

This informality was still no substitute for the permanent presence of political power in the OEEC which was what Harriman wanted; neither did it meet with Spaak's wishes.[53] Harriman's worst feelings about Britain's attitude were confirmed on 11 August 1948 when Spaak told him that he had been warned off by the British ambassador to Belgium and told that British policy was to oppose any strengthening of the OEEC. Spaak recommended that the ECA refuse to accept the report of the Committee of Four and hold back the next Marshall Aid allocations until the OEEC had agreed to appoint a 'personality' and with this drastic course of action Harriman agreed.[54] He had now come to see Britain as the villain thwarting all his plans and his views were so influential that British-American relations sank to a still lower level of suspicion and sometimes contempt.[55] He was suspected of being behind an anti-British press campaign on the subject of the OEEC and the only relief

[50] These grounds certainly were important for Harriman T 236/824, Franks to London, 11 June 1948.

[51] FO 371/71827, UK delegation to London, 1 August 1948.

[52] FO 371/71867, UK delegation to London, 1 August 1948.

[53] FO 371/71868, Conversation between Hall-Patch and Spaak, 9 August 1948.

[54] ECA, 1, Harriman–Spaak Conversation, 11 August 1948.

[55] 'I suspect that what Harriman really feels is that the organisation lacks not "political direction" but "international political figures" with whom he could hobnob and so foster his personal publicity both in Europe and America.' Hall-Patch in FO 371/71869, UK delegation to London, 11 September 1948.

the Foreign Office could see was that Truman would lose the presidential election and Harriman would be replaced. Harriman, however, intended to have Hall-Patch out of office before that. Bevin stuck most loyally by his subordinate on this occasion, as on later ones. Hoffman's views on Britain were no less menacing, although more politely expressed, and after he had aired them in the State Department the Department cabled Douglas in London for advice in grimly threatening form, 'We consider that solution may well involve steps on our part affecting whole range of US-UK relations beyond those arising directly from ERP.'[56]

It was against this background that the Committee of Four struggled with the intolerable burden. Had the Committee merely had to pronounce on an acceptable level of imports from the United States for each country its task would have been difficult enough. But there was no way of separating the problem of each country's imports from the dollar zone from the problem of its overall import programme. If less international credit were extended to any country for the purchase of imports from the United States, that might immediately affect in a significant way the pattern of trade between two Western European countries. Because the rough measure of the need for Marshall Aid was the dollar payments deficit, most countries, unless there were overriding considerations of domestic economic policy, had an interest in presenting more extensive import programmes than they might otherwise have done. But the fact that the planned quantity of imports varied with national economic policy itself forced the Committee to pass some judgement on those policies. Furthermore, if ERP aid was to be used to finance intra-western European trade, almost the whole trade balance of many of the countries was in consideration.

Should a country such as France, which planned for substantial trade deficits and where high inflation rates increased the propensity to import still further, have its balance of payments deficit funded in the same proportion as a country such as Italy where deflationary policies were aimed at reducing imports?[57] How many dollar imports should be allowed for Belgium where recovery had been so rapid and where imports fuelled exports to Western Europe which were becoming increasingly difficult to sustain? On the basis of the British calculations, for example, Belgium was entitled to $150 million in aid to cover her import surplus from the United States. The Belgian request which came before the Committee of Four, however, was for $378 million. The other three members were all agreed that they could not sacrifice their own or any other country's direct dollar aid to fund so large a quantity of Belgian imports. Spierenburg, indeed, took the view that Belgium was not

[56] SD 840.50, 534, Washington to London embassy, 20 August 1948.
[57] The French trade deficit with North America fell by 50 per cent between 1947 and 1948, to $400 million; but there was an increase of almost the same dimensions in the trade deficit with the sterling area.

entitled to any aid at all since even $150 million would finance either excess domestic consumption or raw materials for exports which would soon become unsaleable on European markets.[58] Unemployment in August reached 4 per cent of the registered labour force and was growing. For this, the high price of Belgian exports was the main cause. In textiles, glass and leather, where alternative sources of supply were now becoming available, Belgium's situation was noticeably weakening and only the continued world shortage of steel was sustaining her steel exports, roughly half the total value of all exports in autumn 1948. The British delegation thought this would 'probably be the ultimate showdown with Belgium in OEEC'.[59] But the major issue was soon to be revealed, in spite of the continued progress of the London conference, as the relative rates of economic recovery of the French and German economies.

The Committee of Four emerged from seclusion and submitted its report on 12 August 1948. The report did not take into consideration any proposed contribution by the participating countries to funding a European payments scheme. That was still to be settled, but since the Committee had based its discussions on the assumption that there would be such a scheme the proposed aid allocations were not completely finalized but were liable to marginal adjustments to cater for its subsequent introduction. This was in the event to provide just sufficient flexibility for the Committee's work not to be rejected out-of-hand. But this outcome did not at first look possible. There was a two-hour discussion on whether the report should even be discussed.[60] Greece, Ireland, Iceland, Norway and Turkey refused at first to accept it and Denmark accepted only on condition that she could later appeal against it to the OEEC Council. Those countries with membership of the Committee accepted it, as they were more or less bound to do, providing that the adjustments in aid allocation to support an intra-Western European payments system could be made. The only hope therefore lay in a further negotiation to settle that issue. After an acrimonious debate this work was delegated to a Committee of Five, Britain, France, Belgium, Greece and Norway, which was to report by 26 August. Neither Greece nor Turkey, however, was prepared to accept the reduced import programmes as they had emerged from the Committee of Four as a preliminary basis for these subsequent operations.

At this stage came the most ironic, although scarcely unforeseeable, complication. One large economy, the Bizone, had not been represented in the Committee of Four, and the representatives of the American Military Government attacked the report furiously and appealed to Washington against its recommendations. It had always been probable that the other countries would try to solve their problems by minimizing the cuts in their own dollar aid and cutting aid to Germany more. It was mainly the representatives of the

[58]   ibid., UK delegation to London, 28 July 1948.
[59]   T 232/11, UK delegation to London, 28 July 1948.
[60]   Van der Beugel, *From Marshall Aid*, p. 151.

American Military Government who presented the Bizone import programme. When the programme came back again from the Committee of Four, the Americans found it had been reduced much more severely than those of the other countries. The quantity of aid which should be made available to the Bizone had already been seen as a central problem in the CEEC. Britain was, for example, liable to finance a proportion of the Bizone's imports, so that any increase in the Bizone import programme to meet the terms of the ERP would mean not only increasing the strain on Britain's resources but at the same time increasing that part of the total congressional allocation of aid which went to Germany, presumably in part at the expense of Britain itself. Worse, aid to the Bizone beyond a certain limit meant putting the German recovery before the French. Even with Marshall Aid the Bizone was judged to have no prospects of reaching a balance of foreign trade before 1953 or 1954, so the issue was financially an important one.[61] The Bizone programme when submitted to the OEEC represented a significant departure from the levels of German production previously agreed. The upward revision of the level of industry agreements for Germany in 1947, which itself had almost wrecked the CEEC before it had met, had been based on an annual level of imports into the Bizone of about $2000 million. The Bizone's proposals foresaw imports running at $2818 million, a level higher than that of 1936 for the comparable area. It had already been obvious in the level of industry discussions that Germany's exports would have to be higher than from the same area in 1936 if it were not to be too great a burden on the Allies, but these proposals implied a level of exports about 60 per cent higher than in 1936, and as far as exports of machinery went, the estimated increase was much greater.

This higher volume of exports to OEEC countries was intended to finance the forecast of dollar deficits and in this sense the Bizone was only stating what every other European country was stating, that recovery in the post-war world depended on exports. And like every other OEEC member it was planning to export more goods to other OEEC members than they were intending to buy. But it was unacceptable in London and Paris that the agreements on the level of industrial output should once more be revised upwards by this backdoor method.

General Clay, who had from the outset believed that the European organization would exist to the economic detriment of West Germany, decided that it would be better for West Germany not to be a member of it and to receive its ERP aid directly from ECA.[62] Such a solution being politically out of the question the State Department and the ECA ruled that the decision of the OEEC would have to be overturned by an overriding decision of the American

[61] T 236/708, London Committee, 'Report of Working Party on West German and European Recovery Programme', 8 February 1948.
[62] J.E. Smith (ed.), *The Papers of General Lucius D. Clay: Germany 1947–1949* (Bloomington, 1974), vol. 2., pp. 790–1. (Cited hereafter as 'Clay Papers'.)

government. It thus turned out that even when all sixteen Western European countries did agree on a common recommendation about the size of West Germany's permitted import deficit it was unacceptable to the United States because it seemed to set a rate of German recovery less than that wanted in Washington.

Harriman did not support the State Department's attitude and Hoffman, who initially did so, almost immediately regretted it.[63] Clay argued that the actions of the Committee of Four were an attack by the United Kingdom on the financial basis of the fusion agreements which had created the Bizone. From his viewpoint they corresponded with the contemporary refusal of the British to allow convertibility of their sterling contribution to the JEIA. He would, however, have been prepared to accept the Committee of Four's report, had Washington insisted that it was a matter of higher national policy to do so.[64] But the State Department did not so insist. When it subsequently emerged that the Committee of Five, in devising the payments scheme to make the aid allocation acceptable, was intending to treat the Bizone as a potential creditor country rather than as a debtor, Clay's opinion and that of the Department of the Army hardened. Harriman, too, then began to support a position where the recommendations of the Committee of Four would be overturned in Washington and the Bizone given an aid allocation large enough to support its original import programme as submitted to the Committee.

On 26 August the British government refused to participate in a joint Anglo-American request to restore the original allocation to the Bizone. Two days later Clay told Robertson that he was under instructions from the Department of the Army not to accept the new allocation.[65] As all waited for the report of the Committee of Five on the payments scheme other European countries began to hedge on their provisional acceptance of the Committee of Four's decisions. On the eve of the submission of the report of the Committee of Five, Snoy, Marjolin and Hall-Patch met Harriman and told him that its acceptance by Council at the meeting on 1 September 1948 was unlikely.[66] In desperation and without as yet having consulted Washington Harriman suggested that a small extra sum of aid might be allocated by means of 'over-programming'. After an all-night session arguing the position of Britain and Belgium in the payments scheme the Committee of Five eventually reported on 31 August just in time for the deadline for submission to the OEEC Council. Washington instructed Clay that the Bizone could only abstain on the presentation of the report, not cast a negative vote, because the public unity of OEEC must be paramount. But the damage had been done. Harriman and the ECA were determined to get more aid for the Bizone than the final

[63] SD 840.50, 5671, Correspondence between Harriman, Hoffman and Washington, *passim*.
[64] *Clay Papers*, II, pp. 770–1.
[65] T 232/11, Robertson to London, 28 August 1948.
[66] ibid., UK delegation to London, 30 August 1948.

decisions of the two Committees recommended. They were especially displeased with the extent to which the proposals permitted further large French import deficits. Harriman asked,

> Was not France a sponge, which was absorbing these vast resources and giving practically nothing in return to European recovery? ... All the Americans who came to France to see him [e.g. Senator Connally] were asking was not this aid that America was giving merely designed to allow French politicians to avoid facing the real issues.[67]

In effect Harriman had moved to a position where he was prepared to override the whole exercise on the German question and impose the American will directly. He persuaded Cripps not only to give up a portion of the British allocation in favour of the Bizone but to try to persuade the French government to do the same. In the middle of these pressures the Schuman government fell. The recommendations of the Committee of Five then went forward to the OEEC Council. There the United States and the Bizone insisted that if any of the newly created drawing rights in the payments scheme[68] were unused they should be transferable, implying that if the Bizone did not turn out during the operation of the scheme to be a creditor its imports would be funded under the scheme by funds provisionally allocated for the imports of others. This was to run into even worse trouble with the British who were determined that under no circumstances would there be any but the most strictly limited amount of currency transferability in the payments scheme. There was a flat refusal in London to allow Bizone sterling debts to be transferable, even in this very limited way, into any other European currency.

With the small concessions made by Britain, and with a general understanding that, if the forecast patterns of intra-Western European trade against which the Committee of Five had made the allocations for the payments scheme should prove seriously wrong they could be adjusted during the year, the recommendations for aid allocation were accepted by Council on 11 September and the payments agreement signed on 16 September. It had been done, but at what cost! The attempt to force a genuinely integrative and supra-national process on the OEEC had been strenuously resisted by the European nations, not finally accepted by them except in such conditions as to make it seem very doubtful whether it could be repeated, and, most ironically, as soon as it touched on the question of Germany, rejected by the United States as well.

As far as the ECA was concerned, however, it would have been a public abandonment of its policy had it accepted the implications of what had occurred and allowed the OEEC to lay down the intolerable burden, unless the attempt to give stronger executive powers to the Council or a Director-General

---

[67] T 232/13, UK delegation to London, 3 September 1948.
[68] See pp. 271–6.

succeeded. There was, therefore, no change in policy and having barely survived the task of recommending the allocation of aid for the financial year 1948–9, the OEEC had to take up the burden again for 1949–50. At the same time Harriman and Hoffman persevered in their attempts to change the constitution so that the organization could exercise direct powers of its own.

The total value of congressional allotments of aid for the financial year 1948–9 had eventually been $4636.7 million which was $239 million less than the OEEC had finally requested. The total allotments for the next financial year would obviously be smaller and in fact when the sums allocated to the payments system were deducted, amounted only to $3510.7 million. As the sum diminished, so did the problem grow of getting any general agreement within the OEEC as to how it should be allocated.

At first, however, the burden was easier to bear, because the two tasks of drawing up the recovery programme for the coming year and of deciding the allocation of aid were this time separated by a wide space of time. The national programmes were to be screened by the OEEC in December 1948, theoretically within the wider context of a common European medium-term programme, the actual allocation of aid did not have to be made until mid-summer 1949. But Congress ultimately voted only $3780 million as a total appropriation for 1949–50, whereas the national programmes, when first presented in January 1949, amounted to $4347 million. The extent by which the Committee of Four in 1948 had had to reduce the programmes for 1948–9 to make them fit the sum of aid actually allocated was thus far less than what was now to be required of the OEEC in 1949.

The chances of the OEEC emerging from an even more drastic exercise of the same kind as a more supra-national body were not worth considering; the likelihood was that the OEEC would fail to survive the process in any form. Yet the congressional debate on the Marshall Aid appropriations showed how much political support there was in America for the policy of European unification. At the joint session of the Senate Foreign Relations Committee and the House Foreign Affairs Committee the administration found itself under attack for its over-cautious progress towards producing European unification and in particular for the emphasis which it placed in its testimony to the Joint Foreign Relations Committee on the preliminary necessity of working towards economic unification through an earlier stage of co-operation. The administration had to resist considerable pressure to make the next round of Marshall Aid funds conditional on certain specific acts of integration. This discontent emerged more strongly in the subsequent debates. There was long and bitter haggling over the allocations and when the annual Authorization Act was passed it contained the additional phrase that 'it is further the policy of the United States to encourage the unification of Europe'.

Much of the congressional criticism was levied precisely at the fact that the OEEC had so far turned out to be much less of a step towards integration than the administration had originally claimed it would be, and yet both to the Joint Foreign Relations Committee and on the floor of the Senate and House the administration continued to paint too rosy a picture of the Organization. This was to become unavoidably obvious in July 1949 when the OEEC began again on the task of allocation. The task was again finally achieved, in a fashion, but with so much public discord, so many unsatisfactory last-minute compromises, and so much national acrimony on every side that it became obvious that the allocation of aid by the OEEC was a step, not towards integration but towards disintegration. Since Congress did not finally pass the appropriations until 6 October it had plenty of time to observe that this was so. Although, therefore, the OEEC was forced once more to lift the intolerable burden, this was a Pyrrhic victory for the ECA whose outcome was the almost immediate abandonment of the policy of creating through the OEEC a common organ of European economic government. The period from July to October 1949 was the grand climacteric of the first American attempt to bring European economic integration into being. The political struggle coincided with a sharp recession in the United States whose international repercussions on the European economies exacerbated their differences with each other and made the allocation of aid within the OEEC an even more divisive function. Thenceforth the OEEC faded rapidly from the forefront of European politics and began its transition to honest statistical toil.

In October 1948, before the task of programming the import needs for the next financial year began, Harriman personally approached Spaak about the possibility of installing him as 'Director-General' of the OEEC 'otherwise there would be difficulties with Congress'.[69] Harriman and Hoffman decided to base their manoeuvres on the resentments of the smaller power in the state system against Britain and France. When Hoffman had demanded constitutional reform in his summer speech he had received support from the Irish representative, MacBride, whose proposals for reform still lay before the OEEC. It was not hard to recruit similar support from Italy. In November 1948 the Italian government produced a fulsome memorandum, in tone like the contemporary communications between eastern Europe and Moscow, referring to 'the complete disinterestedness of the Government and people of the United States' and advocating that the OEEC should be no longer an assembly of experts but that it should push towards 'complete union'.[70]

Prompted by the Americans Spaak tried to insist that the Council should hold a meeting at ministerial level, as it could constitutionally now be asked to do at the Chairman's request, in order to discuss these proposals for changes in the organization's structure. Britain and France managed to put off the meeting until February 1949 giving them time to agree on alterations to the constitution which would still retain it as an effective barrier against American

---

[69]   SD 840.50, 535, Brussels embassy to Washington, 11 October 1948.
[70]   ibid., 5676, Italian memorandum to the OEEC, 23 November 1948.

policy. These agreements were presented to Spaak at an informal dinner given for him in London by Cripps and Schuman on 28 January 1949.[71] MacBride's proposals had called for full meetings at ministerial level at least every two months and the institution of a full-time executive President. Cripps and Schuman proposed that an inner group of four ministers from Britain, France, Italy and one other country, if possible a Scandinavian country, would meet four times a year for one week and together with a President take all the political decisions necessary for carrying on the business of the OEEC.[72] Spaak's own counter-proposals for a steering committee of five, subordinate to a full-time executive President, which would present all decisions for discussion and approval by the Council were, like MacBride's ideas, 'quite unacceptable' to the French.[73] All such proposals would mean modifying the OEEC convention which had been settled only with such great difficulty less than a year ago. Marjolin let it be known that he would probably resign the secretary-generalship if executive powers were given to a President or Director-General.

When the new proposals were laid before the Council the opposition of the Netherlands, Sweden, Switzerland and Turkey to the idea of a permanent inner management core in line with British and French ideas was so vigorous however that it had to be agreed that the President should be able to call meetings of the Council at the ministerial level and that ministers of all seven countries represented on the Executive Committee should take part.[74] This, although it gave a better position to the smaller powers, did not seriously weaken the Anglo-French position, while getting the Americans virtually nowhere. When the ministers met they would be called the Consultative Group. In so far as the Consultative Group would be ministerial the Americans had achieved their objective of getting ministers to regular meetings in Paris, but the Council still reigned supreme. The difference in function between the Consultative Group and the Executive Committee was not easy to perceive and they were made up of the same countries.

The changes were only thought of as a staging-post by the ECA and the pressure to foist a Director-General with real executive powers on the OEEC continued, 'Superman' as the post was referred to in the British documents. In August 1949 the Belgian government fell and Spaak lost his post as Foreign Minister which also meant the loss of his position in the OEEC. In American eyes this set him free for the neutral task of full-time executive. Schuman now sought a way too of keeping Spaak in the organization, partly because he did not want it to be dominated too much by Britain and Spaak had been a useful counterweight, partly because the French interest in 'Greater Benelux' had

---

[71] FO 371/77778, Foreign Office to UK delegation, 29 January 1949.

[72] FO 371/77733, Conversation of Cripps with Italian ambassador, 29 January 1949.

[73] FO 371/77735, Proposals by M. Spaak, 8 February 1949; ibid., OEEC Committee of Nine, 14 February 1949.   [74] FO 371/77734, UK delegation to London, 15 February 1949.

strongly revived.[75] But this was a difficult manoeuvre too. It was no more possible for France than for the United States to achieve its ends by relying on the interest of the smaller powers and MacBride's plans to give 'The Council of Ministers the same relationship to meetings of officials as a Government bears to its civil servants' were far from what Schuman had in mind.[76]

In late September Bevin and Cripps, no longer able to count on France, both vetoed Spaak's appointment when approached by the new chairman, van Zeeland, as mediator, but the State Department refused to accept their right to do so.[77] The question was referred directly to Truman who gave a presidential decision to proceed with Spaak's appointment.[78] On 14 October 1949 Spaak went to London to see Cripps, expecting the appointment now to be confirmed, and Dean Acheson, appointed to be Marshall's successor as Secretary of State, sent a message to Bevin asking for this confirmation.[79] Bevin 'wanted to know whether the Belgians were to be president of everything' and 'said that the Labor Government could not under American pressure accept the appointment of Spaak or any other continental to a position of control in the OEEC.'[80]

In the first two days of November Harriman and Hoffman reiterated their demands to Cripps and Bevin until Bevin appeared to weaken and agreed to arrange an informal meeting of those relevant ministers who were attending the Council of Europe at that time. Hoffman, asked by Bevin to attend the meeting, and under the impression that it would recommend Spaak's appointment waited for two days only to discover that Bevin had indeed called the meeting, mainly about other business, and introduced the topic of Spaak's appointment so off-handedly as to cause the Dutch and Scandinavians no qualms in opposing it. Schuman's opposition to this manoeuvre was so mild as to be insignificant.[81] Harriman, that power-loving capitalist tycoon, had been duped by the power-loving trade union leader and with a tactic that Bevin had surely remembered from his past.

In reality it scarcely mattered any longer, the whole focus of the OEEC's work was shifted to other, less contentious tasks in October. But so long as the ECA persisted Britain and France were bound to resist, because 'Superman' would be supra-national and that was the unacceptable point. In December van Zeeland was persuaded to call a further meeting of the Consultative

[75] SD 840.50, 5683, Harriman to Washington, 21 August 1949.
[76] ibid., MacBride's correspondence with van Zeeland and Spaak, 24 August 1949, 6 September 1949.   [77] SD 840.50, 5684, Webb to Hoffman, etc., 27 September 1949.
[78] ibid., Memorandum of meeting with the President, 1 October 1949.
[79] FRUS, 1949, IV, Acheson to London embassy, 14 October 1949, p. 429.
Dean Gooderham Acheson, 1893–1971. A lawyer of wealthy family. Educated at Yale and Harvard. Under-Secretary of Treasury 1933. Entered Department of State 1941. Under-Secretary of State 1947–9. Secretary of State 1949–53, an office he filled with distinction. A prolific and stylish writer about foreign policy, the Democratic Party, the American political system, and his own life.   [80] ibid., London embassy to Acheson, 18 October 1949, p. 430.
[81] ibid., Harriman to Acheson, 6 November 1949, p. 440.

Group to consider the appointment. Harriman had arranged for a secret message, which van Zeeland helped to compile, explaining the strength of American feeling, to be sent to each of the ministers. On 20 December the Consultative Group met to consider the proposals before their discussion in Council. To Harriman's fury Schuman and Cripps jointly set about the task of emasculating them so that the duties of the 'personality' who was to be appointed should mainly be 'dynamic liaison'.[82] Under American pressure the proposals were more or less restored to full health and sent to the Council. But as van Zeeland realistically summed up, 'general enthusiasm for proposal to appoint special representative could be indicated as zero'.[83]

Spaak's moves after Christmas 1949 must have been such as to make even Harriman pause. He attacked British policy in Western Europe publicly and privately while in the United States.[84] He also published an article, critical of Britain, on the subject of European integration in *The Daily Telegraph*, a paper militantly opposed to the Labour government. On 20 January Acheson was told by Franks that whatever happened Spaak was absolutely unacceptable.[85] It would, Acheson realized, be a mistake to push the candidacy any further.[86] What is extraordinary is how far the United States had in fact pushed it. No doubt this was in part due to Harriman's vanity and intemperance. Acheson himself does not seem to have been very impressed with Spaak's recommendations on practical ways to achieve Western European integration when he met him in January.[87] As soon as the candidacy was dropped the way was clear for the Dutch Foreign Minister, Dirk Stikker to be placed in a similar position.[88] A Dutchman in that position was obviously more acceptable to Britain and Scandinavia. Stikker was one advocate of economic integration who managed to bridge in his outlook the idea of a free-trade area and the idea of regulated markets. He offended no one's economic views too much, was a pragmatist, and had been a respected member of the Dutch delegation to the OEEC. He had not been associated, as Spaak had been, with agitation for political federation.[89] On 31 January 1950 he was appointed, on an experimental basis only, and while still retaining the post of Dutch Foreign Minister, as 'Political Conciliator', his task no more than 'dynamic liaison'.

[82] FRUS 1949, IV, Katz to Hoffman, 21 December 1949, p. 464.
[83] SD 840.50, 5686, Brussels embassy to Washington, 22 December 1949.
[84] Acheson Papers, 65, Conversation with Spaak, 17 January 1950.
[85] ibid., Conversation with Sir O. Franks, 20 January 1950.
[86] FRUS 1950, III, Acheson to Harriman, 24 January 1950, p. 616.
[87] Acheson Papers, 65, Conversation with Spaak, 17 January 1950.
[88] Dirk Uipko Stikker, born 1897. A banker and director of Heineken Breweries. Member of the Dutch delegation to the round table conference on the West Indies 1946–8. Chairman of the Peoples' Party for Freedom and Democracy 1948. Foreign Minister 1948–52. Ambassador in London 1952.
[89] Stikker's views are discussed in A.F. Manning, 'Die Niederlände und Europa von 1945 bis zum Beginn der fünfziger Jahre', *Vierteljahrshefte für Zeitgeschichte*, 29 (1), 1981.

The constitutional reform of the OEEC to make it the instrument of European integration had failed. Even before that the political task thrust on the organization to make it function as an integrative instrument, the allocation of aid within a programming and planning exercise covering the whole of Western Europe had also in effect been taken away. Neither by American standards nor by European had the OEEC been able to provide a·satisfactory framework for European reconstruction. Although the first reason for this, the fact that the Western European countries did not accept American views on Europe's reconstruction, is obvious, to ignore the other reasons, as they were revealed in the collapse of the OEEC, would be to fail to explore what was really needed if such a framework was to be created.

THE COLLAPSE OF THE OEEC

American policy started from the assumption that there was a need for dramatic, total and relatively sudden political change in Western Europe. The undeniable need was for something much less, an international institution which would reduce the friction which was bound to arise at the international level if Western European economies continued to pursue the same expansionist policies which had brought them to the crisis of 1947. Marshall Aid resolved that crisis between Western Europe and North America. But by openly inviting the Europeans to continue in the same economic direction it brought forward the time when similar problems would arise between Western European economies. The national economic programmes submitted to the CEEC had left no doubt that the invitation extended by the ERP had been accepted. With so many countries aiming for an increase in output and all aiming for a large increase in exports it could only be a short time before a substantial measure of international co-operation was needed to attain these goals. But the problem was that the only framework which did exist in Western Europe through which the problems of economic interdependence could be handled was no more than the fragmentary remains of a pre-war order in which domestic and international objectives had often been very different. Any attempt at expanding exports, for example, would at once fall foul of the fact that there was no mechanism through which international payments settlements could be made in Western Europe other than highly restrictive bilateral trade agreements.

The Bretton Woods settlement had not done much to remedy this, the ITO was unborn, GATT would be too general and the IMF too weak. All that survived the crash of 1947 was the commitment to fixed exchange rates which did exert a certain influence on governments' attitudes towards the internal price level. However, even this commitment was not held very firmly between 1947 and 1951, especially in France and Italy where multiple exchange rates were practised and a change to floating exchange rates openly canvassed. The need for a minimum level of international economic agreement in Western Europe to fill this vacuum was obvious after the narrow escape of summer 1947 and in many respects the OEEC fitted the bill. It embraced almost all the relevant countries, it was bound by its functions to concentrate particularly on questions of foreign trade, it was similarly bound to compile and rationalize the necessary data from which the real problems could be exposed, and it was excellently staffed at the technical level.

Yet at this level it was prevented from functioning effectively because of the much greater and more dynamic political and economic functions which the United States tried to attach to it. The member states were well aware that its real purpose in American eyes was not so much the mediation of intra-European economic problems but to serve as a political instrument for the reconstruction of Western Europe in ways which the United States regarded as Europe's only salvation and the European states themselves intended to resist. Although therefore at a technical level much useful work could be done in the OEEC, it could never be given the political links with national governments or attain the influence there which alone would turn it into the international institutional framework which would suit Europe's needs. It was a striking example of the way in which the gap between ambition and feasibility deprived American policy of all effectiveness in the period.

Yet, even had the European states, great and small alike, had the will to begin the process of economic and political integration by accepting the constitutional changes to the OEEC which the United States so persistently demanded, it would not have made it any more effective as an instrument of European reconstruction. The precise nature of the economic activity which the United States had thrust on the OEEC was one which focused political argument not only on a major area of difference but on one where national sovereignty was most staunchly upheld, the choice of domestic economic policy.

Intense argument was concentrated on the one narrow issue of balance of payments deficits and surpluses over what were really very short periods of time, because the payments imbalances were dollars. Persistent imbalances, whether deficits or surpluses, were inevitably the subject of recrimination and the blame for them was quickly laid on what were seen as defects of domestic economic policy. In this way the differences in economic policy which did exist were blown up out of all proportion and the fact that differences in policy might not mean differences in objectives often overlooked. Of course, the prime reason for the Western European countries to have refused the political implications of the American conception of the OEEC was that it was based on asking them to accept an immeasurable risk in the interests of a set of political and economic ideas to which they did not subscribe. But had the dollars come from heaven and not America the economic activity which was the OEEC's prime task would still have put it asunder.

Belgium was under constant attack for its surpluses, so much so that the documentary history of the OEEC might convince the reader that Belgium always had intra-European trade surpluses in the reconstruction period and that that was because its economic policies were fundamentally different from the other members. Although Belgian policy could be reasonably described as making hay while the sun shone, governments had none the less, while seizing the main chance, not been uninfluenced by the reaction against the unemployment and depression of the 1930s. It is true that it was external rather than internal demand that was sustaining the economy in the second half of 1948, and that the weakness of the latter was the first origin of the increase in unemployment which manifested itself before the end of the year, and persisted more strongly throughout 1949. But these tendencies were mitigated by a conscious policy of deficit financing and government expenditure on public works. None of this made Belgium any more popular with her OEEC partners, but the differences between them were differences of scale, not of ideology as might often have been supposed from the denunciations emanating from London and Oslo. After the immediate post-war trade surpluses, which were the direct result of the earlier liberation of Belgium and the greater damage done to industrial capacity elsewhere in Western Europe, Belgium's trading balances with Western Europe were very volatile and the high level of dependence on steel exports a very dangerous position. Had Belgium restricted consumption more imports would have been lower, but trade surpluses when they occurred would have been higher. And what would have been the attitude of the British to the deliberate diversion of funds away from consumption to investment in Belgium? Judging from their response to French economic plans, unhelpful and no more encouraging. In the light of the general range of economic objectives of the European countries, was it so outrageous to demand aid to sustain existing export surpluses rather than planned import deficits?

The only country where economic policy in 1948 and 1949 was so obviously different as to call the immediate economic objectives into doubt was Italy. Rigorously balanced budgets, a sharp deflation, a steep rise in registered unemployment, and the control of the economy as far as possible by merely monetary and fiscal measures set Italy quite apart from the other OEEC countries. Not surprisingly, this was to prove more alarming to the ECA than the persistent inflationary tendencies in France. As unemployment increased between September 1947 and the end of 1948 the foreign reserves rose from $70 million to $440 million.[90] It had not been intended that Marshall Aid

---

[90] G.H. Hildebrand, *Growth and Structure in the Economy of Modern Italy* (Cambridge, Mass., 1965), pp. 44 ff. argues that this was the first stage of 'the Long Boom' lasting until 1961 and largely attributable to the government's monetary policy. But ECA and Italy's OEEC partners can hardly be blamed for seeing it in a different light because their judgements were necessarily comparative ones. Hildebrand's demonstration of the stability and consistency of the Italian boom is not unfair, but by the side of it must be set the fact that the rate of increase of output in 1948 over 1947 was significantly greater in all other Western European countries except Belgium and Sweden, and that in these last two as in all the others (except Germany and Austria) industrial output was, even in the lowest case, more than 10 per cent above that of 1938, whereas in Italy it was still below that level.

should be used to increase foreign exchange reserves and the ECA was severely critical in public of the Italian government's policies.[91] Hoffman's discontent was expressed in a letter written in January to the head of the Italian mission.

> I am, therefore, in full agreement that there is need to press the Italian Government for more action, more and better co-ordinated plans, and more means and more energy for implementing them. In particular, I am thinking of the need for working out jointly with the Italian Government in some detail an annual national investment budget, involving both the use of counterpart funds and investments by the Italian Government out of its own resources.[92]

As output began once more to rise in Italy in 1949 and as the interests of the ECA turned more towards slowing the rate of inflation, Italy ceased to be the prime target of ECA criticism. But as the trade surpluses which Luigi Einaudi's monetary policies were intended to produce strengthened it became a target of British criticism. With a greater degree of co-ordination inside the OEEC, however, the problem of coping both with Italy's different policies, which for example had as a necessary component the ability to export surplus labour to Western Europe, as well as with its trade surpluses would not have been unmanageable. But in fact more attention was devoted to quarrelling with Belgium, because Belgium was at the centre of so many of the arguments about the relationship of ERP dollars to intra-Western European payments mechanisms.

Finally, any effective institutional framework for intra-western European co-operation would have depended absolutely on a reasonable degree of Anglo-French agreement about the nature and purposes of that co-operation. The close agreement between France and Britain within the OEEC, however, existed largely for negative purposes. The Labour government in London had very little sympathy with the economic objectives of post-war French governments, even when they were also of the left. It is true that full employment and better welfare were not the purpose of French policy, but labour markets were at least as tight in France as in Britain and in retrospect it is easy to see that the direction in which the French economy was being steered led towards higher welfare levels. The official targets of French policy as expressed in the Monnet Plan struck no chord of sympathy in London, so that the only claim the French could make for economic support was the claim of common economic and political interest against Germany. As we have seen, this would have committed the British government until summer 1948 to supporting policies in Germany entirely different from those which it judged to be in its own and Europe's best interests. After summer 1948 France was seeking a

---

[91] ECA, *Country Report, Italy* (Washington, 1949).
[92] Hoffman files, 269, Hoffman to James D. Zellerbach, 11 January 1949.

Franco-German association so that there was no possibility at all of Anglo-French co-operation in the OEEC on the greatest unsolved problem of European reconstruction.

Yet it was their national economic decisions which would mainly determine the parameters of a realistic and feasible recovery programme within the OEEC for any other participant, as well as having by far the greatest effect on the size of the OEEC's total dollar deficit. When over every area where there had to be an attempt to reconcile French and British economic policies there hovered this larger political issue where total disagreement still prevailed, the consequence was inescapable. It made the British suspicious of all French attempts at economic policy harmonization, because they saw them as attempts to inveigle them into support for French political objectives in Europe. It made the French increasingly sceptical about the extent of the British government's commitment to any economic reconstruction of the continent, because the pursuit of its domestic economic objectives within the protective framework of empire or in closer association with the United States seemed always so present as alternatives.

When the French national programme was submitted to the OEEC preliminary programming exercise in late 1948 it was based on a much higher level of exports, particularly food exports, to Britain than the British were prepared to incorporate into their own programme. The French proposal was that Britain take 1 million tonnes of its wheat imports from France by 1952/3, but the British were not ready to make any greater commitment than the 100,000 tonnes which they intended to take in 1949/50, about a fortieth part of their total wheat imports in that period.[93] The British programme, it was argued in Paris, did not give France the opportunity to earn sufficient sterling. But behind this complaint lay the French wish to co-ordinate more closely the foreign trade sectors of the French and British economies so as to guarantee a certain level of exports, as a safeguard for the higher levels of output envisaged by the Monnet Plan. It had proved impossible to interest the British in any such co-ordination in 1946 but with the creation of the OEEC the French had returned to the charge. The insistence on the production of a common European programme within the OEEC seemed to strengthen the position of the French and it was eventually to be made even stronger when, by the terms of the Consultative Group's resolution on 8 March 1949, countries were required to prepare a list of industries which might be suitable for international co-ordination.

The long-term European plan at which the French aimed was based on the important political consideration that Anglo-French economic co-ordination would provide safety against Germany. In British eyes this could be seen as merely asking British economic support for the Monnet Plan, and by late autumn 1948, as the first serious criticisms of the inflationary aspects of the

[93] FO 371/71982, Cabinet working paper on long-term programmes, 4 December 1946.

Plan began to emanate from the ECA, this seemed even more the case. The British, too, regarded the French plan as a dangerously inflationary venture. Nor were they prepared to make it possible by accepting a much larger quantity of French food exports. The Foreign Ministry's support for the Plan as a basis of European foreign policy was only strengthened by the danger that the lack of external support might cause its external objectives to be modified. As Alphand expressed it,

> At the same time, as the French Government is making every effort at London to secure control and limitation of German industrial potential, the main argument used against us, especially by the Americans, is to say: German production and particularly steel production must be developed in order to meet Western Europe's needs. Our best answer is to reply: France is partly capable of substituting for Germany especially as far as steel is concerned. How can such an argument convince our questioners if, at the same time, the Government in Paris decides that France does not have the necessary force to stick courageously to the path along which it has been going up to now.[94]

The British delegation to the OEEC had to plead that a French programme showing the continuation of the balance of payments deficit for two more years be accepted in London.[95] The French delegation proposed to their British counterparts that the issue be settled informally outside the OEEC, either between the two or in conjunction with Benelux and Italy. In the British delegation's words,

> For instance, Monnet, who had admittedly a rather 'simplist' approach to problems, had said that if Plowden and some of his collaborators could come over and work for two months with the French planners to produce a scheme for production, which should leave out of account all the difficulties of financial transfer and country boundaries, he believed something very useful might come of it.[96]

Plowden was the Chairman of the Economic Planning Board, which for all its impressive title had no more powers over economic planning in Britain than the Labour government had real interest in the subject.[97] Its political and economic influence was negligible by the side of that of the French Commissariat. None the less the French suggestion caused real alarm in London. It was followed by a French attempt to send a full-scale official delegation to the proposed talks between the two governments in February to straighten out

[94] FJM, AMF 22/2/1, Alphand to Schuman, 29 November 1948.
[95] FO 371/71982, UK delegation to London, 9 November 1948.
[96] FO 371/77741, Ellis-Reeves to Berthoud, 2 February 1949.
[97] Edwin Noel Plowden, subsequently Baron Plowden, 1907– , became permanent civil servant during the war, Chairman of the Economic Planning Board, 1947–53 and then of the Atomic Energy Authority. Subsequently a director of several companies.

their OEEC programmes. The talks were postponed by the British and the French were told to leave their planners at home and appear only in the person of Alphand and his officials.[98] Nevertheless Monnet and his deputy in the Commissariat, Etienne Hirsch, met Plowden privately on 17 February and proposed that the harmonization of the two programmes should first be undertaken by the two teams of planners each of which would separately report back to their national governments.[99] Plowden declined on the grounds that it was unconstitutional, but when the second official inter-governmental meeting took place at the end of February the French pressed the case once more.

The grounds for this were the talks between Cripps and Petsche, the French Minister of Finance, about co-ordination of the programmes, held on 23 February.[100] Cripps had accepted that there should be an agreement on long-term food purchases by Britain. When the officials met again six days later they made better progress and in the much better atmosphere that prevailed it was agreed to let the two planning staffs jointly examine the programmes during April 1949. On the conclusion of the official meetings Plowden twice met Monnet to listen to Monnet's proposals, once with Cripps present.

> M. Monnet explained that in his view western Europe was a vacuum, on either side of which were the two great dynamic forces of communism and American capitalism. He felt that this vacuum could be filled either by one of these two outside forces or by the development of a western European 'way of life'.[101]

He went on to plead for informal talks between the two sides with no agenda in order to settle a common policy on Germany which he regarded as the basic issue at stake.

To what extent Cripps and Monnet shared a common way of life might be a rich subject for irony but the British objections to the Monnet Plan as the basis of European reconstruction went deeper than that. When Plowden was briefed for the talks between the two planning staffs the limits of Britain's commitment to any such policy were made very clear. 'We should obviously not agree, however', his instructions read, 'to anything which would render us incapable of sustaining an independent resistance if France were overrun.'[102]

[98] FO 371/77931, Correspondence on proposed French-British discussions in London, 11/12 February 1949.

[99] FO 371/77932, Meeting of Plowden, Monnet and Hirsch, 17 February 1949.

[100] Maurice Petsche, 1895–1951. Began his career as a teacher at the Ecole des Sciences Politiques but became a civil servant in 1920. Served as a financial expert at the London conference 1921, in the negotiations for the Franco-German restitution treaty at Wiesbaden in the same year, and in the Dawes Plan negotiations. Deputy 1925. Variety of minor government posts 1929–32. Secretary of State for Finance 1948. Minister of Finance 1948–51.

[101] FO 371/77933, Plowden's notes on his conversations with Monnet, 3 and 7 March 1949.

[102] ibid., Briefing for Sir E. Plowden, 2 April 1949.

They were not, however, spelled out so clearly to the French who had been encouraged to discuss their European plans more extensively than before. No real misunderstanding had been allowed to occur but the basis for one had been laid and later in the spring Bevin's general sympathies for a greater British commitment in Europe expressed to Schuman appeared more encouraging to the French precisely because the technical task of harmonizing the two programmes in the OEEC had now been set in the context of the Monnet-Plowden talks.

When in spring the OEEC began to involve itself with the details of the next attempt at a European payments system the British position became more isolated because the ECA insisted that the payments system include a genuine element of currency convertibility. The more the United Kingdom strove to defend the sterling area against the threat of a convertible pound the more the gap between Britain and the continent became apparent. At the same time the American recession, through its impact on sterling area trade, had a much more drastic effect on the payments position of Britain and the sterling area than on that of France and several other continental economies, and this both increased the ambivalence of the Franco-British alliance and also created a wholly new problem for the OEEC by making the deficit calculations made in the programming exercise look too small as a basis for aid allocation.

Hoffman's address to the OEEC Council in July 1948 had asked for a long-term European recovery programme to be prepared in common, so that the separate annual aid allocations would be tied into an overall plan for European recovery. In late 1948 the production of a plan of this kind was supposed to be part of the work of the OEEC while it was beginning the task of collating the national aid requests for the financial year 1949/50. The Monnet-Plowden conversations were officially held within the context of preparing this long-term plan. The chances of its ever being produced as a document which would please Congress were obviously not high. The disputes between France and Britain were echoed by similar disputes between Britain and other member countries.

The Norwegian government also approached Britain with a view to coordinating their two programmes. Norway wanted Britain to provide the market for its proposed increased level of iron ore, ferrous alloy, aluminium and magnesium exports and to participate in its planned steel works in northern Norway, the project which was most frequently singled out in the ECA as an example of the predilection of European countries for autarchy over the principles of comparative advantage. Britain, however, wanted, for strategic reasons, to control its own magnesium production and preferred Canadian aluminium to Norwegian because it was cheaper and because exports to Canada earned hard currency. The United Kingdom was not interested in the steel works project because it could not envisage being able to provide the necessary coke exports.[103]

[103] FO 371/71982, Meetings of European Economic Co-operation Committee, 22 November 1948, 23 November 1948.

When the Danish programme revealed an export total to the United Kingdom $100 million above Britain's intended imports from that source the possibility was at once discussed of breaking most of the traditional trade links with Denmark on the grounds that Denmark, because of its high demand for fodder imports, was less efficient a supplier of primary products than Commonwealth countries.[104]

The totality of the separate national programmes when looked at as a common long-term plan is revealing. By 1952/3 Western European countries were collectively intending to produce about 20 per cent more than in 1938. Their imports would, however, be about a third higher and all were budgeting for a substantial dollar deficit which they intended to finance as far as possible through exports to other OEEC countries, exports which those countries were not intending to take. The projected level of intra-European trade was at least a third higher than in 1938, although no adequate European trade and payments system had yet been reconstructed. Only Britain's projected level of trade within western Europe was lower than in 1938. Even if these European export targets were reached the estimated total imports from all sources would still be about 15 per cent more than could be covered by the exports, no doubt because the forecasts were intended to maximize national claims to aid for dollar imports. Thus the programme indicated even at the end of the planning period an intended deficit of about $1000 million with the dollar zone.[105] No document coming to these conclusions could be passed off as a long-term plan, much less one which would be acceptable to the ECA and Congress.

The realization that insistence on the publication of the long-term programme would probably generate more opposition than support in Congress, firstly, because of the programme's obvious defects as a piece of common European economic planning and, secondly, because it would show that large sums of American aid would still be needed after the end of the ERP stopped the idea in its tracks. At the end of the year the national programmes collated in the OEEC as a long-term programme were published as an 'Interim Report', which stated firmly, 'It should be stressed that this report is not a joint European recovery programme.'[106]

At its first meeting, in early March, the Consultative Group agreed on and announced a so-called Plan of Action which was supposed to be an agreement to enforce the long-term programme, but in reality was a series of economic statements of mixed origins about the future based on no co-ordinated programme at all, much less intending to enforce any such programme. The Plan of Action was a curious political compromise. Harriman managed to get it established as the first point that economic policy should aim at financial and monetary stabilization. The other points were that there should be an

[104] ibid., 20 October 1948. [105] FO 371/71876, The economic problems of Western Europe.
[106] OEEC, *Interim Report on the European Recovery Programme*, 2 vols. (Paris, 1948), vol. 1, p. 14.

increase in exports, a curtailment of non-essential dollar imports, an expansion of intra-European trade, some concerted action for investment together with an exchange of investment information, and an attempt to tackle the problem of 'surplus manpower' in some countries. The statement was an ill-looking amalgam of American and European policies and the European elements were precisely the same incompatible ones which it had proved impossible to combine into the common programme.

When the OEEC began its task in late 1948 of screening the national requests for aid for the financial year 1949–50, anxiety had been at first much less than in the previous year. The task of recommending specific allocations of dollars was still distant and the economic programming could thus be conceived as a more abstract activity, not having, as it had had on the previous occasion, immediate relevance to actual dollars. The job of making recommendations on the allocation of aid only began six months later. Indeed the annual programmes for the sixteen countries had to be drawn up without any good knowledge of what the likely total of aid appropriated by Congress would be. Hoffman had told Marjolin that the programmed deficits should not be more than $4000 million in total, but other advice had differed. When compiled the programmes came to $4700 million and after screening to $4347 million, $347 million more than the American suggestion. The screening of the programmes involved no greater a degree of interference in the sovereign liberty of any participant to submit any programme it cared to, so long as it was not too blatantly inconsistent with that of all the other participants. To criticize a country's import programme for the financial year 1949–50 in late 1948, when it was well known that many of the important national economic decisions which alone could give such statistics real force and meaning had not yet been taken, seemed pointless. The screening that did take place to reduce the total programmed deficits was deliberately based on a method of avoiding detailed criticism of national submissions. The same specific percentage decreases were imposed on particular dollar commodity imports for all participants.[107]

The British claim had been for a deficit of $940 million, a sum which the OEEC Committee had had difficulty in accepting. But in London by May 1949, as the American recession began to have its effect, it was not looking enough.[108] On 22 July the United Kingdom submitted a revised estimate of its deficit as a basis for aid allocation, putting it this time at $1518 million. Because the ECA had now announced the withholding of a sum of direct aid in order to support a new payments system, the total sum available, even if Congress did pass an appropriation of the size which the ECA was suggesting, would not be more than $3850 million. There was no way the aid allocation could cope with a situation in which 40 per cent of the aid was claimed by one country and the French suggested putting off the revised British bid for separate discussions between Britain and the

[107] FO 371/77823, Coulson to Bevin, 13 January 1949.
[108] CAB 134/238, Minutes of the European Economic Co-operation Committee, 4 May 1949.

United States.[109] But this would have been for the United States to accept the incapacity of the OEEC and so the new British request went forward into the mutual screening process of the allocation recommendations.

Why the British claim on the next round of aid was revised upwards so far remains a mystery. Treasury forecasts of the likely dollar deficit in 1949/50 revised it upwards from the originally submitted estimate of $940 million only to $1081 million, and in fact the British delegation was given secret instructions to accept a reduction of their claim to $1000 million.[110] The import programme was about the same in value as in the previous year, although because of the drop in import prices this meant a noticeable increase in the volume of imports. In fact about two-thirds of planned dollar imports would still need aid. The dollar value of forecast expenditure of British oil companies operating abroad was equal to about half the total foreseen dollar import deficit and this, plus the forecast dollar expenditures by colonies and the need to close the dollar deficits of dominions, may well have led the British government to submit so high a bid. They may have wished to leave no doubt that in their own eyes American aid was expected to support sterling as an international currency across the whole sterling area.

Spaak considered the new British submission 'ill-timed and difficult to comprehend' and, together with Marjolin, suggested that the OEEC should examine the whole range of Britain's economic problems and report on them in the hope of imposing common action. The common European programme, he pointed out, had been ignored by the OEEC and was now likely to be forgotten because 'the impending British crisis hangs as a pall over the whole of Europe'.[111] There was not the slightest chance that the British government could be made to accept any course of action imposed on it by the OEEC[112] and the OEEC had no other resort than the screening process. This was done as a purely technical exercise leaving the decisions on recommendations and implementations to the Council.

When the screening committees had done their work and produced their suggestions on aid allocation the effort made to meet the increased British demands meant that everyone was left unsatisfied. Italy asked the United States to intervene as it had done the previous year in the case of the Bizone and reject the recommendations.[113] Austria declared that the sum allocated would mean its inability to meet its obligations as an independent country.[114]

[109] SD 840.50, 5682, Katz to Harriman, 26 July 1949.

[110] The Treasury estimates are in CAB 134-242, Revised UK 1949/50 Programme. The instructions to the delegation are in CAB 134-239, Meeting of European Economic Co-operation Committee, 17 August 1949.

[111] SD 840.50, 5682, Brussels embassy to Washington, 30 July 1949.

[112] This was reserved for politically weaker countries as in the case of West Germany's deficits with the EPU in 1950.

[113] SD 840.50, 5682, Italian ECA programme, Conversation between Luciolli and Unger, 3 August 1949; Rome embassy to Washington, 5 August 1949.

[114] ibid., Conversation between Kleinwächter and State Department officials, 8 August 1949.

When the OEEC Council met on 19 August 1949 only one country, Belgium, accepted the report. After ten days of fruitless argument the task of producing an agreement was delegated to two people, the Secretary-General and the head of the Benelux delegation, Baron Snoy. When the Snoy-Marjolin report was finished it recommended a British allocation of $962 million and this was accepted in London. The OEEC as a whole, however, accepted the Snoy-Marjolin report only with resentful acrimony and did so only because the report made no allowance for the $150 million reduction in total aid to cover the sum which the ECA intended to withhold as support for the payments scheme. When Hoffman accepted the OEEC recommendations he made it clear that this sum would none the less be withheld and that the recommendations were therefore in excess of the sum of Marshall Aid available.

During the whole wrangle France had been remarkably indifferent to the British case. Schuman's interests, like those of the planners, were beginning to turn elsewhere. The disputes between advocates of controls on trade and advocates of decontrol had persisted and become symbolic of disputes over a much wider range of issues. In the involved arguments over the payments system for instance Belgium's open espousal of the cause of currency convertibility was seen by other countries, Norway in particular, as an attempt to enlist American support in demolishing one of the main props of demand management. No one had a good word to say for Italy, where deflationary monetary policy was blamed for the substantial trade surpluses which were being built up with other countries and making a payments system more difficult.

The 'intolerable burden' had broken the OEEC. The committees responsible for programming and aid allocation had not been able to produce agreed decisions and the task had had to be undertaken in the end by two men only. Their report had been accepted only in the most unwilling fashion and even then they had only been able to produce it through a deliberate overestimation of the sum available. We may agree with Gordon that, at the last moment 'responsible European ministers ... could not afford to carry disagreement to an ultimate breaking point'.[115] But the operative word in that judgement is 'afford'. The purpose of making them divide that aid had been to build in the process an integrative European organization which would survive the end of the ERP and go from strength to strength. Nothing held it together in July and August 1949 but the scramble for dollars and even that worked no further than to produce an unsatisfactory report in an unsatisfactory way leaving practically no hope that the exercise could be done again next year and not the slightest hope that, if it were, it would advance the cause of integration. No sooner had the exercise been completed than there was a sweeping readjustment of all European exchange rates, done with no co-operation and no reference to

[115] L. Gordon, 'The Organization for European Economic Co-operation', *International Organization*, February 1956.

the OEEC, making nonsense of the forecast deficits and the programmes of aid to finance them which had taken the OEEC nine months to hammer out. The 'intolerable burden' had proved almost purposeless.

Hoffman did not transmit his official acceptance of the Snoy-Marjolin report until the middle of September. He accepted the recommendations only for the first half of the fiscal year 1949–50 and even then only in principle. The devaluations were likely to make the forecast trade balances different from those foreseen. They were certainly soon to make the British forecast which had finally broken the organization far too gloomy a one. But at the same time as Hoffman partially accepted the aid recommendations he brought to an end the whole system. In future the ECA itself would decide on the allocation of Marshall Aid and its decisions would be 'directly related to the performance of the participating countries, acting both individually and collectively through the OEEC'.[116] The 'intolerable burden' had been lifted. It remained only for the OEEC Council to take the decision that all future programming should be based on the assumption that aid would be needed in exactly the same ratios as in the programmes finally drawn up by Marjolin and Snoy. The shares of aid between the participants were thus permanently fixed. The further assumption would be that the total sum of aid in 1950–1 would be 75 per cent of the total for 1949–50, and in 1951–2 50 per cent of the total for 1950–1. Even the programming thus was reduced at once to a technicality. It was no longer intended that the OEEC should merge the fierce and complicated clash of national wills and policies in an integrated, supra-national entity. It was accepted that the results of such a policy had been more or less the opposite of what had been intended.

*   *   *

Within three years from its foundation the OEEC evolved from an experimental standing political conference with a rudimentary staff to a highly formalized, bureaucratized body with constitutional provision for regular meetings of important national ministers and a permanent staff of 1000. Although it had been forced into being by America as a bold attempt to overcome the limitations of the European system of nation states, within the same three years it had become so depoliticized that it served only as a forum for registering international agreements made elsewhere, increasingly of a minor kind. In so far as historians and political scientists have interested themselves in it at all they have taken two opposing views of it. Political scientists seem generally to accept the statement by Lincoln Gordon, an ECA official, that, 'At no time either in conception or in operation, has there been any attempt to give the OEEC a supra-national or federative character.'[117] Assuming this was indeed

---

[116] Van der Beugel, *From Marshall Aid*, p. 164.

[117] L. Gordon, 'The Organization for European Economic Co-operation' in *International Organization*, 10 (i), 1956.

so, they have not given much time to the history of an organization which could only seem a dull, uninteresting prelude to the more politically exciting organizations which soon followed, such as the high authority of the European Coal and Steel Community, which did embody important new principles of international political organization, especially the concept of supra-nationality. Historians, however, have tended to assume that the creation of the OEEC must, nevertheless, have been in some way a prelude to what came afterwards, even if it served only as a learning process, and have thus tended to describe the OEEC as a step on the path to the more genuine integration which did follow. Because the United States insisted on a common effort to plan the deployment of Marshall Aid, so runs the implication, this explains a small part of the origins of the European Economic Community. Both these interpretations, as the evidence in this chapter has shown, are wrong.

The OEEC was called into being at the insistence of the American government as the first stage in the attempt to build a United States of Europe. No one was entirely sure what 'integration' or 'supra-national' meant, so that the attempt was a clumsy, inadequate mixture of elements of forced international co-operation with elements of what has certainly since been considered as supra-nationality. The role of the 'Director-General' or of the Ministerial Committee which the United States never succeeded in bringing into being would certainly have been supra-national, because some of the ministers acting as a committee would have been taking decisions for all the countries, as would Spaak also had he been finally jobbed into position. Indeed, the Committee of Four, the Committee of Five, and the Snoy-Marjolin committee were forced very close to the boundaries of supra-nationality themselves, even though their very purpose was to defend the OEEC against any such concept. They could always rightly claim that the final decisions lay with the OEEC Council on which all countries were equally represented, but in each case the refusal of their recommendations by the Council would have been tantamount either to a refusal of Marshall Aid or to the acceptance of a system in which the smaller economies would have had to bargain directly and bilaterally with the United States for their aid, something which the United States was presumably not prepared to accept.

As for the OEEC Council itself, it was sometimes seen by the ECA as a very early prototype of a western European federal government, a hopeful view, and to that extent there were federative as well as supra-national elements in the creation of the OEEC. Had the long-term programme been approved and acted on or even had the principles which were set out in the Plan of Action been applied, the OEEC Council would have been harmonizing fiscal policies across Western Europe within much the same political and economic rationale as a federal government does in relationship to its constituent states. From the viewpoint of the political theorist therefore the beginnings of the American attempt at a United States of Europe would seem a confused, theoretical jumble likely to be condemned by this very weakness to failure, and the historical evidence would fully support such a condemnation. But there was such an attempt, however bungled, and therein lies the importance of the OEEC to the story of reconstruction.

But this does not mean in any way that the historians' interpretation of it is acceptable. The OEEC does explain part of the origins of the EEC, not, however, because it was the first stage in a progress towards greater economic co-operation or integration, but because it was a total rejection of integration within that particular political framework. And where there was effective politico-economic co-operation within the OEEC it was as a defence against the type of integration which the United States desired to impose as an essential element in Western European reconstruction.

At the start this was mainly Franco-British co-operation to thwart American policies, although there was always a sufficient number of smaller states on which the Franco-British front could rely. Norway's opposition to integration was, for example, throughout the whole period, even more prominent and outspoken. As the politico-economic interests of the United Kingdom and France in European reconstruction began to diverge, and France began to pursue its own quite distinct concept of integration, it was still possible to rely on Britain if the main issue at stake was to thwart American ideas of European reconstruction, and at the same time the extent to which France could also rely on the support of Benelux increased as the direction of British policy became more evident. Outside the boundaries of the OEEC, and with only occasional echoes and reverberations inside it, France was pursuing from summer 1948, after the second stage of the London conference, the possibility of an entirely different form of European integration in order to resolve the Franco-German problem. This was necessarily aimed at retaining an extensive battery of controls on markets and production very different from the ECA's vision of the complete freedom of movement of factors. It would also be within geographical boundaries much less widespread than those envisaged by the ECA. Therein might lie a safer road to national security as well as a better chance of realizing national reconstruction objectives; in the ECA's version of the United States of Europe lay only danger. The OEEC did therefore bring nearer the integration of some of the Western European economies, but only as a reaction to the all-embracing, liberal common market, and an integrated Western Europe under a supra-national body with a wide range of economic powers, which the OEEC had been intended to inaugurate.

The barriers which the system of nation states presented to the implementation of American policy proved so many and so high that the question really needing to be answered is how such a policy was ever conceived. Briefly to recapitulate the more important of these barriers, they were the following. No decisions had been made by the great powers about Germany and when they began to be made their repercussions on the other European nation states were inevitably such as to emphasize the different national interests of those states rather than their areas of agreement. Because the nature of the reconstruction of Germany was likely to determine much of the nature of the reconstruction of Western Europe the differences were of extreme importance to the political and economic future of those states, of much too great an importance to be resolved within an experimental, possibly temporary, international political organization. Secondly, the capacity of any alliance between the two major, intact nation states, the United Kingdom and France, to dominate the OEEC and resist American policy was very high. Thirdly, the chances of the United States forming sufficiently strong and stable alliances of interest with the smaller states to push through any parts of its policy were negligible. The differences of interest between these smaller states were too great for them to support anything but a free-for-all forum where all were equal in spite of their manifest inequalities and none of them, in any case, were in favour of the whole package of American policy, only little bits of it where it suited their own interest. Where it did not, they ran for shelter in separate alliances of interest with the larger European states. Lastly, the United States simply did not have the economic or political leverage to achieve such grandiose ambitions or even to leave Western Europe at the end of the ERP within distant sight of their achievement. How, then, did such a mismatch between policy objectives and the means of attaining them arise?

Part of the answer to this question has been given in chapter 1. The American diagnosis of Europe's economic difficulties in 1947 was wrong. It exaggerated the weakness of the European economies and in doing so led to a great exaggeration of the scope of the political and economic action needed as well as to an overestimation of the power and influence which Marshall Aid would exert. Because Marshall Aid was measured and provided in the very form in which it was most useful to solve the economic crisis of 1947, as finance for balance of payments deficits with the dollar zone, it solved the technical aspect of the crisis very efficiently. Because it was provided in a way which did not insist on any change in economic policies in Western Europe, it did not interfere with the rapid expansion of these economies which was taking place and which had only been blocked by the payments crisis to which the technical solution had now been found. Ironically, the success of Marshall Aid was itself therefore a major obstacle to the implementation of American policy. But starting from a much graver diagnosis of Europe's economic ills in 1947 that was hard for American policy-makers to see.

Accepting, however, that false diagnoses are the natural, inevitable hazard of all major international policy-making it remains the case that the ambitions of American policy were curiously grand, too grand to be entirely explained in this way. After all, the economic analyses of the malfunctioning of the international economy and the variety of advice put out were just as varied in the United States as elsewhere and these variations were equally marked within the State Department, Treasury and ECA. Underlying policy-formulation was a sort of puritanical, missionary zeal to put the Old World to rights. The basis was a deeply held liberal persuasion that in some way the development of the Old World had been blocked while still in a state of sinful imperfection and thus had not reached, yet, the competitive heaven of high productivity which the United States had now attained. These underlying quasi-religious, quasi-nationalist assumptions influenced the choice of policy at critical moments and, when the strategy of making the OEEC itself allocate Marshall Aid was abandoned, were to do so again decisively in the choice of a substitute policy. They were, naturally, much less influential in the world of professional foreign service officers in the Department of State, but much more influential in Congress. Economic integration was seen as a part of the march of history and history as the march of progress with the United States in its vanguard. The real role of integration in European reconstruction was to show how glibly superficial such ideas were. But they were zealously held and like many zeals kept hidden they motivated policy all the more for being so deeply buried. It proved, not for the last time in post-war American history, that policy choices pursued with fervent zeal and derived from a simplification of America's own history turned out not to be real policy choices at all but just over-vaulting ambitions.

In this case American policy produced a shifting set of common fronts against it in Western Europe, as well as a set of deeply ambivalent political and economic relationships between Western Europe and the United States. Western Europe became an object of thwarted American love and America the dominant lover whom it was always necessary to deceive because, although much admired, he was too possessive, by no means wholly admirable, and through a different upbringing had come to believe different things. This became part of the fabric of post-war history. Before the ERP came to its appointed end it was to be merged into the more solemn commitment of military alliances. The beloved enemies would be unable to part. America's decision to integrate Europe through Marshall Aid and the OEEC ultimately produced not only a different form of European integration as a defence against America but strengthened that bitter-sweet European emotion, anti-Americanism.

VI

FOREIGN TRADE AND PAYMENTS AND EUROPEAN RECONSTRUCTION

From the mid-nineteenth century, at the latest, foreign trade has been of fundamental importance in determining the levels of prosperity and welfare in most Western European countries. Relatively small national units with limited resources could not have sustained the process of industrialization and economic development which they then experienced in full had there not grown up between them a complicated network of international economic relationships of which the most noticeable was the rapidly increasing volume and value of the goods which they exchanged. Superimposed on this was their tendency to exchange people on an equally impressive scale. Superimposed in turn on both these processes was the flow of investment, information and services between these national units which by 1914 meant that in some cases their invisible transactions with each other amounted to about a third of the value of their visible commodity transactions. Although there was a temporary divergence from this trend in the 1930s it was seen in most Western European countries as a regrettable, necessary adaptation to harsh economic and political circumstances and one which offered few enticing long-term prospects. Only in Germany, and among certain influential circles for a brief period in Italy, was there any conscious attempt to justify this interruption of the trend as a turning-point in Western European history and to advocate a more self-sufficient and autarchic policy as a sound basis for future economic development. The economic facts as well as the performance of the German economy over those years did not suggest that these were well-founded ideas, at least within the 1938 or even the 1939 frontiers of the Third Reich. For Italy they were apparent nonsense as soon as any attempt was made to put them into practice.

Nevertheless, the inter-war experience had imposed distinct limitations in practice on the ease with which trade, people and capital could flow across national boundaries. The importance of such phenomena to the economies of even the smaller national units was not greatly different in 1947 from what it had been in 1913 and the mechanisms through which such flows had passed had been largely destroyed. Attempts after the First World War to recreate a multilateral framework for international trade and payments based on a commonly accepted set of practices in international payments and a stable pattern of currency exchange rates along the lines of the gold standard of the decades before 1914 had not been very successful. One reason, perhaps the most powerful one, had been the increasing variation in domestic economic policies between the different countries. New and powerful political interests were not prepared in many cases to accept changes in the external value of the currency as signals to change domestic economic policies. These ideas persisted into the reconstruction period. There was a constant tension in all Western European countries between, on the one hand, the widely accepted idea that in the long run prosperity depended on a return to more open economies with a relatively free multilateral system of trade and payments, and, on the other hand, the determination to reconstruct the economy and society in the way in which the purely national mandate for change demanded. Had these national mandates always led in similar directions the tensions might more quickly and easily have been resolved, but although there were certain observable common trends the differences remained important.

Furthermore, the immediate economic importance of international transactions to the different economies was very different, a function of their history and size. The *per capita* value of foreign trade as a percentage of *per capita* national income in 1949 in Belgium was 71.3, in the Netherlands 63.3 and in Denmark 50.6. For France it was only 30.3 and for Britain 39.4. Most of Belgium's foreign trade was with Western Europe so it was hardly surprising that Belgium should have been an advocate of an immediate return to a multilateral payments system in Europe based on convertible currencies as the indispensable backing to any domestic recovery policy. Countries such as France and Britain could hope to see established their own national recoveries and even persuade others to accept the main principles of them as the principles of future *international* economic agreement before the need for a multilateral trade and payments system had to be finally accepted. The principle that there should be such a system had been almost universally accepted in British and French financial circles in 1944 and 1945 at the time of the Anglo-American Financial Agreements and the Franco-American Lend-Lease negotiations. But the date by which the British Treasury hoped to see it in practice varied wildly and vaguely over the post-war years according to the state of the British balance of payments and in France its importance as a policy objective fluctuated in subordination to other policy objectives like the Monnet Plan.

These inherent conflicts of economic interest were made worse by the great differences in the pattern of distribution of the western European countries' exports. The high demand for reconstruction imports and the substantial losses of invisible earnings meant allocating an exceptional priority to exports as a vehicle for recovery. This would have been so even had the ambitions of domestic economic policy been no more than a return to the levels of pre-war output and activity. But in most countries they were much higher. To employ the resources left idle in the 1930s would make an even more daunting demand on the capacity of increased exports to pay for increased imports. In such circumstances there was no glossing over the fact that in the immediate recovery period countries such as Britain and France could hope for rapid export gains outside Europe, particularly in their own protected currency areas, whereas countries like Italy or Denmark could realistically only hope for immediate relief of their problems in intra-European trade.

In 1947 intra-European trade was still a smaller proportion of total European trade than in the inter-war period, but this was much more because of the decline in imports by European countries from European suppliers. Imports from Europe were only 37 per cent of total European imports when, generally, since the late nineteenth century they had been rather more than a half (table 25). This cannot by any means be explained entirely by the virtual elimination of Germany, although Germany accounted for only about 4 per cent of intra-European trade in 1947 compared to about 20 per cent in 1938 (table 26). There were other causes keeping intra-European trade at a lower level than it might otherwise have reached. The high domestic demand for certain kinds of manufactures may well have held back exports in spite of the effort made by several countries to divert output into exports. But the propensity to import from two other sources, the United States and associated territories outside Europe, was very marked. The first was encouraged, as we have seen, by the immediate post-war shortage of capital goods in Europe and the extensive

Table 25   Intra-European trade as a proportion (%) of
Europe's foreign trade

	Exports	Imports
1913*	68.7	57.5
1927*	73.2	52.4
1938	63.0	55.0
1947	55.0	37.0

Sources: W.S. Woytinsky and E.S. Woytinsky, *World Commerce and Governments* (New York, 1955), pp. 74–5 (for 1913 and 1927); UN, *A Survey of the Economic Situation and Prospects of Europe* (Geneva, 1948), p. 31 (for 1938 and 1947).

* The six major foreign traders only (Belgium, France, Germany, Italy, Netherlands, United Kingdom).

Table 26 German and West German trade as a proportion (%) of total Western European trade

	Imports		Exports	
	Altreich	'West Germany'*	Altreich	'West Germany'*
1937	14.6	11.8	23.7	18.1
1938	19.3	15.8	23.8	18.5
	West Germany		West Germany	
1946	6.2		6.8	
1947	3.0		5.4	
1948	5.5		8.4	
1949	8.6		10.5	
1950	14.0		13.8	

Source: OEEC, *Statistical Bulletin of Foreign Trade*.

* Pre-war 'West Germany' calculated as consuming 71 per cent of the imports and providing 67 per cent of the exports of the 'Altreich'. For imports of all other countries the German component reduced by 29 per cent and for exports by 33 per cent.

provision of dollars in various forms, especially by relief programmes and troop pay in 1946. The second came from the elimination of European food surpluses and the policy of purchasing primary imports as far as possible from other areas than the dollar zone so as to save hard currency.

Such major shifts in the pattern of world trade altered the terms of trade to European countries. The underlying trend was unavoidable, even though for most Western European countries it had not yet emerged. A sustained increase in manufactured output in Western Europe would end the phase of excessively low primary prices which had prevailed in the inter-war period and shift the terms of trade against European countries by increasing the prices of their extra-European primary imports in comparison to those of their manufactured exports. But the difference in the rates of recovery in Europe meant that this underlying trend had not yet emerged for many continental economies, whereas for Britain, the value of whose extra-European trade in 1947 was more than twice that of Belgium's total trade, the adverse movement in the terms of trade was a serious addition to the international difficulties of 1947. The volatile price movements in the recovery period as well as the arbitrary pricing policies under controlled trade and bilateral trading agreements make it almost impossible to say with any accuracy by how much Britain's terms of trade had deteriorated compared to the 1930s and many government calculations exaggerated the extent of the adverse movement. Cairncross's statement that over the period 1948–50 the United Kingdom's terms of trade were 13 per cent worse than over the period 1936–8 tallies, however, with the evidence.[1]

[1] Sir A. Cairncross, 'The post-war years 1945–1977', in R. Floud and D. McCloskey (eds) *The Economic History of Britain since 1700* (Cambridge, 1981), vol. 2, p. 390.

To a government faced with the need, as it had calculated, for a 75 per cent increase in commodity exports even to compensate for the impact of the loss of invisible income on the balance of payments this was a serious extra charge in terms of the increased price of imports to produce these exports. The one indubitable success of British economic policy in the first three years after the end of the war was that exports rose by even more than the daunting target set for them. But this did not prevent balance of payments crises in 1947 and 1949 and among the complex causes of these was the underlying need to adjust to a different trend in world commodity prices which were responding to domestic reconstruction policies in Europe.

For many countries on the continent, and particularly for the two potentially largest producers, Germany and France, the impact of this trend was deferred by the lower levels of production. French output in 1947 was still below its low level of 1938 and German output at barely a third of the same level. It was also deferred by the very high prices which certain categories of exports could command. The price of Belgian steel exports, for example, was for some categories almost twice those of the United States, but in a situation where American steel was scarce and still controlled, and where price might sometimes matter less than the currency in which the price had to be paid, such high price levels could be maintained. For the continent as a whole, although this was not the case for each country, the adverse movement in the terms of trade was not apparent until 1949, when its extent is even harder to measure because of the currency devaluations of that year. But within that underlying global trend the rapidly changing patterns of intra-Western European politics and trade also had their effect on international trade prices. In 1947, for example, France still had access at very low prices to primary imports from Germany.

From the inception of the ERP American policy was to increase as rapidly as possible the volume of intra-Western European trade. The underlying motive was the assumption that economic integration was an inescapable and beneficent tendency of the process of capitalist economic development and that foreign trade was one of the main mechanisms through which both economic development and integration proceeded. The function of foreign trade was to increase the possibilities of division of labour thereby increasing economic efficiency and improving productivity. A higher level of intra-Western European trade would therefore bring nearer 'viability', or, at least, the capacity of western Europe to survive within a world-wide multilateral trade and payments system without the need of dollar aid from the United States. It would also lead to larger, less restricted markets, to the decay of protectionism, and would bring nearer the desirable political objective of Western European integration.

Such ideas meant that the methods by which European countries conducted their international economic transactions stayed on the front of the political stage from 1947 onwards and thus assumed an even greater importance to

European recovery than they would in any case have had. Eventually, after the failure of the OEEC to cope with these problems, a different solution emerged, the European Payments Union (EPU). Like the European Coal and Steel Community (ECSC) it was an organization different in principle from what the United States had originally hoped for in trying to promote European integration as the basis of reconstruction. Where the OEEC failed as an instrument of political reconstruction the EPU succeeded. The reason was that it corresponded, in a way that the OEEC failed to do, to the realities of Western European economic and political circumstance. Although much less so than the ECSC, it was an assertion of European economic and political will as a reaction against American policy. This can only be demonstrated by examining the development after 1945 of the pattern of European payments and trade.

MULTILATERAL AND BILATERAL TRADE IN WESTERN EUROPE

In the two decades before the First World War the existence of a multilateral trade and payments network embracing western Europe and America had been based on the fact that national currencies were readily convertible against each other on the basis of their values against gold, which remained remarkably stable. After 1918 the major western European currencies, although still traded on free markets, fluctuated wildly against each other. There had been a great increase in public borrowing and in credit expansion between 1914 and 1918, but it had not been on an equal scale everywhere and the differences had been exaggerated by differences in fiscal policy. The First World War bequeathed a severe threat of inflation to all European countries in the immediate post-war period, but the attitudes of governments to that threat were very variable according to the political circumstances in which they found themselves, so that the differences in internal price levels which had developed during the war became yet wider in the war's aftermath, provoking, and in turn eventually being provoked by, rapid fluctuations in exchange rates. This contrasted so sharply with the virtually stable exchange rates of the period before 1914 that the 'stabilization' of post-war Europe came to mean above all the return in 1925 and 1926 to a period when once more, even if only briefly, European currencies came to have a relatively steady and predictable relationship to each other and to gold. These more stable relationships were accompanied by an expansion in output and trade. The depression of 1929 was accompanied, however, by another series of rapid alterations in currency relationships leading to the introduction of drastic trade and exchange controls almost everywhere and most especially in the economy which had been the fulcrum of European trade, Germany.

Foreign transactions during the 1930s in most European countries were closely supervised and controlled. Probably as much as a third of Europe's foreign trade was conducted by short-term bilateral trade agreements between two countries, usually covering no longer a period than one year, to exchange specific quantities of goods at specified prices. About four-fifths of Germany's foreign trade was conducted and controlled in this way. Such agreements were constructed to equalize the total flow of foreign transactions and payments between pairs of countries, so that they usually also included other forms of currency transactions, such as interest payments on investment, shipping earnings and losses, and all forms of inter-governmental loans and credits. Exchange rates thus lost much of their significance as indicators of international economic movements and became increasingly arbitrary. Although the growing extent, complication and sophistication of controls on foreign trade and payments was such as to cause many commentators to see in them a new form of aggressive mercantilism, they were for the most part, even in Germany, desperate defensive measures, the need for which arose from the primacy given to domestic recovery policies. It was, however, always possible to mount a more powerful critique of them in as much as where economic recovery did take place it seldom occurred as vigorously in the foreign sector as in the domestic sector. European trade, and in particular intra-European trade, did not again reach the levels of 1928/9 and foreign investment within Europe scarcely recovered at all. In recent history, therefore, expanding trade was associated with a stable multilateral trade and payments system, stagnating trade with bilateral trading mechanisms and 'artificial' exchange rates.

During the 1930s the Department of State, under Cordell Hull, had vigorously championed the cause of a restoration of multilateral trade and the re-creation of an international payments system which would support it, although the barriers to foreign trade erected by the United States were not such as to lend to this policy any great power of conviction. The startling increase of American national product, output and foreign trade during the Second World War, however, made it much more apparent on the domestic political scene that America's vital national interest lay in pursuing still more vigorously the restoration of an internationally agreed multilateral system of foreign trade. Unless United States exports were maintained not far below the level they had climbed to with the aid of Lend-Lease financing it seemed possible that the high levels of employment and income to which the war had shifted the American economy might not be preserved, and this in turn meant making room for more imports than in the 1930s. The creation by international agreement of a new mechanism for multilateral trade throughout the world became a priority amongst American objectives for the peace. The promise to co-operate in the creation of such a mechanism was a condition of the Anglo-American Financial Agreement of December 1945 under which the line of credit was made available to the United Kingdom. Likewise it was a condition of the master agreement providing Lend-Lease to France.

One underlying idea, ratified by the agreement at Bretton Woods to create the IMF, was that countries would seek to maintain stable exchange rates for long periods of time and alter them only in an 'orderly' way through the international mediation of the IMF, with which they would register a 'par rate' for their currency against the dollar, which was itself convertible at a stipulated price into gold. There was widespread agreement on the usefulness of maintaining external values of currencies within a relatively narrow band of fluctuation against each other and what has subsequently been one of the most criticized aspects of the 'Bretton Woods system' was one of the least disputed aspects of it at the time, although, as we shall see, it was soon to be called into question by European events. In spite of this comprehensive international institutional attempt to eliminate exchange controls and establish a sound basis for currency convertibility and multilateral payments in the post-war world, the arrangements to promote an increase of international trade were exceedingly vague. They turned on the creation of a world-wide International Trade Organization (ITO) whose members would renounce 'discrimination' in international trade as well as on a series of international conferences aimed at bringing about a reduction in tariffs and other barriers to trade. The ITO never came into being. The curious position of the United States in international payments in the immediate post-war period, when it had such massive payments surpluses, went a long way towards making the IMF ineffective. Its currency holdings were never intended to be so large as to cope with so persistent a demand for one currency, the dollar. In the event Marshall Aid was in part designed to meet this particular problem and the IMF was pushed into the background under the assumption that it could once more become effective when post-war recovery was complete, of which the measure would now be the elimination of 'the dollar gap' between Western Europe and America, 'viability' in the language of the ECA. The United States' surpluses would otherwise have only encouraged the maintenance of trade and payments controls in Europe unless other positive measures had been taken to make the dollar a less scarce currency.

The ERP was thus thought of at first as an emergency measure, which, by ensuring Western Europe's economic recovery, would by increasing European dollar earnings enable the Bretton Woods agreements, the basis of the world-wide peace settlement, to be brought into operation in their full panoply in spite of the setback of 1947, even though the communist bloc would be excluded. With full economic recovery in Western Europe would come a payments equilibrium between Western Europe and North America, the dollar would cease to be in such excess demand in international payments and the IMF could begin to function fully as a regulatory agency of a world-wide multilateral payments system. It was therefore inherent to the ERP that European countries should use Marshall Aid from the outset to move towards a multilateral system of trade and payments and away from the methods by which they had increasingly been trading since 1929. Otherwise, if this

American analysis were correct, the IMF could only be brought into operation for intra-European trade.

The recovery of intra-European trade in 1946 and 1947 had taken place within circumstances which had tended to encourage discrimination and certainly made the possibility of a multilateral payments system between western European countries, even if dollar trade and payments were temporarily to be excluded from such a system, seem remote. The different rates of recovery, related to differences in wartime economic experience and to differences in the capacity to adjust to the changed pattern of economic activity in Europe after the war, meant that the pattern of intra-western European trade was markedly different from that which had prevailed before the war. British trade surpluses with the continent, German exports at the level of the smallest European trading nations, massive import surpluses into all countries from the United States, all were formidable and recently added barriers to any relaxation of trade controls, and even more to the free convertibility of currencies.

The consequence was that as intra-European trade revived it did so even more within the framework of those very bilateral trade and exchange agreements which were being denounced for the economic woes of the 1930s. In unsure and unpredictable circumstances bilateral trade protected the chosen domestic economic policies of the separate countries by removing the need to stabilize exchange rates by drastic policy alterations. It was seen, by governments intent on policies of sustained development of the economy, of high employment or demand management, as a safeguard against the danger of having to maintain stable exchange rates through deflation. The aspirations to a better world, for which the war had been fought, thus served in western Europe to strengthen the controlled and relatively inflexible system of trade and payments which had been held responsible for the disappointingly low levels of intra-European trade in the 1930s.[2] After the payments crisis of summer 1947 only the Italian government sought to diminish its current account deficit by deflationary policies in the domestic economy. The other countries, whose growing current account deficits lay at the heart of the crisis, sought a way out through more selective types of trade control. Even though bilateral trade agreements were thought of in principle in most countries as only a temporary safeguard until a more stable and 'normal' pattern of international trade and payments should emerge, by the end of 1947 a far greater proportion of western Europe's trade was being conducted through such restrictive devices than at any time in the 1930s.

---

[2] 'In sharp contrast to prewar German bilateralism, it will be seen that the postwar Western European bilateralism is actually a multilateral system of considerable consistency and flexibility. It is, in fact, the most extensive multilateral system feasible for Western Europe in the absence of a solution to the current dollar shortage.' G. Patterson and J. Polk, 'The emerging pattern of bilateralism', *The Quarterly Journal of Economics*, vol. 62, 1947/8, a conclusion which subsides into accuracy.

This was a double threat to American plans and hopes. If western Europe, which was much the greatest generator of international trade, showed no perceptible movement towards a greater degree of multilateralism and if Western European governments regarded the possible advent of a multilateral payments system with suspicion and apprehension, America's global policy was doomed to failure. Secondly, once the focus of immediate interest had switched under Marshall Aid to the economic integration of Western Europe as a means of supporting America's international strategy it appeared obvious that the existing trading arrangements were a severe obstacle to that integration. If the freest possible flow of factors promoted efficiency and integration, anything which restricted that flow had to be construed as an obstacle both to Europe's recovery and America's strategic safety. The mechanism through which intra-Western European trade was financed and grew after the war was in fundamental conflict with American policy and aspirations. Nor was it one with which European countries themselves could be content in the long run.

The restrictions imposed by bilateral agreements were practical and immediate. All such agreements strictly limited the volume of debt which any country could accumulate against another in either of their currencies over a short period of time. They were usually, however, more flexible than before the war, permitting a small degree of 'swing' beyond strict balance. The margin of permissible debt once reached, it was necessary to make all further payments in gold or hard currency. In the post-war world this normally meant dollars or Swiss francs, both of which were jealously hoarded. As foreign trade between European countries expanded after the war it tended therefore to be increasingly subject to sudden interruptions when particular countries reached their agreed margins of debt against others and cut off all further imports from the supplier in question rather than have to part with gold or hard currency. On the abstract level of theory bilateral agreements also appeared restrictive even when operating uninterruptedly, in the sense that perfect freedom of choice for importers and exporters would have implied lower transaction costs as well as a greater degree of maximization of comparative advantage and thus of efficiency in international trade. Whether these theoretical considerations did actually apply in Europe in the two years after the war and whether the bilateral framework did actually restrict the growth and volume of trade are, however, another matter altogether.

The pattern of intra-Western European trade after Germany's defeat did not make the transition to a multilateral payments system seem acceptable or even possible to many European countries. On the other hand the inherent rigidity of bilateral trade, it could be argued, was such as to set Europe's foreign trade firmly within the mould formed by the bilateral agreements and thus actually to prevent any transition to an equilibrium pattern of trade from which an equilibrate multilateral payments system could emerge. Once, however, intra-Western European trade was set in the context of the trade of

Western Europe with the rest of the world, this argument in turn looked somewhat remote from reality. Almost all Western European countries had very large current account deficits with the United States and the dollar zone, so that even were it possible to move to an equilibrium in intra-Western European payments by freeing foreign trade progressively from controls, it was not easy to see what difference this would make to Europe's trade with America. There might still be a disequilibrium in trade with the United States so great as to prevent the emergence of a multilateral payments system linking Western Europe and the United States. To believe that an intra-Western European equilibrium would reduce the European demand for dollars and help to produce 'viability' and a Western European-American equilibrium it was necessary to share the assumptions that maximizing the division of labour implied maximizing foreign trade, and that this would so alter Western Europe's international position as to permit the restoration of a multilateral payments system with currency convertibility and stable exchange rates embracing both Western Europe and the dollar zone. Such bold assumptions depending on theoretical analyses of international trade which were often very remote from its practice were not the intellectual stock-in-trade of most European economic ministries. Many of them could see no connection between the possible advantages of a Western European payments equilibrium in themselves and the advantage of such an equilibrium in bringing about a transatlantic or world payments equilibrium. There is not much to say that their scepticism was misplaced.

As America's needs for an international ideology of its own became so acute from 1947 onwards the theoretically greater economic efficiency of large markets and a multilateral payments system came to be seen also, however, as a fundamental aspect of political democracy and 'a free society' by many in Washington. Harriman and Hoffman, in particular, appear to have been entirely unable to distinguish between the possible theoretical advantages of a multilateral payments system from the standpoint of economic efficiency and such a system as one of the pillars of a free, democratic society based on fundamental human liberties. Underlying the long and tedious arguments over the technicalities of European trade and payments systems from 1947 onwards was an important and complex political struggle. It was a struggle firstly to construct a payments system which would replace the highly con-trolled system of the 1930s, but which, nevertheless, would still allow countries to pursue domestic economic policies based on sustained economic growth. Secondly, it was a struggle to make that system acceptable to American, as well as European, political interests. Thirdly, it was a struggle to arrive at a framework for European foreign trade which would reflect the important political and social changes which the war had brought in Europe and allow them to be preserved.

THE POST-WAR PATTERN OF WESTERN EUROPE'S TRADE

Figures 8–12 show the inherent difficulties in establishing a multilateral payments system in post-war Western Europe. Many of these difficulties had their origins in the changes in the pattern of trade produced by the war and its aftermath. The largest pre-war European contributor to intra-Western European trade, Germany, had been reduced in 1947 to insignificance, its total exports less in value than those of Denmark, much less than those of Switzerland, and largely made up of raw materials, whereas before the war they had consisted mainly of manufactures. Britain's exports now accounted for two-fifths of the total value of all Western European exports (table 27). Before 1939 trade surpluses with Britain had allowed Western European countries to settle many of their deficits in extra-European trade in sterling. Most of them now had import surpluses from Britain (table 28). Until 1949 only Italy had a persistent export surplus with the United Kingdom.

The pattern of German trade changed violently over the period. Because of the very low levels of consumption and output in occupied Germany for the first three years after the war the western zones still generated an export surplus in intra-European trade. But instead of manufactured goods making the major contribution to this surplus it was mainly made up of raw materials, in particular timber and coal. In 1946 coal accounted for 83.4 per cent of the value of all exports from the British zone, in which was included the greatest share of pre-war German manufacturing output.[3] As German economic recovery began to lift the economy towards pre-war levels of output trade became more evenly balanced, until in 1950 West Germany developed a deficit on intra-European current account, largely explained by the increase in imports of food and semi-manufactures. By the first months of 1951 Western Europe's greatest manufacturing exporter was accumulating massive import surpluses. In early summer this pattern again reversed itself and West Germany began once more to pile up trade surpluses, but this time on the basis of manufactured exports.

One of the countries which had set out to increase the importance of the industrial sector in its economy as a part of the reconstruction process, the Netherlands, showed persistent import surpluses in intra-Western European trade. The Netherlands was a debtor throughout Western Europe on merchandise trade until 1949, after which the pattern became more varied, but still leaving the Netherlands an overall debtor because of its very large deficits with Belgium. The export surpluses with the Netherlands kept Belgium as a surplus country in Western European trade after 1946 and the largest intra-Western European deficits throughout the period were those of the Netherlands to Belgium. Even in 1950 they showed no sign of diminishing. By contrast Italy, after 1947, where the domestic demand for reconstruction

---

[3] F. Jerchow, *Deutschland in der Weltwirtschaft 1944–1947* (Düsseldorf, 1978), p. 341.

Table 27 The trade of the United Kingdom and Western Europe compared, 1937–1951 (million current dollars)

	Imports			Exports		
	Total Western European imports	*Total UK imports*	*UK imports as % of Western European imports*	*Total Western European exports*	*Total UK exports*	*UK exports as % of Western European exports*
1937	13,006.5	5,087.7	39.1	9,374.0	2,950.4	31.5
1938	11,674.8	4,496.4	38.5	8,539.9	2,602.8	30.5
1946	13,773.3	5,236.6	38.0	8,250.3	3,884.0	45.4
1947	20,818.7	7,232.0	34.7	12,215.0	4,828.3	39.5
1948	24,123.1	8,374.5	34.7	15,903.5	6,635.4	41.7
1949	24,237.3	8,443.8	34.8	18,453.6	6,834.6	37.0
1950	23,441.4	7,303.1	31.1	19,375.6	6,317.0	32.6
1951	32,786.0	10,959.8	33.4	26,720.3	7,578.3	28.4

Source: OEEC, *Statistical Bulletins of Foreign Trade.*

Table 28   Annual balance of United Kingdom trade with the countries of western
Europe, the United States and the whole world; 1937, 1938, 1946–51

| Year | Million US dollars (current) | | |
	Total trade	Western European trade	United States trade
1937	−2136.29	−280.35	−355.91
1938	−1893.55	⋅305.67	−436.73
1946	−1352.68	+495.31	−764.07
1947	−2403.74	+178.52	−950.08
1948	−1739.10	−266.66	−453.73
1949	−1609.15	−141.78	−598.21
1950	−986.08	+23.80	⋅234.70
1951	−3381.49	−664.27	−636.99

(− deficit;   + surplus)

Source: OEEC, *Statistical Bulletins of Foreign Trade*. Before 1951 the whole of Germany and
not western Germany is used in the calculations.

goods was deliberately held back and whose agricultural exports were in high
demand everywhere showed persistent surpluses in Western European trade
except, from 1949, with Belgium/Luxembourg.

Thus if a tendency for pre-war patterns of intra-Western European trade to
reassert themselves could be discerned it was slow and uncertain and the
pattern as it existed in 1949 still hardly seemed one which could serve as the
basis for a multilateral payments system. Where certain countries were
creditors on a substantial scale to almost all the rest of Western Europe and
others debtors on an equally substantial scale the limitations of multilateral
payments were obvious, especially when, because of the trade deficits with
the United States, a global balance could not be reached either to right the
intra-Western European imbalances.

It has already been pointed out that the degree of importance of foreign
trade and of intra-Western European trade to the Western European economies
was very different. In Belgium-Luxembourg and in Denmark intra-Western
European trade alone had been the equivalent of about a fifth of national income
in 1938; in Britain and France less than a twentieth (table 29). The real interest in
an expansion of intra-Western European trade of those smaller economies
above the broken line in table 29 was markedly greater than that of the two large
national economies which dominated the OEEC. Full economic recovery, in
the smaller countries, to say nothing of the growth of income and welfare to a
higher level than in the pre-war years was inconceivable without the full
recovery and further growth of intra-Western European trade. Whatever the
difficulties and dangers of the prevailing situation, in the long run nothing very
much could be achieved in such countries under trade and exchange controls.

Thus, in spite of the manifest difficulties, there were certain practical common interests, between Western Europe and the United States in developing a more flexible system of trade and payments in intra-Western European trade, even if the ultimate implications of such a system for a world-wide payments equilibrium or even as a step towards Western European integration were not accepted. But the pattern of intra-Western European trade was too far from equilibrium for the gap between reality and equilibrium to be breached by an extension of export credits in the form of increases in the permitted 'swing' on bilateral agreements, and in any case what surplus countries like Belgium wanted was not other inconvertible European currencies but hard currency. The real interest of any country in that position was to try to get some portion of Marshall Aid allocated as backing for a multilateral payments scheme for Western European trade.

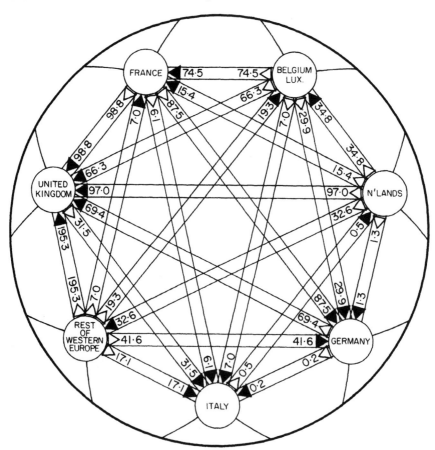

Figure 8   Balances on intra-western European commodity trade, 1946. (Arrows show direction of deficits. Germany = whole of Germany.)

Table 29   Intra-western European foreign trade as a percentage of
national income, 1938–51

	1938	1947	1951
Belgium/Luxembourg	19.2	17.3	23.6
Denmark	21.7	11.5	22.5
Netherlands	14.5	12.8	28.3
Norway	14.9	15.0	18.8
Switzerland	10.5	11.2	14.1
United Kingdom	4.3	3.3	7.2
France	4.3	2.5	5.3

Source: OEEC, *Statistical Bulletin of Foreign Trade. International Financial Statistics.*

That there should be an attempt to produce such a scheme had been a condition imposed by Benelux on the CEEC and to discuss the Benelux proposals for it had been one of the CEEC's first tasks, bequeathed to the OEEC. The original Belgian proposals had been based on the assumption that American aid would be specifically allocated to supporting an intra-Western European multilateral payments system as a transition to a world-wide system, but because the United States had not been prepared to make such a specific commitment in 1947 and because even had it been the proposals would not have been acceptable to the other members of the CEEC, no progress at all had been made in this direction when the OEEC took up the burden of allocating aid. From that moment the problems of Marshall Aid allocation and of the transition to multilateral trade were inextricably mixed, each in turn complicating the other and serving as a constant forcible reminder that European recovery and reconstruction might not, in fact, be a step towards the successful implementation of the Bretton Woods agreements nor a reinforcement of the first post-war peace settlement.

Yet, for all the political turmoil which they caused, the actual agreements negotiated between Western European countries to facilitate international payments remained before 1950 very cautious in their implications and in their duration. What was talked about was often grand in conception, payments unions, free-trade areas, customs unions and economic unions, replacing the harsh facts of the 1940s with the progressive dreams of the 1850s. What was done, by contrast, remained petty. These grander conceptions were all aimed first and foremost not so much at an economic basis to Western Europe's reconstruction as at a political one. They were dependent, however, on a measure of economic agreement which was not there. The only three countries which had it in their power to produce so grand a reconstruction of the economic basis of Western European life, America, Britain and France, disagreed entirely about which grand solution should be chosen. This was to

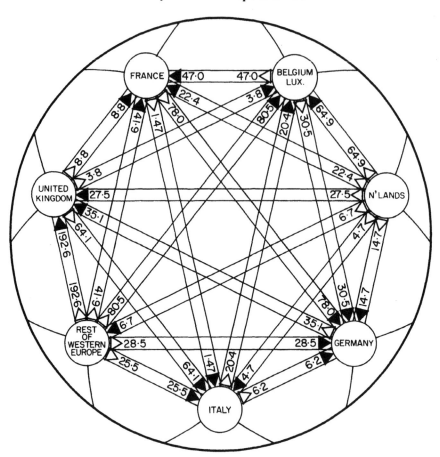

Figure 9   Balances on intra-western European commodity trade, 1947. (Arrows show direction of deficits. Germany = whole Germany except for deficit with the rest of Western Europe where it is West Germany.)

become clear when France responded to the American proposals for the integration of the whole of Western Europe in a liberal framework with proposals for a smaller and much more closely regulated western European customs union.

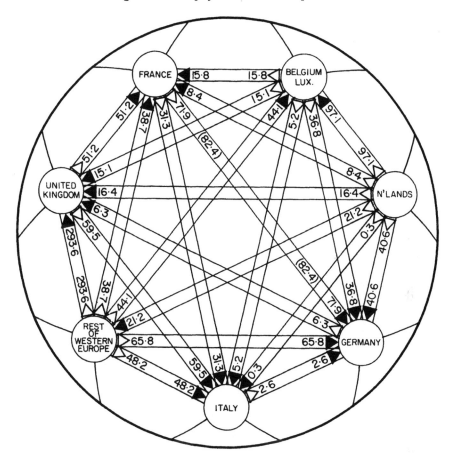

Figure 10   Balances on intra-West European Commodity Trade, 1948. Million US dollars. (Arrows show direction of deficits. The trade between Germany and Belgium–Luxembourg, France, and the rest of Western Europe, respectively, is for 'Western Germany'.)

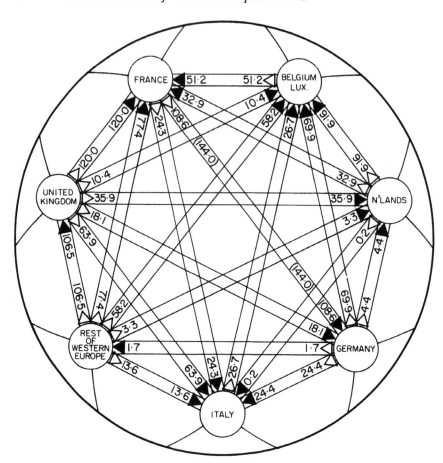

Figure 11   Balances on intra-West European Commodity Trade, 1949. Million US dollars. (Arrows show direction of deficits. The trade between Germany, Belgium–Luxembourg, France, and the rest of Western Europe, respectively, is for 'West Germany'.)

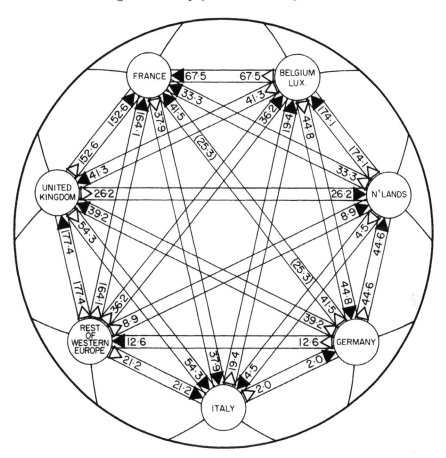

Figure 12   Balances on intra-West European Commodity Trade, 1950. Million US dollars. (Arrows show direction of deficits. The trade between Germany, Belgium–Luxembourg, France, and the rest of Western Europe, respectively, is for 'West Germany'.)

VII

THE ADVENT OF
THE CUSTOMS UNION

The ambitious scope of American plans for a free-trade customs union in western Europe had to be met by a European response of equal scope; dogged opposition to them within the OEEC was not enough. The issue for the European states was whether their response should be made merely for publicity purposes to appease public opinion in America, and where it supported the American initiative in Europe also, or whether there was an alliance of real interests in Europe for some other form of economic integration. A publicity gesture might be made which avoided the German problem by postponing it, but any alliance of real interests would have to meet it head on.

Even before the beginning of the change in the direction of French policy towards Germany in summer 1948 there were political groups in France which openly advocated European unity as a way of avoiding another punitive and failed peace. These, although not strong in 1947, represented a wide spectrum of opinion, many members of the socialist parties, liberal idealists, European federalists, militant anti-communists who now saw the first priority as western European unity against the Soviet Union, and a wide spectrum of those who had, for a variety of reasons, adopted radical views, usually while in the resistance movements, on the necessity for weakening or eliminating the European state system.[1] The idea that the alternative to another and more swingeing Versailles was some form of European integration was thus often voiced in French political life, especially by socialists, even though it had had no impact on official policy by summer 1947. The image of European unity as the guarantee of an entirely new and peaceful European order had an

[1] W. Lipgens, 'Innerfranzösische Kritik der Aussenpolitik de Gaulles, 1944–1946', *Vierteljahrshefte für Zeitgeschichte*, 4, 1976; id. (ed.) *Europa-Föderationspläne der Widerstandsbewegungen 1940–1945: eine Dokumentation* (Schriften des Forschungsinstituts der Deutsche Gesellschaft für Auswärtige Politik, Bd. 26, Munich, 1968). W. Loth, *Sozialismus und Internationalismus. Die französischen Sozialisten und die Nachkriegsordnung Europas 1940–1950* (Stuttgart, 1977).

understandable appeal in the post-war world and when presented, as it was by American policy-makers, not simply as a noble cause but as the best possible economic way forward into prosperity, its appeal was considerably strengthened. Yet, viewed in a more sceptical light, no country's welfare was more threatened by such proposals than France. Even setting aside the profound gulf between France's political intentions in Germany and those of America and Britain, a customs union or some other form of free-trade association between the Western European states as a response to the ERP would mean abandoning the possibility of implementing the Monnet Plan before it had begun to establish even the bases of future French economic welfare and security. But as soon as Marshall had spoken the chances of success for France's German policies had obviously diminished and the British-American proposals to increase the permissible levels of industry there, which France discovered just before the opening of the CEEC, emphasized this. A fall-back position was essential for France in case the French plans to deal with Germany were entirely disregarded. It was clearly necessary to explore other possibilities of action, even if only as a second best solution.

Three weeks after the start of the CEEC Alphand gave a private luncheon to the Benelux delegation and proposed that Benelux should form within the next five to seven years a customs union with France and Italy.[2] The British delegation had been forewarned of this move, but in their first judgement Alphand's proposals were only a gesture in public relations, motivated by a desire to stand well with the Americans so as to get more aid, rather than having any more serious European intention.[3] This was to prove a misjudgement.

The proposals were not in fact the first moves in the direction of a customs union. There had already been some more tentative discussions between France and Italy. The invitation had apparently come from Italy as an attempt to return to the comity of respectable European nations. Both the Prime Minister, Alcide de Gasperi, and his Foreign Minister, Carlo Sforza, were advocates of some form of European unity and if the first step to this could be a French alliance this would mean considerably greater support for Italy in the continuing wrangles over her north-eastern frontier and her colonies. At no time, however, did France have any serious interest in a customs union with Italy alone and the long negotiations over that issue were essentially for the purpose of keeping alive the much more promising idea of a customs union with Benelux and Italy together.

The original scepticism of the British is not surprising. To seek to contain Germany by a customs union appeared to be a reversal of French policy in the pre-war years. Both Aristide Briand's proposal for a united Europe and the Tardieu plan had been based on the mutual extension of preference schemes or

[2] FO 371/62522, UK delegation to London, 2 August 1947.
[3] ibid., 4 August 1947.

most-favoured-nation clauses envisaging not only a much larger European association in which Germany would be contained but also one which would be much less closely knit.[4]

The French proposals clearly envisaged a Germany of some form or other being included in the union, otherwise the union would be meaningless because the Ruhr would remain under British control. But on the evidence of autumn 1947 the customs union might well have been thought of as having to cope only with a severely truncated German economy, minus the Saarland, parts of the Rhineland, west and east Prussia, and Silesia, with the Ruhr area under some form of common international control, and with no central political organization. It was in that sense that the French proposals were a reaction to American policy, not an attempt to curry favour but to erect an extra defence against it.

The Benelux delegates made no immediate reaction to the French proposals other than to indicate that for them the recovery of Germany was a prerequisite for the sustained recovery of their own economies and that any such union must therefore hold the possibility that western Germany should be able to join. In addition they suggested Switzerland also be invited. Hirschfeld himself felt that this might be the historic moment to embark on such a course but the difficulties seemed overwhelming. Could Germany be brought into the scheme without a major crisis in Europe? Would a recreated Germany accept no tariffs after their earlier importance in German history? Were not the French tariff proposals at the Geneva trade conference themselves higher than previous high French tariffs? Above all, would Britain join?[5]

Hirschfeld's instructions were to go no further and no faster than the United Kingdom in the customs union discussions.[6] It was of no interest to Benelux to join a French-dominated customs union, although for Belgium alone the case might well have been different. For the Netherlands either Britain had to be a participant, or that as yet unborn political entity, West Germany. They were its two most important trading partners and no customs union which did not enable the Netherlands to take at least the same share of the trade of Britain and Germany it had had in the 1930s offered a very enticing prospect.

The Italian government took the opportunity to issue a general statement to the Executive Committee of the CEEC in favour of a regional customs union as a first step towards a larger European union.

We would conclude that customs unions are the most generally accepted form for and the one which best meets with the project for a better

---

[4] J. Bariéty, 'Der Tardieu-Plan zur Sanierung des Donauraums (Februar-Mai 1932)', in J. Becker and K. Hildebrand (eds) *Internationale Beziehungen in der Weltwirtschaftskrise 1929–1933* (Munich, 1980).
[5] MBZ, 610.32, Netherlands delegation to The Hague, 3 August 1947.
[6] FO 371/62552, UK delegation to London, 11 August 1947.

international organization of trade. Can we prepare to finalize an agreement which unites in one single customs area the countries subscribing to the Marshall Plan?[7]

This was followed by a further declaration in the same tone on 18 August 1947.[8] Such rhetoric entirely glossed over the fact that earlier customs unions in Europe had had only a small impact on international trade and that in any case the more important obstacle to the flow of international trade in Western Europe was not tariffs but the proliferation of non-tariff barriers to trade. The French initiative and the Dutch and Italian responses nevertheless demanded an immediate appraisal of British policy.

BRITAIN AND THE CUSTOMS UNION

There had been a certain amount of talk about the possibility of some form of common Franco-British economic co-ordination since 1945 and this had even led to a request by Bevin, not handled seriously, for a study of the economic implications of a Franco-British customs union. None of this had been treated as of any practical importance in London outside the immediate circle of Bevin and his advisers.[9] It was thought to arise out of Bevin's anxieties about the future defence of the United Kingdom in Europe, and also to be an echo of the fact that on the eve of the French surrender in 1940 the British government had itself proposed a Franco-British union to prevent the surrender. The dominant assumption in London was that as both nation states settled into a post-war world from which the German menace had been removed such complications would not be necessary. Both states would become stabilized and able to solve most problems in Europe by nothing more complicated than occasional collaboration.

The French initiative in the CEEC focused the debate on a real choice of economic policy rather than an abstract theoretical position. At the highest levels in the Foreign Office opinion swayed against any British participation in such a customs union and in the economic ministries it was very firmly negative. Under the pressure of Soviet reaction to Marshall Aid and of his close advisers, Bevin, however, came briefly to see a European customs union as not merely a desirable but a necessary basis for the western European defensive alliance which had assumed such high priority in his policy. Between August 1947 and February 1948 he gradually shifted his position from the stern opposition to any closer European association which he had manifested so

---

[7] OECD, CCEE/26, Déclaration du délégué italien faite au Comité Exécutif, 5 August 1947.

[8] MBZ, 610.32, Déclaration du délégué italien au Comité de Coopération Economique Européenne, 18 August 1947.

[9] Monnet, however, told the French President in March 1947 that he would soon produce a Franco-British federation 'with a federal authority and the partial abandonment of sovereignty which would be completely independent of the USSR and the USA'. V. Auriol, *Journal du septennat 1947–54*, vol. 1, 1947 (Paris, 1970), p. 145.

vigorously to Clayton to ardent advocacy of a European customs union as the basis for a military alliance and a step towards his greater vision of a trans-atlantic western union. The opposition of the economic ministers in the cabinet remained implacable. There thus opened up a fundamental divide between the apparent political advantages to Britain of membership of a western European customs union and the apparent economic disadvantages, a divide which was to dominate the formulation of British policy towards the common market for the next thirty years and which perhaps still dominates it.

Eventually, in April 1948, Bevin let the matter drop. The opposition in cabinet was too great and in any case the defensive and cultural union which was his prime interest became associated with the Brussels Pact and NATO and also developed with reassuring speed. The British decision not to partici-pate in a European customs union was effectively made in April 1948, although it was not officially made clear to Britain's allies, nor even formulated as official policy for more than another year. In retrospect questions about the wisdom of this decision cannot be avoided. Our main interest in it here is in its impact on European reconstruction, but it was a moment at which the first decision on an issue in Britain's post-war history which has not ceased to be discussed since was taken, and for that reason too the way the decision was taken merits exploration.

It was the almost unanimous opinion of civil servants, as well as of the few academic economists who were consulted, that customs unions automatically led to much closer forms of political union as well as to the harmonization of economic policy. The historian may well take a more cautious line here. The history of the Zollverein, as of the Dual Monarchy, shows that customs unions may very well survive for long periods of time while their constituent parts retain certain quite different internal economic policies and a wide range of political powers. Nor does it show that these differences are necessarily eroded over the duration of time; whether they are or not depends on the nature of continuing political choices. Once the nature of the customs union and the political powers with which it has been endowed are defined, historical example suggests there is not necessarily any inherent irresistible dynamic for further development along these lines. The recent history of the EEC has been a severe disappointment to liberal federalists just for that reason. None the less the conviction that membership in a European customs union would be an irreversible political step, irreversible, at any rate, except by a dangerous and certainly final act of policy and thus by a political decision as far-reaching as any in the history of the country, was almost universal. In those circum-stances the attraction of the existing economic state of affairs was naturally strong. The United Kingdom's almost great power status, the Commonwealth, the Empire, the sterling area and, not least, the greater apparent possibilities for increasing trade and exports which all these represented – and thus the long-run continuation of existing expensive domestic economic policies and even perhaps of eventual independence of political and economic action from the United States – did not then seem to the British as fragile as they now seem in retrospect.

The London Committee had been well aware that the CEEC might bring with it the need to take a stand on the question of a European customs union and it had appointed a sub-committee to determine the line to be taken in Paris should the issue arise. The sub-committee received negative advice from the Board of Trade and the Treasury. It is important, however, to distinguish between the negative opinions on the customs union of these two ministries.

In the Board of Trade's attitude there was no real merit or intelligence. It was devoid of the most rudimentary elements of proper economic analysis and amounted to no more than a statement of outright and unthinking protectionism.

> It would mean (as would *ex hypothesi* be its intention) the decline of industry here in favour of its competitors elsewhere with all the attendant dislocation. All the difficulties in fact, but on a larger and wider scale, that our own development area policy is aimed at minimising. This seems politically unthinkable in a European world in which all Governments are increasingly feeling their way to methods of planning aimed at mitigating the effect on their citizens of the more extreme rigours of the free interplay of economic forces.[10]

Even as this opinion was being formulated the government in France must have been moving towards a consideration of how French plans for the future, much more comprehensive than anything in Britain, could be integrated into a European tariff union. Underlying the Board of Trade's attitude was not merely the successful experience of wartime planning and controls in Britain but a deep-seated fear that important sectors of British capital goods production, particularly steel and chemicals, would need permanent protection once the limits on the volume of German industrial production were removed, together with a total unwillingness to consider how this could be put to rights.

The Treasury's objections, on the other hand, were not so much based on considerations of domestic policy. The central consideration was that British reserves were also the sterling area reserves. Anything which might endanger the size of these reserves would endanger British recovery and world recovery, the more so as extra-European trade was more important than intra-European trade to that recovery. Deeper than that lay the suspicion that one aspect of United States policy was an attack on the position of the City of London and an attempt, not just to gain access for United States exports on easier terms to markets where British goods had formerly dominated, but also to secure much of London's international business in invisibles for New York. The clash of policy over the post-war existence of the sterling area and its common

[10] FO 371/62552, BOT note, 'Customs union for western Europe', 30 June 1947.

pool of dollar reserves had left bitter memories from 1944/5 and, for the Treasury, British membership in a European association turned first and foremost on the question of how well those sterling area reserves would be safeguarded. From their standpoint the sterling area was an expansionary force in world trade and a way of overcoming the international structural disequilibria. It offered the possibility of multilateral settlements to a group of nations representing a significant part of total world trade.[11] British imports in 1947 were by themselves almost the equivalent of United States imports. What was more, most British purchases of primary goods were carried out through bulk purchasing agreements over several years and Britain thus offered what underdeveloped primary exporters most required, guaranteed longer-term markets. By contrast private trade in the United States offered no such guarantees.[12] From the standpoint of the United States, however, the sterling area was the big obstacle in the way of European integration. It encouraged the flow of trade of Europe's largest international trader away from the continent itself. It was, furthermore, associated with the structure of British imperial preferences, which were seen both as a fundamental barrier to American trade and, by 1947, as a fundamental barrier to Britain's taking the lead in producing an economically integrated Europe.

In London the sterling area seemed an indispensable foundation stone of Britain's post-war edifice. It would have been strange had it been otherwise, for as the world shortage of dollars squeezed ever tighter on expanding international trade the idea was inescapable that Britain had an important advantage in being part of a large multilateral trading area, which facilitated access to a variety of foodstuff and raw material imports not needing to be purchased in dollars. The economic interest of the Labour government in the Empire and Commonwealth was fired by the possibility which the sterling area seemed to offer of economic independence from the United States. In the post-war world its possible advantages seemed even greater than in the 1930s because of the disappearance of European food surpluses and because of the alleged structural alterations in the pattern of world trade.

What the Treasury most wanted from Western Europe was a stable pattern of trade and exchanges. Once this arrived it was assumed that it would be eventually followed by a return to the convertibility of Western European currencies. This once attained, there might be a general lowering or perhaps even removal of intra-western European tariffs. For the Treasury, therefore, a European customs union in 1947 was at best irrelevant, at worst a threat to the

[11] There are two accounts of the pattern of sterling area trade and settlements: P.W. Bell, *The Sterling Area in the Post-War World* (Oxford, 1956) and USA, ECA, *The Sterling Area, An American Analysis* (London, 1951).

[12] These guarantees were the better in as much as primary exporters probably had more confidence in the British government's expressed intention to maintain full employment than in that of the American government. The American downturn in 1948 saw both a steep increase in unemployment and a sharp reduction in primary imports.

British position, and almost certainly unworkable. In the longer run, however, once the sterling area was safe from American diplomatic pressures, it might prove a logical step linked to a similar process beyond the boundaries of Europe itself.[13]

The advice which the London Committee received from its special sub-committee on the question reflected these opinions. 'We see', the sub-committee wrote, 'many and insuperable objections to any proposals for a customs union of which the United Kingdom would be a member.'[14] The chief of these were, that unless the Commonwealth were a member the whole structure of British–Commonwealth trade would be destroyed, that British trade might decline, that insufficient political thought had been given to the question, that it would mean the harmonization of British economic policies with those of Western Europe, and that it would create strategic problems. The sub-committee's advice, which was in essence the brief for the British negotiators at Paris and, later, Brussels, was 'We conclude, therefore, it is not in our interest to encourage the idea of a European Customs Union of which the United Kingdom would be a member, and that in any case a general Western European Customs Union is out of the question as a matter of practical politics.'[15]

Only six days after this opinion had been minuted Alphand proposed to the Executive Committee of the CEEC that discussions should now begin among the members on the formation of a customs union. The deputy leader of the British delegation, Hall-Patch, was, although he had the opposite reputation amongst the Americans, sympathetic to the idea of British membership in such a customs union. 'There is', he wrote to Bevin, 'a well-established prejudice in Whitehall against a European Customs Union. It goes back a long way and is rooted in the old days of free trade. It is a relic of a world which has disappeared probably never to return.'[16] In Hall-Patch's view, with which it is difficult to quarrel, the Board of Trade had developed a technique for blocking all rational discussion by stating the choice as though it were between two opposites and that a European customs union would have to mean the dissolution of *all* imperial trading arrangements. Bevin should, he suggested, initiate a more thorough enquiry into how far this was so and he concluded with a direct personal appeal to his minister.

> Now, as a result of the Marshall proposals, European imaginations have been fired. The financial position of Europe is so desperate that there is a chance, which may never recur, to break down the barriers which are hampering a trade revival in Europe. It may even be possible to go some way towards the integration of the European economy comparable to the

[13] Treasury opinion is summed up in the replies to the request from the Foreign Office for guidance on advice to ministers in T 236/808, London Committee, Sub-Committee on Integration of Europe, 1947.　　　　　　　　　[14] ibid., 23 July 1947.　　　[15] ibid.
[16] FO 371/62552, Hall-Patch to Bevin, 7 August 1947.

vast industrial integration of the United States which Soviet Russia is busy trying to emulate. If some such integration does not take place Europe will gradually decline in the face of pressure from the United States on the one hand and Soviet Russia on the other. The possibilities of European integration were revealed by what Hitler was able to do in four short years for his own nefarious purposes. If we can achieve for peaceful purposes what he attempted to do, with some success, for warlike purposes, we may set in motion an economic renaissance in Europe which will go far to solve our own difficulties. The stakes are high and the problems to be solved are enormous, but if there is one chance in a hundred of doing something effective we should not let the chance go by.[17]

This minute was followed by an urgent visit from Franks to London to seek more exact instructions in the new circumstances. Franks listed to the London Committee the various possibilities of action which he thought might satisfy the United States and suggested that a customs union was not necessarily the worst option in so far as Britain, by joining now, might be able to retain empire trade preferences, even though this would be against American wishes. He got short shrift. The Board of Trade's chief representative insisted that the necessary conditions for a customs union were political and economic stability, stable exchange rates, and a large measure of agreement on economic and political questions. 'The lack of these conditions made a European customs union in the foreseeable future quite impracticable.'[18] If this totally depressing view of Europe's future was not exactly in accord with the fears on which the argument for protection was based, the contradiction was made more apparent by the Bank of England's revelation in the same meeting that yet another large British industry would be threatened by such proposals. The textile industry would not be able to compete against revived Italian production. Ministers decided that Britain should participate in the talks but avoid any commitment.[19]

Accordingly the British delegation proposed the formation of a European Customs Union Study Group which would meet in Brussels away from the American influence in Paris and have an independent life of its own. The French were reluctant to accept this procedure. Monnet, who took part in this discussion, insisted that it would not satisfy the United States.[20] The British government sought to reassure itself in Washington that State Department opinion was divided and that not all Clayton's colleagues believed in the practicability of an immediate customs union as he did.[21] Ambassador Douglas gave his opinion that both Britain and western Germany should be members of the proposed customs union and thus make it acceptable to the other members.[22] Eventually the British decided to place their proposal for a

[17] ibid.   [18] FO 371/62565, Minutes of the London Committee, 9 August 1947.
[19] FO 371/62552, Minutes of ministerial decision on 8 August 1947 on UE 7194/5132/53.
[20] ibid., UK delegation to London, 10 August 1947.
[21] ibid., UK delegation to London, 15 August 1947.
[22] ibid., Record of conversation with Douglas by Makins, 15 August 1947.

separate European Customs Union Study Group before the full conference and it was discussed in plenary session of the CEEC on 23 August. Norway had already indicated its opposition.[23] At the plenary session of the CEEC the Norwegian delegates, supported by Sweden, maintained that extra-European trade was as important for recovery as increasing intra-European trade and that any discussion of a customs union fell outside the scope of the conference and should be conducted only within the framework of the United Nations Economic Commission for Europe, which was a less politically divisive organization. The Swiss were clearly not carried away with enthusiasm either and their delegation spoke guardedly only in favour of 'freeing intra-European trade'.[24] The consequence of this lack of unity was that the invitations to the Study Group were not confined to the CEEC participants but went also to all who had received the invitation to the original conference, including Byelorussia. This was intended to strengthen the Study Group's position by giving it an apparent independence from the more direct American pressures, although in the event the only outsiders to attend were certain 'observers' from Commonwealth countries.

In the previous summer Bevin had asked for an exploration of the economic possibilities of a Franco-British customs union which other countries might eventually join, but the Board of Trade had not properly responded to the request. In January 1947 the cabinet had decided to review the whole range of policy options in case the proposals for an international trade organization (ITO) eventually miscarried. As a result of this a brief report under very circumscribed terms had been commissioned from a small group of economists under Sir Denis Robertson. It was completed at the end of August. Its conclusions were that if an ITO did fail there would be better means of achieving such measures of economic integration with Europe as the United Kingdom might desire than a full customs union. If an ITO succeeded these means would not be permitted, whereas a customs union might, and within that proviso the report was not unenthusiastic about the possible gains from a European customs union. A smaller western European customs union without Britain, it concluded, would be harmful to British interests. The report encouraged the idea that the United Kingdom had, however, more to gain economically from a customs union with less-developed economies. The Board of Trade was able fairly to draw from it the conclusion that, 'a Customs Union consisting of a number of primary producing countries with a wide diversity of unexploited resources would be likely to be to the advantage of the United Kingdom; likewise a Customs Union consisting of countries whose industries were primitive compared with those of the United Kingdom.'[25]

[23] UD, 44.2/26 IV, Oversikt over arbeidet pr. 11 August 1947, 12 August 1947.
[24] FO 371/62550, UK delegation to London, 23 August 1947.
[25] FO 371/62554, BOT Memorandum, 'A European customs union or unions', 10 October 1947.

This was taken as confirmation that there was little point in a customs union with continental western Europe unless the western European countries were to threaten to form a union from which Britain would be excluded, but also as an incitement to pursue an entirely different strategy, to try to turn imperial preferences and the sterling area into a more systematic and formalized trade association. Any hint of this kind to the Labour cabinet was likely to be seized on avidly. Independence of economic action from the United States and safety from American international economic policy for their own domestic experiment could go with taking up the white man's burden in a nobler way than in the past. That this might be anachronistic was not likely to be noticed by many in the cabinet or party. On 3 September 1947 Bevin addressed the Trades Union Congress at Southport and in vague terms advocated a customs union which could embrace the Empire and perhaps other states.

His motives were made clearer in a personal letter to Attlee two days later. He wished to re-establish Britain's position in the world, he wrote, and to free it from financial dependence on the United States. One way to do this was, he suggested, to draw on the raw material resources of the Commonwealth and Empire, either through a customs union or a Commonwealth economic council. It might seem that such a letter would indicate that the die was cast against the increasing arguments from the Foreign Office, but this was not so. What Bevin was moving towards was an association of western European states with all their empires and overseas territories and the reason was made clear at the end of the letter.

> I fear, however, we shall not achieve this purpose solely by selling manufactured goods to a world which is becoming increasingly industrialised and that multilateral trade may not suffice. It may come too late or not be wide enough to help us. We must have something in the way of raw materials as well as manufactured goods with which to buy our own food and other requirements in other countries.[26]

In short, a customs union in which Britain and other European countries retained imperial preferences would admirably serve Britain's diplomatic aims, providing both security and independence from the United States.

Nowhere in the opinion which had come from the economic ministries was there any hint that there might be advantages to be won from concentrating a greater proportion of foreign trade on the developed economies. Long-run studies of the pattern of foreign trade show that one tendency of the foreign trade of developed economies is that an increasing proportion of their exports flows to other developed economies. One measure in the post-war world of the competitiveness of developed economies has been the relative rate of increase of the proportion of their manufactured exports which goes to such markets and, conversely, it might be suspected that a tendency for manufactured

[26] FO 371/62554, Bevin to Attlee, 5 September 1947.

exports to be concentrated on less competitive, protected, colonial markets does not augur well for the future. Even seen strictly from the contemporary viewpoint of the British government, the financial and economic problems of the United Kingdom were only to be solved by a long-sustained increase in exports. There was a rapid growth in extra-European exports in the immediate aftermath of the Second World War and, what is more, given the payments and exchange problems which prevailed in Europe, the mechanisms of exporting within the sterling area were easier than those of exporting to Europe. But it is not easy to envisage how the growth of Dominion and colonial imports from Britain could by themselves have satisfied quickly enough the target for export growth provisionally set in 1944, whatever the importance of the supply of primary imports obtained from the same source, to say nothing of the composition of exports to sterling area markets.

Be that as it may, the cabinet decided on 25 September 1947 to set up an inter-departmental committee to consider the feasibility of a customs union with the colonies or even with the Commonwealth.[27] In the cabinet discussions Cripps insisted that such a study should get first priority over any study of a European customs union. Both the Minister of State for Commonwealth Relations, Arthur Henderson, and the Parliamentary Under-Secretary for the Colonies, Ivor Thomas, brought in for the occasion, pointed out that neither Dominions nor colonies were likely to be too interested in these proposals and the whole cabinet appears to have agreed that the idea was unlikely to be a realizable one.[28]

The same issues were considered by the Economic Policy Committee of the cabinet, essentially the cabinet without its less important members, on 7 November. Bevin laid out the Foreign Office viewpoint and indicated that the policy of opposing a European customs union was disappointing to them. He gave his opinion that it was 'essential that Western Europe should attain some measure of economic unity if it was to maintain its independence as against Russia and the United States'.[29] The tenor of the ensuing discussion was that multilateralism in the framework of an ITO was better than any more restrictive solutions and that, if anything was envisaged in the form of special imperial economic links, it would be wiser to keep any efforts in this direction secret from the United States. Bevin's desire for some form of western European association met with no sympathy at all from the heads of the economic ministries. Harold Wilson, President of the Board of Trade, thought that the British delegation in Paris should try to divert discussion away from the concept of a customs union and Cripps actually argued that 'as far as it concerned the United Kingdom, the first stage should be the creation of a Customs Union with the colonial Empire'.[30]

[27] FO 371/62554, Memorandum of cabinet discussions, 25 September 1947.
[28] CAB 129 10 77 (47), 25 September 1947.
[29] FO 371/62740, Meeting of the cabinet Economic Policy Committee, 7 November 1947.
[30] ibid.

It is hard to see how any Commonwealth or Empire country would have welcomed such a policy and this was the conclusion already emerging from the inter-departmental committee which had been set up. Not only did most such countries want higher levels of protection for their manufacturing sectors but their primary exports already usually entered Britain duty-free under imperial preference schemes. If an ITO were to succeed these preferences would have to be renounced but the United States would probably oppose an imperial customs union as old preferences writ large. 'Balancing the considerations set out above', the committee concluded, 'we feel bound to conclude that a Commonwealth Union, while probably desirable in itself, is unlikely to be realisable under existing conditions.'[31]

There was nothing to suggest, however, that, if the ITO never came into existence, the United Kingdom would have to renounce all imperial preferences in opting for a European union. The threat to imperial preferences came not from the CEEC but from the Geneva trade negotiations. The situation in autumn 1947 was that most French colonies received tariff preferences from France, although for some this did not apply to all goods. Their own tariff policy towards French goods varied through almost every possibility. Portugal had lower duties on all colonial imports and received the same preferences in return virtually throughout its empire. Belgium was still a duty-free market for its colonies; the Netherlands imposed tariffs against colonial imports. The future Benelux tariffs were to be a compromise between their two positions.

The only way in which the tariff adjustments to make a closer economic association with Western Europe possible could be discussed in time with all Commonwealth and Empire countries was at the continuation of the international trade talks in Havana in November. The only country not to indicate unease there when the discussions took place was Canada. Otherwise 'suspicion was the keynote of a very lukewarm meeting'.[32] The British government was unable, of course, to give the slightest indication of what degree of Empire preference might still be retained in a European customs union. The French were anxious to acquire British support to amend the proposed ITO charter at the last moment in order to keep the door open for preference schemes which would be part of a European customs union. Their attitude was that 'the Americans would find it easy to fall in with an extension of preferences in the sacred cause of forming a Customs Union'.[33] When these discussions were also taken up informally at Havana the French 'appeared to take it for granted that, if the United Kingdom entered a Western European Customs Union, it would be a *sine qua non* that the Imperial preference system should be continued in one form or another'.[34]

[31] FO 371/62723, UK Study Group on Customs Unions, 3 November 1947.
[32] FO 371/62754, Havana delegation to London, 29 November 1947.
[33] ibid., Stevens to Marton, 6 December 1947.
[34] ibid., Havana delegation to London, 14 December 1947.

In spite of the perfect willingness of France to support Britain in maintaining Empire trade preferences, no matter what undertaking both countries had given to end 'trade discrimination' in their respective financial negotiations with America, such a policy had no real future. It is mainly interesting for the light which it sheds on the intellectual heritage of the British Labour Party. But Bevin was reluctant to abandon the idea of a European customs union linked to imperial preferences as a way to independence from the United States. At the latest, by February 1948 he had fully espoused the cause of Western European customs union. On 22 January 1948 he spoke on the subject in the House of Commons. On 28 January it was decided to draw up a Foreign Office paper 'forcefully stating the political and strategic arguments for a Western European Customs Union.'[35] The paper seems to have been drawn up by Roger Stevens, one of the Foreign Office supporters of a customs union.[36]

Strategic safety depended, it was argued, on a closer Western European association. It was essential to aim at building a powerful association of democratic states linked by traditional affinities and by a common determination to resist any attempt on their independence. The purpose of this association was to halt and possibly even turn back 'the flow of the Communist tide'. But by itself such an association, he argued, would be ineffective unless the economic situation of all countries involved, including the United Kingdom, improved. This depended on establishing secure sources of raw material supply and on a harmonious development of all the Western European economies on that basis.

> In western Europe itself we cannot hope to find any substantial alleviation of our food import problem. On the other hand, the Colonial resources of the United Kingdom, France, Belgium, Holland, and Portugal, can in time be mobilized so as to constitute a valuable addition to our sources of supply. In the industrial field, moreover, we cannot afford to contemplate unregulated growth, if for no other reason than our concern for the future of the German economy. ... In my view, our best hope of securing the political future of western Europe – above all of France and Germany – better even than through treaties and mutual defence arrangements is to help to construct so closely woven an economic pattern that the constituent elements in it simply cannot afford to fall apart.[37]

But what sort of arrangements would best achieve this end? He reviewed all existing arrangements and rejected them as insufficient. The 'European organization' was the best of them but, it was claimed, it could well break apart as soon as 'the lure of the American dollar has ceased to exercise its spell'.[38] An extension of imperial preferences and a Western European customs union were the only satisfactory alternatives. The first by itself would be only a

[35] FO 371/71766, Minute by R.B. Stevens, 11 February 1948.
[36] ibid., Note filed 24 February 1948.   [37] ibid.   [38] ibid.

half-way house, apart from being a breach of the ITO. There were certainly difficulties in the way of the second. But its advantages outweighed them. No other solution would contribute the same political and economic strengthening of western Europe, none had the same permanence, none would produce the same measure of economic integration, even union. Such a customs union would allow medium-term planning, it would have a favourable effect on the United States, it would prevent the formation of regional unions which might not be based on a genuine reduction of trade barriers such as the French proposals and, above all, it would establish the United Kingdom once more as the leader in Europe. He concluded,

> I propose, therefore, that the United Kingdom should take the lead in promoting and inspiring a European Customs Union on the broadest possible basis. Such a Union should comprise at least the United Kingdom, France, Benelux, West Germany and Italy; the addition of Scandinavia, Switzerland, Portugal and perhaps later Spain would be desirable but may be impracticable.[39]

When the formation of the European Customs Union Study Group was determined in September 1947 the attitude of the British delegation under the influence of this debate was not at all negative. Roger Stevens, who was to be the chief of the British representation there, was a supporter of British participation in a European customs union, and it was Hall-Patch who had to deal with the affairs of the study group on behalf of the 'European organ-ization'. The British attitude, irrespective of their judgment of France's intentions, was not to regard the whole affair as just an exercise in window-dressing for the Congress of the United States. Thirteen European countries participated, including Iceland. Norway and Sweden joined only at a later date and Switzerland was present only as an observer.

The Swiss Federal Council's policy appears to have been to change the terms of reference of the study group so that it should also consider all other ways to increase the level of intra-European trade. The hope was that in this way it would be diverted towards what might be the more immediately attainable goal of a more flexible payments system and thus not force Switzer-land to choose between neutrality and a customs union. Furthermore, Switzerland's position as a hard currency creditor meant that its immediate problem, like that of Belgium, was to fund its own exports. There began in Switzerland an internal debate on this question whose outcome was not to be known until October.

On 7 October the Federal Counsellor for Foreign Affairs issued a long statement reflecting the Swiss dilemma. Switzerland did not dare not to take part in the study group because it could not risk economic isolation but

[39] ibid.

it would be to give ourselves up to dangerous illusions to imagine that the creation of a customs union would bring health in Europe. To wish to make an economic unity of Europe in the shape of a customs union would contribute nothing to its economic reconstruction. It would only be a centralization, a sort of levelling downwards, whose drawbacks would quickly show themselves to be greater than its benefits. From the economic viewpoint as well Europe's strength lies in its diversity. It is necessary to try to harmonize the national economies, not to unify them.[40]

Even in Scandinavia the tone was more moderate than that, and although neither Norway nor Sweden participated at the start the Scandinavian countries were in fact busy with their own customs union discussions. In September a French delegation went to Rome to take part in official discussions on the Franco-Italian customs union and when the Customs Union Study Group held its first meeting in Brussels on 10 November 1947 the other delegations were surprised to be encouraged by the British to take up a thorough study of the way in which the national European tariff rates might be harmonized into a common external Western European tariff.

This was a tactic which admirably suited the British position; it kept open the possibility of British participation while obviating the need for any rapid decisions. On the other hand it immediately raised inside the Customs Union Study Group the question of the internal regulation of the common market. The British position was that the study group should study the potential effects of a low external tariff and what the British delegation called a 'pure' customs union, a union without any internal taxes on trade or factor movements. This was also what the Benelux countries wanted the study group to pursue. The French, by contrast, wanted to see an external tariff sufficiently protective to prevent too rapid a shift in existing shares within the market. They also wanted the study group to consider the impact of fiscal policies within the union so that such policies could be used to control the structural adjustments which, they argued, would be necessary.

In spite of these contradictions in its early work the study group advanced more purposefully than had been expected because, on the British side, Bevin's pressure on the Foreign Office caused the delegation to push the other delegations, to their surprise, towards an analysis of the effects of complete tariff removal. The indecision in British policy, the fact that remarkable changes from the British position in the 1930s were at least being considered in London, had in turn an encouraging effect on the other members who had expected an entirely negative British attitude. But there was nothing Bevin could do against the weight of opposition in the cabinet nor against the steadfast conviction, which he himself seems to have shared, that the Western

---

[40] Département Politique Fédéral, Information et Presse, Exposé de M. le Conseiller Petitpierre sur l'attitude de la Suisse vis-à-vis du plan Marshall, 7 October 1947.

European countries themselves would never seriously contemplate so bold a step as to form a customs union without Britain. That, it was thought, was the only danger to Britain in deciding against participation and it was a danger which was unreal.[41] The dangers of participation were not only seen as real but were also greatly exaggerated.

Cabinet and economic ministries thus remained unmoved and by April 1948 Bevin had turned his attention to the more realizable aspects of the Brussels Pact, with its associated cultural and economic links, and to the vague and large dream of western union, which few of his civil servants could understand. His interest in a European customs union as an economic arrangement had always been low. The economic arrangements were only intended to stop the strategic alliance falling apart and he was much happier with and more interested in the idea that a common cultural and spiritual heritage could be expressed in a set of common defence and cultural organizations which would serve the same strategic purpose as a common market. This idea also pleased him more because it implied an alliance bridging the Atlantic. The Customs Union Study Group was left floundering and neglected behind these major issues of the global defence and cultural affinity of the western world. The British government did not, however, properly define its official policy on a European customs union, even to itself, until early in 1949 and the British delegates in Brussels pursued the technicalities of tariff discussions without indicating that the issue, for them, was now a dead one.

There is certainly much to support and little to contradict the argument that membership in a European customs union had nothing immediately to offer to the process of economic reconstruction in Britain. But why should British policy have been formulated on such short-term considerations? The longest period of future time the Treasury envisaged during the whole process of decision-making was four years and its image of what it expected to find on that horizon was extraordinarily wishful, a mirage made of optimism and complacency. The common critique of bureaucratic policy-making, that it is never based on principles of long-term action but only responds erratically to immediate contingencies, applies with force to the way the decision on so important an issue was made, a decision which in fact the United Kingdom has since been obliged unceasingly to discuss and reconsider from all angles and which even gave rise to that extraordinary event for British democracy, a national referendum. The long-term conceptions and plans of politicians may

[41] In March 1948 A.D. Marris, a member of the British delegation to the CEEC gave a fair summary of the official Treasury position in a public lecture at the Royal Institute of International Affairs. 'At present, as I see it, none of the governments or peoples of Western Europe is prepared to face the economic, financial and social consequences of any real measure of integration. ... Yet if the United Kingdom does not lead the movement, it will not occur. For no other country in Europe has the moral authority, and the organizing capacity to bring it about.' A.D. Marris, *Prospects for Closer European Economic Integration* (London, 1948). That was the way the government and most of his colleagues in other ministries saw it too.

have been on the whole founded on dreams, ignorance and prejudice, but it was surely no help that important ministries should have countered this by narrowing the focus of decision down to the immediate present. What was at stake was the long-run future of a country and a continent.

That long-term future was analysed only in the generalities of rhetoric, supposition and opinion. The comprehensive, detailed, factual information and estimates on which such a decision should have been based were confined to questions of the present. What it might mean for the British economy in ten or fifteen years' time to join or not to join a European customs union was set out for decision-makers in a way so generalized and imprecise as to be derisory. At the highest levels of the three ministries mainly concerned with the decision advice was often formulated in self-indulgent memoranda in an outmoded literary vein in which the subtleties of opinion and the elegance of expression do not hide the almost complete absence of knowledge of the things that needed to be known or the extraordinary prejudices about national character which influenced the generalizations. The records do not permit us to know whether politicians did any better at cabinet level.

That is not to say that the decision was wrong. Whether a western European customs union in which all the colonies of the member states received some form of preference would in fact have been acceptable to American diplomacy in 1948 was never put to the test. But even without those preferences, was the customs union, given the powerful influence which the United Kingdom would have exercised in the negotiations, such a threat to British industry in 1948 as to make it a *dangerous* policy? Surely it was not. The defensive cast of mind in which British policy was formulated is unmistakable, particularly in contrast to the approach of the French government in a much weaker and more dangerous position. It was not just a high level of exports which was indispensable to the success of British economic policy, it was also a question of what kind of exports and that was a question of the direction of exports. Seen in those terms future safety did not lie in the sterling area. Of course, it did not necessarily lie in Western Europe either, but in the next decade high rates of growth of national income in Western European economies were closely correlated with high rates of increase of exports of manufactured goods to those economies, and those manufacturing industries which showed the highest proportion of such exports to total output also tended to show the highest rates of growth of productivity. Should that have been so difficult to forecast in 1948? There were also positive dangers to the maintenance of full employment and the welfare state in eschewing the customs union, as well as in joining it. And history was to show very soon that the assumption that the customs union could not happen without Britain was one which should also have raised many questions about the methods of decision-making.

At the heart of British policy-making was a lack of awareness, firstly, of how far a customs union might have an electoral appeal on the continent as a way of drawing a definitive line under a lamentable period in the history of western Europe and, secondly, and much more importantly, a lack of awareness of how possible the creation of such a union by an act of political will actually was. Of course these criticisms cannot be separated from the failure to foresee the advantages of a western European customs union in a period of sustained growth of output and trade. It was these favourable background economic conditions which would eventually make the European customs union such a success and which would make the British decision look like one which had not taken all factors fully into consideration. Furthermore, it was, in the end, going to be much easier for industrialists and farmers in France, Italy, the Benelux and West Germany to agree on a set of complicated economic deals which made a common external tariff possible if they did not have the British to bother about. After all no one in Britain doubted that the eventual recovery of German industry was certain. If it were to recover it had to do so in some framework of common agreement with French and Belgian interests, a common agreement which might well ignore British producers in order to make the necessary agreement possible.

FRANCE AND THE CUSTOMS UNION

For Benelux the Customs Union Study Group had, as their delegation intimated privately in March 1948, 'a more far-reaching and a longer-term purpose' than the 'European organization'.[42] By summer the nature of the British decision could scarcely have been in doubt in The Hague although in the study group the British delegation persisted with the official line that no final decision had been made and all options were open. When the autumn came the Benelux representatives were privately canvassing the suggestion that they might now be prepared to consider a purely continental customs union. It was more than a year after the creation of the study group that anyone told the selected German politicians in the Bizone *Verwaltungsrat* what was going on. When they were told in October 1948 they were 'barely restrained from making an immediate demand for the adoption of a Customs Union at once'.[43] It was the first premonitory rumble of the *deus ex machina* whose eventual descent would so cruelly expose the mixture of defensive anxiety and complacency which had underlain the British decision.

Until the Netherlands was sure of the British decision the French proposals could go no further with Benelux, nor until the Dutch could get some clearer idea of what was going to emerge in Germany. Italy was not held back by any such considerations and the problem for France was to keep the customs

[42] T 236/780, Meeting of the Preparatory Commission for the Economic Committee of the International Customs Union Study Group, 6 March 1948.
[43] T 236/781, Third Meeting of the Economic Committee of the International Customs Union Study Group, 19/23 October 1948.

union negotiations with Italy going while the idea of 'Greater Benelux' waited on the future. At the same time as the Franco-Italian negotiations continued, the Scandinavian countries, alarmed by the apparent speed with which Western Europe was threatening to become a strategic bloc, met to consider their own attitudes as well as the possibilities for a common Scandinavian economic bloc.

The origins of the Scandinavian talks were the agreement between Norway and Sweden in August 1947 that both the CEEC and the customs union proposals were threats to the United Nations framework of security which they themselves preferred to support. Both agreed that the question of a possible European customs union should only be discussed within the already existing United Nations international organs.[44] The Danes objected that this would put Scandinavia in the position of having to carry the burden of American disapproval for the failure of the Paris conference. The Norwegians insisted that their attitude was 'the outcome of mature considerations and could not be changed'.[45] The Danish representatives said the same. At this point Halvard Lange, the Norwegian Foreign Minister, played the card of Scandinavian co-operation and suggested they discuss how far they could nevertheless co-operate economically and put forward a common policy. In these hopeless circumstances the idea of a Scandinavian association, perhaps even a customs union, was put forward. It was no more than a way of saving face and refusing to admit to the world the reality of profound Scandinavian disunity.[46]

Denmark's comparative advantages in processed food exports would be useless were it to be excluded from a European customs union, although to be of value to it such a union must embrace Britain or Germany or both. A Scandinavian union made little difference. Indeed, merely removing tariffs on intra-Scandinavian trade would have made very little difference to Sweden either.[47] Denmark joined the European Customs Union Study Group. Norway, impelled by the logic of its own national economic development, still sought a different direction. Norwegian history suggested that an open economy might well run grave dangers of arrested development and might incur very severe regional problems in the less favoured areas. To lower Norwegian tariffs, Lange feared, would be to flood the country with Swedish manufactures and Danish food. In his opinion, 'This would ruin Norwegian farmers and create industrial unemployment necessitating large-scale population

---

[44] UD 44.2/26, V, Møte den utvidede utenrikskomité, 1 September 1947.   [45] ibid.
[46] There are only the briefest accounts of the proposed Scandinavian customs union. G. Stolz, *Tollunioner* (Bergen, 1948) discusses the possibilities.
[47] Tariffs were very low in both Sweden and Denmark, the real barriers to trade being non-tariff barriers, and the proportion of their foreign trade with Scandinavia was also very low. Norway's level of tariff protection was distinctly higher. The market created by a Scandinavian customs union would only have had 14.4 million consumers and intra-Scandinavian trade amounted to only about 12 per cent of the total foreign trade of the three countries.

shift to fishing, shipping, woodcutting which, even if ultimately successful would be a long disheartening process.'[48] The split between the Scandinavian countries was not to be healed by further considerations. When they met again in February 1948 their positions were further apart. Unden, the Swedish Foreign Minister, still insisted that a customs union had got nothing to do with the ERP and Hammarskjöld insisted that Sweden could never agree that the United States should be the arbitrator in intra-European questions. The Danish government disagreed completely and wanted the others to send full representatives to the Customs Union Study Group.[49] These positions were not to change. The Danish interest in a Western European customs union remained high, the opposition of Norway and Sweden did not abate.

As for the French they were well aware that either the British tactics in the Customs Union Study Group at Brussels were delaying tactics or that, if they were not, they would produce a customs union significantly different from what the French government sought. In an official statement to the CEEC they criticized the study group as being on too low a level and called for action by the governments themselves,

> If Europe can become 'viable' we are absolutely convinced that that must be in an economic framework very different from the one we have known so far. It would serve no purpose to revert to exactly the same conditions. We are utterly convinced that we should arrive in the end at the same problems, the same dangers and perhaps the same cataclysm.[50]

When the CEEC broke up a further declaration in the same spirit, echoing the earlier Italian declaration, announced French willingness to take part in inter-governmental negotiations about a customs union with any of the participating countries.[51] As the alarmed British delegation to the first meeting of the Customs Union Study Group recorded, the French now appeared 'genuinely to have reached the conclusion that the only real salvation of Europe in the long run lies this way'.[52]

By Christmas a Franco-Italian Joint Commission had produced a report on the possibilities of a Franco-Italian economic union. It was absolutely different in principle from the 'pure' customs union whose study the United Kingdom had insisted on in Brussels. It is well characterized by Diebold as making only 'rare acknowledgements of the role of competition'.[53] It was based on the idea of the protection of domestic markets by non-tariff barriers for national

[48] SD 840.50, 532, Oslo to Washington, 6 February 1948.

[49] UD 44.2/26, VII, Ekstraktgjenpart av referat fra Utenriksministermøtet i Oslo 23–24 februar 1948.

[50] OECD, CCEE/54, Déclaration du délégué de la France au Comité de Coopération sur les unions douanières, 27 August 1947.

[51] CEEC, *General Report*, vol. 1, chapter IV, paragraph 98.

[52] FO 371/62755, UK delegation to London, 'First meeting of Customs Union Study Group', n.d. (UE 11362/11295/53).

[53] W. Diebold Jnr, *Trade and Payments in Western Europe* (New York, 1952), p. 361.

production except where market sharing agreements to allow measured quantities of exports would be allowed to come into force. There were sections on how to form market sharing agreements in third markets for agricultural and industrial exports, on how to avoid competition between similar sectors of manufacturing industry, on the sharing and regulation of merchant shipping services, on the limitation of competition between ports, and on the need for controls on the movement of labour and capital. In February 1948 both cabinets accepted the report as a basis for future co-operation and on 20 March Bidault and Sforza staged a dramatic meeting in the former house in Turin of that devoted free-trader and founding father of the Italian State, Count Camillo di Cavour, to initiate a series of detailed commissions to plan the customs union sector by sector.

These commissions consisted of associations of the leading producers in both countries for each sector who were allowed to cobble together whatever suited them best with no interference from government on high. As Mancel says of the meetings of industrialists, 'In general they were in favour of a customs union, but only on the condition that it changed nothing in the existing state of things'.[54] Even so the proceedings created considerable anxiety in France because they seemed to be going ahead quite independently of the views of the National Assembly. But the government had no intention of committing itself to an agreement for a customs union with Italy alone; it would have been 'of no great practical interest to France'.[55] It therefore referred the agreement with Italy to the Conseil Economique, a purely consultative body, as a delaying tactic and allowed that body to fight for greater constitutional importance in demanding government documents about the whole affair and debating and passing motions critical, in several contradictory senses, of government policy.

In a series of debates from March 1948 to May 1949 the Conseil Economique voiced the whole range of possible disagreements to the work of the Franco-Italian commissions while the government kept the various proposals away from the National Assembly.[56] The most frequently voiced objection was to the existence of at least two million unemployed men in Italy and the danger this implied to France if movement of labour were uncontrolled. But there was also vociferous opposition, from industrialists who saw even in such arrangements a weakening of protection, from farmers' organizations fearing competition from Italian agriculture, from industrialists and parliamentarians claiming that the union might strengthen the hand of government against vested interests or parliament, from free-traders who wanted to begin with the removal of quotas and other non-tariff barriers to trade rather than with

[54] Y. Mancel, *L'Union douanière ou le mariage des nations* (Paris, 1949), p. 103.
[55] FO 371/62554, UK delegation to London, 'Statement by Alphand', 17 September 1947.
[56] France, Conseil Economique, *Etudes et Travaux*, no. 7, *Union Douanière France-Italie (I)*; no. 14, *Union Douanière France-Italie (II)*; no. 16, *Union Douanière France-Italie*.

tariffs when there were so many other obstacles to efficiency and competition, and from advocates of a wider union who saw an agreement with Italy alone as an obstacle to its achievement. Among these last the French agricultural associations were especially prominent.

When the report of the joint sectoral commissions was eventually published at the start of 1949 its recommendations for both agriculture and industry were such as to strengthen this opposition. It recommended the creation of a common agricultural market by a series of compensatory taxes. For industry its recommendations implied the end of price controls in France, the harmonization of manufacturing and export subsidies in both countries, and the harmonization of all direct and indirect controls. Labour migration would be allowed, but only under strict control by the Office National d'Immigration Français on the basis of quarterly requests for specific jobs to be filled. A customs union must not lead to the 'disorderly installation of immigrants and the exercise of functions reserved for nationals'.[57] In fact, a complete customs union was inconceivable until Italy had solved the problem of its labour surplus. It was difficult to find two countries in Western Europe with more different economic policies and not hard to see that the lack of controls and central direction in the Italian economy offered little possibility of the acceptance of the principles and methods of French reconstruction. This report ran into even heavier waters in the Conseil Economique, even though as Schuman pointed out in his testimony there, 'we can stop on the way at any time'.[58]

In any case American pressure for a European customs union had by now been dropped in favour of an onslaught on non-tariff barriers to trade, so that the whole set of proposals was even less welcome in Washington and was nullified by the fact that both governments were now committed by the ERP to removing a large proportion of their non-tariff barriers to trade and were much too alarmed by these new commitments to consider any longer the removal of tariff barriers as well.[59] The whole project had passed beyond the possibilities of effective action.

But that was what the French had wanted. The aim had been throughout to keep the possibility of a Franco-Italian customs union in the forefront in order to preserve the other possibility, in which France was more genuinely and increasingly interested, a customs union with Benelux and Italy as the basis of a European economic bloc whose terms a revived West Germany would have to accept. The likelihood of any worthwhile agreement on joint economic policy with Italy was small and the opposition of French agricultural interests, as well as of Italian industrial interests, to such a union hardly to be avoided. But in a wider union the chances of final arrangements more in harmony with French domestic policy were greater and, as far as coming to terms with Germany was concerned, only the wider union would do. As the

[57] France, *Compte-rendu de la Commission Mixte Franco-Italienne d'Union Douanière* (Paris, January 1949).   [58] ibid., p. 57.   [59] See pp. 283–97.

West German economy and state emerged and as the British position did not change, interest in the Netherlands in the French version of a reconstructed Europe grew.

The British decisions had cut the arteries of the Customs Union Study Group as an international organization, but even the seemingly anodyne studies of the theoretical effects of a standardization of tariff rates on the separate countries or of a standardized tariff nomenclature kept the political issue in the forefront. This was perfectly apparent to the British delegation at the study group's meeting in March 1948.

> As the study progresses, the eventual outcome will develop essentially into a crucial issue of our relations with Benelux, France and Italy (leaving aside the United States and the Continent at the moment). We cannot hope to shelter behind the indifference or the delaying tactics of the periphery countries. The big three are not much disposed to take them seriously. All three are fundamentally sceptical of a wide Union, and would really much prefer a smaller party. If there is obstruction on the outskirts, they are likely to propose such a party.[60]

This was a prescient remark, but in the early months of the OEEC the effective counter to it would have been that it was a lot easier to agree on the size of the party than on the games to be played in it. The economic disputes in the OEEC showed just how divided on important issues the 'big three' actually were. To overcome their divisions a major external force was necessary, the emergence of the German Federal Republic as a political entity and a powerful economy, and in spring 1948 that external force was lacking. By May and the end of the second stage of the London Conference on Germany, however, as we have seen, French policy options had been dramatically narrowed, and a Franco-German economic association was coming to seem the only logical way forward for French reconstruction. Two months after the idea of positive steps towards a Western European customs union had been buried in Britain, Greater Benelux, the Little European customs union, became not so much an alternative possibility for achieving France's objectives in Germany as a serious necessity for guaranteeing national security. Without the Netherlands it made no sense. Without Britain was it not too risky? And in summer 1948 Western European integration without Britain was unacceptable in Washington. To make Little Europe feasible required not only the emergence of the German Federal Republic but bold changes of direction by politicians in the United States and the Netherlands. These, however, would not have occurred had it not been for the subsequent pattern of economic events.

---

[60] FO 371/68940, Report on third meeting of the European Customs Union Study Group, 2 April 1948.

VIII

PAYMENTS AGREEMENTS AND POLICIES IN WESTERN EUROPE 1946–9

If there is one thing more than any other which illustrates the proposition that reconstruction after 1945 was not reconstruction from the aftermath of the Second World War alone but from the problems left by the failure of reconstruction after 1918, it is the concentration of international effort on rebuilding a method of conducting international trade and payments which, for the developed economies at least, would function as easily and successfully as the one which had existed before 1914. Before 1914 the assumption that international trade and exchanges would continue to expand had been almost universal. Yet there had been only a brief period in the 1920s in Europe when this had been so. The expansion that took place then scarcely regained the volume lost between 1914 and 1924, and in the 1930s the volume of international trade, investment, and other forms of exchanges remained lower than before 1929 in spite of the fact that many countries, Germany most notably, greatly increased their national output and income.

After 1945 the desire to link expanding output with expanding exports was given compelling urgency by the high demand for imports emanating from high levels of capital investment and the loss of earlier means of paying for them. In 1945 British exports paid for only 30 per cent of imports. If full employment was to be maintained imports were not likely to be reduced much below pre-war level. The loss of invisible earnings and the increase in foreign debts meant that to maintain the flow of imports exports would have to rise by about 50 per cent by 1950. If foreign debts were to be repaid, the reserves to be built up, and a certain amount of investment in the Empire undertaken, they would have to rise by 75 per cent. And if the terms of trade deteriorated as much as they were likely to, exports would have to be increased by even more. The earliest versions of the French Modernization Plan supposed that, by the time an equilibrium had been reached in the balance of payments in 1949, exports would have to be 10 per cent higher than their inter-war peak in 1929. These estimates, however, were made on the assumption of a reconstruction loan from the United States similar in size to that made to Britain. When that did not eventuate later versions of the Plan assumed a much greater increase in exports to make up for it.[1] When the government of the Federal German Republic came into office the situation for them was still clearer. There was higher unemployment and a lower level of productivity than elsewhere in Western Europe and a more rapidly increasing population. If American aid was to end with the predicted end of ERP West Germany would have to double its exports within two years to maintain its population even at the standard of living of 1949, which was below that of the rest of industrialized western Europe and below that of 1929 as well. The motivation within Western Europe for seeking a more flexible trade and payments system was itself very strong, irrespective of the pressures of American world policy, because someone had to take these exports as imports. Over the steps to be taken and the ultimate nature of the system, however, there was not so much agreement.

In spite of the disequilibrium in intra-western European trade, the continued proliferation of barriers to trade, and the inflexibility of bilateral trading mechanisms the growth of western European exports was sustained and vigorous until 1949. Table 30 shows the unbroken trend of export expansion in almost all Western European countries. In spite of this success in a world where exports were vital to reconstruction most European countries were

Table 30   An index of the growth of Western European exports (1948 = 100)

	1938	1947	1948	1949	1950	1951
Belgium/Luxembourg	110	81	100	108	123	149
Denmark	139	92	100	130	172	195
France	125	87	100	147	200	237
West Germany	481	38	100	188	435	622
Ireland	136	95	100	121	136	135
Italy	124	67	100	113	140	175
Netherlands	156	69	100	151	204	242
Norway	124	100	100	104	137	161
Sweden	111	91	100	115	144	147
Switzerland	79	91	100	99	113	136
United Kingdom	73	79	100	110	127	129

Source: UN, *Economic Survey of Europe Since the War* (Geneva, 1953), p. 255.

[1] F.M.B. Lynch, 'The political and economic reconstruction of France 1944–1947: in the international context' (PhD thesis, University of Manchester, 1981), pp. 276 ff.

reluctant to run any risk of unpredictable movements in payments. The period was dominated by the tension between, on the one hand, the impossibility of attaining domestic reconstruction goals without an increase in foreign trade and, on the other hand, the desire to relegate the balance of payments to a subordinate position in determining economic policy, a tension which was to be maintained for two decades. But this tension, although present everywhere, was resolved at a different point along the scale of policy in the separate countries and it was just these differences which emerged in the attempt to build a multilateral framework for trade. Would not Belgium's relatively *laissez-faire* policy undo British policy if allowed to influence it through the balance of payments mechanism? Would not Italy's deflationary policy have the same impact on France? Once these fears, bred out of the clashing disharmonies of domestic economic policies, were brought face to face with the American insistence that a Western European multilateral trading system should not be protected against the dollar zone but competitive with it and a part of one multilateral world they could not help but be enormously enhanced.

TRADE AND PAYMENTS AGREEMENTS IN WESTERN EUROPE, 1946–9

The first concrete European proposal made to the CEEC when it met had been the Belgian proposal to make the credit margins, the 'swing', of the existing Western European bilateral trade agreements multilateral and support them with dollar aid as a step towards making Western European currencies fully convertible. In rejecting this scheme the other countries had agreed that discussion of alternative schemes to multilateralize European payments would be a precondition for the creation of the OEEC. Unless American aid, however, was specifically used to support intra-western European trade any similar proposals to the Belgian ones seemed certain to remain ineffective. And even had the United States agreed to support a scheme which, in the case of the Belgian proposals, would have implied helping the exports of a country which was one of the least in need of American aid, the exchange crisis in August, especially through the shock it administered to British opinion, would probably in any case have meant that western European countries would have rejected the scheme. Until August 1947 the United Kingdom Treasury had officially argued and, it seems, for the most part believed that it was progressing within the spirit of the loan agreement with the Americans towards a date at which the Western European currencies could be made convertible.

There was no firm horizon for that event and the assumption seems to have been that it would in any case take place under British leadership and guidance. There seems at the same time, however, to have been another school of opinion which assumed that the United States had not done enough to guarantee economic recovery after the war, that dollar trade would as a consequence remain very difficult, and that the United Kingdom might mitigate these difficulties for itself by bringing some of the western European economies and their empires into the sterling area. This would have been accompanied by freedom of trade, or something close to it, within the area and, in order to make it work, active, if temporary, discrimination against dollar imports. The main method of discrimination would, presumably, have been by extending the common control of dollar earnings which already existed within the sterling area, the dollar pool, to the much enlarged area.[2]

This in itself would have doomed these proposals for future reconstruction to failure in the Anglo-American Financial Negotiations, because the operations of the dollar pool turned out to be in American eyes the prime example of the discrimination in international trade which they insisted on the United Kingdom ending as part of the price of the reconstruction loan. What the attitude of the other western European economies was likely to be to such proposals seems to have been a matter of supreme indifference in 1945 to both sides of the argument in the Treasury. Although such ideas got nowhere in the Anglo-American negotiations and were vigorously opposed by Keynes who led the negotiations for most of the time on the British side, they resurfaced in a circuitous way in Bevin's response to the French proposals for a customs union in August 1947. His ideas for a counter-proposal had quickly escalated to the idea of a customs union including the sterling area, Western Europe and the other Western European empires. This was seen as a defence against American domination, against the dangers to British domestic policy from the next American depression, and as a secure foundation for a western European strategic alliance against the Soviet Union. These ideas had been rejected by the Treasury which, although the horizon had receded further after the convertibility crisis, remained faithful to the position taken in 1945. But they remained just below the surface of official policy, appearing more or less strongly according to the strength of the United Kingdom reserves. This did not contradict incessant declarations in favour of multilateralism, the British government being adept at using the argument that the sterling area was in any case the world's largest multilateral trading area and that extending it could but bring the one multilateral western world nearer.

It might rather, in effect, have created two large, separate international trading systems, a dollar one and a sterling one. But it could not have done much to insulate, as its advocates suggested it would, the sterling area reserves and the United Kingdom's balance of payments against the effects of the feared depression in the United States. As the events of 1949 were to show,

[2] For the dispute between Sir Richard Clarke, a prominent advocate of these views, and Keynes in 1945, Sir R. Clarke (Sir A. Cairncross, ed.), *Anglo-American Economic Collaboration in War and Peace 1942–1949* (Oxford, 1982), pp. 126–36. Clarke did not change his views after 1945 and tried to influence the London Committee in their direction in 1947.

one of the most severe effects of even a short American recession was to reduce the earnings from exports to the United States of the rest of the sterling area outside Britain, and so in turn reduce British exports and dollar earnings.

The main tendency in British policy towards Western Europe's trade problems after summer 1947 was therefore to postpone any steps towards multilateral trade and fiercely resist any step towards currency convertibility until the moment was judged to be ripe. Underlying this was the alternative tendency, always visible at times of crisis, to consider pulling into the sterling area payments mechanism low-tariff countries which had extensive trading links with Britain, such as the Netherlands, Norway or Sweden. In neither case was there any encouragement to proceed with the construction of a multilateral trading mechanism in Western Europe out of the mesh of bilateral agreements.

But to blame British discouragement, as the Americans did, for the failure to move more rapidly towards a more flexible trading system in Europe was unjust. The differences between other Western European governments were sufficiently wide to have impeded any such move even had the British attitude to it been more favourable. The proper cure for the intra-Western European payments disequilibrium depended on an accurate diagnosis of its causes and about that the European countries were in great disagreement. The nature of the diagnosis tended to reflect the nature of domestic economic policy choices.

Taking a strictly neo-classical view of the problem it could be argued that it was not so much caused by changes in the pattern of world trade and payments stemming from the war and its aftermath but by monetary phenomena.[3] Deflationary pressures in the United States in the 1930s, inflationary pressures in Europe during the war, the failure of several European countries after the war to mop up the over-liquidity caused by the rate of increase of money supply remaining ahead of that of GDP, all created sharp differences between the relative rates of monetary expansion in the United States and western Europe and between Western European countries. In so far as inflation in Western European countries represented an excess of demand for goods over the volume of national production it could result, particularly where rationing had been abandoned, in import surpluses. An obvious example was the superimposition in France of the Monnet Plan on an economy in which monetary reform had been rejected on political grounds. A return to roughly similar rates of monetary expansion in Western Europe through a deflationary policy on the part of those countries with larger import surpluses might therefore, it could be argued, be all that was necessary to end the disequilibrium in payments. Pursued everywhere in Western Europe it might cure the disequilibrium between Europe and America and establish Western Europe's 'viability'.

The Belgian proposals to the CEEC partly reflected this analysis, because

[3] R. Triffin, *Europe and the Money Muddle* (New Haven, 1957).

a speedy return to currency convertibility would mean beginning to bring down at once the inflation rate in a country such as France by monetary policy. Belgium had imposed a currency reform after liberation, although not of the drastic kind which the Federal Republic was later to impose. Reconstruction investment had been mostly left to private initiative and the high profit rates prevailing from autumn 1944 left some scope for this. These profit rates were very much dependent, like most Belgian business and manufacturing, on exports. Overall, Belgium was not in an unfavourable trading position. The problem was that the deficits with the United States could not be compensated by surpluses earned elsewhere, because the surpluses were not earned in convertible currencies. The 'viability' of Western Europe would presumably solve this problem by leading more quickly to convertibility between the dollar and western European currencies.

The trading situation of most other western European countries was by no means so favourable and in their eyes to have put the Belgian proposals into effect would probably have made it even less so. In 1947 they were supported by the United States which was not prepared to see Marshall Aid used to support deflationary policies which, although they might accelerate the closure of the dollar gap, would hardly be in consonance with America's political objectives. When the Belgian proposals were submitted it had, in any case, already been decided that to allow the ECA to finance a separate payments scheme was impossible in that year because it would mean having to admit to Congress that the IMF had failed as an instrument of reconstruction.[4]

If the IMF itself, however, was to play any part in promoting a movement towards currency convertibility in Western Europe it could only be by supporting deflationary policies. Its resources were entirely inadequate to support the reconstruction policies which most countries were bent on pursuing and at the same time to maintain stable exchange rates. The American decision to create a specially funded separate agency to handle Marshall Aid was a major political decision to support initially the more ambitious reconstruction plans of Western European countries and this had to imply eventual support for a payments scheme. Against this strategic necessity the desire of the IMF itself to play an active role in European reconstruction was judged and found wanting. In any case the integration of Western Europe as conceived in Washington must surely ultimately mean currency convertibility, perhaps indeed one currency. This might only be attainable if special dollar aid was allocated for this purpose by the ECA, if it were not to be achieved by deflation.

The Belgian initiative had raised another embarrassing aspect of such a policy. Should the first step be to allocate aid to support the trade of creditors such as Belgium and thus stimulate their exports further, or should it be to

---

[4] President's Committee on Foreign Aid, 11, 'Second memorandum concerning the financial program to be elaborated by the European Economic Cooperation Committee', 26 July 1947.

allocate aid to enable deficit countries to import still more goods? These were difficult political questions too and it is not surprising that in summer 1947 they were shelved. But when the dollar gap did not look like closing in 1948 and currency convertibility had not been brought any nearer the fundamental policy issues remained and had to be faced.

They were issues which were just as internally divisive in Western Europe as in the United States. Even in Paris the pressures for a more liberal framework and claims for the advantages of a speedy move to multilateral trade and convertible currencies were never entirely subdued by the acceptance of the Monnet Plan at the start of 1947 as, in Blum's words, the 'pièce essentielle' of economic recovery.[5] They were to reappear in 1949 in an attempt to unseat the French Planning Commissariat from its influence over French economic policy. In London the Treasury was not unwilling to see a modified version of the original Belgian proposals go forward to the CEEC including the phrase, 'An end shall be put to all inflationary expansion of credit.' The sentence, the Treasury indicated, was aimed at France. But Cripps minuted on the proposal, 'No. This is on the slippery slope of servitude,' and that the phrase in question was 'totally unacceptable'.[6]

Two IMF representatives served on the Committee on Payments Agreements established by the CEEC. The Belgians did not hide from this committee the ultimate scope of their appeal to America. They spoke of an eventual pooling of European central bank reserves and of a European Bank, modelled on the Federal Reserve System, to manage them.[7] A more hopeless initiative in August 1947 is hard to imagine. But since no decisions on the form which Marshall Aid would take had yet been announced from Washington the committee was able to discuss a wide range of hypothetical possibilities whose common feature was the hope of using each unit of American aid twice over, firstly to finance intra-Western European trade deficits and then to finance Western Europe's overall deficit with America.

It was not only the prior American decision that made this love's labours lost, the events of August cast doubt over whether it would be of any use for future years. Colbjørnsen summed up the situation for the American experts in the Washington conversations which followed the break-up of the CEEC.

> Then came the 20th of August with its lesson. The thirty five days period of convertibility from the 15th of July to the 20th of August had finished and we saw the whole question more in the light of the realities of the situation. So, if the United Kingdom has certain doubts now with regard to going too far and too quickly, it is the same or corresponding consideration which was already in the minds of several delegations during the Paris conference and in the meetings of financial experts there.[8]

[5] R.F. Kuisel, *Capitalism and the State in Modern France* (Cambridge, 1981), p. 235.
[6] T 236/794, Memorandum by Sir D. Waley, 29 July 1947.
[7] T 236/799, Proceedings of the Committee on Payments Agreements, n.d.
[8] President's Committee on Foreign Aid, 3, Washington Conversations, 22 October 1947.

In fact only France and Italy supported the Belgian proposals and since their support was conditional on British agreement this was no great commitment.[9]

The CEEC report rejected the idea that changes in policy in Western Europe could correct the lack of equilibrium either in intra-Western European or in world trade.[10] The Committee on Payments Agreements could not come to any agreement until 18 November and the agreement which it did produce, the First Agreement on Multilateral Monetary Compensation, was of little importance.[11] The full agreement covered only France, Italy and the Benelux.[12] These countries agreed to make settlements between themselves automatically out of surpluses and deficits in each others' currencies for one year, the period of the agreement. Most other CEEC countries agreed that they would also make such settlements, but not automatically. An agent was appointed under the scheme to make proposals to these other countries for such settlements and they agreed to 'entertain' these suggestions. The only international organization which appeared capable of managing such settlements, the IMF, was not chosen. A direct link with the pre-war period was established, the task was passed to the Bank of International Settlements created to plan the last desperate attempt to collect German reparations. The IMF seems to have been originally chosen for the role but either through carelessness, as its official history implies, or, more likely, through some kind of chicanery, its representatives were not present at the relevant meeting![13]

The volume of settlements, automatic or otherwise, which could be made under the agreement was very small. This can best be seen from figure 10. Of the full members of the agreement, the Netherlands had a deficit on commodity trade with all others in the calendar year 1948 and Italy a surplus with all others. In Western Europe as a whole Italy had a deficit on commodity trade only with West Germany, and the Netherlands had a deficit with every significant trader. In the ten months of the agreement's existence, until it was replaced at the end of September 1948, automatic compensation covered no more than about $1.7 million out of payments debts totalling $762.1 million.[14]

In February 1948, as soon as it began to look likely that the OEEC would be allowed to come into existence, the Belgians began once more to press for a multilateral payments scheme. There were fears that countries would deliberately reduce imports from Belgium and that Belgium itself would not be generously treated under Marshall Aid, because of its relatively favourable overall trading position. But the growing dangers to the economic relationship

[9] T 236/798, Waley to Hall-Patch, 27 September 1947.

[10] CEEC, *General Report*, vol. 1 (Paris, 1949). 'But the action which the participating countries can take is limited. The power to correct the maladjustment is not theirs alone. ... The solution of the world problem is decisive for the participating countries' future' (p. 57).

[11] The text is published in BIS, *18th Annual Report* (Basle, 1948).

[12] The Bizone joined when the agreement was close to expiry.

[13] J.K. Horsefield *et al.*, *The International Monetary Fund* (Washington DC, 1969), vol. 1, pp. 213–14.

[14] R.W. Bean, 'European multilateral clearing', *Journal of Political Economy*, vol. 56, 1948.

of Belgium and the Netherlands in the first stages of the Benelux customs union now gave added urgency to Belgian policy. The most persistently striking aspect of intra-Western European trade flows in the years after 1945 is the size of the Dutch deficits with Belgium (table 31). This was in itself one of the major causes of the postponement and eventual abandonment of the

Table 31   Trade surplus of Belgium–Luxembourg with the Netherlands, 1937, 1938, 1946–51 (million current dollars)

1937	+ 18.34
1938	+ 18.08
1946	+ 34.78
1947	+ 64.92
1948	+ 97.10
1949	+ 91.94
1950	+174.10
1951	+196.22

Source: OEEC, *Statistical Bulletins of Foreign Trade*.

projected complete economic union between the two countries. The demand for discrimination against Belgian exports in the Netherlands threatened to escalate into policy measures which could scarcely be hidden from the public eye no matter how much they contradicted the avowed aim of political union, unless Belgium continued to provide credits to alleviate pressures on Dutch reserves. At the same time Belgium had to maintain strict controls to prevent imports from the United States, paid for in dollars, being re-exported to the Netherlands, where they would have earned only inconvertible guilders.[15]

The question had an added importance because of the rush in spring 1948 to conclude the Brussels Pact. Bevin's idea that the Brussels Pact countries must be so knit together economically that they could not fall apart may have cut little ice with the United Kingdom Treasury, but the very act of military association and the important non-military clauses of the Brussels Treaty which were then under negotiation inevitably gave an impetus to trade and payments discussions between the Pact members themselves and they decided to meet in April to try to devise a scheme which dealt with the problem of their mutual payments relationships. The Netherlands, naturally, wanted Marshall Aid to be allocated directly to debtors in intra-Western European trade or more generous export credits in the form of an extended 'swing' from its allies. Belgium made the expected objection that this would mean that creditors in intra-Western European trade would be transferring aid which their deficits

[15] The range of obstacles to the completion of the Benelux union is discussed in J.E. Meade, H.H. Liesner and S.J. Wells, *Case Studies in European Economic Union. The Mechanics of Integration* (London, 1962), pp. 59–195.

with the United States might otherwise have entitled them to receive, not from the standpoint of international economics a very well-founded argument.[16] The Belgians would have been prepared to go ahead to negotiating a second and more flexible payments agreement on multilateral compensation without a specific provision of dollars to back it up, but the others were adamant that American funds were indispensable.[17] In fact the five signatories of the Brussels Pact had less chance of constructing a satisfactory payments agreement amongst themselves than the sixteen potential members of the OEEC because the disequilibrium within the smaller group was even more marked. There was even a threat that the British might refuse to finance France's forecast deficit with the sterling area, which the British estimated might reach as high as £75 million ($302.25 million) in 1948.

France's deficit with the United Kingdom alone was relatively small and the British attitude towards the total French sterling deficit revealed once more the ambiguity of Britain's position. When Treasury officials had argued in 1945 for a fallback position in the Anglo-American negotiations in which, should the terms of the American loan prove unacceptable, Western Europe would be brought into the sterling area, there had been no calculations as to whether this would improve or worsen the area's dollar position. Those who continued to hanker after the same policy in 1947 were not so prepared to transfer the burden of French reconstruction to the sterling reserves.[18] Any set of multilateral arrangements in Western Europe which might occasion the loss of sterling to Western European countries was regarded as particularly threatening in London because the position of the sterling area had proved so frail in 1947.

As the shortage of dollars squeezed tight on expanding international trade the sterling area came to have an immediate practical usefulness to Britain in so far as it facilitated access without dollars to a variety of primary imports.[19] This sentiment was particularly strong in Cripps who became the prime architect of economic policy after 1947 and it seems to have been reinforced in his breast by a certain paternalistic imperialism which he may have inherited from the Fabian wing of the Labour Party. Such ambiguities of sentiment were not infrequent in other members of the government and in the civil service. There was in fact a great deal of unclear thinking about the real advantages and disadvantages of the sterling area. Partly this was a reflection of unclear thinking about the future of the whole country, but it was also based on a false assumption that the existence and development of the sterling

[16] T 236/814, Notes of informal Treasury discussions 20/21 February 1948.

[17] SD 840.50, 5658, Paris to Washington, 18 April 1948.

[18] There is a fuller analysis of the United Kingdom government's attitude to these conflicts in C.C.S. Newton, 'Britain, the dollar shortage and European integration 1945–50' (PhD thesis, University of Birmingham, 1981).

[19] British imports from the sterling area in 1947 were 31 per cent of total imports, exports to it 47 per cent of total exports.

area did offer a secure defence against economic events in America. The British government, mainly urged on by Cripps, was determined not to allow any link of convertibility between the sterling area trading mechanisms on one side and a Western European payments mechanism on the other. Since it was Belgium which pressed most strongly for such a mechanism and such a link, because Belgium tended in the post-war world to accumulate sterling surpluses, and since the conversion of Belgian sterling holdings into dollars had been a significant cause of the run on the pound in 1947, the clash between British and Belgian policies was a central obstacle to a more ambitious multilateral payments scheme either for the Brussels Pact countries alone or for the whole of the OEEC. Worse, the Belgians could not avoid being seen in London as tools of American policy in Western Europe, especially as the background to the argument was the foolish American intrigue to make Spaak 'Director-General' of the OEEC.

In fact, the question of the degree to which the sterling area was a discriminatory trading area did not disturb governments and officials in Brussels or Paris, even though British opposition to the Belgian ideas was seen in Washington as symptomatic of the United Kingdom's unwillingness to abandon discrimination at the world as well as the Western European level. The relationship between Belgium and the Congo was much more discriminatory. In all probability, the management of the sterling area dollar pool did not need to involve much more than a process of consultation. As the willingness with which most of the countries remained in it and the increase in the size of the sterling balances in 1950/1 showed, the sterling area brought considerable advantages to most of its members, particularly for primary exporters the long-term guarantees of quantities and prices given by British state purchase contracts. The European proposals for a multilateral payments system in Western Europe certainly did not preclude effective safeguards for sterling held outside Europe. But it was the sterling held inside Western Europe which worried the British and they watched the occasional adverse movements of their current account with Belgium, Denmark or Italy with an almost morbid sensitivity, ready to defend their world-wide interests and the sterling reserves at the expense of reconstruction in much weaker European nations.

All the United Kingdom wanted out of the payments negotiations with the Brussels Pact countries was a short-term solution to its immediate payments problems with France and Belgium which would sustain French imports at less cost to Britain, while the whole question of future convertibility or even of multilateral settlements was buried until such time as London wished to see it resurrected. Belgium agreed to provide £5 million to France out of its sterling balances and Britain matched it with a further £10 million. The price of this agreement, however, was that Britain would join with the others to exert pressure on the United States to back up a further payments agreement covering all the OEEC countries with Marshall Aid dollars.

An approach had been made along these lines in March 1948, when the main American reaction had been to tell the Europeans to keep it quiet and play down the whole matter until the ECA was safely in the saddle.[20] Nevertheless when the Executive Committee of the CEEC met at the start of May the question had received so much publicity that Harriman decided that it was better it be discussed in that forum.[21] Hall-Patch warned the United States that unless the ECA backed a payments scheme important trading relationships 'would come to complete standstill by June 1'.[22] The essential element of the Belgian proposals was still that it should be the surpluses in intra-Western European trade which were financed by dollars, although the assumption was that this would be done through the IMF. If, for example, any European country had a deficit with Belgium, Belgium would provide the extra credits to cover it against, firstly, the creation of a credit of the same size on special account in national currency in the receiving country, and, secondly, the withdrawal of the same sum in Belgian currency from the IMF. The withdrawal of Belgian francs would then permit Belgium to increase its dollar borrowings by the equivalent amount from that source, providing the dollar funding to the IMF was increased.[23] The staff of the Fund proposed to the IMF Board that it should fund a multilateral payments agreement in Europe along these lines, but the American representative on the IMF Board objected to the Fund's participation.[24]

By 1948 three members of the OEEC had already exhausted their borrowing rights on the Fund, two others were disbarred from borrowing, and three were still not members. The American representatives on the Fund 'questioned whether the Brussels plan was multilateral in its aspects or whether it merely took care of Belgium'.[25] The State Department was reluctant, however, to slam the door shut on any such plans and the ECA was entirely willing to support a policy of vetoing the Belgian proposals while suggesting that the OEEC produce something better based on more credits for debtors. The solution the ECA would have most wished was that of a European clearing pool, about which the Belgians had talked in the CEEC, but that being out of reach, both the ECA and the State Department strove to persuade the Treasury and the IMF that the ECA itself should use Marshall Aid to finance a certain percentage of the deficits and surpluses on intra-Western European trade beyond the 'swing' of the bilateral agreements by effectively guaranteeing in dollars further imports in intra-western European trade beyond those limits. The IMF representative in the National Advisory Council maintained a high level of scepticism about such a procedure, which would have been much

---

[20] T 236/815, Washington embassy to FO, 12 March 1948.
[21] T 236/816, FO to Paris delegation, 4 May 1948.
[22] SD 840.50, 5661, Paris to Washington, 5 May 1948.
[23] FRUS, 1948, III, Hebbard to Douglas, 10 May 1948, p. 439.
[24] Horsefield, *The IMF*, vol. 1, pp. 220–2.
[25] NAC, Staff Committee Meetings, meeting no. 127, 11 May 1948.

more liberal than IMF rules, and was obviously unconvinced that intra-Western European trade would cease to grow were something of this kind not done.[26] The Federal Reserve Board stuck to the original principles of American post-war policy and tried to insist that whatever agreement was engineered in Europe be a part of a 'universal, automatic multilateral clearing system'.[27] In that way the agreement would be a long-term one strengthening Bretton Woods, whereas of course the ECA's objective, and that of the State Department too, was to strengthen Western Europe by a short-term agreement backed by aid. Any short-term agreement would still mean the retention of a plentiful array of exchange and trade controls to make it work, 'a Schachtian plan, designed to control by financial device the trade of Europe' as the United States Treasury deemed it.[28]

Before the Committee on Trade and Payments could meet under the new aegis of the OEEC the decisions on the first round of Marshall Aid allocations were announced. Some countries were to receive only loans and this squashed on the spot one persistent European idea, which had not been without support from the Federal Reserve Board, that the Marshall Aid counterpart funds might be used to provide backing for a payments scheme. Suddenly, on 17 June 1948, the deadlock was broken by a deliberate leak by Richard M. Bissell Jnr,[29] an ECA officer, that the American administration had decided that it must after all inject dollars into an intra-Western European payments scheme, although it had not yet come to any decision on a method.[30]

This news inspired the British to a further effort to take the European lead. By the start of July they had put forward proposals which involved extending the limits of credit made available by creditors and had mobilized French support for them. But Belgium remained adamantly opposed.[31] At that point Cripps intervened to prevent the plan going to the OEEC Council for discussion, because in the course of the negotiations the proposed limits to the credits which countries might make had been, he claimed, effectively removed.[32] The arrival of Cripps at the Exchequer had at once made British policy more cautious and his decision foreshadowed all his subsequent refusals to take the risk of any payments plan which allowed a possible loophole for sterling to be converted.

Worse followed immediately. The United States Treasury had not given up its struggle against ECA policy and by continuing to insist that the ECA

[26] ibid., meeting no. 131, 29 May 1948.   [27] ibid., meeting no. 132, 2 June 1948.
[28] ibid.
[29] Richard M. Bissell Jnr, 1909– . Professor of Economics at MIT. Member of War Shipping Administration, then an executive officer of the Harriman Committee and so to Assistant Deputy Administrator of the ECA. Became operations director in the CIA and played an important part in planning the attack on Cuba at the Bay of Pigs in 1961. His hobby was memorizing railway timetables.
[30] T 236/817, Washington embassy to FO, 17 June 1948.
[31] T 236/818, UK delegation to FO, 9 July 1948.
[32] ibid., Memorandum by Chancellor of the Exchequer, 13 July 1948.

would merely be using dollars to support a country like Belgium, which was in a healthy overall position, managed to postpone the implementation of the ECA decision. Likewise the IMF refused to consider itself as a supplementary back-up to the scheme 'which would create an additional financing mechanism that would divert attention from what European countries should do themselves'.[33] The discussion dragged on throughout August and, when resolved in September, was so only uneasily. The political objectives of the ECA and the State Department in Europe were not in fact in harmony with the global multilateralism of official American policy. Marshall Aid now meant providing dollars to support a controlled bilateral trading system to which European countries were clinging in order to support expansionary reconstruction plans. This could still be presented as merely tactical, a short-term policy to prepare the way for real 'viability', and eventually this argument was accepted. But it was wearing thin and was by no means universally accepted even in the ECA.

When in July 1948 the Committee of Four took up 'the intolerable burden' of recommending the allocation of Marshall Aid it followed Bissell's hint and did make the preliminary assumption that there would be an injection of Marshall Aid dollars into intra-Western European payments in the form of direct ECA support for a payments scheme. Within such a scheme there was no sensible way of distinguishing economically between the need for a country to run an import surplus from the dollar zone and an import surplus in intra-western European trade. In general, for the strategic dimension of American policy, as well as to reduce the massive dollar deficits, it could have been seen as more desirable that European countries should import from each other than from the United States. But in any case it was obvious that the allocation of Marshall Aid to individual countries, by determining their capacity to import from the United States would also be a powerful determinant of the extent of their imports and exports in intra-western European trade. Had, for example, Belgium been allocated the sum of money requested to finance its intended dollar deficit rather than the sum (less than half of the original Belgian request) which the Committee of Four felt would cover its *necessary* imports from the United States, this would have financed raw material imports to sustain its exports to Western Europe, if other European countries had been able to find the currency or credits to buy them. Reducing Belgium's export potential allocated more dollar aid to other Western European countries. Some of them, however, may have preferred a greater liberty of choice of supplier. The complexities were seemingly endless, but all referred back to the original programmes submitted to the OEEC and they reflected in their turn domestic economic policy choices which were unacceptable to other Western European countries once their consequences for intra-Western European trade were worked out in this way.

[33] NAC, Staff Committee meetings, meeting no. 139, 8 July 1948. Presumably they should have deflated.

Throughout 1948 criticisms had mounted, especially from those economies, such as Britain, Norway and the Netherlands, where consumption was more firmly restrained than in Belgium, of Belgian trading practices and these came to a head as soon as the OEEC committees had to allow for the transfer of Marshall Aid dollars within a Western European payments scheme, even though the calculations were only hypothetical. It was alleged that essential capital goods imports from Belgium, which were in any case more highly priced than comparable American products, could only be obtained at the price of including unwanted luxury consumer imports in the bilateral trade agreements. From the viewpoint of a highly controlled economy Belgium was asking for Marshall Aid against a dollar deficit made up of imports of eight-cylinder cars from America and then asking for a further transfer of aid to sustain exports of azaleas and hot-house grapes to Western Europe. Given the trend of national economic policies it was understandable that the OEEC committees would favour the funding of import deficits in capital goods and attempt to fund Belgium's export of steel and capital goods in Western Europe at the expense of its imports from the United States. They deleted requests for dollar imports and thus potentially transferred the aid to western European takers of Belgian exports, sustaining some Belgian exports at the expense of Belgian consumption. In theory what Belgium lost in finance for American imports it gained in the added dollar capacity of European countries to take its exports. Whether the United States would accept the method and the sums was not known, so Belgium's displeasure was not unreasonable. In fact, as we have seen, in the case of the Bizone the sums were to be rejected. On the other hand, the OEEC had to come up with agreed proposals while the United States government continued to dispute internally about the nature of American aid for intra-Western European trade.

To allocate dollar aid to a general clearing pool which could be used once the limits of the 'swing' on the bilaterals had been reached appeared to divorce the aid used in that way from the careful planning by which the rest of Marshall Aid was allocated to the national economies. Worse, it would avoid any element of integrated planning and allow trade flows to continue purely on the basis of national decisions. There was another way which had been used in the first year of Marshall Aid. This had been to allow importers to use their dollar aid for imports not of United States provenance, so-called 'off-shore purchasing'. The ECA had resorted extensively at first to such off-shore purchasing arrangements and the value of intra-western European trade financed in this way during the first Marshall Aid year was greater than that of the trading debts compensated under the Agreement on Multilateral Monetary Compensation.[34] The procedure was also, however, open to the political objection that it did nothing to advance the cause of European economic integration. Nor was it too popular with Congress, which kept a watchful eye

[34] W. Diebold, *Trade and Payments in Western Europe* (New York, 1952), p. 30.

on the origins of imports financed by Marshall Aid.[35] Once the European countries finally agreed on a second payments scheme in October permissions to use Marshall Aid for off-shore purchases within Europe dropped away steeply.

Using the projected trade balances which the Committee of Four had had to construct as a means of recommending to the OEEC Council a just distribution of the next year's allocation of Marshall Aid, the Committee's successors, the Committee of Five as they were called, were able to present a draft payments scheme to the Council in October whose principles were acceptable to the United States. It was that the countries which showed a projected surplus on intra-western European trade over the coming Marshall Aid year should provide this surplus against 'conditional' aid. At the same time the settlements machinery in intra-Western European trade would be improved to cover a greater quantity of non-bilateral settlements. The Agreement for Intra-European Payments and Compensations which embodied these principles was signed on 16 October.

All participants in the OEEC except Switzerland and Portugal now agreed that 'first category compensations', the cancellation of equivalent debts and surpluses in a third currency other than their own, could be made automatically. After this the conditional Marshall Aid would come into play in the form of drawing rights. An agreed estimate of the balance of payments between each pair of countries as it might look on 30 June 1949 was struck and the forecast deficit of the debtor country became its drawing rights on the creditor. About two-fifths of these drawing rights turned out to have been allocated to France and more than two-thirds of those allocated were against Britain and Belgium. The drawing rights were then backed by aid allocated from the existing congressional appropriations and thus either potentially added or taken away after a half-year's trading from the final sum of dollar aid which each European country could have expected to receive on the basis of the recommendations of the OEEC Committee of Four. The net effect of drawing rights was, to use the Bank of England's phrase, 'a second Marshall Plan'. Were, for example, all the drawing rights on Belgium to be taken up it would mean that about four-fifths of its aid allocation, as recommended by the OEEC, would be allocated to other countries to pay for Belgian exports.[36] To what extent this was, in fact, taken into account when the ECA eventually announced its national allocations of dollars for the corresponding aid year is not clear and will perhaps only be cleared up by a complete history of the operations of the ECA.[37]

[35] In 1948 54 per cent of the commodity shipments financed by the ECA were purchased in the United States; in 1949 70 per cent. G. Patterson, *Survey of United States International Finance, 1949* (Princeton, 1950), p. 21.
[36] For a concise and comprehensive statement of the distribution of drawing rights and the extent to which they were taken up, Patterson, *Survey, 1949*, p. 19.
[37] There seems to be a suggestion in BIS, *19th Annual Report* (Basle, 1949), p. 202, that countries did not get more dollars than they would otherwise have been entitled to under the recommendations of the Committee of Four.

The forecast balances of payments did not prove a very accurate statement of the actual trade and payments flows over the period in question. Some impression of the rapid changes in trade flows over the period can be gained by comparing figures 10 and 11. These made the task inherently difficult, but some of the forecasting was wrong. The Committee of Four's version of what would happen in the Bizone proved better than the American version, which had been substituted for it. German exports to Britain increased instead of declining. Likewise the drawing rights established by Britain in favour of Italy were unused because the Italian surplus with Britain persisted. In the end drawing rights financed about 10 per cent of total intra-Western European trade over the period of the agreement. Automatic 'first category compensations' as a means of settlement covered, however, no bigger a proportion of intra-Western European trade than under the first (1947) agreement, because the pattern of trade flows still permitted only a very small number of such automatic compensations to be made. Furthermore, the whole structure still rested firmly on the basis of the bilateral agreements and indeed probably strengthened that basis by giving it greater flexibility and appropriateness to a period of rapidly expanding trade. It provided no incentive to reduce inflation and on balance favoured the deficit countries in the agreement, which was bound to limit eventually the degree of satisfaction with which it could be regarded in America. It depended on the inherently implausible procedure of forecasting trade flows for a year in advance in a period of rapidly changing economic circumstances. The settlements were made at the end of each month, so that countries were using drawing rights to finance successive monthly deficits and surpluses in one bilateral agreement, and thus preventing in some cases what would have been their ultimate annual cancellation against each other. Lastly, it depended absolutely on Marshall Aid and without it would collapse. In American eyes it was altogether a high price to pay. Unless the movement towards 'viability' was a very noticeable one during the course of the agreement, integration and even its herald, multilateralism, would be brought no nearer.

When the ECA decided to give dollar backing to this procedure it had in fact intended to make it the start of a process towards a more genuinely multilateral system by making the drawing rights transferable between countries. Should a forecast surplus, for example, not eventuate the forecast debtor should, it was proposed, be able to use its drawing rights elsewhere. To this the United Kingdom objected, seeing transferable drawing rights as a step towards convertibility, which indeed they were intended to be.[38] When Cripps visited Washington in September 1948 this was one of the two most crucial aspects of his talks, the other being the attempt to persuade the United States to allocate dollar aid against the sterling area, rather than just the British, dollar deficit. His brief was unyielding, proclaiming 'we cannot go

[38]   T 236/819, UK delegation to FO, 7 September 1948.

into a payments scheme with undefined liabilities to pay gold. This is what brought the loan agreement to such a sorry end and if the Americans insist on it it will bring European co-operation to the same end'.[39] In this attitude the United Kingdom was not standing alone. Sweden would not have joined the payments agreement on the same grounds and if Sweden had not joined, Norway, to which Sweden was a major creditor, would not have joined either.[40] Final consideration of any payments plan by the OEEC therefore had to be postponed until Cripps's return from Washington. On 1 October Hoffman withdrew the proposals for transferability of drawing rights, while insisting on the right of the ECA to supervise the use of the conditional aid at all times and so, presumably, maintain its conditionality until the end of the trading period covered by the agreement.

Hoffman's withdrawal had been only tactical and the proposal that drawing rights should be transferable could not fail to be put forward much more strongly as the Agreement for Intra-European Payments and Compensations approached its expiry date in midsummer 1949. The hope in the ECA was that transferable drawing rights might be the prelude to a European clearing union. About this, the United States Treasury was as sceptical as it had been about special dollar aid for intra-Western European trade. Any such union would raise the spectre of a separate soft-currency trading bloc covering a large part of world trade and discriminating against the United States, a sad end to the policy of a multilateral world.[41] On the other hand it could not be denied that the existing payments arrangements themselves tended actually to discourage the transition to multilateralism. Ways of improving them were discussed before the National Advisory Council in April where the ideas put forward by Belgium in summer 1947, for a European central bank, a common monetary policy and a pooling of reserves, re-emerged. It had to be admitted that these goals were at present unattainable, but the ECA was encouraged to raise them 'as a strategy to obtain other ends'.[42] If the assumption, however, had been that the period of the Agreement for Intra-European Payments and Compensations would show a steady progress either towards a Western European payments equilibrium or 'viability' it was to be rudely disturbed by the severe deterioration in the British balance of payments which first became worrying in May 1949 and which was to make the idea of transferable drawing rights or any other approach to convertibility even more alarming to the British government than in 1948. Furthermore, the mounting deficit in dollar trade was accompanied by a large Belgian export surplus to Britain in the first half of the year which could only exacerbate the policy disputes within Western Europe.

[39] T 236/28, Brief for Chancellor's visit to USA, 14 September 1948.
[40] T 236/820, UK delegation to FO, 27 September 1948.
[41] ECA, 42, McCullough to Bissell, 'Attitude of US Treasury staff to European Clearing Union', 5 January 1949.
[42] ECA, 33, Record of action, Advisory Committee, 24 April 1949.

In spite of the apparently healthy tendency to produce surpluses in intra-Western European trade the difficulties of sustaining this position had been very present in the minds of Belgian politicians in pressing so hard for a multilateral payments system in western Europe. The circumstances prevailing had been those of high demand for Belgian steel exports which by 1948 had risen above their pre-war level. This growth had then begun to falter, not because of any weakening of demand, but because of payments difficulties. The creation of the drawing rights had had an immediate effect so that in the first half of 1949 the export boom was renewed. One consequence of the renewed boom was a sharp movement into surplus on current account with the United Kingdom just as sterling area reserves were again coming under pressure internationally (table 32). By the middle of the summer Britain was renouncing contracts for imports of Belgian steel and these quarrels could hardly be kept separate from the animosity between the British government and Spaak over the constitution of the OEEC.

Table 32   Estimated quarterly deficits (−) and surpluses (+) on current account of Belgium/Luxembourg with the United Kingdom (thousand current dollars)

1948	
1st quarter	−2500
2nd quarter	−8600
3rd quarter	−2790
4th quarter	+100
1949	
1st quarter	−250
2nd quarter	+6510
3rd quarter	+980
4th quarter	−4710

Source: OEEC, *Statistical Bulletins of Foreign Trade*, Belgium/Luxembourg as reporting country. There are wide discrepancies between the Belgian figures and the United Kingdom figures, as also between quarterly figures and subsequent annual revisions.

From a Belgian standpoint it seemed from the experience of rising un-employment in 1948 that any interruption in the flow of exports to the rest of Western Europe would be a serious affair. But although the payments agreement of 1948 appeared to have produced an upward movement in Belgian steel exports it did not by any means follow that the same thing would occur in 1949, in spite of the British actions. The causes of the volatility of Belgian steel exports were deeper. They lay in high prices and these in turn were related to the lack of modernization in the industry in the inter-war years. The industry was in need of a long period of investment designed to cut prices on the international markets. Whatever the payments system, 1949 steel output fell to a level only a little higher than at the end of 1947, and employment levels fell with it.[43] Weakness of demand in the domestic market contributed to this drop and made it a reasonable claim on the part of the other OEEC members that they could hardly be expected to devise a payments system which remedied the defects of Belgium's internal policies.

Cripps went so far as to propose to Spaak in May that Belgium be left out of any future European payments agreement. This was only one, probably the least helpful, of a series of compromise proposals as the existing arrangements drew to their end. The gist of most of these was that Britain would only make dollar and gold payments against claims arising from multilateral or transferable drawing rights on a sliding-scale up to a certain limit.[44] At the same time each of the other participants would set aside a proportion of their conditional aid into a pool to fund Belgium's surpluses. Where this did not suffice Belgium would fund the remainder of its surpluses through export credits which would be redeemable only in the case of its running into deficit with the sterling area.

It seems, however, as though the ECA never intended anything so drastic as making *all* drawing rights transferable and that the main question for Hoffman and Harriman was what proportion of the total drawing rights could be made transferable. After all, to make a portion of them transferable would enunciate the principles of multilateralism and convertibility and to make the whole of them transferable would not do very much more to put those principles into practice. Furthermore, if countries failed to use all their drawing rights, they would probably insist on some dollar compensation when asked to transfer them and that, too, was one argument for limiting the extent of transferability. The extra weight which the allocation of drawing rights had added in 1948 to the intolerable burden of allocating Marshall Aid had done so much damage that to increase it by increasing the amounts of aid gained or lost nationally through foreign trade was also something about which the ECA had many reservations. On 23 May Hoffman set out the real objectives of the ECA; half of the drawing rights should be made multilateral and those countries benefiting from them should be able to convert half of that proportion automatically into dollars and the other half only with the ECA's approval.[45] To achieve this there would be a special congressional appropriation distinguished from the general appropriation, as Belgium had originally

[43] Index of total steel production in Belgium (1938 = 100).

	1947	1948	1949
January – June	126.1	164.2	193.7
July – December	138.7	186.3	144.7

Source: Banque de Belgique, *L'Economie belge en 1949* (Brussels, 1950), p. 62.

[44] Some were conditional on Britain not losing gold or dollars at all. ECA, 42, 'Meeting at the UK Treasury on new British proposals for intra-European payments for 1949/50', 27 May 1949.

[45] P. Melandri, *Les Etats-Unis face à l'unification de l'Europe 1945–1954* (Paris, 1980), p. 210.

suggested at the start of the CEEC, which in turn would require European countries to accept the transferability of drawing rights.[46] Harriman's eventual proposal was that as much as 10 per cent of the total congressional appropriation might be set aside for this purpose. Not only did this reduce still further the amount of direct Marshall Aid available at a time when the OEEC could not even agree on the disposition of a larger quantity, but it introduced a new form of political and economic leverage which was likely to be applied most directly to Britain.

A special working group of the OEEC Payments Committee failed to find any basis in May for a renewed payments agreement and the question was shifted up to the Council and the Consultative Group in June. Harriman was present almost throughout the meeting of the Consultative Group, although the illusion of independence was preserved by his not being invited to the first two hours of their discussion. It was in fact the first occasion on which he was able to test the efficacy of the constitutional reform on which he had so long and stridently insisted. The group tried to assess how much of the estimated future Belgian trade surplus with Western Europe was in their view deserving of dollar backing, so that those exports which were inessential could be left to be funded by purely Belgian export credits. The motivation for this procedure was to meet the critique of the existing arrangements that Marshall Aid was being used to fund non-essential imports for non-essential exports, a critique which had been forcefully made by Norway since the start of the year. Norway had demanded a full-scale debate in the OEEC in February over the issue of whether countries should in future subscribe to a payments agreement which sustained Belgium's pattern of trade to debtor countries.

Attempting to break down the composition of Belgian exports in this way was inherently difficult and in any case the official British position was that they would still refuse to guarantee any settlement with Belgium in gold and dollars beyond a certain limit, except in the circumstance where Belgium went into deficit with the sterling area. The United States, on the other hand, would not accept any of the British compromise proposals, regarding them as designed to minimize competition and incentives in intra-Western European trade and to create a soft-currency area in western Europe protected against the more competitive world of the dollar zone.[47] On the eve of the meeting of the OEEC Council Cripps told Harriman that Britain would refuse to join any new payments scheme if the United States continued to insist on the transferability of drawing rights. The Council agreed that if no solution were found within two weeks Cripps, Harriman, Petsche, the French Minister of Finance, and Spaak would be allowed to decide the issue amongst themselves.[48] They argued that there must be a special provision to cope with the forecast

[46] FRUS, 1949, IV, Hoffman to Harriman, 21 April 1949.
[47] CAB 134–238, Minutes of European Economic Co-operation Committee, 22 June 1949, 24 June 1949.   [48] SD 840.50, 5682, Harriman to Washington, 6 June 1949.

Belgian surpluses, but Cripps was not prepared, even though he was in a weak position in the group, to accept transferability of drawing rights. In the outcome what the ECA obtained was much less than Hoffman had proposed in May as the aim of the negotiation.

On 28 June 1949 the Consultative Group met again to consider special provisions for handling the forecast Belgian surpluses. There were only two days to go before the expiry of the existing agreement. They disagreed for two days and nights. In Washington the ECA was now genuinely afraid, against the background of the rapidly deteriorating sterling position, that the British opposition to any form of convertibility was such that the United Kingdom might withdraw into an isolated soft-currency bloc with the sterling area and finally abandon the pursuit of a multilateral world.[49] Just before the Consultative Group was due to report its final inability to agree to the Council in the early evening Harriman made a compromise proposal that only 40 per cent of the drawing rights should be multilateral and that all rights so transferred should be covered up to 60 per cent by conditional aid and the remaining 40 per cent by credits from the exporter. In effect this meant that only about a quarter of the total drawing rights would be convertible. Belgium then agreed to these proposals, but only on condition that a relationship be established between the amount of credit it now would be expected to grant to its European partners and the size of its deficit with the dollar zone. The forecast Belgian surplus on intra-Western European trade was about $400 million and the forecast deficit with the United States about $200 million. Belgium agreed to provide credits of $38 million to the Netherlands, $28 million to Britain and $21.5 million to France, and a further $112.5 million of the forecast export surplus in intra-Western European trade was to be covered by additional drawing rights to the same three countries. A limit, $352.2 million, was then set on the total drawing rights which could be used against Belgium. So before gold and dollars would be used to make settlements Belgium would have to have a surplus in intra-Western European trade of $440 million. In the event only the Netherlands used up the provision made. The new provisions came into operation in time to cope with the problems caused by the end of the old ones, although the actual agreement (Agreement for Intra-European Payments and Compensations for 1949–50) was not signed until September.

It lasted for a year and financed about the same proportion of intra-Western European trade as its precursor. The fact that agreement was reached was testimony to the unwillingness of the Western European countries to abandon the idea of multilateral settlements in Europe in spite of the extreme difficulty of actually bringing them into practice. All had an interest in adapting the institutional machinery to cope with the persistent growth of foreign trade and much of the argument was really more directed at not losing sums of dollars in direct Marshall Aid because of domestic economic policies elsewhere.

[49] ECA, 2, 'Suggested basis for an agreement with the British', 27 June 1949.

The sums of money represented by Belgium's surpluses were not so very large, but that relatively prosperous Belgium should be sustained at the cost of less prosperous countries which might get in the end a smaller sum of dollar aid than they might otherwise have been allocated was naturally hard to accept.

The logic of expanding foreign trade triumphed in the end, it may be said, but the political effort it required worsened relationships between the nations in the OEEC in Paris to the point of impossibility, accelerated the collapse of the OEEC as an integrative body, and led more surely to the defeat of American policy there. In that sense the agreement did more harm than good to American policy, whatever principles for the future it managed weakly to enunciate and whatever it demonstrated about the readiness of Western European countries to make a certain small measure of sacrifice to sustain the expansion of their foreign trade with each other. Like the process of aid allocation by the OEEC it brought the divisions between European countries rather than their points of agreement to the forefront and this time for very little political gain.

ONE WESTERN WORLD, OR TWO?

It has no doubt been impossible to hide the fact that the negotiations about the framework of Western Europe's foreign trade after the announcement of Marshall Aid were intricate and tedious. Countries fought with remarkable tenacity over the loss of what were often only small sums of aid. What were at stake, however, were important principles of national and international policy. If an unacceptable move towards multilateralism or, a greater cause for anxiety, convertibility, was forced by the massive pressures from the United States (and the Belgian proposals increased the chances of this happening), the political choice might be made to reject the promises of Bretton Woods in the interest of more urgent domestic needs. After all, given the fact that Britain had been the pivot of the international trade and payments mechanism for so long and that this mechanism had itself been a formative force of great importance in British history and culture, an astonishing number of members of parliament of different political views had been prepared to vote against the American loan and for what Keynes called 'a siege economy', even before the crises of 1947 and 1949.

It is true that the commitment of policy-makers and politicians in the two major Western European economies to multilateralism had been strong since 1945. Nothing in the Monnet Plan had changed that. Indeed, the basic intention of the Plan was to enable the French economy to function competitively in a multilateral world in the way it had been unable to do after 1932. As for the smaller economies, 'a siege economy' offered them very little. But the collapse of Bretton Woods, the failure of convertibility, the sight of the

IMF and the World Bank turned into mere organs of American foreign policy, the sight of the proposed ITO tottering towards rejection opened up again the same range of discussion about the future as at the end of the war. At the point where arguments about the European payments system impinged on the role of sterling in the world economy they raised problems, not just of the future Western European economic order, but of the economic order of the whole western world.

This was the area of contact where the ERP came into conflict with what was still officially American world policy. Having been forced to abandon sterling–dollar convertibility the United Kingdom had no intention of seeing it reintroduced by the circuitous route of a European payments agreement. If convertibility of European currencies was to start even in the most limited way in 1949 it was only likely to be acceptable in London if Western Europe and its dependencies were merged with the sterling area in one soft currency area protected from the dollar zone and discriminating against it. Although the support which Marshall Aid had given to ambitious reconstruction plans in European countries meant American toleration of discrimination against dollar imports into Western Europe, this was thought of as only a temporary stage on the road to 'viability'. A future western world divided into two currency and trading areas was abhorrent in Washington.

Sterling area trade was so large a part of world trade and the sterling area multilateral payments system itself so useful to its participating members that the bargaining position of the United Kingdom was a very strong one. This was why at the desperate close of the negotiations for the 1949 payments agreement the ECA, as it had foreseen, had to abandon its insistence on a larger degree of convertibility of drawing rights. It was afraid that the United Kingdom would simply refuse to participate at all and, while still claiming to be in pursuit of one multilateral world, try to take several of the European countries with it into a soft currency trading area. This would have implied the defeat of all the political aims of the ERP.

Histories of the period assume attachment to the sterling area was one of the fundamental reasons for the United Kingdom's opposition to the idea of a European union of which it would itself have been a member. But as the negotiations in the Customs Union Study Group showed this was not so; the existence of the sterling area was perfectly compatible with a customs union including the dependent territories of other European countries which would have functioned as a soft currency area. This would have provided in the eyes of many ministers and civil servants a sufficient degree of independence from the United States and a sufficient measure of future economic security. A free-trade or low tariff area covering Western Europe and its empires was an option looked on with favour. The sterling area was only a reason for not supporting the Little European customs union, Greater Benelux, on which French policy had now become fixed. Until this became the goal of French policy the sterling area was not necessarily an obstacle to European integration within a much wider world framework. The obstacles to this wider concept were in Western Europe and the United States. Some countries could not have accepted the reduction of trade and exchange controls which that implied, some could not have accepted the low tariffs, some could not have accepted the political implications of British or Franco-British domination which were implicit, and some, unlike the first majority left-wing government to be elected in Britain, did not believe that colonies could offer in the post-war world such promise of security and stability. As soon as the idea of a Little European customs union became central to French policy the sterling area did become an obstacle to European integration. The struggle over the 1949 payments agreement was primarily between Britain and the sterling area on the one side and the United States on the other, but it was noticeable that French support for Britain was barely lukewarm, no more than needed to defend western Europe and the OEEC against American ambitions.

The forecast balances of payments on which the 1949 Agreement for Intra-European Payments and Compensations was based were even less accurate than the year before. A great surge of growth in the West German economy sucked in imports from all over Western Europe, the flow of West German payments was reversed, and the forecast West German export surplus ended up as a large import surplus. Equally striking, the French deficits which had been a constant feature since the end of the war were reversed. French exports grew with remarkable rapidity and France became a surplus country on intra-Western European account. Although the allocation of drawing rights could be and was altered to take account of the currency readjustments in autumn 1949 it could not take account of the major changes in trade. The devaluation of most European currencies in autumn and the swings in trade not only exposed the inadequacy of the 1949 payments agreement and the whole system of drawing rights, they forced to the forefront the serious issues about the unity of the western world and about the economic basis of that unity, showing the inadequacy of the earlier payments agreements to be very much the result of the way they had fudged such issues. It is simply not true that Western Europe progressed gradually through a series of increasingly sophisticated and liberal payments agreements to the EPU. The EPU, as well as trade liberalization, was born out of the failure of what had gone before, not out of a gradual, successful evolution towards multilateralism and integration.

Less than two months after the signing of the 1949 payments agreement Hoffman officially proclaimed that the path forward to integration would now no longer lie through strengthening the political machinery of the OEEC. Before this the ECA had broken by administrative decision the institutional and political link in the OEEC between aid allocation and payments schemes. But this did not imply any renunciation of the belief that foreign trade led to integration, quite the contrary. What replaced the policy of concentrating on the OEEC as a force for political integration was what was thought of as a more apolitical route to the same goal, the use of Marshall Aid to force European countries to remove legislative and administrative barriers to trade, the trade liberalization programme. If concentrating on the improvement of payments mechanisms had only led to serious confrontations over policy which did not even increase European economic co-operation and made integration seem further away, the integrative force of foreign trade could still perhaps be liberated and all these political clashes avoided by simply removing quota restrictions and lowering tariffs. Trade liberalization could be made the price of Marshall Aid, particularly as this was a price which the United Kingdom might be willing to pay. To set a price, such as convertibility, which the United Kingdom was unwilling to pay might end the hope of one multilateral world as well as of Western European integration. Those two goals might not prove ultimately reconcilable, but a minimum condition for reconciling them was that the sterling area should not become a separate western economic system.

IX

DEVALUATION AND THE SEARCH FOR A NEW AMERICAN POLICY

Taking stock in summer 1949 of America's attempt to reconstruct Western Europe it can only be judged at that stage as a near-complete failure. The bold policy of the Marshall Plan had succeeded only in confirming and strengthening the western Europe of independent, competitive nation states which had emerged from the war. It had added to them another one, the German Federal Republic, whose future relationships to Western Europe were obscure and even menacing. The Western European international framework into which West Germany was to be integrated was tenuous and inadequate – a military alliance from which Germany was excluded, a vague and powerless Council of Europe, and the OEEC, which not only made evident the independence and lack of co-operation of the nation states but might endure no longer than Marshall Aid. Faced with the problem of disembarrassing itself of the Ruhr Authority, the Occupation Statute and western tutelage, West Germany might go into limbo and thence eventually into the Russian bloc.

The grand European customs union had been a mirage, Greater Benelux an unrealizable French idea which the United States would not even have supported, and smaller customs unions had been only paper castles. The European payments agreements had clawed their way painfully forward to multilateralize tiny percentages of intra-western European trade while the basis of Europe's trade remained even more restrictive and protective than in the 1930s. The common Western European long-term plan which was supposed to emerge from the OEEC had sunk without trace. The United Kingdom now threatened to block not only economic integration in Western Europe but a multilateral framework for world trade. Of the European framework which had been the first step in its reconstruction virtually nothing had been built. The end of Marshall Aid was approaching and not even 'viability' was in sight, while the sterling crisis made it seem an even more remote possibility. There was nothing in any direction other than the congealing fear of the Soviet Union to hold western Europe together or make it a more stable area than it had been four years after the First World War. And whatever power Marshall Aid had given to the United States was already much weaker and would soon run out. American discontent had been made increasingly clear over the life of the 1948 payments agreement. From spring 1949 onwards there was an increasingly anxious reappraisal and re-examination of American policies. Throughout this reappraisal ran the persistent question, 'What will happen when Marshall Aid ends?' It was the task of the ECA to provide an answer, for it was the political and economic objectives in Western Europe on which they themselves had most insisted which had so far provided most of the rationale of the ERP.

It had become evident that the European countries would not adjust their economic policies to a common horizon. Nor were they striving to reach a payments equilibrium with the dollar zone by 1951–2. Nor would they co-operate in the OEEC to create the economic or political machinery which would serve to integrate, still less that required to unify, Western Europe. If the hopes originally placed on OEEC as an instrument of economic and political integration were abandoned or postponed, what other economic policy could, in the short time now left, succeed in producing sufficient change in the European economy to bring about 'viability' and at the same time advance, even if not so quickly as had once been hoped, the cause of integration.

From early 1949 a group within the ECA began to press hard for a different policy which would reduce the degree of direct political confrontation with the European countries but in the end might achieve more success. The group had its origins not only in the realization that the OEEC had put up a successful opposition to American aims but also in discontent with the extent to which the ECA had so far favoured policies of intervention, control, and maintaining import surpluses in European economies. These they considered to produce merely national recovery and to be unsoundly based because they were beyond the true capacity of the countries concerned. Such policies, they agreed, made the integration of Western Europe itself less likely and impeded, instead of furthering, the integration of Western Europe into a multilateral world system. Marshall Aid, it was argued, was permitting, even encouraging, a Europe of nation states full of economic irrationalities which would continue in the foreseeable future to require American aid. The leading exponent of these views was Richard Bissell. He was himself convinced that the economic integration of western Europe was indispensable if 'viability' was to be achieved and that by insisting on a rapid advance towards integration the more objectionable aspects of post-war European economic and social policy could also be altered.

The position of the group was strengthened by the vociferous opposition in Congress to ECA policies which were thought, firstly, to be encouraging governments of distinctly left-wing tendencies to waste American money on the pursuit of their own objectives and, secondly, not to be bringing sufficient pressure to bear to force the political integration of Western Europe. Congress, Bissell thought, would insist that before the next round of Marshall Aid appropriations the European countries would have to give a firm commitment to form either one or two integrated economic units. There would have to be a surrender of sovereignty over monetary and fiscal policy to a central agency and over trade and tariff policy to another central body. His ideas were a restatement of the simpler ideas of Hoffman, but allied to a different programme of action. There was a direct, immediate correlation, he argued, between larger markets and higher levels of productivity. The way to 'viability' still lay through the application of customs union theory and the creation of a United States of Europe. But Bissell was able to make much more cogently the links to economic theory which sometimes eluded Hoffman, and his sense of political urgency was strong. He wrote:

> This coincides with our own belief that, over long term, attainment and maintenance of economic viability as well as political stability and military security require West European union or unions. As ECA aid declines in future, we will be less able to cushion shocks and ease adjustments of unification. Time is running out to accomplish this work in many ways, not least of which is Soviet possession of atomic bomb so much ahead of schedule.[1]

The group which Bissell gathered round himself, Theodore Geiger, Harold van B. Cleveland, his brother Harlan Cleveland, and John Hully,[2] the Planning Group as they were styled, was able to display Bissell's theoretical convictions on a pedestal of comparative economic history and thus convince at least themselves that a refusal by European countries to go along these lines was not only against America's interests but even more against their own and the larger good. They compared the differences in economic development between Europe and the United States in the nineteenth century and identified the crucial difference as the creation at that time in the United States of one large national market. Unless Europe were to achieve the same degree of economic unification it would continue to fall behind the United States in

---

[1] ECA, 33, Bissell to Katz and Gordon, 2nd draft, 10 May 1949.

[2] It is on the work of this group that M. Beloff lays so much emphasis in his pioneering study, *The United States and the Unity of Europe* (Brookings Institution, Washington DC, 1963), although, presumably because he had no access to earlier documentation and other archives, he greatly exaggerates the extent to which ECA policy in 1949, in insisting on European integration, was a new departure. Integration was central to Marshall Aid from the outset and the new policies in 1949 were only a restatement of an old theme. Harlan Cleveland coined the phrase 'the revolution of rising expectations'.

terms of output per head and the competitiveness of its manufactures. 'Viability', therefore, did depend ultimately on a major political reconstruction of the continent and not on the minor economic and political adjustments which the ECA had so far achieved, and without that major reconstruction Marshall Aid would either prove to have been wasted within its forecast term or would have to be continued in some form or another, perhaps indefinitely, if the United States were not to lose sight of its original global objectives for the post-war period.

Looking back on these views most people are now likely to be first impressed by the thinness and superficiality of the academic justification for such massive interference in the complexities of other areas of the world as well as the unquestioning assumption that the history of the United States itself provided some higher guide to the path of economic development. They are likely to see indications of the links between parochialism, complacency and arrogance which later were to mar American policy-making in more helpless parts of the world. But at the time these intellectual justifications for a new policy were the most unquestioned aspect of it. Identifying what Europe had failed to borrow from the history of the United States was easy and met with wide acceptance; how to graft it on to European history was a more controversial matter.

It was here that the Planning Group came to a tactical solution that was eventually to be espoused by Hoffman and Harriman themselves, and was to have close resemblances to the tactical solution later urged by ardent European federalists and elevated by political scientists to the level of theory under the name of 'functionalism'. It was necessary to create, they argued, such institutional machinery as would by its very functioning produce different patterns of economic and political thought and behaviour in Europe. The difficulty with the OEEC was that this was just what it could not do because it had been designed as a coping-stone to cap the whole edifice of an economically integrated Western Europe before that edifice had itself been built. Better to design institutions which would be on no higher a level than the bureaucratic and technocratic and allow them to be operated by non-political actors, who would then see themselves as solving technocratic problems in unison rather than as representing a particular combination of purely national interests. Such institutions would then be the breeding-ground for further institutional, procedural and behavioural changes leading to an expanding network of similar institutions and eventually to the formation of a new economic framework and a new political community in Western Europe. If by an act of political will Western Europe could put one or two such institutions in place they would, like yeast, work their own ferment. The institution to which the Planning Group gave pride of place was an inter-European commerce commission, designed along the lines of the Interstate Commerce Commission in the United States. Secondly they proposed a European central financial institution with similar powers to the Federal Reserve Board. Europe's problems and the problems of the international economy, they concluded, were not being solved by aid because as far as Europe was concerned they were 'structural problems' inherited from the nineteenth century and they necessitated 'structural' changes. 'This is, in effect, the road to economic union and probably the only practicable one.'[3]

Even if this act of political will were to be achieved there would still have to be continuing direct aid to cope with an anticipated dollar deficit of somewhere between one and two thousand million dollars in 1952–3. Precisely because the real problems were long-run historical ones they could not be cured quickly. When Harlan Cleveland undertook the task of persuading the State Department to accept the new policy he assumed a slowing-down in the rate of growth of output and productivity in Western Europe after 1950 which would be only gradually reversed again as these institutional changes took effect. He argued:

> Unless means can be found to accelerate the normal rate of growth of productivity in western Europe above its pre-war level and even above the level of the last year of the ERP period, the longer range prospects for European self-support at politically tolerable living standards are not bright.

This task was 'one of the most difficult ever to be faced by the western world'. It could only be achieved by attacking the most fundamental reason for the alleged slow rate of productivity growth, 'the stifling effect on the process of economic growth, on competition and on the spirit of enterprise of the restrictive policies and practices of the participating countries, particularly economic nationalism'. The first step in this process was to eliminate all barriers to trade and payments across the area of Western Europe and to do this an inter-European commerce commission and afterwards a single currency and a unified banking system were necessary.[4]

None of this, however, had been accepted as official ECA policy when that policy was submitted to the NAC in August, although the sentiments which underlay it, strengthened by disappointment over the 1949 payments agreement, had produced certain significant modifications. Dollar aid was to be made more selective between countries as a preparation for the possibility that it might still be necessary to continue to provide support after the official termination of Marshall Aid to what were now considered as 'weak spots', Austria, Greece, Italy and West Germany. The main new ideas for producing 'viability' were two. First there were proposals for further stabilization loans to the United Kingdom and France, which would only be made against guarantees of less inflationary domestic policies. Secondly, every effort was to

---

[3] ECA, 10, Memorandum by Geiger, Cleveland and Hully, 19 July 1949.
[4] SD 340.50, 5863, Cleveland to Perkins, 15 August 1949.

be made to stimulate a great increase in private American investment to Western Europe and the rest of the sterling area.[5] This, of course, meant removing 'obstacles' to such investment. But although this represented significant changes of principle from ECA's earlier policies, ECA was still locked in the struggle to obtain agreement in the OEEC Council to the recommendations on aid allocation for 1950.

Elsewhere in Washington there was a powerful undertow of opposition to any further policy measures which concentrated on Europe alone or created further specifically European institutions. There was, for example, one apparently much simpler and more appealing route to 'viability'. This was to force the Europeans to devalue their currencies against the dollar and thereby return to something like the Bretton Woods agreements by establishing a more realistic set of currency parities which would increase the volume of European exports. Why continue to provide Marshall Aid to allow Western European countries to maintain overvalued currencies? Did not America's real economic interest lie in world-wide trade liberalization and world-wide multilateralism? If devaluations produced 'viability', these objectives were again in sight. To create a specific Western European supra-national body which would be first and foremost concerned with trade might only encourage the Europeans to create a large, and in terms of economic negotiations very powerful, soft-currency trade bloc which would never attain international competitiveness with the dollar zone and would continue therefore to discriminate massively against America's foreign trade. From spring 1949 the possibility of devaluation increasingly dominated the stage in policy discussions outside the ECA, while inside the ECA, although the struggle to make the OEEC the instrument of European integration continued, the new policies advocated by the Planning Group came to the forefront.

Within the OEEC itself the subject of devaluation had always been an extremely touchy one. Although several currencies, including the French franc, had had their value against the dollar adjusted downwards since the IMF had begun operations, it was understood that the key exchange rate was that of the pound against the dollar and that any talk of readjusting European currency values against the dollar meant first devaluing sterling. The fact that the leadership in the ECA did not see such a devaluation as a panacea for attaining 'viability' did not mean that they were opposed to it, rather that they increasingly saw it as a necessary first step towards providing a sound basis for subsequent political acts of integration. Some European countries saw it as a necessary step towards improving Western Europe's position and one which might be taken in concert in the OEEC to avoid the 'competitive devaluations' which were held to have marred the 1930s. In November 1948 Sweden had approached the United Kingdom to try to bring up the issue in the OEEC because it was under pressure from its own exporters. The Swedes had been

[5] ECA, 33, 'The ECA program for the fiscal year 1951', 10 August 1949.

firmly told to forget the whole subject. But with opinion in the American Treasury and the Federal Reserve Board running the way it was, seeing devaluation as a step back towards Bretton Woods and a more useful approach to the world payments problem than that of the ECA, it was not likely to be forgotten for long.

One of the more curious aspects of the story is that there seems to have been very little proper analysis in the United Kingdom after the war of the serious long-term question of what the optimum sterling–dollar exchange rate should have been. The amount of direct competition in international trade between British and American goods was not great. It was certain that a lower exchange rate would worsen the terms of trade for Britain. But there was a plausible argument, nevertheless, that in the long run, given the great productivity gains in the United States during the war, a lower rate of exchange against the dollar would be a better reflection of the relative levels of costs and prices in the two countries and might permit a safer accumulation of reserves. Whatever the better decision would have been, one thing is clear. When the devaluation did come, in spite of its sweeping nature its timing was dictated by the pressure of outside events and was in no way the outcome of political forethought. It came because the loss of reserves was accelerating so rapidly that the pound was forced off the existing exchange rate. Even when the decision had been taken its timing was dictated and delayed by personal considerations relating to Cripps, who had firmly opposed it, and diplomatic considerations which were scarcely relevant. The extent of the devaluation appears to have been even less the product of careful analysis than the setting of the first post-war dollar exchange rate, having been decided in personal agreement by Bevin and Cripps at the last moment as though it were a matter of subsidiary importance.[6]

In fact the issue only became seriously discussed in 1949. The discussion was muddled. Opinion was very divided and eventually ministers took the jump because the only alternative policies they were being offered, cuts in public expenditure and deflation, were exactly what they had been elected to avoid and also evoked horrible memories of 1931. A longer-term appraisal of the problem in the calmer circumstances of 1945, or even 1948, would in fact have enabled the issue to be decided more rationally by stripping it of the accompanying and often irrelevant squabbles about what sorts of cuts in public expenditure should be made.

In February 1949 John W. Snyder, the Treasury Secretary, told the Joint Congressional Committee on Foreign Relations in a public hearing that exchange rates in his opinion should be reviewed in the course of the next financial year.[7] But when Sweden raised the issue again it was informed that

[6] I am grateful to Sir Alec Cairncross for providing me with a draft of his own work on this question.

[7] John Wesley Snyder, 1895– . A banker. Served in Office of Controller of Currency 1931–7. Director of Defense Plant Corporation 1940–3. Director of Office of War Mobilization and Reconversion 1945. Secretary to Treasury 1946–53. Returned to private business.

the British view was that devaluation should never be discussed at Paris, as it was not an appropriate question for an international forum.[8] When some ECA officials managed to insert into the draft annual report to Congress that a discussion of devaluation should be put on the OEEC agenda for 1949 the British insisted that it be taken out. Thus the Plan of Action mentioned only an 'examination of costs and prices'. Cripps sent Snyder a personal message objecting strongly to the American government attempting to raise the issue through the alternative channel of discussion in the IMF. Nevertheless, the IMF voted on 6 April to ask the Director to start an enquiry into European exchange rates. Over the next two months Camille Gutt pursued a series of conversations with European governments on this theme.

The ECA was convinced of the need for more realistic exchange rates. What ECA opinion now thought of as an overvaluation of European currencies against the dollar could, it was argued, only increase the danger of the emergence of a soft-currency area in international trade and of trade discrimination against the United States. Within the shelter of that soft-currency area European countries would probably fall even further behind United States levels of productivity.[9] Gutt, too, was personally in favour of devaluation.[10] By May the Treasury, the ECA and the NAC all believed the devaluation of the pound 'an urgent necessity'.[11] The British-Argentinian trade agreement of 1949 came in for particular criticism as did the exports of British oil companies to former American markets in Sweden, Egypt and Argentina. The shortage of dollars, it was argued, was still such as often to nullify the comparative advantage of lower American prices and allow British exports to compete unfairly but without any long-run advantage to Britain, Europe or the world. In these circumstances the United Kingdom was really, in trying to prevent all discussion of devaluation, attempting to stop a dam which was being breached in several places. In the NAC Acheson defended the view that realism demanded some British discrimination against dollar imports and a place in potential American markets for British exports, but by the end of June the NAC was seriously discussing whether to make devaluation of the pound a pre-requisite for approval of the British trade liberalization proposals in the OEEC.[12] The ECA for a time considered making devaluation of the pound a pre-requisite for the concessions which the United States made in the 1949 Agreement for Intra-European Payments and Compensations.[13]

At the high-level diplomatic consultations of the first two weeks of July, which were primarily concerned with defence issues, the awareness of Britain's deteriorating dollar balance of payments, like Banquo's ghost, appeared at all

[8] T 232/88, Note by Hall-Patch, 7 April 1949.
[9] FRUS, 1949, IV, p. 377, Hoffman to Harriman, 17 March 1949.
[10] SD 340.50, 5680, Memorandum from Knapp to Thorp, 4 April 1949.
[11] T 232/88, Washington embassy to FO, 12 May 1949.
[12] NAC, meeting no. 131, 28 June 1949.
[13] ECA, 2, 'Suggested basis for an agreement with the British', 27 June 1949.

the most inopportune moments. The British hope was that some comprehensive settlement of the relationship between sterling and the dollar could be obtained in the context of a general settlement. Such a settlement involved tariff reductions by the United States and an increase in American imports from Europe, extra American support for those sterling area countries whose dollar earnings were falling in the recession, and an increase in American investment in Europe and European colonies. When Bevin and Cripps met Schuman and Massigli, the French ambassador to London, on 4 July, Bevin explained that he regarded the problem as a European one and was opposed to any separate resolution of it purely between Britain and the United States. Devaluation was, in his view, 'no final solution'.[14] Schuman was prepared to agree that the question of devaluation be handled at a government level and kept out of the OEEC. When Bevin and Cripps, however, then moved on to sketch out their proposed joint European approach to prevent devaluation Schuman remained unmoved. He 'said that in France there was a good deal of mistrust of plans for large-scale investment of American capital. The French were always afraid that if the Americans got a major share in an enterprise they would seek to exercise political control.'[15]

When Snyder arrived in London on 8 July for scheduled talks with Cripps, he was every bit as damping about the one other positive British proposal. This was that the United States should increase its purchases from the sterling area of strategic materials for stockpiling in order to build up sterling area dollar balances. The British government then proceeded to formulate cuts in dollar imports of as much as $400 million and struggled unavailingly to make Snyder agree to a joint communiqué that neither government considered devaluation 'an appropriate measure'.[16] Devaluation had not, in fact, been officially discussed, which was in the end what the communiqué said.

Less than two weeks later the cabinet was informed of the more rapid loss of British reserves, and the increased bid for Marshall Aid which added the last straw to the intolerable burden on the OEEC was submitted at Paris.[17] Bevin told Schuman in Paris that 'there was general realisation that the choice lay between the establishment of one common financial system outside the Russian area or the development of two rival currency areas.'[18] And if Bevin was always careful to stress his own support for the former outcome Snyder had left London feeling that Cripps inclined towards the latter. Within the United Kingdom Treasury opinion remained divided, certain Treasury officials being now attracted to the idea of a currency union or even a customs union with the United States to guarantee the 'one common financial system', while others inclined towards the view that the United Kingdom would be

[14]   T 232/90, Record of a conversation at the Foreign Office, 4 July 1949.   [15]   ibid.
[16]   FRUS, 1949, IV, p. 801, Snyder to Acheson, 10 July 1949.
[17]   See pp. 204–6.
[18]   T 232/91, Record of a conversation at the Quai d'Orsay, 23 July 1949.

better off as the leader of a separate non-dollar world.[19] On all these dramatic matters Schuman remained very guarded and obviously still unconvinced by Bevin's protestations that within his global proposals for the resolution of the dollar problem he either intended or would be able to negotiate a solution which would preserve the Franco-British front in western Europe.

The British cabinet took the decision less than a week later that a devaluation was unavoidable, but Cripps, who was ill in Switzerland, seems to have delayed the final ratification of the decision and, furthermore, insisted that it should not be announced until 18 September 1949, after the return meeting with Snyder in Washington to discuss the proposals which the British had put forward in the July talks had taken place. A round of tripartite technical discussions including Canada starting on 27 August had been arranged to precede the main talks of 6 September. Both sides prepared the ground carefully. The American starting-point was that devaluation was the only possible solution to the sterling area's and Europe's problems and that the devaluation must be done through the IMF to preserve its authority. Beyond that they wished to turn the meetings into a full-scale review of earlier European trade and payments agreements and of how some better system might be reconstituted.[20] There were few illusions in Washington about the difficulty of the United States' position. The cuts in British imports were already being implemented and opinion in Washington even envisaged a declaration of national emergency in London and the proclamation of a moratorium on gold and dollar payments. A drastic break in British-American relations could be foreseen which might mean the end of all American plans for multilateralism and also, perhaps, for European reconstruction. The opinion of the ECA was that 'it is evident...that we will be in an extremely difficult position at the September meetings.'[21]

On any balanced view the United States had to accept that its role as a creditor country implied extensive responsibilities if it also wanted the corresponding political and economic advantages. Remedies for the situation began to be discussed with some rapidity as the talks came nearer, the lowering of American tariffs, the simplification of customs procedures, a more favourable attitude towards sterling oil sales by British oil companies, as well as the British suggestion of stockpiling raw materials. The idea of bargaining these possible concessions against the introduction of convertibility faded in the cold light of political feasibility, rather as it had done in the early stages of negotiating the Agreement for Intra-European Payments and Compensations. Convertibility, on ECA estimates, implied a sterling devaluation

[19] See the discussions in T 232/92, passim.

[20] ECA, 33, 'United States proposals on agenda for discussions with British and Canadians', 15 August 1949.

[21] ECA, 2, 'Implications of the sterling area crisis to the United Kingdom and the United States', 18 August 1949.

of more than 25 per cent and both the internal and external effects of that seemed likely to be drastic and not too easily foreseeable.[22]

When the British delegation arrived they informed all those of ministerial level on the American side of the fact and date of devaluation, although not of the new exchange rate which appears to have been decided rather vaguely by those present in the British delegation in Washington. The suspicion was inevitably aroused in France that devaluation had been the result of an Anglo-American agreement in the talks and this suspicion continues to be voiced even now.[23] The Director of the IMF was told privately on 15 September. France and the Commonwealth countries were informed on 17 September, one day in advance of the announcement; other European countries learned from the announcement itself.

What the United Kingdom did agree to in the Washington talks was to make proposals for the gradual drawing down of the sterling balances which were now larger than they had been at the time of the 1947 crisis; to participate in a trade liberalization programme within the OEEC and also in the formation of a European payments union; to embark on a joint 'productivity programme' with the United States in order to raise productivity levels in British industry; to study ways of providing incentives for exports to the dollar zone; to enter into negotiations on the problem of oil sales; and to give a higher degree of priority to the negotiation of a commercial treaty with the United States which would include British colonial territories.[24] Each of these concessions of course did much to banish the spectre of two separate international trade and currency zones in the western world and with one exception each dealt with issues where there was a specific Anglo-American interest distinct from that of the other western European economies. In return the United States agreed to consider providing support for the reduction of the sterling balances once British proposals had been received. It agreed to embark on a relaxation and simplification of its tariffs and customs procedures. It agreed to take stronger action against the domestic shipping lobby which had been able to get such a high proportion of ERP goods shipped in American bottoms at high dollar freight rates. And finally it agreed, although the commitment was rather vague, to look for ways of increasing its stockpiles of certain strategic goods, of which natural rubber was the most in question.

On 18 September it was announced that the pound would be devalued by 30.5 per cent against the dollar. So severe a devaluation was inevitably followed by a wave of European currency readjustments of which the only one to be delayed by serious political disputes was that of the West German mark.

[22] ibid., 'A Study of effects to be expected from the devaluation of sterling', 22 August 1949.

[23] T 232/97, Correspondence between the Paris embassy and the Foreign Office, passim. Melandri ambiguously implies that the tripartite talks 'led to' (*aboutit à*) the British decision to devalue (P. Melandri, *Les Etats-Unis face à l'unification de l'Europe 1945–1954* (Paris, 1980), pp. 225–6).

[24] ECA, 3, 'Six-Month evaluation of progress on the dollar–pound Problem', n.d.

In August Schuman, Petsche and Alphand had been hoping that France might be in some way included in the Washington talks. In the event they went to Washington at the same time, but for separate discussions and were there, but excluded, while the British-American-Canadian talks took place. Three days after their conclusion Acheson, Snyder, Harriman and Hoffman gave the French delegation what on all the existing documentation seems a frank and fair account of what had transpired without breaching the secret of devaluation. They stressed that with the chief exception of the agreements on sterling balances the agreements reached in the tripartite talks would be beneficial to France and the OEEC also.[25] Neither on that nor any subsequent occasion is there any evidence to support the view that Schuman or other important members of the French government felt that there had been an Anglo-American conspiracy against France, although Bonnet, the ambassador in Washington, did try to represent it in that light. Nor is there any evidence that Schuman or Petsche regarded the British-American-Canadian conversations as a serious breach of understanding with France or as an event so drastic as to promote changes of policy by reaction in France.[26] Bonnet cabled that

Table 33   The extent of European currency devaluations relative to the dollar, September 1949

	%
United Kingdom	
Denmark	
Iceland	−30.5
Ireland	
Norway	
Sweden	
Netherlands	−30.2
France	−21.8
West Germany	−20.6
Portugal	−13.0
Belgium/Luxembourg	−12.3
Italy	−8.0

Source: *International Financial Statistics*, 3 (1), 1950.

the talks were 'a historic breaking-point'.[27] Reynaud, the Prime Minister in 1940, described the British action as a breach of understanding and Gaston Palewski, speaking for de Gaulle's new movement, said that Britain should

[25] FRUS, 1949, IV, p. 654, Memorandum of conversation prepared in the Department of State, 15 September 1949.
[26] This does not seem to be the opinion of Melandri who implies that the tripartite talks were a crucial turning-point in French policy (Melandri, *Les Etats-Unis*, pp. 225 ff.).
[27] ibid., p. 226.

not now be surprised to find France in a *tête-à-tête* with Germany. The Council of Ministers protested about the failure to consult, although the French record of consultation with Britain over earlier French post-war devaluations scarcely justified such a complaint. There is no evidence that Schuman or Petsche regarded the matter in this light. The evidence is rather that Schuman gave no ear to these somewhat hysterical exaggerations.[28] He seems to have been neither taken aback by the talks nor by the subsequent devaluation, because he had already come to the conclusion, no matter how loud and frequent the sympathetic European noises made by Bevin, that the realities of Britain's position in the international economy implied not only the need for a measure of separate economic agreement between the United Kingdom and the United States, but independent action in Europe by France. His main efforts in the Washington talks were in fact devoted to the idea of a separate payments association covering 'Little Europe', France, Benelux and Italy, for which negotiations were taking place at the same time, and to eliminating dual prices for German and British coal in order to get cheaper coal imports.

Naturally, the French government would have preferred to have been consulted about the exchange rate readjustments and was not particularly impressed by the British story that the need for secrecy forbade it. Bevin's repeated but vague assurances of Britain's concern to act together in Europe with France, and the Monnet-Plowden conversations whose importance Monnet may have exaggerated in French governmental circles,[29] had certainly given an impression that the United Kingdom was still interested within certain limits in common economic action with France to reconstruct Europe. There is little to be said in defence of Bevin in this respect. He was making vague promises of things of great moment to France which he could not fulfil. Nothing, of course, could mitigate the fact that the United States had been told of the devaluation two weeks before France. But there is no evidence that this changed the direction of French policy in Western Europe or blurred the fact that, as far as France was concerned, the crucial British decisions had been made more than a year earlier.

It was the British, not the French, government which attributed to the talks in Washington too great an importance. The talks did mark the end of the American pressure to force Britain into taking the lead in the economic and political integration of Europe, although their lesson was accepted reluctantly in Washington and only fully driven home in the negotiations for the EPU six months later. The importance of the trade of Britain and the sterling area to

[28] FRUS, 1949, IV, p. 338, Acheson to Webb, 26 September 1949.

[29] As he did in his memoirs. The description given of the second round of discussions between Monnet and Plowden in April in the memoirs gives that impression of simple-minded vagueness and unworldly misunderstanding that in other circles would be considered ridiculous yet which is often conveyed by politicians' memoirs and which can only contribute to public unease about their activities. J. Monnet, *Memoirs* (London, 1978), p. 278 ff.

the real world interests of the United States had emerged as a priority for American policy beyond that of the role of Britain in European integration. But the British government drew a further and quite unwarranted conclusion from what had occurred. They assumed that the scales had so far fallen from the eyes of the American government that the previous two years of tension and misunderstanding were now to be replaced by a special relationship between the United Kingdom and the United States which would give the United Kingdom a higher place in world affairs than other European countries.

When in October the discussions about a possible European payments union seemed to raise once more the threat of a merger of British sovereignty into Europe, Bevin opposed this in a personal message to Dean Acheson, the new Secretary of State, suggesting that Britain could now 'do nothing which is incompatible with the objectives' of the tripartite talks.[30] Acheson's reply spelled out precisely what these talks had meant for America. It was no longer expected that Britain should take the initiative in promoting European integration nor that it should necessarily have to be a part of whatever integrated economic or political unit emerged. But he added that he was unable to see how the tripartite talks 'could be considered incompatible with any steps towards closer European unity'.[31] Britain would be expected not to oppose and as far as possible to encourage any such steps. Although the United States had been forced to recognize Britain's bargaining strength at the international economic level, even if some of it was due to America's own policies, it had in no way acknowledged or sought to create the special relationship for which the British government yearned as a way of defending its role as a world power.

The real limits of America's economic power and influence were once more discovered to be set narrower than its ambitions. The sterling area had to be accepted with all its implications and so did support for the pound as part of the world payments mechanism. Yet the British treated devaluation as a purely national decision, showing a contemptuous disregard for both the IMF and the OEEC which the United States, too, could only accept. For the realism with which this was gradually accepted and for understanding its implications for subsequent American policy in Europe much credit must go to Acheson. The documentary evidence speaks loudly of the critical detachment, pragmatism and deeper awareness of the rest of the world which he brought to American policy. But events work more powerfully than the influence of men; the 1949 economic crisis did even more to dispel those illusions which had survived the 1947 crisis and had in the interval gathered strength again under the optimistic impulse of Marshall Aid and the excitement of the New World remaking the old.

If Britain could no longer be made to remake Europe, if the existence of the

[30] FRUS, 1949, IV, Bevin to Acheson, 25 October 1949.
[31] ibid., Acheson to Bevin, 28 October 1949.

institutions and operational methods of the sterling area had to be accepted as a fact of the post-war world for some time to come, if the OEEC had come to the end of the road as an instrument of European integration, what could now be done to salvage something from this wreck of the political aspirations of the Marshall Plan? There were two possible solutions to hand. One was to encourage France rather than Britain to remake Europe. That had the most serious and worrying implications for American policy in Germany. The other was to take up the ideas of the Planning Group in the ECA, write off the OEEC as a burgeoning political institution, and hope that trade liberalization and the functional institutions that were proposed would bring both 'viability' and integration.

By October the ideas of the Planning Group had been linked to a stage-specific timetable running to July 1952, when it was assumed Marshall Aid would no longer exist. The stage-specific proposals were apparently put together after discussions with the economist Robert Triffin, and his fellow-economist Albert Hirschman drew up the specific proposals for a European central bank.[32] The timetable progressed through the formation of a currency union controlled by a European monetary authority by the end of 1951, to the introduction in July 1952 of a European currency, the ecu, which would float against the dollar, and the simultaneous removal of all quantitative controls on dollar trade.[33] The national currencies would then be stabilized against this common currency. To all this would be added the central commercial authority. The final goal remained unaltered, 'a regeneration of Western European civilisation'.[34]

Of these ideas Hoffman had begun to accept progressively more after August. In mid-September he transmitted to the OEEC his acceptance of the Snoy-Marjolin report and the implicit decision that there should be no more intra-European agreements over the allocation of aid. In future the ECA itself would decide on aid allocation. By early October he was recommending a more active interest in national investment policies and attempting to standardize that part of them subject to ECA control through the counterpart funds. He had accepted the idea of obtaining a firm commitment by European countries to create the two supra-national bodies recommended in the

[32] If Hirschman was committed to the Planning Group's proposals he accepted their eventual defeat with commendable grace and realism. See his article, A.O. Hirschman, 'The European Payments Union; the negotiations and the issues', *Review of Economics and Statistics*, 33, 1951.
[33] Its alternative proposed name was the Europa. Both the two current favourite names for the future European currency were thus happy American inventions, ecu apparently suggested by Triffin as a way of keeping the idea of integration alive (ECA, 42, 'Stages of economic unification', n.d.). These proposals are suspiciously like those put forward in October to the British government as Marjolin's own and at the British request not circulated within the OEEC. (FO 371/78002, 'Draft memorandum by Marjolin for the Consultative Group', 27 October 1949.) He was 'the only foreigner' to have seen the Planning Group's October drafts, SD 540.50, 5685, Memorandum of conversations with Lincoln Gordon, 15 November 1949.
[34] ECA, 10, 'The economic integration of western Europe', Memorandum by Geiger *et al.*, 15 October 1949.

Planning Group's memorandum. He had also accepted the need to begin to force the whole range of policy on Europe, 'to overcome customary inhibitions impressing Europeans actually to do those things now which both we and they know they must undertake sooner or later.'[35] He decided to announce those policies to the OEEC in an important speech on 31 October 1949.

It was the threat of this policy speech which provoked the flow of personal messages between Bevin and Acheson. The British government had got wind of what was now in Hoffman's head and were hastily trying to define the outcome of the tripartite talks in Washington as one which would remove all danger to Britain from anything Hoffman might say. They feared that the terms for Marshall Aid might be made wholly unacceptable by Hoffman's forthcoming address.

Before Hoffman left he lunched with Snyder, Acheson and James Webb, Acheson's deputy. The two State Department members discovered to their alarm that he was intending to demand in his speech almost the full range of the policies in the Geiger memorandum. He 'expressed the feeling that he should press with great vigor for substantial efforts and accomplishments along the lines of the unification of Europe in the economic field as a pre-requisite for further ECA appropriations.' Acheson specifically warned him against raising the question of a central banking structure because it would imply the surrender of national sovereignty in return for aid. It took the combined efforts of the alarmed Acheson and Webb some way into the afternoon before Hoffman could be persuaded to tone down his speech. They were afraid that 'he might place the United States Government in the position of foreclosing fund requests to continue the ECA except on performance of certain conditions which might prove on analysis and discussion to be impossible of achievement.'[36] It was thus only at the last moment that the wilder shores of ECA planning were prevented from becoming the destination which Europe must reach.

When Hoffman did address the OEEC he demanded only specific commitments to trade liberalization. The arguments for liberalization remained those he had taken from the Planning Group memoranda and their purpose remained the same, 'nothing less than an integration of the western European economy'.[37] A large European market must be created by the removal of quantitative restrictions. Fiscal, monetary and investment policies must be anti-inflationary and harmonized. By 'early' 1950 the OEEC should have come forward with a plan to achieve these goals and a programme that would take it 'well along the road to economic integration'. The later specific stages of the timetable and the insistence on a central monetary authority and an

[35] ibid., Hoffman to Harriman, 6 October 1949.
[36] Acheson Papers, 64, ECA Administrator Hoffman's forthcoming trip to Europe, 25 October 1949.
[37] There is a full text of the speech in *New York Times*, 1 November 1949.

international commercial commission were omitted, although they remained as ECA objectives tied in to the trade liberalization programme.

The interval between abandoning the allocation of Marshall Aid through the OEEC and beginning another assault on the problem of European economic integration by demanding that the OEEC undertake the harmonization of national economic policies through the more liberal medium of freeing trade and exchanges was thus very short, and trade liberalization had European integration as its objective every bit as much as did the earlier policy. But outside the ECA much had changed. America's world-wide economic interests were reasserting themselves. In the State Department the unsolved problem of Germany was beginning to dominate. European integration had to make a contribution on both these fronts and it was by no means clear, given French policy, what the new ECA policies could do to solve the German problem. Coming back to the attack in this new way could scarcely hide the fact that the ECA had lost the first round when its position was stronger and a realistic view of the future from October 1949 could only be that Western Europe might also successfully resist the full programme of trade liberalization, or at least make what it wanted of it. At every stage the new policy would be tested against its capacity to deal with the problem of West Germany, and to have to admit that the United Kingdom could not be forced to reconstruct western Europe at the same time as West Germany sprang into existence did not augur well for the ECA's chances of success. The European central bank and its currency, the ecu or the Europa, these names originating in the all-American ambiance of the ECA, are very little nearer to reality now than in 1949, and for much the same reasons.

X

THE EUROPEAN
PAYMENTS UNION

THE TRADE LIBERALIZATION PROGRAMME AND THE
AMERICAN PAYMENTS PROPOSALS

To suppose that the OEEC countries could still be integrated in a free-trade framework by a programme of trade liberalization leading to a multilateral payments system was to commit a double error. In the first place events had already shown that any framework for economic integration would have to be smaller and more restrictive. In the second place, the method now proposed did not in fact avoid the direct political confrontations of the earlier method. To suppose that it would overlooked the extent to which quantitative trade restrictions represented a hard-won balance of real political interests. If they were to be removed as fast as the ECA intended the point would soon be reached where it became a question of removing protective devices whose purpose was to uphold the political balance of power within the nation states.

Since 1929 the need for protection in Europe had increasingly been met by non-tariff barriers to trade, of which import quotas had been one of the commonest and most effective. Almost all pre-war German and Italian imports were governed by quotas, about half of those of France and Switzerland and about a quarter of those of Belgium and the Netherlands. Most of these restrictions had arisen from immediate political pressures on governments struggling to hold economy and country together in the stormy waters after 1929. Only some of them had lost their relevance after 1939. The spread of bilateral trading agreements which had accompanied these controls, followed by the violent price movements during and after the war, had made the pre-war tariff rates meaningless in many countries. French tariffs were in suspension after 1945 because their specific rates were so out of step with post-war prices. Italy's pre-war tariffs, too, had mostly been specific ones. The pre-war German tariff, still waiting on the statute book for the departure of the Military Governments was equally irrelevant. The Franco-Italian customs union negotiations had imposed no threat to protection by discussing the removal of tariffs.

It did not necessarily follow, however, that gains to trade would be greater by the removal of a large proportion of the quota restrictions. Many were so badly judged as neither to be effective limitations on the expression of domestic demand nor, in the circumstances prevailing after 1945, on foreign supply. Nevertheless, because the expansion of intra-Western European trade after 1945 was so strong, it inevitably became the case by 1949 that quota restrictions which had been mainly imposed for the purpose of saving foreign exchange, either in the 1930s or just after the war, came to have as their main effect the subsidization of import-substitution and an almost accidental renunciation of the gains to efficiency through trade expansion. The enthusiasm with which the ECA took up the cause of trade liberalization instead of customs union thus reflected an attunement to the reality of four years' rapid recovery of European output and trade. Yet, although it would be possible to remove a proportion of all quota restrictions without materially affecting the levels of protection, and in some cases the process would be seen by all to be mutually beneficial, after that would come the point when countries would be faced, not with removing administrative irrelevancies, but with altering policies which had become firmly established. And if those were altered the immediate economic relevance of tariffs would be increased. There had been practically no national public discussion of the proceedings of the Customs Union Study Group. Trade liberalization might begin in the same obscurity, but the more successful it was the sooner it would have to emerge into the full light of national public debate. The concept of a European customs union would then also have to leave the shadows of discussion by national and international civil servants and stand under the arc-lights of parliamentary assemblies.

So it was to prove. Trade liberalization made rapid initial progress while it was still a matter for technical bargaining and as long as it did not touch any reasonably powerful entrenched economic interest in a vital spot. As soon as such interests were touched the discussion spread like a fire beyond all control and then the concept of a restrictive customs union as a way of regulating, in some cases stopping, the changes which further trade liberalization would promote, received a new surge of support.

What is more, the policy of trade liberalization had been forged in the ECA with virtually no consideration of the rift which had appeared between Britain and France over the economic nature and political purpose of a larger European market. It could not, even for a brief period of time, appear as a politically neutral position in the disputes over the international framework of western European reconstruction. It was too opposed to French conceptions of a European common market and too close, at least in its initial impact, to British conceptions of a future Europe. Indeed, the first concrete proposals for a general programme of removal of quantitative restrictions in Europe came from Britain in May 1949. The diversionary purpose of the British proposals was obvious. They were made as soon as Belgium had refused to be excluded from any payments agreement in that year and were intended as an alternative programme to multilateralism and convertibility and one which would pre-empt any contradictory French initiative.[1]

The use of quotas and other forms of quantitative restriction on international trade had been much less extensive in Britain in the 1930s than in most continental countries. To take up the cause of trade liberalization made good sense tactically and economically. It would make the creation of a customs union excluding Britain much more difficult and open an easier route into Europe for British exports while requiring very little adjustment in other areas of the United Kingdom's foreign trade. Furthermore, such an action would be well-received in Washington and it might divert American wrath away from British opposition to American proposals for a more multilateral intra-Western European payments system.

By now, however, French policy was firmly set on resolving the German problem by a Franco-German association in a framework more protective of French needs. The aim was to produce a framework for trade and a payments agreement with Benelux and Italy which might absorb the West German state or, at least, erect a barrier against it. These countries had been at first the only full members of the First Agreement on Multilateral Monetary Compensation and immediately after its conclusion had considered signing a wholly separate agreement from the other Western European countries. This tentative move had been vetoed in Washington on the grounds that the United Kingdom would have to be a full member of any payments agreement in 1948.[2] Nevertheless, as the London conference pursued its way, French policy moved to the idea once more of a 'Greater Benelux' linked by its own programme of trade liberalization and by a payments system both multilateral and convertible, but in which tariffs would be retained as a mark of national sovereignty and as a device by which the economy could be regulated as the protective value of quotas was reduced. This idea was strongly encouraged by Harriman who foolishly promised it American government support.[3]

The idea was given a further impetus by Harriman's announcement in June that the ECA would reserve $150 million out of the congressional appropriation for 1949/50 to promote a more rapid liberalization of trade and payments. If 'Greater Benelux' could come up with a payments scheme implying a greater degree of integration than the rest of the OEEC it might hope to secure the whole of this American financial backing for its own scheme. In August the project of a separate 'Little European' payments scheme was put forward to the ECA by France, but in the circumstances the French proposals were more

[1] CAB 134/238, Meeting of European Economic Co-operation Committee, 30 May 1949.
[2] NAC, Staff papers, 20 January 1948.
[3] FJM, AMF 22/2/2, Note by Alphand, 15 April 1949.

of a dilemma than a help to the United States. If the new powers of financial leverage which the ECA had taken were used in this way, would not that do even more to encourage a separate, isolated sterling area? Also, it seemed all too possible that a Little European payments area might liberalize trade more slowly than the OEEC as a whole, even though its payments arrangements were more flexible.

The only way to know this was to extract from the OEEC a commitment to a uniform level of trade liberalization by all countries and to test both the British and the French words and deeds against that standard. A multilateral payments system would not advance the cause of integration unless it were combined with a genuine commitment to the removal of non-tariff barriers to trade. So a set of trade 'rules' accepted by all would have to be a part of a new payments agreement. At some point on the road towards such a comprehensive agreement the ultimate intentions of the British and the French would be discovered. The outcome would determine for some time to come the future framework of European trade, the nature of European integration, if any, and the trading relationships of western Europe and the United States.

No trade and payments agreement in Western Europe which meant that British trade was less liberalized and sterling settlements less multilateral in one part than in another of Western Europe could be tolerated because it was a retreat from the aims of the ERP. The problem of Britain's trade and payments with the sterling area could not be separated from that of Western Europe's trade and payments and British opposition to transferability of sterling had to be allowed to set the pace for Western Europe's progress away from bilateral trade. This situation prevailed until the devaluation of the pound and the Anglo-American talks which preceded it. After that the United States had more flexibility of action in so far as Britain was thenceforward no longer required to take the lead in promoting European integration, and thus the sterling area itself was no longer seen as a fundamental obstacle to European integration. But the contemporaneous adoption by the ECA of trade liberalization as the new road to integration meant that it was still the case that the sterling area would have to be brought into a multilateral payments system in Western Europe and, indeed, that the pressure to do this would be much fiercer. Similarly, the liberalization of British trade would have to be part of a common Western European programme. Because Britain now seemed to be taking the lead in that direction, that looked less problematical. For Britain, however, it meant that the problem of European integration was not entirely solved by the tripartite financial talks in Washington and that the British trade liberalization proposals could not be effective as an *alternative* policy.

The ECA's policy was to back both British and French proposals on liberalization and both were agreed as a possible basis for action in June 1949 by the OEEC Council.[4] The British proposal was that by 1 October each

---

[4] FO 371/77744, UK delegation, 'Note of discussion with Harriman on 18 July 1949'.

country should have presented a list of goods on which it would unilaterally remove quota restrictions, the French that countries should present lists of commodities for negotiation leading to the common removal of quotas. Until the moment of devaluation the French still hoped that there would be mutual consultation with Britain beforehand about these lists as a basis for a renewal of their mutual co-operation within the OEEC, but the British refused any such mutual discussion, which emphasized the complete lack of consequence of the Monnet-Plowden conversations.[5] The unilateral procedures, which were in fact followed, meant that by 1 October the countries could report the removal of quotas on about 30 per cent of the level of their 1948 private trade with each other. For Britain the figure was 66 per cent, for France only 18 per cent, but the effective difference was probably much less than these figures suggest because a large part of Britain's import trade was still carried out under state auspices. The main contributor to liberalization was, not unexpectedly, Belgium, which removed quotas on 78 per cent of its imports.[6] But very few restrictions were removed anywhere on manufactured goods or domestically produced foodstuffs and the removals were frequently not universally valid. Britain did not remove quotas, for example, on imports from Belgium, Switzerland or Germany. The Netherlands and the Scandinavian countries also continued to discriminate against Germany.

Not many restrictions had therefore effectively been removed before Hoffman's speech on 31 October. Although the State Department succeeded in taking out of Hoffman's speech the demands for new political and economic institutions he was intending to make, he used the word 'integration' thirty-one times and linked it emphatically to demands for an agreed timetable of further trade liberalization. He demanded, in much the same terms as the Planning Group, the creation of a single large market without quantitative or 'monetary' barriers to trade and through the creation of a more dynamic, expanding economy, 'nothing less than' Western Europe's economic integration. This was the first time that this insistence had been officially proclaimed in a public statement of policy by the American government. By early 1950 the OEEC would be required to produce a plan that would eliminate most quantitative trade restrictions as well as dual pricing policies for domestic consumption and exports. Any arrangements between smaller groups of participating countries would be encouraged, Hoffman suggested, provided they were in harmony with the wider possibilities of European unity and did not raise trade barriers any higher than those otherwise existing.

In his official reply Cripps went out of his way to restate the official British policy of not integrating the British economy into Western Europe in any way that would prejudice British responsibilities elsewhere, but he also went out of his way to declare that Britain would encourage 'regional' schemes.

[5] FO 371/78087, UK delegation to FO, 17 September 1949.
[6] W. Diebold, *Trade and Payments in Western Europe* (New York, 1952), p. 161.

Hoffman was then shown in confidence the full British proposals for liberalization of trade and unwisely pronounced himself 'thrilled', for in the cooler light of Washington after his return they did not look so thrilling.[7] Acheson, in his personal exchanges with Bevin, provided a definition of integration which incorporated Hoffman's demands, 'the freest possible movement of goods and persons in Europe involving the removal of quantitative restrictions, free movement of funds, and the use of tariffs as a cushion and not as a form of quantitative restriction'.[8] This was confirmed by Harriman and left the Foreign Office much relieved and with the feeling that it was 'only like going back to before 1929'.[9]

But as November went its way it became apparent that so much relief was misplaced. French newspapers were bitterly critical of Cripps's speech and some said it represented the end of Franco-British collaboration in European reconstruction. The decision had been taken by the OEEC Council immediately after Hoffman's speech that each member would remove quotas on half of its private imports at their 1948 level from the rest of the group by 15 December and that this reduction would be achieved in each of the three major categories of imported goods, primary goods, semi-finished goods, and manufactured products. The ECA accepted this as the first step in the timetable towards a European payments union, a central commercial authority, and integration. The final date for the completion of a payments union in the ECA's planning was still 1 July 1950.[10] But these further ambitions, Cripps said, were 'a fifty-year programme'.[11] He went out of his way in a press conference on 17 November to explain that any such proposals would be a danger to the sterling area and to policies of full employment. He was not alone in his attitude. When Harriman dined in Oslo with Lange and Brofoss the 'conversation took turn which made appropriate a direct question whether Brofoss did not feel liberalization of trade and payments within Europe important to achievement economic objectives Norway. Brofoss replied bluntly, "No".'[12]

When the American proposals for the payments union were made available in the second week of December 1949 they were for full intra-Western European currency transferability in payments settlements on current account, with settlements to be made in gold. They thus required the freeing of a wide range of invisible payments as well as payments on commodity account by the end of the current Marshall Aid year. Quantitative restrictions were also to be much further reduced by the time transferability was to be introduced in July 1950. There would be provision for closer associations between smaller groups of countries providing they liberalized trade and payments faster than

[7] FO 371/78022, Speech of Sir S. Cripps to Council of OEEC, 1 November 1949.
[8] FO 371/78023, Berthoud to Makins, 17 November 1949.
[9] ibid.   [10] ECA, 10, Foster to Paris embassy, 20 November 1949.
[11] SD 540.50, 5685, Memorandum of conversations with Lincoln Gordon, 15 November 1949.   [12] ibid., Harriman to Washington, 1 December 1949.

the OEEC as a whole. No more was said in the proposals about a European monetary authority. But the Planning Group was still busy drawing up detailed proposals for just such a body.[13] The intra-European commerce commission now, however, began to appear in the guise of a 'supervisory board' to oversee the operations of a payments union, 'consisting of permanent representatives of the principal participating countries and rotating representatives of other participating countries'.[14] Unlike the decisions of the OEEC Council, decisions by this board were not to require unanimity.

The idea was that the United States would contribute financially from the ERP appropriations to the proposed European payments union. One way would be by making payments to help overcome 'structural deficits'. These were no more than the familiar, unavoidable problem for the ECA that there was no possibility of engineering an equilibrium of settlements purely in intra-Western European trade. A 'structural deficit' was no more than a persistent deficit in intra-Western European trade not balanced by surpluses in extra-European trade with hard-currency areas. A country in this position would presumably be unwilling or unable either to settle partly in gold or hard currency within the Union or to repay its borrowings from the Union. The American contribution would therefore make up the difference between debtors' gold payments to the Union and creditors' receipts. But for this contribution not to be soon exhausted it would be necessary for the terms of settlement to be hard, that is to say that debtors, as their deficits grew, would at an early point have to settle the larger part of their debts in dollars. This was precisely the point at which the scheme might be unacceptable. It was necessary, therefore, that the American contribution should also be used as a cushion of working capital to permit the terms of settlement to be rather less hard. To allow persistent debtors in inta-Western European payments seemed no great sacrifice to pay for a settlements mechanism which would still inject a sufficient measure of gold and dollar settlements into intra-Western European trade to prevent the emergence of two separate western trading systems. The ECA intended to seek permission from Congress to allocate up to $600 million of the next appropriation, which would amount to more than a quarter of the total, to support for a European payments union.

The proposals were not definitive and were produced as guidelines to the OEEC before going for discussion before the NAC in January 1950. But the OEEC was still faced with the situation that it must accept or refuse an agreement along these lines by the summer, when the 1949 payments agreement expired. It must also agree to a further stage of trade liberalization, or refuse Marshall Aid. Less than two months after Hoffman's speech the new American programme seemed to be in place and no further temporizing

[13] One of these is reproduced in the thesis by M.J. Colebrook, 'Franco-British relations and European integration 1945–50' (Doctoral thesis, University of Geneva, 1971), pp. 255 ff.
[14] E.H. van der Beugel, *From Marshall Aid to Atlantic Partnership* (Amsterdam, 1966), p. 198.

possible. Europe must take what the ECA judged to be the road back to Bretton Woods, by way of integration, and now in a framework which made the real barriers to integration seem even higher.

FINEBEL

By the time of the tripartite talks in Washington in September 1949 the French Finance Minister, Maurice Petsche had prepared a set of proposals which he hoped would secure American backing for a radically new payments system. While the United States, Britain and Canada were discussing the problems of Britain's balance of payments and the sterling area, the finance ministers of France, Italy and Benelux agreed to free capital flows and exchange rates, something which perhaps puts into better perspective the exaggerated importance usually laid on the fact that the British did not discuss their September devaluation beforehand with the French! Petsche's proposals were that the exchange rates for both current and capital transactions be freed, that all capital movements between the countries should likewise be freed, that there should be a complete removal of all quantitative barriers to trade, but that the tariffs should remain as a method of economic control and symbol of sovereignty, and, lastly, since it appeared the only way that such a programme could be achieved, that the currencies should float against each other. This would have the necessary implication that neither France nor Italy would revert to officially supporting the cross-rate of the pound against the dollar on their own exchanges, nor allow the exchange rates between their currencies to be governed by the par rates against the dollar registered with the IMF.[15] France had in fact continued to maintain, against all IMF rules, differential exchange rates for imports and exports throughout 1949, although modified by the changes made in October 1948. The French proposals assumed that even the principle of fixed exchange rates, which historians have seen as the hallmark of 'the Bretton Woods system' could now be discarded.

Italy was in a difficult position because the growth of its export surpluses with Britain meant it was holding large sterling balances. Suspecting an imminent sterling devaluation, Italy therefore postponed all consideration of the proposals until the conclusion of the tripartite talks.[16] At the meeting with the Americans on 15 September 1949, at which the French delegation was told what had occurred at those talks, Petsche arrived briefed to obtain American support for the payments plan. However the American team were at best non-committal. The $150 million appropriation for the 1949 payments scheme

[15] FO 371/78111, Washington embassy to London, 17 September 1949.
[16] SD 840.50, 5684, Perkins to Acheson, 'Conversation with Mr van Zeeland on the economic integration of Europe', 14 September 1949.

had not yet been voted and the plan was first, they said, a matter for the IMF.[17]

The Dutch attitude to Petsche's proposals was more positive, although not more welcoming. Since the Netherlands was in deficit with all parties to the possible agreement, but in surplus with the sterling area, it insisted that it must have the freedom within any agreement to settle its payments deficits in sterling. This would necessarily mean discussions with Britain before the Dutch sterling holdings could be used for such a purpose. Secondly, it demanded that all parties should first agree on a common programme of restricting dollar imports. The second objection was unacceptable to all and the first re-emphasized the earlier Dutch objection to the proposed customs union, that without Britain or Germany it was more likely to do harm than good to the Dutch economy while leaving it susceptible to the domination of French foreign policy. The persistent large Dutch deficits within Benelux would only be made larger, while the Netherlands would be cut off from the two major markets, Britain and Germany, with which it was in surplus. The insistence that the partners should first negotiate a common dollar import programme was in fact aimed at Belgium in the hope of using French and Italian leverage to induce the Belgians to substitute Western European imports for their dollar imports. The Dutch view was that they would be prepared to break up the Benelux union if Belgium accepted the French proposals without providing better safeguards for the Netherlands.[18]

The French payments proposals were therefore in difficulty from the start and the suggestion, frequently made at the time, that the British devaluation by impeding them had blocked a step towards European integration was absurd. Once the dust from the devaluation had settled it could be seen that neither it nor the tripartite talks had put any new fundamental obstacles in the way of the French plans, but had even made them slightly more feasible. The United States, as it digested the lessons of the tripartite talks, began to look for a French rather than a British initiative in Europe. And devaluation, by removing the artificiality of the pound–dollar cross rates, made the proposals technically easier to implement. The conversations were pursued throughout October. 'Greater Benelux', the tactful phrase of 1947, was first replaced by 'Fritalux', in spite of its sounding like a proprietary brand of cooking fat and then by Finebel.[19]

As far as ECA was concerned Finebel was a desirable development in the direction of trade liberalization and integration providing Petsche could be dissuaded from the idea of floating exchange rates, which would inevitably

[17] FRUS, 1949, IV, United States-French conversations, 15 September 1949, p. 654. The proposals had been accepted only in a general sense by the US Treasury in late August (SD 840.50, 5683, Washington to Paris embassy, 25 August 1949).
[18] FO 371/78111, Washington embassy to Foreign Office, 15 September 1949.
[19] More pessimistic circles in the Foreign Office suggested 'Benefritz'.

308   *The Reconstruction of Western Europe 1945–51*

mean a head-on clash between American policy in Europe and in the world. Two potential members of Finebel, France and Italy, had never shown any great conviction in the post-war attempts to fix exchange rates. When the franc had been devalued in January 1948, a floating exchange rate which applied to exporters to hard-currency areas had been encouraged as well as a new fixed rate. The avowed purpose was to discover on the market what the optimum new par rate should be. In fact the free rate acted as an export subsidy because exporters to the dollar zone were allowed to retain half their earnings and sell them on the free market. The experiment was virtually a copy of similar actions by the Italian government from summer 1947. In both cases the sterling–dollar exchange rate on the free market had fallen well below the official par rate and it was this problem of the cross rates between the two major foreign trading currencies which led the IMF to refuse to sanction the French multiple exchange rates and disbar France from use of the IMF facilities. In October, while preserving its multiple rates, France took some of the sting out of them by stipulating that all commercial transactions should be carried out at the middle rate between the two, although there was still no firm commitment to support the pound–dollar cross rate. The two rates were only unified in September 1949 when the franc was devalued to meet the British devaluation. After the devaluation the ECA was more than ever insistent that the new pound–dollar relationship would have to be supported and the European exchange rates would have to be fixed. On 6 October 1949 ECA officials asked the British to support the United States in insisting that the Western European countries maintain fixed exchange rates, in return for the ECA's insistence that the Finebel countries in turn continue to support the new pound–dollar cross rates.[20]

The implication appeared to be that future support for sterling might be contingent on Britain not discouraging the Finebel union. Once Bevin had abandoned the idea of a customs union the opposition of the economic ministries to any closer association with Europe was strengthened by weightier considerations of national security. The customs union was no longer needed to hold together a Western European military alliance. The American forces would stay in Europe and would, it was now sure, associate themselves with the Brussels Pact countries in the defence of Western Europe. The continent might be temporarily occupied by the Soviet Union, Britain would not be. British economic decisions, therefore had to be taken with this ultimate consideration of national security in mind. The United States would be committed to the defence of Britain, even if the continent were overrun, and the decision to build the nuclear bomb would make Britain an element of much greater importance in American strategy than the other Western European countries.

That this had become the general opinion emerged from a special discussion in January 1949 between senior officials.

[20] FO 371/78111, Washington embassy to London, 6 October 1949.

The means to this is now the Atlantic Pact. We hope to secure a special relationship with USA and Canada within this, for in the last resort we cannot rely upon the European countries. ... However, we must in practice establish the position that US will defend us, whatever happens to the Europeans.[21]

The inevitable consequence of this was that the United Kingdom could neither surrender any element of sovereignty within a European association nor provide any financial or economic aid to Europe which might weaken the British economy. The definition of policy was then approved in cabinet.

> The present policy approved by HMG early in 1949 is that the United Kingdom should not go beyond the point of no return in its participation in schemes for greater unity between the countries of Europe. The Treasury consider that we have now gone as far as we can under this policy in the economic field, particularly after our liberalisation of trade decisions.[22]

Even had considerations of national defence pointed in another direction, it was now agreed in the London Committee that Commonwealth ties, the 'special relationship' and the insularity of public opinion would still have prevented any further initiative. Of course, 'insularity of opinion' might have been altered to some degree by the same strenuous efforts that the Department of State had made in converting the American public to support for Marshall Aid two years before.[23] But, 'the general atmosphere of the London Committee' was 'that we cannot afford to entangle ourselves further in Europe, particularly in the light of the tripartite talks'.[24]

There was, Bevin now argued to the cabinet, no strategic case any longer for a closer European association. It would be ten years before Western Europe could hope to defend itself and at any time in the interval the Soviet Union could reach the Atlantic coast of the continent unless stopped by America. Safety only lay in closer association with the United States and as the economic storms were weathered dependence might slowly change to interdependence.[25]

Hall-Patch was taken aback in the OEEC on 17 October by 'a most peculiar luncheon party with our friend Hervé Alphand' at which Alphand announced that it was France's firm intention to go ahead with Finebel.[26] The immediate British response was the cautious one that the new payments group must neither discriminate against sterling area exports nor break the sterling–dollar cross rates. But a more official and considered statement was now necessary. Hoffman was due to make his important policy speech to the

[21] Sir R. Clarke (Sir A. Cairncross, ed.), *Anglo-American Collaboration in War and Peace 1942–1949* (Oxford, 1982), p. 208. Document no. 27.
[22] FO 371/78111, Washington embassy to London, 6 October 1949.
[23] Two decades later at the time of the referendum the Foreign Office was far from regarding public opinion as a force which it could only passively obey.
[24] FO 371/71804, Berthoud to Makins, 1 October 1949.
[25] CP (49) 208, Memorandum by Bevin, 'European policy', 18 October 1949.
[26] FO 371/78020, UK delegation to London, 17 October 1949.

OEEC at the end of the month and well-founded rumours were circulating that he was considering demanding a European currency and a European central bank. It was certain that he would speak in favour of closer trade and payments links. It was crucial that Britain make its disclaimer before Hoffman spoke.

The policy conclusions reached three weeks before were thus submitted to the Foreign Secretary. He and Cripps consulted and agreed a definitive statement on Britain's position. They had before them the cabinet decision in January that Britain would not involve itself in any European association beyond the point at which it could withdraw. To this they added several further limitations. Britain must not surrender its sole responsibility for its own budgetary policy and its own reserves. Nothing must be undertaken which might hinder the attainment of equilibrium between the dollar area and the sterling area. In this, Cripps simply took over the opinion which the Treasury had already expressed to the Foreign Office, that, 'we cannot sacrifice opportunities for dollar-earning (or dollar-saving) in order to make it easier for other European countries to earn or save dollars'.[27] Britain could not engage in any form of joint European planning which might imply the reduction in size of any dollar-earning industry. Lastly, imperial preferences must be retained.[28]

When all these things were taken together it was obvious that the limitations on Britain taking part in any European association had been set more narrowly than in 1948, when certain forms of European association had at least been considered theoretically possible in the future. There is no doubt that the resolution of the Washington talks, the realization that in Washington the position had now been accepted that Britain could not be dragooned into close economic integration with Europe, together with a changing view of Britain's defence, made union with Europe seem less desirable than it had done even when the cabinet had defined Britain's European policy in January. As the Bevin-Cripps memorandum put it, 'as a result of the Washington talks … we have established or are establishing a new relationship with the United States'.[29]

The French plans for floating exchange rates were soon abandoned in the face of American objections. But the Belgians showed no sign of allowing their import programmes to be redistributed to accommodate the Dutch, and the French showed no public sign of being prepared to include West Germany in Finebel from its start. Discussions got nowhere through October. This was the opportunity which the Planning Commissariat and the Ministry of Foreign Affairs wanted. In November the latter came forward with further proposals

[27] FO 371/78103, The Council of Europe and the OEEC, 30 September 1949.
[28] FO 371/78021, Memorandum by the Secretary of State for Foreign Affairs and the Chancellor of the Exchequer, 23 October 1949.
[29] ibid. The distinction between past and present tenses is not, unfortunately, so easily blurred.

for an association which implied a much firmer degree of control of the economies. They were aimed at producing a series of international agreements for industrial management which would harmonize major industrial sectors in the five economies as quotas were removed. Monetary and fiscal policy would be harmonized by two ministerial committees under the aegis of another committee of the ministers of foreign affairs. Quotas and quantity controls on trade would be removed, but not the tariffs. A European investment bank would be created to help in the adjustments needed by particular industries. Payments for all current transactions would be freed, although the control mechanisms would not yet be dismantled. Capital transactions would be freed more gradually in order to prevent outflows of capital to Belgium, the surplus country in the group. The removal of quotas would make a large measure of agricultural co-operation necessary. There would have to be a common agricultural policy embracing marketing, exports outside the union and a joint rationalization of production. The union would have its own political machinery, regular ministerial meetings and a common ministerial organization. The proposals were obviously aimed at making the inclusion of West Germany in the arrangements safer and providing an alternative framework to the International Ruhr Authority.

> The Governments invited [to the proposed conference] will have to consider if it is convenient to approach Western Germany to ask it to co-operate as part of the Group. The association of Germany, which is in accordance with the aims of the European policy of the French Government, would perhaps facilitate the solution of the difficult problems of outlets, especially in the agricultural sector.[30]

This was the paragraph which enabled the Dutch to attend the conference.

The Dutch were in agreement with the value of studying the integration of the Western European economies on a sectoral basis, as an alternative to trade liberalization. But their enthusiasm at first was more for this as an industrial than an agricultural policy. The necessary expansion of agricultural output, the Dutch argued, must be achieved first of all by genuine trade liberalization and this meant tariff removal as well. Only this would permit the necessary specialization in agricultural production.[31] At the GATT negotiations in Annecy both France and Italy had submitted very high tariff proposals as initial bargaining positions and this could not help but alarm the Netherlands, which had traditionally not only maintained low tariffs itself but now saw itself in danger of being cut off from rapidly expanding markets for its agricultural exports. Nor was the projected timetable for the removal of quota restrictions fast enough for the Dutch. Their counter-proposal was that

[30] ibid.
[31] ECA, 60, 'Memorandum for the discussion to be held in Paris on the initiative of the French government', 24 November 1949.

three-quarters of quota restrictions should go by the start of 1951 and the whole lot by 1 July 1951. Yet within this framework provision was to be made for the Dutch industrialization programme and infant industries were to receive special protection! Lastly, the Dutch wanted a further effort to be made to bring in the British and, as they made clear, the inclusion also of West Germany and the German market in any final agreement was indispensable.[32]

A dynamic growth of Dutch, Belgian and French exports to the West German market had been taking place throughout 1949. West Germany experienced two powerful surges of consumer demand in that year, and they exerted an immediate influence outside its borders and especially on the primary and processed food exports of the Netherlands and Denmark. Although the ultimate intentions of France towards West Germany could be guessed to be not discouraging to this trade, the speed with which it grew meant that the smaller countries were hardly prepared to wait on the timing of French foreign policy adjustments. For them the West German market was crucial now. And the Dutch, furthermore, must have had extremely low hopes of any British participation. When the parties met in conference in Paris at the end of November to discuss the proposals they were therefore still a long way apart. In spite of the French willingness to concede the usefulness of German participation in any common agricultural policy, France was not ready to lower her tariffs or reduce her non-tariff trade controls against Germany, much less accept the political consequences at home of the participation of West Germany in Finebel.

At the outset of the conference the French reduced their proposal for a European investment bank into one for an investment 'bureau' which would vet, rather than undertake, industrial investment within a common industrial programme. Neither France nor Italy was prepared to discuss tariff reductions, which for Benelux was essential. At the same time the Dutch argued that debtors within the scheme should be liable to settle only up to 25 per cent in gold whereas creditors should have to settle in gold up to 75 per cent.[34] Even supposing that the scheme did secure to itself the whole of the special ECA appropriation of $150 million, such a set of rules would soon have exhausted that fund and presented the ECA with an open-ended commitment. The conference also showed that France could not easily impose its own sectoral planning concepts on the much less *dirigiste* regimes in Italy and Belgium, even if it could persuade the Dutch to join. Brussels was no more enthusiastic about a European investment bank than Rome and although it wanted to see a harmonization of economic and social policies it wanted to achieve that harmonization by the removal of as many restrictions and industrial agreements

[32] SD 540.5686, The Hague to Washington, 22 November 1949; FO 371/78112, The Hague to London, 26 November 1949.
[33] FO 371/78113, UK delegation to FO, 30 November 1949.
[34] ECA, 10, Comments on original Fritalux proposals, 29 November 1949.

as possible, including the complete liberalization of capital movements (which was unacceptable to everyone else).[35] American pressure for payments liberalization within the OEEC would, if successful, in any case produce much the same state of affairs as the Belgian proposals seemed to aim at and in fact the Belgian negotiators were opposed to the creation of any new institutions other than regular meetings of the ministers of finance of the participants. The payments transfers themselves, they argued, should be handled by the BIS.

The French negotiators were thus left facing the stark reality that if Finebel were to solve their future problem with West Germany it would only do so in a much more uncontrolled and liberal framework than they wished to contemplate. As soon as the ECA proposals for a European payments union based on multilateralism and convertibility and sweeping removals of quantitative trade controls were promulgated in December the danger for France came nearer. What made it worse was that the country which showed most eagerness to join Finebel was of course West Germany itself! On 10 November 1949 the Minister of Economics, Erhard, told Petsche in Paris that the Federal Republic wished to be included.[36] At the close of the Paris meeting the countries agreed a communiqué that 'The Ministers considered it appropriate to support and foster the progressive integration of the German people into the European Community.'[37] But events were to prove that the French cabinet was not in fact prepared to do so within a framework as liberal as the one likely to emerge in Finebel.

The initial enthusiasm with which the ECA had welcomed Finebel began to cool rapidly after the Paris conference. On the French side it had become more protectionist than when first mooted. It showed no signs of producing economic co-ordination through central supra-national authorities, nor did it seem likely to provide for the alternative policy, automatic economic adjustments through the effect of the balance of payments on the reserves, of the kind which the gold exchange standard had imposed. It was neither supranational enough for the ECA nor liberal enough. 'We believe', as the Deputy Administrator, William C. Foster, put it, 'that if elimination of QRs is to be permanent there must be really effective machinery for direct co-ordination of national policies by agreement or by some international control over

[35] FO 371/78113, Rapport des experts de la Belgique etc. concernant l'établissement d'une association économique et financière en Europe occidentale, 10 December 1949.

[36] T 232/148, Western Germany in relation to European regional groups, 5 December 1949.

Ludwig Erhard, 1897–1977. Severely wounded in First World War. Worked as economic and industrial analyst in unimportant organizations, 1928–45. Did not join Nazi Party. Economic Adviser to Military Government in Bavaria 1945–6. Head of the Joint Economic Administration of the Bizone, 1948–9. A liberal, he joined the CDU before the 1949 election. Minister of Economics 1949–63. Vice-Chancellor 1957–63. Federal Chancellor 1963–6. In myth, a founding father of his country, in reality a man of but moderate talents representative of the mediocrity of political life in the first decade of the Republic's history.

[37] FO 371/78113, Rapport des experts.

actions of governments and central banks.'[38] There seemed little point in supporting Finebel if it fell short of the mark which the ECA hoped to persuade the whole of Western Europe to reach.

On 23 December Bissell told Alphand that Finebel would not get the $150 million because it did not go far enough along the path of supra-nationality.[39] Furthermore the ECA, he indicated, was unhappy about any progress towards European integration based on international industrial agreements. The payments union which the ECA contemplated was designed to eliminate all possibility of such protectionist cartels. The union would be required to start at the minimum level of trade liberalization acceptable to the United States. In private the French did not think that the ECA's refusal to fund Finebel with dollars made it technically unworkable, providing that once the level of trade liberalization did reach the 60–75 per cent mark which the ECA was demanding that the OEEC eventually reach, American financial backing would then be provided.[40] What made it unworkable was the insistence that West Germany be included from the outset and the parallel insistence within the OEEC on a programme of trade liberalization which cut the ground from under the French proposals for a co-ordinated and managed sectoral integration to cope with the German problem.

Faced with the proposal to accept the trade liberalization programme of the ECA and, at least formally, its implications for the reconstruction of a liberal, integrated western Europe, and faced at the same time with the failure of Finebel to produce a safer alternative, the French government had to recognize in January that another way forward was needed to integrate the Federal Republic into the new framework. The economic and financial risks of Finebel were greater than the political gain. The actual proposals emanating from the Finebal conference were only that the group should remove restrictions on 75 per cent of its intra-trade by the end of June. In the eyes of the British government it had become 'a rather milk and water affair'.[41] But in the context of American demands on the OEEC it opened the split in France between liberals and planners and on the very issue where no error of policy could be risked: future relationships with West Germany.

Not only did Finebel provide no protection against West Germany but, as several ministers objected, it would tie France, with its policy of high employment and expansion, to the three countries in Western Europe with the highest rates of unemployment and the most deflationary policies. The Ministry of

[38] ECA, 10, Foster to Paris embassy, 20 November 1949.

William C. Foster, 1897– . Businessman in the steel industry. Under-Secretary for Commerce in the Department of State 1946–8. Deputy Special Representative in the ECA 1948–9, then Deputy Administrator 1949–50. Succeeded Hoffman as Administrator 1950. A businessman again in the 1950s. Chief United States representative at the Disarmament Conference 1962–9.

[39] SD 540.5686, Memorandum of conversation between Bissell and Alphand, 23 December 1949.   [40] ibid.

[41] CAB 134/248, Fritalux, 14 January 1950.

Finance supported the Belgian plans for multilateralism and a return to gold settlements in intra-Western European trade and saw Finebel as it had emerged from the Paris conference as a useful financial discipline, combined with the ECA payments proposals, both for France and Western Europe.[42] Petsche himself certainly showed a tendency to accept this policy, which was also that of the Bank of France, all through the subsequent negotiations over the EPU.[43] He was, however, not consistent, probably through never having entirely mastered the technical intricacies of the advice he was receiving and thus tended to accept the last advice given. The planners were very consistent, particularly in their opposition to the return of any form of gold standard or subservience to the balance of payments and it was they who won the day.

Marjolin had submitted a set of proposals based on the OEEC trade liberalization programme. These were that the OEEC, instead of liberalizing trade entirely by the end of 1950, as the ECA hoped, should proceed to the removal of only 75 per cent of the quantitative restrictions by that date. Since the Dutch proposals for Finebel had been that it should achieve the same target by the end of June 1950 this could also be accepted, with the implication that until the end of June Finebel would amount to no more than an acceleration of the OEEC trade liberalization programme within one group and after that date would have no separate existence. Marjolin's argument, which carried the day, was that this was the only effective defence against American pressure for total liberalization of trade and more rapid moves towards convertibility.[44] These decisions were linked with two important provisos. One was that West Germany and Britain should end their dual pricing policy for coal which made their coal exports to France more expensive than the price to their domestic consumers. The other was that the OEEC should insist on the possibility of the reintroduction of quantitative trade restrictions to defend the balance of payments if necessary. On 17 January Alphand formally asked for British government support for these decisions. In spite of the resurgence in France of liberal economic opinions the ECA's last great push to integrate Western Europe through trade liberalization had succeeded only in bringing France and Britain together again in combined opposition to the whole idea.

Schuman supported Marjolin's proposals.[45] Finebel had proved not to be a sound political basis for the attempt to harness West Germany safely to the French bloc in Western Europe. It raised too many fears in France. But it was now up to the French planners to provide Schuman with an alternative policy to achieve the same end. They had driven away the spectres of floating exchange rates, gold settlements and deflation. What could they put in their place which would clinch their own position within France and also be backed

---

[42] T 232/149, Discussion with M. Monnet on 1 February 1950. Monnet had been present at the ministers' meeting.

[43] FO 371/86995, Note of a discussion with Mr Katz on June 23, 24 June 1950.

[44] FO 371/87083, Hall-Patch to Berthoud, 13 January 1950.   [45] ibid.

by a strong enough consensus to serve as the policy which Schuman was looking for? The answer was to emerge four months later in the proposals for a coal, iron and steel community.

UNISCAN

So far most authors who have ventured to comment on the Finebel proposals have contrasted them with the contemporary discussions for a trade and payments area between Britain and Scandinavia, Uniscan.[46] They happened at the same time and had equally insensitive and unappealing names. Otherwise they had little in common. Uniscan had only the most limited bearing on European reconstruction, although it is not without importance as a signpost to Britain's ultimate reaction to the Treaty of Rome.

Uniscan had its origins in the OEEC's abortive attempt to arrive at a long-term European economic programme. The Norwegian government had been an even more ardent opponent of integration in the OEEC than the British but its diplomatic weight was, of course, very small. Throughout the whole period the Norwegian Labour Party became increasingly fearful that the conjoint pressures of American and European liberals would create a Western Europe which would be so inimical to Norway's own centrally planned and controlled reconstruction programme as to render it inoperative. Every attack on trade and exchange controls was seen as an attack on the very basis of Norway's own reconstruction and consistently the worst relationship in the OEEC was that between Norway and Belgium, for to the Norwegian planners Belgian policy, about which they were by no means expert, symbolized every thing they abhorred about inter-war Europe. With very few illusions about the British Labour Party they naturally saw it as the one possible strong ally. On almost every issue at Paris, Britain and Norway were in fact firm allies.

On the side of the British Labour Party, illusions were rife about Scandinavia in general. Too complacent and too much a product purely of British history to understand what was happening in France, and, in any case, divided from the French by serious issues of foreign policy, the Labour Party looked beyond France and saw only a yet more hostile European world of revived and vigorous neo-liberalism, supremely indifferent to what they thought of as their own uniquely successful experiment in modern governance. Where else could they turn for consolation other than to Scandinavia? Having turned their eyes in that direction they soon exaggerated certain similarities of economic and social policy into a common model of a controlled, egalitarian, welfare state. When therefore the Norwegian government put forward tentative proposals in 1948 for co-ordinating its long-term programme with that of Britain they were received diplomatically with almost effusive goodwill.

[46] Or 'Ukiscan', as the British sometimes preferred to call it.

There was much less real economic goodwill. The United Kingdom had no interest in investing in Norway's long-term development projects and money was not as available as pleasant feelings. The approach gave rise only to an Anglo-Norwegian Economic Committee, meeting for regular discussions in the same way as the parallel Anglo-French Economic Committee. The Norwegians had wanted to place the Minister of Commerce, Brofoss, on the Committee but the British declined to have anyone so important, and obviously did not intend the Committee to operate on so high a level. One year later, as British anxieties about Finebel reached their peak, Norway came forward with further tentative proposals, this time to create an alternative payments association linking the United Kingdom and Scandinavia.

The Norwegian motives were complex and bound up with the dangerous isolation in which Norway feared it would end. The abortive Scandinavian customs union negotiations had shown how few points of economic agreement there were between Norway and its neighbours. Moral and even perhaps some financial support for Norwegian reconstruction might be discovered in Britain. The British motives were much simpler and less ambivalent. A payments association with Scandinavia would make Finebel seem more isolated and emphasize to Washington the danger that American support for Finebel might split the western world and leave Britain the leader of a soft-currency area. Scandinavian countries already held sterling in considerable quantities and formalizing the agreements into a payments association starting with a Norwegian agreement might even bring Scandinavia into the sterling area.[47] With the rebirth of German exports to Europe that would be a particularly opportune development. And if that were to happen, might it not also prove possible to pull the Netherlands into the sterling area? The Economic Co-operation Committee, the new title of the London Committee which had controlled the delegations to the CEEC and OEEC, even went further and speculated on whether the Federal Republic might not also be brought into the sterling trade network thus ending permanently all talk of Little Europe.[48]

There was no reason unduly to fear competition from Scandinavian industries, even if they had to be offered concessions beyond the level of trade liberalization on which the ECA was now insisting, although as it turned out the Board of Trade, true to form, was most unwilling to allow any such concessions. Even without the Scandinavian countries becoming full members of the sterling area Britain could offer freedom of current transactions and a greater freedom of capital movements. The currencies could be held without limits thus permitting a more vigorous and less interrupted growth of trade between the two areas. There was no question of any disagreeable supra-national political implications and, besides, as the paper

[47] FO 371/78136, UK delegation to London, 1 November 1949.
[48] T 232/148, Meeting of European Economic Co-operation Committee, 5 December 1949.

submitted to the Economic Policy Committee of the cabinet put it, 'The Scandinavians have reached a comparable stage of social and political development to our own.'[49]

In comparison with Finebel, Uniscan did not much matter to world trade, nor even to British trade. Three of the seven countries which spent the largest share of their national income on British exports were Norway, Denmark and Sweden.[50] But as markets they were too small to offer the prospect of important export gains. In 1950 British exports to Scandinavia were 9 per cent of all exports. The proportion going to Little Europe (Finebel) was only 11 per cent (table 34), but what had to be considered was the difference in potential growth of demand between an area with a total population of 14.4 million and an area of 156.0 million. In return for such

Table 34   Trade with Scandinavia (Denmark, Norway and Sweden) and Little Europe as a proportion (%) of United Kingdom trade

	Exports		Imports	
	Scandinavia	Little Europe	Scandinavia	Little Europe
1910/13	4	22	8	25
1935/38	7	14	8	13
1948/50	8	11	7	11

Source: F.V. Meyer, *United Kingdom Trade with Europe* (London, 1957); OEEC, *Statistical Bulletins of Foreign Trade*.

small potential economic gains economically there was in fact very little that the United Kingdom in its turn could offer to Scandinavia. When the British concessions were formulated they amounted only to the removal of more restrictions on imports from Scandinavia than from the rest of western Europe and much less strict terms for the use of sterling than were applied to the other Western European countries.

Table 35   Trade with the United Kingdom as a proportion (%) of Scandinavian trade, 1948–50

Exports			Imports		
Denmark	Norway	Sweden	Denmark	Norway	Sweden
39.6	17.5	16.1	29.8	20.7	18.1

Source: OEEC, *Statistical Bulletins of Foreign Trade*.

[49] FO 371/78137, Closer economic association between Scandinavia and the sterling area, 30 November 1949.
[50] F.V. Meyer, *United Kingdom Trade with Europe* (London, 1957), p. 159.

Even these concessions raised the awkward debate in Britain about the future relationship of the sterling area to Europe. If the idea that West Germany might eventually be included had any future at all, might it not simply mean that it would be easier for West Germany to capture the British markets in Scandinavia? Even leaving Germany outside and attracting the Netherlands, although it would scotch French plans, ran into severe objections because it would transfer to the sterling reserves the problem of the Dutch deficits with Belgium and how they could be settled. In January it was decided, however, that encouraging the international use of the pound was a more important objective than protecting Scandinavian markets against German exports.[51]

In the face of the Scandinavian reactions these large considerations were to remain theoretical. In Norway Lange and Brofoss secretly discussed possible membership of the sterling area with the relevant Storting committee and seem to have got a favourable response for continuing the discussions with Britain.[52] But opinion in Denmark and Sweden was hostile. Britain's earlier readiness to consider throwing over food imports from Denmark if a cheaper source had been available had already underlined the indifference in London to Denmark's position. A closer association with Britain would only make Denmark's position riskier and Prime Minister Hans Hedtoft was against it.[53] In Sweden the future trading relationship with West Germany was considered more important than that with Britain.[54]

By the time the first Uniscan talks were held in January 1950 the news of the rejection of Finebel by French ministers was filtering into Whitehall. The inference that in the impending struggle with the ECA over the nature of a European payments union the United Kingdom would now after all be able to rely on French support in the OEEC against any proposals that seemed too dangerously liberal was correctly drawn. Uniscan looked even less worth straining for. All that emerged from the January talks was an easing of foreign exchange restrictions on tourists, which was not fully applicable in Norway, and the removal of certain other restrictions on payments on capital account.

Although Uniscan died down almost as soon as it had begun to produce a flare of enthusiasm, the brief light cast by it on European reconstruction was a disturbing one for the United States. A range of possible western European futures still existed in spite of Marshall Aid and might still exist even when the ECA had secured its agreement on a Western European payments union. The meaning was not lost on Washington where the rest of the administration took an increasingly cautious view of the ECA's ambitions for the payments union.

[51] CAB 134/246, Economic Co-operation Committee, 13 January 1950.
[52] FO 371/78137, Ellis-Rees to Rickett, 25 November 1949.
[53] SD 540.5686, Harriman to Washington, 22 December 1949.
[54] ibid., Stockholm embassy to Washington, 20 December 1949.

THE EUROPEAN PAYMENTS UNION

Marshall Aid had insulated both Western Europe and the United States against the collapse of Bretton Woods. While all energy had been concentrated on righting what was thought of as a disastrous situation in Europe no clear thought had been given in 1948 to the question of what would replace the first post-war economic settlement. This was mainly because the glib assumption still prevailed that Marshall Aid, by restoring Western European 'viability', would soon allow the Bretton Woods agreements to become operative. But the reality in 1948 was that the underlying assumptions of those agreements had had very little impact on European economic policies. In the agreements themselves, and just as much in all the earlier rejected or modified plans put forward in the process of negotiation by Keynes and White, the assumptions had been axiomatic that the concept of an equilibrium in world trade and payments was a valid one and that because most international trade in the post-war world would be the business of the private sector its reactions to economic signals would always tend to restore that equilibrium. It was only on those assumptions that the IMF could be expected to work properly and the same assumptions underlay all the ECA schemes for a purely Western European payments organization. The reality was a disequilibrium in international payments so large as to cause many even of the most convinced liberals to doubt the validity of the equilibrium theory of international trade and to call for government intervention of all kinds to remedy the 'structural' problems. If the disequilibrium in Western European payments looked irremediable to many, it was only a pale reflection of the disequilibrium between Western Europe and the United States. But with trade conducted so extensively by governments themselves, armoured with trade and exchange controls and, in many cases, relegating the balance of payments to as low a priority as possible as an economic signal, most European countries had shown themselves singularly unresponsive to payments disequilibria. What relevance did the Bretton Woods agreements then have to the future? In 1948 it was not an unreasonable view to suppose that the future of Western Europe would be one of government trading and controlled economies, 'mixed economies' in which the government was a much bigger part of the mixture than allowed for in that phrase of the 1950s.

In the event the world of the 1950s was not like that at all and the complicated apparatus of state trade controls crumbled away in Western Europe after 1949 at least as much by European volition as through American pressure. All agencies of the American government were united in seeking the restoration of a system more responsive to international pressures and so a barrier to inflationary trading practices by governments and a conduit to integration, and more representative of the society which they wanted to produce in Europe. All this applied every bit as much to a European payments union as to the world-wide arrangements of Bretton Woods. If responsiveness to trade disequilibria was the heart of the matter, the degree of hardness of the terms of the settlements was the crucial issue in the negotiations. At what point should deficit countries have to pay their debts in gold and so be brought to heel? But this was a divisive question in the American administration. If that point was set too soon would not European countries persist with the arrangements of 1948?

Finebel, the British reaction to it and flirtation with Uniscan, the apparent equanimity with which the British government, in response to the ECA's new policy, took the position that if the terms of the European payments union were unsatisfactory Britain would not join and would make its own arrangements in a separate soft-currency area, showed that whatever commitments to the post-war order Britain and France had made before the end of 1945 they were now no longer thought of as binding before the primary objectives of domestic and European reconstruction. In Washington the Bretton Woods agreements were thought of as a sleeping beauty, in suspended animation and awaiting the kiss of completed European reconstruction to awake to a happy future; in Western European capitals they were either moribund or a corpse.

These differences could no longer be dodged. The problem for the ECA was to continue to convince opinion in America that European integration was still the handsome prince who would wake Bretton Woods to full life. When the ECA proposals went for discussion in the NAC in January 1950 Hoffman embarked on a series of propaganda speeches in the Mid-West, returning for the Council discussions, and he carried on the debate outside Washington in a further series of public speeches through the first two weeks of February. His theme was always that recovery was not only recovery from the effects of the war but from the erroneous path of European economic history over the last fifty years, which had led to 'indulgences in economic practices that are basically unsound'.

> Instead of thinking in terms of expanding markets, too many of Europe's businessmen took the more comfortable route of dividing markets. Instead of competing, they cartelized. Instead of battling for increased volume with a lower unit profit, they followed the will-o'-wisp of a low volume and high profits.

It was not 'an impractical dream' to seek to reverse this long-term trend. Rather it was 'a practical necessity'.

> It is, in our view, quite impossible for Europe to become enduringly self-supporting, with a reasonably high standard of living for its people, unless Western Europe's 270 million consumers are welded into a single great market.[55]

[55] MBZ, 45/50.1, Speech of Hoffman before the Junior Chamber of Commerce at Peoria, 21 January 1950. He must have been including Spain to get such a number.

The proposal that the ECA should contribute to an automatic settlements mechanism in Western Europe ran immediately foul of the IMF which represented the surviving interests of the world-wide Bretton Woods system. So far the claims of the IMF to operate the Western European settlements had been kept on the sidelines by the American government, but the rapidly improving payments balance between Western Europe and the dollar zone after the devaluations suggested that the equilibrium for which the Fund was supposed to be waiting before becoming fully operational in Europe might now be arriving. The Director insisted that the IMF now play a full part in the discussions and that it should itself be responsible for any new regional payments union.[56]

In the NAC the United States representative on the Board of the IMF, Frank A. Southard Jnr, argued forcefully against acceptance of the ECA proposals. They would, he suggested, postpone world-wide convertibility by continuing to divert Western Europe's exports to Western Europe and away from the dollar zone and would also be a serious infringement on the world-wide authority of the IMF. No such regional clearing unions had been countenanced elsewhere in the world. The International Bank argued that United States participation in the payments union by providing dollars would mean that America would find itself sponsoring a payments union which would discriminate against American exports. The proposed union would prevent the arrival of convertibility and of non-discriminatory trade. This was also the view of the Department of Commerce, the Export-Import Bank and the Federal Reserve Board. Underlying some of these views was also the unease, expressed in particular by the Export-Import Bank, that America was now proposing to become even more deeply, perhaps inextricably, involved in Europe's economic reconstruction whereas one original purpose of Marshall Aid had been to set a time limit to that involvement.

Hoffman's counter-argument that 'the only limit to American exports was the number of dollars European countries could earn' was less than convincing given the persistence of discriminatory trading practices in Europe. The State Department's arguments that, 'if one thought of the union as a temporary arrangement carrying out operations parallel to those the International Monetary Fund carries out, but is not doing for Europe at present, that kind of responsibility might well revert to the Fund after 1952 when ECA had withdrawn from Europe', can only be described as specious, since the hope was that an integrated Western Europe would preserve, if not the same, at least a very similar arrangement. The NAC was not convinced that this was 'the historic moment' which Hoffman claimed it to be, nor by the bathetic prophecy that:

[56] J.K. Horsefield *et al.*, *The International Monetary Fund* (Washington DC, 1969), vol. 1, p. 289.

If there were a second collapse in Europe as a result of our inability to figure out the technical aspects of recovery, Europe once more would become an easy prey for Communist propaganda, the United States would become a garrison state, and there would be no chance of having a balanced budget.[57]

The proposals were referred back to a special meeting of the senior representatives to try to harmonize them with the machinery and intentions of Bretton Woods.[58]

It was not possible to lay down any fixed rules about what was acceptable. A major international negotiation was to begin and the negotiators could only be given guidance on what an acceptable goal should be. That goal was defined in such a way as to imply the minimum of difference between the operations of a European clearing union and the IMF. If American funds were to be put into the clearing union, rather than into conditional aid in support of the drawing rights, the funds had to be used to support multilateral trade. Within the clearing union all currencies would have to be transferable. This did not mean that currencies would be convertible in the sense in which the word has been used since, but all settlements in the union would have to be automatic and it was precisely this which had led to so many earlier objections on the grounds that it was already either a form of convertibility or too positive a step on the road to it. Over the current fiscal year of the $800 million of conditional aid most had not been in the form of multilateral, but only of bilateral, drawing rights. The sum now suggested to back the union was less than this because the assumption was that if all settlements were automatic and multilateral the total value of final settlement transactions would be less. Debtors running up excessive deficits in the union would have to pay their debt in dollars in an increasing ratio as the deficit mounted; creditors would receive a diminishing proportion of their surpluses in dollars. There would therefore be built into the settlement rules a mechanism for directing the members towards an equilibrium.

The ECA had always firmly retained the final powers to determine aid allocations to individual countries and indeed had demonstrated this very clearly in overriding the OEEC in 1948 on the question of aid for the Bizone. Most members of the NAC would have preferred the ECA to continue in this way and, if need arose, simply make its own settlement with any creditor country with a claim on the payments union. The argument against this was, of course, that the union itself was intended to be a piece of functional machinery to promote European integration. Hoffman insisted that he should be allowed to listen to advice from the union on the disposal of dollars and on occasion take it after consultation within the government. The NAC refused, however, to allow this financial commitment to be in any way open-ended;

[57] NAC, Minutes, meeting no. 146, 19 January 1950.
[58] NAC, Staff Committee Papers, Minutes of an executive session of the senior representatives, meeting no. 46, 20 January 1950.

dollar funding for the union would be entirely dependent on congressional allocations to the ERP and when the ERP ended in two years there would have to be a financial settlement with the union to account for any initial dollar funding which had been provided. If the EPU survived beyond that date it would be on European support alone. The potential clash of powers with the IMF was largely, it was hoped, eliminated by these restrictions; at least the realistic possibility was left that IMF would replace the union in 1952. But it was still the case that the ECA would hardly be able to allocate aid according to 'merit' without making important statements about the nature of European domestic economic policies and their effect on national balances of payments. It was agreed that this should also be done in consultation with the IMF.[59] The idea of a central European monetary authority was obviously fading to the more distant horizons of policy even before the Europeans themselves had had to mobilize their own opposition to it.

Before the ECA proposals were given a full consideration by the OEEC the first troublesome economic effects of trade liberalization seemed to be appearing in some of the smaller economies. Mainly, as chapter 13 shows, this was because of the inequitable nature of the method used to measure liberalization. But where trade liberalization seemed to be producing balance of payments deficits the alarm about the European payments union was the greater. Because the trade liberalization procedures, for example, did not apply to a large proportion of Danish exports Denmark was already faced with the possibility of having to deflate to regulate its balance of payments and was more likely to opt instead for trade controls. The arguments inside the NAC had reinforced the ECA's conviction that debtors in the payments union would have to be forced by the rules to take sterner measures than in the past if the system was going to work. Full employment must now definitely take a lower priority than 'viability' and debtors must now realize that 'present investment programs no longer sufficient justification for continuation present levels overall deficits, particularly when contribution to attaining viability by 1952 doubtful, as in case Norwegian investment program'.[60] As European countries were forced towards a less secure balance of payments position by the trade liberalization programme they would also be forced by the proposed payments system to unpopular domestic economic measures to rectify the balance of payments.

The OEEC Council in January 1950 issued only a general statement of principles in reply to the American proposals, saying that any European payments union would have to be reconciled with the existence of the sterling area and would have to retain certain bilateral elements. In early February the decision was taken in Washington to apply for permission to withhold as much

[59] NAC, Minutes, meeting no. 147, 23 January 1950.

[60] ECA, 10, Hoffman to Paris embassy, 'Disadvantages of the pro-debtor proposals – clearing union', 24 January 1950.

as a third of the congressional appropriation for the fiscal year 1950/1 for use in supporting the process of trade liberalization. The sum would be composed of a flat-rate percentage reduction to each country in the sums of Marshall Aid that would otherwise have been awarded according to the Snoy-Marjolin formula.[61] A small part would be allocated to joint investment projects in Europe's dependent territories if they could be shown to be likely to contribute to improving productivity and closing the dollar gap. Otherwise, as Hoffman told the Joint Foreign Affairs Committee of Congress, the sum would be used in accordance with the expressed wish of Congress in the 1949 amendment to Public Law 472 'to encourage the unification of Europe'.

Once it had been established that so large a part of the appropriation was to be used to reward 'merit', the ECA sought to force the hand of the British government by reviving Finebel, hinting that the whole sum might now go to support the Little European payments union.[62] Triffin suggests that this was a successful negotiating tactic.[63] But the Finebel participants and the British government knew well enough that Finebel had died. Only Belgium and Italy were now prepared to back the Finebel plan. The French position was that it was no use without West German inclusion but that it was not possible to include West Germany in the plans as they stood. The Dutch remained adamant that they could not consider a clearing union without German membership, and especially if Britain objected to Dutch participation.[64] The final report on the Finebel negotiations submitted in February to the Dutch government indicated that agreement had only been reached on further discussions on the basis that either the United Kingdom would be invited to participate or that it would co-operate closely with the member states.[65] At the start of March Acheson could only agree with Stikker that raising the spectre of Finebel was in no way likely to bring trade liberalization and the EPU any closer.[66]

The ultimate success of the negotiations was not dependent on such intricacies of negotiating tactics, which so fascinate negotiators themselves, but on major concessions on each side, as well as on the repercussions of external events. The terms of the EPU were eventually agreed by the OEEC on 18 August 1950 and the treaty establishing it signed on 19 September. Negotiations were concluded therefore only after Schuman had proposed the European Coal and Steel Community, after the negotiations for the ECSC had made important progress and after the outbreak of war in Korea. 'Rarely', Triffin, who observed this long drawn-out process at close quarters, tells us, 'has an

[61] ECA, 59, 'ERP Strategy', Draft, 10 February 1950.
[62] T 232/149, Telegram to Paris delegation, 3 February 1950.
[63] R. Triffin, *Europe and the Money Muddle* (New Haven, 1957).
[64] MBZ, 6204/50.1, Bespreking inzake Finebel te Parijs op 9.2.1950, 13 February 1950.
[65] ibid., Rapport des experts de la Belgique etc. concernant l'établissement d'une association économique et financière en Europe occidentale, 16 February 1950.
[66] Acheson Papers, Memorandum of conversation with Stikker, 1 March 1950.

international negotiation been so successful in reaching its objectives.'[67] The judgement here depends on the standpoint of the observer. The historian is likely to agree that what emerged was realistic, practical and durable. But it was only so because it fell so far short of ambitions on the American side while still producing an important change of attitude and policy on the British side. For America it marked a defeat for the new policy of the ECA, and the end of any idea that the EPU would lead to further functional machinery for European unification. For Britain it marked a definite commitment of the sterling area to a pattern of multilateral settlements on a world-wide basis and the end of the lingering hopes of leadership of a soft-currency area including parts of Western Europe.

There was no chance that deficit countries would accept to make settlements entirely in gold. To impose complete gold settlements would in any case probably multiply restrictions to trade, whereas the whole purpose was to reduce them. Settlements would therefore be made, it was agreed, in a mixture of credits and gold. Each country would make an initial deposit into the EPU of its own currency and credits in settlements would be allowed up to 60 per cent of the size of each country's deposit ('quota'). The size of the quota was fixed as 15 per cent of the country's visible and invisible transactions with all other members. A surplus or deficit up to 20 per cent of the size of quota could be covered entirely by credits. Between that point and the 60 per cent mark the relative proportions of gold and credits in the settlements increased on a sliding-scale.

The EPU thus resembled in principle in its operations the functioning of the IMF, the members offering an overdraft facility of 20 per cent to the central authority in return for overdraft rights of the same magnitude. These rights could be exercised in the currency of any Union member and were thus, unlike the drawing rights of the previous two payments agreements, fully multilateral. All compensable deficits were thus cleared automatically irrespective of the currencies and the number of transactions involved. Once the 20 per cent automatic credit barrier was passed any member could continue to overdraw up to 60 per cent providing it met the requirements of the sliding-scale by purchasing for gold (or dollars) from the Union the stipulated proportion of its foreign currency requirement. In theory the gold (or dollars) which the Union would obtain in this way could be balanced by gold and dollar payments to those members from which it obtained the foreign currencies being purchased in this way by the first member. The Union could, in effect, also draw on a member in excess of 20 per cent and up to 60 per cent of its quota by purchasing for gold or dollars the appropriate proportion of its extra requirement of that country's currency.

The effect of the sliding-scale was such as to encourage a member with an increasing deficit position to correct the deficit, as the proportion of the total

[67]   Triffin, *Europe*, p. 161.

foreign currency requirement which had to be purchased from the Union in gold (or dollars) increased. The United Kingdom would in fact permanently lose gold (or dollars) through its deficits with Belgium and Italy unless it subsequently ran a surplus big enough to recover it. The net positions were calculated at the end of every month by the BIS, so that a member could begin to win back gold even on a monthly surplus without having to wait until the whole of an accumulated deficit was first wiped out.

In practice, of course, in spite of this incorporated encouragement to member countries to correct deficits, the disequilibrium in intra-Western European trade was still such as to make it improbable that the EPU would effectively balance its operations. From the standpoint of a potential creditor country it may seem there was no great incentive to support such a scheme. Such countries were given first claim, by the terms of the agreement, on the Union's gold and dollar resources should it go into liquidation. But the greater incentive was the desire of the creditor countries to find some trade and payments mechanism which would sustain their exports, even at the risk of some eventual financial loss.

Even so, the final outcome was highly displeasing to Belgium and the cabinet apparently decided at one stage to refuse to join the Union. But the Belgian position was too isolated to bring anyone else along in so extreme a course of action. The last-minute deadlock was broken by a concession that any outstanding Belgian credits, if the Union broke up, would have to be repaid within two years. Italy would probably have preferred more hardness in the settlement arrangements too, but the British opposition to this was supported without wavering by the Scandinavian countries and the Netherlands, forcing the United States once more to recognize the real limits of its international economic power. On 15 June the Staff Committee of the NAC decided to use the last-minute Belgian opposition to the proposed agreement in order to try to obtain terms more satisfactory to the United States, but when only Belgium opposed the agreement as presented by Stikker to the ministers assembled in the OEEC on 16 June there was nothing further that the Americans could do.

One thing above all decided the issue, the financial support which the United States provided in terms of a dollar contribution to the EPU's initial funds. Without this no potential creditor country could reasonably have supposed, no matter how great the need to sustain exports, that the arrangements would have been worthwhile, because they would have provided insufficient opportunity to translate surpluses on intra-Western European payments into gold or dollars. This financial support took various forms, however, and the terms and conditions under which it was provided emerged only in the course of a long negotiating process. Merely to describe the way in which the EPU operated does not show how several of the central issues of European reconstruction were in fact subsumed in the agreement. Of these, two were of crucial importance, the relationship of the sterling area to western Europe and the functional capacity of the EPU to produce western European integration.

It is through the outcome of the agreement in these two areas that it became one of the pillars of the post-war economic settlement. Had it not enabled the trade of the sterling area to be linked in a common payments mechanism to that of Western Europe, the trade expansion of the next decade would scarcely have been feasible and the threat of two separate western trading worlds would have continued to hover over American-European relations. Had America not abandoned its attempt to dissolve the sterling area in the interests of an integrated Western Europe, the new international framework of interdependence would have been unachievable. Had the agreement not at the same time put a firm end to the idea that the payments union would only be the first step towards a monetary and then a political union, it would scarcely have been possible to create a framework of integration appropriate to a durable peace settlement. Agreement on the EPU on those terms came at an important moment in the negotiations for the European Coal and Steel Community, for whose success the abandonment of the ideas of the ECA Planning Group was essential. The conclusion of the EPU agreement on those terms, representing as it did a major policy retreat by the United States, together with the agreement on a coal and steel community, laid the foundations of an effective reconstruction of Europe, closing one period and inaugurating another.

In February the British government was still flatly opposed to participation in automatic multilateral clearing in Western Europe. The division of opinion inside the British government was still as it had been in 1947, some hoping for agreement on a modified version of the American plan which would allow Britain to participate and others much more reluctant to countenance anything resembling the ECA proposals. One difference on this occasion seems to have been the greater role played by the Bank of England. But every part of the British government was opposed to the principle, still central to the ECA's plans, that the managing board of the EPU should have powers to influence and harmonize national financial policies. Until March the British government had an acceptable excuse for inaction, the approaching general election, in which it almost fell from power. Only at the start of March did it indicate that it would be putting forward its own proposals.[68]

That these proposals would be unacceptable to the United States was made plain six days later in a personal handwritten plea from Cripps to Hoffman. 'I hope', wrote Cripps, 'you will not hustle us unduly in this matter or encourage others to insist upon provisions which it is not and never will be possible for us to accept.'[69] Hoffman's reply was discouraging. The American proposals, he intimated, were less than the American people wished for and could not be

[68] Acheson Papers, Memoranda of conversations, 'Exchanges of views between the Secretary and the Netherlands Foreign Minister', 1 March 1950.
[69] Hoffman Papers, 26, Cripps to Hoffman, 7 March 1950.

modified. The programme of trade liberalization, including the end of dual pricing, had been agreed to and could not be weakened, otherwise, 'the restoration of a cordial relationship between the United Kingdom and the United States will be difficult of achievement'.[70]

Just how unacceptable the British proposals would be had not been foreseen; the ECA had never anticipated a British proposal that multilateral settlements should be confined to the continent. But that was more or less what the proposals implied.[71] The United Kingdom would preserve intact its bilateral agreements but would pay off to a limited extent its bilateral debts through the payments union either with gold and dollars or with bilateral claims. Claims on Britain beyond the bilateral credit margins would be settled in gold but only after a transfer to the clearing system of all British claims on other countries in excess of the bilateral 'swing'. Combined with the maintenance of import controls this meant that the United Kingdom would be protected against all risk of losing gold but in a good position to gain it, and therefore sheltered from those forces of competition which were the essence of the scheme. 'Loss of gold', as the ECA now argued, 'should be a signal for fundamental economic readjustments.'[72]

The only concession which the ECA was prepared to make at this stage was to consider as structural, and thus as warranting special aid, any British deficit to the EPU beyond an agreed point at which Britain would be allowed to reimpose quantitative controls.[73] If the divide between the European area and the sterling area was not to open up this could hardly be avoided. When the NAC considered the position on 5 April it could offer nothing more constructive than the justified, but futile, comment that 'the scaling down of the [sterling] balances should have been done in 1945'.[74] The sterling balances hovered now over the proposed EPU with more deadly weight than over convertibility in 1947. The problem was difficult enough at a technical level but the British desire to defend sterling as an international currency was increased by fears that the EPU would not only reduce the use of sterling in international trade but might yet even give birth, as indeed the ECA hoped it would, to a new, rival, European international currency unit.

This fear was intended to be strengthened by the bogus resurrection of Finebel in February, but even while this febrile manoeuvre was under way a set of compromise proposals was emerging in Washington which would eventually permit agreement on the issue of the sterling area. Continental holders of sterling balances, it was eventually agreed, would be allowed to negotiate to have them repaid over a two-year period from the start of the EPU and if the negotiation failed the United Kingdom would still have a further two

[70] ibid., Hoffman to Cripps, 15 March 1950.
[71] ECA, 3, 'European payments scheme', 20 March 1950.
[72] ECA, 2, United Kingdom participation in European unification, n.d.
[73] ECA, 3, Katz to Hoffman, 23 March 1950.
[74] NAC, Minutes, meeting no. 153, 5 April 1950.

years to pay them off if necessary. A continental country in surplus to the EPU would be allowed to exchange its claim for credit against sterling balances which would be usable for settlements within the Union. Britain would then be reimbursed by the ECA for any gold payments made to the EPU as a result of this arrangement. The sterling balances held within the Union, such as the sterling surpluses on bilateral trade accumulated by Italy, would thus be multilateralized while the threat of gold loss which this posed to Britain would be much diminished. At the same time any country with a sterling surplus could avoid having to accumulate sterling balances or having to face the imposition of British import controls against its exports. In fact over the first years of the EPU Britain was on balance a creditor, so the provisions scarcely applied and the use of sterling in intra-Western European trade was much the same as in the previous year.

As late as March Cripps's position was that the payments union should only begin to function once the bilateral agreements were exhausted, financing trade beyond the point at which bilateral agreements could not go. At the same time he had demanded full freedom of action to reintroduce at any time exchange controls and quantitative restrictions on a unilateral basis if the sterling reserves were under serious threat. Even to accept these new American proposals was thus a major shift of opinion, especially as it was accompanied by an acknowledgement that quantitative restrictions and other controls would only be reintroduced on a multilateral basis. On the American side it meant accepting a further financial commitment, to redeem European sterling balances if necessary out of the earmarked portion of the congressional appropriation.

In themselves the terms of this compromise between the sterling area and the continent were such as to block the path to integration, but it was just as firmly blocked by other aspects of the Union. As far as the Planning Group was concerned the next stages were currency convertibility and a monetary union. The Planning Group advocated floating exchange rates as the best basis for convertibility and the surest way to integration and 'viability'. The idea of abandoning fixed exchange rates was not, as the early stages of Finebel had shown, without support in Europe and after the devaluation the Belgian government had considered adopting floating exchange rates. Although they were soon forced by international pressures to revert to a fixed rate, the decision to do so was apparently gained, even with American pressure, 'only by a hairsbreadth'.[75] Italy in 1947 and France in 1948 had had dual exchange rates and the Bank of France was in favour of convertibility on the basis of floating rates. But after January the official position of the French government throughout the negotiations was to insist on fixed exchange rates and to oppose all elements of currency convertibility other than those embodied in the automatic transferability of currencies within the Union to make the

[75] T 232/148, Washington embassy to London, 23 September 1949.

settlements. In January the Dutch representative on the IMF demanded that it reiterate its policy of fixed rates. During the EPU negotiations, however, Petsche came increasingly under the influence of the Bank of France and the split between planners and liberals in the French government reappeared. The planners, represented by Marjolin, continued to argue for fixed exchange rates and softness in settlements as the best backing for further economic expansion.[76] Petsche increasingly saw this as inflationary, but never adhered to this opinion long enough or firmly enough for it to affect the outcome of the negotiations.

In March, after what seems to have been a tense debate, the Board of the IMF was pushed to a vote on the nature of what settlement terms it would approve. The principles it did approve were considerably stricter than the eventual provisions of the EPU agreement. The official history tells us that 'as the negotiations progressed a note of disillusionment crept into the Board's discussions'.[77] Many of its members did not think the EPU would in fact, with the terms of settlement it would allow, advance the cause of convertibility. And, furthermore, it was clear that many of the Europeans, seeing the IMF as a mere instrument of American foreign policy, wanted to keep it entirely out of the new European agreement. The United Kingdom was not even prepared to consent to the presence of IMF observers on the EPU board of management.[78]

The preamble to the agreement stipulated that its purpose was to facilitate a return to the general convertibility of currencies, but the terms of settlement fell well short of this goal and even further short of the goal of monetary union. Of course, the settlement terms were multilateral – even that European sterling balances were made available for multilateral settlements – which would reduce in the future the effective range of policy instruments at the disposal of governments. Furthermore, for the first time since 1947 there was now a mechanism which actively discouraged deficits and in that sense the EPU also implied restrictions on the future scope of policy choice. But pushing national policies into a narrower frame of choice was far from the close harmonization of policy which a monetary union would have demanded. The tendency was to push policies into a middle range of choice, mildly inflationary and expansionist, but dependent nevertheless on quite different mechanisms of intervention and control and often expressed in strikingly different public affirmations of purpose. The more extreme illusions of national independence of action had to be abandoned, and the payments arrangements made for the sterling area were the most striking example. But this was far from meaning that European economies in the next decade were to be committed to pursuing similar economic goals through similar policies of Keynesian demand management.

The only irreversible commitment (irreversible, that is, without yet another

---

[76] FO 371/86995, 'Note of a discussion with Mr Katz on June 23', 24 June 1950.
[77] Horsefield, *The IMF*, vol. 1, p. 290.
[78] ibid., vol. 3, pp. 325 ff.

new beginning to the task of European reconstruction, which would have meant inconceivable changes in foreign and defence policy), was to a multilateral payments system in Western Europe embracing sterling area trade. The commitment that this multilateral trading area would also be linked to the dollar trading zone was firm but not irreversible. It depended on American financial support for the Union. This was large, but in principle existed only until the end of Marshall Aid or, alternatively, a dissolution of the Union.

Out of the congressional ERP appropriation $600 million was reserved to further the cause of trade and payments liberalization. Of this, $350 million was placed into the Union as initial working capital. For the guarantee to the United Kingdom against possible gold losses incurred in allowing the European sterling balances to be used in multilateral settlements, a further $150 million had to be set aside. Even with such large dollar sums in the Union's initial working fund and the rapid progress in the first six months of 1950 towards reducing Western Europe's dollar deficits as well as the more persistent deficits in intra-Western European trade, the disequilibria were still such that complicated arrangements had to be made with the Union's initial working balances to try to minimize the risk that they would be inadequate to enable countries to make the gold and dollar settlements even on the relatively 'soft' terms which had finally been agreed. The countries were not all started in an equal financial position at the beginning of the Union's operations. The same exercise as with forecasting 'conditional' aid was performed to try to forecast which countries would be more persistent creditors and which debtors to the Union. Belgium, Britain and Sweden were presumed to be likely to be persistent creditors, and they were therefore started off in a debtor position to counteract this. Contrariwise the four presumed persistent debtors, Austria, Greece, the Netherlands and Norway were started off in a creditor position. Those allocated a debit balance at the start were in effect receiving conditional aid, the old drawing rights, as compensation for the grants they were thus making to the other members. The countries started in a creditor position got $279 million in grants and $35 million in long-term loans through Marshall Aid allocations, thus increasing still further the potential of the others to earn dollars in intra-Western European trade.

It required a great faith in the power of multilateral trading arrangements to suppose that for this great financial commitment the ECA's dream of European unity had been brought closer. Of the 'functional' political machinery nothing was in place except a 'Managing Board' of the EPU and a new OEEC committee, the 'Control Group', which superintended and reported on the progress in trade liberalization. It is true that the Managing Board of the EPU could exercise its executive powers by majority vote, a principle which had never been permitted in the OEEC. Not even Britain, however, opposed that, because the Managing Board was ultimately entirely dependent on the OEEC Council where the same rule of unanimity as before still prevailed.[79] In reality

[79] CAB 132/247, Meeting of European Economic Co-operation Committee, 28 June 1950.

the Board had been given no jurisdictional or executive powers beyond those of the OEEC itself. The dream of a European monetary authority survived in only one respect. The EPU kept its accounts in a special unit, defined at the start as having the equivalent gold content of the 1950 United States dollar. No country would subsequently be able to veto any change which was the same as or smaller than the subsequent appreciation or depreciation of its own currency in terms of gold. The EPU unit of account therefore would effectively be defined in the future as whichever member currency remained most stable in terms of gold. Triffin argued for this definition to preserve the idea of a European monetary unit that might be available when integration did come.[80]

The narrative of this book can have left few doubts that the ECA was inspired by a great faith, too great to be abandoned. William Foster predicted in a speech at the University of Washington that in spite of its many compromises the EPU would eventually lead to a European central bank and a common European currency.[81] The Finance and Payments Division of the ECA, which had done much of the work in the negotiations, was also optimistic. 'Undoubtedly', it claimed, 'EPU is a step towards the economic unification of Europe.'[82] Bissell's judgement was more cautious. The EPU, he said, was 'a major negotiating achievement' in what he called 'the longest, toughest, most exasperating assignment yet undertaken by ECA'.[83]

In reality, what the United States had to settle for was the highest common factor of agreement which would preserve one trade and payments system in the western world, a limited form of multilateralism, continued dollar aid to make that possible, and the persistence throughout the 1950s of discrimination by powerful economies against the dollar. For three years, since the crisis of 1947, the ERP had gone ahead on the assumption that it was building a road to the re-establishment of the Bretton Woods agreements. In 1950 this assumption could no longer bridge the growing complexities of America's policy goals. The ECA's position weakened in Washington precisely because it was not at all clear there that European integration and a return to Bretton Woods were necessarily compatible objectives and in those circumstances the larger world-wide hope of Bretton Woods prevailed at the expense of the ECA's faith. That great faith still, even in 1950, presumed a relative economic weakness in Western Europe's position which, from more realistic viewpoints in the American government, was by no means visible.

The decision to accept the payments union on these compromise terms followed the decision to accept the French initiative in the Schuman Plan to create an integrated Little Europe. In the EPU it was the strength of Britain's position which had to be acknowledged, in the Schuman Plan that of France. In either case the terms on which European reconstruction was finally settled

[80] Triffin, *Europe*, p. 173, p. 9.
[81] MBZ, 45/50.4, Text of speech by William C. Foster at the University of Washington, 15 June 1950. [82] ECA, 33, 'The European Payments Union', 8 July 1950.
[83] ECA, 10, Administrator's Staff Meeting, 12 July 1950.

were more European than American. The much stronger economic position of Western Europe in 1950 compared to that of 1947; the realization, especially after the economic crisis of 1949 and the outbreak of war in Korea, that European integration was by no means the answer to many of America's economic and strategic problems; the deeper understanding of the variety and complexities of the politics and economies of the European nation states acquired over three years, all played their part in this. The limits of America's power to reconstruct Europe were reached in the construction of an economic interdependence whose form was less determined by American policies than by Europe's resistance to them.

'Why do we always support the British against the continental countries?' asked Arthur Marget, one of the Governors of the Federal Reserve, as the EPU agreement was reluctantly accepted in the NAC, only to receive the convincing answer, 'We did our damnedest to isolate the British on every single issue. We couldn't do it.'[84] The real weakness of America's tactics was unavoidable. 'There was', as the ECA representative explained, 'a conscious decision by the interested people in the Executive Branch to try to get the British in.'[85] What other policy would have made economic sense for the future?

But it was not only because of the terms which the United Kingdom obtained that a rueful discontent rumbled in Washington. The IMF complained that it was only in the year after the agreement came into force that there would be any real degree of hardness in the settlements, yet western European foreign trade was already more than 25 per cent above its pre-war level and production was rising every year.[86] The Federal Reserve Board grumbled that an attempt to restrict the expansion of credit in the European economies had ended in a set of arrangements which would facilitate more than restrict credit expansion. Two years later when the term of America's financial contribution to the EPU expired Harriman had to plead desperately for the retention of any American support for it. At that time Treasury Secretary Snyder cast a bleakly accurate, prophetic Treasury eye into the future.

> It could be said there was no problem about the dollar now, [he argued,] but there may be a day before too long when we may be concerned about its position in world trade, and we do not want to build up an organization that would place us at a complete disadvantage in future world trade.[87]

---

[84] ECA, 3, Transcript of NAC staff committee meeting, 15 June 1950.   [85] ibid.

[86] NAC, Minutes, meeting no. 158, 29 June 1950.

[87] NAC, Minutes, meeting no. 190, 13 March 1952.

XI

THE 1949 RECESSION
AND THE DIVERGENCE
OF BRITAIN
AND LITTLE EUROPE

In chapter 8 it was emphasized how vigorous was the expansion of western Europe's foreign trade from the nadir of 1945. The expansion of exports, however, was by no means equal even between countries which had had similar experiences during the war. Given the difference in emphasis in national economic policy and the erratic nature of the trade and payments mechanism, especially in the first three post-war years, this is not surprising. But the overall powerful upward trend of growth of western European exports is unmistakable. Even so, in 1948 only the United Kingdom and Switzerland had a higher level of exports than in 1938, which had itself been a year in which exports had been at a relatively low level. Much, therefore, depended on the continuation of this vigorous upward trend through 1949 and beyond.

So vigorous an expansion of western Europe's exports necessarily implied a vigorous expansion of British exports too, because of the large weight of British foreign trade in western Europe's foreign trade. In 1937 the total value of British foreign trade had been 31.5 per cent of that of Western Europe. In 1946 it was 45.4 per cent of that of Western Europe and even in 1950, when it was 32.6 per cent, its weight was still greater than before the war. At first glance table 36 presents a rosy picture of British export performance. This was one area where at the time there were no lamentations about the performance of the British economy and few criticisms of British economic policy. The balance of payments crises which dogged the British economy in 1947, 1949 and 1951 were attributed mainly to the unforeseen level of imports and to the unfavourable change in Britain's terms of trade from the pre-war years.

Table 36 Value of exports of the United Kingdom and Little Europe, 1928–50 (million current dollars)

	1928	1938	1946	1947	1948	1949	1950	1950 at pre-September 1949 dollar exchange rates
Little Europe	6,387	4,243	2,163	4,718	6,475	8,244	9,295	11,007
United Kingdom	3,520	2,603	3,884	4,828	6,635	6,835	6,317	8,244
Exports of Little Europe to United Kingdom	1,768	1,065	735	1,215	1,700	2,226	2,879	3,222
Exports of United Kingdom to Little Europe	523	371	563	505	735	712	776	1,013

Source: OEEC, *Statistical Bulletin of Foreign Trade*. Germany has been calculated on the territorial area of the Federal Republic throughout. See Appendix.

British foreign trade had not declined so steeply during the 1930s from its 1928 level as that of the other major Western European economies. If the experiences of the 1930s and the post-war world are directly compared, however, it can be seen that after 1946 the foreign trade of Little Europe reversed this comparative trend and showed a more vigorous tendency to growth than that of the United Kingdom. But at the start of the trend this could accurately be put down to the lower levels from which the trade of the continental countries had begun to grow in 1946, especially when the extraordinarily low level of German and Italian trade in that year is considered. This explanation, however, was made to do duty for much longer than it should have done, perhaps because the tendency was greatly to exaggerate the damage caused by fighting and occupation to the continental economies. By 1949 it was no longer valid. There were serious short-run and long-run weaknesses in the United Kingdom's foreign trading position. These played their part in the balance of payments crisis of 1949 as much as did the steep rise in imports and the deterioration in the British terms of trade (regarded at the time as merely unlucky). More significantly, they continued to be prominent over the next two decades.

These weaknesses are revealed by the marked divergence in the rate of growth of exports of the United Kingdom on the one hand and Little Europe on the other to the rapidly-growing Little European market. Recalculated to allow for the price changes caused by the 1949 devaluations, British exports to Little Europe grew by 38 per cent over the period 1948–50 while the exports of Little Europe to the same market grew by 90 per cent. This divergence is important in explaining the events which this book seeks to explain. It may also explain something of the economic success of the continental countries as compared to the United Kingdom in the 1950s. In 1947, a Western European customs union without Britain seemed economically pointless, dangerous, even impossible. In spring 1948, as the payments situation and the reserves improved, it still seemed in London likely that in spite of the 1947 setback the United Kingdom would achieve its objective in setting the timing for the return to multilateralism and convertibility in Western Europe. By autumn 1949 none of these hopes were realizable. British dollar earnings and the dollar position of the sterling area reserves were severely damaged by the American recession of that year, through its impact on exports from the rest of the sterling area to the United States. Meanwhile France, West Germany, Benelux and Italy remained much less disturbed by these American events and, except for Belgium, achieved through the rapid growth of their own intra-trade an export expansion much more vigorous and also much more promising in the long run than that of the United Kingdom. For France the customs union without Britain, which had before seemed dangerous, now appeared feasible and even, as German exports began their dramatic upward surge, necessary. The devaluation of the pound in September and the way in which it was carried out did no more than provide confirmation of this situation. Now was the proper economic moment for decisive political action; Greater Benelux, an apparently impossible idea in 1947, could become Little Europe, in French eyes a step towards safety and, as it now began to look, prosperity as well.

The growth of the economies of Western Europe and of their intra-trade in manufactured goods was to be intimately related in the next decade through productivity changes. The growth of manufactured exports was mainly to be between those economies with the highest levels of industrialization and national income *per capita*. Those manufacturing industries which had the highest ratios of exports to total output showed also in general the highest rates of productivity improvement. To the successful the wherewithal for further success through foreign trade was given, providing they could continue to make the productivity improvements necessary to grasp it, and as in previous sustained boom periods in western Europe the expansion of foreign trade tended to be faster than the expansion of output. But the 1949 balance of payments crisis in the United Kingdom showed the weakness of Britain's position for the future, because the distribution of its foreign trade meant that these trends operated on it with less beneficial force than on the trade of most of the other Western European countries. The failure of British exports to grow as fast as those of Little Europe was partly due to the fact that so many of them went to extra-European markets, whose behaviour, because they were more susceptible to movements in demand in the American economy, was more volatile in the 1950s than that of Western European markets, and where there was, too, much more threat of losing the market through import-substitution policies. The geographical distribution of British manufactured exports raised a further question as to whether the markets to which they were directed were as competitive, as technologically demanding, and thus as capable of exerting the same upward pull on productivity levels in the exporting country, as those to which Little European exports were increasingly directed.

This is by no means to suggest that the difference in the direction of British exports compared to those of Little European exports was an important cause of the comparatively slow rate of growth of national product in Britain in the 1950s compared to that of Little Europe, either through its effects on productivity levels or on the balance of payments. The causes of the difference in growth rates were surely much more complex and probably at least as much related to domestic as to foreign considerations. But the fact that, having established a higher rate of growth than Britain in the recovery period, the Little European countries were then able to maintain it was probably related to the continued rapid expansion of their intra-trade throughout the period 1949–51, when the growth of British export trade was much less rapid. Their exports continued to grow when those of Britain, aimed at less rapidly expanding economies, did not.[1] Subsequently in the 1950s British manufactured exports took a declining share of the extra-European markets to which they mainly went. The 1949 balance of payments crisis which led to so drastic a devaluation of the pound against the dollar was only a crisis in most other Western European countries in so far as any crisis involving a country which was responsible for a third of Western Europe's foreign trade inevitably had its impact on them too. But from all its more serious effects on the growth of trade and the balance of payments they were insulated by the accelerating upward spiral of their own intra-trade.

The year 1949 thus became a watershed. The British balance of payments crisis and the relative ease with which the other Western European countries rode the storm were symptomatic of the potentially healthier foreign trade position of the Little European bloc, the more vigorous expansion of their intra-trade, and the already apparent advantages in terms of productivity increases and maintaining the growth rate of national income which these factors would create. The political and institutional framework which would further maintain this difference began to be put into place in 1950. Until summer 1949 the Labour government still was in sight of a Western European reconstruction which could set the seal of prosperity on its domestic social and economic policies without their having to be significantly modified. After summer 1949 the United Kingdom had lost all capacity to reshape Western Europe in its own interest, a just reward for the low level of priority it had given to the problem. The pattern of Britain's external economic relationships was set throughout the prosperous 1950s in the unsatisfactory mould to which exigency had shaped it before 1949.

THE AMERICAN RECESSION AND THE BRITISH AND WESTERN EUROPEAN ECONOMIES

The circumstances in which the initial expansion of British exports took place at the end of the war were to some extent advantageous. The more important European competitors were at low levels of output and American competition was hampered by dollar-saving policies. Against this should be set the inadequacy of Britain's manufacturing base to take full advantage of the situation. No matter how drastic the controls which diverted goods to thirsty markets the United Kingdom could not hope to fill the gap left by the elimination of Germany. As chapter 1 showed, this was a crucially important aspect of Western Europe's mounting dollar needs and of the exchange crisis of 1947.

[1] The case for the stimulation of industrial investment by expanding exports is a very strong one. The overall ratio between the increase of trade and the increase of GNP does not sufficiently show the higher share of exports in the output of manufactures in the 1950s, and when, as was then the case, exports of manufactures rise faster than output, the incremental dependence of new industrial investment on export markets will be much higher than its average dependence, at least twice as high. GATT, *International Trade 1968* (Geneva, 1969), p. 11. The case for the correlation of higher investment rates and higher rates of growth of national income is of course altogether more complex and arguable.

Against this, too, should be set the fact that the causes of the weaknesses of the British economy in the 1930s were still there. In that decade the difficulty of paying for imports out of income on current account had increased. That the external value of sterling had been maintained may well have been more due to the existence of the sterling area than to domestic recovery. It is hard to avoid the conclusion that there was a higher demand for sterling than that emanating from visible and invisible trade transactions, and this may have been due to countries recouping their severe sterling losses over the period 1929–33 in order to conduct their foreign trade in sterling. One cause of the declining capacity of foreign earnings to pay for imports was the decline in invisible earnings from foreign investment. This decline had gone much further during the war. Income from foreign investment still paid for about 21 per cent of British imports in 1938; in 1950 it paid for only about 6 per cent.

Although the original domestic and international basis of Britain's free-trade policy had been entirely corroded away when it was finally abandoned in 1931 it had not been replaced by anything more satisfactory. The diversion of exports to Commonwealth and colonial markets had been only a port of shelter in a storm. As the years after 1945 in particular were to show these markets would be much more affected by import-substitution policies than European markets. A realistic appraisal of the 1930s would have suggested the need for a further geographical reorientation of Britain's exports and a concomitant restructuring of their commodity composition as soon as the storm was weathered. The drastic protectionism practised in Germany and Italy and the stagnation of the French economy made this very difficult to do, however, and even had the problem been posed in these terms its solution would have had to await the end of the war.

In 1945 and 1946 there were still large difficulties in the way of such a policy. The most evident were the high level of immediate demand from outside western Europe, the greater ease of satisfying that demand emanating, as it did, from previously well-established markets with comfortable trading connections and a functioning payments system, and the urgency to earn dollars scarcely to be earned in Europe. The urgency of immediate need dictated that British exports should flow in the direction they could. The existence of the sterling balances strengthened this tendency and following the force of historical circumstance British foreign trade – although its commodity composition showed, as did that of almost all other Western European countries in the reconstruction period, a shift towards more capital goods exports – adhered to its former geographical pattern.

The most obvious change in the composition of British exports from the pre-war period was the much higher proportion of machinery, vehicles and aircraft in their total value. Machinery, electrical machinery and apparatus and vehicles, including locomotives, ships and aircraft, made up 37 per cent of exports in 1951, compared to only 22 per cent for the two years 1937–8.[2] By 1947 there was only one significant western European export market, Italy, where this marked change in the composition of British exports did not obtain. By 1951, as German competition was felt, there was a significant shift away from this new balance in the composition of exports to Switzerland and the Netherlands. This was compensated, however, by the steady trend towards a higher proportion of capital goods in exports to Italy (table 37). These changes were particularly at the expense of coal exports which had accounted

Table 37　The proportion (%) of machinery and transport equipment* in British exports to certain destinations, 1938–51

	Belgium/ Luxem- bourg	Denmark	France	Italy	Nether- lands	Norway	Sweden	Switzer- land
1938	19.9	12.8	14.4	13.7	26.7	13.3	18.0	16.1
1947	37.2	29.7	43.1	5.5	65.2	33.3	36.8	29.1
1949	41.5	26.1	34.3	19.2	39.8	51.3	49.6	37.6
1951	38.1	25.5	33.2	31.1	39.9	49.6	38.0	21.0

Source: United Kingdom, Board of Trade, *Annual Statement of the Trade of the United Kingdom.*

* Categories III F, III G and III S. Electrical goods and apparatus, machinery, vehicles, including locomotives, ships and aircraft.

for 7.5 per cent of the total value in the earlier period and were almost absent in the post-war period. This switch towards machinery and vehicle exports was comparable to similar tendencies elsewhere. French exports in these categories rose, for example, from an average of 10.5 per cent of total exports in 1937–8 to 15 per cent in 1951.[3] Nevertheless, in spite of these notable changes the total output of the capital goods sector of British industry remained too small and insufficiently varied to replace pre-war German capital goods exports. What is more the growing demand for such goods inevitably focused on the still relatively empty order books of West German industry rather than on the overfull books of British manufacturers. None the less the shift in production during the war, whose continuation was helped by the post-war reconstruction policies on the continent and elsewhere, was beginning to produce by the end of 1947 the needed shift in the composition of British manufactured exports. In the metals, engineering and vehicle manufacturing sector production had risen by 30 per cent at the end of 1948 over its average level for 1946.[4]

[2] United Kingdom, *Annual Statement*, 1937, 1938, 1951.
[3] France, Direction Générale des Douanes et Droits Indirects, *Tableaux du commerce extérieur de la France*, 1937, 1938, 1951.
[4] UK, *Annual Abstract of Statistics*, no. 86, 1938–48, p. 119.

Yet the base for this increase in exports and output was insecure. Steel output had greatly expanded during the war, from 10.56 million tonnes in 1938 to 15.1 million in 1948 and German output had been reduced by three-quarters, from 21.8 million tonnes to 5.7 million. But much of the increase in engineering and vehicle output was in motor vehicle output, where Britain already had a large pre-war lead over Germany. Differences in machinery output are exceptionally difficult to measure because of the lack of comparability between machines but, weight for weight, in fixed motive power machinery Britain had a pre-war superiority only in internal combustion motors, and over the total sector a marked inferiority. In machine tools the comparison was overwhelmingly in Germany's favour. In this area the world's export markets had been dominated by Germany and the United States. Even had world capital goods imports remained at their immediate pre-war level and even had British exports had price advantages over those of the United States, the expansion of output in Britain could not have taken place sufficiently rapidly to meet the level of demand arising from Germany's elimination. But as we have seen already demand was much higher. What this meant for Western Europe can be seen from table 38 which shows that the increase in imports of British capital goods fell short of the increase in those from the

Table 38   Changes in the sources of Western Europe's capital goods imports, 1938–49 (excluding United Kingdom and Germany) (million current dollars, fob)

Source	*Increase (+) or decrease (−) in 1949 as compared to 1938 at 1949 prices*
Germany*	−832
United Kingdom	+598
United States	+665

Source: UN, *Economic Survey 1949*, p. 88. Recalculated to 1949 prices.

* The comparison is between Greater Germany (not Bohemia and Moravia) in 1938 and West Germany in 1949 and thus overstates the decline.

United States. The general implication of this also applied to Britain; British capital goods imports also had to be purchased in dollars. In 1938 44.2 per cent of British machinery imports had come from America, while in 1947 the proportion was 65 per cent. The corresponding figures for imports from Germany were 25 per cent and 3 per cent.

Although the question of the ability of British manufactured exports to compete with American exports was much studied in the post-war period and although the impact of the September 1949 devaluations on foreign trade prices was highly relevant in this context, the preceding figures suggest that this was neither the most central nor the most relevant question for the future of Britain's foreign trade. After all, although the United States took a larger share of the German capital goods market than did Britain, in spite of such widespread discrimination against dollar exports, the British performance in comparison to the pre-war years was a good one and one which was laying the basis for a long overdue change in the composition of British exports in favour of more rapidly expanding sectors. The central problem was surely the ability to compete in the future against German exports. That this was not so clearly understood appears to have been because it was assumed that the recovery of German exports would take place much later and much more slowly than it actually did. In spring 1948 the German economy was still prostrate and the West German state only to be allowed to emerge under the strictest tutelage. The Federal Republic was still not in the OEEC, the levels of industry agreements still prevailed and, indeed, were beyond what the German economy could actually attain, and Germany's foreign trade was firmly under the control of the Allied armies. Two years later the Federal Republic would be in the course of a boom in output and trade as remarkable as any in history, the political and diplomatic constraints on its economy would be weakening visibly and constantly, and its foreign trade would be free of controls. Whatever advantages in foreign trade the United Kingdom gained from devaluation came too late to cope with the central problem of retaining the place it had gained.

Germany's markets for manufactured exports were and always had been mainly in Western Europe, whereas of all the Western European countries Britain was the one with the smallest proportion of its exports going to Western European markets. Only two other Western European exporters on a significant scale, France and Italy, sold less than half their exports in Western Europe. Britain, after 1946, sold only slightly more than one quarter of its exports there, a smaller proportion even than in the 1930s. This may in part have been due to occasional sterling shortages in some markets such as France but this could hardly have been important. Exports were directed to paying for imports of food and raw materials and they came mainly from outside Europe. With very high levels of domestic demand, so high that companies often had to be forced to export by a range of restrictions on domestic sales, it was understandable that there should have been no particular effort to increase the proportion of sales to Europe. Furthermore, trade within the sterling area was technically easier. There seems therefore no reason to argue that Britain's failure to compete effectively in Western Europe in this period with German or American exports was an indication that the manufacturing base of the economy was too small, or that the level of final costs of British goods was higher than that of German or other European manufacturers because of lower levels of productivity in manufacturing, attributable to lack of technical progress or any other cause. Of course, had the manufacturing sector been capable of a yet more rapid expansion than it actually experienced the level of export penetration in Western Europe would no doubt have been higher. But from the standpoint of output and exports the manufacturing sector was experiencing more success than in any period since before the First World War while competing for scarce resources in a fully stretched economy. That this made any change in the geographical distribution of British exports unlikely appears only in retrospect as a weakness.

Within this tendency could be observed a parallel tendency for the proportion of British exports sold within Little Europe to drop more steeply than the proportion sold within Western Europe as a whole (tables 39 and 40). In 1946

Table 39   Exports to Western Europe as a percentage of all exports, 1937, 1946–51 (by value)

Exporting country	1937	1946	1947	1948	1949	1950	1951
Belgium/Luxembourg	62.5	66.1	61.8	58.2	60.4	60.9	59.3
Denmark	88.4	75.4	70.2	71.2	79.3	80.5	76.0
France	46.6	48.5	38.9	37.2	35.8	41.0	36.7
West Germany	48.2*	–	94.4	85.6	75.6	63.8	58.2
Italy	37.4	47.1	44.4	37.0	43.2	48.2	47.4
Netherlands	63.7	71.0	62.6	62.5	61.0	59.9	62.4
Norway	68.0	63.4	60.2	58.1	59.4	61.2	61.4
Sweden	63.8	57.7	54.4	58.0	60.5	61.3	61.1
United Kingdom	30.5	30.1	26.0	26.5	25.0	27.7	25.9

Source: OEEC, *Statistical Bulletins of Foreign Trade*.
* Whole of 1937 Germany.

British exports to Little Europe were only at about the proportionate level which had prevailed in the pre-war period. As the growth of Little European imports continued Britain's share in them fell to below its level of the pre-war period. The French example is the most telling. In spite of the rapid growth of French imports they accounted between 1947 and 1953 for only about 2.2 per cent of United Kingdom domestic exports. In the 1930s they had accounted for 4.5 per cent and in the previous decade, when the French economy was at a more fairly comparable level of production, for 5 per cent. By 1947 British exports to Little Europe were only 11 per cent of total domestic exports, half the proportion of the period before the First World War.

Table 40   Percentage of United Kingdom domestic exports sold in Little Europe and the United States 1910/13–1952

	1910/13	1927/30	1935/38	1950	1952
Little Europe*	22	17	14	11	11
United States	6	6	6	5	6

Source: F.V. Meyer, *United Kingdom Trade with Europe* (London, 1957), p. 122.
* Before 1950 all Germany, 1950 and 1952 the Federal Republic.

The immediate post-war expansion of Western European exports to extra-European markets did not include an increase in exports to the United States. Most countries, notably France, exported a smaller proportion of their total exports to America than before the war. Britain only maintained its share. The bulk of the expansion was in sheltered markets with previous connections and mostly consisted of British and French exports to territories where they had previous and present political connections. The surge of reconstruction demand from these areas was coming to an end by summer 1949 and the fall in American imports from the same areas in that year meant that the increase in Western Europe's extra-European exports was much less than it had been in the previous year.

The drop in American imports was the immediate consequence of the sharp recession which began in the United States in autumn 1948. Post-war planning for reconstruction had never been free from the idea that there would be a fierce post-war restocking boom which would be followed by a depression transmitted from the United States as the expected inventory boom came to an end there. There was no sign of any such downturn in America in 1947 and, as we have seen, Marshall Aid could have been of only small significance in preventing such a movement in the American economy or in preventing its transmission to Europe when it came. The American decision to permit European expansion to continue in 1947 and 1948 only postponed the threat of post-war depression. The fear of such an event had very much influenced British trade and payments policy since 1944, because it seemed the most obvious and identifiable threat to full employment as an economic objective. Ironically, it was only after the collapse of the Bretton Woods system that the American recession eventually arrived. When it did its effects on Western Europe, although not on Britain, were imperceptible. If the recession had not arrived in 1947 that might have been for many reasons, none of them more than a postponement of the evil hour. When it did eventually arrive in autumn 1948 it turned out not to be the much-feared repetition of the disaster of 1920, but an event so mild that in retrospect, for Western Europe as a whole even if not for each of the individual countries, the whole of the reconstruction period appears as one continuous boom. That Western Europe should have survived virtually unscathed the end of the post-war inventory boom in the United States was so contrary to all expectations as to make it necessary to pay more detailed attention to the exact nature of an American recession which, compared to the scale of many pre-war movements in the United States economy, was of no great significance. The reasons why the American recession itself was relatively short are of great relevance in understanding the movement of the Western European economies in the same period. Its main consequence for Europe was, in fact, to produce the marked divergence in the rate of growth of British and Little European exports which has already been observed and which had such important consequences for the future political framework of Western European reconstruction. But that framework was sustained by the same underlying economic realities which made the end of the American restocking boom so short-lived an experience.

The most evident aspect of the depression was the fall in inventories. Manufacturing output fell by 8.5 per cent from July 1948 to May 1949 because goods were supplied by running down inventories.[5] This has been variously explained. Hamberg attributes it to the return to a 'normal' proportion of savings to consumption.[6] The background to the restocking boom of 1945–7 had been a high level of consumption as the potentially much higher level of purchasing power which people had accumulated during the war, but which had been pent up by the absence of goods, was unleashed on the economy. But there is no evidence that 1948 saw any shift in the relative importance of consumption and saving. In 1943 and 1944 about 77 per cent of disposable income had been allocated to consumption; over the years 1946–8 the figure remained constant at about 95 per cent.[7]

Brett and Ondrichen attribute the change in inventories to the end of the fierce inflation of 1947, the fall in prices causing, they argue, a change in expectations.[8] If this had occurred, it would have resembled more closely the events of 1920, when the peak of the boom saw a great increase in stock exchange speculation followed by a bursting of the bubble. Not only was this type of speculation noticeably absent in 1947 and 1948 but there seems to have been no expectation of a downward movement in prices. What fits the facts much better is Fels's hypothesis that restocking after 1945 was in fact a much more cautious business than in 1919, perhaps because of the memories of 1920, and that inventory investment was one of the last components of output to reach its peak.[9] Its decline represented a prior fall in real fixed investment.

Hamberg's argument that this was a response to a fall in consumption and a fall in exports is far-fetched. The most noticeable aspect of the recession and probably the principal reason for the shortness of its duration was that consumption did not fall. It continued unrestrained in 1948 and 1949 and was boosted in some respects by government action, so that the marginal propensity to consume increased as output fell. American consumers had begun to liberate their pent-up, wartime purchasing power in 1946–7 at a time of high and rising prices and shortages of goods. Until the second half of 1947 the increase in expenditure on consumption was greater than the increase in disposable incomes. The situation was then reversed and the biggest part of the gain in real earnings between the end of the war and the end of 1948 came

[5] C.A. Blyth, *American Business Cycles 1945–50* (London, 1969), p. 137.
[6] D. Hamberg, 'The recession of 1948–49 in the United States', *Economic Journal*, 12 (245), 1952.
[7] L.V. Chandler, *Inflation in The United States 1940–1948* (New York, 1951), p. 242.
[8] E.C. Brett and J.P. Ondrichen, 'The 1948–49 recession re-examined', *Economic Journal*, 63 (249), 1953.
[9] R. Fels, 'The US downturn of 1948', *American Economic Review*, 55 (4), 1965.

in 1948 itself with the end of inflation. Employers granted large wage increases between 1945 and 1947 and increased their profits by passing on their extra costs to consumers who continued to consume, and when prices fell this unleashed a further wave of consumption which pushed the economy back into an upswing.

One particularly important aspect of this was the increase in residential construction. It had fallen as interest rates peaked at the end of 1947, but in early 1949 as interest rates followed prices downwards it revived again strongly. The fall in the demand for steel from capital goods manufacturers led to the removal of controls on steel supply to car manufacturers and for the first time since the end of the war cars became freely available. The consequence was not only a rise in car purchases during the recession but also that, apart from a small wavering in summer 1949, output in the steel industry did not fall, because the increased demand from car manufacturers compensated for the fall in demand from other steel-consuming industries. The wonderful grain harvest of 1948 brought agricultural prices down from their previous high levels and, although at first this reduced farm incomes, by summer 1949 lower food prices were helping to maintain expenditure on consumer durables. To some extent the persistence of high consumption levels may have been aided by the tax reductions in the 1948 Revenue Act and at the very least the reaction of the government to the recession, even if it may not have been particularly effective, was in a quite different direction from that of governments in the 1920s.

Defence expenditure had been rising from the middle of 1947 and continued to rise throughout 1948 and 1949. Foreign aid also continued. The disequilibrium in world trade and the rapid growth of Western Europe's exports meant a fall in American exports from their high level of 1947, which probably did contribute to the recession in the capital goods sector of manufacturing. But in a wider sense the continuation of foreign aid through the recession was supporting America's position as a creditor country and preventing a much worse drop in the value of exports and this, too, was in striking contrast to the period after the First World War when that task had been left to the sporadic, unsystematic actions of private American investors.

The short duration of the American recession may therefore be attributed to the much longer period of high and rising earnings which Americans experienced in the Second World War as compared to the First; to the fortunate timing of price changes in 1948 of which one component, the drop in food prices, was autonomous; to certain marginal effects of government policy which tended in a quite different direction from that after the First World War; and possibly to differences in the pattern of consumer behaviour which may have become fixed in the post-war world in a different mould from that of the inter-war period, in a way that has not been satisfactorily incorporated into the economic theory through which such phenomena are normally explored.

Similar economic trends maintained the buoyancy of the Western European economies. There were only three, Belgium, Italy and Germany, where full employment did not prevail from the end of the war. High employment levels were accompanied by higher levels of real earnings so that the increase in real earnings was greater over a comparable period of time than for any period since before the First World War. Even in Italy, in spite of persistent unemployment and a large low-productivity sector, the gain in real earnings for those in employment was comparable with those elsewhere, probably because inflation was brought under control more firmly there. But the extent to which these gains in disposable purchasing power could be translated into increased consumption was much more limited than in the United States. Shortages of consumer goods due to low levels of production, rationing of consumption in controlled economies by a variety of direct and indirect methods, discrimination against consumer goods imports as a method of foreign exchange saving, all meant that the claims which European consumers accumulated against the economy were liberated later than in the United States. They were often liberated, too, at a time when inflation was slowing down whereas in America they were first liberated during the hectic period of decontrol and inflation in 1946–7. The other phenomena present in the American economy were also all there to a varying extent in Europe. Residential construction was at a much higher level than during the inter-war period in Belgium, Denmark, Sweden and the United Kingdom and was on the point of becoming so in West Germany. As in America the 1948 harvest, after the disasters of 1947, was a good one and food prices fell as supply eased. On top of all this the level of investment and output in capital goods industries did not fall away except in Belgium/Luxembourg and France.

The relative stagnation of the Belgian economy was caused by one industry, steel, which dominated the export trade and influenced the growth of exports adversely no matter what the tendency of other exports to increase, whereas in France it was domestic demand which stagnated while the export sector sustained the growth of the economy. The stagnation in the rate of growth of industrial output in France began after the second quarter of 1949, so that it coincided with the recovery in the United States. It did not resume its upward trend until the last quarter of 1950. The prevailing impression in most of the literature that the Modernization and Re-equipment Plan guaranteed a steady flow of investment into selected sectors in the French economy is surely wrong. The ratios of investment were not higher in France than in Western Europe as a whole and were less consistently maintained. Indeed it was in Western Europe's most planned economy that internal economic growth was weakest in 1950 and this may well have been due to the cuts in the officially planned investment targets in 1949 and 1950.[10] At the end of 1950 the value of

[10] J. Bouvier, 'Sur l'investissement de réconstruction-modernisation au temps du Plan Monnet', paper presented to a colloquium at the Fondation Nationale des Sciences Politiques, 1981.

output in the French engineering industry was still below the level reached in the last quarter of 1948 and steel output remained far below the target envisaged in 1946 when the Modernization Plan was first formulated. There was in fact a contraction of steel output in the first half of 1950.

If we except Belgium's problems, which had dogged the reconstruction period and were only to be finally solved when the inflow of foreign investment after 1958 reduced the dependence on steel and the less-sophisticated engineering sectors, all that was needed to sustain the boom conditions in western Europe was a framework which permitted a high rate of growth of foreign trade. In this respect western European economies and the United States were in fundamentally different situations. An American recession could be overcome even in a period of falling exports; sustaining a European boom required an expansion of exports. In fact even to a large economy the export sector was important enough to sustain the growth of national income, as in France, when the domestic springs of growth were inadequate. The realization that this was so had, no doubt, been important everywhere in the conclusion of the EPU.

Yet, when it is considered that the volume of private imports into the United States probably fell by as much as 8 per cent in the recession and that European exports to the United States fell by about a third, dropping back to their level of 1947, the situation could be seen to be still frail. In comparison with the total value of Western Europe's foreign trade, or even with its total trade deficit with the United States, the decline in exports to the United States was not very great in absolute terms, only about $170 million. But coupled with slackening demand elsewhere and contrasted with the continued vigorous growth of demand in most Western European countries, it helped in changing the force behind Western Europe's export expansion from extra-European to intra-European trade.

The total value of Europe's extra-European trade in the last quarter of 1949 had not grown beyond that of the last quarter of 1948, although it had made a good recovery from the much lower level of July–September 1949. Intra-European trade, in contrast, attained its 1938 level for the first time in the last quarter of 1949 after still being at only four-fifths of that level at the start of the year. In 1949 the increase in the value of intra-Western European exports over the previous year was 27.65 per cent.[11] Over the three years 1948–50, of all the Western European countries only the exports of Austria grew more strongly to the rest of the world than to Western Europe. Western Europe's export boom was being saved by Western Europe's own economies.

Yet from this process Britain was largely excluded. The increase in the value of British exports to Western Europe in the same period was a mere 4.96 per cent. That of French exports was 41.19 per cent, so that in spite of the high proportion of extra-European exports in French foreign trade the American

[11] The calculation omits Portugal.

recession left French foreign trade unscathed. All other Western European countries had a higher proportion of their exports going to Western Europe than had France and Britain. Britain's overall balance of payments deficit increased over the year whereas that of France fell by a half. Of the total decline in the foreign exchange reserves of Western Europe and its associated territories and dependencies between April and September 1949, the sterling area was responsible for about 130 per cent (table 41). Whereas in 1947 the payments crisis had by no means been a purely British affair, in 1949 it was so

Table 41   Estimates of changes in foreign exchange reserves of hard currency over the period April–September 1949 (gold and dollars in million dollars)

United Kingdom and sterling area	−493
Belgium/Luxembourg and dependencies	+48
Denmark	−12
France and possessions	−37
West Germany	−40
Italy	+43
Netherlands and possessions	+39
Norway	−23
Sweden	+1
Switzerland	+81

Source: UK Treasury estimates made in November 1949. T 232/152.

almost entirely. This was the familiar problem from the 1930s. In an American depression imports of raw materials from the sterling area fell more than from elsewhere. The percentage fall in United States imports by value from the sterling area over the years 1948–9 was 17 per cent.[12] The drop in American imports of rubber, wool and jute was especially marked and this affected particularly Malaya, Ceylon, Australia, New Zealand, South Africa, India and Pakistan, a roll-call of important British markets.

This did not mean that British exports to the rest of the sterling area could not grow, whatever its impact on their dollar-earning capacity. Most of the countries whose exports to the United States dropped so sharply had large sterling balances in London. Obviously the behaviour of British exports to the rest of the sterling area is only to be explained by a study of the economic history of those diverse societies themselves. The trade deficit of the whole sterling area with the United States in the second quarter of 1949 was twice its average size for the four quarters of 1948. The imports of the sterling area excluding Britain scarcely increased, although British imports from the United States increased very steeply. In the third quarter of 1949 this growth of imports from America was checked and for the sterling area as a whole was well below the level of the previous year, but export earnings in dollars fell

[12] Sir D. MacDougall, *The World Dollar Problem. A Study in International Economics* (London, 1957), p. 49.

even more. The increase in British exports to the rest of the sterling area in 1949 was heavily concentrated in the first quarter of the year.

The argument can only be a relative one. The American recession was not particularly harmful to the British economy. It was only the occasion, not the cause, of the British devaluation, and there were persuasive arguments in favour of an earlier devaluation as an act of policy. The geographical distribution of British exports to extra-European markets both in 1949–50 and afterwards was only relatively less favourable to exports and to productivity growth than the concentration of other economies on intra-Western European trade. For twenty years after the war British exports not only consistently grew but grew at a remarkably even rate of growth. The argument is that the rate of growth of exports of the economies which were to form Little Europe stayed higher because the geographical distribution of their foreign trade led to a more vigorous expansion of manufactured exports, albeit for a commensurate increase in imports; and that the markets to which these exports were increasingly directed were more competitive and encouraged a higher level of productivity in manufacturing industry. This pattern emerged in 1949–50 when the vigorous growth of intra-Western European trade sheltered Western European economies, but not Britain, from the effects of the American depression and in particular from the payments crisis which it might have provoked.

THE ECONOMIC FOUNDATIONS OF LITTLE EUROPE

The total value of Little Europe's export trade over the period 1948–51 is shown in table 42 alongside that of the United Kingdom. Over the period it grew by 114.5 per cent, that of the United Kingdom by 14.2 per cent. The year 1951 witnessed a powerful resurgence of extra-European demand based on the rapid increase in imports of raw materials triggered off by the purchase

Table 42   Total value of the exports of the United Kingdom and Little Europe to Western Europe and the rest of the world, 1948–51 (million current dollars, fob)

	To Western Europe		To rest of the world	
	from United Kingdom	from Little Europe	from United Kingdom	from Little Europe
1948	1755.95	3356.90	4879.45	3118.39
1949	1709.65	4162.57	5124.96	3861.91
1950	1752.96	5033.74	4564.06	4260.82
1951	1962.93	7107.64	5615.39	6780.43

Source : OEEC, *Statistical Bulletin of Foreign Trade.*

of stockpiles for the Korean war. This rescued British exports from the doldrums in which they had been wallowing since 1948. Over the period 1948–50, before that demand arrived, British exports stood still, at least in current prices, while Little Europe's exports to Western Europe increased by a half, and by more than a third to the rest of the world.

The growth of capital goods exports from the major Western European producers to Western European markets in particular showed no sign of faltering (table 43). In the last quarter of 1949 intra-Western European trade in foodstuffs received a major impulse from the new import policies of the West German government, which began to remove some of the draconian restrictions previously applied by the JEIA. From this surge of German imports the Netherlands was a particular beneficiary (table 44). This resurgence of what had always been one of western Europe's major trade flows was of considerable importance in weaning the Dutch government at the strategic moment towards the concept of a customs union in which Britain might not be a participant. The trading circuits of Little Europe were fitting into place as Britain struggled to cope with the trading problems of a wider world.

The most striking aspect of the growth of Little Europe's trade in 1948–50 was the revival of German trade. The steep increase in West German imports

Table 43   Estimated increases in the value of capital goods exports to Europe and the rest of the world, 1948–9 (million current dollars, fob)

	Europe	*Rest of world*
Belgium/Luxembourg		
1948	628	256
1949*	713	268
France		
1948	224	370
1949*	302	499
Italy		
1948	130	170
1949*	157	151
Netherlands		
1948	170	49
1949*	209	89
Sweden		
1948	235	43
1949*	258	38

Source: UN, Department of Economic Affairs, *Survey of the European Economy in 1949*. Derived from tables 59 and 78.

* Extrapolated annual rate from first nine months.

Table 44   Exports to Germany* from the
            Netherlands, 1948–9 (million
            current dollars, fob)

1948	
1st quarter	7.08
2nd quarter	22.98
3rd quarter	12.36
4th quarter	17.79
1949	
1st quarter	20.85
2nd quarter	24.69
3rd quarter	27.15
4th quarter	57.18

Source: OEEC, *Statistical Bulletins of Foreign Trade*.
* All Germany.

in the last quarter of 1949 produced a deficit of more than $1000 million.[13] Even then imports were still only equivalent to their 1936 level, and the population was increasing with no sign of that dramatic increase slowing down. The incentive to export could not have been more compelling. In the event exports increased more than threefold over the first two years of the Federal Republic's existence and 60 per cent of the increase was absorbed by Western Europe, a total of $1172.5 million, or two-thirds the total value of British exports to the same area. Nothing could more tellingly illustrate the final weakness of Britain's position, which was also, at the same time, one of the great strengths of Little Europe's trade, always providing, of course, that Europe could continue to absorb such a volume of exports.

Before the war German exports had been about 27 per cent of western Europe's total exports, German and British exports together about 56 per cent. In terms of pre-war intra-western European trade West Germany's exports (the exports of the Third Reich recalculated to allow for the reduction in territorial size and output to the equivalent of the Federal Republic) would still have amounted to 18.3 per cent of all intra-western European exports. In 1949 they only amounted to 10.15 per cent. By the end of 1951 this proportion had risen to 16.5 per cent and West German exports were surpassed in value among western European countries only by those of Britain and France (table 45). As a proportion of western Europe's total exports West German exports were still in that year only 13 per cent. If the central problem of Western European recovery, enabling the Federal Republic's export trade to return to levels sufficiently approximate to those of the Third Reich to permit a reasonable level of income and employment there, was well on the way to being solved, that, too, was mainly a function of intra-western European trade and not of western Europe's trade with the outside world.

[13] Of which 70 per cent was with the United States.

Table 45   Rank order of main western European exporters (by value) (values in million current dollars)

1946	1947	1948	1949	1950	1951
United Kingdom (3883.97)	United Kingdom (4828.26)	United Kingdom (6635.40)	United Kingdom (6834.61)	United Kingdom (6317.02)	United Kingdom (7578.32)
France (849.63)	France (1871.43)	France (2002.11)	France (2717.48)	France (3079.38)	France (4225.30)
Belgium/Luxembourg (680.88)	Belgium/Luxembourg (1406.97)	Belgium/Luxembourg (1691.44)	Belgium/Luxembourg (1770.12)	West Germany (1980.51)	West Germany (3473.57)
Sweden (644.82)	Sweden (899.92)	Sweden (1105.27)	Netherlands (1292.43)	Belgium/Luxembourg (1645.21)	Belgium/Luxembourg (2633.45)
Switzerland (622.32)	Switzerland (760.14)	Italy (1076.66)	West Germany (1123.04)	Netherlands (1390.03)	Netherlands (1926.47)
Denmark (333.31)	Netherlands (700.77)	Netherlands (1006.13)	Italy (1121.41)	Italy (1215.41)	Sweden (1774.14)
Netherlands (295.79)	Denmark (476.42)	Switzerland (798.86)	Sweden (1074.62)	Sweden (1098.68)	Italy (1629.28)
West Germany* (280.00)	Italy (424.02)	West Germany (698.95)	Switzerland (803.23)	Switzerland (904.87)	Switzerland (1078.23)
Norway (240.75)	Norway (364.66)	Denmark (599.03)	Denmark (657.86)	Denmark (653.71)	Denmark (825.49)
Portugal (183.92)	West Germany (315.15)	Norway (413.27)	Norway (394.63)	Norway (389.38)	Norway (619.29)
Italy (175.97)	Portugal (172.28)	Ireland (198.80)	Austria (285.81)	Austria (326.18)	Austria (453.83)

Source : OEEC, Statistical Bulletins of Foreign Trade.

* An estimated figure. The figure probably exaggerates the value of West German trade in as much as parts of the estimate are made up of other countries' recorded imports which are occasionally made up from the whole of Germany.

If we assume that the share of total intra-western European trade taken by the area equivalent to the Federal Republic before the war was in some way the normal situation, it is then possible to estimate the degree to which the lower level of intra-western European trade in the immediate post-war years was due to the severely depressed level of Germany's foreign trade. Such an assumption is by no means unquestionable, since it implies that substitution of German exports by other European exporters, in particular Britain, was not significant, whereas the commodity composition of post-war British exports suggests this was not the case. On the other hand it could reasonably be argued that a calculation based on the contribution of the Third Reich to intra-Western European trade over the years 1937–8 underestimates Germany's normal share of that trade, especially Germany's normal capacity to absorb imports from Western Europe, because of the import-saving policies of the National Socialist government. In either case the implication is that such a calculation can do no more than suggest rough orders of magnitude. What these orders of magnitude indicate is that the actual level of total intra-Western European imports in 1947 would have been 24.5 per cent higher had West German trade been at its normal pre-war level, 18.4 per cent higher in 1948, 13.1 per cent higher in 1949, 4.5 per cent higher in 1950 and still 4.1 per cent higher in 1951.[14] On this basis 1950 appears as the year in which West Germany's re-establishment in intra-Western European trade proceeded far enough to effect not only a remarkable increase in that trade, while world trade tended to stagnate, but also to create a set of trade and payments circuits between the countries of Little Europe which, for all too obvious reasons, had not been possible in the pre-war period.

A lagged linear regression examining the growth of Western European manufactured exports over the period 1946–51 shows a much stronger correlation with the growth of output than with any other phenomenon, such as, for example, the incidence of payments agreements or of trade liberalization policies. Although such an exercise does nothing to establish in which direction the chain of causation ran, there seems no reason to suppose that what applied to Western Europe as a whole did not apply to West Germany. The surge of output there was always likely to be accompanied by a concomitant surge of exports unless West Germany's recovery were to take place in some other framework than that required by the Marshall Plan and OEEC. From producing only four-fifths of its 1936 level of output at the start of 1949, in the last quarter of the year the Federal Republic regained its 1936 level and in 1950, the 'miracle year', surpassed it by more than a third (table 46).

The resumption of manufactured exports at first took place to neighbouring

[14] The assumptions are that P1 is the percentage of the pre-war (1937–8) intra-West European imports into 'West Germany'. Pre-war 'West Germany' is calculated for trade purposes as given in the Appendix. P2 is the percentage of post-war imports actually generated. The calculation is P1 − P2 + P3, where P3 is the difference, omitting the potential dynamic effects on all intra-West European imports of the growth of P2.

Table 46   An index of industrial production in West Germany, 1947–51 (1936 = 100)

	Bizone	French zone
1947		
1st quarter	34	39
2nd quarter	44	46
3rd quarter	46	48
4th quarter	50	48
1948		
1st quarter	54	50
2nd quarter	57	54
3rd quarter	65	61
4th quarter	79	67

	Federal Republic
1949	
1st quarter	83
2nd quarter	87
3rd quarter	90
4th quarter	100
1950	
1st quarter	96
2nd quarter	107
3rd quarter	118
4th quarter	134
1951	
1st quarter	129
2nd quarter	137
3rd quarter	133
4th quarter	146

Sources: W. Abelshauser, 'Probleme des Wiederaufbaus der westdeutschen Wirtschaft 1945–1953', in H.A. Winkler (ed.) *Politische Weichenstellungen im Nachkriegs deutschland 1945–53*, Sonderheft 5, *Geschichte und Gesellschaft* (Göttingen, 1979). The figures for the French occupation zone are from M. Manz, *Stagnation und Aufschwung in der französischen Zone von 1945–1948* (dissertation, University of Mannheim, 1968).

countries and it was only later that they began to appear in quantity on more distant markets. There was throughout the period a constant trend towards the wider dissemination of German exports, a gradual return to the earlier pattern. The share of total West German exports going to Little Europe for example dropped from 44.5 per cent in 1949 to 29.5 per cent in 1951. If, however, the trend in the geographical distribution of the more important manufactured exports is examined it will be found that although the trend was in the same direction it was much less marked. Table 47 lists a sample of the manufactured goods exported in the largest quantities and whose rate of growth over the period was high. Although it is confined to manufactured goods it represents more than a quarter of total exports in 1949 and 45 per cent in 1951. The decline in the proportion of these goods being exported to Little Europe over the period 1949–51 was much less than in the proportion of all exports going to the same destination. The more important and the more rapidly growing exports still depended on these neighbouring markets to sustain their explosive quantitative growth.

Table 47   The growth of West Germany's manufactured exports 1948–51 (million dollars)

Increase in the value of West Germany's 20 most rapidly growing manufactured exports, 1948–51	1388.6
Value of exports of the same products, 1948	26.9
Amount of the increase going to Little Europe	317.8
Total value of West German exports in 1951	3473.9

Source: German Federal Republic, *Der Aussenhandel der Bundesrepublik Deutschland.*

The growth of intra-Western European exports in 1949 was of scarcely less significance for France. It accounted for more than 40 per cent of the increase in French exports over the level of 1948. The level of French exports in the last quarter of 1950 was more than double that of 1938 and more than 50 per cent higher than the average for the four quarters of 1949. West Germany's exports over the same period were three times their average volume in 1949 and more than a quarter above their level of 1928. There is every indication that if the pause in the boom in France was due to a faltering in domestic demand, perhaps connected to a fall in public investment, the resumption of high rates of growth of output in 1950 was export-led.

This does not mean that it continued to be export-led and a reasonable argument could be made out that after 1952, with the removal of many restraints on investment through the planning mechanism which had been imposed in 1949, the rise in domestic investment and demand again took over, at least until 1956, as the driving force in the French boom. But in the period of restraint on the Modernization Plan and of a return to a more parsimonious management of the public finances which began in 1949, the impetus given to the economy by the boom in exports in intra-Western European trade was of crucial importance. The importance of the Little European bloc and of West Germany's pivotal role in its trade to the continued success of the Modernization Plan was therefore only enhanced by the domestic difficulties into which the Plan ran in 1949. Faced with the possibility of Finebel and with the government's increasing unwillingness to incur the costs of meeting the Plan's investment targets, the Planning Commissariat could only struggle the harder to regulate the international environment through which its ambitions might still be realized. When, with the collapse of Finebel, the Modernization Plan again returned to the forefront as a guide to foreign economic policy, it had now, because of the demonstrated importance of the intra-Western European trade boom and the fact that Germany was the main element in that boom, compelling economic as well as political reasons to deal with Germany first and not last.

The rate of increase of manufactured exports from Western European countries over the two crucial years 1949–50 is shown in table 48. The three countries showing by far the fastest rates of growth are West Germany,

Table 48   Quantum index of manufactured exports of Western European countries, 1938–50 (1948 = 100)*

	1938	1947	1948	1949	1950
Austria	216.7†	55.8	100	132.0	170.8
Belgium/Luxembourg	95.5	77.2	100	111.6	116.1
France	84.3	96.3	100	165.8	204.0
West Germany**	–	–	14.4	33.1	100
Italy	121.3	63.7	100	106.1	129.9
Netherlands	152.5	71.7	100	147.1	207.2
Norway	132.4	96.0	100	108.1	144.0
Sweden	131.2	100.8	100	107.9	134.6
Switzerland	89.8	94.8	100	106.7	114.3
United Kingdom	75.2	78.8	100	110.0	127.8
United States	58.2	125.6	100	93.4	77.3

Sources: Austria, Österreichisches Statistischen Zentralamt, *Statistik des Aussenhandels Öster-reichs*; Belgium, Institut national de statistique, *Bulletin mensuel du commerce extérieur*; France, Direction générale des douanes et droits indirects, Statistique mensuelle du commerce extérieur de la France; Germany, Statistisches Reichsamt, *Sondernachweis der Aussenhandel Deutschlands*, Statistisches Amt, *Der Aussenhandel der Bundesrepublik Deutschlands*; Italy, Instituto Centrale di Statistica, *Statistica di commercio con l'estero*; Netherlands, Centraal Bureau voor de Statistiek, *Maandstatistiek van den In-Uit-En Doorvoer van Nederland*; Norway, Statistisk Sentralbyrå, *Månedsoppgaver over Vareomsettningen med Udlandet*; Sweden, Sveriges Officielle Statistik, *Handels Berättelse*; Switzerland, Eidgenössische Oberzolldirektion, *Jahresstatistik der Aussen-handels der Schweiz*; United Kingdom, Board of Trade, *Annual Statement of the Trade of the United Kingdom*; United States, Department of Commerce, *Foreign Commerce and Navigation of the United States*.

* For details of index see Appendix.
† 1937
** 1950 = 100.

France and the Netherlands. Italy's performance is roughly comparable to that of the United Kingdom and that of Belgium/Luxembourg is worse. The deflationary policies of the Italian governments from summer 1947 onwards had produced a dramatic improvement in the balance of payments by stimulating primary exports, especially to Western Europe which now took a much bigger share of Italian foreign trade than before the war. They did very little, however, to increase the proportion of manufactured output going on to the export market and this prevented Italy from sharing in the export boom in quite the same way as the other Little European countries. As for Belgium, the structural weaknesses of her manufacturing sector in terms of providing competitive exports were, as we have seen, already reasserting themselves in 1949. The comparison with the increase in French manufactured exports since 1938, shown in table 48, is stark. It would be foolish to attribute it only to obvious differences between the two countries in the influence of government policy on investment and foreign trade, but in both the Italian and Belgian cases government policy, or the lack of it, was surely not without influence in maintaining the rate of growth of manufactured exports nearer to the British level than to the higher level of the other countries of Little Europe.

The growth of intra-Western European trade was accompanied by a remarkable improvement in the trade balance of Western Europe with the United States, an improvement which was as marked for Britain as for Little Europe. In the second half of 1950 American imports were 15 per cent higher than in the first half of the year but to attribute the improvement in the trade balances solely to the Korean war would be erroneous. Just as the upswing in the American economy clearly predated the outbreak of war in Korea so did the upswing in American imports. In the first three quarters of 1949 the gold stocks of the United States grew by $219 million, while in the last quarter of the year and the first two quarters of 1950, that is to say until the outbreak of the war, they fell by about $400 million in spite of a reduction of 25 per cent in grants and 50 per cent in loans over the same period.[15] The surplus on goods and services account of the United States with Western Europe in the first six months of 1950 was only half what it had been in the first six months of 1949.

The most frequent explanation given at the time was that devaluation had produced the expected immediate gain in exports and the penalty of increased import prices had not yet been paid, but there is some evidence to suggest that this may be too facile an explanation. The average devaluation of Western European currencies was only just greater than the fall in American export prices produced by the recession. Furthermore, much of the improvement in Western Europe's dollar trade balance was attributable to a fall in imports, (dollar imports fell by a third in the first half of 1950), and this reflected essentially an improvement in the supply position in Western Europe. That devaluation may have made only a marginal contribution to this sudden, rapid progress towards 'viability' is suggested by Polak's study of the comparative export performance in the United States' market of countries who made large devaluations and those who made only a small or no devaluation, such as Belgium, Italy and Switzerland. The first group showed a 13 per cent increase in their exports to the United States in the first half of 1950 as compared to the first half of 1949, the second group an 8 per cent increase[16]. The difficulty with

[15] UN, *Balance of Payments Trends and Policies, 1950–51* (New York, 1952), p. 8.

[16] J.J. Polak, 'The contribution of the September 1949 devaluations to the solution of Europe's dollar problem', *IMF Staff Papers*, vol. 2, 1951–2.

this method of analysis, however, is that the Italian and Belgian devaluations were sufficient to make substantial export gains in theory. Only 5 per cent of the devaluing countries' gains in exports to the United States is attributed by Polak to devaluation. Although this may be an underestimate the evidence does suggest that it was in fact a combination of devaluation and the return of Western Europe to pre-war levels of production (which in the context of 1949–50 meant the return of West Germany to pre-war levels of production), together with the cyclical upswing in the American economy, which was responsible for the fall in Western Europe's dollar deficit. The greater importance of devaluation may have been in reducing the competitiveness of American goods in Europe.

The balance of payments of OEEC countries with the United States in 1949 showed a deficit of $2700 million. In 1950 this was reduced to $1000 million. The total drop in imports was of the order of $1300 million, the increase in exports about $300 million, and the increase in invisible earnings of about the same dimensions. This was still some way from the 'viability' which the ECA sought, but when broken down into its component national parts it presented a picture fundamentally different from that of 1946–9. For most Western European countries the balance of payments deficit with the United States was becoming compensable without further special aid; on these grounds in fact the United States was to end Marshall Aid to Britain. What had emerged was a small number of countries, Austria and West Germany above all, whose dollar deficits were still too large to be met other than by continuing aid and too large, also, to be run down without serious damage to American policy.

Providing, therefore, that American aid to the German Federal Republic was sustained, the external economic position of Little Europe had been strengthened by the same tendencies which had strengthened that of Western Europe as a whole, and the greater confidence brought by the benefits from the surge of intra-Western European trade was matched by the greater confidence brought by the improvement in the payments position with the dollar zone.

In 1947 the exports of West Germany, Italy and the Netherlands were each less than those of Switzerland. By 1950 the countries of Little Europe were the five largest Western European exporters after Britain. In 1947 the total value of their combined exports was less than that of British exports, while in 1950 it was roughly 30 per cent more. Their exports went very largely to Western European markets and such markets dominated the export trade of three of them, Belgium, the Netherlands and West Germany. In this growth circuit Britain played only a small part and the consequence was that the movement of foreign trade over the two years 1949–50 produced a radical alteration in the relative scope for political action in Western Europe, weakening Britain's position, greatly strengthening that of France, greatly strengthening the ties of economic interest between the Netherlands and West Germany, and finally making a Little European bloc seem not only feasible and desirable but also attractive to the other European economies, Italy not least.

The expansion of output and trade did not, however, exactly keep pace with each other. If we plot the quantum indices of exports of manufactured goods (table 48) against the index of industrial production it emerges that in almost every Western European country in either 1948 or 1949 the rate of increase of exports of manufactured goods began to exceed the rate of increase of industrial production. The most notable exception was Italy where the upward movement of industrial production in 1948–9 coincided with a slackening of the rate of increase of exports so that the two expanded at similar rates until the end of 1950. In Austria the rate of growth of industrial output and exports also remained closely similar. Elsewhere, the trend is clear. The need for great export increases had been seen as a pre-requisite of recovery and reconstruction. This was incorporated into government policies, of which the various fiscal devices by which the West German government encouraged exports and the direct intervention of French planning to encourage certain export industries were the most striking. The tendency for exports of manufactures to grow faster than production was already observable in 1949, although since so high a proportion of the exports were in intra-Western European trade it probably could not have been sustained without the subsequent growth of extra-European exports which the American recovery and subsequent surge of growth permitted.

Of course, what became all too visible by 1960 was only just perceptible in 1950 and certainly anything but irreversible. But once 1947 and 1949 had been surmounted and had not repeated the disaster of 1920, Little Europe was already travelling along a more hopeful path towards future prosperity than the United Kingdom. The political settlement between France and Germany was to acknowledge the differences between these paths and to erect the first political and institutional barriers to their convergence.

XII

THE SCHUMAN PLAN

In 1983, when miles of major steel works are being closed down all over Europe, it may seem superfluous to remark that the manufacture of steel is one of the most volatile of all industries. Steel is the basic constructional material of the modern economy, its level of output immediately affected by any fluctuations in sales and investment. The peculiar problems of the steel industry derive from the instability and uncertainty arising from this extreme sensitiveness to economic trends conjoined with the massive scale of most of the manufacturing plant necessary. Since the invention of the Bessemer process in the mid-nineteenth century, a small number of huge investments, for the most part privately owned, have struggled to modify and equilibrate the effect on the steel industry of the fluctuations of the economy. In so doing in every western European country they have called into question the relationship of private ownership of the industry both to the state and to the common good, as well as the relative merits of free and controlled markets. The European steel industry has since its birth been at the heart of the controversy over the nature of the capitalist economy and the dramatic ebb and flow of its economic fortunes has been accompanied by insistent and far-reaching national and international political controversy.

In singling out the steel industry as a basic industry, an indispensable foundation of the economy, the French Modernization Plan did no more than incorporate into the formally planned pattern of investment a surge of investment in the steel industry which took place everywhere in western Europe after 1945 except in Germany. Public investment in the reconstruction of railways, mines, factories and housing meant a rapid rise in the demand for steel. When the Western European countries had to present national recovery programmes to CEEC they all incorporated into those plans proposals for a substantial increase in steel output. If the output of all the countries shown in table 49 (which comprises all the large and most of the small Western European steel producers) in their peak inter-war year is added together, it can be seen that they were still intending to exceed that quantity by a substantial margin even in 1948 and to have left it far behind by the time Marshall Aid should have come to a close.

Table 49   European steel plans, 1948–51, as presented to the CEEC in 1947 (crude and semi-finished steel, thousand tonnes, crude steel or ingot equivalent)

	Peak year in inter-war period	Actual output 1947	Planned output			
			1948	1949	1950	1951
Belgium	4,275	2,815	4,250	4,250	4,850	4,850
France	9,711	5,812	10,400	10,890	11,700	12,690
Italy	2,328	1,600	2,500	2,670	2,830	3,000
Luxembourg	2,696	1,800	3,000	3,000	3,000	3,000
Netherlands	57	207	303	393	473	503
Norway	65	57	67	72	92	92
Sweden	995	1,195	1,300	1,500	1,760	2,060
United Kingdom	13,192	12,700	13,970	14,200	14,480	14,990
Total	33,319	26,186	35,790	36,975	39,185	41,185
Western Germany and Saarland	20,782	3,562	5,725	8,188	10,188	12,688
Total	54,101	29,748	41,515	45,163	49,373	53,873

Source: CEEC, Vol. 2, *Technical Reports*, Appendices C(i), C(ii), C(iii).

For such ambitious programmes to be justified it would be necessary for the high domestic level of demand for steel to be sustained once the immediate reconstruction boom was over and for that boom not to turn into a period of contraction. The American administration was sternly critical of the programmes, seeing them as mercantilistic and nationalistic, inasmuch as each Western European country was interested in maximizing its own output of steel irrespective of the optimum distribution of the industry in Western Europe as a whole. This was the period in which the first major Dutch and Norwegian steel works, at Ijmuiden and Mo-i-Rana, were planned. Congress expressed the view, at the prompting of the ECA, that at a time when demand for steel in the USA was so high that in spite of record output levels steel rationing had nevertheless to be maintained, it would prove impossible for European countries to obtain the inputs to make so much steel.

The second underlying assumption of these European plans, however, was that the resources would be obtained at the expense of the reduced and restricted German steel industry. Table 49 shows that even when West German output would have reached the revised maximum limit imposed by the western Allies in 1947, total Western European output would still be lower than at the peak level of inter-war production. The targets set for the growth of the other Western European steel industries were in fact predicated on the restrictions to be maintained on the German steel industry.

This had a double advantage; if domestic demand proved insufficient the large pre-war German export markets would be left for Germany's European competitors. This process, for example, was originally intended to account for about 3 million tonnes of the planned increase in steel output under the French Modernization Plan. In this light the objectives of the Western European governments in this sector were not so expansionist as they seemed in Washington, but they none the less assumed a regularity of demand for steel such as had been far from obtaining in the inter-war period. There might, the CEEC report suggested, be a slackening-off in demand in the early 1950s due to a weakening in the demand arising from the immediate needs of post-war reconstruction, but this would prove only a temporary phenomenon and continued prosperity would produce new sources of demand for steel. It was as though the Western European countries had taken a model of their economies in the inter-war period, injected into it full employment as a permanent factor and then simply read off the quantity of steel consumption which altering that variable would imply. *Per capita* steel consumption in France in 1951 was thus estimated at 234 kg ingot equivalent of finished steel compared to 162 kg in 1929, and in Italy at 87 kg compared to 59 kg in 1938.[1]

Most of the investment to meet this presumed demand was concerned with the modernization and rationalization of existing plant. The major, dramatic, single new projects which were launched in these years – the two continuous strip mills in France, the hot-rolled strip mill in South Wales, and so on – were only a part of a much more widespread programme of mixed private and public investment in the modification of existing plant sustained by boom conditions. Taken as a whole investment in the steel industry was not fitted into a rational programme of action but responded to the immediate situation where order books were full and steel sold at high prices. French steel investments were, of course, channelled through the Modernization Plan and this certainly contained a greater element of rationalization than was seen elsewhere, such as the linking of clusters of steel works to new, single, common electricity-generating stations. In a less rationalized framework the British steel manufacturers were also obliged to prepare a common development plan, but, as might have been expected from such a procedure, the plan seems to have contained something for almost every manufacturer.[2] The export capacity of the Belgian steel industry was so great that there was less anxiety that it might fail to meet the increased demand from the home market. In relation to the total output of the industry investment was lower in Belgium than in France and Britain, but in comparison to the previous thirty years it was at a high level.

[1] The actual levels attained in 1951 were France, 185 kg, and Italy, 75 kg, crude steel equivalents, UN, *Quarterly Bulletin of Steel Statistics*. Crude steel equivalencies based on suggested method in OEEC, *Industrial Statistics*.
[2] D. Burn, *The Steel Industry 1939–1959. A Study in Competition and Planning* (Cambridge, 1961).

The fact that government did no more than encourage and try to facilitate the modernization of the steel industry in Belgium was, however, exceptional in Western Europe. Elsewhere, no matter how unsystematic its actions, it was much more intimately involved in the process. In fact after 1914 there had been few years anywhere in western Europe where the steel industry's fortunes had been left to the untrammelled influence of the market. The scale and importance of the capital investments meant that even when governments did not regard the industry as being of such peculiar strategic and economic importance as to involve themselves closely in its fortunes the firms themselves protected the position of their investments through an intricate network of national and international agreements. Even after the great depression, the seizure of power by the Nazi government, and the rapid increases of steel output in Germany caused by reflation and rearmament there, the second

Table 50   Estimated values of investment in the iron and steel industry, 1947–51

| | France | United Kingdom | Belgium | West Germany |
	(million 1952 dollars)		(million current dollars)	
1947/8	190.4	305.2	24.6*	n.a.
1949	184.8	201.6	42.2	78.5
1950	246.4	212.8	41.0	90.4
1951	221.2	198.8	28.9	142.7

Sources: E. Baumgart, R. Krengel and W. Moritz, *Die Finanzierung der industriellen Expansion in der Bundesrepublik während der Jahre des Wiederaufbaus* (Berlin, 1960), pp. 51 ff.; D. Burn, *The Steel Industry 1939–1959. A Study in Competition and Planning* (Cambridge, 1961), p. 395; C. Reuss, E. Koutny and L. Tychon, *Le Progrès économique en sidérurgie. Belgique, Luxembourg, Pays-Bas 1830–1955* (Louvain, 1960), p. 290.

* 1948 only.

International Steel Cartel still regulated the export markets of European producers. These were allocated not so much on the basis of rationality as of previously established positions, traditions and business connections. Over the period 1925–9 steel exports in Europe had been about 38 per cent of total output of which exports to non-European countries had formed about 16 per cent. In the 1930s exports were of less importance, about 22 per cent of output over the period 1935–9.[3] Steel exports had been an important foreign currency earner for western Europe from the mid-nineteenth century onwards. They were closely tied to European investments in railways, harbours and other infrastructural developments in the underdeveloped world. In spite of the political fragmentation of Europe in the 1930s, co-operation within the International Steel Cartel was not found wanting in the face of attempts by

[3] UN, *European Steel Trends in the Setting of the World Market* (Geneva, 1949), pp. 7 ff. For American producers exports were relatively insignificant, about 5 per cent of output, and about four-fifths of world steel exports originated in western Europe.

less-developed economies to develop their own steel industries. It was the Cartel's policy to keep export prices low, often at the expense of domestic prices, in order to maintain a hold on these markets.[4] The national domestic markets were, except for the well-established trades in semi-finished metals and in certain special steels, amply shielded from competition by outside producers.

The view of future policy which emerged from the national steel production programmes submitted to the CEEC was not significantly different in this respect from what had gone before. At higher levels of output exports would be more important, but they would be possible because of the absence of German exports and, except for Belgium and Luxembourg, they would continue to be seen essentially as useful regulators of the level of activity, a way of minimizing the fierce impact of cyclical fluctuations on the industry. The elimination of German exports would make the re-establishment of the Cartel easier. The outside world had, however, changed considerably. The war and its aftermath had stimulated the development of protected iron and steel industries in numerous markets which had been important in the inter-war period. It had also enormously increased the level of United States steel output, from an annual average of 44.1 million tonnes over the period 1936–9 to 80.3 million tonnes in 1948. In spite of the tightness of the home market, which meant that most United States steel exports only took place in the immediate post-war years through special licensing and controls, it was nevertheless implicit in all America's post-war international economic policy that this level of steel output would eventually imply a substantially greater volume of American steel exports than before. The steel output of the rest of the world, omitting Europe and North America, had run at an annual average of 9.2 million tonnes over the period 1936–9. The United Nations estimated its likely volume by the end of the Marshall Plan at 15 million tonnes. The submissions to the CEEC took little or no account of these changes in the extra-European world. In this light the objectives of the Western European countries looked much more ambitious, whatever happened in Germany.

In 1948 no significant producer in fact reached the forecast output. The reason for this, however, was certainly not a weakness in domestic demand. If Germany is excluded from the calculation, 1948 was a record year for steel consumption on the domestic markets of Western Europe. Exports had now fallen to a share of only about 18 per cent of total output and most countries maintained export quotas to ensure the availability of steel at home. Belgium suffered from export difficulties, but these were mainly attributable to high prices and to payments problems. The main reason for the failure of output to match the targets was the acute shortage of inputs, of which the most telling was the coke and coking coal shortage in France. Joined to this was the shortage of scrap. Before the war the United States had been a major exporter

⁴ E. Hexner, *The International Steel Cartel* (Chapel Hill, 1943).

of steel scrap for use in European blast furnaces, but the growth of output in America had stopped this trade and the increased use of scrap in European furnaces in order to economize on coke meant that every European country, again with the exception of Germany, had by 1948 run into a bottleneck with supplies of steel scrap. Connected with both these causes, because due essentially to the same reasons, was the shortage of semi-finished steel imports from the United States.

If, however, the failure to reach the forecast level of output was caused until the end of 1948 by a bottleneck in the flow of inputs, in 1949 and 1950 it was due to a new and worrying cause, a noticeable slackening in the demand for steel everywhere except in Germany. The trend of rising output which had remained unbroken from the end of the war until summer 1949 then began to fall. The sudden downturn in production put the steel production targets in a quite different perspective. The end of the post-war restocking boom, which had not materialized in 1947, seemed now to be arriving. What made this even more alarming was West Germany's immunity to it. The backlog of demand for steel was so great there and there was so much spare capacity which could be taken up cheaply that the situation was entirely different.

German steel-making capacity had remained a long way above the limits set for it after Potsdam. When the report of the Humphrey Committee was accepted existing capacity was estimated at 19 million tonnes a year. The subsequent dismantling activities still left capacity far beyond the agreed output limit of 11.1 million tonnes. A comparison of plans with output achieved in Western Europe can be made by comparing tables 49 and 51,

Table 51   Crude steel output in Western Europe, 1946–52 (million tonnes)

	Belgium	Luxem-bourg	France	Saarland	Italy	Nether-lands	United Kingdom	West Germany
1946	2.26	1.27	4.34	0.29	1.13	0.13	12.70	2.72*
1947	2.84	1.69	5.64	0.70	1.66	0.19	12.72	3.12*
1948	3.86	2.41	7.12	1.21	2.09	0.33	14.88	5.47
1949	3.79	2.24	9.01	1.73	2.02	0.42	15.55	9.01
1950	3.72	2.41	8.52	1.87	2.33	0.48	16.29	11.93
1951	4.97	3.03	9.68	2.56	3.01	0.55	15.64	13.29
1952	4.99	2.95	10.70	2.78	3.48	0.67	16.42	15.56

Source : OEEC, *Industrial Statistics*.

* All Germany.

although the basis of calculation of the two tables is slightly different. Before 1950 all Western European countries were not keeping pace with their objectives as stated to the CEEC. By 1951 they had all reached those objectives except France. The shortfall in French output was, however, by that date made up by the great increase in West German output. In 1950 West German steel output passed the limits foreseen by the CEEC, passed the limits imposed on it by the Allies, and passed that of France. From the start of 1948 to the end of 1950 steel output doubled in the Federal Republic and its rate of increase did not slacken as output began to dip in the last quarter of 1949 in the other Western European countries. In 1951 it was only West Germany's contribution to the Western European total which finally justified the CEEC estimates of 1947!

In 1949 German steel exports made their re-entry into European markets and in that year they were about one quarter the value of British exports. In 1951 they were to exceed them. How this remarkable recovery in the German steel industry came about can be explained both by the general nature of the economic recovery in West Germany and by the specific situation of the steel industry relative to other industrial sectors.

Until the end of 1948 the recovery of output in the iron and steel industry in western Germany was further behind the level of recovery of the industrial economy as a whole, compared to pre-war levels, than that of any other significant industrial sector. From spring 1948 output in steel-consuming sectors rose vigorously, although unevenly, and sustained the demand for iron and steel when it was beginning to flatten out or even decline in other countries. At the end of 1948 when the index of total industrial production in the Bizone as compared to 1936 stood at 79 per cent, that of the iron and steel industry was still only at 55 per cent (table 52). Only one other industrial sector, the closely related 'other metallurgical industries', stood at a lower

Table 52   Index of industrial production in the British and American occupation zones of West Germany (1936 = 100)

	Industrial production	Iron and steel production	Iron and steel construction	Engineering and optical industries	Motor vehicles	Electrical industries
1946	34	20	42	35	15	33
June 1947	41	21	42	40	17	64
Dec. 1947	44	26	50	40	18	68
Apr. 1948	53	31	59	46	27	93
Sep. 1948	70	47	84	60	52	130
Dec. 1948	79	55	99	73	69	165

Source: W. Abelshauser, *Wirtschaft in Westdeutschland 1945–1948*, p. 43.

comparative level. Germany entered 1949 in potential boom conditions for the steel industry with a rapidly accumulating demand which remained unsatisfied only because of the need to repair plant and because of the bottlenecks in the supply of inputs. These two problems dealt with, as they largely were in 1949, the only restriction was that imposed by international agreement. This was already itself being relaxed in the course of 1949. In November, for example, the Petersberg protocols relaxed the limits on German shipbuilding and so opened up another domestic market likely to grow rapidly.

The combination of rapidly growing output and ample reserves of spare capacity and spare labour was an especially favourable one on the export market. Whereas other European steel manufacturers had full order books German manufacturers could accept immediate export contracts at less than profitable prices because of the gains they brought in economies of scale and in bringing idle plant into utilization. After the quota restrictions were eased on French steel exports in October 1948 actual exports over the ensuing twelve months fell about a third short of the newly permitted level.[5] For the first three quarters of 1950 they showed a slightly declining trend. If there was a sufferer from the increase in West German exports, however, Belgium/ Luxembourg was the more probable candidate. In terms of national currency, exports of iron and steel products from Belgium and Luxembourg fell by more than 50 per cent between the third quarter of 1949 and the third quarter of 1950. No doubt some of this was due to the exchange rate readjustments in September 1949 when Belgium devalued by less than most of the other Western European countries and thus left her overpriced steel exports especially vulnerable. Although the dollar value of British steel exports, for example, fell by $27.5 million in the last quarter of 1949 their sterling value increased by £3.6 million. The fall in Belgium/Luxembourg's steel exports to the Netherlands in 1949 was roughly the equivalent of the increase in West Germany's exports to that destination (table 53). The Monnet Plan, however, had given an important place to steel exports; when output of crude steel reached 12.5 million tonnes a year, exports were to account for about three million tonnes. A double shadow of the failure of the domestic and foreign markets to absorb the Plan's output was thus thrown over the French economy.

From 1945 onwards the problem of Western European reconstruction had increasingly crystallized into the problem of future Franco-German relationships, and that of Franco-German relationships into the relationships of the coal and steel industries. The disindustrialization of Germany, the removal of most of its industrial capacity, had never been accepted as wise or feasible. The ceilings imposed on industrial output by the Levels of Industry Agreement had been calculated in order to make reparations out of current production possible. But the Soviet Union had wanted its reparations at once before output reached those limits (not an unreasonable interpretation of the Potsdam agreements), reparations had become meaningless as a guide to action, and the real interest of the western powers, even France, soon no longer lay in enforcing general limits on industrial output. That policy had in any case originally been devised without French participation. French interests had been more specific and focused on the control and regulation of the Ruhr

[5] M. Fontaine, *L'industrie sidérurgique dans le monde et son évolution depuis la Seconde Guerre Mondiale* (Paris, 1950), p. 160.

Table 53 Total steel exports 1946–52, Belgium/Luxembourg, France, United Kingdom and West Germany (thousand tonnes)

	1938	1946	1947	1948	1949	1950	1951	1952
Belgium/Luxembourg	2314.3	1572.3	2268.9	3446.0	3745.5	3580.7	5160.9	5020.3
of which to Netherlands	287.0	319.6	357.3	586.2	521.1	727.2	856.5	646.1
of which to United Kingdom	300.3	12.8	71.4	238.3	511.0	142.2	262.8	489.0
*France**	1336.3	165.4	319.1	897.9	2117.1	3630.3	4537.8	3007.1
of which to Germany†	1.8	n.a.	0.7	157.7	92.9	203.6	105.6	297.1
of which to Italy	42.4	n.a.	1.3	8.8	44.4	261.4	298.7	157.5
of which to United Kingdom	206.9	n.a.	1.9	22.4	121.6	176.0	85.0	107.2
West Germany	‡2300.9	0	n.a.	**124.0	**608.5	1952.7	2345.6	2061.4
of which to Netherlands	315.8	0	3.0	101.8	91.9	196.3	217.1	198.8
United Kingdom	1549.8	2254.0	1919.6	2117.0	2493.9	2596.6	2142.2	2089.4

Source: British Iron and Steel Federation, *Statistical Yearbooks*. Includes all steel products.

  * After April 1948 includes Saarland.
  † After 1947 West Germany.
  ‡ Including Austria.
  ** Bizone.

industrial area. If at first this was acting under the strong influence of history and trying to force to a successful conclusion policies which had not been successfully enforced after 1918 it soon came to have a more modern rationale as well, since the success of the Modernization Plan seemed also to depend on the disposition of the Ruhr's resources. In this context the Ruhr meant coal, coke and steel. The Modernization Plan's targets depended on the allocation of the Ruhr's coal and coke resources and on what was to happen to the German steel industry.

When, after the second stage of the London conference, the Quai d'Orsay began to manoeuvre policy towards a Franco-West German economic association, the relationship between the French and German coal, iron and steel industries became even more central to the most crucial areas of foreign policy. It was precisely in these sectors that attempts at such an economic association had been made after the manifest failure of the Versailles treaty. In one sense, although at a very low level, the firm adherence of both France and Nazi Germany to the International Steel Cartel had been just such an association, but it fell far short of anything that the French had hoped might be produced by the occupation of the Ruhr in 1923. The problems requiring to be resolved could hardly be so by any agreement which avoided the whole question of regulation of domestic markets. The formation of the West German state, the long and detailed struggle over the powers of intervention of the International Authority for the Ruhr in those markets, and the enormous ambiguities which were left about the exact status and duration of the Ruhr Authority, had brought that question into a position from which it could hardly be removed by another unsatisfactory compromise like that of the Cartel. When the West German government took office the international bonds which restrained the Promethean strength of Germany's steel industry were already being tested and broken. Some new policy was needed if a Franco-German settlement was to become a reality and reconstruction to be achieved.

COMPARATIVE PROSPECTS OF THE FRENCH AND GERMAN STEEL INDUSTRIES

German steel output in 1938 had been more than 40 per cent of Western Europe's total output, most of it produced in the area which had now become the Federal Republic. In 1949 the Federal Republic's output was only 18.2 per cent of Western Europe's. Would the organized defence of Western Europe and the integration of the Federal Republic into the strategic bloc be accepted by the United States while so much steel-making capacity still lay idle or underutilized there? Had the occupying powers in fact succeeded in removing most of that capacity from Germany or replacing German output by their own the situation would have been different.[6] But they had not. An increase of defence expenditure in Western Europe would certainly increase once more the demand for dollar imports, and to expect the United States to provide increased aid which would logically be construed as payments to keep West German manufacturing capacity idle was hardly feasible. By autumn 1949 the American army seems to have espoused the cause of limited rearmament in West Germany; the rumours which tremulously ran on that subject in France were not without foundation. At the end of April 1950 the United States Joint Chiefs of Staff pronounced in favour of German rearmament.[7] There were several barriers to its becoming official American policy, not least the consternation it would cause in Western Europe if it were adopted. In September formal proposals for German rearmament were in fact made by the United States. At the start of March 1950 Konrad Adenauer asked for a raising of the limits to German steel output and in that month the quantity of steel produced passed one million tonnes, suggesting the international limits might in any case be broken. Supposing all international regulation of the German coal and steel industries, including the International Authority for the Ruhr, to be ineffective, what would be the respective situations of the French and German steel industries now and in the likely future?

No entirely satisfactory answer could be given to that question at the time. Nor is it any easier to answer in retrospect. All that can be done is to strike a balance of probabilities, but in striking it a much more accurate appreciation of the two steel industries emerges. One of the reasons why the balance of probabilities is so hard to strike is because the patterns of comparative advantage in steel-making between Western European countries had been increasingly distorted for more than thirty years by government action. Any calculation of the relative production costs of the two industries shows that a more important part in production cost differences was played by government intervention than by differences in the overall balance of factor input costs. The relative difference in the prices of coke and ore to the two industries did of course contain an important element representing the natural comparative advantages of the two countries; German reserves of coking coal and French reserves of iron ore were each among the world's largest and most easily accessible. Even here, however, government intervention through freight rates and tariffs formed a substantial part of the final cost difference. And in this respect the immutable fact was that whereas France depended on German coal Germany consumed insignificant amounts of French ore.

---

[6] In Rhineland-Westphalia six blast-furnaces, forty-seven Siemens-Martin furnaces and two Thomas converters were dismantled entirely. Almost all the electro-steel capacity was removed, as were the rolling mills of the Hörder Verein and the one continuous wide strip mill at Dinslaken. K.H. Herchenröder, J. Schäfer and M. Zapp, *Die Nachfolger der Ruhrkonzerne* (Düsseldorf, 1954), p. 8.

[7] P. Melandri, *Les Etats-unis face à l'unification de l'Europe 1945–1954* (Paris, 1980), p. 291.

In comparing the relative costs of coke and ore the differences in the steel-manufacturing processes and the possibility of adjusting the mix of inputs within the blast furnace have to be considered. The French industry was less diversified than the German, a much greater proportion of its output coming from the relatively undifferentiated basic steel industry which had grown up in Lorraine on the low-grade minette ore field from the 1890s. The open-hearth process, which accounted for the greater part of West German output (table 54), was more capable of flexibility both in the mix of inputs and in the final product. On the other hand its costs were, except in very favourable

Table 54   French and German crude steel output by process, 1950 (thousand tonnes)

	France	Germany
Gilchrist–Thomas basic	5449.3	5129.0
Open–hearth, acid and basic	2587.9	6661.0
Electric arc, induction and crucible	539.6	331.0

Source: British Iron and Steel Federation, *Statistical Yearbooks*. The French figures are not comprehensive since they omit a small part of output not under the scope of the Chambre Syndicale de la sidérurgie française.

circumstances, higher than those of the Gilchrist-Thomas basic process. Because the Gilchrist-Thomas process is the best approximation to a standardized mass-production process in the industry the comparison of costs is easier there. It is, however, not possible to draw worthwhile comparisons between the cost structure of the Gilchrist-Thomas process and the open-hearth or other process. Indeed, even in respect of the Gilchrist-Thomas process it is only on the basis of an exact comparison between individual enterprises that the real situation could be accurately determined, since a global comparison has a manifest inapplicability to important individual cases. And this is to consider only the difficulties of comparing factor input costs at any moment in time. The way in which those costs could be adjusted in the final sale price, which was the crux of the matter, is a question of comparative productivity and the growth trend of comparative productivity. Although several ingenious methods have been devised for attempting such international productivity comparisons it must be said that there is still no econometric method satisfactory enough to justify its employment to take the issue further at this stage.[8] Not the least important reason for this is the purely political one that almost every element of the price structure of factor inputs into the two industries could be subject to radical alteration through

[8] The most satisfactory, especially as it was devised precisely for the steel industry, is that suggested by R.C. Allen, 'The peculiar productivity history of American blast furnaces, 1840–1913', *Journal of Economic History*, 37 (3), 1977, but in respect of the problem considered here the remark still applies.

unpredictable political interventions at any moment, and that the aim of French diplomacy could be no more than to modify and control that political intervention in its own interests. A dubious comparison of relative levels of productivity in 1949/50 would be more or less worthless for establishing the relative final cost pattern of the two industries in 1952.

That having been said, it must also be said that the level of knowledge of and enquiry into the two industries by governments on the eve of embarking on extremely serious negotiations on the subject appears to have been quite astonishingly amateurish. That remark cannot exclude the Commissariat au Plan. As yet no written evidence has been discovered that they were really in a position to forecast with any reasonable accuracy the likely impact of their policies on the steel industry. There seems no reason why a historian should refrain from what may be blundering judgements when governments received advice which could be no more accurate.

In December 1951, six months before the European Coal and Steel Community entered into force, the material input costs of one tonne of Gilchrist-Thomas steel plate were estimated to be lower in West Germany than in France by almost 16 per cent.[9] The largest elements in the difference were the input price of coke in France, which exceeded the advantage France obtained from cheaper ore inputs by more than a thousand francs a tonne, and the greater cost of energy inputs into the manufacturing process, which reflected the higher cost of coal in France as compared to Germany. To this calculation, to establish final production costs, would have to be added wages and social security payments, any other incidences of national taxation which fell on the firm, internal transport costs, and an allowance for interest and depreciation on the capital. However, the costs of raw material inputs in Gilchrist-Thomas steel manufacture are by far the greater part of production costs, as much as 70 per cent of the total in some cases.

Differences in wage and social security costs ought theoretically in the conditions of 1950 to have been in West Germany's favour also, but in fact there is no evidence that wage rates in the West German steel industry were lower than in France, although the burden of social security payments on French producers made the total payment which the employer had to make considerably higher in France. The spread of wages in German steel works in 1950 seems to have been much wider than in French ones but this is the only indication that in West Germany there were 1.8 million unemployed in March 1950 whereas in France full employment still prevailed. The retrospective wage figures given in the Community's bulletin indicate that German steel workers' wages in August 1950 varied from 21.88 cents an hour to 30.91 cents; in France a skilled worker's wage was 29.99 cents.[10] It may emerge that

[9] J. Chardonnet, *La sidérurgie française. Progrès ou décadence?* (Paris, 1954), p. 102.
[10] Communauté Européenne de l'Acier et du Charbon, *Evolution des salaires et politique salariale dans les industries de la Communauté 1945–1956* (Luxembourg, 1960), p. 74.

the reason for this similarity was the maldistribution of the unemployed labour force in West Germany. The population of North Rhine-Westphalia had not increased, but had fallen in the immediate aftermath of the German surrender, and the influx of refugees into the Bizone had been mainly into the more rural Länder of Schleswig-Holstein and Bavaria. The metal-workers union, endowed with a remarkable gain in factory negotiating powers by the Allies, had been able to establish wage rates relatively free from the influence of the flood of unemployed *Ostvertriebene*, and the German steel industry did not gain the advantage of low wages common to almost all other West German industries, except of course coal, at the time.

Whatever the reasons for the similarity in wage levels it is clear that the social security element of the wage payment falling on the entrepreneur was much higher in France, especially because of the more generous family allowances paid there. The total burden of non-wage payments in the first quarter of 1950 in France was 53 francs, or another 50 per cent on the wage bill, and only 32 francs, or less than a third of the wage bill, in Germany.[11]

The nominal incidence of fiscal policy was quite different between the two industries, mainly because of the higher levels of direct taxation in the Federal Republic. The total fiscal burden on domestic steel prices in France was estimated in spring 1950 at about 23 per cent, in West Germany at 33 per cent.[12] Both countries, however, had a system of export rebates on turnover tax, but at different rates so that the incidence on export prices was entirely different. This was to be one of the most fiercely-fought issues of the Schuman Plan negotiations, especially when taken with the difference in protective tariffs. Finished steel sold in Germany paid a tax of 6 per cent; sold abroad it attracted a 6.5 per cent rebate. Imported steel had to pay a compensatory levy of 6 per cent. French steel sold on the domestic market paid taxes equivalent to 19 per cent of the price, while the corresponding export rebates and import levies were about 16.5 per cent. Thus the price relationships of German and French steel in their respective markets after tax were substantially different from those before tax. Although Gilchrist-Thomas plate f.o.b. the steel mill in Germany, discounting the difference in labour costs, was about 16 per cent cheaper than the equivalent product in France, this price advantage would be lost if it were exported to France. The same French Gilchrist-Thomas plate would then sell in West Germany at about 6 per cent less than the sale price of the equivalent German product in France.[13]

By the side of this scale of difference, differences in internal transport costs, capital costs and depreciation allowances could not have been especially

---

[11] FJM, AMG 22/5/4, Commissariat Général, 'Note relative aux effets du Plan Schuman sur les industries du charbon et de l'acier en France', 8 February 1951.

[12] C.H. Hahn, *Der Schuman Plan. Eine Untersuchung im besonderen Hinblick auf die deutsch-französische Stahlindustrie* (Munich, 1953), p. 80.

[13] See the prices given by H. Mendershausen, 'First tests of the Schuman Plan', *Review of Economics and Statistics*, 35 (4), 1953.

significant. Everything we know about the period implies that capital must have been more expensive in Germany. Depreciation allowances, on the other hand, were set at a generous level by the Federal government. The extent to which capital costs and replacement were to be taken into account in deciding the future relationships of the two industries was by no means a negligible one; none the less it can be set on one side for the moment, because so much the main determinant of production costs were raw material inputs and fiscal policy.

Simply taking the most easily comparable sections of the French and German steel industries into account in this way suggests very strongly that in terms of basic input costs Germany was at a marked advantage. But this does not seem to have been the view of the Planning Commissariat, which seems rather to have believed that in any regulation of the European markets the Lorraine basic steel industry would be favoured.[14] Of course everything in such a comparison depended on the future growth of productivity and on what would be done about the element of government intervention in determining costs, for the variation in the government element was greater than that in factor input costs. Once fiscal and tariff policies, for example, were taken into account, Germany's cost advantages did not appear as an international comparative advantage, indeed some French Gilchrist-Thomas steel could be sold marginally more cheaply in West Germany than the equivalent German steel in France. But setting aside these matters the Planning Commissariat still took the view that the 16 per cent difference in material input costs between French and German Gilchrist-Thomas plate was due to lack of rationalization in the French industry and thus made this industry not only susceptible to being closed by planning but on the way already to being so.[15]

Once we widen the comparison to try to include the open-hearth producers and other producers of specialized steels the economics become even more problematic. The German industry, because so much more of it used the open-hearth process, required greater quantities of scrap and other iron inputs, and scrap prices were high after 1945. In this respect only the steel industry of Belgium and Luxembourg, 90 per cent of whose output was made by converters, was more favourably situated than the French. At the opposite extreme was Italy's small steel industry which was concentrated very heavily on special steel production. France used on average in 1949 312 kg of scrap combined with other inputs to produce one tonne of crude steel compared to West Germany's 429 kg, Britain's 629 kg, and Italy's 875 kg.[16] The input cost of scrap was about 20 per cent higher in France than in West Germany, because of the large amounts of scrap still lying around in the Federal Republic, but this still left the French industry's total scrap costs per tonne of steel produced considerably below the West German level.[17]

---

[14] FRUS, 1950, III, Acheson to Washington, 12 May 1950, p. 697.
[15] FJM, AMG 22/5/4.   [16] Hahn, *Der Schuman Plan*, p. 73.
[17] Although surely not 40 per cent lower as calculated by K.W.F. Zawadzki, 'The economics of the Schuman Plan', in *Oxford Economic Papers*, N.S., v, 1953.

An approximation of the average costs of material and labour for all steel-making was made by the United Nations Department of Economic Affairs in 1951. This shows that even when the open-hearth industry is included the principal differences in factor input costs betwen the French and German industries were still, on the French side, dearer coke and higher labour costs, and on the German side the higher costs of imported ore, and that the difference in labour costs balanced the difference in imported ore costs leaving the much greater relative cost of coke inputs the principal French disadvantage (table 55).

Table 55 Approximate costs of labour and main raw materials for steel making, 1951 (dollars)

	France		West Germany	
	Per hour or per tonne of raw material	Per tonne of steel	Per hour or per tonne of raw material	Per tonne of steel
Labour (inc. maintenance services)	0.63	21	0.63	16
Imported ore	0	0	20	5
Domestic ore	11	7	19	4
Scrap purchases	24	4	20	5
Coke	16	12	10	6
Costs per tonne of steel	44		36	

Source: UN, *Economic Survey of Europe Since the War* (Geneva, 1953), p. 228.

A national assessment of the economic situation would therefore point to the following conclusions. The West German industry had significant cost advantages over that of France, of which the most significant was the input price of coke. The French government could hope to remedy this, as indeed it had been struggling to do since 1944, because West Germany was by far the most important foreign supplier of coke to the basic steel industry in France and France was West Germany's biggest market for coke exports. Given the relatively low level of investment (which, if the figures could be calculated net of the disinvestment which must also have taken place, would be even lower) in the West German steel industry since 1944 compared to its French counterpart, and given the high cost of capital in the Federal Republic, the view of the Planning Commissariat that differences in final sales prices to France's disadvantage would be eliminated or very much reduced by higher rates of productivity growth in the French industry was not necessarily wrong. Lastly, governmental pressures in any direct inter-governmental negotiations were likely to bring final sales prices closer together because government intervention, especially through fiscal policy, was so important a component of the final price in each country.

It was better for France to negotiate now while the West German state was in tutelage, before the extent of the Ruhr Authority's powers were finally discovered, and before the Federal German Republic was admitted more fully into the system of military alliances. But what form should the negotiations take? Certain issues relating to the regulation of the German steel industry and its domestic markets had already been hotly debated in the London conference and its aftermath. One was the difference made to final costs by the size of the firm. All the Allied powers, even though they had started from different philosophies, had made a facile identification of 'big business' with the Nazi regime. Powerful vested business interests and cartels were publicly branded at Potsdam as enemies of democracy and the trials of prominent German firms and industrialists at Nuremberg for war crimes were intended as a part of the process of 'democratization'.[18] Large, integrated firms were held to have exercised a malign influence on German history since the late nineteenth century and irrespective of the economic considerations involved there were powerful political pressures to break up the Ruhr firms into their component parts. Similar pressures had been exercised by French negotiators throughout the long discussions on the International Ruhr Authority and on dismantling. At least a third of Ruhr coal output was controlled by integrated steel firms. Such firms consumed coal and coke, not at market prices, but rather at more favourable transfer prices. Production costs may have been lower because in the larger integrated concerns economies of scale were greater and coal and coke input prices lower.

Another issue which had been important in the negotiations for the International Authority for the Ruhr was discrimination between domestic and export coal and coke prices. That is not to say that France and others did not also discriminate in the same way in respect of iron ore. But once the Saarland had been attached to France, Germany scarcely used French ores at all. The relatively high cost of imported ore in West Germany arose from the high transport charges on Swedish ores.[19] The price of German metallurgical coke delivered in Lorraine in spring 1950 was about 46 per cent higher than its price in the Ruhr, before compensatory fiscal adjustment in France.[20] The United Nations estimated that about 15 per cent of the delivered price was due to transport costs.[21] If this estimate is correct, using the rates of dependence of the French industry on German coke calculated in chapter 4, the difference made to final production costs in the French steel

[18] Two major steel manufacturers, Krupp and Flick, were prosecuted.
[19] Swedish Kiruna ore at 60 per cent fe. content retailed at $4 per tonne at the mine-head but at $7 per tonne fob Narvik in spring 1949. UN, *European Steel Trends*, p. 65.
[20] Zawadzki, 'Economics'.
[21] UN, *European Steel Trends*, p. 55.

industry by dual pricing of German coke could be estimated at about 2 per cent.[22]

During the Schuman Plan negotiations much evidence emerged that the freight rates charged by the railways through the Palatinate were highly discriminatory. Removing this further element of discrimination might therefore reduce the production costs of Lorraine steel by as much as 2.5 per cent. On the basis of 1950 steel prices this would have brought the price of Gilchrist-Thomas merchant bars in France down to equality with the equivalent German product although it would by no means have closed the gap between actual French and German prices for Gilchrist-Thomas plate, nor for open-hearth steel. The possible gain was, however, by no means negligible, for it might also preclude price discrimination in the future against the French steel industry, while the West German industry stood to gain little or nothing from the possible removal of French ore price discrimination against it.

If to this possible gain could be added a breaking-up of the integrated Ruhr firms the gains might be still greater. The average size of the producing unit was much larger in West Germany than in France. The assumption underlying the Modernization Plan's major investment projects in the French steel industry was that the optimum output level for unspecialized steel-producing plant which would be internationally competitive was one million tonnes of crude steel a year. No French plant was producing at that level in 1950; in September of that year three German works were operating at a higher level. In 1949–50 about half of German ingot output came from plant whose output was greater than 900,000 tonnes a year.[23] Most such firms were integrated upwards as far as the rolling mill and many owned their own coal supply, thus increasing the cost advantages which their greater steel-making capacity provided. The original Bizone proposals for 'deconcentration' made in February 1947, whose implementation had been postponed because of the dispute with the French government over ultimate ownership, had indicated that the major German steel companies would be broken up into twenty-five single firms. The French government could hope to develop the basic idea of these proposals while accepting in return the Allied *fait accompli* on the question of ownership. In this matter at least small might seem more beautiful to all except the Germans.

What, however, is by no means established is that the French coal and steel industries were any less integrated than the German. What seems more likely to have been the case is that integration brought greater savings in production costs in Germany because of the assembly on one continuous site by the larger firms of so many aspects of iron and steel-making and processing, with the

---

[22] The estimate of 4.8 per cent made by the UN, *European Steel Trends*, p. 65, is based on a set of coke prices which are not confirmed elsewhere and on inexact assumptions about the other elements in the calculation.   [23] Burn, *The Steel Industry*, p. 402.

consequent saving in transport costs. These savings would not be lost through breaking up the ownership of the capital in the enterprise. This would probably only reduce the advantage the German firms had, if any, in the external economies arising from the greater scale of management or the possibility of more flexible financing. There were numerous examples of similar forms of integration in France, which, even if the gains in productivity were less and the form of integration less direct and binding, no doubt brought similar internal price advantages to those in Germany. Of the thirty-seven companies which Lauersen lists in the French iron and steel industry, eight had the same degree of integration as the major German firms except that they had now lost control of their coal resources to the French state. A further five firms combined steel production with rolling mills and other finishing processes but had no blast-furnaces.[24] Before nationalization of the coal-mines at least ten of the French steel firms had owned their own coal supply and the Lorraine mines in particular had been intimately linked to particular steel works. This is to say nothing of the links between steel-makers and iron ore mines in France which were every bit as extensive as those between coal-mines and steel works in the Ruhr; sixteen of the French firms owned their own supply of ore.[25]

The issues discussed in this section may seem rather fine, even trivial, by the side of the grandiose language in which politicians wrapped the initial proposals for the Schuman Plan and beside the undoubtedly high ideals of some of its proponents. Variations in the price of coke and differences in productivity in steel works are not, it must be admitted, themes so apt to raise the enthusiasm as the waning of the nation state or the reconciliation of bitterly divided enemies. The intention of dwelling at such length on such uninspiring subjects is not to insist on the primacy of the economic objectives of the Schuman Plan. Far from it, the objectives of the Schuman proposals were overwhelmingly political. It is to explain precisely what the real possibilities for political initiative were, what their implications, and, above all, to show how the Schuman proposals, far from being a change of economic and political direction, evolved logically from the consistent pursuit of France's original domestic and foreign reconstruction aims.

THE POLITICAL ORIGINS OF THE SCHUMAN PLAN

The European Coal and Steel Community is sometimes criticized for having created so tangled a web of economic and political relationships between the member states as to have destroyed from the outset all possibility of economic

---

[24] W. Lauersen, *Ausmass und Formen vertikaler Verflechtung in der Eisen- und Stahlindustrie der Vereinigten Staaten, Grossbritanniens, Frankreichs, Belgiens und Luxemburgs* (Kiel, 1951).

[25] ibid., pp. 85–6.

rationality. But such a criticism disregards the previous history. To arrive at anything simpler the Community would have had to unravel a skein of politico-economic relationships which had already become almost untraceable in their complexity. There are certainly many justifiable economic criticisms of the Coal and Steel Community, but it was not more complex than what went before. It was in certain respects a simplification. In April 1950, on the eve of the Schuman proposals, the ECA confessed itself unable to understand what the effect of the French proposals to the coming foreign ministers' meeting to modify the relationship between the Allied High Commissioners and the International Ruhr Authority would be.[26] When Dean Acheson took over as Secretary of State he found American policy on the different issues negotiated so interminably at the London conference to be so piecemeal that 'he did not understand either how we ever arrived at the decision to see established a West German government or State. He wondered whether this had not rather been the brainchild of General Clay and not a governmental decision.'[27] A special sub-committee of the National Security Council was set up to review the whole range of American policy on Germany. It was through this procedure that the American army in Germany was eventually brought to heel and a final settlement with France on the uncompleted details of the London conference reached. Even this did not clarify the extent of French and Allied powers over the West German economy.

The deadline towards which events moved was set by the projected arrival of the Foreign Ministers in Washington to negotiate the North Atlantic Treaty Organization on 31 March 1949. Ten days before this Schuman met Clay and gave him the clearest indication that France was no longer especially interested in elaborate controls and control boards over the German economy, of the kind that the British government had favoured, and which the London conference had laboured so long to include in the preliminary versions of the Occupation Statute. French interest was now, Schuman indicated, more in the general principles by which French and German economic recovery might be harmonized.[28] The State Department had of course only accepted unwillingly the future operation of these complicated control boards and was glad to see them go. The agreed policy statement left with Truman on the eve of the NATO conference therefore sketched out an Occupation Statute much simpler and less restrictive than the London conference had discussed. It would contain the necessary security safeguards, the stronger because the North Atlantic Pact would mean that United States forces would remain in Germany 'until the present tense and insecure situation in Europe has been replaced by a satisfactory measure of international confidence and balanced

[26] ECA, 61, 'Problems of the International Authority for the Ruhr', 12 April 1950.
[27] FRUS, 1949, III, p. 102, Memorandum of conversation by Murphy, 9 March 1949.
[28] FRUS, 1949, III, p. 115, Caffery to Washington, 22 March 1949.

normal relationship'.[29] The Occupation Statute would now be only a short document reserving certain vital matters, such as foreign affairs and external security, to the Allied powers. The reign of the army would come to an end and with the birth of the Federal Republic the Allies would appoint civilian High Commissioners to deal with a government which would be entirely independent except for those matters reserved in the simpler Occupation Statute.[30] The occupying powers would surrender all their administrative controls over the German economy to the West German government except where the Occupation Statute or the International Authority for the Ruhr took precedence.

This still left much to settle about the relationship between the Moscow sliding-scales, the OEEC, and the Ruhr Authority, as well as about the continuation of dismantling and 'decartelization' in Germany. The Moscow scales stopped at a level of 330,000 tonnes output of coal daily and France wanted them extended upwards so that at higher levels of output the same percentage of Ruhr coal would have to be made available without the possibility of any discretion being exercised by the Ruhr Authority. It also wanted the sliding-scales to cover coking fines and coke at this higher level. The European Coal Organization had been wound up, but coal availabilities still had to be listed to the UN Coal Committee of the Economic and Social Commission for Europe, a vestigial trace of the earlier attempt at a world-wide peace settlement, so that there were other possible complications on the question too. Furthermore, it was unforseeable what France's allies would be prepared to support when the Ruhr Authority first met in Düsseldorf, although the decision had been quite firm that the Authority's decisions could not contradict the annual economic programmes approved by the OEEC.

At the first meeting of the International Ruhr Authority the French representatives had their worst fears more than confirmed. The total budget of the Authority was to be only about $280,000 annually. It was not to have its own statistical services. It would have no direct contact of its own with the German firms, but only through the offices of the Allied High Commission. It would rarely be able to make inspections. It would have no say in the formulation of the West German programmes tabled at the OEEC.[31] There was very little France could do there except ensure that the relevant powers vested with the High Commissioners were not given away before they might be inherited by the Authority, a somewhat long-term course of action which was now only marginally relevant to French policy.

Until the Federal government entered into office its votes on the Authority were exercised by the occupying powers. There was no certainty that the new

[29] FRUS, 1948, II, p. 122, US Policy respecting Germany, 22 March 1949.

[30] Clay's verdict was, 'We have lost Germany politically and therefore it really does not matter except that history will prove why there was World War III.' Clay Papers, II, p. 1063.

[31] Y.62.3, Account of first meeting of the Ruhr Authority. Telegram, Dejean to Paris, 1 June 1949.

government would agree to serve on it or accept its rulings. The first Bundestag of the German Federal Republic was elected on 14 August 1949. On 20 September Konrad Adenauer came into office as Federal Chancellor, by the narrowest possible margin, and at the same time the Economic Council (Wirtschaftsrat) and the Administrative Council (Verwaltungsrat) for the Bizone were dissolved and the three civilian High Commissioners entered office as the Allied High Commission, replacing the separate Military Governments.[32] In opposition in Bonn the Social Democratic Party clamoured against the Ruhr Authority and pressed the government not to join it. On 16 September the High Commissioners agreed that Germany should be represented on the Authority by full voting members. The real problem for the High Commissioners was not whether to ratify this decision but how to disguise the fact that, in sharp contrast to the view of it taken by the Social Democratic opposition in Bonn, the Authority had few real powers anyway! As the British High Commissioner put it,

> Germans now think of IAR as a very powerful body and if they join they will soon discover that real powers lodged in other agencies. Therefore Germans likely go other extreme with impression that Authority has no important job to do and not to bother to work with it except in perfunctory way.[33]

It was not until 28 October that the Federal Republic took its seat in the OEEC and three days later a German representative attended the Council meeting. The problem was that although a seat on the Executive Committee had been kept warm for Germany when that Committee was first set up, any German representative now occupying it would mean an immediate breach in the Occupation Statute's prescription that the Federal Republic could not control its own foreign policy! Robertson suggested he might speak for Germany when the Executive Committee met at ministerial level, but that might have presented the Americans with the perfect excuse for insisting that their High Commissioner should also be involved in the OEEC.[34] In September the French High Commissioner, André François-Poncet, cut the tangled knot by suggesting that this one exception to the rule that the West German government be excluded from the sublime heights of foreign affairs be allowed, and the Federal Republic attended in October its first international conference as an equal.[35]

[32] The British High Commissioner was the same person, Sir (rather than General) Brian Robertson. General Koenig was replaced by André François-Poncet, a former ambassador to Berlin. The American High Commissioner was John J. McCloy.

John J. McCloy, 1895– . A lawyer. Educated at Harvard. Assistant Secretary of State 1941–5. President of World Bank 1947–9. United States High Commissioner for Germany 1949–52. Chairman of Board of Chase National, then Chase Manhattan Bank, and of the Ford Foundation, 1953–61. Disarmament adviser to Secretary of State Dulles. Co-ordinator of US Disarmament Activities 1961–3. An energetic and strong-willed person who exercised much influence.

[33] FRUS, 1949, III, p. 486, Riddleberger to Acheson, 16 September 1949.
[34] FO 371/76937, Robertson to Kirkpatrick, 23 February 1949.
[35] ibid., UK High Commission in Bonn to London, 13 September 1949.

The new government chose well its first ground to fight. Although at first it declined to send full members to the Ruhr Authority, this was not in protest against the Authority but against the continuation of dismantling activities. It was on those grounds that the occupying powers were weakest; there was as much dismantling of German firms in 1949 as in the earlier years and the Americans had scarcely disguised their wish that it should end. With a change of heart in this direction by the occupiers Adenauer made it clear that the Federal Republic would accept its place in the Ruhr Authority.

The status of the specific controls on the level of output in West Germany had been decided in a set of separate negotiations in London which culminated on 31 March 1949. The United States had agreed to the continuation of the Potsdam limits as revised in 1948 on the annual output of steel in West Germany until the end of the ERP. The Bizone's limit was raised from 10.7 million tonnes to 11.1 million to allow for the incorporation of the French zone. The list of 'prohibited and restricted industries' had also been maintained in principle with only a few significant differences from the list first drawn up after the Potsdam conference. But as far as individual works went there were great changes. Of the 167 plants originally scheduled for dismantling whose removal from the list the Humphrey Report had recommended, 159 were removed from it. Yet among the six which were conceded to the British and French opposition and remained on the dismantling list was the Thyssen steel works at Hamborn, and the six between them represented as much as 30 per cent of the total employment provided by the full 'Humphrey list'. The insistence by Britain and France on putting up a harder fight in respect of the list of prohibited industries reflected the fact that domestic political opposition to relaxing the restrictions on the German economy would obviously focus on questions of future strategic security.[36] All shipyards with a capacity of more than 277,000 tonnes a year were also prohibited. The limits on the size and speed of new German ships remained. All these limitations were to apply until summer 1952 at the earliest. France had wanted them to be of indefinite duration.

In September both Adenauer and Kurt Schumacher, the leader of the Social Democratic Party, jointly urged John McCloy to try to end the dismantling activities, before Germany joined the two international organizations. Adenauer offered as a bait a willing acceptance by his government of 'some form of internationalization if such works as Thyssen could be preserved.'[37] The Americans agreed that they would try to persuade their allies at talks scheduled for that month in Washington, although Acheson thought there was little chance of success. Bevin knew well enough, as did the British

[36] In the United States the argument ran the other way; should works which contributed to Germany's strategic strength be dismantled? The American negotiators insisted against strong British and French pressure on removing the electro-steel works, Deutsche Edelstahlwerke, from the dismantling list.   [37] FRUS, 1949, III, p. 595, McCloy to Acheson, 13 September 1949.

cabinet after the Humphrey Report, that dismantling was coming to an end because it was impractical politically, but that seemed to him all the more reason for going ahead at an accelerated pace while it was still possible. Bevin wanted until April 1950 to knock down, for it now did not really come to much more than that, the remaining plant he was entitled to claim as the outcome of the March agreements on the Humphrey Report.[38]

This was not a very sensible policy, in so far as it made an intensification of the dismantling programme coincide with the Soviet moves to establish a government in their own zone of Germany. The effect of the Soviet actions on the western powers was a very powerful one, for it institutionalized a direct rivalry for the future allegiance of Germany. The wait to see whether the Federal German government would subscribe with some reasonable degree of conformity to the Western European institutional framework which had been devised, in the face of the very strong domestic opposition to that policy which it was encountering, was an anxious one and seems to have given many in Washington the feeling that they had lost control of the situation in spite of the ERP. Demonstrations against the dismantling squads in the British zone,[39] where most of the dismantling had to be undertaken, pressure from the United States, and agitation within the Labour Party against the policy worked to change Bevin's mind and on 28 October he proposed a compromise solution to be worked out through the High Commissioners, which would establish a definitive final programme with only a small remaining number of plants for dismantling. It was to be the last Allied attempt to grapple with the problem from a position of relative strength.

Accordingly the High Commissioners met in closed session in Paris with their three foreign ministers on 10 November. The main problem was the French anxiety about the level of German steel production. Providing the West German government gave an understanding to work with the Ruhr Authority and the Military Security Board France was prepared to remove from the list of prohibited industries, and thus from the list of works to be dismantled, synthetic oil plant, synthetic rubber plant, all factories in Berlin, and all major steel works including the Thyssen factories in Hamborn, but excepting the Hermann Goering works in Salzgitter and the Krupp works in Essen. As far as steel was concerned Schuman insisted, however, that all steel plant should be placed under a special statutory authority so that it could not exceed the permitted limits of production.[40] All Schuman could obtain was that the High Commissioners would be empowered to put any or all of the steel works now to be retained out of action once more if in fact German steel output did exceed the permitted limits.[41] Any further extension of German

[38] ibid., p. 599, Memorandum of conversation by Acheson, 15 September 1949.
[39] In March 1950 a serious riot stopped the dismantling of the Watenstedt plant of the former Reichswerke Hermann Goering at Salzgitter.
[40] CP (49) 237, Memorandum by Bevin, 'Germany: meeting of British, United States and French foreign ministers', 16 November 1949.
[41] When this happened, in 1950, they did not do so.

steel-making capacity would require a licence from the Military Security Board. These terms were then embodied in the Petersberg agreements signed on 22 November, and thenceforward the German representative on the Ruhr Authority served as a full representative. To the embarrassment of all other member countries, who had appointed technical personnel, the German government nominated Franz Blücher, the Vice-Chancellor.

The possibility of a Franco-German association had not therefore been ruled out by the first actions of the West German government and the French government had pursued a careful, conciliatory path towards its objectives. French anxieties were more about the tendency of American policies to eliminate the bargaining advantages France still had over Germany. The Americans had given no support to France in the Ruhr Authority and in almost the first independent economic action of the West German government, the devaluation of the Deutschmark, France found only lukewarm support from the United States. The outcome was a further slight weakening of the French position.

The devaluation of the pound took place three days before Adenauer presented his government and its policy to the Bundestag. The first decision of any consequence which the Federal Government was called on to make, to establish a new exchange rate for the Deutschmark against the dollar, thus bore immediately on all issues which concerned the French government. Too large a devaluation would increase the competitiveness of German exports in Europe. The pound had been devalued by 30.5 per cent, the official export exchange rate of the franc by 22.5 per cent. The French proposed the mark be devalued by only 15 per cent. The German government proposed 22.5 per cent.

When the French ministers were in Washington in September Schuman had made a particular plea for direct American pressure to be brought to bear on the German government on the question of coal export prices.[42] The French government now insisted that the question of a new value for the mark should be tied by the High Commissioners to the end of dual coal and coke pricing by Germany. If the domestic and export prices of German coal and coke were equalized the French government would reluctantly accept a 20 per cent devaluation of the mark against the dollar.[43] Ironically, this was the level at which Erhard had originally wished to establish the mark, but he had been overruled by bankers, financial advisers and the Chancellor on the grounds that such a rate would cripple Germany's export capacity.[44] The French protest was followed by one in similar terms from Belgium and Luxembourg claiming that the new exchange rate proposed in Germany would 'wreck the

[42] ECA, 5, 'US-French conversations on economic problems', 15 September 1949.
[43] FRUS, 1949, III, Bruce to Washington, 22 September 1949, p. 451.
[44] ibid., McCloy to Washington, 22 September 1949, p. 452.

economies of France and the Benelux countries'.[45] America was not, however, prepared to tie the question of coal export prices to the new exchange rate.

There were good grounds for the American resistance. America's policy was to end dual pricing throughout Europe, not to enforce on the Federal Republic the abolition of a practice which was still standard in Britain. Nevertheless McCloy was now ordered to urge on Bonn a devaluation of only 20 per cent. At the High Commissioners' meeting on 24 September François-Poncet, the French High Commissioner, refused to agree to ratify any rate without an agreement to terminate dual coal pricing.[46] Once McCloy had persuaded the Bonn government to change its mind to conform to Erhard's original suggestion Acheson and Schuman met again for the second time in three days and Schuman agreed to the new rate on the understanding that American policy would actively pursue the ending of dual pricing by both West Germany and Britain.[47] The High Commissioners did not formally agree to the new German exchange rate until 28 September, by which date a further procedure had been established. A study group was to be set up to enquire into disparities in German coal prices with a view to eliminating them by the first day of 1950, 'if possible'.[48] Adenauer objected vigorously; he 'could not see what relation the internal price of coal had to the purposes of the occupation'.[49]

Needless to say the British cabinet had no intention of ending the dual price for British coal. They flatly declined to do so in December leaving the United States once more face to face with the Franco-German problem.[50] On 1 January 1950 the West German government did not abolish the dual pricing system but reduced the official differential between export and import prices from DM8.00 a tonne to DM5.82, later readjusted to DM5.46. As part of the readjustment domestic coal prices were increased, but by an amount which still left them well short of French domestic coal prices. This could be seen as a concession in view of Adenauer's categorical statement to the Bundestag in September that he would not increase the domestic coal price.[51] The German government, while insisting that the question of the price of coal exports was not, in its view, one to be settled either through the High Commission or the International Ruhr Authority, implied that it would be amenable to settlement through a more general European agreement which would change the status of the Federal Republic.

The worst tensions likely to emanate from the International Authority for

---

[45] ibid., Memorandum of conversation between Schuman and Acheson, 23 September 1949, p. 454. [46] ibid., McCloy to Washington, 24 September 1949, p. 458.
[47] Acheson Papers, 27, Visit of M. Schuman, 26 September 1949.
[48] FRUS, 1949, III, McCloy to Washington, 28 September 1949, p. 471.
[49] ibid., McCloy to Washington, 1 October 1949, p. 472.
[50] FRUS, 1949, IV, Kenney to Harriman, 13 December 1949, p. 460.
[51] F.R. Willis, *France, Germany and the New Europe, 1945–1967* (Stanford, 1965), p. 64.

the Ruhr were in fact avoided at the start of its existence by the sluggish performance of the French economy in 1949 and the fact that steel output in West Germany, although rising rapidly, was still so low. In the conditions briefly prevailing on the Western European coal market in winter 1949–50 German coal producers were by no means reluctant to see their output allocated a secure niche in a large export market by an international organization! The opportunity was taken to end the interest which the UN Economic Commission for Europe still had in the allocation of German coal. By summer 1950 the situation would again have changed completely and in the coal shortage which the 1950 steel boom once more produced France would invoke every power it could inside the Authority to obtain supplies of coal in a time of coal penury in Germany. Before that, however, the possibility of an economic understanding was brought nearer by the sudden, temporary relaxation of the fierce scramble for coal and coke and the postponement of the struggle expected inside the Ruhr Authority.

Three days before the Petersberg agreements France had embarked on a last attempt to get the full powers of the Allied Coal and Steel Control Boards transferred intact to the International Ruhr Authority. America, however, was determined that they should remain in the hands of the High Commission, thus giving the American High Commissioner the decisive voice.[52] When this attempt failed the French government followed it with an attempt to vest some of the powers of the High Commissioners themselves in the Ruhr Authority. These proposals, which were to go to the foreign ministers' conference in May 1950, were that the final decision about allocation be transferred to the Authority and that the commission should give a firm guarantee at once that when its powers on decartelization were transferred these too would go to the Authority and not to any other agency. The French proposals were both vague and complex, vague because numerous hints seem to have been dropped that if these powers were transferred France might in turn agree to the Ruhr Authority being extended in some way to cover the Saarland, Benelux and France. Although the State Department and the ECA readily agreed that this would make the Authority more palatable to Germany, it was not a suggestion which the ECA looked on with favour. An extended Authority of this kind 'could hardly fail to become engaged in the maintenance of prices and the restriction of production in the interests of producers'.[53] And

[52] FRUS, 1949, III, p. 295, United States interests, positions and tactics at Paris, 5 November 1949.
[53] ECA, 61, Problems of the International Authority for the Ruhr, 12 April 1950. 'Can one' asked the State Department briefing for the May meeting, 'confidently hope that a new organization consisting of the present members of the Ruhr Authority could undertake investment planning with respect to their steel industries (or their coal industries) in a manner which would be less open to objection than the only organized inter-governmental attempt in this field that has actually taken place? This would appear to be extremely doubtful since the OEEC at least has the advantage of including in its membership countries whose interests are primarily those of consumers of steel rather than producers.'

since it meant weakening the powers of the American High Commissioner the State Department could not ultimately agree to it either. All roads to a Franco-German settlement through the Ruhr Authority seemed to be closed politically, in spite of the temporary peace which prevailed there.

Yet the international scope for a direct French initiative towards Germany outside the sphere of the Authority had increased. Adenauer's foreign policy left no doubt of his desire for a close co-operation with France. After September 1949 the United States had been obliged to accept that its policy of integrating western Europe through British political and economic leadership was neither possible nor, indeed, necessarily in American interests if it were to provoke British actions which would prevent the achievement of a wider multilateralism. In spite of the prevailing view in the ECA that to extend the Ruhr Authority's powers to Benelux and the Saarland would be against American interests, in so far as it would open the door to the return of the coal and steel cartels, the fact of the matter was that the integration of Western Europe was now only likely to be obtained through supporting a French initiative, and that this was the area where the scope for a French initiative was not diminishing.

Although the Occupation Statute contained a promise that within eighteen months it would be revised to extend West German jurisdiction, the areas in which it imposed limits on the freedom of action by the Federal government made up a forbidding list; defence, foreign affairs, occupation costs, matters relating to the federal and land constitutions, reparations, foreign trade and exchange controls, and international borrowing, as well as the powers over decartelization, the power to restrict ownership of Ruhr industries and the power to allocate Ruhr coal between domestic and foreign markets which was retained by the International Ruhr Authority. From the moment Adenauer was elected Chancellor he made it the prime objective of his foreign policy to have these restrictions on the full sovereignty of the Federal Republic removed. The path he chose was one of the closest possible collaboration with the western powers, probably in the hope that German economic strength would fairly soon establish the country as an indispensable and perhaps even the strongest member of the Western European bloc. Whatever the variety of public arguments put forward to defend this policy, Adenauer's basic assumption seems to have been that no short-term solution to the problem of German reunification was now possible. Once the time came when such a solution might be envisaged it would only be a satisfactory one if the Federal Republic could act from a position of strength, and this it could only obtain within the western bloc. If the time did not come, it would be even more dangerous to abandon the closest possible co-operation with the western powers.[54] It was

---

[54] For an analysis of Adenauer's motives see W. Besson, 'Die Anfänge der bundesrepublikanischen Aussenpolitik' in G. Lehmbruch (ed.) *Demokratisches System und politische Praxis in der Bundesrepublik* (Munich, 1971).

this policy which offered the political opportunity to the French government which the Schuman Plan proposals were to seize, and without Adenauer's autocratic imposition of his own foreign policy on the Federal government these proposals would surely not have been made.

While tenaciously disputing the questions of dismantling and the mark exchange rate, Adenauer hinted at a solution on the largest possible scale. This was, even more strikingly, his attitude towards French actions in the Saarland. The Saar Landtag had approved in November 1947 a constitution instituting a monetary and customs union with France and effectively making the Saarland independent from Germany. Over the course of 1949, as the Federal Republic emerged, these earlier decisions proved increasingly displeasing to a broad spectrum of political opinion in the Saarland and it no longer looked as though France could rely on them as a way of retaining control of the Saar's resources. In February 1950 the French began to negotiate a convention by which the Saarland would receive autonomy but remain separated from Germany. The outcome of the convention, signed in March, was that France retained financial and customs authority in the Saarland and was given a long-term lease on the Saar coal-mines which would thus continue to operate in a French administrative framework and contribute to French supply, even though the rest of the area became independent of France in matters of day-to-day administration. The mines would remain under French control until a peace treaty was signed and in return the French government would pay a rent of 400 million francs ($1.14 million) annually. The convention also agreed on an attempt to equalize production costs in the coal and steel industries between the Saarland and France. The origins of this attempt were that the earlier proposals for a complete merger had not been at all welcome to the Lorraine steel industry, subjected to full competition on its own market from a steel industry operating at production costs nearer to the German than the French level.[55] The day after the convention was signed Adenauer described it as 'a decision against Europe'.[56] The West German government then announced its decision to delay its entry into the recently formed Council of Europe. At the same time Adenauer repeatedly offered through various unofficial channels to negotiate an association of French and German industries on equal terms or even a Franco-German economic union. He left no doubt that any initiative in this direction would be welcomed. This had been the attitude of several German politicians in the Ruhr itself to the Ruhr Authority. During the last debates on the 'socialization' bill in the Landtag of North Rhine-Westphalia the Minister-President, Karl Arnold, had publicly held out the hope that the bill would not be killed but serve as the basis of an equal agreement between

[55] J. Freymond, *The Saar Conflict 1945–1955* (London, 1960), pp. 61 ff; P. Fischer, *Die Saar zwischen Deutschland und Frankreich: Politische Entwicklung von 1945–1959* (Frankfurt, 1959), pp. 81–90.
[56] Willis, *France*, p. 76.

France, the Benelux and West Germany on the coal industry, and in a new year broadcast after the publication of the Ruhr Statute he repeated the wish.[57]

In the United States the opinions of the new Secretary of State, Acheson, had moved strongly in one direction. He had come to believe that negotiations over Germany's role in Europe had been so long and tortuous, and even by November 1949 had still not clearly produced the result that America wanted, because it was not really in the power of the United States alone to produce such an outcome. It was in the end only France which had the power to fulfil America's ambitions. German economic recovery was indispensable, but 'the goal of ERP is fundamentally political and France is the keystone of continental Western Europe'.[58] This conviction was finally established by Britain's actions in the 1949 sterling crisis.

On 21 October the more important American ambassadors in Western Europe, together with Harriman, McCloy and Admiral Alan G. Kirk, from Moscow, were brought for two days to Paris to discuss the whole range of American policies in Europe. Acheson provided them with an analysis of his own thinking. He asked them to recognize the limits on British actions and on American power and to accept that 'the key to progress towards integration is in French hands'.[59] But what could France specifically be expected to do? The answer came in the conclusion of his letter.

> By progress towards integration, as mentioned above, I have in mind the earliest possible decision by the Europeans as to objectives and commitments among them on a timetable for the creation of supra-national institutions, operating on a less than unanimity basis for dealing with specific, economic, social and perhaps other problems.[60]

The ambassadors thought this unrealistic.[61] Three days after they had told Acheson so he received Bevin's statement of the limits of Britain's commitment to Europe, that Britain could not 'accept obligations to western Europe which would prevent or restrict the implementation of our responsibilities elsewhere'.[62] Five days later Acheson decided, in spite of the ambassadors' pessimism, to reject their advice and make a personal appeal to Schuman to take an initiative along the lines he had suggested to the ambassadors' meeting and thus reconcile West Germany to Western Europe.

> I believe we would be wise to give an 'advance' of good will to the Germans in view of the strength of the safeguards which we have erected and our ability to call upon the powers we have reserved. Although we have these powers we cannot reasonably hope to recreate a German will to co-operate if we once permit it to die for lack of nourishment.

[57] D. Hüwel, *Karl Arnold. Eine politische Biographie* (Wuppertal, 1980), pp. 179–80.
[58] ECA, RG286, 53A 405, 1, State Department briefing papers, 'France', 31 December 1948.
[59] FRUS, 1949, IV, p. 470, Acheson to Paris, 19 October 1949.   [60] ibid., p. 472.
[61] ibid., p. 342, Bruce to Acheson, 22 October 1949.
[62] ibid., p. 347, Personal message to the Secretary of State from Bevin, 25 October 1949.

I believe that our policy in Germany, and the development of a German Government which can take its place in Western Europe, depends on the assumption by your country of leadership in Europe on these problems.[63]

If France were now to come forward with a specific plan coupling a solution of the Franco-German problem to the idea of European integration, that plan could fly in the face of all the former, grander, more liberal American ideas of economic integration. In the interests of American foreign policy the State Department would now support it. When Acheson next left for Paris in May 1950 Congress still refused to delete from the appropriations bill the statement that the object of Marshall Aid was the economic unification and federation of Europe. For France, it was now or never. Before the Federal Republic burst its economic shackles asunder it might be brought, in return for entry into the western European community on more equal terms, into the sort of regulated market sharing agreement on which the United States government had so far looked with abhorrence as a basis for the economic reconstruction of Europe. In Washington, too, the way was suddenly open for the Schuman Plan.

But once we pass to the question, why did the Schuman proposals take the precise form they did, it becomes obvious that this analysis confined to the international level is insufficient. The nature of the proposals was also determined in Paris by purely domestic considerations, both political and economic.

Very little is said anywhere in this book about the various European political movements advocating some form of European political integration, because they exercised so little influence on policy decisions and on events. But as a political constituency they were there, particularly in France, Italy and West Germany, and to their ideals could be attached powerful, if transient, political emotions. The strength of these emotions brought these disparate groups from many countries together in 1947 in the European Union of Federalists, and from the conjoint pressures of this and associated groups there met in 1948 The Hague Congress of the European Movement where so many resounding speeches proclaiming the ideal of European unity were made by politicians of no little prominence.

When Count Richard Coudenhove-Kalergi polled European parliamentarians, albeit in an unsystematic way, to discover whether they approved in principle of European federation, 57 per cent of the Italian deputies and 44 per cent of the French replied in the affirmative before Marshall's speech.[64] It was evident in 1949 that a settlement between France and Germany might be more pragmatic if it could obtain the support of all those diverse groups who pinned

[63] FRUS, 1949, III, pp. 624–5, Personal message from Acheson to Schuman, 30 October 1949. Melandri, in his otherwise thorough account of American attitudes and policy towards European integration, seems not to have noticed that Acheson rejected the advice of the ambassadors' meeting. He emphasizes rather the ambassadors' own conclusions.

[64] W. Lipgens, *A History of European Integration 1945–1947*: vol. 1, *The Formation of the European Unity Movement* (Oxford, 1982), pp. 437 ff.

their hopes on some form of supra-national European organization. It would probably be a great mistake to underestimate the changeability and fluidity of political opinion in occupied Germany, but public opinion surveys there showed a high and consistent level of support for the idea of a western European union.[65] It was seen chiefly as a barrier to any further war and to the spread of communism, and a smaller proportion of respondents saw it as a barrier to undue American influence over western Europe. But the rapidity with which the idea developed in 1949 and 1950 probably drew on deeper wells of emotion. Sacrifice of national interest in a united Europe offered redemption from the awful sins of the past. A month after the Schuman Plan was proposed, before any of the details were negotiated, it met with a greater degree of approval in Germany than at any time in the subsequent six years.[66]

This strand of political opinion in both countries was brought into greater prominence by the formation of the Council of Europe. The Hague Congress had made the creation of a European council, a prototype European parliament, its main demand and had instituted a working party to devise a scheme under the former French Prime Minister, Paul Ramadier. The French government had then taken up the idea at the Consultative Council of the Brussels Pact countries, seeing it as yet another possible route to supporting a reconstruction which provided security against Germany. The British government had reluctantly accepted, determined that the Council of Europe should remain entirely powerless. The negotiations over its constitution between July 1948 and January 1949 had thus been disputatious. The French government wanted the Council of Europe to exercise certain parliamentary functions in order to make it a credible political framework into which West Germany could be inserted – and held. France wanted more members in the Council, wanted them to be elected or chosen in some way other than by government nomination, and wanted them to vote freely.[67] The British government, on the contrary, was determined to avoid any suggestion of a popular European assembly.[68] Had it not been for a threat by France to take the initiative and create such an organization unilaterally the Council of Europe might never have come into being. The long wrangle did however serve to keep the idea of a 'European' solution before parliamentary and public opinion and the outcome was yet another loose association between Western European countries, one more buffer poised for the shock of the encounter with the politics of the Federal Republic.

When the Assembly of the Council of Europe met it was, not surprisingly,

[65] A.J. Merritt and R.L. Merritt, *Public Opinion in Occupied Germany. The OMGUS Surveys, 1945–1949* (Urbana, 1970), pp. 217, 296–7.
[66] K.W. Deutsch and L.J. Edinger, *Germany Rejoins the Powers. Mass Opinion, Interest Groups, and Elites in Contemporary German Foreign Policy* (Stanford, 1959), p. 157.
[67] FO 371/79214, Paris embassy to London, 21 January 1949.
[68] 'We must avoid creating a kind of chamber of echoes where cranks could make their voices heard,' Ernest Bevin in ibid. Events have shown this to have been an impossible ambition.

inundated with a variety of motions calling for European integration. One proposal was that it should set up a powerful economic department, formed out of sections transferred from the OEEC and the UN Economic Commission for Europe, which would draw up proposals for the progressive integration of the economies of the member states. This was supported by both Guy Mollet and André Philip for the Section Française de l'Internationale Ouvrière (SFIO) and by Schuman and Bidault for the Mouvement Populaire Républicain (MRP) as well as by a bizarre collection of other people including the first post-war Prime Minister of Italy, Ferruccio Parri, a future Prime Minister of Britain, Harold Macmillan, and a future President of Sénégal, Léopold Senghor. The British government's view was that they 'would be opposed even to the study in Strasbourg of the many subjects covered by the Resolution'.[69] None the less, the debates on the succession of motions with similar implications, even if no commitment was involved, demonstrated the growing variety of groups to whom an economic solution of the problem of a Franco-German settlement which embodied a supra-national approach to European integration would appeal.

The interest in such a policy was emphasized by the re-emergence in 1949 of a school of opinion among both French and German steel-makers which repeated one idea of the Seydoux proposals for a Franco-German settlement in 1920, that there should be French investment in the reconstruction of the German steel industry.[70] The chairman of the board of trustees appointed under Law No. 75 to supervise the decartelization of the German industry and its transfer back to private ownership, Heinrich Dinkelbach, publicly espoused such a solution. So did Robert Lehr who was widely regarded as the spokesman in the CDU for the Iron and Steel Association and who, before the conclusion of the European Coal and Steel Community treaty, became a minister in the German government.

In February and in April 1949 the two congresses of the European Movement in Brussels and Westminster singled out the coal and steel industries as one area in which a common European organization could be created. But about what type of organization it would be they were not so clear. The impression given by the debates is that it would have been mainly controlled and managed by the firms themselves although there would have been an 'intergovernmental board' and, to retain the support of French socialists like André Philip who backed it enthusiastically at both conferences, trade union representation on the management committee.[71] Philip became chairman of the Basic Industries Sub-Committee of the Economic Committee of the Council of Europe and from this position he persuaded the Economic Committee of the Council to

[69] FO 371/78101, London to UK delegation in Strasbourg, 29 August 1949.
[70] The Seydoux proposals are analysed in M. Trachtenberg, *Reparation in World Politics. France and European Economic Diplomacy, 1916–1923* (New York, 1980), pp. 174 ff.
[71] FO 371/76694, Memorandum of conversation between Sir Harold Butler and Roger Stevens, 18 February 1949.

pass a resolution in December 1949 calling for a public authority for the European steel industry, to advise on investment, prices and production as the first step towards similar sectoral planning in coal, oil, electricity and transport.

Lastly, the argument in France over the status of the Modernization Plan and the Planning Commissariat has to be considered to understand both why the proposals took the form they did and why they were formulated in the way they were. Throughout 1949 the position of the Planning Commissariat had looked increasingly frail. The successful recovery of output in 1947 and 1948 followed by the faltering in 1949 had first soothed the anxieties about French recovery which had given the Planning Commissariat its initial opportunity and then raised doubts about whether the Modernization Plan could either achieve its economic targets or was necessary any longer as a basis for national reconstruction. In November 1949 the cabinet refused to give responsibility for the investment of public funds to the Planning Commissariat and prominent associations of employers launched a public campaign to abandon the principles and methods of the Modernization Plan on the grounds that a 'normal' situation had now been reached and persistence with the planning targets could only encourage over-investment.[72]

In the event the planners won the day and one reason for their victory was that the French cabinet could not face a future in which it was tied within Finebel to a much more liberal trade and payments relationship with West Germany. The opportunity had to be taken to reinstate the Monnet Plan as a guideline for foreign policy if it was to be safe as a guideline for domestic policy. The Schuman Plan was invented to safeguard the Monnet Plan.

The implication of the descriptions of the way the Schuman proposals were formulated is that the new policy was created in a daring and highly original way inside the Planning Commissariat and outside the normal channels of foreign policy formulation in the Ministry of Foreign Affairs. This is the view which Monnet and his colleagues and disciples have assiduously propagated.[73] A small cabal led by Monnet himself, it is suggested, acting in speed and secrecy, prepared the proposals, which were ignored by Bidault but then eagerly taken up by Schuman who was looking for a new policy. For fear that so revolutionary a departure in policy and in policy-making be stopped at the outset by vested interests Schuman, it has been implied, deliberately kept it secret from all but his most important cabinet colleagues, rushed it through cabinet with the Prime Minister's help, and announced it the same day. The new policy thus appears as the work of an enlightened cabal who by acting boldly and secretly changed the continent's history. This view, which owes much to Gerbet, has been accepted lock, stock and barrel by subsequent writers.[74]

[72] R.F. Kuisel, *Capitalism and the State in Modern France* (Cambridge, 1940), pp. 241 ff.
[73] Monnet, *Memoirs*, pp. 288 ff.
[74] P. Gerbet, 'La Genèse du Plan Schuman des origines à la déclaration du 9 mai 1950', *Revue française de science politique*, vi, 1956; Willis, *France*, pp. 83 ff.; R. Mayne, *The Community of Europe. Past, Present and Future* (New York, 1962), pp. 90 ff; W. Loth, *Die Teilung der Welt 1941–1955* (Munich, 1980), p. 249.

A certain saintliness has been conferred on all those who touched the Schuman proposals from Monnet and Schuman down to the professor of law who drafted a version of them, Schuman's *directeur de cabinet*, and Adenauer's chief of staff. Even now they do not lack their hagiographers, often from the ranks of those on whom the light shone. But from where else but the Planning Commissariat was policy likely to emerge? That the text was prepared in consultation with Monnet and other high officials of the Planning Commissariat was not at all exceptional. From Monnet's first proposals for an economic plan the Ministry of Foreign Affairs had sought to use the Plan as a justification of French policy in Europe to their allies. The common interest of the Ministry of Foreign Affairs and the Planning Commissariat had not weakened and, if there was no possibility of further advance to a settlement through .the Ruhr Authority, it was up to the planners to think of something else.

How far the text of Monnet's first proposals was amended in the Ministry of Foreign Affairs is difficult to establish until all the relevant archives are made available. The versions of parts of the statement and the account of its preparation given by Monnet suggest there was considerable alteration. There were also alternative proposals which had to be rebuffed, such as the idea that at first only the Ruhr and Saar should be placed under a common regime.[75] That the substance of the proposals came from Monnet and the Planning Commissariat need not be doubted and the timing of their submission reflects Monnet's shrewd sense of the stage at which French policy had arrived. Alphand and indeed the Foreign Ministry as a whole had been in search of some such policy since June 1948. Civil servants have not been able to organize the same level of publicity for their actions since, and they were not so free to claim public credit at the time, but it would not be unfair on the evidence to say that some of them, who are never numbered in the gallery of European saints, had as much claim to the new policy as Monnet and his circle. The first origins of the Schuman Plan were really in the Ministry of Foreign Affairs during the London conference.

But the ultimate credit for the Schuman plan must go to Schuman himself. He had the courage to act quickly. Britain had not even been consulted and the proposals were made in the full knowledge that they might mean the end of the Franco-British co-operation in western Europe on which French policy towards Germany had been based since the end of the war. Such an outcome was not certain and was definitely not desired, but the risk was large. In taking it Schuman had the courage to seize the moment and translate into reality a complexity of vague interrelationships, suggestions and ideas which the fearfulness of others had left trembling on the brink of actuality.

[75] FJM, AMG 1/2 bis/1, Contre proposition pour une autre procédure, 6 May 1950.

On 8 May Acheson arrived in Paris on his way to the foreign ministers' meeting in London. Schuman mentioned to him 'quite casually' and in general terms that he might, if he could, persuade the cabinet at its meeting the following morning' to make a foreign policy initiative of some importance towards Germany.[76] That evening Monnet explained the full importance of what was happening to McCloy who had also come to Paris and McCloy told Acheson who, however, was obliged to keep the matter secret. The following day the proposals were approved by the cabinet and at six o'clock Schuman gave a press conference at which he read out his proposal, 'that the entire French-German production of coal and steel be placed under a joint High Authority, within an organization open to the participation of other European nations.' This would provide some real immediate function for a supranational political body.

> By pooling basic production and by creating a new High Authority whose decisions will be binding on France, Germany and the other countries who may subsequently join, this proposal will create the first concrete foundation for a European federation which is so indispensable for the preservation of peace.[77]

The functions of that High Authority were then specified; to modernize production, to supply coal and steel on equal terms within a common market, to develop joint exports, and to equalize working and living conditions. This meant an investment plan, price equalization, a reconversion fund to permit closures in the cause of rationalization, and the standardization of freight rates. The setting up of the High Authority would not prejudge the question of ownership, but the Authority would take into account all the powers conferred on the International Authority for the Ruhr.

Although Schuman's statement was received at the time without many signs that it was an event of special importance, within a very short space it came to be thought of as a watershed in the post-war world, a moment when things going badly were reversed, a new vision of hope for post-war Europe, and it has been generally so considered since. Much of the emotion which was so quickly attached to it was attracted because it seemed to offer some prospect of European unity and peace at the very moment when those ideals seemed no longer to have any political force. After the disillusionment of the return of familiar national governmental figures and systems, after the worse disillusionments of 1947 with the division of Europe and the Cold War, after the failure once more to produce any real promise of a settlement acceptable to Germany, after the failure of pressure groups for European unity, Schuman

---

[76] FRUS, 1950, III, Acheson to Washington, 10 May 1950.
[77] There is a full text of the proposal in *Le Monde*, 11 May 1950.

specifically linked the settlement with Germany to the hope of a united Europe. In so doing he tapped a vein of hope and idealism which had been buried even more deeply under the common earth of post-war history and associated a diplomatic initiative with a cause. Thus 9 May 1950 and the Schuman proposals soon came to be seen as the starting-point of a united Europe. Especially was this so in the 1950s and 1960s, when large numbers still believed the process of European integration to be progressive and irreversible and the Schuman proposals to have been the first date of a new historical epoch.

The immediate danger, however, was that the proposals would appear in America as the first step in an attempt to revive protectionist cartels as a framework for European industry. Thus into the proposal was inserted the statement:

> Unlike an international cartel whose purpose is to divide up and exploit national markets through restrictive practices, and the maintenance of high profits, the projected organization will insure the fusion of markets and the expansion of production.[78]

This, nevertheless, was the aspect of the proposals which Acheson was least convinced about when he was told about them and it remained the one major worry which they presented to Washington. Well aware that this would be the case, Monnet's group had presented a memorandum to McCloy on the eve of the announcement setting out the reasons why the proposals would result in an arrangement entirely different from the pre-war cartel.[79] McCloy, as American High Commissioner in Germany, was a key figure because without the permission of the members of the Allied High Commission West Germany would not even be able to embark on the negotiations. The memorandum stressed that what was at stake for France was a policy which would permit the continuing increase of output and productivity by enlargement of markets and rationalization of production. This was certainly the point at which French and American conceptions of the economic future coincided. As the Cold War became more frightening, as the rate of increase of output in the French economy slowed down, and as more conservative voices were heard in France, it became a matter of great concern to the Planning Commissariat that the momentum gained in the first three and a half years not be lost through a relapse into the defensive attitudes of the 1930s especially in the face of the rapid German revival. If the means by which it sought to achieve this aim were not so unremittingly liberal as the ideology which served America's ends, the coincidence was sufficient to make it plausible that the Schuman Plan might

[78] FRUS, 1950, III, p. 694.
[79] CAB 134/295, Plowden to Makins, 10 May 1950. Almost certainly the same document passed on to Acheson and translated in FRUS, 1950, III, Acheson to Washington, 12 May 1950, p. 697.

eventually be firmly directed against restrictions on output. The existence of the High Authority would mean that all decisions taken would be open and public and those decisions would not be taken purely by representatives of the industries concerned. Later, France and America were to make joint representations to Adenauer not to appoint representatives of the steel industry to take an official part in the negotiations. In so far as price fixing and market sharing agreements would continue they would be only transitional.

Neither Acheson nor the State Department were ever entirely convinced by this view of the matter in spite of Dulles's enthusiastic recommendations. Dulles, it seems, had discussed similar ideas with Marshall at the Moscow Council of Foreign Ministers.[80] The State Department had three 'major difficulties' with the proposals – that they would result in a protectionist cartel, that Germany's association with it would slow down the pace of technological advance there, and that ultimately political considerations would override economic rationality.[81] From the documentary evidence at the moment available it seems these hesitations, which did not prevent the State Department from welcoming the proposals, were overcome by a change of heart and an almost wholly favourable verdict on the part of Harriman and the ECA. The proposals were now judged by the ECA to be an 'important step' towards trade liberalization and the concept of a single competitive market.[82] They implied the removal of tariffs, which of course was one of the ECA's main concerns, and the same ultimate goal of higher productivity which the ECA wished to achieve. The danger of a protectionist cartel was not absent, the ECA considered, but without the proposals it was surely greater.[83]

The American attitude was thus resolved, although a careful eye was kept on the course of the negotiations themselves. As they proceeded American anxieties began to develop again. The weakening of the powers of the High Authority in favour of those of the Council of Ministers which was added to it, the complicated price fixing for coal, the retention of coal distribution organizations, and above all the artificial coal prices fixed to allow subsidies to be paid to the Belgian mining industry, all confirmed some of the earlier fears.[84] But by this time the situation had radically changed. The Korean war and the rumour of West German rearmament had raised the possibility that the Federal Republic might not now have to accept the Schuman proposals as a way of getting rid of the limitations on its sovereignty. Whether the United States should back the French proposals for a European defence community became the determining question and when Washington decided to give full support to the concept of a European army it not only could no longer

[80] FRUS, 1950, III, Webb to Acheson, 10 May 1950, p. 695.
[81] ibid., Webb to Acheson, 11 May 1950, p. 696.
[82] ibid., Harriman to Acheson, 20 May 1950, p. 702.
[83] ECA, 33, Simons to Jeffers, 26 July 1950.
[84] FRUS, 1950, III, Byroade to Perkins, 9 September 1950, p. 747; Webb to Paris, 3 October 1950, p. 754.

withdraw support from the Schuman Plan on economic grounds, but it had to back it and even cajole Germany to join it if the chance of West German rearmament was not to be irretrievably lost. All the United States could do after the outbreak of the Korean war was to try to salvage from the Schuman proposals whatever it could of the original American conception of a free-trade union in Europe. There was not much that could be saved and acceptance of the Schuman Plan meant a reversal of thirty years of American foreign policy.

In the 1920s the United States, like Britain, had had a vague vision of European unity as emerging, if it ever did, as the outcome of a network of most-favoured-nation clauses – just as the optimistic liberals of the 1860s had hoped – because this seemed the only way that European unity could be a stage towards world unity. This was the basis of American objections to proposals such as the Briand Plan or the Tardieu Plan, which in their attempts to create a European economic framework to contain Germany had foreshadowed the Schuman Plan. All this was now thrown over. In the face of such momentous issues the querulous voice of the American steel industry complaining that it would now be faced with a government-backed European steel cartel from which it would be excluded went unheeded. Thirty years later, at the moment of writing, its complaints are much louder, largely justified, and very much heeded.

When, in answering the few questions at the press conference where he made his proposals, Schuman agreed that they were 'a leap in the dark', the deepest obscurity was that which lay on the other side of the Channel. If the American government could be convinced that the proposals could be presented as in accordance with America's own interest in integration, if the German government could be convinced that the proposals were an offer to treat on almost equal terms, the voices in both countries which had been clamouring for some similar solution would be raised in enthusiastic support. But nothing could disguise the fact that France had this time taken a bold step towards creating her own Western Europe without regard to Britain and in the full knowledge that official British policy was opposed to such ideas. Acheson tells us that when Bevin was informed he flew into 'a towering rage'.[85]

Independently though the French had acted, however, they spared no effort of diplomacy to bring Britain into the proposed European framework on their own terms. Schuman travelled to London immediately after the announcement and on 14 May Monnet with other members of the Planning Commissariat arrived to explain and persuade. The task of finding out exactly what the implications were for Britain was delegated to Plowden, so that the meeting appeared in a rather ironical light as a continuation of the Monnet-Plowden talks of the previous year. Plowden was told to discover whether Britain would be able to go into the proposed talks 'without

[85] D. Acheson, *Sketches from Life of Men I Have Known* (New York, 1961), p. 39.

commitment'.[86] Monnet's own version of his approach to these talks, a version which seems to be borne out by the record, is that the one point on which he would make no concession was that all parties to the talks must accept beforehand the principle of the existence of a High Authority whose decisions would be binding. The political principles involved in the proposals were sacrosanct; the technical details were all negotiable, for the simple reason that none of them had yet been decided. As Monnet explained at the beginning of the talks France intended to reach an agreement with Germany anyway whatever the British reaction, so that great flexibility in the economic details was essential.

The talks with Plowden showed that the enthusiastic ideas of the Planning Commissariat were considerably removed from future political realities as they were to emerge from the negotiations. Monnet thought the appointment of a United Nations observer would be essential.[87] Hirsch, who was to be his successor as head of the Planning Commissariat, said that it would be a matter of indifference whether steel production were located in Germany or France since national frontiers would be wiped out. Members of the High Authority, he said, would be appointed for their technical expertise and nationality would be irrelevant. They could be British, or Swiss, or even American.[88] That last possibility, no doubt, was some way from the mind of Schuman and Adenauer.

Plowden's advice, based on these rather vague conversations, was that participation was likely to be economically advantageous to Britain and that Britain should therefore try to take part in the discussions. The Foreign Office did not, however, want Britain to do so 'unreservedly'.[89] Meanwhile the views were sought of the National Coal Board and of the British Iron and Steel Federation, the owners' association of the steel industry. At his final press conference before he left Britain Schuman seemed to leave open the possibility that Britain might indeed be able to be associated with the proposals without an entire acceptance of their political implications. This was the policy endorsed by the Economic Policy Committee of the cabinet on 23 May[90] and expressed in the official British notes of 25 and 27 May.[91] The French ambassador, René Massigli, in a conversation with Kenneth Younger, the Minister of State at the Foreign Office, on 28 May, did not rule out this possibility, but when the official French reply came back on 30 May it left no room for manoeuvre; the political negotiations must be begun by all on the basis that there would be a High Authority and a transfer of sovereignty.

[86] CAB 134/293, Meeting of Committee on Proposed Franco-German Coal and Steel Authority, 15 May 1950. [87] CAB 134/295, Minutes of a meeting at the Hyde Park Hotel, 16 May 1950.
[88] CAB 134/295, Minute by Berthoud of conversation with Hirsch, 19 May 1950.
[89] CAB 134/293, Report by Plowden to Committee on Franco-German Coal and Steel Authority, 17 May 1950. [90] CAB 134/293, Economic Policy Committee, 23 May 1950.
[91] Cmd. 7970, *Anglo-French Discussions Regarding French Proposals for the Western European Coal, Iron and Steel Industries*, May–June 1950.

402   *The Reconstruction of Western Europe 1945–51*

The outcome of the consultations with the relevant industrial bodies, with other industries, and with the leaders of the trade unions concerned justified the French stance, which seems to have stiffened after Schuman's return to Paris. The British Iron and Steel Federation was all in favour of an agreement to limit competition and feared exclusion from any such agreement, especially in so far as it might endanger ore supplies from Sweden and North Africa. On the other hand it would have wished any such agreement to preserve the home market and allow imports on equal terms only when there was 'excess' demand in the domestic market, like the pre-war International Steel Cartel. This seems to have been very much the view taken by its European associates also. All would have preferred to see a return of the Cartel, secure home markets, and no increase in governmental supervision. The steel manufacturer Hermann Reusch later resigned his post as economic adviser to the German government during the negotiations, publicly demanding a return to the pre-war Cartel as official policy. The dangers of competition on the domestic market and of ultimate government or international control over the industry were the chief subjects of attack in the national campaign launched against the proposals by the French owners' association.[92]

Although the British Iron and Steel Federation did not foresee a future without any agreement with its European rivals, exclusion from the proposed arrangements was scarcely a dangerous threat to sales. Western Europe accounted for less than 5 per cent of British steel exports (table 56). If the

Table 56   Proportion of total steel exports to future members of the ECSC (%)

	1938	1946	1947	1948	1949	1950	1951	1952
Belgium/ Luxembourg	27.0	22.2	19.3	19.4	18.9	26.3	20.7	27.9
France	15.2	–	–	23.4	11.3	17.3	12.1	18.3
West Germany	17.5	–	–	91.0*	22.2†	15.7	13.9	15.0
United Kingdom	3.8	n.a.	4.8	0.6	6.1	4.4	4.9	6.8

Source: British Iron and Steel Federation, *Statistical Yearbooks.*

* Includes Austria.   † Bizone.

political implications of the proposals did have to be accepted in full the Federation would on balance have preferred to stay out, in spite of the strong British competitive position, because it regarded the defence of a large acquired position outside Europe as more important than the possible opportunity of expanding a small position inside Europe.

Prices were lower and it was believed that productivity was higher in the British steel industry than in any of its continental competitors in 1950

[92] The campaign is analysed in H.W. Ehrmann, 'The French trade associations and the ratification of the Schuman Plan', *World Politics*, 6 (4), 1954.

(table 57) and it was at least as well equipped to withstand the revival of the German steel industry as was the French.[93] If wage levels were to be equalized

Table 57   An index of comparative domestic prices of steel (January 1950)

	Britain	France	West Germany	Belgium	Luxem-bourg	Italy	Nether-lands
Angles	100	127	109	121	129	200	145
Joists	100	107	100	–	123	–	–
Plates	100	134	104	119	125	222	145
Hot rolled strip	100	112	103	–	117	–	130
Rails	100	126	112	133	140	–	–
Sheets	100	124	115	–	–	–	–
Merchant bars	100	111	91	101	109	176	127

Source: CAB 134/295, Report of Working Party, 'Schuman proposals for an international coal and steel authority in western Europe', 16 June 1950. The prices are those supplied by the British Iron and Steel Federation.

it would be even better equipped, because this would mean a relative increase in production costs outside Britain. Britain had as much to gain, economically, in participating in any agreement as the other countries. When Schuman made his proposals steel markets were slack, which was some justification for the British manufacturers' response, although in the end the question resolved itself into one of Britain's willingness to compete in the future on relatively equal terms in its own as well as in export markets with the German steel industry.

Here we are touching on the unwritten and seldom spoken fears in Britain. The experience of the Labour government had been to start in a situation where only a seemingly impossible increase in exports could permit them to carry through their chosen domestic policy. That increase had been all but achieved, but only in a world market from which two of the most important competitors had been temporarily removed. The same anxieties for the future as governed the policy on international payments governed the attitude to the return of Germany to international markets. The natural reaction of the industry was to hold on to what it had and in a wider context the government's reaction was the same.

The National Coal Board's attitude was less ambiguous. For the coal industry anything resembling the Schuman proposals was a quite unwanted departure. Orders to reallocate output or to close pits emanating from a High Authority, as well as the apparent intention to give that Authority power over investment policy, were unacceptable because 'the NCB is sure of getting a fair hearing from His Majesty's Government.'[94] The shortsightedness of this

[93]   CAB 134/294, Views of the British Iron and Steel Federation, June 1950.
[94]   CAB 134/294, Views of the National Coal Board, 2 June 1950.

view may be compared with that of the General Secretary of the Iron and Steel Trades Confederation, who argued that British steel workers would not wish in future to lose the wage benefits accruing from the generally higher level of productivity in the British steel industry than in the French and German industries.[95]

These unfavourable opinions were put forward as the close wrangle over whether Britain could alter the terms of participation came to a head. The French government obtained the initial acceptance of the terms of the negotiation from Germany, Italy, Belgium, Luxembourg and the Netherlands, although the Netherlands reserved the right to leave the negotiations at any time. This agreement was in the form of a draft communiqué and on 31 May the British government offered to put its name to the same communiqué providing there was still no firm commitment to the High Authority but instead a commitment to negotiate 'in a constructive spirit'.[96] It seems that at that stage Schuman still sought a compromise to allow Britain to join the talks. The Planning Commissariat made sure that in trying to amend the communiqué the French government did not alter the text in such a way as to abandon its original position, otherwise there would have been 'only some kind of OEEC'.[97] Thus, when it arrived in Britain the amended text made none of the hoped-for concessions and was accompanied by an ultimatum requiring a definite answer by 8 p.m. on 2 June. The British government made one last effort by proposing a meeting of the ministers of all the countries concerned to devise a different way of going about the negotiations, but this was certain to be declined.

The cabinet met on 2 June and there seems to have been a general, resentful agreement to give a negative answer. 'No British government could be expected to accept such a commitment without having had any opportunity to assess the consequences which it might involve for our key industries, our export trade and our level of employment.'[98] There was some foolish discussion about whether the Allied High Commission might not be used to stop the West German government taking part in the negotiations, followed by the conclusion that 'it should be made clear to the French government that we were surprised to receive such summary treatment in a matter of this importance.'[99] Britain had in fact already used its voice in the Council of the Allied High Commission to suggest that West Germany, since it was in economic and political tutelage, ought not to be freely allowed to negotiate and that an observer from the High Commission should be appointed.[100] But that suggestion had been firmly put down by McCloy and François-Poncet.

[95] ibid., Views of Lincoln Evans, 3 June 1950.   [96] Cmd. 7970.
[97] FJM, AMG 24/1/24, 'Note confidentiel pour le Gouvernement' by Pierre Uri, 1 June 1950.
[98] CAB 128/17, Cabinet conclusions, 2 June 1950.   [99] ibid.
[100] FRUS, 1950, III, McCloy to Acheson, 23 May 1950, p. 705. In Monnet's version the objections were made by Robertson, but in fact they were voiced by Sir G.N. Macready, his economic adviser, who stood in for him at the meeting.

There was no possibility of blocking the route in that way, although the High Commission did assert its right to be fully informed of the progress of the talks. As a last, ill-considered gesture the Foreign Office published its final secret compromise proposal for a ministerial meeting, even though that proposal had already been firmly declined in Paris. The idea, presumably, was to wean the other participants towards the British way of doing things.

There can be no doubt at all, reviewing the historical record, that the final French ultimatum was fully justified. There is ample evidence that the British government had no intention of accepting the High Authority or any surrender of sovereignty and that had Britain been allowed to join the negotiations they would have been of such a fundamentally different kind as to nullify completely the French initiative. There was a general acknowledgement in the British government that an international agreement on the organization of the Western European coal and steel industries was desirable. But it was felt that this should be essentially devised by the firms themselves, subject only to a loose supervision by consultative bodies of responsible ministers. This was the system that had applied in Britain since 1931 and the British government seems to have thought it more effective as a method of control than what was happening in France.[101] It is some indication of the lukewarm attitude of the government towards its own policy of nationalizing the steel industry that it was so concerned to preserve the powers of the entrepreneurs to make decisions. Industry and government together conspired to avoid a situation in which mandatory powers conferred on a special Authority and the surrender of national sovereignty which that involved might mean the disappearance of discriminatory practices and non-tariff barriers whose function was to preserve the home market and full employment.[102]

There is no need to do anything but briefly summarize the subsequent actions of the British government. It had taken a collective decision which was fully in accord with the principles of its foreign policy towards Europe and America as they had been finally determined in 1949 and the Conservative Party, vociferous in its opposition, adhered to the same principles once in office. The only question was whether Britain would help or hinder the negotiations. It helped in two ways. Firstly, it did not make public the alternative plans for European coal and steel which it began to prepare and refused to make any rival bid for the allegiance of the other negotiating partners who

[101] 'It is very difficult to mix countries which for national reasons must exercise a large degree of state control over their economy with countries which for various reasons cannot do so even if they want to. ... France after the war, even under a socialist government, found she was incapable of doing so because the country did not have the necessary level of civic responsibility' (Mr Denis Healey in H.F. Havilland Jnr (ed.) *The United States and the Western Community* (Haverford Pa., 1957), pp. 41–2, exactly reflecting the views of the Foreign Office.) Five years later there would begin a spate of enquiries about why France was able to control its economy so much more effectively than the United Kingdom.
[102] See the discussion in CAB 134/293, First Report of Working Party on Schuman's Proposals, 19 June 1950.

had such reservations about Monnet's proposals. Maurice Petsche, Monnet's opponent since 1949, more or less invited London to intervene with rival proposals, but this was wisely declined. Whereas the essence of the negotiations was to start by taking away all barriers to equal competition and then gradually replace some of them or devise new ones to allow the negotiations to succeed, the essence of the alternative British plan was to take the barriers away over time by a series of gradual and carefully judged separate acts.[103] Secondly, it brought strong pressure to bear on Adenauer not to break off the negotiations as the German position became stronger. The direct and strong help which American officials gave to France by their pressure on the German government was not known in London for some time afterwards. Any attempt to rival the French proposals would have met with strong opposition from the United States, so that the United Kingdom did not have much room for manoeuvre. Nevertheless, most of those concerned in the Foreign Office thought the negotiations would fail, mainly because the single market was to be created too rapidly, and that the British proposals could then be used.[104] When they succeeded the only possibility was 'association'.

History cannot entirely avoid the bias of the moment at which it is written and it is impossible to avoid asking the question whether this was not a critical turning-point in Britain's post-war history. The answer, however, must be that the question is itself too simplified and too dramatic. Whether it was a turning-point economically would only be determined by the future economic relationships with the new economic bloc which was to be created. The events of 1950 and the signing of the Treaty of the European Coal and Steel Community on 18 April 1951 made no difference whatsoever at the time to the British economy and even the opening of the common market for certain of the products on 10 February 1953 made very little. No proper economic answer to the question can be given except by considering almost the whole span of time during which the framework created by the treaty has survived, and in that span of time so many other variables would come into account that the question would lose all precision and force. The decision not to join summed up past economic events and showed their influence, conscious and unconscious, on diplomacy. The deep anxiety about Britain's international position in the 1930s, the protectionism which arose from that, the inability to find any certain way in which the high standard of living which trade and industrialization had created in Britain could be enhanced in the future, the conviction that no risks could be taken with exports, the war effort, the defeat of Germany and the influence which that had in preventing government from coming to terms with the longer view of history in which that enormous event was only a temporary aberration – all these things kept Britain out of the ECSC.

[103] CAB 134/294, Report of Working Party, 30 June 1950.
[104] ibid., 31 August 1950.

Yet the prevailing mood while the decision was being made was more than natural anxiety. It was fear, and it is this which makes the contrast with French actions so striking and marks the event as more of a political than an economic turning-point. In retrospect it is impossible to agree that the High Authority and the Court of Justice were at all as dangerous to the British economy, to full employment, to the principles of British political life, and to British foreign policy and defence as was suggested. They were in fact, for all the fine language about European unity in which they were wrapped, of limited scope and only narrowly specific application. They were certainly less dangerous to the economic and political future of the United Kingdom than the wild ideas of economic association or even union with the United States that were current in some circles in 1950. That the British reaction should have been both fearful and defensive may well have been of much more significance for the country's future than the decision not to join.

THE EUROPEAN COAL AND STEEL COMMUNITY

The political motivation for the ECSC remained paramount throughout the negotiations and because of that the economic implications had to be accepted in Germany. On the day the Bundestag ratified the treaty Monnet telegraphed to Adenauer, 'Europe is born, long live Europe.' 'Big Europe', the far-flung, liberal customs union with a low external tariff still waits to be born. In its stead came 'Little Europe' based on an incomplete, carefully regulated, sectoral integration, which, in the event, has not proved capable of extension to other countries without such serious modification as to call its meaning and its survival into question. Little Europe did involve a surrender to a supranational body of certain formerly jealously guarded activities of the nation state and so was greeted with rapturous enthusiasm by many advocates of the greater union. Yet, seen from the admittedly short perspective of thirty years, its most lasting attribute, one which shows no substantial signs of weakening, has been its solution to a past problem and not its importance for the future. The Franco-German alliance has been the heart of all subsequent developments in the European Community and has taken on as permanent an air as the hostility which preceded it.

By contrast the tree of European integration, apparently planted by the conclusion of the treaty in April 1951, has shown almost every kind of mutation. Some of its branches grew rapidly at first in the same pattern until the sectoral integration of agriculture laid the basis for a common market covering a wider range of products. But their fruits were already different inasmuch as there was less talk about, and much less action to create, democratically representative control of the executive machinery which itself was finally of a different kind. After that growth was stunted by the icy blasts of the 'Europe of the nations'. Recovering from that long winter the tree is proliferating in so diverse a way in the new climate, which is becoming more

Mediterranean, as to become a quite different plant, a sort of dense, impenetrable, rambling undergrowth clinging to the nations and holding them at times so firmly in place as to prevent all movement and at other times tempting them to hack it contemptuously to the ground.

The ECSC eventually emerged with large differences from Schuman's original proposals. Why it changed so much between conception and birth is a necessary appendage to the story. But it is impossible to tell it in any but provisional form at the moment because of the lack of documentary evidence. All that can be done is to round off the relevant aspects of the story and to hazard some suggestions as to why the changes came about.[105]

On the eve of the negotiations the proposals contemplated a wide range of drastic actions. They contemplated the removal of all customs duties within the market on the products covered, the removal of all discriminatory freight rates and export prices, the equalization of wages in the coal and steel industries, together with the appointment of the High Authority and of an 'arbiter' to ensure that its procedures in carrying out these changes were fair.

As they emerged in treaty form the proposals were for a five-year transitional period before the common market became complete. Some arrangement of this kind had always been thought of as necessary but the common market turned out to be much less perfect than foreseen. Italy was allowed to keep full tariffs for this period to protect its small, high-cost steel industry. The Belgian coal-mines received transitional subsidies from the German and Dutch mines and because the subsidies were paid out of sale prices the coal price policy took on straight away what the Belgian delegation called a 'very marked international dirigisme'.[106] The subsidies were to provide a breathing space for the modernization and rationalization of the Belgian mining industry, where productivity levels were lower than in the other countries. When they were due to end, the closure of a large number of mines in the Borinage was announced and the subsidies were hastily renewed to allow the mining of uncompetitive Belgian coal to continue. The production cost of a tonne of Belgian coal in 1950 was about a third higher than for French coal and the chances of closing such a gap over the transitional period could not have been good.[107]

Although coal prices were harmonized and dual coal pricing brought to an end, differential national and international rail freight rates remained in force. A fair transport rate for coal and coke on the German railways through the Palatinate would have made them cheaper in Lorraine than coal and coke from Nord and Pas de Calais! In May 1957 when genuinely equalized freight rates did come into force it was still only for distances of less than 400 miles. Thus

[105] The best general account of the early history of the community is W. Diebold Jnr, *The Schuman Plan, A Study in Economic Cooperation 1950–1959* (New York, 1959).

[106] CAB 134/295, Note of conversations with the Belgian delegation to the Paris negotiations, 20 September 1950.

[107] FJM, AMG 22/5/4, Note relative aux effets du Plan Schuman, 8 February 1951.

the higher priced Italian producers still remained protected. As for the equalization of wages, that was a far too ambitious project once the market included the two lower wage countries of the Netherlands and Italy. The difference made to steel prices by the incidence of turnover taxes, sales taxes and export rebates was not removed, in spite of Erhard's strenuous objections. The Tinbergen Committee appointed to report on the problem allowed France to maintain its equalizing levies on German steel imports, apparently letting its sense of what was politically feasible rule its economic heart. To insist that member countries harmonize their domestic taxation policies was to sail too close to one of the reefs on which American policy in the OEEC had stuck.

The Netherlands and Belgium objected to the great and undefined powers to be invested in the High Authority. The French conception was that the Authority should be set up first in order to create the common market and to define the economic functions and regulatory role which it would itself play. This would have left the other countries too much in the hands of a close Franco-German agreement on the powers of the Authority, so the Dutch and Belgian delegations insisted that the negotiations also define exactly what the economic purpose of the High Authority should be. This seems to have been the biggest blow to Monnet's hopes. The Benelux delegations insisted from the outset that the final treaty should lay down detailed and absolute provisions for the powers of the High Authority, and they were determined that there should be some governmental supervision over its decisions.[108] Both Dutch and Belgian delegations wanted a Council of Ministers to be able to issue directions to the High Authority. From this confrontation between France and West Germany on the one side and the smaller countries on the other the High Authority emerged in company with a Council of Ministers whose task was to review the Authority's decisions (although not to issue directives to it), with a court, with a powerless consultative committee of users, employees' representatives and so on, and with the annual Common Assembly which the French had tacked on to blunt the technocratic edge of the Authority and which was given the power to get rid of the High Authority itself by a two-thirds majority.

The specific economic issues with which French policy on the Ruhr had been concerned were also subject to compromise during the negotiations. Whether the differential export pricing of German coal had been worth the enormous effort France had devoted to the issue could perhaps be doubted. It was a function of the coal shortage and, given the importance of the French market to German producers, was not likely long to survive the moment when the supply of coal again came into equilibrium with demand, which it already showed signs of doing before the Korean war boosted demand again.

---

[108] CAB 134/295, Report of the Working Party on the Schuman Plan, 28 June 1950; ibid., Conversation between Labour attaché in Brussels and M. Vinck, 6 July 1950.

It needed only a small increase of 4 marks a tonne in the price on the domestic market for the differential to be eliminated.

One economic sacrifice which the Planning Commissariat seems to have regarded as inevitable and may, indeed, have actually welcomed, was the Plan's original ambitious target for coal output. The Plan had envisaged an annual output of 62 million tonnes of coal by 1955–6 and from the way Monnet and Hirsch presented the Schuman proposals in London they seem to have resigned themselves to reducing this target by about 10 million tonnes.[109] This would have been only a small increase over the 1949 output. The proposals were conceived at a time when the European coal shortage seemed to be disappearing and when, as a consequence, the coal targets of the Modernization Plan, if they had ever been justifiable, no longer looked so. Output in fact fell in 1950 when it was still more than 11 million tonnes below the Plan's target, whereas the increase in output in West Germany continued unabated. Stocks of coal in France at the time of the proposals were higher than before or after.[110]

It was estimated that by 1953/4 Germany would have about 31.6 million tonnes of coal available for export. If transport rates were equalized France would nevertheless be able to export coal to areas south of Karlsruhe, which would compensate for the inevitable increase in non-coking coal imports from Germany. The agreement was eventually written in such a way that French output would never have to fall by more than one million tonnes a year in the transition period. The national distribution organization, Charbonnages de France, was allowed to maintain zonal prices. Furthermore the High Authority could, if it wished, levy a tax of up to 10 per cent of the value of net deliveries to France above the level of 1950 in order to reduce the price of French coal in the dearer zones. Since France had already decided to reduce coal output by one million tonnes the maximum possible theoretical decline in output under these arrangements, 5 million tonnes, was, even should it occur, not such a burden. It was only possible if coal was in very plentiful supply and it would be accompanied by a reduction in coal prices to producers. There would also be the readaptation fund which would help to cover the costs of any reduction in the labour force below the reduction of between four and five thousand already planned.

The extent of control of coal-mines by integrated steel works in Germany was, at least temporarily, much reduced, not in the Schuman Plan negotiations but by the contemporaneous exercise of the powers of the Allied High Commission implementing the 1947 Bizone plan for decartelization of the industry. It was made clear that this was a pre-requisite for the entry into power of the High Authority. Whatever the belief of the French planners in rationalization and modernization they did not for one moment take the view

[109] CAB 134/295, Meeting of Monnet, Makins etc. in Hyde Park Hotel, 16 May 1950.
[110] Coal stocks held at mines were 1.17 million tonnes in May 1948, 3.6 million tonnes in May 1950, and 1.8 million tonnes in May 1951. UN, *Monthly Bulletin of Statistics*.

that the large size of the German steel companies was a laudable example of either of these processes. Deconcentration of capital holdings in the German coal and steel industries thus went ahead, even though it meant reducing the annual crude steel output of some of the larger German firms below the one million tonnes level which the Planning Commissariat itself had regarded as the minimum level for optimum efficiency in a large integrated steel works. Ironically, this was achieved by insistence on the decartelization programme originally developed by the American and British Military Governments, the very programme which had originally been developed as a way of returning the German industries to private ownership and to which the French government had so strenuously objected.

Eleven days after the Schuman proposals were made public the High Commission approved Law No. 27 which re-enacted all the provisions of Law No. 75 of the Bizone Military Government, the law which had come close to breaking up the London conference in 1948.[111] It introduced a few modifications which would before have been even more offensive to the French. The absolute ban on works being returned to persons punished for political offences was replaced by the imposition of 'a reasonable and appropriate indemnity'. When the executive orders to the law were published in September 1950 the directors of the firms to be broken up were themselves appointed as overseers of the process. The six largest steel companies were broken up into twenty-four separate firms, with only a few variations from the original plans of the Military Government. Between September 1950 and March 1951 the United States brought pressure to bear on the German government to make it accept the separation of coal-mines from steel works. The twelve largest steel works, which had produced before the war about 90 per cent of the total output, were only allowed to own coal-mines up to 75 per cent of their required coal supply. In theory this should have left only 16.5 per cent of West German coking coal under the ownership of the German steel industry, instead of the pre-war proportion of at least a third. The coal companies were to have a separate management and were to sell to steel works only at established market prices. On this particular issue, therefore, the outcome was much more acceptable to France than what was likely to be achieved by the International Authority for the Ruhr.

Once the High Authority was functioning questions of concentration of capital, except where they concerned persons with a blatantly Nazi past or of especially unpleasant repute in France, did however come to be handled more as questions of economic convenience or rationality. The consequence was that the economic advantages of concentration reasserted themselves very quickly over the more political considerations which had prevailed in the decartelization programme. The amalgamations of the newly created

[111] The French High Commissioner placed a suspensive veto on the law which delayed it for one month, but during that month Schuman made his proposals.

Dortmund Hoerder Hütten Union with Howald shipyards, as well as of the two very large Belgian coal, steel and engineering companies, Cockerill and Ougrée, were both permitted by the High Authority in 1955 on the grounds of rationalization. The smaller companies into which the central German coal and sales agency, Deutsches Kohlen-Verkauf, was broken up by the executive orders of February 1951 remained associated by numerous personal and business links, the common device of interlocking directorates which normally thwarts political interference of this kind.[112] The real powers of the High Authority to supervise and regulate business practices within large and diverse enterprises had obvious limitations. In 1954 a series of spot checks found serious irregularities of business practice in thirty-five of the forty-eight firms investigated.[113]

The fate of the Ruhr Authority depended on German willingness to reach a settlement. It remained in place throughout the negotiations and in November, against strong German protests, as the demand for coal again increased, resumed the compulsory allocation of German coal to France, even though there was a serious bottleneck in supply in Germany. This provoked a demand from Germany that a definitive decision be made about the Ruhr Authority in the light of the new negotiations. Monnet gave assurances to Hallstein,[114] the chief German negotiator, that if the Federal Republic accepted the gist of the Schuman proposals France would press for the International Ruhr Authority to be wound up.[115] Towards the end of the negotiations the Federal Republic obtained a formal written undertaking from the French Ministry of Foreign Affairs that this would be their policy. Until then the struggle within the Authority was every bit as discouraging as its opponents had foreseen. Over the first six months of 1951 the German representatives voted against every decision on allocation and the representatives of the other countries voted for them until finally in August Franz Blücher, the Vice-Chancellor, resigned from the Authority in protest. The background to the negotiations for the ECSC could scarcely have been further from the international idealism which Monnet had preached.

There was an acute energy crisis in the Federal Republic in 1950 and 1951.

[112] The nationalized coal industry in France retained its own national coal importing and sales organization. The national sales organization of the French steel industry, the Comptoir Français des Produits Sidérurgiques, was proclaimed dissolved in 1952, but there is considerable evidence that a very similar control mechanism was retained with tacit government encouragement (W.G. Baum, *The French Economy and the State* (Princeton, 1958), pp. 265 ff).
[113] H.L. Mason, *The European Coal and Steel Community, Experiment in Supranationalism* (The Hague, 1955), p. 76.
[114] Walter Hallstein, born 1901, university teacher of law at Berlin. Professor of law at Rostock 1941, where he wrote a book not uncritical of legal tendencies under the Nazi regime. Army officer 1942–5. Professor of Law and Rector of the University of Frankfurt, 1946. State-Secretary in the Office of the Federal Chancellor, 1950. President of the Commission of the EEC, 1958. President of the European Movement, 1968. Author of books on law and, later, on European unity.
[115] FJM, AMG 22/4/23, Monnet to Schuman, 3 February 1951.

In the third quarter of 1950 West German industry only received about half the average quantity of coal it had received for the first two quarters. About a quarter of Ruhr blast furnaces were not working because of coke shortages.[116] The operations of the International Authority for the Ruhr contributed only marginally to the situation. Nevertheless its actions and those of the Allied High Commissioners in breaking up the firms, together with the intervention by the OEEC to direct and control West German imports in order to save the EPU,[117] all showed the real nature of the choice before Germany. A spasmodic and haphazard economic regulation and intervention by the international diplomacy of the occupying powers was hardly to be preferred to whatever pressures might emanate from what was likely to be a more predictable and possibly more sympathetic source. Erhard's dislike of the ECSC as a needless restriction on German industry took little account of the other restrictions on the German economy which would persist unless the ECSC was accepted. Adenauer insisted throughout on the prime political priority for the Federal Republic of the removal of the Ruhr Authority and the weakening of the Occupation Statute.

Very little is yet known of what must have been a hard struggle inside the government of the Federal Republic. In August the representatives of the German Iron and Steel Manufacturers' Association were in Paris and Heinrich von Brentano, the CDU Party Chairman, was sent by Adenauer to impress on them that 'the political aim was in the foreground, and economic aims were more or less subordinate to it'.[118] The German steel industry had to agree to French steel-makers supplying the south German markets for two to three years and over that period sales to Germany made an important contribution to French exports.[119] The expansion of the German car industry provided, before Germany had reacquired the same technology, a market for products from the new wide strip mills whose construction the Modernization Plan had financed. At the same time the strength of domestic demand in Germany diverted German steel away from the export markets where France had most feared competition.

The reappearance of the coal shortage in 1950 benefited the French steel industry in a tangential way. Not only did Germany have to share the coking coal shortage but the special investment funds under the control of the High Authority were exclusively allocated to the coal industry until 1955, and by the end of 1958 High Authority loans had financed $205 million of investment in French coking plant. If West Germany had had any thought that the institution of the investment fund would ease the problems of capital investment

---

[116] W. Abelshauser, 'Korea, die Ruhr und Erhards Marktwirtschaft: Die Energiekrise von 1950/51', *Rheinische Vierteljahrsblätter*, 45, 1981.

[117] See below, pp. 431–2.

[118] CAB 134/295, Views of the German Iron and Steel Association, 21 September 1950.

[119] French steel exports to West Germany

1952 243,000 tonnes	1953 486,000 tonnes	1954 855,000 tonnes

in the reconstruction of the German steel industry those hopes had to be deferred. Investment had to come either from self-finance or from government short-term credits under the special programmes instituted in 1951, and that meant higher prices.[120] In 1952 German steel prices were raised twice so that when the common market came into operation the gap between French and German selling prices for a wide range of products had been almost eliminated.

It cannot be said that France came badly out of the negotiations. Negotiating from a position of political strength had proved as advantageous as Schuman had thought. Nevertheless, when the French negotiators presented the project of the draft treaty to ministers in Paris in December 1950 several important ministers demanded alterations which would have ended the negotiations on the spot. René Mayer wanted unilateral obligations to be imposed on Germany over the question of the ownership of the firms if the Ruhr Authority was to go. Petsche wanted the High Authority to have no greater powers than to receive reports about cartels and other forms of business association in French firms. He was opposed to allowing Italy to maintain its tariffs for a longer transition period and also to giving Italy access to North African ore on favourable terms. Ministers recommended to the Planning Commissariat that the existing rules covering business associations in France should not be affected by the treaty and that firms, presumably only French firms, should be protected against the powers of the High Authority to allocate all raw materials in times of scarcity.[121] In the circumstances Monnet's original insistence that the negotiators on the French and German side should not be ministers but men free from the weight of previous policy or of party politics had obviously been wise. The negotiators provided a buffer between the numerous members of both French and German cabinets who were increasingly opposed to what was going ahead.

Yet, assuming the original plans for French coal output to have been too ambitious, ministers were only being asked to make one major concession. That was over the Saarland. The protests from Germany over the conventions signed between France and the Saarland government in spring 1950 did not die down. The lukewarm enthusiasm of America and Britain for France's interest in the Saarland and the increasingly repressive nature of the unrepresentative Saarland government, as opposition to its policy of association with France mounted, so seriously weakened France's position there that the Bonn government felt strong enough in the negotiations to demand some change. This led the French government through various shifts of policy. Firstly it was proposed that the Saarland government should have its own representation in the ECSC or that both its autonomy and French control of its foreign

[120] The methods of financing are discussed in H.R. Adamsen, *Investitionshilfe für die Ruhr. Wiederaufbau, Verbände und Soziale Marktwirtschaft 1948-1952* (Wuppertal, 1981).
[121] FJM, AMG 22/4/2, Documents relatifs aux observations des ministres. The concession that allocation within national boundaries should be a matter for national governments was made in February (ibid., AMG 22/5/3, Letter by Monnet, 9 February 1951).

relations be recognized by France signing every part of the ECSC treaty twice, once for itself and once for the Saarland. There was a lot of discussion emanating from proposals made by Adenauer that the Saarland should become the first 'European' state, its territory governed by a special European legal status, and that Saarbrücken should become the headquarters of the ECSC. The Saarland elections of 1952, which were not fairly held, produced a substantial majority vote for the Saarland government and its policies of autonomous association with France and effectively ended the chances of this solution. The West German government, however, did not allow a position to arise where it would seem to be recognizing the post-war status of the Saarland, and in 1951 the French and West German governments exchanged letters in which it was expressly stated that the West German signature of the ECSC treaty would be in the full recognition by both governments that the current status of the Saar was not recognized by the German government, which would only accept a status determined by a treaty of peace.

When the treaty was presented to the French national assembly for ratification the government was obliged to accept further commitments which limited the force of its application. Among them was one to regulate the status of the Saarland. The others were that it should press for the canalization of the Moselle (which, it was thought, would reduce costs to French steel producers), that it should turn all loans made to the steel industry since 1947 into loans on the same terms as those to the nationalized coal industry, and that it should further pursue the harmonization of international transport costs, social service payments and indirect taxes so as to minimize the difficulties under which French producers would find themselves. In special steels the opening of the common market was delayed for three months at the last moment, a violation of the treaty by the High Authority's own rules.

In fact the sum total of concessions made to the Federal Republic during the negotiations not only scarcely modified the original French negotiating standpoint, but what the Federal Republic eventually accepted was considerably less than what Schuman had at first offered. Where France itself made concessions from the original proposals they were not to Germany but concessions which had to be made to secure the adherence of the other member countries to the bloc.

Once the complexity of the interests of the other countries, which were closely tied to conditions prevailing in the French and German steel industries, had to be taken into account, the more sweepingly simple ideas of the Planning Commissariat did not stand up to the test. Tariff policy, prices and freight rates had to take account of problems of regional adjustment and vested interest in areas long protected, and the difference between the ECSC and the concept of a single competitive market became wide.

Belgium and Luxembourg were more dependent on that market for their steel exports than the other members. Furthermore, steel was a fifth of their

Table 58   Exports of iron and steel as a proportion (%) of the value of Belgium/Luxembourg's total exports, 1937–51

	%	Total weight (000 tonnes)
1937	19	3909.0
1938	16	2314.3
1946	27	1572.3
1947	23	2268.9
1948	30	3446.0
1949	28	3745.5
1950	19	3580.7
1951	21	5160.9

Source: British Iron and Steel Federation, *Statistical Yearbooks*.

total exports (table 58). For them the issues, economically, were more crucial than for France or Germany. The Belgian industry was all in favour of sharing out exports but had no wish to sacrifice any part of its domestic market and aimed at a set of arrangements like the pre-war International Steel Cartel.[122] The reduction in the export price of Belgian merchant bars to a level about a third below that of British prices in February 1950 had been interpreted as an attempt to force the reconstitution of the Cartel.[123] For some time Belgium held out against giving the High Authority powers to co-ordinate investment, but received no support from the Dutch and, with so high a level of dependence on ECSC markets was not in the end in much of a position to argue.[124] The Netherlands was an importer on a large scale from the other countries, about 80 per cent of its steel imports coming from the ECSC. Its own small steel industry was highly competitive and it could hardly lose from the proposals unless the external common tariff of the ECSC was set too high. At this point the industry's interest coincided with that of the Dutch government which was afraid a high external tariff would preclude subsequent British membership.[125] Eventually the tariffs were set higher than those of the Benelux countries but lower than those of France. Only in the Netherlands were the economic advantages to the steel industry indisputable. It gained a safer access to imported raw materials and the new steel works at Ijmuiden which dominated the industry was protected from the price cutting and other discrimination which the International Steel Cartel had habitually employed against all

[122] FJM, AMG 3/3/1, Compte-rendu de la séance restreinte du jeudi 22 juin.
[123] *The Iron and Coal Trades Review*, vol. 160, p. 285. It could only have been effective for purchasers holding Belgian francs.
[124] MBZ, 602/50.6, Verslag van de Vergadering van de Commissie van Advies voer het Plan Schuman, 19 October 1950.
[125] MBZ, 602/50.9, Verslag van de Vergadering van de Commissie van Advies voer het Plan Schuman, 9 December 1950.

newcomers. But although the economic arguments were persuasive the reasons for accepting the ECSC were, as everywhere, political.[126] The ECSC was regarded as a decisive, long-term political choice and therefore not one to be lightly made. The Council of Ministers was added to the arrangements in order to meet Dutch objections that the high authority had handed power over to a group of officials who would be independent of elected government, and the addition to the original French proposals of a Common Assembly with the power to dismiss the High Authority was designed to meet objections of the same kind from the same source.

The Italian government did not object to the surrender of sovereignty and control 'in view of the relatively small scale of the Italian steel and coal industries'.[127] But it was nevertheless determined to bargain hard to mitigate the removal of protection from industries protected from birth. In the bargaining the Italian steel industry not only obtained a special protective regime during the transitional period but also obtained special treatment for ore and scrap. The Italian steel industry was different in nature from its partners because of the very high proportion of its output made up of special steels and steel made by the electric arc process. A quarter of the total output of steel in 1950 was made in electric furnaces compared to 6 per cent in France and less than 3 per cent in Germany. It was thus overwhelmingly dependent on scrap inputs. Its whole life had been spent behind very high protective tariffs and its cost structure bore no comparison to those of the other steel industries. The second post-war steel boom which arrived in Europe in the last quarter of 1950 threatened to recreate the acute shortage of steel scrap of the immediate post-war years. In those years western Europe had maintained a price for scrap lower than world scrap prices, mainly because of the rich stores of scrap left in Germany and the strict price and export controls covering the scrap trade. Italy insisted, to preserve this situation, that the common market should include scrap as well as coal, coke, ore and manufactured iron and steel. The ECSC emerged with a maximum price for scrap still artificially kept below the world price in order to keep the cost structure of the Italian steel industry within politically acceptable parameters. The excess demand for scrap within western Europe was met by an agreement to import from outside the ECSC at higher prices and to share between the other industries the cost of maintaining lower scrap prices to Italian manufacturers. Furthermore Italy was also guaranteed special access to ore from French territory in North Africa which France originally appeared to be hoping to exclude from the common market.

Although the ideas of the French architects of the Schuman Plan were very much influenced by their interpretation of France's own recent history, one

[126] MBZ, 602/50.6, Ministerie van Economische Zaken, Stand van de Besprekingen voer het Plan Schuman per 28 October 1950.
[127] FO 371/87167, Conversation between Makins and Grazzi, 13 July 1950.

of their weaknesses was their historical insensitivity, their assumption that the future could be cleansed of the influence of the past. In the formation of the ECSC history gave them a sharp reminder of its persistent influence. The High Authority emerged from the negotiations presiding over a highly imperfect single market in raw materials and manufactures, with powers to interfere in transport, with the capacity to make some decisions of its own about capital investment, and presiding over a common labour market which existed only in theory. Where the economic distortions of the nation state were replaced, it was less by the neutral, anonymous efficiency of the free market, or of an expert technocratic decision-making body, than by a set of complex regulations arising from the careful balancing and adjustment of the interests of the various nation states to allow them to achieve particular national objectives. The future political economy of the Treaty of Rome, the analysis of which by any neo-classical formulations is likely to reduce the analyst only to a state of bewildered despair, had already taken shape.

Yet in many respects this was a big improvement on what had gone before. It not only made a set of economic issues which had been closely intermingled with the causes of war and peace the subject of permanent government regulation but it provided a permanent international governmental organization, with some public appearance of neutrality, to regulate them. How well all this worked out in practice in the 1950s is another story, not yet known. But it survived, and the Franco-German alliance survived with it unweakened, thus providing the central tie in western European reconstruction which was so conspicuously missing in the 1920s. At no time after 1918 had any German government found itself able honestly to accept any French proposals for a settlement of the coal and steel problem or for a general western European reconstruction. In that sense the treaty of the ECSC ended eighty years of bitter and deadly dispute and made the reconstruction of western Europe possible. It did so by avoiding all major questions of war and peace and creating instead a formalized network of institutional economic interdependence. International regulation of the economy was institutionalized as the alternative to the formal diplomatic resolution of major areas of political conflict.

In this light it is hardly surprising that the national industrial associations failed in their opposition. They were asking to be allowed to regulate at an international level matters where their uncontrolled power to decide even on the domestic level had become unacceptable. The understanding by national governments of what was at stake was superior to that of the economic interests which opposed them, just as in most cases it already had been in the first two years of reconstruction when policies had been pursued in a purely national setting. The tensions between government and industrial interests over who was in control of economic policy, which had emerged at the end of the war in the various national battles over planning and nationalization, spilled over into the international setting in the battle over the Schuman Plan. The only industrial groups to support it everywhere were iron and steel users, who generally assumed that it would bring them lower prices. The steel industry in France was deeply divided, eventually embarking on a disunited campaign of public opposition. The divisions in the German steel industry were scarcely less. The Belgian coal industry bitterly opposed its own government during the negotiations and the Belgian steel industry, which wished to keep its own business associations and cartels sacrosanct, put up a fierce opposition to the extent of the High Authority's powers.

In retrospect these campaigns by industrial associations against arrangements which proved eventually to be more in their own economic interests than against them can be seen as the culmination of a struggle for political power in the reconstruction period. They were the last fierce resistance to the acceptance of real government power over the mixed economy in western Europe in peacetime. The alliance between government and industry could only be cemented if industry was prepared to concede that government had an over-riding political interest to which industry must subscribe. This had not been accepted, for example, by either the French or German coal and steel industries between 1918 and 1924. In the immediate aftermath of the Second World War the issue hung in the balance. The Monnet Plan had seemed to promise to French industrial interests a much more established and important position in policy-making than they had previously had, providing their weaker members accepted the implications of rationalization and the sanctions by which the Ministry of Finance and the Planning Commissariat could enforce them. But the intentions of the Plan were not ultimately protectionist, no matter how much the policy of the first years did provide a certain extra measure of protection. When the Plan had to be translated into the international setting which could alone guarantee French security the difference in objectives between industry and government could no longer be hidden. The ECSC represented the triumph of government in that struggle and the eventual reconciliation of the two industries to the domestic and international political realities of the post-war world. An external body backed by international hopes and itself an integral part of the peace settlement carried more force in bending industry to the will of government than any purely domestic body.

No durable framework of international interdependence could have been built without this domestic struggle for political power having been first decided. It was a major attribute of the importance of the Schuman proposals, as well as a decisive factor in their success, that they took a form which not only insisted on the primacy of an *international* regulation of the future of the French and German economies, but that they were able to use the international framework to force a solution in government's own interest to the purely internal national struggle for control over the economy. What the French and German steel industries could never be made to accept in the 1920s they were forced to accept in the 1950s.

In April 1951, the month when the treaty was signed, the other controls on the German steel industry, apart from the decartelization programme, were drastically modified. Britain delayed the assent of its High Commissioner until October for tactical reasons. The new Foreign Secretary, Herbert Morrison, was determined against the advice of the Foreign Office to make the agreement depend upon Germany fully accepting its obligation to continue to supply steel scrap to Britain. The High Authority was left, almost, face to face with the national governments. It was to be its great good fortune that for most of the first twenty years of its operation it would never be called upon to deal with one problem with which it was manifestly unequipped to cope, a severe and lasting contraction in the market for steel, for that would have torn apart its flimsy supra-national finery.

Keeping that finery in place meant that the ECSC was never so simple a basis for European reconstruction as its numerous enemies – left, right and centre – claimed, not the 'Europe Inc.' of Schumacher, not a charter for unbridled government intervention in the economy, and not the triumph of an undemocratic, uncontrolled, technocratic bureaucracy. It was a proto-plasmic organization able to take any shape it wished according to the pressures on it from the nation states. What other kind of organization could have resolved so complex and so long a historical problem? It was firmly based, as much as any previous European peace treaty, on the real interests of the nation states which signed it. Whether one of its protoplasmic attributes was that it could lead to a federation of Europe can only be judged by its subsequent history, and that remains to be written.

The Franco-German association which it created was in many respects a shotgun wedding. The German bride, although her other choices were not very enticing, had nevertheless to be dragged protesting by her aged father to the altar while numerous members of her family staged noisy protests on the way and an equally large number of the bridegroom's friends and relations prophesied disaster. Yet the knot once tied this surprising union soon settled into a safe bourgeois marriage in which the couple, rapidly becoming wealthy and comfortable as passions cooled, were held together, as such couples are, by the strong links of managing their complex joint economic affairs. To all those associated with the marriage and brought into the house the same bourgeois prosperity was vouchsafed. The United Kingdom was left in the position of a prim spinster who, having earlier rejected the bridegroom because of the lack of promise of his stormy adolescence, was later allowed into the household on not very flattering terms as a rather acidulous baby-sitter. If she leaves it will not make much difference, except to her. But if the marriage breaks up it will be the end of the peace settlement and perhaps of us all.

XIII

TOWARDS
THE COMMON MARKET

THE IMPACT OF TRADE LIBERALIZATION

The success of the negotiations for the ECSC pointed out a possible solution to the problems raised for Western Europe by the programme of trade liberalization – sectoral integration. Not that the Schuman proposals themselves were in any direct or important way a response to the trade liberalization programme. As far as the iron and steel industry was concerned it was scarcely conceivable that a business of such fundamental industrial and strategic importance should have been swept into that programme. In the event, however, the ECSC provided a timely barrier against the issue ever being raised. In many other sectors the pursuit of trade liberalization was running into real difficulties by the end of 1950, difficulties which were made only more painful by the agreement on the EPU.

Commentators surveying the movement towards economic integration in western Europe have not infrequently come to the conclusion that what Tinbergen, in his early economic analysis of the possibilities, called 'negative integration', the removal of discriminatory instruments of economic policy between economies, was much easier and therefore more in evidence than a 'positive policy of integration', the agreement on common new economic policies for the future.[1] But the historical evidence hardly bears this out. Rather it suggests something entirely different, that countries were readier to accept the path of 'negative integration' because they *thought* it was easier, but that not very much progress down that path could be made before it was

[1] J. Tinbergen, *International Economic Integration* (Amsterdam, 1954), pp. 122 ff. With a slight shift of meaning of the phrase 'positive integration' Pinder, one of the more lucid commentators on the subject, takes this view. J. Pinder, 'Positive integration and negative integration: some problems of economic union in the EEC', in F.R. Willis (ed.) *European Integration* (New York, 1975).

discovered to be extremely difficult to go any further. At that point further progress depended on whether the interaction of national interests revealed a sufficient degree of common interest to produce some policy of 'positive integration'. 'Negative integration' was not the easier route because the removal of discriminatory policies threatened to undermine just as many entrenched interests as more positive policies would have done. So it was with the trade liberalization programme.

The first target date set for removing quotas under the programme was 31 March 1950. By that date the OEEC countries were to have removed 50 per cent of their import quotas on private intra-Western European trade as they had existed in 1948, and this measure was to have applied to each of three major areas of commodity trade, food and fodder, raw materials, and manufactures. When that date arrived most had got reasonably near the target in terms of their total imports from the area but many were a long way away from the target in particular sectors. They reached the overall target by removing more than half their quotas on raw material imports, but fell well short of the 50 per cent mark when it came to taking off quotas on food imports and imports of manufactured goods. Austria, for example, was adjudged to have removed quotas on only 26 per cent of its relevant food and fodder imports, Italy on 11 per cent of its imports of manufactured products, Norway on 27.5 per cent, and Denmark on 33.8 per cent.[2] Norway had not in fact deviated from its policy of maintaining strict controls on consumer goods imports to achieve a higher level of domestic investment and Denmark, faced with a balance of payments crisis, had arrested the whole process.

A short consideration of what was involved shows how little had in fact been achieved. Countries were only liberalizing their private imports. Imports under government contracts were exempt and these were about a quarter of total British and French imports. Furthermore they were only liberalizing imports from other OEEC countries, so that the effect on the total import trade of Britain and France was very limited. It amounted to the removal of quotas on only 10 per cent of their total imports in each case and in the case of Italy and West Germany on only about 15 per cent. Once this is stated in terms of GNP it meant that France and West Germany had removed quota restrictions on imports equivalent to about 1 per cent of national product and Britain and Italy to about 2 per cent.[3] The quotas removed were those which had been in place in 1948. Many of these had lost their relevance, so that their removal often had no effect whatsoever on the movement of goods. Tariffs remained inviolate – in fact the Italian tariff was greatly increased in summer 1950. Quotas which protected powerfully represented domestic interests had not been touched, the quotas on cars, for example, not having been modified in any way. Until the EPU, therefore, the process of trade liberalization more

[2] W. Diebold, *Trade and Payments in Western Europe* (New York, 1952), p. 164.
[3] ibid., p. 182.

resembled a sweeping away of legislative debris of the 1930s and the immediate post-war years than a programme positively designed to increase trade.

Foreign trade did, as we have seen, increase very vigorously in 1950, but also very unequally as between the different members of the OEEC. The influences operating on the growth of Western Europe's foreign trade were so numerous and the actual detailed implementation of the liberalization programme at the frontiers so varied and complicated that the increase in foreign trade cannot be attributed to the removal of quantitative restrictions. The effects of this must, for example, have been very small compared to only one other cause, the increase in West Germany's foreign trade. Although the rate of increase of intra-Western European trade in 1950 was 60 per cent higher than in 1949, there is no reason to accept the OEEC's own judgement that it might, from the viewpoint of 1949, have been expected to decline.[4] Quite the contrary – the more rapid expansion of output compared to the previous year would, given the persistence of the relationship between output and foreign trade prevailing since 1946, have led to a greater rate of expansion of foreign trade.

None the less, the removal of quotas did give rise to complaints that it was altering the expected pattern of intra-Western European trade to the disadvantage of certain countries. The main reason given was the inequitable nature of the rules for quota removal. That the process was inequitable can hardly be disputed. Although the impact on Britain, France and West Germany was insignificant, on small economies this was not necessarily so. Although by March Britain had achieved a substantial compliance with the rules by having to remove quotas on only about 10 per cent of its total imports, for Denmark even falling short of the rules had required the removal of quotas on 28 per cent of total imports, for Switzerland meeting them had liberated 40 per cent of total imports, and for Belgium-Luxembourg going beyond the target to 60 per cent removal also meant freeing 40 per cent of the total. Such differences were very large in absolute terms. The total value of Belgium's imports from Western Europe and its dependencies was as much as half that of the United Kingdom; it was three times that of Italy's imports from the same sources. Furthermore, the imbalance between government and private trade in Western Europe was likely to preserve these inequities. Danish imports were almost entirely private, while, for example, British imports from Denmark were almost wholly on government contract. Furthermore, because quotas were not removed equally on all categories of imports and in particular tended to be kept on food imports, countries such as Denmark and the Netherlands where foodstuffs were an important part of total exports found themselves giving away far more concessions than they were receiving.

In January 1950, under pressure, the OEEC Council had agreed in principle

[4] OEEC, *Third Annual Report. Economic Progress and Problems of Western Europe* (Paris, 1951), p. 147.

to explore ways of going beyond the 50 per cent mark, but only once an agreement on the EPU had been reached. When the EPU was ratified the process of trade liberalization had to advance further, this time in conformity with the 'trade rules' agreed as part of the EPU to prevent trade discrimination from impeding the functioning of multilateral settlements. They forbade discrimination in the process of quota removal against any member of the EPU. Up to March five countries had in fact kept all their quotas against the Federal Republic and they now had to abandon these defences against the country whose exports were growing most rapidly. It also became necessary to liberalize controls on invisible transactions. To some extent these changes were mitigated in the ensuing round of quota removals by the proviso that the target would now only apply to total imports and not separately to each of the three categories of imports as it had before. Nevertheless as soon as the EPU was ratified the new trade rules entered into force, so that from mid-September the countries were committed to removing 60 per cent of their 1948 quotas by the end of December, and eventually a target date of 1 February 1951 was set for the removal of 75 per cent of them.

Although the process did at first go a little further it was well behind target in December 1950, and by February of the next year there had been scarcely any change at all from the situation as reported in December. In fact several of the EPU trade rules had not been brought completely into operation. Trade liberalization was not turning out to be a politically neutral process, a universally beneficial process, or the route to integration. Nor, once the American concessions in the EPU agreement had been made, was there the same sense of political urgency on the American side. Examples of recalcitrant or even backsliding countries were plentiful. Norway, for example, had still by February 1951 only liberalized about a quarter of the relevant manufactured imports. The severity of the objections to the process can best be understood from its effect on three countries in particular, West Germany, Denmark and the Netherlands. Its effect on West Germany raised yet again the central question of the relationship of German economic recovery to that of the other European economies. Its effect on the others stimulated the idea of controlled sectoral integration in another sector of the economy, agriculture.

The way in which the EPU quotas were allocated suggests that it was assumed that West Germany would run an export surplus in 1951 and this may have been the German expectation too. In fact the opposite happened and it was the size of the Federal Republic's import surpluses which posed the worst problems at the first EPU clearings. Over the first three months of the EPU West Germany used up more than half of its annual quota and in the next month the problem was even worse. If the EPU rules were to be adhered to, the Federal Republic would almost immediately have to start paying for its imports from Western Europe in dollars. Special dollar aid to the Federal Republic alone was not likely to enhance the cause of either trade liberalization or integration. The only clear alternative was the reimposition of trade controls.

Large German import surpluses proved no more welcome than the export surpluses of cheap manufactures which some countries had feared. The coincidence of rapidly rising output and consumption in West Germany with large balance of payments deficits revived bitter memories of a defeated Germany once more not paying the costs of the war while living at the expense of its neighbours and the United States. The fact that the swing from surplus to deficit in the West German current account coincided with the onset of the trade liberalization programme served to point up more sharply to the Europeans the implications of the ECA policy if carried out to its full extent. Yet the rapid expansion of Western Europe's foreign trading sector not only demanded the removal of many of the existing barriers to trade but also meant that the expansion of trade with West Germany was an imperative. How could it be managed?

For those who believe the relatively liberal policies of Erhard and the CDU/FDP government to have been the foundation of West Germany's remarkable economic success and prosperity over the next twenty years, the removal of so many controls on German trade in 1949 is seen as a courageous and ultimately justified profession of faith. The success of the Federal German economy, measured in terms of output and growth of national income, has been usually attributed in glowing terms to Erhard's early liberal economic policies and to the boldness of the currency reform which preceded them.[5] The currency reform itself was much modified from the original American plans so that it was socially much more inequitable than the occupying forces wished, and these modifications were energetically supported by Erhard. The apparent success of Erhard's own policies, represented so well by his well-fed figure and opulently modern style of living, became as much the founding political myth of the Federal Republic as the resistance movement became that of the post-war French republics. The first signs of a more systematic historical exploration of the first years of the West German economy do not augur well for Erhard's reputation, nor for the alleged importance and significance of his policies, which may not have been a very good fit for what was actually occurring in the German economy.[6]

From the start of 1948 bilateral trade negotiations on behalf of West Germany were increasingly undertaken by German officials of the Verwaltung für Wirtschaft, although they remained under the direction of the JEIA and the Allied Military Governments. The pressures on these negotiators from the

[5] The best example of this view is H.C. Wallich, *Mainsprings of the German Revival* (New Haven, 1955).
[6] See, for example, Abelshauser 'Korea, die Ruhr und Erhards Marktwirtschaft: Die Energiekrise von 1950/51 in *Rheinische Vierteljahrsblätter*, 45, 1981; *ibid.*, 'Ein Briefwechsel zwischen John McCloy und Konrad Adenauer Während der Korea-Krise' in *Vierteljahrshefte für Zeitgeschichte*, 30 (iv), 1982.

Netherlands, Denmark and Switzerland to pursue a more liberal policy in respect of imports into Germany were very strong and were favourably received, even to the extent of negotiating agreements which were unacceptable to the occupying authorities. This was the case with the list of extra Dutch imports into the Federal Republic agreed in March 1949 which was disapproved by Clay as 'non-essential'.[7] The Danish government had submitted an official note of protest about the low level of Danish-German trade in July 1949. From the German viewpoint all food imports from the Netherlands and Denmark were dollar-saving, but while German exports had to be purchased in dollars the trade was unlikely to grow. There were also political reasons, quite apart from the obvious economic advantages or any ideological grounds, for breaking free from the straitjacket which JEIA control had imposed on the Federal Republic's trade with its Western European neighbours.

Before the EPU, however, liberalization had largely to be confined to an increase in the range and quantity of goods covered in bilateral agreements for which import licences would not be required, or an extension of the size of the permitted 'swing'. Within these constraints the German negotiators had pursued as liberal a policy as possible. From the start of 1949 private trade was allowed in the export of goods which the JEIA deemed to be 'non-scarce', and the trade agreement with the Netherlands, although Clay disallowed some of the specified imports, made an important breach with the principle of maximization of dollar earnings on which the JEIA had always insisted. Not only was it the first step towards resuming the pre-war Dutch-German trade, but it allowed for a much higher level of exports paid for in guilders. After 15 October, when the JEIA handed over all its administrative functions except those concerned with trade with the communist bloc, the German negotiators could pursue an even more liberal policy, although the JEIA retained its supervisory powers in reserve pending a decision to be taken later by the High Commissioners. The policy which the German negotiators had followed in 1949 was wholeheartedly endorsed by Erhard in January 1950 in an article in *Die Neue Zeitung* where he described trade liberalization as a step on the path to European reconstruction. Access to European markets was a matter of life or death for the German economy and it was understandable that there should be no firmer advocate of trade liberalization than the Federal Republic.

Yet there were also German, as distinct from Allied, limits to liberalization and these were already becoming apparent even as Erhard added a political rationale and a theoretical consistency to what had in any case been an obvious practical response. When the trade agreement between France and West Germany was negotiated at the end of January 1950 it called forth strong American objections to two of its clauses. One was a clause which permitted the sudden reintroduction of quotas should things go wrong. The other was

---

[7] OMGUS, H.G. Schmidt, *The Liberalization of West German Foreign Trade 1949–1951* (Historical Division, Office of the Executive Secretary, OMGUS, 1952), p. 19.

the so-called 'entente' clause, put in by the French but willingly accepted on the German side, which called for regular negotiations between industrial and agricultural groups within the two countries to request adjustments to the agreement whenever necessary. This second clause had to be qualified by a series of letters before the United States would allow the Federal Republic to accept it and it was not long before the American government uncovered a Franco-German cartel in abrasives and protested strongly at Bonn.

One area which gave rise to no difficulties at all in the Franco-German agreement was agriculture. Here both countries pursued a blatantly protectionist policy. In spite of the enthusiasm with which the Federal Republic pursued liberalization in other sectors it was by no means a matter of universal agreement in the OEEC that Germany had attained the initial 50 per cent stage of quota removal in March 1950 as far as agricultural products were concerned. Throughout 1949 there was a system of price equalization in force for food prices. Food importers paying over the established domestic price levels were reimbursed and those paying less had to surrender to a central fund part of their realized profit. This system was reinforced and extended later in the year by one of the first acts of the Federal Government and one which was officially 'questioned' by the American High Commissioner, so that it could not be published until 20 February 1950. Between May 1950 and December 1951 a series of laws on the importing and marketing of food created several semi-governmental commodity import monopolies to implement the system of price equalization, all of which were opposed by the American High Commissioner but not by his French counterpart. In June 1950 McCloy asked the West German government 'to reconsider this entire program of legislation'.[8] It was not possible to resist flatly a request of this kind and in the summer there were signs of a tactical withdrawal on the German side. This, however, was in a wider context. A new German tariff had to be submitted to the GATT conference in Torquay and the Allied High Commission had also objected strongly to the levels of agricultural protection proposed by the new tariff law. The High Commission demanded instead that West Germany allow the free import of wheat and rye, and make reductions in the proposed duties on bread flours, butter, margarine, fruit and vegetables.[9] The outcome was a compromise set of proposals, which, to appease the Allied High Commission, were accompanied by modifications in the price equalization system in the Federal Republic. But the consonance of interest between the Federal Republic and France was unmistakable and, because America's central concern was with intra-Western European trade, there seemed a good chance that it might be turned into a political agreement similar in form and purpose to the proposed coal and steel community.

[8] OMGUS, Schmidt, *Liberalization*, p. 82.
[9] F. Jerchow, 'Aussenhandel in Widerstreit. Die Bundesrepublik auf dem Weg in das GATT 1949–1951', in H.A. Winkler (ed.) *Politische Weichenstellungen im Nachkriegs-deutschland 1945–1953* (Göttingen, 1979), p. 272.

In 1949 West Germany's trade with Western Europe had still been in surplus because of the low levels of consumption and the continuation of the Allied policy of squeezing out German primary goods to pay as far as possible for the occupation. In the last quarter of the year this began to change and West Germany did not again consistently produce trade surpluses with Western Europe until 1951, when they were composed of quite different goods, being mainly manufactured commodities of all kinds. The Federal Republic's trade with the whole world, however, continued in 1949 to show

Table 59	Balance of trade of West Germany with Western Europe, 1949–51 (monthly average, thousand current dollars)
1949	
1st quarter	+22,640
2nd quarter	+17,790
3rd quarter	+12,260
4th quarter	−5,070
1950	
1st quarter	−10,190
2nd quarter	+13,700
3rd quarter	−4,500
4th quarter	−8,650
1951	
1st quarter	+8,950
2nd quarter	+82,930
3rd quarter	+55,430
4th quarter	+78,260

Source: OEEC, *Statistical Bulletins of Foreign Trade*.

massive deficits which were compensated almost entirely by American aid, a little more than half in the form of GARIOA funds and a little less than half in the form of Marshall Aid. Thus over the year the Federal Republic had a deficit of $956 million on current account in the balance of payments with the dollar area and a surplus of $32 million with the OEEC excepting the sterling area. The balance on capital account with the dollar zone was $915 million. The total import bill rose from $1588 million in 1948 to $2237 million in 1949.[10] On the other hand the proportion of it covered by exports and other commercial transactions rose from about a third in 1948 to 57 per cent. In 1950 it would be as high as 82 per cent. The West German economy was clearly on the right

[10] Smuggling was so rife in the West German economy that the recorded quantities of foreign trade are probably substantial underestimates. This also partly accounts for the great discrepancies in the statistics, although it cannot entirely account for the wide difference between German figures and others. The figures given here are those recorded by the Bank of International Settlements and the OEEC.

track to emancipate itself from the vast sums in dollar aid it was absorbing in 1948, although, at an import level of $2704 million in 1950, total American aid was only $120 million less than it had been in 1947.

The problem was the short term. The almost complete reversal in the commodity structure of German exports between 1949 and 1951, back to what it had been since the late nineteenth century, could not possibly be achieved without a very rapid increase in the size and variety of imports. This increase is reflected in the overall balance of trade deficit in the last quarter of 1949. In the first half of 1950 the balance of trade with Western Europe moved into surplus again, this time on the basis of an export structure much more akin to that which had prevailed in the past. This too, however, was only temporary. The outbreak of war in Korea produced a world-wide run on raw materials which shifted the terms of trade against the Federal Republic at the very moment when it was most vulnerable to such a movement, because it was in no position economically or politically to reduce its imports. The effects of this were exaggerated by the panic consumer purchasing which followed the outbreak of war and by the ruthless scramble for raw materials by German firms sensing an export boom. In the second half of 1950 overall import deficits increased to three times their level in the second quarter and trade with Western Europe also moved firmly into deficit and stayed there.

The import surpluses from Western Europe were small by the side of the overall trade deficit. But the overall trade deficit was largely a function of dollar aid; the Western European deficit had to be funded within the EPU. It meant that either the Federal Republic would have to pay in gold, which it could not do, or accept the implication of the EPU rules, deflate its economy, and stop the recovery. The effects of such an action on European recovery would have been catastrophic. About half of the increase in intra-Western European trade since 1948 was accounted for by German imports, by far the most rapidly growing element in Western Europe's foreign trade, and, as chapter 11 showed, France as well as West Germany's immediate neighbours would have been severely hit by their reduction.

Like those of any highly developed, industrial economy the imports of the Federal Republic in 1950 covered a bewildering range of goods, such that it is certainly not easy, nor entirely convincing, to attribute the trade deficits with Western Europe in 1950 to increases in imports of particular commodities or from particular countries. Nevertheless, the violent shift in the commodity structure of German trade had perforce to be accompanied by an equally violent shift in the sources of German imports in order to cater for the coming reduction in dollar aid. The value of imports in 1949 from the dollar zone was about the same as that from Western Europe; in 1950 it was less than a third. Doubtless this resulted in a considerable reduction of expenditure on invisibles such as shipping and freight charges, but for the infant EPU it was a large lump to swallow. From the general increase of all kinds of German imports from Western Europe one particular category can be singled out here for its political significance, the remarkable increase in imports of food from the Netherlands and Denmark. This, of course, was the most obvious form of dollar-saving available and one for which the Dutch and Danes had long been clamouring.

As a proportion of total West German imports, imports of food and agricultural products reached their peak in the last quarter of 1949 and the first quarter of 1950 (table 60). This was the *Fresswelle* in which West German

Table 60   Agricultural imports of West Germany as a proportion of total import trade, 1949–51 (million current dollars, cif)

	Total value of all imports	Percentage formed by agricultural products*	Value of all imports from OEEC	Percentage formed by agricultural products
1949				
Average of first three quarters	495.6	46.34	158.4	29.67
4th quarter	635.4	56.88	232.1	45.54
1950				
1st quarter	592.4	50.83	290.8	49.17
2nd quarter	528.1	41.37	250.1	40.62
3rd quarter	669.9	46.59	348.0	45.89
4th quarter	913.2	41.04	470.8	38.89
1951				
1st quarter	885.2	38.73	434.3	39.04
2nd quarter	761.4	41.71	248.4	36.84
3rd quarter	946.1	42.05	391.3	38.59
4th quarter	910.4	39.36	372.8	37.63

Source: OEEC, *Statistical Bulletins of Foreign Trade*.

* Including fish and fish products and excluding forestry and wood products.

consumers spent their increases in purchasing power so heavily on food that patterns of consumer expenditure showed a remarkable distortion from those more normally observed. At the same time the average diet showed a drastic change from cereals and potatoes towards dairy products and meats, that is to say in exactly the direction of the main agricultural exports of the Netherlands and Denmark. The *per capita* consumption of pork meats in 1950 was almost the same as its pre-war level, whereas in 1949 it had been at only about half that level.[11] Although the proportion of foodstuffs in West German imports fell slightly after the first quarter of 1950 it remained very high, more than 40 per cent of all imports for the next two years.

The effect of these changes on the export trade of the Netherlands and

[11] UN, *Survey of the European Economy in 1950*, p. 99.

Denmark over this period was, at least in terms of volume of exports, much what they had hoped for, although as we shall see later Denmark reaped no benefit from this after the end of 1949. In the first half of 1950 West German imports from the Netherlands were over 12 per cent of total imports and although this represented a wide variety of goods, some of which no doubt did not originate in the Netherlands, the difference with the comparable figure of 3.2 per cent in the first half of 1949 scarcely needs comment. Roughly half the deterioration in West Germany's trade balance with Western Europe between 1949 and 1950 was accounted for by Dutch-German trade.

The first round of settlements within the EPU thus coincided with a West German balance of payments crisis in September and October 1950. The adverse trade balance was in fact responsible for only half the total deficit in the third quarter of 1950 but it was inevitably on trade that the anxieties over Western European reconstruction focused, for it was precisely in that area that Germany was seen either as a sponger on the European system or, alternatively, as an impossibly formidable competitor. In October the West German government was faced with a barrage of protests that the excessive speed with which it was decontrolling trade was wrecking the EPU. In fact the increased deficit represented a great increase in import licences issued in the three months before the OEEC decisions on further trade liberalization in October 1950. The response to the Korean war had been a reckless issuing of import licences to meet the demands of manufacturers for raw materials to supply new orders. When it is considered that this was superimposed on an economy whose total output grew in 1950 at a rate almost unprecedented, and when it is also considered that this increase in raw material demand was in turn superimposed on the remarkable increase in demand for food in the same year, it is the small size of the German deficits with Western Europe that is more striking than their occurrence. But coming so hard on the start of the EPU they directly threatened the first successful step towards Western European economic interdependence.

Yet, if the threat was the worse for coming from West Germany it was also the easier to cope with politically. It was possible to intervene in the Federal Republic's foreign trade in a way that would have been unacceptable to another state. The Managing Board of the EPU appointed two 'advisers' to vet West Germany's import policy and to make suggestions in Bonn as to how it might be amended. The advisers upheld the basic principles of that policy but recommended certain changes in the issuing of import licences. In their view, which was subsequently borne out as correct, the import surpluses were but the prelude to a much higher level of West German exports, which were rising throughout the deficits. In the event, however, it was to be later than the advisers had forecast before German trade swung again into its traditional pattern of large export surpluses with Western Europe – not until the second quarter of 1951.

In October the Federal German government restricted credit by raising the discount rate. It cancelled a range of import licences already issued and demanded from all importers that they first deposit half of the foreign exchange cost of the imports with the central bank. In November the government was obliged to guarantee to the OEEC the continuation of its existing import controls. In December, when it received a special additional credit of $120 million from the EPU, it was obliged to accept an agreement to repay a third of each month's deficit in dollars. All these measures, combined with the impact of fiscal and monetary policy, brought the deficit on the balance of payments down in November and December. But in spite of them it suddenly rose again and produced a second payments crisis within the EPU in February 1951. Trade liberalization, which had to all intents and purposes been halted in November, was now replaced by a period of drastic trade controls followed by a longer period of what were still, in effect, planned imports.

The failure of the measures taken from October 1950 to right the payments imbalance is partly explained by the persistent weakness of all monetary policy instruments, their inability to control every form of money. Short-term credits and liquidity appear to have increased throughout the period of restriction. By the end of February three-quarters of the special credit granted by the EPU had been used up. On the last day of the month all import licences were stopped. The managing board of the EPU, acting through the OEEC, obtained a complete control by the OEEC of all West German imports until 1 June. This was to be followed by a comprehensive plan for future imports which embodied a gradual phased reduction, still under OEEC supervision, of import controls.

It was fortunate that the crisis developed when French policy was wholly directed to creating a Franco-German association. The French government made no attempt to take advantage and sought to sustain as far as possible the West German position in the EPU. They had no reason to do otherwise. Erhard's vision of Europe was going down to visible defeat as the idea of sectoral integration, with which he had displayed a marked lack of sympathy, was going from strength to strength.

The effect of the collapse of West German trade liberalization on Dutch and Danish exports to Germany was immediate. Their level in the second quarter of 1951 was less than half that of the last quarter of 1950. As far as Denmark was concerned this was an aggravation of a burden which was already making the country's external position in that year almost insupportable.

The threat to Denmark's external position posed by trade liberalization had raised directly the question of whether trade liberalization could effectively be extended to agriculture. About 75 per cent of Danish exports by value were foodstuffs or other forms of agricultural produce, and over 80 per cent of them were to countries in the OEEC. On average by the end of March 1950 the OEEC members had removed 51 per cent of their 1948 quotas on private

Table 61   Combined value of Dutch and Danish exports to West Germany, 1949–51 (million current dollars, fob)

	Value
1949	
1st quarter	8.07
2nd quarter	10.38
3rd quarter	10.21
4th quarter	24.57
1950	
1st quarter	33.18
2nd quarter	27.36
3rd quarter	35.51
4th quarter	41.56
1951	
1st quarter	32.54
2nd quarter	19.28
3rd quarter	33.89
4th quarter	29.08

Source: OEEC, *Statistical Bulletins of Foreign Trade*.

agricultural imports, but this nominal conformity to what was required could not hide the fact that several major importers, such as Britain, did not allow many private agricultural imports. In the case of Danish-French trade, for example, as Diebold points out, by the end of the year only 5 per cent of French imports from Denmark had been liberalized against three-quarters of Danish imports from France.[12] Furthermore, Britain continued to buy Danish food exports at medium-term contract prices while the price of liberalized raw material imports into Denmark rocketed upwards in the second half of 1950. The import price of coal, for example, increased by 25 per cent between summer 1950 and April 1951. Unless Western European countries liberalized agricultural imports and also changed their trading methods Denmark's comparative advantage in food production could not shield it from severe balance of payments difficulties as the trade liberalization programme proceeded.

The exact extent to which the mounting deficit in the Danish balance of payments was caused by the inequalities of the trade liberalization programme is impossible to estimate. There were other causes, too. The adverse movement in Western Europe's terms of trade in 1950 absorbed about a third of the increase in exports in that year and Denmark was worse hit by this movement than most others. In August, however, the Danish government announced that it would reverse its trade liberalization measures and reimpose quotas on a range of imports. In fact the government fell before it could do so, but by the

[12] Diebold, *Trade*, p. 193.

end of the year Denmark had still only removed 50 per cent of its 1948 quotas and on manufactured imports far less. Over a wide range of agricultural products Denmark was the most competitive Western European producer. But the leverage which so small an economy could exert in trade bargaining was very small. The opening of the German market to Danish exports had provided compensation for these difficulties. Its closing meant that the political choices over which the country had temporized since 1945 now had to be faced.

The idea of a Scandinavian customs union had never had much appeal there. Danish policy had been rather to move the other Scandinavian countries towards the idea of a European customs union. However, the genuinely competitive free-trade area within which Denmark's exports would have expanded had proved unattainable as far as the agricultural sector was concerned. A closer adherence to Little Europe might mean the sacrifice of comparative advantage within a complicated process of sectoral integration and might cut the country off from its main export market, Britain. It was certainly not likely to induce the United Kingdom to pay better prices for Danish exports. For this reason the Social Democratic government had decided in August to reverse the trade liberalization programme and begin the reimposition of quotas, reasserting whatever bargaining power it could muster in defence of full employment and increased government expenditures. When it fell from power, it was succeeded by an opposition coalition which demanded deflation and reduced rearmament expenditure as a way of correcting the balance of payments deficits, but which was by no means united over the issue of import controls.

These were serious enough events and showed just how quickly the repercussive effects of increased economic interdependence in Western Europe spread to domestic politics, forcing political parties to take up positions on the nature of intra-European economic relations about which they had previously been noticeably vague. The current impact of the same divisive forces on the Labour Party in Britain illustrates the point perfectly. But as soon as we turn from the Western European country most dependent on agricultural exports to the next most dependent, the Netherlands, it is the relative width of policy choice discussed in Copenhagen which is apparent. In The Hague matters were considered much more defensively.

Dutch agriculture was considered to be less competitive internationally than Danish and the Dutch economy to be much more dependent on Little Europe. While almost every issue of international political and economic choice was raised by the political debate in Denmark, in the Netherlands the debate was driven towards concentration on the answer to one question. How could Dutch agricultural interests be accommodated in the process of European integration as it had developed in 1950? The only answer seemed to lie in treating agriculture as the Schuman Plan had treated coal, iron and steel.

Anything else was too risky. If the *dirigiste* economic framework which the French had proposed for Western Europe had initially aroused fears for the ultimate success of the Dutch Industrialization Plan these were increasingly stilled by the realization that the French attempt to control their own immediate international economic environment left them open to a fairly wide range of bargaining possibilities, as the concessions made to the Netherlands over the Schuman proposals showed. Trade liberalization had not taken long to bring Western Europe face to face with the realities of history and politics which Bissell and his group had hoped to circumvent; what was now at stake was a set of long-standing domestic agricultural policies in Western Europe about which very few seem to have had any doubt. It was only trade liberalization which was divisive; otherwise the policies pursued in the agricultural sector were pursued with remarkable unanimity.

POST-WAR AGRICULTURE IN WESTERN EUROPE

Without discussion or argument there was one matter on which all national reconstruction plans were in agreement, the maximization of agricultural output. The prevailing world food shortage after the war and the fact that a large part of the available food surpluses had to be purchased in dollars might have been enough in themselves after 1945 to still all political argument. But to their persuasive weight have to be added the lessons drawn from the Second World War in those countries such as the United Kingdom and Switzerland which had previously adopted more liberal policies towards the agricultural sector. Any sacrifice of agricultural output on the altar of international efficiency now appeared as strategically dangerous and politically disastrous, as well as a threat to the balance of payments. Furthermore, since all countries aimed at a higher standard of food consumption than in the 1930s, as well as at one that would continue to improve with economic expansion, the level of domestic agricultural output below which strategic and political safety was endangered was thought to be higher than before the war.

The reconstruction years were therefore a period of remarkable political opportunity for farmers. The costs of maximizing national food output could be plausibly argued to be less than the alternative costs of dollar imports, and the farming community to be so strategically indispensable a part of the nation as to merit specially favourable treatment. For the first time since the 1870s the gap between countries pursuing agricultural protection, such as France and Germany, and those with relatively low or no agricultural tariffs, such as the Netherlands and Britain, was closed, and a seventy-year period of fundamentally conflicting policies in Western European agriculture came to the definitive end which the movement back to protectionism in the 1930s had foreshadowed.

How justified this unquestioned trend throughout Western Europe was is an interesting question. It can be readily agreed that the damage done by the Second World War to Western Europe's agriculture was much longer-lasting, and may even have been absolutely greater, than the damage done to industry. In four countries, the United Kingdom, Denmark, the Netherlands and Switzerland, the output of food went up during the war. Elsewhere acute shortages of labour, machinery, fertilizer, seed and other inputs amounted to a four-year period of disinvestment whose effects, after the depressed conditions of the inter-war years, were especially difficult to overcome. Even the Danish and Dutch agricultural sectors lived off their relatively high pre-war levels of productivity, which alone enabled them to support the experience of occupation better than the rest of Western Europe. On balance they too suffered from substantial net disinvestment. The worst damage was done to livestock, the quantity of cattle and sheep in several countries being reduced by about 30 per cent. But there was also a large loss of arable area to military activity of all kinds from airfield construction to fighting. In France, for example, about 1.4 million hectares of arable land fell out of cultivation during the war.

The consequence was that European agricultural output regained its pre-war levels much later than industry. It was not until 1949/50 that it did so and even then in West Germany it was still well below its pre-war level. By that date, however, the proportion of total supply of some foodstuffs coming from indigenous production in most Western European countries was already much higher than in the 1930s, and only in the United Kingdom could this be associated with productivity gains. This was especially the case for bread

Table 62   An index of agricultural production in western Europe, 1946–50 (1934/38 = 100)

	1946/7	1947/8	1948/9	1949/50	Share of European output in 1949/50 (%)
Belgium/					
Luxembourg	84	86	92	112	2.1
Denmark	97	90	97	117	2.5
France	82	77	96	96	16.4
West Germany	69	64	77	84	8.6
Ireland	100	92	97	97	1.3
Italy	85	89	97	102	11.1
Netherlands	87	88	104	117	3.1
Norway	98	91	100	106	0.7
Portugal	99	109	95	101	1.6
Sweden	104	100	109	109	2.3
Switzerland	107	101	110	99	1.4
United Kingdom	117	108	124	121	7.7

Source : UN, *Economic Survey of Europe in 1950, (Geneva, 1951)* p. 43.

grains in Belgium, Denmark, France and the United Kingdom, for other cereals in Belgium, the Netherlands and the United Kingdom, for root crops in West Germany and the Netherlands, for sugar in Belgium, Denmark and the Netherlands, and for fats and oils in Denmark and France (table 63). This trend was even more marked in the next crop year, 1950/51, when total output was well above its average of the 1930s. By the end of that year, for example, Belgium, Denmark, France and Italy were all producing sugar in quantities well above the levels of domestic demand and the meat surpluses of both Denmark and the Netherlands were much larger relative to domestic consumption than they had been before the war. Only West Germany was producing less of its own food than in the pre-war period. The earliest versions of the Monnet Plan had aimed at agricultural self-sufficiency in France; by the end of 1948 the Plan aimed at food exports.

The net imports of food into Western Europe in 1951, nevertheless, were not so much smaller than they had been in the 1930s and imports of two commodities in particular, wheat and wheat flour, were 25 per cent higher (table 64). A larger population whose average annual earnings were higher than before the war kept up the pressure for food imports in spite of the persistent efforts of trade controls and rationing systems to keep them in check. There was a major reduction in imports of maize and also a fall in imports of animals and raw meat, but otherwise the pattern was much as it had been.

These imports now came much more from the dollar zone than they had before the war. In the inter-war period eastern and south-eastern Europe had still had large food surpluses to export to western Europe but these had mostly disappeared during the war and Western Europe was now much more dependent on food imports from the dollar zone. Over the period 1949–51 four-fifths of the wheat imports, two-thirds of the cane sugar and almost a half of the maize and barley imports were dollar imports compared with pre-war proportions of 39.2 per cent, 42.6 per cent, and 11.8 per cent respectively (table 65).

This was not simply because Marshall Aid provided the dollars. The striking preference of countries for using dollar aid to purchase non-food imports even in the hungrier circumstances of 1947 has already been noted. This preference increased, so that with the exception of those countries which had been neutral during the war only the United Kingdom allocated a large proportion of Marshall Aid to American agricultural imports. The causes were much deeper. American agricultural surpluses continued to form a major proportion of traded world food surpluses, and foodstuffs, processed and unprocessed, were still 15.1 per cent of United States exports by value in 1951. Dollar zone exports of wheat and wheat flour in 1950 were about 71 per cent of world exports of those commodities, of maize the same proportion,

Table 63   Indigenous production of food in Western European countries as a percentage of gross supply

Country	Crop year	Bread grains	Other cereals	Root crops	Sugar	Meat	Fats and oils (fat content)
Belgium/	1934/5–						
Luxembourg	1938/39	44	40	97	99	93	39
	1948/49	42	48	97	93	67	34
	1949/50	56	50	93	119	87	38
	1950/51	50	52	102	160	98	39
Denmark	1934/5–						
	1938/39	60	91	102	101	192	127
	1948/49	104	95	106	165	135	143
	1949/50	93	93	107	185	190	155
	1950/51	85	90	105	194	259	141
France	1934/5–						
	1938/39	99	88	105	86	99	39
	1948/49	99	90	100	110	100	43
	1949/50	109	86	98	83	102	47
	1950/51	103	91	100	112	103	46
West Germany	1934/5–						
	1938/39	77	80	93	49	92	53*
	1948/49	61	69	97	57	93	59*
	1949/50	69	71	98	48	93	49*
	1950/51	66	79	104	66	90	42*
Italy	1934/5–				.		
	1938/39	94	93	102	99	95	77
	1948/49	76	86	99	90	98	62
	1949/50	85	93	98	90	97	72
	1950/51	89	92	94	106	96	59
The Netherlands	1934/5–						
	1938/39	62	29	110	84	110	56
	1948/49	51	45	110	70	92	50
	1949/50	62	48	119	100	109	58
	1950/51	46	46	110	102	120	51
United Kingdom	1934/5–						
	1938/39	24	41	97	21	48	12
	1948/49	33	77	100	28	45	12
	1949/50	33	72	99	26	45	11
	1950/51	39	67	99	37	49	9

Source: FAO, *Yearbook of Food and Agriculture Statistics*, I, *Production*.

* Omitting fats and oils for industrial use.

Table 64   Net imports of foodstuffs into Western Europe* (thousand tonnes)

	1934–8 average	1946	1947	1948	1949	1950	1951	1946–51† average
Wheat and wheat flour	10,067	11,860	13,979	16,426	13,892	9,258	12,878	13,186
Rye	708	385	492	764	1,195	579	712	712
Bread grains (wheat and rye)	10,775	12,245	14,471	17,190	15,087	9,834	13,590	13,736
Barley	2,249	684	854	1,809	1,761	2,057	2,541	1,629
Oats	678	720	581	748	847	633	663	700
Maize	8,222	1,385	3,276	3,501	4,619	4,052	3,498	3,444
Non-bread grains	11,149	2,789	4,711	6,058	7,227	6,742	6,702	5,773
Rice	860	7	48	115	103	284	165	126
Sugar	2,532	2,055	2,144	3,100	2,882	2,722	2,755	2,610
Tobacco	336	319	307	260	342	337	366	320
Cattle**	171	(+3)‡	(+125)‡	(+12)‡	26	23	(+45)‡	(+30)‡
Pigs**	709	11	65	38	103	400	238	142
Raw meats	1,201	1,259	1,247	1,118	1,063	1,028	681	1,066
Cheese	87	226	191	138	146	86	111	150
Eggs	182	143	116	118	81	85	60	99

Source: FAO, Yearbook of Food and Agricultural Statistics, II, Trade and Commerce.

* Includes Finland.
† Includes average 1948–51 for Austria.
‡ Net exports.
** Thousand head.

Table 65   Proportion of Western Europe's* food
imports originating in the dollar zone (%)

	1934–8	1949–51
Wheat	39.2	81.7
Maize and barley	11.8	47.1
Cane sugar	42.6	64.9
Fats and oils	5.1†	16.8
Meat	7.1	8.8
Crude tobacco	54.2	63.5

Source: UN, *Economic Survey of Europe Since the War* (Geneva,
1953), pp. 284 ff.

* The six major food importers, Belgium/Luxembourg, France,
  Germany (1934–8 all Germany, 1949–51 western zones),
  Italy, the Netherlands and the United Kingdom.
† 1938 only.

and of sugar 62 per cent.[13] These were three of the four main agricultural
imports into Western Europe and to this pattern the contribution of Marshall
Aid was insignificant.

Dollar-saving thus persisted as a long-term motive for increasing national
agricultural output and it was the external position of Western European
countries which was the first cause of the continued unquestioning acceptance
of expensive policies of agricultural protection. To the role of the agricultural
sector in domestic economic recovery not very much attention was paid. The
Monnet Plan, it is true, singled out agricultural machinery as one of its 'basic
sectors' for investment but even that was chosen more in the context of
long-term modernization than short-term recovery; the aim was to remedy
the comparatively low level of mechanization in the French agricultural sector
in the inter-war period. Indeed the steering by one method or another
throughout Western Europe of investment towards industrial production
may have been one of the causes of the much slower recovery of the agricultural
sector compared to the industrial. Policy in the agricultural sector was to
allow guaranteed high prices to solve the investment problem. Whether they
did so or not would make an interesting study.

However, as so often, once governments had embarked on a policy of
protectionism and subsidization the need for exports itself became a further
justification of that policy. There was therefore no reason why the policy
should weaken once pre-war levels of output in the agricultural sector had
been once more attained and surpassed. The Steering Group of the Food and
Agriculture Committee of the OEEC was unanimous, when considering the
implementation of the trade liberalization programme, that liberalization

[13] W.S. Woytinsky and E.S. Woytinsky, *World Commerce and Governments* (New York,
1955), p. 137.

could only be acceptable in the agricultural sector if the expansion of agricultural production continued apace and European farmers were at the same time assured of markets.[14]

Within Western Europe itself the countries were in a very varied position. There were two very large net importers of agricultural products, the United Kingdom and West Germany, and one net importer on a large scale, France, for which agricultural exports were also important, being 18 per cent of total exports. There was one large net exporter, Denmark, for which agricultural exports were of overwhelming significance. The Netherlands was both

Table 66   Gross exports and imports of agricultural products (excluding forestry products) as a proportion of total exports and imports – 1951 (%)

	Exports	*Imports*
Austria	1.5	47.0
Belgium/Luxembourg	14.7	44.4
Denmark	74.9	34.1
France	18.3	57.4
West Germany	4.3	67.9
Iceland	98.9	22.6
Ireland	83.6	38.7
Italy	23.6	53.6
Netherlands	41.0	38.7
Norway	30.0	25.5
Portugal	35.4	40.2
Sweden	6.5	27.3
United Kingdom	8.8	69.8

Source: FAO, *Yearbook of Food and Agriculture Statistics*, vol. VI, part 2, 1952.

importer and exporter on a substantial scale. But agricultural exports were over 40 per cent of total exports and on balance the Netherlands had a surplus on agricultural trade second only to that of Denmark. Ireland's exports were almost entirely agricultural but the surplus was small. Belgium, Italy and Sweden were all heavy importers on balance but for Italy agricultural exports were almost a quarter of total exports. In spite of the similarity in domestic agricultural policy the interests of the Western European countries in what external provision to make for the agricultural sector were by no means the same. The situation was further complicated by the fact that not even the relative positions of Denmark and the Netherlands were similar. Dutch agricultural exports were similar in composition to Denmark's but over most of the products where there was direct competition the Netherlands was

[14] Sunnanå Archiv, 2, OEEC, AG(5) 14, Liberalization of trade in agricultural products, 19 April 1950.

extremely apprehensive about being able to compete. Complete liberalization of agricultural trade, therefore, was considered in Copenhagen to be to Denmark's advantage, but in The Hague to be a dangerous move for the Netherlands which would be directly exposed to superior competition from Denmark in the two main European markets for each country, Britain and West Germany.

Whether this apprehensiveness was justified is doubtful in the light of the producers' prices as they existed after devaluation, compiled by the Dutch Food Production Directorate itself. They show that although over the general range of agricultural prices Denmark did indeed have an advantage, Dutch prices for milk and fodder grains were lower.[15] Of Denmark's total agricultural exports slightly more than a third consisted of oils and fats, mainly butter, and rather less than a quarter was meat. The third biggest item was eggs. Dutch agricultural exports were more varied. Butter was again the biggest item, just less than a fifth of the total, but potatoes came in second place and after that cheese and dairy products. Meat, eggs and fruit each accounted for about a tenth of the total, so that, since Danish potato exports were negligible, over the most important export items it is anything but obvious that the Netherlands was in no position to compete. Not only that, but Denmark's agricultural exports were much more heavily concentrated on a few products and Denmark's risk therefore the greater. None the less, the conviction prevailed in The Hague that Denmark was a dangerous competitor and that sectoral integration in a regulated market was safer than European free trade provided the regulation did not eliminate the Dutch advantage over France.

The overall tendency in Western Europe to support increases in domestic production at almost any price was a common threat to both the Netherlands and Denmark. If trade liberalization was to fail in agriculture, as it showed every sign of doing, the first aim of Dutch and Danish commercial policy would have to be security of access to what otherwise would be firmly closed markets. This was likely to bring the real interests of both countries into conflict with powerful vested political interests in other states unless this interplay of interest could be compromised at the international level. Because opinion in the Netherlands was so apprehensive of trade liberalization in agriculture and of competition with Denmark, this was a specific Dutch aim before it was a Danish one. The obvious compromise to attempt, as soon as Schuman had made his proposals on coal, iron and steel, was to propose sectoral integration in the agricultural sector too as a way of avoiding trade liberalization while retaining markets. In Denmark, the debate could hardly be so quickly resolved, because the economic advantages of complete liberalization were greater and because the debate called into question one of the very bases of Denmark's economic success since the mid-nineteenth century.

[15] MBZ, 6202/50.5, Directie van de Voedselvoorziening, Belangrijkste Producentenprijzen.

THE ORIGINS OF THE COMMON AGRICULTURAL POLICY

French agricultural interests had not shown many signs of contentment at the prospect of a customs union with Italy. As expressed in the negotiations their discontent was particularly focused on the prospect of increased Italian wine imports. Italy had produced about 38.4 million hectolitres of wine annually in the 1930s but the agricultural committees of the OEEC assumed an Italian production of 42 million hectolitres by 1952. This implied a level of wine exports of about 2.5 million hectolitres, twice the pre-war level. French intentions were not to go beyond the output level of the 1930s but to drink much less of it and export about seven times as much. To have any chance of acceptance a customs union would require an agreement on the control of new plantings and an agreement on the compulsory distillation of output beyond a fixed level. When to these difficulties was added the threat of higher levels of Italian vegetable and fruit exports to France, French agricultural interests could see no satisfactory solution except in a wider European customs union.[16] In November 1949 the Confédération Générale de l'Agriculture expressed its strong objections both to the liberalization of agriculture and to the Franco-Italian customs union and demanded a customs union which offered France the possibility of more agricultural exports in return for any greater access by other countries to French markets.

Competition, they argued, between complementary economies such as France and Italy was unacceptable. What was needed was a trading area which embraced countries less immediately competitive with France. In any case it was necessary to regulate agricultural exports on a product-by-product basis by setting prices and quantities for each. In the crisis of autumn 1947 the French Minister of Agriculture, Pierre Pflimlin, had obtained large increases in state funds for the expansion of food production. This expansion was then incorporated into a fundamental revision of the Modernization Plan in 1948, aiming to turn France into a permanent net exporter of wheat, dairy products, sugar and meat. Monnet's first idea was to export these surpluses to Britain but when the British refused to contemplate any real change in their supply arrangements he turned to Germany, the only major market whose prices were likely to be high enough to make such exports possible, supported by smaller quantities which would be sold to the Benelux countries. For Monnet and Pflimlin another layer in the construction of Little Europe which also met the needs of French economic reconstruction was appearing. There was, the Confédération argued, now 'only one solution: the opening up to France of another regulated market which imported foodstuffs, namely Germany.'[17] That was also the argument made by the Charpentier Report to the Economic Commission for Europe,

[16] France, Conseil Economique, *Compte-rendu de la Commission Mixte Franco-Italienne d'Union Douanière* (Paris, 1949), p. 22. [17] T 232/148, Paris embassy to London, 14 November 1949.

which, because of the forum in which it was presented, lacked all political weight, but showed none the less what French agricultural interests wanted from European reconstruction. It was certainly taken in The Hague as a sign that the French now wished to exclude Britain from agricultural integration as well as from that in coal and steel.[18]

When the French and Italian trade liberalization proposals in March 1950 were presented to the Conseil Economique as though they were a step on the road to Franco-Italian customs union, the agricultural interests there demanded that the Conseil refuse to ratify the agreement of March 1949 to proceed towards a customs union. They asked for the immediate suspension of the March 1950 liberalization proposals and presented their counter-proposals for a larger customs union.[19] In June the International Federation of Agricultural Producers met at Saltsjöbaden in Sweden and the French and German delegations agreed to begin talks on a Franco-German common market in agriculture, resembling Schuman's proposals for coal and steel.

These talks were an almost total failure. Apart from wheat, German farmers were more interested in excluding French exports. Both sides, though, could agree that trade liberalization in agriculture was impossible and that a close regulation of Western Europe's intra-trade in agricultural products was essential. When early in 1950 Dirk Stikker persuaded the Dutch ministers that an overall European plan for 'sectoral integration' was the only way that trade liberalization could be achieved he said that a special arrangement had to be made for agriculture. This was left to the Minister of Agriculture, Sicco Mansholt, to devise and so was born the first of many Mansholt Plans for West European agriculture, a Plan which although much modified by the liberal opposition in the Dutch government was to reappear after the signature of the Treaty of Rome as the basis of the Common Agricultural Policy. From summer 1950 onwards Mansholt made a determined effort to reach as comprehensive a regulation as possible of all the food products traded in Western Europe. The method was another, or the same, High Authority. Pflimlin unsuccessfully tried to persuade the French government to introduce a similar proposal into the Schuman Plan discussions. Monnet was opposed, but only because he wanted agricultural regulation to be the second stage of a united Europe lest it impede the achievement of the first based on coal and steel.[20] There followed, nevertheless, much active discussion between the Dutch and French Ministries of Agriculture, some of it kept secret from ministers in both countries who were hostile, with a view to reaching a common plan. The issues raised closely foreshadowed those which would be raised after the signature of the Treaty of Rome and so did the solutions which were some-

[18] MBZ, 61/50.5, Bespreking met Charpentier, 11 August 1950.
[19] France, Conseil Economique, *Etudes et Travaux no. 14, Union Douanière France-Italie (II)*.
[20] FJM, AMG 58/1/2, Monnet to Pflimlin, 28 December 1950.

times found. Stikker's proposals were presented to a meeting of ministers at the end of May. They included a second High Authority, parallel to that for coal, iron and steel, which would superintend the removal of all quantitative restrictions on agriculture, determine a uniform European price for agricultural products, determine the levels of compensation for higher-cost producers and work out a common policy to be applied to all non-Western European products and producers. The proposals were to be presented as encouraging competition in the sense that it should be possible for the proposed Authority to determine a plan, providing the prices were correctly set to favour the most competitive producers, in which 'shifts of production will practically never occur'.[21] The idea underlying the proposals was that a reduction in inequalities of production costs and final prices would ultimately stimulate competition. That it might also raise prices was readily admitted. The instrument by which inequalities would be reduced – and this caught the imagination as the most distinctive aspect of the proposals – was a European integration fund, which would make loans to less competitive producers to help the transition to competitiveness. Although the fund was conceived primarily to help in the task of bringing a common agricultural policy into being, there was no reason why it should be limited to the primary sector and it could be presented as an addition to Schuman's proposals, an additional supra-national organization to reinforce the one, or two, High Authorities.

A draft of the proposals was then passed confidentially to Hall-Patch who accurately assessed them as proposals for the abandonment of the process of liberalizing trade by percentage stages. The purposes of the European integration fund had now been specified so that it neatly combined both Dutch and French economic interests. It could use its funds for modernizing selected industrial sectors or, establishing an affinity with the Monnet Plan, for developing entirely new sectors. Otherwise the fund would be used to compensate sectors for damage done by the process of sectoral integration. It would make compensation payments to the firms themselves, or to the workers displaced by the process, or it could establish worker retraining schemes.[22]

It was easier to bridge the difference in economic policy between the Netherlands and France than the difference in their foreign policy. The Stikker proposals were evasive on the question of Britain's inclusion. They said that the integration fund should remain under the control of the Council of the OEEC and thus, presumably, involve the whole of Western Europe. On the other hand the Dutch had now made the important transition to the principle of supra-nationality; the Council of the OEEC, it was proposed, should be able to determine the policy of the fund by a three-quarters majority, a position which would certainly be unacceptable in London.

[21] MBZ, 6117/50.1A, Integratie plan voor de landbouw, n.d.
[22] FO 371/87161, Paper handed confidentially to Sir E. Hall-Patch by Dr Stikker on 1 June 1950.

There is not much a small power can do to influence the course of history. If the moment is well chosen and the interplay of national interests correctly judged, however, the small power is not helpless. The change in Dutch foreign economic policy, the abandonment of the firm liberal stance taken after 1945, the acceptance of European reconstruction through integration even if the degree of regulation involved meant the exclusion of Britain, might be judged as only an acceptance of necessity, a response to powerful external pressures. But this would be to ignore the extent to which after 1945 foreign policy had for some time failed to take into account the much more positive spirit of direction and intervention in domestic economic policy. Compared to what was going on at home foreign policy had in fact an anachronistic air in the first post-war years and only began to lose it in 1949. By judging well both the timing and the form of the change of direction Stikker was able to lever the reconstruction of Western Europe into a direction which was more appropriate to what were now the interests of the Dutch economy.

The one thing Stikker could not do was to straddle the widening rift between Little Europe and the OEEC. In an attempt to hold on to the OEEC framework he gave the ideas behind his proposals their first public hearing in Oslo. He had been invited to address a meeting of Staatsøkonomisk Forening, a national association which met to discuss general problems of political economy. There were important matters to discuss.[23] Norway was considering reimposing quotas on Dutch exports because of the slow pace of Dutch liberalization. Neither the Netherlands nor Norway were at all content with the liberalization programme and Norway had felt aggrieved after the last allocation of drawing rights. The occasion was a perfect one and Stikker, without specifying the details of the Netherlands proposals, in effect revealed the whole scheme and spoke strongly in favour of a planned European market as a substitute both for protectionism and for the current process of trade liberalization. He made it clear that the Netherlands was now not only backing sectoral integration but wanted speedy action to 'create a strong, balanced European market, before overproduction and unemployment will force us again to withdraw into our own shells, with a lower standard of living as a result'.[24]

A week later, on 15 June, the Stikker Plan was announced under the title 'Plan of Action'. It stipulated an industry-by-industry approach to Western European integration, beginning with 'the basic industries, agriculture and those processing industries which by their specialization can particularly contribute to Europe's viability and the products of which play an important part in international trade both intra-European and inter-continental.'[25]

[23] 'In a not unusual alcoholic ecstasy my Norwegian colleague told me that the whole of Oslo was in an uproar over the coming visit of Minister Stikker and even the King was involved.' MBZ, 6202/50.12, Van Tuyl to The Hague, 27 May 1950.   [24] Diebold, *Trade*, p. 205.
[25] MBZ, 6205/50.1, Essential points of the Netherlands government's memorandum on European integration, n.d.

The objectives were specified as an increase in living standards, a balance of payments equilibrium between Western Europe and the world, and stable, high employment levels. The actions to be taken were even more specific.

The 75 per cent stage of trade liberalization was only to be achieved on the basis of an idea which had always been present from the start of the liberalization programme but never entirely accepted, the so-called common list. Hitherto the commodities on which quotas were to be removed had never been stipulated and countries were free to remove them where they wished. One result had been that at the 60 per cent stage there were still virtually no commodities free of quota restrictions across the whole of Western Europe. France had always been opposed to this piecemeal policy, because specifying categories of goods on which all countries would have to remove restrictions would have been a step towards the common sectoral regulation of the market which France desired. In January the OEEC had accepted that in the progress towards the 75 per cent stage some attempt should be made to harmonize the lists. The Dutch now backed that position wholeheartedly by stipulating that further trade liberalization must be tied to sectoral integration and this necessarily meant drawing up a 'common list'.

State trading would still be excluded from liberalization providing the state purchasing contracts were long-term and offered guaranteed markets. Progress from 60 per cent to 75 per cent and onwards was to be attained within the framework of sectoral integration which would proceed, like the Schuman proposals, with the intention of removing all tariffs, as well as non-tariff obstacles, within a particular sector. The sectors in question would each be studied by special technical committees and would be entitled to have access, if needed, to the European integration fund. As far as the agricultural sector itself was concerned everything started from the assumption that Western Europe need be deficient in only one important item, bread grain. For all other items European production should expand to fill the gap currently filled by imports. Surpluses of agricultural products in Western Europe created by imports from outside Europe would be unacceptable, because of their depressive effect on purchasing power in the agricultural sector.[26]

The first impact of the Stikker Plan was on the long-unresolved negotiations for the Franco-Italian customs union. It behoved the Italian government to do something quickly because the balance of bargaining advantage within Little Europe had shifted so suddenly in favour of the planners. The response was the Pella Plan. While it can be readily accepted that the Pella Plan also aimed at an accelerated pace of European economic integration, that only shows how relatively meaningless in the historical context the word integration had become. What mattered was the form and type of integration, the precise next

[26] MBZ, 60/50.13, Ontwerp-Considerans van de Landbouw-paragraaf in het Nederlandse Plan van Actie, 27 June 1950.

steps required. On these counts the Pella Plan was not a reinforcement of the Stikker Plan, it was fundamentally opposed to it.[27]

It started from the assumption that there were permanent differences in factor endowment between European countries which must be permanently compensated. Tariffs were one necessary compensatory device and would have to be retained. Over the Western European area, however, it should be possible, Pella argued, to extend a series of common preference agreements which could soon allow a common external tariff for the preferential zone to be established. Once this had been done other forms of compensation for the inequalities of factor endowment in Western Europe would then be needed. Italy's agricultural exports would thus be protected within Western Europe from the only competition they need fear, for that came from outside the area, while her own agricultural sector would be protected on the domestic market without the stricter regulation which the Dutch idea of a common market assumed. There were very few sectors on which Italy was prepared to envisage the removal of internal forms of protection, differential tax rates, export subsidies and so on, and if the procedure followed in the Schuman Plan negotiations was to be followed for agriculture every one of these protectionist devices would be questioned, bargained over, and susceptible to control by a new High Authority. The Italian delegation at the OEEC let it be known that their government was 'not at all in favour' of the Stikker Plan and that there would be no results from it.[28] The Italian government took the same attitude to the proposed European integration fund. A European investment fund, Pella suggested, rather than an integration fund, would certainly be a useful and acceptable idea if it channelled investment into those areas which did suffer from a permanent disadvantage in factor endowment, but if it were specifically geared to making sectoral integration work it was of no interest to Italy.

The Pella proposals also took up again what had been from the start a central plank of Italian policy. In order to eliminate some of the inequalities of endowment, Pella argued, it was essential to improve the freedom of factor movements. This meant, of course, primarily the movement of Italian labour to other Western European countries and, the necessary corollary, the liberal-ization of invisible payments. The inflow of foreign capital, the inflow of migrants' remittances, and the earnings of Italian banks and shipping companies abroad had all played an important role in Italian economic development before the fascist period had demoted them in importance by seeking a

[27] Giuseppe Pella, 1902–81. A self-made man. Began his political life in the Popolari, but gave up politics in the Fascist period. An accountant who worked for a woollen business, he was a representative at numerous international conferences 1932–9. Deputy 1945. Under-Secretary for Finance and Treasury 1946. Minister of Finance 1947. Minister for Treasury 1948. Minister for Budget 1951, 1953, 1960. Minister of Foreign Affairs 1953, 1957, 1959. Chairman of the interministerial committee for reconstruction. Governor of the IMF.

[28] FO 371/87161, Paris delegation to London, 28 June 1950.

different path to development. The ambition was to return to the original path and the Italian government still sought to modify the European economic framework to make this more possible.

The French attempt to act as a broker between these conflicting positions produced a third set of proposals, the Petsche Plan, so that within one month the OEEC was faced with three different sets of proposals for progressing towards economic integration in Western Europe, all designed to slow down the speed and blunt the force of trade liberalization. The Petsche Plan, however, failed to catch anyone's imagination except its author's. It was designed not only to adapt the Stikker proposals a little more closely to Italian interests but also to modify their *dirigiste* nature lest they should provide too much support for the planners in the French cabinet. Petsche's uneasiness with his own government's policy during the EPU negotiations has already been noted as well as his tendency to lend a ready ear to central bank advocacy of a floating franc. He did not like the idea that the cash in Stikker's European integration fund appeared to be intended to come from central governments and that the decisions of the fund were thus likely to supplement and strengthen those of domestic planners. On the other hand the Petsche Plan did not differ in its objectives from the ultimate objectives of the Monnet Plan. Indeed it sought to enhance them by ensuring that the integration fund was used more for purposes of modernization than for compensation. But at the same time Petsche sought to transform the fund into something more in the nature of a private investment bank which would bring American capital into Western Europe to support the transfer of American technology and the process of industrial modernization.

He accepted Pella's proposal that it should be an investment fund rather than an integration fund and proposed in turn that it should raise dollar loans on American private capital markets. Similarly, instead of drawing on the meagre foreign exchange reserves of governments, the fund would operate by raising capital on private European markets.[29] If the decisions were taken on banking principles, the loans, Petsche hoped, would necessarily be channelled into the modernization and development of expanding high-technology sectors, some of which would be viable only on a European scale. This idea led to the addition of a proposal for a common European organization to co-ordinate scientific and technological research to help in the modernization of European industry. This too required immediate European co-ordination because once the separate national programmes of technological development had been achieved they would no longer be able to be co-ordinated.

The Petsche Plan was not only an effort to bridge the gap between the Dutch and Italian proposals, but also to bridge the gap between the warring economic philosophies in the French cabinet. This was one reason why it was

[29] MBZ, 6117/50.1, OEEC, Groupe de Travail No. 6 du Comité Exécutif, Tableau Synoptique des Plans Stikker, Pella, Petsche, 26 July 1950.

not favourably received in Italy and therefore, on a simple tactical level, did not resolve the problem of what the OEEC could do. The Stikker Plan had one immediate pre-requisite; the OEEC was faced with the need to agree on the way in which the 75 per cent mark for quota removal could be reached and the Stikker Plan made it clear that, although some progress towards this target might be made in the same way as before, there had also to be a commitment that in the sectors specified in the Plan trade liberalization would take on a fundamentally different meaning. In particular this next stage would have to be accompanied by the removal of some tariffs and by the start of joint planning in some agricultural sectors. The Pella Plan had its pre-requisites too; Italy was not prepared to go to the 75 per cent mark without an agreement on the liberalization of invisibles which would help to provide for labour migration.

The Stikker Plan was sternly opposed by the ECA, which regarded it simply as an attempt to wriggle out of the trade liberalization commitment and also the trade rules of the EPU.[30] The British could see no way forward in their own interests except to persuade Stikker to give up his proposals and to persist with the trade liberalization programme. London was altogether more sympathetic to the Pella proposals, which were seen as coinciding with the British conception of a low tariff area.[31] But Stikker, when presenting his proposals to the OEEC Council on 7 July, requested an immediate meeting of all the ministers of agriculture to 'unify the market'.[32] Denmark, unwilling to accept any longer the unfair working of the trade liberalization programme on its own economy, supported the request.[33] But would integration into Little Europe make the external position better? If the OEEC as a whole rejected the Stikker Plan the next Dutch move was easy to foresee, whereas for Denmark the same move would very likely mean the loss of the British market. The French, it seems, did approach Denmark to ask the government to consider the equivalent of a Schuman Plan for agriculture as the way out of its problems.[34]

The Council of the OEEC and Working Group No. 6 of the Executive Committee, to which all aspects of the conflicting proposals other than that of quota removal on agricultural produce were referred, tried to devise a time-scale at whose more distant points the Stikker and Pella Plans might not look so different. The British were vigorously opposed, however, to this effort at compromise. They saw the Stikker Plan as an alarming extension of the Schuman Plan which must be stopped. They defended the view that, as Roll expressed it, 'shocks which occur through the continuing process of liberalization can and must be taken up through EPU and Marshall Aid which are

[30] FO 371/87161, UK delegation to London, 29 June 1950.
[31] ibid., The Stikker Plan, 29 June 1950.
[32] ibid., Report of discussion in OEEC Council, 7 July 1950.
[33] FO 371/87162, Dudley to Hall-Patch, 18 July 1950.   [34] ibid.

intended for just this very purpose.'[35] The European integration fund, in the form in which Stikker had proposed it, disappeared rapidly from view in the working group. Only Norway gave it real support. The French watered down the proposal even more than the Petsche Plan had originally done, so that the working group finished its discussions with the idea of a European investment bank operating as a conventional private bank and in no way dependent on government decisions, whether national or supra-national, able to respond only to individual applications for capital from firms or their equivalent.[36]

On the matter of establishing a 'common list' of goods to be used as a basis either of sectoral integration or of the next stage of trade liberalization France and the Netherlands remained insistent, although the working group had endless difficulties in finding even one industrial good which was clearly acceptable to all. Eventually it was agreed that the idea could be put to the test by appointing two specialized technical committees to study how it might be worked out in respect of, firstly, pulp and paper and, secondly, woollens, an area in which Pella was expert. To read the debates even at this early stage is to realize that the chances of a future integrated Europe producing a common industrial policy, outside the domain of coal, iron and steel where such special historical circumstances applied, were utterly negligible. But as far as agricultural products were concerned prospects were altogether more promising, mostly because so few were prepared to accept the consequences of further trade liberalization in that area.

Between March 1950 and the end of the year there had been practically no further liberalization of quotas on agricultural products. Even had there been, most such products would still have encountered formidable tariff barriers. On grain, flour, fresh meat, sugar and many categories of vegetables French and Italian tariff rates were more than 30 per cent *ad valorem*. In Benelux sugar imports faced prohibitive tariff barriers. The manipulation of tariffs and quotas to fit the seasonal movements of production often meant that fresh fruits encountered insurmountable obstacles on all Western European frontiers. Face to face with the unwillingness of countries to remove any further non-tariff barriers to agricultural trade, with the fact that even if they did so this would not mean any effective degree of liberalization unless the tariffs themselves were reduced, and faced, finally, with the fact that after the outbreak of the Korean war there was a still greater emphasis on the need to increase Western Europe's own food production, opinion in the Food and Agriculture Committee of the OEEC, to which the task of liberalization in the agricultural sector had been delegated, was favourable to abandoning

[35] MBZ, 6117/50.1B, De Behandeling de Plannen Stikker, Petsche en Pella, 16 August 1950. They did not take the same view when in a similar position themselves at the end of 1951.
[36] FO 371/87163, passim. FO 371/87166, Projet de création d'une Banque Européenne d'Investissements, 8 July 1950.

trade liberalization in favour of something along the lines of the Stikker Plan. If it was necessary to encourage yet further increases in output in European agriculture, and if the demand for Western European food was so great as to offer to Western European producers a wide range of guaranteed markets for particular products in Western Europe itself, what was the point in quotas and tariffs except as a protection against food coming from outside the region? All that was needed was to guarantee by a system of market regulation increasing levels of output, prices and profit within Western Europe. The guarantees could be provided by the regulation of price and quality. The Committee decided to report by mid-February 1951 on possible ways of 'unifying the market' for dairy products, pork, eggs, fish, fruit and vegetables. After that it would proceed to wine, vegetable oils and fats.[37]

These desultory efforts fell far short of what the highly organized European agricultural interests had already glimpsed in the 1948 revision of the French plan and in Mansholt's ideas.[38] As prices for animal products began to fall after 1950 they demanded a much more decisive intervention in the markets than the Food and Agriculture Committee of OEEC could provide. In France this did not go as far as supporting Pflimlin's wish for an agricultural High Authority. The farmers' organizations wanted guaranteed exports of their surplus crops; a High Authority might also compel them to take imports. This was the standpoint of the Deutscher Bauernverband too. But in the Netherlands there was active support for going further and accepting the principles of the Mansholt Plan by which inequalities in comparative advantage and productivity would be gradually eliminated through investment and improvement financed by an equalization fund which would be financed by a common tariff on all agricultural imports into a Western European common market.[39] Payments from the fund would guarantee stable prices to European producers. Within this protective structure special production plans for the more troublesome items, wheat, sugar, and milk, would be drawn up. For all commodities the equalization of supply and demand over periods of time would be achieved by a European stockpiling programme. The fund would function like Stikker's proposed European integration fund, providing loans to those sectors worst affected by the common policy to enable them to modernize and adapt to new opportunities. Although the internal tariffs and differences in national prices would remain until this was achieved, prices in intra-Western European trade would be equalized before this and maximum tariff levels determined.[40]

[37] FO 371/87164, passim.
[38] Sicco Leendert Mansholt, 1908– . An agronomist. Plantation manager in Java 1931–4; farmer 1934–45. Played a role in the Dutch resistance movement. Minister of Agriculture, Fisheries and Food 1945–8. Vice President of Commission of EEC 1958. President of the Agricultural Working Group of EEC 1958 onwards.
[39] FO 371/87256, Nichols to Bevin, 13 November 1950.
[40] FO 371/87256, European collaboration in agriculture, 14 November 1950.

The Mansholt Plan was intended to apply, supposedly, to the whole of Western Europe. Its applicability, however, to the British economy, with its low agricultural tariffs and its stream of cheap extra-European food imports, was not clear. It would be implemented and controlled by a European board of agriculture and food, responsible to a Council of Ministers and governed by qualified majority decisions of that Council. The administrative mechanism was thus easily assimilable in principle to the administrative apparatus of the Schuman Plan. If Britain did not join, the European board of agriculture and food could without difficulty resemble the High Authority of the ECSC.

In Denmark the minority Social Democrat government fell from power in October partly because of its efforts to shift government policy towards a more overt support for industrial investment. The right-wing parties remained committed to agricultural exports as a pillar of the economy and wanted to try first to remedy the balance of payments crisis while adhering to a trading framework which was as free as possible and from which, they argued, Danish exports must in the long run benefit. Since the mid-nineteenth century that framework had been provided by the British economy. Had markets there been closed the heavy investment in Danish agriculture after 1870 might well never have produced the remarkable economic results it did after 1890. The structure of investment and output in the agricultural sector was in fact geared over a long period of time, the most crucial period in the country's development, to British demand. In the inter-war period, particularly after 1933, the German economy had provided a welcome relief from this prosperous but for Denmark dangerous, symbiosis. But in the circumstances of the 1930s the Germans had offered no alternative long-term solution, however, and the drastic agricultural protectionism of the Federal German government did not look as though it would do so either. For Denmark the Stikker Plan raised an issue of future development which was not a small matter of policy adjustment but a complete change in the pattern of the country's development. From 1945 to 1949 Denmark had stood aside in relative comfort from the problems of Europe's economic reconstruction. In 1950 it had to be recognized that those problems struck at the very roots of Denmark's modern history.

The Danish dilemma was discussed in the Anglo-Scandinavian Economic Committee. The Danish social democrats welcomed the general approach of the Stikker and Mansholt Plans because, whereas quota removal had proved entirely ineffective in the agricultural sector, they would force the reduction and even removal within Western Europe of tariffs on agriculture. The British attitude to the Plans was 'unhelpful',[41] because even from the standpoint of the right-wing Danish parties complete opposition to these ideas by Britain would not lead to their abandonment and a further stage of liberalization as Britain hoped, but might lead to another negotiation like that contemporane-

[41] CAB 134/252, Minutes of the second session of the Anglo-Scandinavian Economic Committee, 23 November 1950.

ously going on for coal, iron and steel. If Denmark participated the gains would be small, perhaps, and, in return, there would be a clean break with the idea of Scandinavian economic association as well as a rupture of the ties with Britain. Throughout the abortive discussions in 1947 and 1948 about the possibility of a Scandinavian customs union the assumption had always been that this would be within the wider setting of 'the European organization', if Sweden would accept that organization. But the affinities between the Stikker Plan and the Schuman Plan were unmistakable and the Mansholt Plan would be obviously easier to implement in Little Europe alone. Norway, it is true, had supported the original conception of a European integration fund as a way of helping government investment cope with disadvantaged sectors and regions, but was opposed to what had now emerged as a private investment fund, and, of course, firmly opposed to either a common industrial or agricultural policy which implied a stage in integration. Needless to say, Sweden, if prepared to consider any further steps in integration at all, would certainly not do so for any lesser area than the OEEC.

The moment when the difficulties and dangers of making this choice had to be faced proved, however, not yet to have arrived. The Pella Plan had already given an indication of how little Italy had immediately to gain from substituting sectoral integration for trade liberalization. The Stikker proposals were intended to bring down tariffs, whereas Italy had high tariffs. German opinion reflected Erhard's antagonism to sectoral integration as a form of protectionism against German interests. Italian agricultural exports had more to gain from continued quota removal than from tariff removal and sectoral integration. Many were not directly competitive with national production elsewhere. Tariffs on citrus fruits, for example, were insignificant in Europe. The political problems of sectoral integration in agriculture compared to those in coal and steel were formidable. Coal and steel were both very small industries in Italy in terms of employment, but there was a larger proportion and number of voters dependent on the agricultural sector for their incomes than in any other occupation or in any other Schuman Plan country. Access to the French market through a Franco-Italian customs union would have been a valuable gain for Italian farmers. But that had never been acceptable in France except in the context of the wider, regulated market which in turn gave French farmers access to British or German markets or both. But there was no economic reason in 1950 for Italy to accept this situation and begin the process of sectoral integration in agriculture. The Danish dilemma was not resolved, but it was postponed by Italy's insistence that the Pella Plan was as far as it would go in modifying the trade liberalization programme.

This left the problem of the French farmers unresolved too. For them the West German market had become and would remain the crucial issue. For French agricultural plans to be realized the Federal Republic would have to admit French dairy products much more liberally than before and both countries would have to undertake an extremely complicated readjustment of their highly protected markets for sugar. All this would have to be done at the same time as Dutch dairy products, and also perhaps Danish, were given guarantees of longer-term access in greater quantities to the German market. The return for all this would be a much longer, perhaps an indeterminate, lease of life for a wide range of inefficient peasant food production in West Germany. At the best this would be a breathing space in which the Federal Republic might cope with the problem of modernizing an agricultural sector which had been sheltered from the reality of international prices and competition by a succession of governments, culminating in the 1930s in the orgy of agricultural protectionism in which the National Socialists had indulged. At the worst it would be an attempt by the new democracy to avoid one of its most urgent responsibilities.

It is impossible at the moment to write with any accuracy or insight about the way the West German government itself approached this aspect of post-war reconstruction. For all its objections to sectoral integration as imposing an unnecessary degree of protectionism on an economy whose future prosperity depended on world markets, the government against Erhard's protests had blatantly excepted the agricultural sector from the process of trade liberalization even before the start of the OEEC programmes. The halt which the OEEC called to the freeing of German imports, followed by their gradual liberalization again from January 1952, did not much affect French or German farmers. Whether the resumption of German trade liberalization after the economy had moved back into surplus within the EPU would have been allowed to reach the agricultural sector is impossible at the moment to estimate. But it is in fact only a hypothetical consideration. Trade liberalization was brought to a more definite stop in Western Europe by the two major countries concerned, France and Britain. Both countries by the end of 1951 were reimposing import restrictions against Western European imports to rectify a rapidly deteriorating balance of payments position. Britain's nominal percentage rate of liberalization in October 1951 was not reached again until 1956, although by that time it covered a much greater quantity of trade because of the privatization of the import trade which proceeded apace in the 1950s.

The origin of the British action was not the increased imports caused by trade liberalization, although these did play a part in the loss of reserves, but the disturbances to the whole complex of trade and payments within which the British economy functioned, caused by the impact of the Korean war together with what appears to be a less than adequate response to those problems by the domestic economy. Over the three years from the outbreak of war in summer 1950 military expenditure in the United States increased threefold. One of the first consequences was a fierce restocking boom of which sterling area raw material exporters were one of the main beneficiaries.

Western European exports to the United States also rose and the background to the first months of the EPU was a continuation of the marked improvement in Western Europe's external position. By mutual agreement Britain and the United States terminated Marshall Aid as the dollars in the sterling area dollar pool began to pile up. It was a false dawn. The instability of the American economy had not yet finished exercising its fierce pressures through the sterling area mechanism on the British balance of payments. This time through the arrangements for partial convertibility which Britain had finally conceded as part of the EPU agreement it made the strain on Britain's payments with Western Europe worse.

Even as Western Europe's foreign trade reaped its initial dollar gains from American rearmament the point of the trade liberalization programme and American pressure for automatic gold settlements in the EPU was beginning to be called into question in Washington. Was it not now in America's strategic interests to try to organize and regulate commodity markets also? By the end of 1950 the National Advisory Council was suggesting that now 'the major problem before the United States was to organize the international allocation of basic materials in the way best calculated to further strategic interests', and that the importance of doing this might mean 'that the trade liberalization program may be de-emphasized and deferred for the time being'.[42] In the event the Council decided that, even though it was now no longer possible to 'assume that freedom of individual choice in a single market will always lead to the optimum direction of resources', the ultimate goal in Europe was still the same. 'We felt that EPU combined with the trade liberalization program was a step towards the US objective of West European unification.'[43] But there was no optimism about achieving this goal now.

American rearmament provoked a sudden and violent deterioration in the terms of trade of the developed economies. An increase in European defence expenditure increased dollar imports and in Britain's case this was exacerbated by the fact that an economy running at high levels of capacity utilization had to be provided with non-capital goods imports postponed in 1950. As the raw material boom slackened off in summer 1951 Europe's external position swung alarmingly in an unfavourable direction, 'viability' again receded and, once more, the deterioration in Britain's external position was worse than that of the other countries, although this time France was not saved by the cushion of intra-Western European trade, because its own and the franc zone's exports to the dollar area had been increased by the American boom. Western Europe's dollar deficit was bigger in 1951 in absolute terms in current dollars than it had been in 1949, although as a proportion of Western Europe's

[42] US Treasury, EUR/4/31, National Advisory Council Staff Committee, 'Financial policy questions re foreign assistance programs proposed for fiscal year 1952', 18 December 1950.

[43] ibid., 'The future of EPU and the European trade liberalization program', 26 December 1950.

combined gross product it was less significant than it had been then and in terms of constant pre-devaluation dollars it had not risen.

Why the impact of this swing was so particularly severe on Britain has not been satisfactorily explained, although the general outlines of the explanation are the same as in 1949. The increase in exports was less than it should have been, given the great stimulus to demand provided by the increased sales of the rest of the sterling area to the United States. On this occasion, unlike the balance of payments crisis of 1949, the geographical distribution of the United Kingdom's foreign trade should have been more advantageous. The reason most frequently given for the sluggishness of British exports is the high level of demand for capital goods in the home market and the lack of spare capacity to expand output.[44] But French exports increased by about 30 per cent over the same period. The proportion of French engineering output consumed on the home market was much higher than that of Britain.[45] Although there was some spare capacity in French manufacturing industry in 1949, it had certainly been mopped up by the end of 1950 and throughout the whole period the labour market was even tighter than in Britain.

Extra-European demand was still heavily for capital goods and steel and in that sector the British manufacturing base does not seem to have been able to take advantage of the brief opportunity offered, which was necessary if the economy was to function as the hub of so large a wheel of payments. The output of crude steel in Britain in 1951 fell, whereas it rose steeply in the other main Western European steel-manufacturing countries. But as table 67 shows there was a spectacular fall in textile and clothing exports from the peak attained in the fourth quarter of 1950, whereas the stagnation of exports of metal goods and machinery after that date correlates with the pattern of manufactured exports overall. There appear to have been two strong surges of British exports, in the final quarter of 1950 and the second quarter of 1951. Except in textiles and clothing the second surge recaptured the ground lost after the first and the subsequent stagnation was at this higher level. The restocking boom in America was initially as beneficial to British exports as might have been predicted, but why did they falter so badly in the first quarter of 1951? And why was the ground gained by textile and clothing exports entirely lost?

Both Britain and the rest of Western Europe had large deficits with the rest of the sterling area in the first half of 1951. The rest of Western Europe could now settle these deficits through the partial convertibility of sterling balances to which Britain had reluctantly agreed in the negotiation of the EPU. The sterling balances of non-European countries grew by $1030 million in the first half of that year. Britain was financing under the terms of the EPU agreements

[44] UN, *Economic Survey of Europe in 1951* (Geneva, 1952), p. 69; A.J. Youngson, *The British Economy 1920–1957* (London, 1960), pp. 173 ff.
[45] UN, *Economic Survey of Europe Since the War* (Geneva, 1953), p. 213.

Table 67   Trends in exports of manufactures from the United Kingdom, 1949–51 (1947 = 100)

Year	Quarters	Metal goods* and engineering products	Textiles and clothing†	All manufactured goods
1949	1st	149	150	145
	2nd	141	138	136
	3rd	136	136	132
	4th	151	131	142
1950	1st	165	145	155
	2nd	165	136	154
	3rd	163	146	160
	4th	176	166	174
1951	1st	159	157	161
	2nd	175	162	176
	3rd	163	148	167
	4th	174	132	170

Source: UK, *Board of Trade Journal*, various issues.
* Groups III C, D, E, F, G, S (excluding rubber tyres and tubes).
† Groups III I, J, K, L, M.

a substantial part of Western Europe's deficit on extra-European trade. At some point, had those agreements not existed in the form they did, some Western European countries would have been obliged to pay gold or dollars to Britain. When the raw material boom ended with the filling of American inventories Britain found itself in the last quarter of 1951 making heavy gold payments to the EPU while countries still in surplus were drawing gold.

Within the EPU the tendency to disequilibrium sharply increased and the pattern of disequilibrium resembled very much that which had prevailed so strongly in intra-Western European trade in 1947 and 1948 and been so large an obstacle to multilateral payments then. France went back into deficit and

Table 68   Average monthly balance of certain EPU members, 1950–1 ($ million = million units of account)

	1950		1951			
	3rd qtr	4th qtr	1st qtr	2nd qtr	3rd qtr	4th qtr
Belgium/Luxembourg	−0.9	+2.9	+27.9	+48.9	+62.7	+59.2
France	+63.5	+9.7	+19.5	−25.2	−35.8	−95.4
West Germany	−59.1	−60.8	−29.6	+57.7	+55.6	+50.2
United Kingdom and sterling area*	+36.9	+135.2	+52.8	−9.0	−171.3	−187.4

Source: UN, *Economic Survey of Europe in 1951*, Appendix Table XXX, p. 192.
* Except Iceland.

Belgium's surpluses mounted (table 68). The Belgian surpluses in the EPU were particularly related to an increase in exports to Britain and France. In the last quarter of 1951 Belgium adopted measures to restrict commodity exports, a small export tax and restrictions on export licences. Belgium's quota in the EPU was comparatively small and surpluses of such a size were as big a threat to the financial operations of the EPU as the deficits of countries with large quotas. But the threat to France's payments position came also from the dollar account. Both France and Britain experienced a 15 per cent increase in 1951 in imports from the United States. The coal shortage returned with the rampant boom and French imports of coal from the United States had to resume. Although on extra-European trade as a whole France had a surplus, it was mostly with the franc zone countries which had benefited like the sterling area from the raw materials boom, and thus did not help to meet the dollar settlements. Like the United Kingdom France took refuge in import restrictions and the trade liberalization programme foundered in the face of war, rearmament, and the further reminder they gave that equilibrium in Western European payments was a chimera and that 'viability' between Western Europe and North America had little meaning.

Ironically, it took the impact of a long and savage war to make it clear that 'viability' and equilibrium were not indispensable elements of a lasting peace. The end of the ERP ceased to be a landmark and Marshall Aid was gradually merged into military aid under the Mutual Security Act to allow the European economies to cope with the problems of international trade that rearmament imposed on top of six years of sustained, heavy investment. The ultimate purpose of trade liberalization became subsidiary, although still a goal of American foreign policy. The immediate purpose of integration became rearmament, particularly German rearmament. The crossing of the thirty-eighth parallel had ended the ECA's dream; German rearmament still meant European integration, but no longer of the kind of which Hoffman, or Bissell, much less Clayton, would have approved.

Had the process of trade liberalization continued to be backed by the United States, would the European Economic Community have emerged as a reaction earlier than it did? There is no reason to argue that the construction of a common market in agriculture was any easier in 1961 than it appeared in 1951. Free trade in Western European agricultural products had gone for good. The Danish and Dutch hopes for an association of the United Kingdom with an agricultural common market were more in the nature of naturally hesitant fears for the future. Had sectoral integration proceeded it would have included a common agricultural policy as well as a common market. Italy's economic objections were no greater in 1951 than later. What was lacking was the political reason to override them and, no doubt, in Bonn too it was the weight of the political factors which would have been decisive. But the idea of sectoral integration in agriculture was displaced into the distant background of policy as soon as the Korean war definitely interrupted trade liberalization and German rearmament and the European Defence Community became the central and overriding issue in Franco-German relations. It was scarcely to be heard of again, even when the foreign ministers of Little Europe agreed in 1956 to accept the recommendation of the 'Spaak Committee' as the basis for proceeding to a common market, until December 1961 when the Council of Ministers met to discuss the passage to the second stage of the transition period to the common market.

Then it proved that the situation had not changed. Agreement on a common agricultural policy was a precondition before either France or the Netherlands would proceed to the second stage. British participation in the 'Spaak Committee' more or less ended in November 1955 when it became clear that what the committee would recommend was a closely-regulated customs union akin to French ideas as they had been since 1947, with a relatively high level of common external protection, rather than a gradually developing and widening free-trade area. The instructions handed down by the governments from the Messina meetings to Spaak's intergovernmental committee neatly encapsulated the ideas and positions which had become clear in the opposition to trade liberalization in 1950 – and in the plans for sectoral integration in agriculture. France insisted on a common external customs regime, Benelux and Italy on a readaptation fund, Italy on the freedom of movement of workers and Germany on the proscription of all discrimination. But thenceforward discussion was entirely about the feasibility of these proposals for industry. There was nothing specifically about agriculture in the Messina instructions. Yet it was axiomatic that if a common market was to be produced an agreement on what to do about agriculture would have to be reached. It had become clear in 1950 that that could only be on the basis of a common agricultural policy and nothing in that respect had changed by 1961. The central issue was still the degree of access to the German market and although the two major contestants there, France and the Netherlands, disputed minor points contentiously, they were, as Edgar Pisani, the French Minister of Agriculture, put it, 'condemned to succeed'.[46]

Whether they would have succeeded in 1951 would have depended on the threat of trade liberalization exerting an equivalent pressure. The obstacles were looming large by the end of 1950, although what was to be the main one in 1961 was smaller then, the strong current of opinion in the West German government that it would be advantageous to import food from the cheapest possible source. In 1950 the scarcity of dollars made that argument weaker. Those who pinned a greater hope in continued trade liberalization in 1950 and estimated its advantages higher than those of a common agricultural policy were also, of course, pinning their hopes on a rather uncertain development.

[46] L.M. Lindberg, *The Political Dynamics of European Integration* (Stanford, 1963), p. 269.

This was the weakness of Italy's position. Of course, the latent disagreements between France and the Netherlands on the precise nature of a common agricultural policy were also just as evident as later. France, judging the degree of its comparative advantage to be less than that of the Netherlands, sought high minimum prices and a high level of external protection. The Netherlands, while insisting on the necessity for a common policy, had to guard against the danger of a Franco-German understanding which would be excessively protectionist and render the Dutch comparative advantage worthless.

As for the Federal Republic, it was never put to the test and the idea of 'unifying the market' with their French counterparts remained a somewhat abstract conception for German farmers for another decade. When it became actual they were more than a little ambivalent over developments they had seemed in 1950 to be encouraging. But even so in 1950, as in 1961, every agricultural interest group in Little Europe outside Italy was close to the conviction that a policy which would favour its interests could be negotiated. The Stresa negotiations were difficult and dramatic, but like the Schuman Plan negotiations they succeeded, because it was another area where reconstruction through the development of a formalized system of economic interdependence was always possible if the external pressures were strong enough. Indeed, the Common Agricultural Policy has become the main business of the EEC. Ninety-five per cent of the European Community's regulations are agricultural regulations and three-quarters of the time of the Council of Ministers is spent on a sector which contributes only about 7 per cent of the Community's GNP and is responsible for only about 12 per cent of its employment.

By 1950 this was not so difficult to foresee. The butter mountains, wine lakes and sugar swamps of Little Europe beckoned enticingly on the horizon. British voices might urge the eye temporarily to more distant world perspectives, but these were blurred and insecure compared to the temptations which that nearer, safer vision offered to the calculating political mind. The more difficult thing to explain is why it took so long to get there. For that, the mirage of the European Defence Community is probably most to blame. Against the economic absurdity of preventing the citizens of Western Europe from choking on butter, drowning in wine and suffocating in sugar only by exporting these commodities at knock-down prices to unfriendly, developed economies, who themselves have only been prevented by their own monumental inefficiencies from pursuing similar policies, there is no defence. But if the post-war reconstruction of Western Europe as it had taken shape by 1951 is a major cause of the longest peace on the European continent, twenty years of tedious argument over the intervention price for wheat and the basic price for pigs might seem a small price to pay.

XIV

CONCLUSIONS

THE ARGUMENT OF THE BOOK

During the years of reconstruction there was a deluge of economic and journalistic analysis on the theme of what ought to be done, most of it characterized by an absence of any longer-term historical perspective to an extent unusual even in hastily written contemporary comment. It is as if in 1947 events had taken so dramatic and inexplicable a turn and moved so quickly as to invalidate the traditional modes of analysis on which most commentators rely. After 1953 this spate of comment stopped short and there was an almost complete absence of discussion of the reconstruction for two decades while Europeans busied themselves with the life of getting and spending for which the reconstruction had prepared the way. Most economics literature was concerned to explain why rates of growth of national income were so high and so sustained, and how they could be maintained. In this discussion the post-war reconstruction made only a very perfunctory introductory appearance. After the Second World War, it was suggested, something called 'the Bretton Woods system' had been created which permitted and even encouraged – other things being equal – economies to pursue similar policies leading to higher rates of economic growth. There had been, it was usually indicated, some initial difficulties in making 'the Bretton Woods system' function, because the United States had at first underestimated the dimensions of the needed recovery from the damage and dislocation wrought by the Second World War. This, however, had been put right by Marshall Aid, which at the same time had produced a certain measure of European economic co-operation lacking after the First World War. Thus by 1950 the foundations had been laid for the bright new world of sustained economic growth. The only alternative explanation was that the two decades of high growth rates which followed were due to high levels of armaments expenditure and were thus the product of the Cold War, an explanation which implied that the reconstruction was either irrelevant or a failure.

Curiously enough, when the end of sustained high growth rates came in 1974 it produced a mass of economic analysis which, by a meticulous enquiry into why 'the Bretton Woods system' had ceased to function (or never had functioned) adequately, only established this superficial view of the reconstruction the more firmly, dividing the post-war world into a Bretton Woods and post-Bretton Woods period. It has been left to historians re-examining the failure of western European reconstruction after 1918 to begin to put the reconstruction after 1945 into the more accurate perspective of European history since 1914. This is where it belongs and to consider it in any shorter perspective defeats understanding. Western Europe was reconstructed, not from the destructive consequences of the Second World War only, but from those of the catastrophic economic collapse of 1929–32 and, in so far as that collapse itself was attributable to the First World War, from the consequences of the First World War too. The economic boom of 1919, which collapsed before the peace settlements of Versailles and St Germain had even been signed, the febrile, uncertain boom engendered by the Dawes Plan, the separate national recoveries in Germany, America, or Britain after 1932 with their severe domestic limitations, brought no proper hope for an international recovery. All appear as very brief episodes compared to the period of, even by the meanest definition, twenty years of uninterrupted growth of incomes *throughout* western Europe which followed the Second World War. At the same time the peace which was never concluded has lasted longer than any other in western Europe. What contribution does this book make to explaining those two things?

It is necessary to begin by recapitulating the warning of the preface. This is a history of the reconstruction written from above, not below. The basis of the argument is that in place of a comprehensive political peace settlement there developed in the reconstruction period an institutionalized pattern of economic interdependence in Western Europe which was a better basis for western Europe's economic and political existence than the comprehensive regulation by treaty of major political issues which was attempted after 1918 and which failed. To some extent this international process defined the parameters within which domestic economic policy could be pursued, but only to some extent. The process would have had no chance of success had there not been a sufficient area of common economic ground. Most of this common economic ground existed because of the similar international situation in which the national economies found themselves in 1945. They had all experienced a severe fall in foreign trade. They were all faced with the threat of inflation. They all wished to attain a higher standard of living. To do that they had to increase their level of exports well beyond that of 1938. And they were all faced with a large trading deficit with the dollar zone and a shortage of the world's most important trading currency. Beyond these similarities, however, there were often striking differences between the situation of the national economies after the war, to say nothing of the even more striking array of different policies with which they tackled even those problems which they had in common. They were driven by the experience of the 1930s and the need physically to reconstruct the damage of the Second World War towards more expansionist policies. This in turn drove them to struggle for a system of international trade and payments which accommodated such policies better than what had existed since 1930. Even at this point great contradictions arose. Which should receive preference, existing levels of domestic output and employment or the *possibility* of expanding foreign trade through a system which might leave levels of national employment and output much more vulnerable to events in other economies? The Bretton Woods agreements had tried to resolve this question by combining a system of fixed exchange rates with a variety of institutional innovations, but the policies which European governments pursued in 1947 showed those agreements to have solved nothing and to have practically no value or use as the basis of post-war reconstruction. If the Bretton Woods system had ever operated it ended in that year.

The idea that a major reason for the success of the European reconstruction after 1945, compared to its failure after 1918, was that countries pursued more similar policies which were more easily harmonizable at the level of international agreement is unacceptable. The differences were not so wide, it is true, as after 1918, but they were far too wide to be accommodated in any agreement as comprehensive as Bretton Woods. In spite of similarities in their international situation the domestic objectives of economic policy in the separate nations could be very different, as they were for example between Britain and Italy. Seen at the national level western Europe was a bold patchwork of distinct national experiments. What was needed after the failure and collapse of the Bretton Woods agreements was a less comprehensive and a more painstaking and accurate construction of a system of international economic interdependence which built on the few interests which the national economies did have in common. This book explores the interconnections between them and tries to show how the nature of these interconnections determined the nature of the durable economic peace settlement which was eventually achieved and which shaped a new western Europe. But it has very little to say about how and why the separate national choices of domestic policy were made. The national foundations and walls of western Europe's house have held it in place every bit as much as its international roof. But defining the shape of the roof will, I hope, help others to explain how the foundations and walls were built.

In some cases the walls had to be altered in the course of construction to meet the roof as its specifications were agreed by the separate architects, while in others the roof had to correspond to the firm determination of the separate architects to put their walls where they wanted them. This rambling, incoherent construction, easy to get lost in, has not, however, proved a ramshackle one and like a more famous house of many mansions it has even, by some, been thought of as a salvation. In a house of that kind the roof was the most difficult bit, particularly where it had to reach the more improbable walls. What does this book say about how it was built?

I have assumed that most readers will read these conclusions only, or first. What immediately follows, therefore, is only a brief series of statements summarizing the arguments, or assertions as some may judge them, which came before in the other chapters and which substantiate the basic arguments of the book. I hope the readers who disagree with them will consider the evidence in the earlier chapters before making their disagreement explicit. The further implications of the arguments summarized here may also interest the disagreeing reader. They come afterwards.

The first proposition of the book is that the economic crisis of 1947 which ended dollar–sterling convertibility and produced the European Recovery Programme was not caused by the deteriorating domestic economic situation of the western European economies. Even less was it attributable to an impending political, moral and spiritual collapse. It was, on the contrary, attributable to the remarkable speed and success of western Europe's economic recovery. It was caused by the widening gap in the first six months of 1947 between increasing imports and increasing exports in some European economies, particularly Britain, Italy and the Netherlands, and the failure of that gap to continue to narrow in others, notably France. Thus the trend towards a restoration of some kind of trade and payments equilibrium, expected and consistently observable in 1946, was reversed. The main cause of this reversal was the sustained high level of capital investment in western Europe expressed in a marked increase in capital goods imports from the United States in 1947. The response of the European economies to their increasing international payments difficulties was not, however, as it had been in 1920, to deflate but, with the exception of Italy to maintain inflationary boom conditions while increasing the level of control over foreign trade.

The elimination of Germany as a capital goods supplier, and the relatively low levels of output elsewhere in the world, however, focused this increased demand for imports on to the American economy at a time when the principal foreign trade problem of all western European countries was a shortage of dollars to balance their external accounts with the United States. The underlying causes of the dollar shortage were more diffuse, but they did not lie, as is sometimes argued, in a reduction of dollar outflows from America after 1946 nor in long-run structural alterations in the pattern of world trade and payments caused by the war. They were all essentially attributable to the short-run problem of world economic recovery from the war. It was the success and vigour of the European recovery, not its incipient failure, which exacerbated this payments problem. Marshall Aid did not save Western

Europe from economic collapse. In order to defend America's own strategic interests it allowed some Western European governments to continue to pursue by means of an extensive array of trade and payments controls the extremely ambitious, expansionist domestic policies which had provoked the 1947 payments crisis and destroyed the Bretton Woods agreements almost at birth. It thus postponed, without resolving, the problem of combining self-sustained recovery with foreign equilibrium.

Practically no Western European government would have been content with mere recovery to the level of 1938. Most sought a fundamental reversal of their experience of the 1930s. It was that which took them to the brink of an impossible external payments position in summer 1947 and, although the danger of this was clear to all, the domestic political imperatives prevented them, except in the case of Italy, from turning back at the last moment. High and increasing output, increasing foreign trade, full employment, industrial-ization and modernization had become in different countries, as a result of their experience of the 1930s and the war, inescapable policy choices, because governments could find no other basis for political consensus. The ERP permitted European governments to continue to translate these domestic political imperatives into economic policy. The fact that European countries did not change direction in 1947, together with all the consequences that followed from this, meant that 'the Bretton Woods system' has largely been an invention of economists. It died in 1947 of infant mortality, or, if a harsher view is taken, of infanticide by its European parent. It follows that any explanation of the subsequent period of high growth rates which implies that they depended on common policies of growth and expansion pursued within the framework of those agreements can have no validity. What came into existence in 1958 when currency convertibility was restored in Western Europe was a different system founded on other economic and historical realities, and by that time growth rates were slowing down.

For the first three years of the ERP the United States was able to reconcile the existence of Marshall Aid to American ambitions for the world-wide multilateral payments system embodied in the Bretton Woods agreements by the argument that in promoting a recovery in Western Europe's output, Marshall Aid was closing Western Europe's dollar deficit with the United States and thus preparing the way for a re-establishment of the principles agreed at Bretton Woods. But the concentration of dollar outflows on Western Europe made it even less likely that this would be the case. So did the sweeping political and economic ambitions of the Marshall Plan.

In spite of its title the ERP aimed at the total political reconstruction of Western Europe, not just its recovery. The goal was the integration of Western Europe into one common economic area before the end of the ERP and its ultimate integration into one common political area. The definition of integration was variable, depending on which part of the United States administration was defining it. But the meaning which it mostly took in the ECA, the body which administered Marshall Aid, was that a free-trade customs union should be created in Western Europe. This, it was thought, would increase the level of output and productivity in Western Europe, eliminate the dollar deficits, and ultimately lead to the merging of the Western European nation states, including part of the whole of Germany, into a United States of Europe. All American objectives were thought to have been reconciled by this attempt to sweep away the nation state as the basis of the European political system, and the ERP attempted a reconstruction of western Europe more radical than anything which had gone before.

The Committee of European Economic Co-operation (CEEC), the grand Western European conference which met in response to the American offer of aid and which the United States hoped would be the first stage in the process of integration, did not, however, result in agreement on a European recovery programme so much as in fundamental disagreement. It did not lay the foundations of European economic co-operation, much less of integration. It revealed how far apart the economic objectives of the separate European countries were and how serious were the international differences between them and the United States. The question of the economic recovery of Germany, which the United States especially wished to resolve through the creation of an integrated Western Europe, proved particularly divisive. From the moment the United States opted for the ERP the French objectives in Europe, which were determined by the desire for national security against Germany, could no longer be ignored. The CEEC report to Congress, on which the Marshall Aid legislation depended, could not have been produced unless the United States had made a substantial concession to France, namely to support in some form or another the French policy of internationalization of the Ruhr.

Until mid-summer 1948, at the very earliest, France's aims in European reconstruction were concentrated on a partition and permanent weakening of Germany and on acquiring a guaranteed access to German coal and coke resources. The goals of French domestic reconstruction were defined by the Plan for Modernization and Re-equipment (the Monnet Plan) and this was closely linked to foreign policy objectives. The intended increase in output of the French steel industry was predicated on the assumption that France would obtain through the post-war reconstruction a sufficient quantity of coal and coke from the Ruhr and the Saarland to make these domestic planning objectives feasible, and also that in the post-war world the French steel industry would be able to supply markets which before 1939 had been supplied from Germany. It was intended in the partition of Germany to create an autonomous international state covering the Ruhr area so as to guarantee French national security in the future, of which guaranteeing the success of the Modernization Plan was one crucial aspect. The opposition between

French policies towards Germany and those of Britain and America was so profound that no worthwhile decisions about European economic co-operation, much less integration, could be taken in the framework of the CEEC or its successor as a standing international conference, the OEEC.

The issue of the respective futures of the French and German economies had to be tackled in the London conference on Germany and what happened there brought about a dramatic change of policy in France, but not in the direction of any greater agreement with Britain and America over Western Europe's reconstruction. The decision by the second stage of the London conference to set up a unitary West German state whose central government would have important powers forced France to abandon its original plans for post-war reconstruction, but only in their international aspect. It was now necessary to devise a different policy in Western Europe which would none the less support the national economic objectives of the Monnet Plan. From June 1948 onwards the Ministry of Foreign Affairs began the task of moving ministers, governments, parliament and people towards the alternative policy of a Franco-German economic association. Because such an association would have to cover the question of France's access to German resources of coke and coal as well as that of the future regulation of steel markets it was conceived as beginning in these relatively restricted but historically important industrial sectors. Thus after more than seventy years of failure to mediate the major political questions which divided France and Germany a Franco-German alliance began to be constructed by confining the mediation to economic issues.

Until such time as policy could be officially changed (and the West German state had not even yet come into existence) it was essential to increase French bargaining power by strengthening the controls and limitations on West Germany's economic life. In particular it was necessary that the internationalization of the Ruhr should still give France power to allocate Ruhr resources in the necessary quantities to the French economy. The long and tedious struggle over the precise powers of the International Authority for the Ruhr, which occupied the last stages of the London conference, was concerned directly with the question of the future allocation of German fuel resources and the size and control of future German steel output. It was indecisive, but at least in the short run proved to have given France the needed bargaining counter. It did nothing, of course, to promote political harmony and co-operation in Western Europe, and even less so in the western world.

The change of policy in the direction of seeking a Franco-German economic association was a direct response also to American pressures for Western European integration in a free-trade framework. Integration in a framework of this kind would not provide for France's future national economic security. Before the Monnet Plan had achieved its ultimate objective of making the French economy internationally competitive, France would be left exposed to the free play of comparative advantages against an economy which seemed in the circumstances of 1947 to be likely to emerge with a great many such advantages. From the moment when Marshall Aid was offered and the CEEC met, therefore, French policy towards Germany had also to be conceived in the light of an alternative Western European economic framework to that which the United States now wished to impose through the ERP.

British opposition to the goals of the ERP was equally adamant. These goals were seen in London as having no relevance to the solution of the world payments problem and as offering an absolutely unacceptable future to the United Kingdom as a part of a united Western Europe, albeit, as the Americans wished, as the creator and inspirer of that unification. Opposition to these American ambitions was equally strong in many of the smaller European nation states. In such circumstances the American policy to create in the OEEC an international economic organization of major importance which would evolve during the period of the ERP into a prototype European economic parliament were absolutely unrealizable. The OEEC was not even in any important sense a stage in European economic co-operation and could not become an effective instrument of European reconstruction. All American policies were thwarted there by a common Franco-British front and the United States could never create a sufficiently strong pattern of alliances with the smaller nations within the OEEC to prevent its complete political and economic emasculation.

The central thrust of American policy was the insistence that the OEEC should itself recommend the allocation of ERP funds. When this had to be abandoned in 1949 an alternative policy of bringing about European integration through the process of trade liberalization was chosen because it seemed to avoid the direct political clashes on specific policy issues which had been inevitable in the process of aid allocation. The abandonment of any genuine process of aid allocation by the OEEC reduced the OEEC at once to a very low level of political importance. But the alternative process of trade liberalization proved not to be as politically neutral as its advocates had hoped. It was to encounter the same fundamental political and economic obstacles as had been present in the OEEC. Chapter 5 explores the failure of America's ambitions for European reconstruction in the OEEC and its collapse as a basis for Western Europe's reconstruction.

Marshall Aid was not in fact important enough to give the United States sufficient leverage to reconstruct Western Europe according to its own wishes. The main economic importance of Marshall Aid over the whole duration of the programme was the imports, particularly capital goods imports, which it permitted. It continued to allow European economies to achieve high rates of capital formation, higher for most of them than for almost the whole of the inter-war period. The essential question, however, is whether they could have achieved similarly high levels of capital formation without Marshall Aid after

1948 by reducing or eliminating the range of commodities other than capital goods which they imported through the ERP. The conclusion is that two of them, France and the Netherlands, could not have done so. The others may have been able to. In its other aspects Marshall Aid was of less importance and its importance diminished more rapidly.

Faced with American intentions France had begun to explore the possibilities from summer 1947 of a more restricted customs union based on regulated and controlled markets which would not threaten the domestic planning mechanism nor the control of domestic economic policy in France, and with which later some form of German state would have to conform. If the more drastic French policies towards Germany failed, as they now looked very likely to do, this might be an alternative way of securing access to German resources and guaranteeing national security. For a brief period over the winter of 1947–8 the British Foreign Office also espoused the cause of a customs union embracing Western Europe and its overseas territories, in which Britain would be the leading power. This policy was never accepted by the government as a whole and after April 1948 it was dead. The British-inspired customs union would have been much closer to the free-trade model than the Little European customs union envisaged by French policy, although it would have been flatly opposed to American policy in as much as it was based on the maintenance and development of the sterling area and imperial preferences. The Little European customs union was no more realizable in 1948. Although the Italian government desired a customs union with France this was not on terms acceptable to economic interests in France and in any case fell far short of meeting the needs of French reconstruction policy. The Netherlands was not prepared to consider a customs union in which neither of its main pre-war trading partners, Britain and Germany, was definitely included and, in 1948, was still opposed to the French conception of closely regulated markets within the union.

From this unpromising, and for France particularly dangerous, situation, Western Europe was nevertheless able to construct an institutionalized pattern of economic interdependence which did serve the separate national interests of the countries concerned and which laid the basis of a successful reconstruction and a durable peace. The pillars of the reconstruction were the European Payments Union and the European Coal and Steel Community.

It was not therefore until 1950 that there were even the beginnings of an adequate international framework for reconstruction. The continued high levels of output and employment and high rates of growth of national income over most of Western Europe before that date cannot therefore be attributed to a better international institutional framework or a greater degree of international economic co-operation. They continued to be the result of separate, often conflicting, national reconstruction policies. One of the unexplained aspects of the reconstruction is how a parallel series of separate national booms based largely on the capital goods sector of manufacturing industry evolved into the common boom of the 1950s and 1960s which drew its strength more from the consumer goods sector and exports. Western Europe's success in creating from 1950 onwards a more appropriate institutional basis for reconstruction based on its own real economic interests was directly related to the persistence of these booms and their relative immunity from the American recession of 1948–9. The booms did not, however, change their character until after the success of the international reconstruction. Some suggestions as to how this may have occurred are made after this summary of the book's argument.

The creation of a successful framework for reconstruction would surely have been impossible without the very rapid growth of the foreign trade of the Western European states throughout the period and especially the powerful surge of intra-Western European trade in 1948–50 which insulated all the Western European economies except Britain against the American recession. That recession had been expected to arrive and to endanger western Europe's reconstruction boom, on the analogy with the post-First World War period, in 1947. Whether the degree of deflation which might have had to be pursued in western Europe after August 1947, had the ERP not been announced, would have seriously interrupted the reconstruction boom is a hypothetical question which need not be pursued since, in the context of the argument, Marshall Aid only postponed the hour of reckoning until an American recession did arrive or the ERP came to an end. The question was, what would happen then?

As the analysis in chapter 11 suggests the factors which made that American recession a much shorter-lived phenomenon than had been expected and in some sectors of the economy a very much milder one were also present in the Western European economies too. Even a recession of such short duration in the United States, however, would have had a severe impact on the growth of Western Europe's exports had it not been for the countervailing tendency exercised by the astonishingly rapid growth of output in West Germany. The intra-Western European trade circuits recreated by West Germany's recovery provided a vigorous export market in 1949–50 for all West Germany's neighbours. Intra-Western European trade grew particularly vigorously in the capital goods sector and this reinforced the patterns of growth already established by domestic demand stemming from national reconstruction policies and in the case of France, indeed, made up for the virtual stagnation of domestic demand from late 1948 to spring 1950. From this circuit of increasing foreign trade the United Kingdom, however, by virtue of the geographical distribution of its exports, was excluded and suffered the full force, through the sterling area pattern of trade and payments, of the sharp reduction in American imports. The recovery of the West German economy was already under way in 1945 but the reabsorption into the Western European trade and payments framework of Western Europe's largest producer was essential for sustaining that recovery, especially to sustaining its astonishing pace in 1950–1. When all credit is accorded to the persistence with which American policy strove to promote German recovery its success still depended on the creation of a framework acceptable to the European states rather than the one which American policy envisaged. That the reinsertion of West Germany into the intra-Western European trade circuits insulated Western Europe, other than Britain, against the effects of the American recession was ultimately therefore attributable to the emergence of a pattern of interdependence acceptable to the European states, which the United States had to accept.

That patterns of trade should have had so powerful an impact on the course of political events is less surprising when it is considered how far the aspirations of the European nations and the United States depended on an expansion of world trade. It was in the various, complicated schemes for breaking out of the pre-war pattern of trade and exchange controls and out of the low level of foreign trade relative to output that the greatest international ingenuity was shown, because it was there that the greatest area of common interest was to be found. The acute differences of national domestic economic policy in Western Europe which paralysed planning in the OEEC were no less an obstacle to general European agreements on trade and payments, but the need and the will to overcome them were the greater.

None the less, using Marshall Aid as backing for intra-Western European payments schemes only made the problems of the OEEC more acute and pushed it the more rapidly towards its final emasculation. The intra-Western European payments schemes before 1950 in no sense foreshadowed the institutional and political principles of the EPU, rather the ingenuity with which they were devised strengthened the bilateral basis of European foreign trade and in doing so built up even greater barriers against the success of American hopes for Europe. It took three things to translate these temporary agreements into the more permanent acknowledgement of interdependence embodied in the EPU.

One was the drastic alteration in the flow of world trade and payments after September 1949 which convinced a sufficient number of Western European countries, most importantly Britain, that a multilateral payments system in intra-Western European trade would not endanger their domestic economic objectives, provided that the terms of settlement agreed on in the EPU were by no means as hard as most branches of the American government or a creditor country like Belgium would have wished. The second was the abandonment by the Americans of their insistence that a multilateral payments mechanism in Western Europe must be only the first step towards economic and political integration. After the collapse of the OEEC in September 1949 as an instrument for producing the economic integration of Western Europe the ECA had tried to achieve the same goal through using Marshall Aid to demand a rapid and progressive removal of quantitative restrictions on intra-Western European trade. This was linked to demands for a multilateral payments union which would become in turn a European monetary union and thus serve to harmonize and integrate the European economies. The evolution and implications of this alternative route to integration are analysed in chapter 9. The agreement on the EPU, however, signified the defeat of all these further American hopes and, indeed, the EPU would not have been achieved unless that had been made clear. The third was an equally drastic change of policy in the United States, the abandonment of the aim of integrating the United Kingdom into a united Western Europe and the acceptance of the existence of the sterling area and of the United Kingdom as its pivot in the post-war world. This change of policy had effectively been forced on the United States by British actions at the time of the devaluation of sterling in September 1949 and was acknowledged in the agreements on the EPU which not only made special arrangements in the form of dollar guarantees against sterling losses through transferability in multilateral payments but laid down the future basis of economic relationships between the sterling area and Western Europe.

The fundamental British objection to multilateral settlements was the threat which they imposed to the sterling area reserves; there must be no return of the crisis of 1947 if Britain's national reconstruction was to be achieved. It was this especially which imposed such severe limitations on European payments agreements before 1950. The American wish to make Britain lead Western Europe into integration could not endure the reality of Britain's position in 1949. The international economic effects of the American recession of that year, like American depressions of the inter-war period, were felt much more severely on Britain's foreign trade than on the foreign trade of the other Western European countries. As the sterling reserves again fell towards danger level and Britain entered its second post-war balance of payments crisis British resistance to American policy in Europe became more absolute. Against American conceptions of European integration as a step towards multilateralism the United Kingdom raised the, at least in American eyes, no longer spectral but substantial threat of complete withdrawal into the sterling area payments mechanism and the division of the western world into two payments systems, a hard-currency system dominated by the United States and a soft-currency system dominated by the United Kingdom. This threat accompanied by the unexpectedly drastic devaluation of the pound forced the United States to accept that its real interests were more affected by the world-wide ramifications of British and sterling area trade than by Britain's role in Europe.

No durable reconstruction could have been possible unless the future terms of co-existence of the sterling area, Western Europe and the dollar trading zone had been defined. So long as they were defined in terms of dismantling the sterling area and forcing Britain into an integrated Western Europe nothing could be achieved, whatever the possible advantages (as some may argue) of such a policy to the United Kingdom may have been. But it was not only in that sense that the EPU created a pattern of institutionalized interdependence. It was a multilateral payments network, no matter how generous the terms of settlement, and it did impose certain restrictions on national policy choices to make it work. The success of this institutionalization of interdependence free from pressures towards integration was immediately seen in the way the EPU coped with the very problem which had proved most disastrous for the OEEC, the economic recovery of West Germany.

At the same time the conjoint international economic consequences of the American recession and the contemporaneous surge of output in West Germany made possible the Franco-German economic association towards which France had begun to move in summer 1948, in the framework of the regulated Little European market at which French policy aimed, and permitted the erection of the second pillar of the reconstruction, the European Coal and Steel Community.

While the fall in America's imports produced a fall in British exports to the non-European world which provoked a sterling balance of payments crisis, the foreign trade of those countries whose exports went mainly to Western Europe grew vigorously and unchecked for two years. The causes were complex but the most important cause of this immunity from the long-feared American slump was the growth of West German imports. The main beneficiary was the Netherlands and this played an important part in changing opinion there in favour of the French plans, providing West Germany would be a founder member of any Little European economic association. This, together with the American abandonment of the idea of making Britain integrate Europe, provided the opportunity for France. If European integration was not to be produced by Britain it could only be produced by France. America was no longer in a position to object to any French initiative, no matter how limited in geographical scope or how protectionist, unless the whole idea of European integration was to be given up altogether, which was too drastic a renunciation to contemplate. If France could find the right policy the opportunity to shape European reconstruction while guaranteeing national security was suddenly there.

In the circumstances prevailing in 1949 the right policy was hard to find. The slackening in the growth of French output, although not of exports, and in particular the stagnation in the steel industry called into question the very premises of the Monnet Plan. As it did so the growth of West German steel output in spite of all production difficulties was driven onwards by the apparently insatiable demand from the domestic market. Foreign trade was in that year the most dynamic sector of the French economy and it was understandable that ideas should turn in France towards a more liberal framework for an integrated Little Europe as a solution to the problem of national security. This would accommodate the Netherlands, further the cause of trade liberalization, be acceptable to the United States in a way that the earlier proposals for a customs union would not have been, and swing the balance of economic power in France away from the planners and in favour of a more liberal order. But the Little European payments union, Finebel, was stillborn. It was unacceptable to the Dutch without German participation and, when it came to the point, the French government itself was not prepared to face the West German economy in so liberal a framework. After January 1950 the only politically acceptable framework was to return to the concept of a regulated market. Although this implied the probable exclusion of Britain, after September 1949 American objections would no longer be absolute and might even have little force. But how could the internal political objections in France, as well as those of France's neighbours, be met?

It followed from the objectives of the Monnet Plan and from the unsatisfactory guarantees provided by the International Ruhr Authority, as well as from the seventy years of dispute over the issue, that any policy for harmonizing French and German reconstruction had to deal directly with the central question of coal and steel resources. By defining the customs union as a common market and by confining that common market at first to those strategic commodities the answer was found. No common market in those products could be created without the most complex agreements on its regulation. The area covered would coincide exactly with that of the Little European customs union unless Britain also became a member. The reduction of the scope of the common market offered some hope of this provided the United Kingdom would accept the political implications. The market would be regulated more in the French than in the German interest, because the Federal Republic would have to make economic sacrifices in return for so dramatic an acknowledgement of its equal political status. And in those sacrifices France would achieve a better guarantee of access to German resources than by any other policy now conceivable. The Schuman Plan was called into existence to save the Monnet Plan.

France substantially achieved its objectives in the ECSC as far as West Germany was concerned, but had to accept large modifications of them to accommodate the other members. These modifications, however, joined together more strongly and intricately the framework of economic interdependence and political alliance on which the rest of the economic peace settlement could then be erected. From the Schuman Plan negotiations emerged an altogether more pragmatic process of integration which resolved the central political problem of Western Europe and became the pattern for the European Economic Community.

The last chapter shows how the possibility of using the same process to incorporate agriculture into that framework as a defence against trade liberalization was immediately taken up. By 1951 the process of trade liberalization had been temporarily stopped and reversed. The most obvious obstacle to its continuation was the high and increasing level of protection which the domestic and international economic situation caused European countries to accord to the agricultural sectors of their economies. Here too American pressure towards integration was eventually to produce by reaction an entirely different form of interdependence and one based more on the economic and historical realities of Europe's situation. The inequalities of the trade liberalization process penalized agricultural exporters. The process as a whole made the accommodation of West Germany into the newly emerging European framework more difficult. West Germany was no less protectionist in its agricultural sector than the other members of the proposed coal and steel community. The European Economic Community and the Common Agricultural Policy now appeared as another, and the most ironical, alternative to the liberal dream of one free European market which had inspired the ERP. The necessary conditions for the Treaty of Rome, the coping stone of the European reconstruction, were already present as Marshall Aid merged into Mutual Security Aid.

The Korean war, the British and French balance of payments crises of 1951, the acceptance in the United States of Western European integration in a geographical and economic framework that would have been unacceptable in 1947 and 1948, ended the illusion that the ERP was a step towards the return of Bretton Woods. By 1949 the policies of the ECA and the objectives of ERP were under direct attack in the United States on the grounds that they were actually impeding a proper solution to the problem of world trade and payments. This was an opinion that the British actions in September 1949 could only strengthen. In place of a liberal unified Europe came a closely regulated Little European common market whose twin purposes were to provide for French national security by containing West Germany and to permit its members to continue to pursue a very limited range of common economic policies in a few specific sectors of the economy, which would otherwise have become impossible. Parallel with this development the whole of Western Europe, by rejecting the economic framework for interdependence which the United States sought to impose on it, was able to build an alternative framework which, although it may not have withstood the storms of that time, was certainly better founded than anything devised in the inter-war period.

Thus by rejecting the task of first regulating the major political questions concerning Western Europe, and then rejecting the constraints on national economic recovery imposed by the agreements signed at Bretton Woods, and finally rejecting the ultimate implications of American policy in Western Europe after 1947, Western Europe made its own peace settlement. In place of the major peace settlement that never came it created an alternative pattern of reconstruction, a restricted but workable institutional framework for economic interdependence which has proved more effective than any previous peace settlement. There is very little to say that this was not in the end the best solution for the United States too.

*   *   *

That, summarized briefly, is the argument of the book. Such an argument leaves much to be explained at the national level. The twists and turns of French domestic economic policy and the erratic behaviour of the French economy do not look consistent with the unswerving pursuit of an indicative plan, even when inspected from above. Neither is the behaviour of the Italian economy after July 1947 entirely consistent with the stern principles of liberal financial orthodoxy to which it is said to have reacted so favourably. The relationships between domestic economic planning and the international economy, of such importance in France, could surely not have been ignored in so trade-dependent a country as the Netherlands. The list of unanswered questions could be very long. But the argument as it stands raises two further unavoidable questions. Why after the First World War did the reconstruction boom end, except in Germany, a year and a half later in a severe depression, whereas after the Second World War it merged into the greatest boom in European history? The second question is of more general import but has constantly been posed in different forms. What has been the contribution of the process of European integration to the durability of Europe's reconstruction? The implications of these two questions are considered in the sections which follow.

RECONSTRUCTION AND THE GREAT BOOM

With few exceptions analyses of Western Europe's greatest and longest economic boom suggest that it was a phenomenon of the 1950s which gradually petered out in the 1960s. The most frequently given starting date for this astonishing period of increasing output and incomes is 1950 itself. There is no justification for this. The trend of growth of national income was unbroken, if diminishing, between 1945 and 1960 and by any possible statistical definition Western Europe's greatest boom began with the end of the war and proceeded without interruption until 1967. There is only a separate 'reconstruction period' in the sense in which the phrase has been used in this book, the period of time taken to create a satisfactory international basis for the *continuation* of the boom. From another standpoint it might be plausibly argued that the economic nature of the boom of the 1950s was fundamentally different in character from that of the immediate post-war years, because it was more apparent in the consumer goods sector and because for much of the time in many countries it was export-led. This change of character came at different dates in different countries. It was not clearly apparent in France until late in the 1950s. And with the possible but dubious exceptions of Switzerland and Sweden it was not firmly established anywhere until after 1951. Nevertheless, if the political nature of Europe's reconstruction permitted the continuation of the boom the question why it continued must also be asked, especially why it continued with the capacity to change its form. There were already certain indications before 1951 that the international framework which was emerging might not only permit but encourage this change of character and in so doing actually help to sustain the boom.

The most prevalent explanation for the boom's persistence is that governments, persuaded by the school of economic analysis of which Keynes is the best-known exponent, became convinced that they were more in control of their economic destinies than they had once believed. Convinced that economic policy could be effective they began to manage economies to produce certain goals, the increase of the national wealth, the growth of incomes, high employment rates and price stability. Because the objectives of economic policy were so similar in different states the task of international economic management to make the achievement of domestic economic policy possible was much simpler. The persistence of the boom is thus attributed to a broad similarity in economic policy resulting in a lower level of international economic friction.[1]

Although the objectives of economic policy in Western Europe were certainly more similar between countries than they had been in the 1920s, this explanation cannot carry much conviction. The objectives of economic policy in West Germany and in Italy were frequently very different from those in France and in none of these countries did Keynesian economics have a noticeably strong influence over policy-formulation in the 1950s. That governments did continue, with considerable differences of method and emphasis, to pursue expansionary policies was perhaps more due to the fact that expansion proved possible without posing political and economic problems which were too great to resolve. In fact the lure of sustained economic growth as a policy objective and as the basis of a new political consensus was still feeble and uncertain in 1951, although national income growth had been sustained at high levels in Western Europe for six years.

Another common explanation is that Western Europe was recouping the growth of national income lost in the wars and the inter-war period and returning to its twentieth-century growth trend. Although, it is often argued, general aspects of the international economy and particular circumstances in individual economies inhibited the growth of national incomes between 1918 and 1945 the basic potential for economic growth was still present. Thus the increase in inputs of education and technology into most Western European

---

[1] This view is most comprehensively expounded in A. Boltho, *The European Economy. Growth and Crisis* (Oxford, 1982).

economies did not diminish over that time so that if the barriers to growth were lifted a surge of growth would be automatically produced. Abelshauser and Petzina, for example, show some favour to this explanation of the long duration of exceptionally high growth rates once the German reconstruction was launched, although their explanation is confined to long-run phenomena operating on the German economy alone.[2] Carré, Dubois and Malinvaud are prepared to attribute some of the explanation for high post-war growth rates in France to similar causes, this time in a purely French context.[3] It is a temptingly simple argument to explain the length of the boom by considering it either as the completion of the unfinished reconstruction boom after the First World War or as the resumption of the growth trend prevailing before 1914.

But the historian is bound to be sceptical about any argument which carries the implication that over the long run investment and growth tend towards a norm. In any case the prolongation of trend lines of growth from the pre-First World War period to the end of the 1960s leaves the growth achieved by Western European economies in the 1960s above the line. Furthermore, the experience of investment or of disinvestment in the world wars and the inter-war period was extremely variable between the separate national economies, too variable to prepare the ground for so similar a common experience after 1945.

There may be grounds for arguing that the restocking boom after the end of the Second World War was likely to last longer than after the First. The physical damage done by fighting during the First World War had been confined to a smaller area and the damage to housing, transport and other forms of fixed capital caused by bombing was far more restricted. The difficulty with this argument is that the high levels of investment which prevailed in western European economies from 1945 onwards were by no means due merely to replacement investment. Much of it was new investment and in some cases replacement investment was deliberately postponed so that new investment would not be too much impeded. One of the most striking aspects of the distribution of post-war investment in Western Europe is that a higher proportion of capital investment was devoted to housing in Britain than in any other economy, although the damage done to the total housing stock there was less than anywhere else except the neutral countries. And if in retrospect it appears that there was over-investment in this sector the comparison would still have to be made with the meagre allocation of investment funds to housing under the French Modernization Plan after a long period of low investment in the same sector before the war. These were fundamental

[2] W. Abelshauser and D. Petzina, 'Krise und Rekonstruktion. Zur Interpretation der gesamtwirtschaftlichen Entwicklung Deutschlands im 20 Jahrhundert', in W.H. Schröder and R. Spree (eds) *Historische Konjunkturforschung* (Stuttgart, 1980).

[3] J.-J. Carré, P. Dubois and E. Malinvaud, *French Economic Growth* (Stanford, 1976), pp. 496 ff.

choices by governments armed with every sort of control over the housing sector and they were to lead to a very obvious difference in social conditions in the two countries over the next twenty years. In Italy, where the damage to housing stock had been even worse, the proportion of investment allocated to its rebuilding was even lower than in France.

The proclamation of Marshall Aid (and the flow of Interim Aid) allowed European countries to continue with the high levels of gross domestic capital formation which had provoked the payments crisis of 1947. Throughout 1948 and 1949 capital formation did not fall off and remained, except in Germany, at much higher levels than in 1938, a year of heavy investment in rearmament (table 69). The pattern observed in chapter 3 in the investment of ERP counterpart funds is observable also in overall investment, a marked fall after 1947 in the proportion of total investment in fixed capital allocated to transport and communications, presumably to their repair. But the completion of reconstruction work on railways, bridges and roads did not lead to any slackening in the total rate of investment, so the share of other sectors increased accordingly.

Table 69   Gross domestic capital formation as a percentage of net national income (at factor cost in current prices)

	1938	1948	1949
Austria	13*	n.a.	26
Belgium	13	17	15
Denmark	22	25	27
France	16	26	24
Western Germany	16	31	
Italy	18	22	24
Netherlands	21	31	33
Norway	37†	44	47
Sweden	31‡	34	32
United Kingdom	17	22	22

Sources: UN, *Survey of the European Economy in 1949* (Geneva, 1950), p. 23. USA, United States Strategic Bombing Survey, Overall Economic Effects Division, *The Gross National Product of Germany 1936–1944* (Washington, 1945).

* 1937   † 1939   ‡ 1938–9

It would be fallacious to assume in fact that, could a neat distinction be drawn between investment determined by the need to recoup war damage on the one hand and new investment on the other, countries switched from replacement investment to new investment between the end of 1947 and 1948. The two kinds of investment are not only virtually impossible to separate but countries had little intention of trying to separate them, because damage done to fixed capital during the war offered an opportunity for a rationalization and modernization in the appropriate sector which almost always implied a different distribution of capital within the sector and also a larger volume of capital investment than was necessary merely to recoup the damage done during the war plus the investment foregone.

The best guide to the pattern of investment in 1949 is in the separate plans which the European economies published at the close of 1948 when they failed to produce the common medium-term plan which had been requested from the OEEC.[4] These show how a mixture of new and war-determined investment was planned for the period 1949–52/3, as well as the large amount of investment which could unambiguously be classed as new. The most ambitious programme was that of Austria. Of the $1200 million estimated investment from the start of 1949 to the end of the Marshall Plan about $900 million could be categorized as new investment. Of the $270 million allocated for railways, most was earmarked for electrification works while some reconstruction of war damage and recoupment of foregone investment during the war was postponed until after 1952 to enable the electrification programme to proceed. Out of the rest of the total sum of investment there were specific allocations to the development of dairy farming, the mechanization of agriculture, irrigation projects, improvement of haulage facilities in forestry, increasing coal-mining capacity, increasing power station capacity, increasing steel output, and building more rolling-mill capacity.

The Austrian example is not typical. There had been less net disinvestment there during the war, if any, but the problem of survival as an independent economic entity was held to demand investment programmes on this scale. Yet some of its aspects are picked up in every country's submission, showing a common base pattern of public investment throughout Western Europe. Industrial output was to be expanded well beyond 1938 levels by the end of the Marshall Plan. Capital goods output was to be increased relative to consumer goods output. The share of public investment was to be higher. In Austria, for example, 'basic' industries and capital goods industries were intended to reach a level of output 60 per cent above pre-war, and consumer goods industries only between 10 and 15 per cent above. Almost every country's investment plans included the mechanization and rationalization of agriculture, the modernization and rationalization (rather than the mere reconstruction) of railway and inland waterway systems, an increase in coal-mining capacity, an increase in power station capacity and oil refineries, and often an increase in the size and variety of steel-making capacity. In all the cases except Benelux a very large proportion of the investment, if not so large as in the Austrian case, was new investment in the sense that it did not arise from the war. The 'basic sector' targets of the different versions of the Monnet Plan did not distinguish between new and replacement investment but swept both into the common task of 'modernization'. Norway had special investment

[4] OEEC, *Interim Report on the European Recovery Programme*, vol. 2 (Paris, 1948).

programmes in electrochemical industries, electrometallurgy and steel which ran together with replacing war damage and represented in each case a major addition to pre-war capacity. The United Kingdom had similar programmes in oil refining, chemicals, cement, steel, precision instruments and ball bearings; the Netherlands in steel and electricity.

Of the total Danish investment target of $1565 million, half was 'war-conditioned'. Yet only about the same proportion of investment over the period 1946–8 appears to have come under that category. Although the merchant marine had been almost completely restored to pre-war size by the end of 1948, less than half the wartime loss in the machine stock had been regained, because other investment priorities had been greater. The biggest slice of Italian investment was to help in the development of poorer agricultural regions and in schemes of land reform. The high proportion of investment in the railway sector was by no means entirely for repairing war damage; the investment target was to double the passenger-carrying capacity of the railway system compared to pre-war as well as electrify long lengths of it. The high proportion of transport investment in Norway was not for railways but shipping. It did not decline much after 1947 because the intention was that the merchant marine should be almost one million gross tons larger by the end of the Marshall Plan than in 1938. In France new investment was about a third of all public investment in 1947 and from the start of 1948 to the end of 1951 about 36 per cent.[5] The part of private investment in this non-replacement investment rose from 38 per cent in 1947 to about a half in 1951.[6]

The estimates submitted to the OEEC, however, were only investment intentions and in some areas in 1949 the climate was decidedly less expansionist. It was, for example, publicly questioned whether the steel industry was not grossly over-equipping itself in the light of future market forecasts. It is sometimes suggested that the reconstruction boom had run out of momentum in 1949 because the task of physical restoration was over, leaving in isolation a set of ambitious investment plans which could not be justified. The timing of the onset of the American recession in late autumn 1948, the fact that one of its principal aspects was a steeper fall in stocks than in output, and the fact that it was especially felt in capital goods industries, all tended to support that view. Sometimes the suggestion is extended into an argument with much more sweeping consequences for an explanation of the post-war period, that the reconstruction boom sustained the capitalist economies to the winter of 1948/9 and that they then began to enter into a period of depression from which they were only rescued by the Korean war, rearmament, and a permanently higher level of defence expenditure. If this were the case there would obviously be no inherent connections between the boom which accompanied reconstruction and the later prosperity.

[5] J. Bouvier, 'Limites et aléas de l'investissement, 1947–52' unpublished paper, 1980.
[6] France, Commissariat au Plan, *Cinq ans d'exécution du Plan 1947–1951* (Paris, 1952).

But it is not the case. Sweden appears to be the only country in Western Europe where total fixed investment fell in real terms in 1949. Industrial production there rose only sluggishly throughout the year. In Belgium and Luxembourg it fell after the first three months of the year so that by the end of 1949 it was again below the 1938 level. In Luxembourg the fall was especially steep and indicates the root of the problem, steel, which dominated Luxembourg's output. The severity with which Belgium and Luxembourg suffered from the slackening in the overall demand for steel was directly related to the foreign trading problems analysed earlier. Their steel industries depended on exports and were a very large part of those exports. Their export prices were too high and as other sources of similar steel became available on export markets the Belgian franc became a hard currency for steel buyers. As in other sectors Belgium's failure to participate fully in the reconstruction boom after mid-1948 appears to be related to the failure of an open economy whose prosperity was geared to foreign trade to make the necessary structural adjustments to fit its situation and policy. Throughout the reconstruction period, as we have seen, the blame was always placed by the Belgian government on the imperfections of Western Europe's trade and payments mechanisms. Had they been more perfect and returned, as the Belgians wished, to something akin to the gold exchange standard, the effects on Belgium's steel industry would only have been harsher and the need for a restructuring of industry yet more urgent. Industrial output in the Saarland, where steel had a comparable weight, climbed throughout 1949.

Setting aside the special problems of the steel industry in Belgium and Luxembourg, we are left with the curious paradox that in two countries where the public direction of investment was most comprehensive and, in theory, co-ordinated into a medium-term programme, France and Norway, the increase in industrial production slowed down compared to 1948. It did so in France in the second half of the year and in Norway earlier, picking up in the last quarter. In neither was there a recession at all comparable to the American experience and in all the other Western European economies growth continued unabated. So powerful were the government influences on the economy in France that the explanation for the slower growth of output there than elsewhere in Western Europe may lie in changes of government policy, perhaps in the attempts of government to reduce the balance of payments deficits which had been the counterpart of high investment levels in earlier years.

For the rest of Western Europe 1949 was a year not only of sustained high investment but also of sustained growth of output and national incomes. The effects of the American recession on the United Kingdom's economy were seriously felt only in exports and the balance of payments. Industrial output increased in every quarter except the third and full employment continued. When the American restocking boom burst it did not reproduce the pattern of

1920/1; Western Europe remained prosperous, growth rates stayed high for the most part and investment did not falter. The reasons why the United States recession was not longer and deeper are themselves pointers to the favourable background conditions in Europe too and show that the economic circumstances were not the same as in 1920. Consumption in the United States did not'fall, with a slight drop in interest rates the domestic housing market soon picked up, and a varied collection of new and rapidly developing industries remained relatively unaffected. None the less, it is still necessary to explain why the American recession, even if it did not have repercussions in Western Europe of the kind that occurred in 1920, did not produce a downturn in European investment.

The upturn in the United States came before the Korean war and the shift to higher levels of defence expenditure. In Norway the steep increase in industrial output which began in the last quarter of 1949 continued even more vigorously into the new year. Luxembourg was recovering rapidly from the start of 1950. It is only in Belgium and France that any case could be made out, on the grounds of timing, for the Korean war as the stimulus which cured the malaise of 1949. This is not very plausible in the French case as the weakness there was in the domestic market, while the export sectors in 1949 and 1950 were the main force for growth. This is not to say that the changes in world demand consequent on the increase of American imports after summer 1950 did not serve as a stimulus to French industrial output in the last quarter of 1950, as they did in the United Kingdom. The effect was similar. But the earlier sluggishness of French output cannot be attributed to the previous reduction in American imports, nor, indeed, to the pattern of international trade in general.

The relative immunity of Western Europe to American conditions in 1949 and the persistence of the boom was not due to public investment alone or to levels of government consumption higher than before the war, combined with the vigorous growth of intra-western European trade to which attention has already been drawn. Table 70 understates the importance of public investment since there were numerous ways, for example in the impact of so large a public expenditure on house building in the United Kingdom, in which the effects of public expenditure were to create a safer climate for private investment. But private investment was buoyant and except in France and Italy it amounted to about two-thirds of total investment. Evidently private investors did not share the fears of some politicians in 1947 that the Russians would soon be in Calais banging away with their guns at Dover. Of course, physical reconstruction encouraged by government aid, extensive nationalization in Britain and France with concomitant investment programmes, and the interposition of numerous intermediate managerial organizations between government and industry, all with more or less positive programmes of action, encouraged a favourable climate for private investment as well. But private investment on

Table 70 The share of private and public investment as a percentage of total investment, 1947–9

	1947		1948		1949	
	Private	*Public*	*Private*	*Public*	*Private*	*Public*
Belgium	69	31	69	31	70	30
Denmark	79	21	86	14	n.a.	n.a.
France	n.a.	n.a.	56	44	44	56
Italy	n.a.	n.a.	59	41	n.a.	n.a.
Luxembourg	96	4	90	10	n.a.	n.a.
Netherlands	n.a.	n.a.	n.a.	n.a.	68	32
Norway	73	27	79	21	77	23
Sweden	71	29	66	34	67	33
Switzerland	n.a.	n.a.	75	25	n.a.	n.a.
United Kingdom	72	28	73	27	77	23

Source: France, INSEE, *Etudes et Conjoncture. Quelques aspects fondamentaux de l'économie mondiale* (Paris, 1951), p. 215.

this scale would not have taken place without very favourable judgements of future market conditions independent of the market provided by government.

The share of national income taken by government consumption in 1949 was almost 50 per cent greater in the Netherlands and Sweden than before the war and about a third greater in Denmark, Norway and the United Kingdom. Elsewhere the difference was insignificant, although it has to be borne in mind that in pre-war Germany (including Austria) government consumption took up about a quarter of national income. This was certainly a characteristic of post-war economies and it was to persist. None the less to explain the persistence of the boom the potential of private markets is needed.

The buoyancy of private investment until late in 1948 is probably best explained by the favourable conditions created by the *persistence* of governments in the face of many international obstacles in maintaining high levels of reconstruction expenditure. Even before the end of 1948, however, the steep increases in real earnings in most countries and the great increase in the total volume of earnings in many were opening up an enticing prospect of a rapid growth in consumer goods markets. There were few countries where these higher levels of disposable purchasing power could be freely translated into consumption. Relatively low levels of consumer goods output, trade controls practised against consumer goods imports, fiscal policies aimed at encouraging investment, and still in many countries rationing and other physical controls on consumption meant that the backlog of consumer demand and the accumulation of unliberated purchasing power were creating a potential consumer goods market capable of very rapid expansion when permitted. In some countries, Britain, Sweden and Switzerland for example, high and increasing real earnings and low levels of consumption had existed together for almost eight years by the start of 1949.

Omitting France and Germany from the calculation the average level of real earnings of industrial or manual workers in Western Europe in 1948 was almost a fifth higher than in 1938. For all countries for which a meaningful calculation can be made the share of wages in the national income had risen markedly compared to pre-war. Only in France was this not the case and, as chapter 1 suggested, there was probably a sharp fall in wage-earners' purchasing power there in 1947. But by the end of 1948 the ground lost in the previous year had been recovered. Between the first quarter of 1946 and the last quarter of 1948 the purchasing power of the hourly wage in France increased by 20 per cent, so that in spite of the vicissitudes of 1947 French wage-earners had achieved a comparable rate of increase in purchasing power to those elsewhere in Western Europe.[7] The general level of wages in France, however, compared to pre-war, was lower in 1950 than elsewhere except where supplemented by family allowances, which were much larger than elsewhere. The slower rate of increase in real earnings after 1948 may explain some of the weakness of domestic demand in France in 1949 compared to the other countries.

Very large wage increases were conceded by many governments as one of their first acts after liberation. Other redistributive policies and full employment improved the income of wage-earners still further as did the fact that the number of potential new adult entrants into the labour market was at first restricted because of the very low birth rates sixteen to twenty years before. Only in West Germany was immigration on a large enough scale to weaken the bargaining position of young adults on the labour market before 1950 and even there the effect of the migrants on wages was regional.

The climate for private, as for public, investment was made more favourable by the economic mechanism of all recoveries of this kind. In a highly developed economy with a low level of utilization of capacity, repairing the damaged infrastructure will quickly set to work underemployed resources of fixed capital and labour for relatively little investment cost. The capital/output coefficients are much more favourable in such circumstances. A small sum of capital, or a small extra expenditure of public effort, will produce astonishing increases in production compared to its effect in other circumstances. Without the force of this inherent recovery mechanism it is impossible to comprehend the speed and magnitude of the West German recovery in particular. There, the high levels of investment between 1933 and 1943, combined with the massive disruption of the last eighteen months of the war and the political and economic semi-paralysis imposed by the division into almost completely separate zones of military occupation, demonstrated this mechanism in its most exaggerated and spectacular form. But beyond the German frontier it is hard to see how this impetus could have lasted beyond 1948–9.

[7] M. Catinat, 'La production industrielle sous la IVe république', *Economie et statistique*, no. 129, Jan. 1981, p. 19.

Superimposed on the will to rebuild the economy was the intention to go much further, to change its method of functioning so that it achieved higher levels of output – especially of manufactured output – and of exports than before the war, and provided higher levels of welfare for the population and, in some cases, higher levels of employment. The length of the post-war boom was not caused by the ambitious similarities of government policy in so many western European countries. Yet the existence of this general will and the belief that it was possible was a constant permissive factor in what occurred. Governments did not have political reasons for stopping the boom, nor even for interrupting it except for short-term adjustments to the balance of payments or the rate of inflation. This in itself was a very different situation from that prevailing in the 1920s and it was a necessary condition of the link between recovery and boom as it was of the subsequent length of the boom. Eventually the boom was to create its own justificatory ideology in the economics of growth and productivity. Once this had become an established orthodoxy it exercised a further narrowing pressure on the choice of government policy. The international framework created by the EPU and the ECSC was designed in each case not just to permit but to encourage policies of expansion and in no way acted as a restraint on the later developments of the 1950s.

The model was already there and, apparently, working. The much higher levels of productivity in the United States had not only preserved its national security but had done so while increasing the level of incomes and consumption there and, it seemed, stilling the fierce social tensions of the pre-war period. When the controls came off and the successive booms in consumer goods and house purchases drove the economy forward, America became the cynosure of European eyes, a land of plenty, safety and democracy where political parties were already arguing most of the time about which minor, short-term adjustments to the economy would make things better. With such a model before its eyes and safe only in a close alliance with it, it is no surprise that European political opinion increasingly emphasized productivity and growth, and thus sustained investment, as the answer to political governance in the post-war world. As the boom did not end in 1949 and as constraints on consumption were gradually released the tendency of governments and policies to refuse to accommodate themselves to the constraints of interdependence became steadily less evident, and the more radical aspirations to change nurtured by war, resistance and revolution were losing their power to influence minds. Western Europe was moving under its own economic propulsion towards a more general consensus from which an astonishingly assorted collection of factions under the common appellation 'extremists' were to be excluded.

But how did it get there? The ERP, while it permitted the sustained high levels of investment in 1947 and 1948, was no antidote to shocks transmitted from the end of the restocking boom in the United States. No matter how short the American recession of 1949 its effects would have been transmitted to other Western European countries than Britain had they not been insulated against them by the timing of the West German recovery and the effect this had on their exports. This was especially important in France between the start of 1949 and the outbreak of the Korean war. Although industrial output stagnated in this period exports of manufactured goods continued to rise, not so much to West Germany but to neighbouring countries whose exports to West Germany were increasing. The effect of the West German recovery was that while British exports stagnated several of West Germany's neighbours moved into the pattern of export-led growth which dominated the boom of the 1950s.

In the 1950s it was in those industries where the highest proportion of output went to exports that productivity rose most rapidly. This may have been related to the economies of scale demanded by rapidly expanding sales, but the nature of the market to which the exports went was also important. Exporting to Western European markets was more effective in raising productivity, because the demand there was for the more technologically sophisticated goods which would allow the importing country itself to stay in the race for higher productivity and higher exports. While British exports stagnated in 1949 in uncompetitive and undemanding markets because of the influence of the American recession, intra-Western European trade continued to grow powerfully, creating an expanding market for high-value exports. From this Britain was excluded by the geographical distribution of its exports and its foreign trade sector was left at the mercy of the movements of the American economy in the same way as in the inter-war period. Furthermore, British manufactured exports were finding their main market in economies where in the next decade they would be most at the mercy of import-substitution policies imposed by governments seeking more rapid development.

This does not mean that by 1949 the difference in rates of growth of output and productivity between continental Western Europe and the United Kingdom, which was observable throughout the great boom of the 1950s, had become irrevocably established. That would be to ignore the multiplicity of other explanations for the relatively slower rate of growth of investment and national income in the United Kingdom over those years and, although none of these seem convincing, discussion of them, as well as of their relationship to the foreign trade sector, would merit another book. It is a large jump from investment to growth rates with many things intervening. Nor is the evidence that technological innovation was weaker in the United Kingdom at all strong, although there is better evidence that the nature of markets may have impeded technological innovation from developing into production technology. Nevertheless, the pattern of the 1950s becomes discernible in 1949. In the two subsequent periods in the 1950s when there was a slight fall in British exports there was also a decline in real fixed investment, although the first was not necessarily a cause, and much less the sole cause, of the second. The more common explanation at the time was government action to damp down domestic demand. Yet it is worth noting that there were several occasions in the 1950s when governments elsewhere in Europe, most notably in France, took similar courses of action without these having similar repercussions on investment.

The sustained growth of manufactured exports and levels of productivity was only one of the parts of the balancing act needed to pass from the reconstruction boom into the 1950s, but it was the part for which Britain's own reconstruction had left the economy particularly ill-equipped. It is not impossible that the rapid and marked shift in the commodity composition of British industrial output and exports between 1945 and 1950 in the direction of newer technologies and more sophisticated capital goods was to be largely in vain because the geographical pattern of British foreign trade did not shift sufficiently over that time to help sustain this change. The international payments difficulties could only serve to encourage British trade with the sterling area.[8] If to the exclusion of Britain from the greater benefits of the pattern of intra-Western European trade created by Germany's dramatic revival is added the fact that there were initially more idle resources and thus higher capital/output ratios in Germany, Italy, the Netherlands and France, and that in the first three of these wages were relatively low, it becomes more understandable that those three countries achieved the highest rates of growth after 1949. Belgium, where there had been much less disinvestment, where wages were high, and where the structure of exports rather than their geographical distribution made entry into the intra-Western European trade boom more difficult, had growth rates more like those of Britain. France came in between, only firmly joining the virtuous circle of intra-Western European trade after 1957. For Western Europe as a whole 1949 was not only, however, the year in which important elements of the future pattern became clear, it was also the year in which the transition from the first to the second stage of the great boom began. The Korean war did not rescue Western Europe from an incipient depression; it interrupted the strongly beneficial impact of the pattern of intra-Western European trade on economic development, and the pattern took some time to reassert itself.

For it to be entirely secure a trade and payments mechanism much more susceptible to trade expansion than that of the pre-war period was needed. It took only three years from the collapse of the unsatisfactory Bretton Woods mechanism to create a more practicable and serviceable one in the EPU. About that no more need be said, not because it was not of great importance, but because it has been said earlier.

[8] Lamfalussy's calculations of the possible causes of gains and losses in commodity trade in the 1950s do not refute this possibility, because his method of comparison eliminates intra-EEC trade from the estimate of gains accruing from 'market-distribution', whereas the argument here is that these gains were crucial and already accruing in 1949. When they are included, as Lamfalussy concedes, 'market-distribution' becomes a major factor in the United Kingdom's loss of trade. A. Lamfalussy, *The United Kingdom and the Six* (London, 1963), pp. 51 ff.

Two other factors need briefly to be taken into consideration. One is the role of defence expenditure. In the years before the outbreak of war in Korea defence expenditure was a smaller part of GNP in most Western European countries than it had been in 1938, although it was by no means insignificant, 6.5 per cent of GNP in France and 5.7 per cent in Britain. Only in the Netherlands and Sweden was it significantly higher than in the pre-war period.[9] On the other hand these levels of defence expenditure were very much higher than those of the 1920s and the question must arise whether they did not have a stabilizing effect on the economies. Similar levels of defence expenditure in 1938 appear to have reduced the severity of the 1937 recession. Defence expenditure at a level of 4 per cent of national income, including expenditure on veterans, had not prevented a very steep fall in manufacturing output in the United States in 1949 and the recovery from that fall is attributable to entirely different influences. At a higher level of national income, defence expenditure in Britain, France and the Netherlands may have exercised a somewhat stronger stabilizing influence, but as we have seen such an influence could not have been very effective, since in France, where commitment to defence expenditure was the greatest, production stagnated. The volume of investment in other sectors was much more influential than that in the defence sector before late 1950 and most of the European economies were already in a powerful upswing before the outbreak of war in Korea produced the upward step in defence expenditure. Indeed, in so far as the persistence of the boom depended on a transition away from government-influenced investment in the capital goods sector towards investment in a much wider range of manufactured output, and in so far as that transition was successfully being made in 1949–50, the Korean war and its effects made the transition harder to achieve, just as they strained the newly created payments mechanism almost beyond what it would bear. To argue that defence expenditures cannot explain the persistence of the post-war boom from 1945 to the end of 1951 is not, of course, to argue that high levels of defence expenditure throughout the 1950s did not exert a stabilizing influence; that is another and much more complex question belonging to a different book.

The other factor which may have had marginal importance in explaining the persistence of high private investment levels was the cluster of technological innovations of the late 1930s and immediate post-war years, which provided opportunities for new investment and the concomitant spread of consumer durables to a larger market. This did not have much influence in Western Europe before 1950, and even after that the growth of consumer expenditures in most Western European countries benefited older rather than newer products. Before 1950 higher levels of disposable purchasing power were mostly spent on increases in consumption of food, clothing and furniture. Some new

[9] J. Berolzheimer, 'The impact of US foreign aid since the Marshall Plan on western Europe's gross national product and government finances', in *Finanzarchiv*, 14 (1), 1953.

products were, however, making their appearance. Television was largely confined to Britain until 1953, by which date there were more than two million sets in use. Between 1948 and 1950 annual sales of washing machines grew from 94,000 to 311,000 in Britain and from 20,000 to 100,000 in France. Sales of refrigerators grew at about the same size and rate in France, although they were lower in Britain.

But the real growth of consumption after 1949 was in older-established goods, radios, vacuum cleaners, sewing machines and cars. Above all the car had become the major target for private consumers and private investors. When it is considered that the passenger car industry and its inputs accounted for about 11 per cent of industrial production in Britain, France, West Germany and Italy in the 1950s and that its output was responsible for more than a quarter of the increase in industrial output in these economies together between 1945 and the late 1960s, the importance of a rapidly expanding car market after 1948 becomes obvious. The rapidity of its expansion was not only a function of the increase in disposable purchasing power but of the severe decline in car stocks during the war. In Germany four-fifths of the pre-war car stock had been destroyed or rendered useless. From spasmodic contracts for repairing the vehicles of the occupying forces in 1948 German car plants passed by 1951 to a level of output of new cars second only in Europe to that of France. In the five countries where cars were produced in significant quantities there were 606,000 new registrations in 1951. Two years later this figure had increased by 30 per cent, in Sweden and the United Kingdom by much more. It was becoming evident that, in spite of the stern upbringing imposed by post-war society the reconstruction, like most parents, was not bringing up exactly the progeny it might have wished.

RECONSTRUCTION AND INTEGRATION

Few would dispute that the prosperity of the 1950s itself contributed to the durability of the western European reconstruction, seeming to confirm the wisdom of its principles. The process of integration, although explained and understood in a great variety of ways, has usually been regarded as making an important contribution to this durability also and the argument of this book supports that view. The nexus of economic and political ties between France and the Federal Republic was what held the second peace settlement together, just as the absence of these ties was a main cause of the ineffectiveness of the first. The various attachments which bound the other European countries into the settlement could not have been completed without those ties and would not survive their breaking. In that sense 'European integration', that phrase capable of so many meanings, depended on a central necessity, a Franco-West German economic association and alliance. But although a simple reassertion of this basic diplomatic reality explains more of the nature of European integration than much of the vague rhetoric on the theme, the concept of European integration was obviously always a larger one and more forward than backward-looking.

To a greater or lesser degree earlier treatments of this theme attribute the movement towards integration to human idealism fortunately triumphing at specific moments over the narrow, anachronistic realism of national governments. The strength of this idealism is usually related to the events of the war itself, as though the experience of National Socialism, of resistance, of the appalling bloodshed and terror and, at the end, of the relative feebleness and helplessness of the European nation state, particularly in the face of the two 'superpowers', had convinced a sufficient number of people that it was an inadequate, unstable basis for a durable reconstruction.

That view of the matter is flatly contradicted by this book. Here the interpretation is that the very limited degree of integration that was achieved came about through the pursuit of the narrow self-interest of what were still powerful nation states. This is not because the book draws heavily on the public archives of some of these nation states. Previous writers have always entirely failed to show through what political mechanism the idealisms which supported western European integration actually influenced governmental policy-making in the nation states, unless it be through the vague suggestion that men like Adenauer, Schuman, Sforza, and Spaak, who themselves shared these enthusiasms, were able to override the massed cohorts of government and bureaucracy whose task it was and is to define and uphold the national interest before all else. Of these idealists Monnet has always been depicted as the most effective just because he deliberately stood outside this apparatus of national bureaucracy and government in order to persuade others of the higher ideals which it was necessary to espouse.

There is no intention in this book to deny a certain welcome leaven of idealism to these men, although the other political ideas which they stood for were not shared by many who also ardently desired a less divisive political framework in western Europe. But the policies from which a limited measure of economic integration did emerge were, so the evidence clearly indicates, created by national bureaucracies out of the internal expression of national political interest, not by the major statesmen who implemented them. The Schuman Plan, for example, was based on two and a half years of the evolution of policy in the French Ministry of Foreign Affairs. The Stikker Plan represented the gradual evolution and convergence of policy in the Netherlands. Policies had to be devised to meet the hard realities that the United Kingdom was prepared to play only a severely limited role in European economic reconstruction and the control of Germany and that, whatever the free-trade inheritance, the future prosperity of the Dutch economy from 1949 onwards was increasingly linked to developments in the West German economy.

To a historian this may not be any great surprise, for although not said before in histories of the subject it must have been very frequently thought! I do not think many serious historians have doubted that this is just what would appear when once the history of these events was written in a neutral way rather than in the full flush of ardent discipleship. Indeed, a large majority of historians, having read what there is to read on the history of the origins of the European Economic Community, have probably dismissed it as myth, and it is no great thing to show to be wrong what few historians ever believed to be right. My intention in attempting to write a more accurate history of the role of European integration in the reconstruction is not destructive but constructive.

Those who explain the movement towards integration as essentially a victory of higher ideals see it also as a progression towards political virtue, reaching a high point between 1950 and 1952, falling back between 1953 and 1954, relaunched in a forward direction in 1955 until it reached the furthermost point of its advance in 1957 with the Treaty of Rome, holding that advanced position until the entry into force of the European Economic Community, and then being beaten back in a series of small but constant defeats, interrupted only by the election of a European parliament, as the nation states reasserted their misguided claim to be able to guarantee the European future. The interpretation of the EEC in this book is quite different. The historical evidence is that it came into existence to cope with certain historically specific and well-defined economic and political problems and, those problems once resolved, there would be no further momentum from the national interest towards any further stage of economic or political integration. Again, this is not intended as a criticism of the role played by the various EEC organizations. Far from it; the obvious implication of this book is that the ECSC, the Common Agricultural Policy and the Common Market were indispensable pillars of Europe's reconstruction. But each was and is designed to resolve a particular and limited, not a generalized and universal, problem. There was no necessary implication in any of these carefully controlled acts of economic integration that the supersession of the nation state was an inevitable continuing process. The process of integration is neither a thread woven into the fabric of Europe's political destiny nor one woven into the destiny of all highly developed capitalist nation states.

This does not mean that integration has come to a stop, only that any further steps in that direction will have to be equally specific to the resolution of economic and political problems not otherwise resolvable. There may well be such problems; the theoretical possibility therefore certainly exists that the pattern of integrative activity of the reconstruction period could be repeated.[10]

[10] The report specially commissioned to identify such problems, Sir A. Cairncross *et al.*, *Economic Policy for the European Community: The Way Forward* (London, 1974), did not come up with many that were neither relatively trivial nor possible to solve by less demanding political means. But the first impression that report would now make on any reader would be of the fearful rapidity with which Western Europe's economic problems have changed.

The historical evidence gives considerable support, in fact, to the theoretical proposition that the validity of the ECSC, as of other examples of sectoral integration, did not lie so much in their vaunted supra-nationality as in their extra-nationality – that they were created as an arm of the nation states to do things which could not otherwise be achieved.

Integration, as it evolved between 1947 and 1951, was a formalization of interdependence significantly different in form and final implication from anything previously seen. Even if the motive which compelled nation states to surrender aspects of the 'sovereignty' they had so jealously guarded over centuries was to prevent the uncompleted arch of western Europe's reconstruction from collapsing in ruins, this in no way diminishes either the importance of the specific acts of integration or their novelty. The durability of western Europe's reconstruction has in part depended on a new kind of international organization. But was that development specific to the time and circumstances of the reconstruction, a historical, rather than a political or economic problem? If the historical evidence will in no way support the theory that integration is the necessary and inevitable end of the nation state, is it possible to comprehend the role of integration in the reconstruction as anything other than a set of specific, unique historical events?

If we demand from the concept of integration no more than the gradual development by nation states of the ability to devise co-operative ways of existing with each other in peace and security, which is essentially what Deutsch implies by 'community', the reconstruction of Western Europe gave rise to a vigorous crop of new international organizations all intended to achieve this result.[11] But the historical records shows that in resolving the problem of reconstruction they were mostly either unimportant or failures. The OEEC, for example, was not only unable to reduce the area of conflict between nations; it actually introduced new areas of conflict, because it could not cope with those problems of reconstruction which required major political decisions and sacrifices by national governments if they were to be solved. Of the Council of Europe more could surely with profit have been said in this book, but it is hard to imagine that anyone will be able successfully to argue that it made much contribution to the task of reconstruction. Of the contribution of the IMF and the other Bretton Woods organizations, 'least said soonest mended' would appear the only appropriate remark. The European organizations which depended on the United Nations could achieve no more than technical collaboration at a low level, and that only by rigorously avoiding every area of political dispute. There was, the evidence suggests, no gradual tendency of nation states, whether as a result of the spread of commerce between them or of common cultural perceptions, to develop a level of international community sufficient to solve problems of the magnitude they were faced with.

[11] K.W. Deutsch et al., *Political Community and the North Atlantic Area* (Princeton, 1957).

In so far, therefore, as other theories of integration place the emphasis less on this progress towards 'community' and more on the primacy of major political actors, the political élites and the machinery of the state, in achieving integration (however it be defined), the history of the reconstruction gives them far more support. The role, for example, of political socialization, of the acquisition of new and more favourable attitudes towards the idea of European political integration by the national voters or populations as a whole, was negligible in producing the ECSC compared to the role of political élites, often concerned with matters of future national security about which the population at large was far from fully informed. Even when a wave of emotional sympathy for the ideas of a European federation welled up in 1947 and 1948 it was no more than a faintly disquieting and soon stilled disturbance for the ships of state, their officer governments and their crews of civil servants. For the populations of the nation states it was only a publicly experienced dream of a better Europe which could not long survive the baleful awakening reality of those years. The growth of political pressure groups advocating European unity which culminated in The Hague Congress, although an interesting study in itself, had very little effect on the major political actors, except when they wished temporarily to use such sentiments for their own ends.

On the other hand, as Pentland suggests, many theorists who accept the primacy of the role of the major political actors in producing integration do so because they envisage the outcome of integration, not necessarily as a specifically new form of political institution, but as 'the growth of certain common values, perceptions and habits'.[12] A 'community' of this kind would be an acceptable goal, no matter what the political process which created it, not only for federalist advocates of integration but for many pluralist advocates of it too. But in fact the major political actors produced in the ECSC, and were seeking to produce in an agricultural common market, a supra-national body from which these ultimate aspirations were distant or in some cases absent. They were primarily seeking a specific, new form of political institution, and the mechanism of integration was not the acceptance of common habits but the enforcement by law of treaties.

Much of the political theory which aims to explain how this type of supra-national integration can come about tends to put the emphasis on the development in the modern world of economic, social or ecological trends which the nation state can no longer cope with inside its own frontiers. To continue to function adequately the powers of many of its institutions have to reach beyond the frontiers. The mechanism of integration is thus a functional one, depending not on the highest levels of governmental decision-making, but on the problem-solving activities of functional institutions at a lower level. This sort of theory is no better a fit with the historical evidence from the

[12] C. Pentland, *International Theory and European Integration* (London, 1973), p. 22.

reconstruction period than the more generalized liberal equation of integration with progress and development as inherent tendencies in the nation state, and obviously has certain shared assumptions with it.

These assumptions dominated the political and economic logic of the trade liberalization programme. But in pursuing that programme Bissell and his ECA colleagues ran at once into concrete examples of the theoretical objections made to these functionalist arguments by many political scientists. For a theory of this kind to explain the process of integration it must be true not only that a clear distinction can be made between political (controversial) and technical (non-controversial) issues of international co-operation, but also that the technical issues should not be at so low a level as to prevent any co-operation on really important issues from which integration would emerge. Quota removals, foreign trade rules, a European central bank, a common currency, were not technical but political, and it was absurd ever to suppose anything else. The functionalist approach to European integration led immediately to intervention by the major European political actors whose interests were substantially different from those of the ECA.

More complex and interesting theories which would explain the process of integration are those which have been labelled 'neo-functionalist'. Here the emphasis is on the tendency of the interaction of political forces such as governments, parties, or interest groups, in promoting their own interests through the medium of international political institutions, to find, nevertheless, that in this pursuit their self-interest is best satisfied in an integrative solution. Thus, Haas would see the process of interaction by all these forces within the ECSC as leading to a gradual move to a new, supra-national centre of authority.[13]

Whether this has in fact been the case seems extremely doubtful, but the historical evidence in this book could be no test of such a theory because it would have to be tested by historical events subsequent to the forming of the Communities.[14] The way in which the Schuman Plan emerged, its causes and motives, the course of negotiations for the ECSC, all suggest, however, that the major political actors have first to make the decisive political step and build the arena in which the neo-functionalist interplay of vested interests can push the process of integration further, if, indeed, they do. Many of those vested interests were firmly opposed to the building of that arena. To suggest, as Haas does, that the emergence of this neo-functionalist interaction of vested interests implies that there is no longer a distinct political function 'which finds its reason for being in the sublime heights of foreign policy, defence and constitution-making' is to attribute a formidable change of

[13] E.B. Haas, *The Uniting of Europe, Political, Social and Economic Forces 1950–1957* (Stanford, 1958).

[14] There has been a useful attempt to do this in H. Wallace, W. Wallace and C. Webb, *Policy-Making in the European Communities* (London, 1977), which suggests that the neo-functionalist approach is not justified by historical evidence.

function and attitude over a very short period to an international institution such as the ECSC, which was created, against the strong opposition of many of those vested interests, to conquer those very heights.[15]

Political theory, therefore, does very little to explain why the process of reconstruction was able to clinch its success by new forms of political and economic organization. Nor is economic theory any more helpful, in spite of the fact that the integrative organizations were mainly concerned with economic affairs. Although it has a great deal to indicate about the effects on trade and national income of integration in the form of customs unions or free-trade areas, according to the extent of tariff cuts, the complementary or competitive nature of the economies involved, and the proportion of their total trade involved in the integrative process, its predictions are mostly based on static equilibrium assumptions. They operate on a given quantity of resources which, if the tariffs are changed, will move to a new equilibrium through the twin processes of trade diversion and trade creation. The motives which inspired the process of integration in European governments were certainly not those of gains to trade. In any case, had they so been it would have been discovered that, on the basis of these static assumptions, for the political effort required the net gains to trade through the process of trade creation would have been only a small, once and for all, gain to national income.[16] Compared to the gains which might be derived from the other, more dynamic effects on national income of the process of integration they might also have been very small. The dynamic effects, however, are obviously less predictable and their political consequences more widespread. Because governments were driven towards integration by political motives, it was with these dynamic effects that they were mainly concerned. They constituted a powerful economic motivation for selecting Western European integration as a goal of American policy, even if the economic reasoning now looks less impressive. They constituted, also, a powerful motivation on the European side for seeking integration through other channels in which the unpredictable dynamic effects, both economic and political, could be more securely confined.

American policy was based on the belief that these dynamic effects would be felt on investment, productivity (because of the potential for greater economies of scale in a larger market), and thus ultimately on the balance of payments. The increase in the potential market would stimulate higher levels of investment and competition, more capital-intensive methods of production and more efficient business habits, leading to higher output at levels of productivity nearer to those in the United States, and would thus solve the major problem in international payments by eliminating Western Europe's

[15] E.B. Haas, 'Technocracy, pluralism and the New Europe', in S.A. Graubard (ed.) *A New Europe* (Boston, 1967), p. 71.

[16] H.G. Johnson, 'The gains from free trade with Europe: an estimate', in *The Manchester School of Economic and Social Studies*, 26, 1958. R.G. Lipsey, 'The theory of customs unions: a general survey', *Economic Journal*, 70 (3), 1960.

dollar deficit. Without Marshall Aid dollar deficits of the size which obtained in Western European countries might have been a severe obstacle to the growth of national income and removing them, as the ERP aimed to do, would have meant much greater gains to income than the static gains from trade creation. Similarly the evidence of many examples from European economic development in the nineteenth century, as well as from the 1950s, suggests that the possibility of large gains in productivity through economies of scale produced by increases in market size is very strong, providing the increase in market size takes place over a short enough period of time and other conditions are propitious. It has also to be said, however, that the distribution of these gains to income through the dynamic effects of integration is unequal between the nations or areas to be integrated, and also unforseeable. They are by no means as generalized as the rather vague theory which demonstrates their presence would imply.[17] This was precisely the ground on which European governments resisted American pressures to integration and particularly the ground on which French governments, once having committed themselves to integration as a solution to the reconstruction problem, resisted American pressures even more fiercely.

The form of integration which did complete Western Europe's reconstruction was based on an attempt by the nation states to control and distribute the gains and losses which might arise in the particular sectors involved in such a way as to determine beforehand the extent to which the national interest of each party to the agreement would be satisfied. Monnet's own original conception of the High Authority would have left more scope to the neofunctionalist interaction of self-interest that Haas believes did actually characterize the ECSC once it began to operate. But this scope was drastically reduced in the negotiating process which set up the ECSC so as to determine as far as possible the extent and direction of national gain and loss before the High Authority began to function. It is often argued that the massive imperfections of the market which were bequeathed by this negotiating process, which was also followed in establishing the Common Agricultural Policy and the Common Market, are in themselves inherently disintegrative, because they increase the inequality of distribution of gains to welfare. Certainly, in these matters the proof of the pudding is in the eating. The history of the EEC has been one of increasing regional (national) divergence of income levels, although not necessarily of growth rates. Its principal politico-economic mechanism, the CAP, actually engenders income divergence at both national and regional levels. If present policies remain this will be experienced in a particularly harsh way by the poorer agriculturally based regions of the Greek, Portuguese and Spanish economies.

[17] Many of the implied gains in changes of psychological or social outlook or business habits of which Scitovsky writes in the fullest statement of this theory are based on no more than casual unsystematic observation, as the author admits. T. Scitovsky, *Economic Theory and Western European Integration* (London, 1958).

But, excluding the United States as a historical example, the history of earlier European customs unions shows no better a record in this respect than that of the EEC. Whether the example of American history and the American economy was a satisfactory basis for European reconstruction was a matter which, superficially, very much divided the major European political actors. Monnet and Spaak held it up as an indication of what could be and had to be achieved, Schuman and Adenauer never appear to have mentioned it. As soon as that example was brought to the level of practical policy-formulation for a future Europe, however, the irreducible complexity of history and national interest made it seem utterly remote and implausible. This is nowhere more evident than in the dichotomy between Monnet's own words and actions.

Even so, there was much support everywhere in Western Europe for a political and economic solution to the problem of reconstruction which would produce the more general dynamic gains which it was believed would arise from integration and market extension, providing their consequences could be controlled and directed as far as possible beforehand, so that they did not stop or reverse the process of integration when they emerged and in doing so destroy the peace settlement. The beneficial nature of these gains in fact became one of the basic tenets of growth theory during the 1950s and a commonplace of political discourse. A way of obtaining these gains had to be found which did not leave scope for the specific limited areas of integration to be extended by either functionalist or neo-functionalist pressures and so endanger reconstruction. It was the lesser risk that the imperfect nature of market integration which would necessarily arise from this might ultimately be so disintegrative as to threaten the same consequences. That was something that might be more easily remedied if need arose.

The historical evidence here which indicates how this way was found cuts awkwardly across the political theory which has tried to explain it. It suggests that, although functionalist theories are indeed not an explanation, it is necessary to combine different elements of the explanatory mechanisms of other theoretical approaches. The acceptance of the primacy of the role of major political actors has to be combined with the neo-functionalist hypothesis to explain an outcome which pluralists and federalists, who are prepared to accept the initial role of the major political actors, have nevertheless envisaged differently, and one with which neo-functionalists would be much less than content since it eliminates most of the predictive force of their model. But if this approach is applied to the way the policy-formulation process did actually function in the nation states between 1945 and 1951 it is not a sterile exercise.

It suggests, for example, that in so far as British policy aimed at creating a series of low-level integrated organizations, which would have no further momentum towards integration as conceived elsewhere but whose purpose was to help to maintain a durable reconstruction in western Europe, it was ill-conceived, because it did not go far enough to establish the durability of that reconstruction. Furthermore, it suggests that each act of integration involves a political decision which can only be taken at the highest level and by weighing the most serious calculations of national gain and loss. Thirdly, it suggests that the determination of these gains and losses is by a process of political bargaining to which, although they are economic gains and losses, economic theory is no guide, because the process is designed expressly to negate the implications and workings of that theory. Neither political nor economic theory serve as more than a verbose encapsulation of a generalized set of desired goals. But when, as in the case of the gains alleged to arise from market integration, there is a consensus on their desirability, theory does have an important political function as simplifier and reminder of what the process is all about.

European integration was not, for example, merely a device to make the Franco-West German tie possible. It genuinely embodied wider and greater aspirations which elevated the Franco-German tie beyond a mere traditional diplomatic alliance. And this in turn gavé the alliance a deeper meaning and a nobler purpose for many in the population of both countries, no matter how frequently these beliefs were traduced at government level. By extension, the same difference was created between the EEC and an alliance. In a period when the extent of political participation was increasing, the process of integration could stimulate participation in its own support and thus attach that support to the complex technicalities of formalized economic inter-dependence on which the European peace settlement was founded. Where in defeated Germany it was indispensable to start once more the processes of political mobilization and participation, while redirecting them towards new goals, the idea of European integration proved a powerful one.

The evidence suggests, furthermore, that in the process of bargaining by the major political actors the calculations about gains and losses must be long-term ones, even if they are unforeseeable with any reasonable accuracy. National bureaucracies, therefore, although they have to take their place as major political actors in the process and were indeed much more important to it than theory suggests, are deplorably ill-equipped for such a task, trained as they are to distil with the greatest possible accuracy forecasts about calculable short-term consequences. Robert Hall, head of the Cabinet Office Secretariat, summing up the British position on European integration at the end of 1949, came to the conclusion that the constraints on British policy-formulation were such that the only appropriate course was to follow the guidance of the hymn *Lead Kindly Light*:

> I do not ask to see
> The distant view – one step enough for me.[18]

The light was not so kindly to those in such a position. This might serve as a relevant cautionary note for those once more engaged in the United Kingdom

[18]   FO 371/87144, Draft note on integration, 19 December 1949.

in approaching the same decision again, this time perhaps in the reverse direction.

But these constraints did not apply to the British national bureaucracy alone; they were the same in every country with a national bureaucracy of the same size and importance. One question has had to be repeatedly posed. How did France, starting from so weak a position in 1945 and pursuing an unrealizable set of foreign policy objectives, arrive at such a satisfactory long-term political and economic solution? The answer must be, not that the French policy-making machine was in any way superior to that in Britain, which largely failed to achieve its own objectives in the reconstruction of Europe, but that the German threat to French national security simply would not go away and, because it was always there, forced French policy-formulation to consider a more distant horizon. In the constant effort of lifting the eyes to that horizon a longer-term solution was eventually found. By contrast, on the rare occasions when the United Kingdom Foreign Office or Treasury had the leisure to switch their gaze to the longer-term, the level of their comment dropped from penetrating and well-ordered expertise to rambling and alarmingly ignorant self-indulgence. No doubt the same traits were present in France on other questions, but not on the question of Germany. There, it had become too dangerous.

In the United States the national bureaucracy was not deficient in long-term considerations but lamentably deficient in establishing any links between them and the immediate practical possibilities of action. Some part of this is explained by the constant pressure from the ECA which was staffed not by permanent civil servants but by figures from the business and academic world brought in for the purpose. The tendency of the American policy-formulation machine not to be bound by a merely short-run perspective because it is constantly refreshed by figures from outside the national bureaucracy was certainly very evident in the reconstruction period. But the long-run objectives which they imposed in the pursuit of European integration were only long-run dreams, which had only an impossibly short term to be turned into realities.

All this in turn suggests that, although the major political actors themselves assume the neo-functionalist role in the process of integration, and may well be able to reduce to insignificance the extent to which others may play that role after integration has been achieved, they are not necessarily very good at it. Consideration of the role played by the Netherlands in 1949 and 1950 shows that by choosing its opportunity well a lesser political actor, for such the Netherlands was in those negotiations, can force the greater political actors to alter the parameters within which they have decided to act, and in a way which, in that instance, left the future much less clear and controlled than they would have wished. Given that the economic future was always much less controllable than the political, Schuman was quite right when he called his proposals a leap in the dark.

There was, as it turned out, nothing in that darkness for a long time that the post-war settlement could not cope with. Both the ECSC and the Common Market were designed for a period of vigorous economic expansion. The extent to which they contributed to sustaining that expansion is only partially measurable. But it is hard to believe that the great boom would have been so vigorous and so long had the reconstruction of Europe had the air of incompleteness and frailty which it had had all through the 1920s, when the major western European economy never accepted its principles and several others waited eagerly for their overturning. Nor is it easy to see how the reconstruction boom could have merged into a continuing post-war boom had political events turned out differently in 1949 and 1950 and the arch of political and economic reconstruction not been completed by the process of integration.

Lastly, it has to be said that, although the process of integration was a Western European solution to a Western European problem, and that Western Europe made its own peace settlement, the external world exerted constant pressures towards a similar solution. Western Europe had much to thank the Soviet Union for, especially its threatening, unremitting hostility throughout the whole period. And without the drive of the United States to impose integration to suit its own strategic goals Western Europe would perhaps not have discovered its own different route to a settlement. Small wonder that from the conception of the EEC its relationship with the United States has been so ambivalent.

The great European boom is becoming a memory of the middle-aged and the ideas which characterized it are being swept into the intellectual dustbin. The ECSC can find no coherent response to entirely different economic conditions. The CAP commands a diminishing number of friends in Europe and only enemies outside it, of whom the United States is becoming the leader. The appropriateness of the present Western European institutions to an enlarged EEC is not easy to see. For the first time the validity of the principles of western Europe's reconstruction is called into question on all sides. Its pillars tremble. The painfully constructed roof of interdependence shakes. The balance of power still depends on the thrust and counter-thrust of the nation states which sustain it. Adjustments of their positions are continually necessary, but even the smallest makes the two great buttresses of the superpowers start to slip and slide and those beneath to cower. Let all those who wish to reconstruct the roof on fundamentally new principles think first that never except beneath that roof has western Europe known so long a peace nor a life so prosperous and so humane.

APPENDIX

Figures 8–12. The basic source is OEEC, *Statistical Bulletin of Foreign Trade, Series 1.* The method adopted was to take the United Kingdom as the reporting country in all transactions concerning that country, Belgium-Luxembourg as the reporting country in all transactions except those with the United Kingdom, Italy as the reporting country in all transactions except those with Belgium-Luxembourg and the United Kingdom, and so on through the Netherlands to France and to Germany, Germany being placed at the end of the chain because its statistics for obvious reasons are the most doubtful. In all transactions with 'Rest of Western Europe' therefore the reporting country is the other party to the transaction. The discrepancies in French and German figures on their current account transactions are so great that the German figure is also given in brackets. 'Germany' is defined as explained on each figure.

Table 36. The weights in the last column (the value of exports of Little Europe at pre-September 1949 exchange rates) are those of the relative share in the value of the exports of the Little European countries to the same markets in 1948.

Table 48. The index is a quantum index (Laspeyres) with fixed weights in which the quantities of trade for each period are multiplied by constant prices (unit values)

$$Qu = \frac{\Sigma\, Poqn}{\Sigma\, Poqo}$$

where Q is the index, P the unit value, q the quantity, o the base period and n the current period.

The weight used is the net value added in the base period. The figures for the United States have been adjusted, in order to make the coverage for that country more comparable to that for the others, on the assumption that items not directly used in the calculation were subject to the same average price changes as all the other items in the traded aggregate of manufactured goods. In standardizing German trade statistics the procedure has been adopted of estimating the territorial area of the Federal Republic of Germany to have accounted for 67 per cent of the exports and 71 per cent of the imports of the Third Reich.

METHOD OF REFERRING TO DOCUMENTS

Documents in the Public Record Office, Kew, are referred to by the reference number of the file and the title and date of each document is given. This applies to Board of Trade, Cabinet, Foreign Office and Treasury documents. The same system is used for records in the National Archives of the United States. For the records of the Department of State the file number is given with a full description, for the records of the Economic Co-operation Administration the box numbers on the catalogue of the Washington Federal Records Center. For documents in the Harry S. Truman Memorial Library the specific collection is identified together with a description of the document and this system is used for the Paul Hoffmann papers at Suitland also. For the records of the Dutch, French and Norwegian foreign ministries the file reference is given and for the OMGUS documents a full description of the document.

BIBLIOGRAPHY

NATIONAL AND INTERNATIONAL OFFICIAL
PUBLICATIONS AND STATISTICAL SOURCES

AUSTRIA

Bundeskanzleramt. Sektion für wirtschaftliche Koordination. *Zehn Jahre ERP in Österreich 1948/58. Wirtschafts hilfe im Dienste der Völkerverständigung.*
Österreichisches Statistisches Zentralamt, *Statistik des Aussenhandels Österreichs.*

BANK FOR INTERNATIONAL SETTLEMENTS

Annual Reports.

BELGIUM

Banque Nationale de Belgique, *Bulletin d'information.*
Institut National de Statistique, *Bulletin Mensuel du Commerce Extérieur.*
   Annuaire Statistique de la Belgique.

COMMITTEE OF EUROPEAN ECONOMIC CO-OPERATION

General Report and Technical Reports (July/September 1947).

DENMARK

Danmarks Statistik, *Statistisk Arbog.*
   Vareomsaettningen med Udlandet.

EUROPEAN COAL AND STEEL COMMUNITY

Recueil statistique de la Communauté Européenne du Charbon et de l'Acier.

FEDERAL REPUBLIC OF GERMANY

Auswärtiges Amt, *Gutachten zu Fragen einer Europäischen Agrargemeinschaft* (Bonn, 1953).

Bundesministerium für den Marshall-Plan, *Berichte der Deutschen Bundes-regierung über die Durchführung des Marshallplanes.*
Statistisches Amt, *Der Aussenhandel der Bundesrepublik Deutschland.*

FRANCE

Commissariat au Plan, *Cinq ans d'exécution du Plan 1947–1951* (Paris, 1952).
Conseil Economique, *Compte-rendu de la Commission Mixte Franco-Italienne d'Union Douanière.*
Etudes et Travaux.
Direction Générale des Douanes et Droits Indirects, *Statistique mensuelle du commerce extérieur de la France.*
Tableaux du commerce extérieur de la France.
Institut National des Statistiques et des Etudes Economiques, *Annuaire statistique.*
Le Bénélux (Paris, 1953).
L'Economie de la Ruhr (Paris, 1947).
L'Economie de la Sarre (Paris, 1947).
Le mouvement économique en France de 1938 à 1948 (Paris, 1950).
Le mouvement économique en France de 1944 à 1957 (Paris, 1958).
Etudes et Conjoncture, Inventaire économique de l'Europe, Economie Mondiale nos. 17, 18, 19, 1947.
Etudes et Conjoncture, Quelques aspects fondamentaux de l'économie mon-diale (1951).
Ministère de l'Industrie et du Commerce, *Statistique de l'industrie minérale.*
Ministère des Affaires Etrangères, *Documents de la Conférence des Ministres des Affaires Etrangères de la France, du Royaume-Uni, de l'URSS tenue à Paris du 27 juin au 3 juillet 1947.*

INTERNATIONAL BANK FOR RECONSTRUCTION AND DEVELOPMENT

The Report of the Economic Commission for Europe 'Economic Survey for 1948' (1949).

INTERNATIONAL MONETARY FUND

Balance of Payments Yearbook.
International Financial Statistics.

IRELAND

Central Statistics Office, *Trade and Shipping Statistics.*

ITALY

Comitato Italiano per la Ricostruzione, *Lo sviluppo dell'economia italiano nel quadro della ricostruzione e della cooperazione europea.*
Istituto Centrale de Statistica, *Annuario statistico italiano 1944–1948.*
Statistica de Commercio con l'estero.

LLOYDS REGISTER OF SHIPPING

NETHERLANDS

Centraal Bureau voor de Statistiek, *Jaarcifjers voor Nederland 1947–50.*
Maandstatistiek van den In-Uit-En Doorvoer van Nederland.
Zeventig Jaar Statistiek in Tydreksen 1899–1969.

NORWAY

Statistisk Sentralbyrå, *Norges Økonomi etter krigen, Samfunnsøkonomiske
Studier 12 (Oslo, 1965).*
Månedsoppgaver over Vareomsettningen med Udlandet.
Økonomisk Utsyn 1900–1950, Samfunnsøkonomiske Studier 3 (Oslo, 1955).
Statistisk Arbok.
Statisk-Økonomisk Oversikter.

OEEC

Industrial Statistics
Integration Studies, Motor-car industry (Paris, 1950, 1951, 1952).
  Textile Machinery (Paris, 1950).
  Wool Sector (Paris, 1950).
Interim Report on the European Recovery Programme, 3 vols. (Paris, 1948).
Intra-European Investments (Paris, 1951).
Private United States Investment in Europe and the Overseas Territories
  (Paris, 1954).
*Report to the Economic Co-operation Administration on the First Annual
  Programme* (Paris, 1949).
*Third Annual Report to the Economic Co-operation Administration. Economic
  Progress and Problems of Western Europe* (Paris, 1951).
*Fourth Annual Report to the Economic Co-operation Administration. Europe
  The Way Ahead* (Paris, 1952).
*Report of the Results of the Bilateral Discussions between Participating
  Countries* (Paris, 1949).
Reports on Internal Financial Stability in Member Countries (Paris, 1949,
  1950, 1952).
Statistical Bulletin of Foreign Trade.
Statistics of National Product and Expenditure 1938, 1947/52.
*The Structure of the European Economy in 1953. Tentative Input-Output
  Table for the OEEC Member Countries* (Paris, 1953).

OECD

From Marshall Plan to Global Independence (Paris, 1978).

PORTUGAL

Instituto Nacional de Estatistica, *Comercio Externo.*

SWEDEN

Statistiska Centralbyrån, *Sveriges Officielle Statistik. Handels Berättelse.*
Statistiska Centralbyrån, *Statistisk Arsbok för Sverige.*

SWITZERLAND

Eidgenössische Oberzolldirektion, *Jahresstatistik des Aussenhandels der Schweiz.*
Eidgenössisches Statistisches Amt, *Statistisches Jahrbuch der Schweiz.*

UNITED KINGDOM

Board of Trade, *Accounts Relating to the Trade and Navigation of the United Kingdom.*
Annual Statement of the Trade of the United Kingdom.
Board of Trade Journal.
British Iron and Steel Federation, *Statistical Yearbooks.*
Central Statistical Office, *Annual Abstract of Statistics.*
National Income and Expenditure 1946–51 (London, 1952).
Foreign Office, *Anglo-French Discussions Regarding French Proposals for the West European Coal, Iron and Steel Industries in May-June 1950* (Cmd. 7970).
Political and Economic Planning, *Britain and World Trade* (1947).

UNITED NATIONS

Department of Economic Affairs, *Balance of Payments Trends and Policies, 1950–1* (New York, 1951).
Coal Consumption Trends in the Western Zones of Germany (New York, 1953).
Customs Unions (Geneva, 1948).
Economic Survey of Europe Since the War (Geneva, 1953).
Economic Surveys of Europe.
The European Coal Problem (New York, 1952).
The European Steel Market in 1953 (Geneva, 1954).
European Steel Trends in the Setting of the World Market (Geneva, 1949).
Financial Needs of the Devastated Countries (Geneva, 1947).
The Foreign Exchange Position of the Devastated Countries (New York, 1948).
Inflationary and Deflationary Tendencies 1946–1948 (New York, 1949).
Major Economic Changes in 1948 (New York, 1949).
Monthly Bulletin of Statistics.
National Income Statistics of Various Countries 1938–1947 (Geneva, 1948).
Post-War Shortages of Food and Coal (Geneva, 1948).
Preliminary Report of the Temporary Sub-Commission on Economic Reconstruction of Devastated Areas (New York, 1946).

The Quest for Freer Trade (New York, 1955).

Recent Changes in Production (New York, 1952).

Relative Prices of Exports and Imports of Under-Developed Countries (New York, 1949).

Salient Features of the World Economic Situation 1945–47 (Lake Success, 1948).

Statistical Yearbooks.

Steel Production and Consumption Trends in Europe and the World (New York, 1952).

Survey of Current Inflationary and Deflationary Tendencies (Geneva, 1947).

A Survey of the Economic Situation and Prospects of Europe (Geneva, 1948).

Yearbook of International Trade Statistics.

Food and Agriculture Organization, International Emergency Food Committee, *Preliminary Appraisal of the World Food Situation 1946–7.*

Report for the Council (1948).

Yearbook of Agricultural Statistics.

Statistical Office, *Statistical Papers, Series E No. 1, National and Per Capita Incomes of Seventy Countries in 1949 Expressed in US Dollars.*

Series J No. 1, World Energy Supply in Selected Years.

UNRRA, *Operational Analysis Papers*, no. 26, *Italy's Balance of Payments in 1947.*

no. 41, *The Food Situation in Continental Europe.*

no. 43, *Agriculture in Italy.*

Survey of Italy's Economy (Rome, 1947).

UNITED STATES OF AMERICA

Council of Economic Advisers, *The Impact of Foreign Aid upon the Domestic Economy* (1947).

European Recovery Program. Report of the Committee on Foreign Relations on S.2202 (1948).

Congress, 80th Congress, *Report on the European Interim Aid Act of 1947.*

The European Recovery Program. Basic Documents and Background Information.

The French Crisis and Interim Aid (1947).

The Italian Crisis and Interim Aid (1947).

United States Foreign Policy for a Post-War Recovery Program. Hearings Before the Joint Committee on Foreign Affairs (1948).

81st Congress, *Extension of the European Recovery Program 1949. Hearings Before the Joint Committee on Foreign Affairs* (1949).

Report to the Joint Committee on Foreign Economic Co-operation on Progress of the Economic Co-operation Administration (1949).

Department of Commerce, *Foreign Aid by the United States Government 1940–1951* (1952).
Statistical Abstract of the United States.
Statistical History of the United States From Colonial Times to the Present.
Department of State, *Foreign Relations of the United States.*
Germany 1947–1949. The Story in Documents (1950).
Economic Co-operation Agency, *Country Studies.*
Report of the ECA-Commerce Mission to Investigate the Possibilities of Increasing Western Europe's Dollar Earnings (1949).
A Report on Recovery Progress and United States Aid (1949).
The Sterling Area. An American Analysis (London, 1951).
Federal Reserve Bank, *Federal Reserve Bulletin.*
High Commission in Germany, *The Liberalization of West German Foreign Trade 1949–1951* (1952).
National·Advisory Committee on International Monetary and Financial Problems, *Foreign Assets and Liabilities of the United States and Its Balance of International Transactions. Report to the Senate Committee on Finance* (1948).
Office of the Military Governor of the United States, *Monthly Report of the Military Governor.*
Ownership and Control of the Ruhr Industries (1948).
Wirtschaftsstatistik der Deutschen Besatzungszonen.
President's Committee on Foreign Aid, *European Recovery and American Aid* (1947).

WIRTSCHAFTSRAT DES VEREINIGTEN WIRTSCHAFTSGEBIETES
Wörtliche Berichte.

NON-OFFICIAL AND SECONDARY PUBLICATIONS

Abelshauser, W. 'Ein Briefwechsel zwischen John J. McCloy und Konrad Adenauer während der Korea-Krise' in *Vierteljahrshefte für Zeitgeschichte*, 30, (iv), 1982.
Abelshauser, W. 'Korea, die Ruhr und Erhards Marktwirtschaft: Die Energiekrise von 1950/51', in *Rheinische Vierteljahrsblätter*, 45, 1981.
Abelshauser, W. 'Wiederaufbau vor dem Marshall-Plan. Westeuropas Wachstumschancen und die Wirtschaftsordnungs-politik in der zweiten Hälfte der vierziger Jahre', in *Vierteljahrshefte für Zeitgeschichte*, 29 (4), 1981.
Abelshauser, W. *Wirtschaft in Westdeutschland 1945–1948. Rekonstruktion und Wachstumsbedingungen in der amerikanischen und britischen Zone* (Stuttgart, 1975).

Abelshauser, W. and Petzina, D. 'Krise und Rekonstruktion. Zur Interpretation der gesamtwirtschaftlichen Entwicklung Deutschlands im 20 Jahrhundert', in W.H. Schröder and R. Spree (eds) *Historische Konjunkturforschung* (Stuttgart, 1981).

Acheson, D.G. *Present at The Creation* (New York, 1970).

Acheson, D.G. *Sketches from Life of Men I Have Known* (New York, 1961).

Adamsen, H.R. 'Faktoren und Daten der wirtschaftliche Entwicklung in der Frühphase der Bundesrepublik 1948–1954', *Archiv für Sozialgeschichte*, 18, 1978.

Adamsen, H.R. *Investitionshilfe für die Ruhr. Wiederaufbau, Verbände und Soziale Marktwirtschaft 1948–1952* (Wuppertal, 1981).

Adler-Karlsson, G. *Western Economic Warfare 1947–1967, A Case Study in Foreign Economic Warfare* (Uppsala, 1968).

Arkes, H. *Bureaucracy, the Marshall Plan, and the National Interest* (Princeton, 1972).

Auriol, V. *Journal du septennat 1947–1954* (Paris, 1970).

Backer, J.H. *The Decision to Divide Germany. American Foreign Policy in Transition* (Durham, NC, 1978).

Backer, J.H. *Priming the German Economy: American Occupational Policies 1945–1948* (Durham, NC, 1971).

Balabkins, N. *Germany Under Direct Controls: Economic Aspects of Industrial Disarmament 1945–1948* (New Brunswick, 1964).

Balogh, T. 'The Crisis of the Marshall Plan', *Finanzarchiv*, N.F.12, 1950.

Balogh, T. *The Dollar Crisis* (Oxford, 1949).

Balogh, T. 'The dollar crisis revisited', *Oxford Economic Papers*, 6, 1954.

Banco di Roma, *Review of the Economic Conditions in Italy. Special Issue. Ten Years of Italian Economy 1947–1956* (Rome, 1957).

Bariety, J. 'Der Tardieu-Plan zur Sanierung des Donauraums (Februar-Mai 1932)', in J. Becker and K. Hildebrand (eds) *Internationale Beziehungen in der Weltwirtschaftskrise 1929–1933* (Munich, 1980).

Baudhuin, F. *Histoire économique de la Belgique 1945–56* (Brussels, 1958).

Baum, W.C. *The French Economy and the State* (Princeton, 1958).

Baumgart, E., Krengel, R. and Moritz, W. *Die Finanzierung der industriellen Expansion in der Bundesrepublik während der Jahre des Wiederaufbaus*, Deutsches Institut für Wirtschaftsforschung, Sonderhefte, N.F. 49 (Berlin, 1960).

Baumgart, E. *Investition und ERP-Finanzierung. Eine Untersuchung über die Anlage – Investionen als Wachstumsdeterminante des Wirtschaftsprozesses in der Bundesrepublik-Deutschland und die wirtschaftspolitische Einflussnahme durch Investitionsfinanzierung aus dem ERP-Sondervermögen in empirischer Sicht von 1949–1956*, Deutsche Institut für Wirtschaftsforschung, Sonderhefte, N.F. 56 (Berlin, 1961).

Bean, R.W. 'European multilateral clearing', *Journal of Political Economy*, 56, 1948.

Bell, P.W. *The Sterling Area in the Post-War World* (Oxford, 1956).

Beloff, M. *The United States and the Unity of Europe* (Washington DC, 1963).

Berolzheimer, J. 'The impact of US foreign aid since the Marshall Plan on western Europe's Gross National Product and government finances', *Finanzarchiv*, N.F. 14, 1953.

Besson, W. 'Die Anfänge der bundesrepublikanischen Aussenpolitik', in G. Lehmbruch (ed.), *Demokratisches System und politische Praxis in der Bundesrepublik* (Munich, 1971).

Bissel, R.M. Jnr 'European recovery and the problems ahead', *American Economic Review*, 42 (2), 1952.

Blücher, F. *Dienst an Deutschland und Europa. Vier Jahre Bundesministerium für den Marshallplan* (Bad Godesberg, 1953).

Blyth, C.A. *American Business Cycles 1945–50* (London, 1969).

Bok, D.C. *The First Three Years of the Schuman Plan* (Princeton Studies in International Finance, 8, 1955).

Boltho, A. *The European Economy. Growth and Crisis* (Oxford, 1982).

Borchardt, K. 'Integration in wirtschaftshistorische Perspektive', in E. Schneider (ed.) *Weltwirtschaftliche Probleme der Gegenwart* (Berlin, 1965).

Borchardt, K. 'Trend, Zyklus, Strukturbrüche, Zufälle: Was bestimmt die deutsche Wirtschaftsgeschichte im 20 Jahrhundert?', *Vierteljahrschrift für Sozial und Wirtschaftsgeschichte*, 64, 1977.

Borchardt, K. 'Die Bundesrepublik in den säkularen Trends der wirtschaftlichen Entwicklungen' in W. Conze and M.R. Lepsius, Sozialgeschichte der Bundesrepublik Deutschland: Beiträge zum Kontinuitätsproblem (Stuttgart, 1983).

Bourneuf, A. *Norway. The Planned Revival* (Cambridge, Mass., 1958).

Bouvier, J. 'Limites et aléas de l'investissement 1947–1952', unpublished paper, 1950.

Brakel, W. *De industrialisatie in Nederland na 1945* (Leiden, 1954).

Bratt, E.C. and Ondrechen, J.P. 'The 1948–49 recession re-examined', *Economic Journal*, 63 (249), 1953.

Braudel, F. and Labrousse, E. (eds) *Histoire économique et sociale de la France*, vol. 4, part 2: *Le Temps des Guerres Mondiales et de la Grande Crise (1914–vers 1950)* (J. Bouvier *et al.* eds).

Brodsky, N. 'Some aspects of international relief', *Quarterly Journal of Economics*, 62, 1947/8.

Brofoss, E. 'The Marshall Plan and Norway's hesitation', *Scandinavian Journal of History*, 2, 1977.

Brown, W.A. Jnr *The United States and the Restoration of World Trade* (Washington DC, 1950).

Brown, W.A. Jnr and Opie, R. *American Foreign Assistance* (Washington DC, 1953).

Burn, D. *The Steel Industry 1939–1959. A Study in Competition and Planning* (Cambridge, 1961).

Byé, M. 'L'union douanière franco-italienne', *Annales d'économie politique*, 1950.

Cairncross, Sir A. 'The economic recovery of Germany', *Lloyds Bank Review*, 22, October 1951.

Cairncross, Sir A. 'The post-war years 1945–1977', R. Floud and D. McCloskey (eds) *The Economic History of Britain Since 1700*, vol. 2 (Cambridge, 1981).

Cairncross, Sir A. *et al. Economic Policy for the European Community. The Way Forward* (London, 1974).

Carré, J.J., Dubois, P. and Malinvaud, E. *French Economic Growth* (Stanford, 1976).

Catinat, M. 'La production industrielle sous la IVième république', *Économie et Statistique*, 129, January 1981.

Chandler, L.V. *Inflation in the United States 1940–1948* (New York, 1951).

Chardonnet. J. *La sidérurgie française. Progrès ou décadence?* (Paris, 1954).

Clarke, Sir R. *Anglo-American Economic Collaboration in War and Peace 1942–1949*, ed. Sir A. Cairncross (Oxford, 1982).

Clayton, W.L. 'GATT, the Marshall Plan, and OECD', *Political Science Quarterly*, 78, 1963.

Colebrook, M.J. 'Franco-British relations and European integration 1945–50' (Doctoral thesis, University of Geneva, 1971).

Coppola d'Anna, F. 'The integration of Western Europe', *Banca Nazionale del Lavoro*, 13 (3), 1950.

Coppola d'Anna, F. 'L'unione doganale italo-francese', *Rivista di politica economica*, 38, 1948.

Daneo, C. *La politica economia della Ricostruzione 1945–49* (Torino, 1975).

de Cecco, M. 'Italian economic policy during the reconstruction', in S.J. Woolf (ed.) *The Rebirth of Italy 1943–1950* (London, 1972).

Despres, E. and Kindleberger, C.P. 'The mechanism for adjustment in international payments – the lessons of postwar experience', *American Economic Review*, 42 (3), 1952.

Deutsch, K.W. *et al. Political Community and the North Atlantic Area* (Princeton, 1957).

Deutsch, K.W. and Edinger, L.J. *Germany Rejoins the Powers. Mass Opinion, Interest Groups and Elites in Contemporary German Foreign Policy* (Stanford, 1959).

Deutsches Institut für Wirtschaftsforschung *Die deutsche Wirtschaft zwei Jahre nach dem Zusammenbruch* (Berlin, 1947).

Dewhurst, J.F. *et al. America's Needs and Resources* (New York, 1947).

Diebold, W. Jnr *The Schuman Plan, a Study in Economic Cooperation 1950–1959* (New York, 1959).

Diebold, W. Jnr *Trade and Payments in Western Europe. A Study in Economic Cooperation, 1947–1951* (New York, 1952).

Dow, J.C.R. *The Management of the British Economy, 1945–60* (Cambridge, 1960).

Ehrmann, H.W. 'The French trade associations and the ratification of the Schuman Plan', *World Politics*, 6 (4), 1954.

Ehrmann, H.W. *Organized Business in France* (Princeton, 1957).

Ellis, H.S. *The Economics of Freedom. The Progress and Future of Aid to Europe* (New York, 1950).

Fels, R. 'Theoretical significance of the 1949 recession', *American Economic Review*, 45 (2), 1955.

Fels, R. 'The US downturn of 1948', *American Economic Review*, 55 (4), 1965.

Fischer, P. *Die Saar zwischen Deutschland und Frankreich: Politische Entwicklung von 1945–1959* (Frankfurt-am-Main, 1959).

Fontaine, M. *L'industrie sidérurgique dans le monde et son évolution depuis la Seconde Guerre Mondiale* (Paris, 1950).

Freymond, J. *The Saar Conflict 1945–1955* (London, 1960).

Gardner, R.N. *Sterling-Dollar Diplomacy* (Oxford, 1956).

Gerbet, P. 'La Genèse du Plan Schuman des origines à la déclaration du 9 mai 1950', *Revue française de science politique*, 6, 1956.

Gimbel, J. *The American Occupation of Germany* (Stanford, 1968).

Gimbel, J. *The Origins of the Marshall Plan* (Stanford, 1976).

Golay, J.F. *The Founding of the Federal Republic of Germany* (Chicago, 1958).

Gordon, L. 'The Organization for European Economic Cooperation', *International Organization*, 10 (1), 1956.

Goriély, G. 'L'opinion publique et le plan Schuman', *Revue française de science politique*, 3, 1953.

Gottlieb, M. *The German Peace Settlement and the Berlin Crisis* (New York, 1960).

Graubard, S.A. (ed.) *A New Europe* (Boston, 1967).

Guglielmi, J.-L. and Perrot, M. *Salaires et revendications sociales en France 1944–1952* (Paris, 1953).

Haas, E.B. *The Uniting of Europe, Political, Social and Economic Forces 1950–1957* (Stanford, 1958).

Haberler, G. 'Some Economic Problems of the European Recovery Program', *American Economic Review*, 38 (2), 1948.

Haberler, G. 'European unification and the dollar problem', *Quarterly Journal of Economics*, 64, 1950.

Hahn, C.H. *Der Schuman Plan: Eine Untersuchung in besonderen Hinblick auf die deutsch-französische Stahlindustrie* (Munich, 1953).

Hamberg, D. 'The recession of 1948–49 in the United States', *Economic Journal*, 62 (245), 1952.

Harris, S.E. *The European Recovery Program* (Cambridge, Mass., 1948).

Harrod, R. *Are These Hardships Necessary?* (London, 1947).

Haussmann, F. *Der Neuaufbau der deutschen Kohlenwirtschaft im internationalen Rahmen* (Munich, 1950).

Haussmann, F. *Der Schuman Plan im Europäischen Zwielicht* (Munich, 1952).

Havilland, H.F. Jnr (ed.) *The United States and the World Community* (Haverford, Pa., 1957).

Herbst, L. 'Ludwig Erhard und die Nachkriegsplanungen am Ende des Zweiten Weltkrieges', *Vierteljahrshefte für Zeitgeschichte*, 25 (3), 1977.

Herchenröder, K.H., Schäfer, J. and Zapp, M. *Die Nachfolger der Ruhrkonzerne* (Düsseldorf, 1954).

Hexner, E. *The International Steel Cartel* (Chapel Hill, 1943).

Hickman, B.G. *Growth and Stability of the Post-War Economy* (Washington DC, 1960).

Hildebrand, G.H. *Growth and Structure in the Economy of Modern Italy* (Cambridge, Mass., 1965).

Hirschman, A.O. 'The European Payments Union; the negotiations and the issues', *Review of Economics and Statistics*, 33, 1951.

Hirschman, A.O. 'Inflation and deflation in Italy', *American Economic Review*, 38 (4), 1948.

Hoffmann, P.G. *Peace Can Be Won* (New York, 1951).

Horsefield, J.K. *et al. The IMF, 1945–1965*, 3 vols (Washington DC, 1969).

Hunold, A. (ed.) *Wirtschaft ohne Wunder*. Volkswirtschaftliche Studien für das Schweizerische Institut für Auslandsforschung (Erlenbach-Zürich, 1953).

Hüwel, D. *Karl Arnold. Eine politische Biographie* (Wuppertal, 1980).

Institut für Zeitgeschichte *Westdeutschlands Weg zur Bundesrepublik: 1945–1949, Beiträge von Mitarbeitern des Instituts für Zeitgeschichte* (Munich, 1976).

Jerchow, F. *Deutschland in der Weltwirtschaft 1944–1947. Alliierte Deutschland- und Reparationspolitik und die Anfänge der westdeutschen Aussenwirtschaft* (Düsseldorf, 1978).

Johnson, H.J. 'The gains from free trade with Europe: an estimate', *The Manchester School of Economic and Social Studies*, 26, 1958.

Jones, J.M. *The Fifteen Weeks (Feb. 21–June 5, 1947). An Inside Account of the Genesis of the Marshall Plan* (New York, 1955).

Jürgensen, H. *Die Westeuropäische Montanindustrie und Ihr Gemeinsamer Markt* (Göttingen, 1955).

Keynes, J.M. *The Economic Consequences of the Peace* (London, 1919).

Kindleberger, C.P. *Europe and the Dollar* (Cambridge, Mass., 1966).

Kindleberger, C.P. 'European economic integration', *Money, Trade and Economic Growth, Essays in Honour of John Henry Williams* (New York, 1951).

Kindleberger, C.P. 'Germany and the economic recovery of Europe', *Proceedings of the Academy of Political Science*, 23 (2), 1949.

Knapp, M. 'Deutschland und der Marshall Plan: Zum Verhältnis zwischen politischer und ökonomischer Stabilisierung in der amerikanischen Duetschlandpolitik nach 1945', *Fünf Beiträge zur Deutschlandpolitik der westlichen Allierten* (Wiesbaden, 1977).

Kolko, J. and G. *The Limits of Power. The World and United States Foreign Policy 1945–1954* (New York, 1972).

Kretzschmar, W.W. *Auslandshilfe als Mittel der Aussenwirtschafts- und Aussenpolitik. Eine Studie über die amerikanische Auslandshilfe von 1945 bis 1956 unter Berücksichtigung sowohl wirtschaftlicher als auch praktisch-politischer Gesichtspunkte* (Munich, 1964).

Kuisel, R.F. *Capitalism and the State in Modern France. Renovation and Economic Management in the Twentieth Century* (Cambridge, 1981).

Lamfalussy, A. *The United Kingdom and The Six* (London, 1963).

Lauersen, W. *Ausmass und Formen vertikaler Verflechtung in der Eisen- und Stahlindustrie der Vereinigten Staaten, Grossbritanniens, Frankreichs, Belgiens und Luxemburgs* (Kiel, 1951).

Lehoulier, J. 'L'évolution des salaires', *Revue d'économie politique*, 7, 1947.

Lindberg, L.M. *The Political Dynamics of European Integration* (Stanford, 1963).

Lipgens, W. *Europa-Föderationspläne der Widerstandsbewegungen 1940–45*, Schriften des Forschungsinstitutes der deutschen Gesellschaft für Auswärtige Politik, 26 (Munich, 1968).

Lipgens, W. *A History of European Integration*, vol. 1: *1945–1947. The Formation of the European Unity Movement* (Oxford, 1982).

Lipgens, W. 'Innerfranzösische Kritik an der Aussenpolitik de Gaulles 1944–1946', *Vierteljahrshefte für Zeitgeschichte*, 24 (iv), 1976.

Lipsey, R.E. *Price and Quantity Trends in the Foreign Trade of the United States* (Princeton, 1963).

Lipsey, R.G. 'The theory of customs unions: a general survey', *Economic Journal*, 70 (3), 1960.

Lister, L. *Europe's Coal and Steel Community: An Experiment in Economic Union* (New York, 1960).

Loth, W. *Die Teilung der Welt 1941–1955* (Munich, 1980).

Loth, W. *Sozialismus und Internationalismus. Die französischen Sozialisten und die Nachkriegsordnung Europas 1940–1950* (Stuttgart, 1977).

Lundestad, G. *The American Non-Policy Towards Eastern Europe 1943–1947: Universalism in an Area not of Essential Interest to the United States* (Oslo, 1978).

Lynch, F.M.B. 'The political and economic reconstruction of France 1944–1947 in its international context' (PhD thesis, University of Manchester, 1981).

McArthur, J.H. and Scott, B.R. *Industrial Planning in France* (Boston, 1969).

MacDougall, D. *Studies in Political Economy*, 2 vols. (London, 1975).

MacDougall, D. *The World Dollar Problem. A Study in International Economics* (London, 1957).

Machlup, F. *A History of Thought on Economic Integration* (London, 1977).

Magnus, K. *Eine Million Tonnen Kriegsmaterial für den Frieden. Die Geschichte der St.EG* (Munich, 1954).

Maier, C. 'The politics of productivity: foundations of American international economic policy after World War II', in P. Katzenstein (ed.) *Between Power and Plenty: The Foreign Economic Policies of Advanced Industrial States* (Madison, 1978).

Maier, C. 'The two postwar eras and the conditions for stability', *American Historical Review*, 86 (2), 1981.

Mancel, Y. *L'Union douanière ou le mariage des nations* (Paris, 1949).

Manderson-Jones, R.B. *The Special Relationship: Anglo-American Relations and Western European Unity 1947–1956* (London, 1972).

Manning, A.F. 'Die Niederlände und Europa von 1945 bis zum Beginn der fünfziger Jahre', *Vierteljahrshefte für Zeitgeschichte*, 29 (1), 1981.

Manz, M. 'Stagnation und Aufschwung in der französischen Zone von 1945–1948' (Doctoral dissertation, University of Mannheim, 1968).

Marjolin, R. *Europe and the United States in the World Economy* (Durham NC, 1953).

Martin, J.S. *All Honourable Men* (Boston, 1950).

Mason, H.L. *The European Coal and Steel Community, Experiment in Supranationalism* (The Hague, 1955).

Mayer, H.C. *German Recovery and the Marshall Plan 1948–1952* (Bonn, 1969).

Mayne, R. *The Community of Europe. Past, Present and Future* (New York, 1962).

Mayne, R. *The Recovery of Europe* (London, 1970).

Meade, J.E. Liesner, H.H. and Wells, S.J. *Case Studies in European Economic Union. The Mechanics of Integration* (London, 1962).

Melandri, P. *Les Etats-Unis face à l'unification de l'Europe 1945–1954* (Paris, 1980).

Mendershausen, H. 'First tests of the Schuman Plan', *Review of Economics and Statistics*, 35, 1953.

Mendershausen, H. 'Foreign aid with and without dollar shortage', *Review of Economics and Statistics*, 33, 1951.

Mérigot, J.-G. and Coulbois, P. *Le Franc 1938–1950* (Paris, 1950).

Merkl, P.H. *The Origin of the West German Republic* (New York, 1963).

Merritt, A.J. and Merritt, R.L. *Public Opinion in Occupied Germany. The OMGUS Surveys 1945–1949* (Urbana, 1970).

Meyer, F.V. *United Kingdom Trade with Europe* (London, 1957).

Mikesell, R.F. *Foreign Exchange in the Post War World* (New York, 1954).

Mikesell, R.F. 'Regional multilateral payments arrangements', *Quarterly Journal of Economics*, 62, 1948.

Mioche, P. 'Aux origines du Plan Monnet, 1942–1947', *Revue Historique*, 538, 1981.

Monnet, J. *Mémoires* (Paris, 1976).

Marris, A.D. *Prospects for Closer European Economic Integration* (London, 1948).

Newton, C.C.S. 'Britain, the dollar shortage and European integration 1945–50' (PhD thesis, University of Birmingham, 1981).

Niclaus, K. *Demokratiegründung in Westdeutschland. Die Entstehung der Bundesrepublik 1945–1949* (Munich, 1974).

Otto, H.-J. *Strukturwandlungen und Nachkriegsprobleme der Wirtschaft Italiens* (Kiel, 1951).

Papi, G.U. 'Myths and realities of the European green pool', *Banca Nazionale del Lavoro Quarterly Review*, 5, 1952.

Patterson, G. *Survey of United States International Finance 1949* (Princeton University, Dept. of Economics and Social Institutions, International Finance Section, 1950).

Patterson, G. and Polk, J. 'The emerging pattern of bilateralism', *Quarterly Journal of Economics*, 62, 1947/8.

Pentland, C. *International Theory and European Integration* (London, 1973).

Perroux, F. *Le plan Marshall ou l'Europe nécessaire au monde* (Paris, 1948).

Pharo, H. Ø. 'Bridgebuilding and reconstruction. Norway faces the Marshall Plan', *Scandinavian Journal of History*, 1, 1976.

Piettre, A. *L'économie allemande contemporaine 1945–1952* (Paris, 1952).

Pohl, M. *Wiederaufbau. Kunst und Technik der Finanzierung 1947–1953. Die ersten Jahre der Kreditanstalt für Wiederaufbau* (Frankfurt-am-Main, 1973).

Polak, J.J. 'The contribution of the September 1949 devaluations to the solution of Europe's dollar problem', *IMF Staff Papers*, 2, 1951/2.

Pollard, S. *The Integration of the European Economy Since 1815* (London, 1981).

Pounds, N.J.G. and Parker, W.N. *Coal and Steel in Western Europe* (London, 1957).

Price, H.B. *The Marshall Plan and its Meaning* (Ithaca, 1955).

Pünder, T. *Das bizonale Interregnum. Die Geschichte des Vereinigtem–Wirtschaftsgebiets, 1946–1949* (Rastaat, 1966).

Reuss, C., Koutny, E. and Tychon, L. *Le Progrès économique en sidérurgie. Belgique, Luxembourg, Pays-Bas 1830–1955* (Louvain, 1960).

Reuter, P. *La Communauté européenne du charbon et de l'acier* (Paris, 1953).

Salvati, M. *Stato e industria nella ricostruzione. Alle origini del potere democristiano (1944/1949)* (Milan, 1982).

Scharf C. and Schröder, H.-J. *Die Deutschlandpolitik Grossbritanniens und die Britische Zone 1945–1949* (Wiesbaden, 1979).

Schuker, S. 'The two postwar eras and the conditions for stability', in *American Historical Review*, 86 (2), 1981.

Schwarz, H.-P. *Vom Reich zur Bundesrepublik. Deutschland im Widerstreit der aussenpolitischen Konzeptionen in den Jahren der Besatzungsherrschaft 1945–1949* (Neuwied, 1966).

Scitovsky, T. *Economic Theory and Western European Integration* (London, 1958).

Sforza, C. *Cinque anni a Palazzo Chigi: la politica estera italiana dal 1947 al 1951* (Rome, 1952).

Simpson, E.S. 'Inflation, deflation and unemployment in Italy', *Review of Economic Studies*, 17, 1949/50.

Smith, J.E. (ed.) *The Papers of General Lucius D. Clay: Germany 1945–1949*, 2 vols (Bloomington, 1974).

Steininger, R. 'Ruhrfrage und Sozialisierung in der anglo-amerikanischen Deutschlandpolitik 1947/48', *Vierteljahrshefte für Zeitgeschichte*, 29 (2), 1979.

Stolz, G. *Tollunioner* (Bergen, 1948).

Stone, D.C. 'The impact of US assistance programs on the political and economic integration of western Europe', *American Political Science Review*, 46, 1952.

Tapinos, G. *L'immigration étrangère en France, 1946–73*, Institut national d'études démographiques, Travaux et documents, Cahier no.71 (Paris, 1975).

Tinbergen, J. *International Economic Integration* (Amsterdam, 1954).

Touchard, J. *Le gaullisme 1940–1969* (Paris, 1978).

Trachtenberg, M. *Reparation in World Politics. France and European Economic Diplomacy 1916–1923* (New York, 1980).

Triffin, R. *Europe and the Money Muddle* (New Haven, 1957).

Trued, M.N. and Mikesell, R.F. *Postwar Bilateral Payments Agreements*, Princeton Studies in International Finance, 4, 1955.

Van der Beugel, E.H. *From Marshall Aid to Atlantic Partnership. European Integration as a Concern of American Foreign Policy* (Amsterdam, 1966).

Wallace, H. Wallace, W. and Webb, C. *Policy-Making in the European Communities* (London, 1977).

Wallich, H.C. *Mainsprings of the German Revival* (New Haven, 1955).

Watt, D.C. *Britain Looks to Germany* (London, 1965).

Wightman, D. *Economic Cooperation in Europe. A Study of the U.N. Economic Commission for Europe* (London, 1956).

Williams, J.H. *Economic Stability in a Changing World* (Oxford, 1953).

Willis, F.R. (ed.) *European Integration* (New York, 1975).

Willis, F.R. *The French in Germany 1945–1949* (Stanford, 1962).

Winkler, H.A. (ed.) *Politische Weichenstellungen im Nachkriegsdeutschland 1945–1953, Geschichte und Gesellschaft* Sonderheft 5 (Göttingen, 1979).

Worswick, G.D.N. and Ady, P.H. (eds) *The British Economy in the Nineteen-Fifties* (Oxford, 1962).

Worswick, G.D.N. and Ady, P.H. (eds) *The British Economy 1945–1950* (Oxford, 1952).

Woytinsky, W.S. and Woytinsky, E.S. *World Commerce and Governments. Trends and Outlook* (New York, 1955).

Youngson, A.J. *The British Economy 1920–1957* (London, 1960).

Zawadzki, K.W.F. 'The economics of the Schuman Plan', *Oxford Economic Papers*, N.S., 5, 1953.

Zeitschrift für die Gesamte Staatswissenschaft *Currency and Economic Reform After World War II. A Symposium*, 135 (3), 1979.

Zotschew, T. 'Die Strukturwandlungen in deutschen Aussenhandel und deren Folgen für die westeuropäische Zusammenarbeit', *Weltwirtschaftliches Archiv*, 66, 1951.

WORKS PUBLISHED SINCE THE COMPLETION OF THE HARDBACK EDITION

Armstrong, P., Glyn, A. and Harrison, J. *Capitalism Since World War II. The Making and Break-Up of the Great Boom* (London, 1984).

Berding, H. (ed.) *Wirtschaftliche und politische Integration in Europa im 19- und 20-Jahrhundert* (Göttingen, 1984).

Bossuat, G. 'L'aide américaine à la France après la seconde guerre mondiale', *Vingtième siècle*, janvier/mars 1986.

Bullen, R. and Pelly, M.E. (eds) *Documents on British Policy Overseas*. Series II, vol. 1: *The Schuman Plan. The Council of Europe and Western European Integration May 1950–December 1952* (London, 1986).

Bullock, Sir A. *Ernest Bevin – Foreign Secretary, 1945–1951* (London, 1983).

Cairncross, Sir A. *Years of Recovery. British Economic Policy 1945–51* (London, 1985).

D'Attorre, P.P. 'Anche noi possiamo essere prosperi. Aiuti ERP e politiche della produttività negli anni Cinquanta', *Quaderni storici*, 20, 1985.

D'Attorre, P.P. 'Il Piano Marshall. Politica, economia, relazioni internazionali nella ricostruzione italiana', *Passato e Presente*, 7 (1), 1985.

Griffiths, R.T. and Lynch, F.M.B. 'L'échec de la "Petite Europe". Les négociations Fritalux/Finebel, 1949–1950', *Revue historique*, 274 (1), 1985.

Groupe de Liaison des Historiens auprès des Communautés, *Histoire des Débats de la Construction Européenne Mars 1948–Mai 1950* (Brussels, 1986).

Kaplan, L.S. *The United States and NATO. The Formative Years* (Lexington, Kentucky, 1984).

Lacroix-Riz, A. *Le choix de Marianne. Les relations franco-américaines de la Libération aux débuts du Plan Marshall (1944–1948)* (Paris, 1985).

Lademacher, H. and Mühlhausen, W. (eds) *Sicherheit, Kontrolle, Souveränitat: Das Petersberger Abkommen vom 22 November 1949. Eine Dokumentation* (Melsungen, 1985).

Lynch, F.M.B. 'Resolving the Paradox of the Monnet Plan. National and International Planning in French Reconstruction', in *Economic History Review*, 27, 2, 1984.

Painter, D.S. 'Oil and the Marshall Plan', *Business History Review*, 58, 1984.

Poidevin, R. 'La France et le charbon allemand au lendemain de la deuxième guerre mondiale', *Relations internationales*, 44, 1985.

Poidevin, R. 'La France devant le danger allemand (1944–1952)', in Hildebrand, K. and Pommerin, R. (eds), *Deutsche Frage und europäisches Gleichgewicht* (Cologne, 1985).

Ranieri, R. 'La siderurgia italiana e gli inizi dell'integrazione europea', *Passato e Presente*, 7 (1), 1985.

Riste, O. *Western Security: The Formative Years. European and Atlantic Defence 1947–1953* (Oslo, 1985).

Wexler, I. *The Marshall Plan Revisited. The European Recovery Program in Economic Perspective* (Greenwood, Ill., 1983).

INDEX